CHOOSING DEFEAT

A truly unique all-embracing narrative of the American war in Afghanistan from the words of its architects, *Choosing Defeat* takes an unparalleled inside look at America's longest war, pulling back the curtain on the inner deliberations behind the scenes. The author combines his own extensive experience in the Army, the CIA, and the White House with interviews with policymakers within the Bush, Obama, and Trump administrations to produce a groundbreaking study of how American leaders make wartime decisions. Transporting you inside the White House Situation Room, every key strategic debate over twenty years – from the immediate aftermath of 9/11, to Obama's surge and withdrawal, to Trump's negotiations with the Taliban, and Biden's final pullout – is carefully reconstructed. Paul D. Miller identifies issues in US leadership, governance, military strategy, and policymaking that extend beyond the war in Afghanistan and highlights the existence of deeper problems in American foreign policy.

Paul D. Miller is Professor of the Practice of International Affairs at Georgetown University. He served as Director for Afghanistan and Pakistan on the National Security Council staff; worked as an intelligence analyst for the CIA; and served as a military intelligence officer in the US Army. He is a veteran of the war in Afghanistan and author of *Just War and Ordered Liberty* (2021) and *American Power and Liberal Order* (2016).

CHOOSING DEFEAT

The Twenty-Year Saga of How America Lost Afghanistan

Paul D. Miller

Georgetown University

CAMBRIDGE
UNIVERSITY PRESS

CAMBRIDGE
UNIVERSITY PRESS

Shaftesbury Road, Cambridge CB2 8EA, United Kingdom

One Liberty Plaza, 20th Floor, New York, NY 10006, USA

477 Williamstown Road, Port Melbourne, VIC 3207, Australia

314–321, 3rd Floor, Plot 3, Splendor Forum, Jasola District Centre,
New Delhi – 110025, India

103 Penang Road, #05–06/07, Visioncrest Commercial, Singapore 238467

Cambridge University Press is part of Cambridge University Press & Assessment,
a department of the University of Cambridge.

We share the University's mission to contribute to society through the pursuit of
education, learning and research at the highest international levels of excellence.

www.cambridge.org
Information on this title: www.cambridge.org/9781009614375

DOI: 10.1017/9781009614382

First published 2025

Printed in the United Kingdom by CPI Group Ltd, Croydon CR0 4YY

A catalogue record for this publication is available from the British Library

Library of Congress Cataloging-in-Publication Data
Names: Miller, Paul David, 1978– author.
Title: Choosing defeat : the twenty-year saga of how America lost Afghanistan / Paul D.
Miller, Georgetown University, Washington DC.
Other titles: Twenty-year saga of how America lost Afghanistan
Description: Cambridge, United Kingdom ; New York, NY : Cambridge University Press,
2025. | Includes bibliographical references and index.
Identifiers: LCCN 2024061362 | ISBN 9781009614375 (hardback) | ISBN 9781009614351
(paperback) | ISBN 9781009614382 (ebook)
Subjects: LCSH: Afghan War, 2001–2021 – Decision making. | Afghan War,
2001–2021 – United States. | United States – Foreign relations – Afghanistan. |
Afghanistan – Foreign relations – United States. | United States – Foreign relations – 21st
century. | Afghanistan – Foreign relations – 2001–2021. | Nation-building – Afghanistan. |
Nation-building – United States. | United States – Military policy.
Classification: LCC DS371.41252.U6 M55 2025 | DDC 958.104/7–dc23/eng/20250228
LC record available at https://lccn.loc.gov/2024061362

ISBN 978-1-009-61437-5 Hardback

This book is dedicated to the people of Afghanistan,

and to the American and Allied soldiers, sailors, airmen,

Marines, diplomats, and intelligence professionals

who deserve better than what history has dealt them.

Contents

Acknowledgments	*page* viii
Dramatis Personae	ix
List of Abbreviations	xv

1	Myths and Mysteries of War in Afghanistan	1
2	2001: Victory	37
3	2002–2003: Neglect	70
4	2003–2005: Refocus	106
5	2006: Insurgency	133
6	2007–2008: Counterinsurgency	161
7	2009: False Start	197
8	2009: The Hinge	227
9	2010–2011: Surge	258
10	2010–2014: Negotiations	297
11	2012–2014: Transition	327
12	2015–2016: Obama's Forever War	358
13	2017–2018: Trump's Forever War	379
14	2018–2020: Doha	401
15	2021: Defeat	435
16	Why Did We Lose?	467

| *Bibliographic Essay* | 496 |
| *Index* | 505 |

Acknowledgments

I would like to thank the Smith Richardson and Sarah Scaife Foundations, without whose research grants I could not have begun work on this project. Thank you as well to George Shambaugh and all my colleagues at Georgetown University who gave me time and showed me patience. Thank you to Clara Cramer, Alex Gibson, Lucile Malone, Charlotte Armistead, Elisabeth Miller, Bergite Musaj, and especially Madison Lockett for their invaluable work as my research assistants on this project. Madison stuck with this project for almost two years and, in addition to being an invaluable conversation partner, helped organize the mass of information, notes, and interviews that became this book, which would likely still be languishing unfinished without her help.

I owe an apology to the students of my spring 2022 and 2023 course, "The Practice of Policy Tradecraft." I was grossly negligent in grading your assignments in a timely fashion. This book is to blame.

This book reuses part or all of the following articles, used with permission: "What Really Went Wrong in Afghanistan," *The Dispatch*, January 29, 2020; "Afghanistan Didn't Have to End This Way," *The Dispatch*, August 13, 2021; "Review," in H-DIPLO Roundtable XXIII-44 on Malkasian, *The American War in Afghanistan: A History*, June 27, 2022; and "Graveyard of Analogies: The Use and Abuse of History for the War in Afghanistan," *Journal of Strategic Studies*, Vol. 39, No. 3 (2016), pp. 446–476.

All statements of fact, opinion, or analysis expressed are those of the author and do not reflect the official positions or views of the US government. Nothing in the contents should be construed as asserting or implying US government authentication of information or endorsement of the author's views.

Dramatis Personae

I sympathize with readers who may struggle to distinguish between dozens of generals and ambassadors with names like McNeil, McKiernan, McChrystal, McKenzie, McKinley, and McMaster, or John Allen, John Abizaid, John Bolton, John Brennan, John Kerry, John Nicholson, John Campbell, and John Gastright. There are several Millers involved in the saga – Laurel Miller, Scott Miller, and myself (to my knowledge, we are not related). Fate seems determined to confuse students and future historians: when a new National Security Advisor took office in 2013, she wasn't even the first African American woman surnamed Rice to hold the position. To aid the reader, listed here are the principal players in each administration and in the military and diplomatic agencies referenced in the text, as well as interviewees who shed special light on different aspects of the story.

THE BUSH ADMINISTRATION

PRINCIPALS

George W. Bush, President, 2001–2009
Dick Cheney, Vice President, 2001–2009
Donald Rumsfeld, Secretary of Defense, 2001–2006
Robert Gates, Secretary of Defense, 2006–2011
Colin Powell, Secretary of State, 2001–2005
Condoleezza Rice, National Security Advisor, 2001–2005; Secretary of State, 2005–2009
Stephen P. Hadley, National Security Advisor, 2005–2009; Deputy National Security Advisor, 2001–2005

NATIONAL SECURITY COUNCIL STAFF

Doug Lute, Assistant to the President and Deputy National Security Advisor for Iraq and Afghanistan, 2007–2009

Andrew Eerdman, National Security Council Director for Iran, Iraq, and Strategic Planning, 2003–2005

Tony Harriman, Senior Director for Afghanistan, National Security Council staff, 2003–2007

STATE DEPARTMENT

Richard Armitage, Deputy Secretary of State, 2001–2005

Richard Boucher, Assistant Secretary of State for South and Central Asia, 2006–2009

John Gastright, Deputy Assistant Secretary of State for Afghanistan and Pakistan, 2003–2008

Eliot Cohen, Counselor to the Secretary of State, 2007–2008

Larry Wilkerson, Chief of Staff to the Secretary of State, 2001–2005

Ashley Tellis, National Security Council Senior Director for Afghanistan, 2003; State Department Policy Planning Staff, 2004; Special Advisor to Undersecretary of State for Political Affairs, 2005–2008

Maureen Quinn, Coordinator for Afghanistan, Acting Chief of Mission (Kabul), 2004–2006

Mitchell Reiss, State Department, Director of Policy Planning, 2003–2005

Zalmay Khalilzad, Special Presidential Envoy for Afghanistan, 2001–2003; US Ambassador to Afghanistan, 2003–2005; US Permanent Representative to the United Nations, 2007–2008

DEPARTMENT OF DEFENSE

Douglas Feith, Undersecretary of Defense for Policy, 2001–2005

Eric Edelman, Undersecretary of Defense for Policy, 2005–2009

James Shinn, Assistant Secretary of Defense for East Asia and Pacific Affairs, 2006–2008

Mitchell Shivers, Assistant Secretary of Defense for Indo-Pacific Security Affairs, 2008–2009

THE OBAMA ADMINISTRATION

PRINCIPALS

Barack Obama, President, 2009–2017

Joe Biden, Vice President, 2009–2017

Robert Gates, Secretary of Defense, 2006–2011

Leon Panetta, Director, Central Intelligence Agency, 2009–2011; Secretary of Defense, 2011–2013

Chuck Hagel, Secretary of Defense, 2013–2015

Ash Carter, Secretary of Defense, 2015–2017; Deputy Secretary of Defense, 2011–2013

Hillary Clinton, Secretary of State, 2009–2013

John Kerry, Secretary of State, 2013–2017

Jim Jones, National Security Advisor, 2009–2010

Tom Donilon, National Security Advisor, 2010–2013

Susan Rice, National Security Advisor, 2013–2017

NATIONAL SECURITY COUNCIL STAFF

Doug Lute, Deputy Assistant to the President and Senior Director for Afghanistan and Pakistan, 2009–2013; US Ambassador to NATO, 2013–2017

Jeff Eggers, Special Assistant to the President and National Security Council Senior Director for Afghanistan and Pakistan, 2010–2015

Peter Lavoy, Special Assistant to the President and Senior Director for South Asia, 2015–2017; Principal Deputy Assistant Secretary of Defense for Asian and Pacific Security Affairs, 2011–2014; Deputy Director of National Intelligence for Analysis, 2008–2011; Chairman, National Intelligence Council, 2008–2009; National Intelligence Officer for South Asia, 2007–2008

Frank Ruggiero, Senior Deputy Special Assistant for Afghanistan and Pakistan, 2010–2012; Senior Civilian Representative in Kandahar, 2009–2010

STATE DEPARTMENT

Barnett Rubin, Special Advisor to the United Nations Special Representative of the Secretary General for Afghanistan, 2001–2005; Senior Advisor to the Special Representative of the President for Afghanistan and Pakistan, 2009–2013

Tony Wayne, Coordinating Director for Development; Deputy US Ambassador to Afghanistan, 2009–2011

DEFENSE DEPARTMENT

Michèle Flournoy, Undersecretary of Defense for Policy, 2009–2012

Vikram Singh, Deputy Assistant Secretary of Defense for South and Southeast Asia, 2012–2014; Deputy Special Representative for Afghanistan and Pakistan, 2009–2011

Chris Kolenda, Senior Advisor to the Undersecretary of Defense for Policy, 2010–2014; Strategic Advisor to Commander, International Security Assistance Force, 2009–2010

OTHERS

John Brennan, Homeland Security Advisor, 2009–2013; Director, Central Intelligence Agency, 2013–2017

THE TRUMP ADMINISTRATION

PRINCIPALS

Donald Trump, President, 2017–2021

Mike Pence, Vice President, 2017–2021

Rex Tillerson, Secretary of State, 2017–2018

Mike Pompeo, Secretary of State, 2018–2021; Director of the Central Intelligence Agency, 2017–2018

Jim Mattis, Secretary of Defense, 2017–2018

Mark Esper, Secretary of Defense, 2019–2020

H. R. McMaster, National Security Advisor, 2017–2018; Deputy to the Commander for Planning, International Security Assistance Force, 2010–2012

John Bolton, National Security Advisor, 2018–2019

Robert O'Brien, National Security Advisor, 2019–2021

NATIONAL SECURITY COUNCIL STAFF

Victoria Coates, Deputy National Security Advisor for the Middle East and North Africa, 2017–2021

Lisa Curtis, National Security Council Senior Director for South and Central Asia, 2017–2021

DEFENSE DEPARTMENT

Colin Jackson, Deputy Assistant Secretary of Defense for Afghanistan, Pakistan, and Central Asia, 2017–2019

Fernando Lujan, NSC Director for Afghanistan and Pakistan, 2014–2016; NSC Senior Director for South and Central Asia, 2017; Special Advisor to Ambassador Khalilzad, 2018–2020

THE BIDEN ADMINISTRATION

Joe Biden, President, 2021–2025

Kamala Harris, Vice President, 2021–2025

Tony Blinken, Secretary of State, 2021–2025

Lloyd Austin, Secretary of Defense, 2021–2025

Jake Sullivan, National Security Advisor, 2021–2025

COALITION AND ISAF COMMANDERS

Dan McNeill, Commander, Coalition Forces – Afghanistan, 2002–2003

David Barno, Commander, Combined Forces Command – Afghanistan, 2003–2005

Karl Eikenberry, Commander, Combined Forces Command – Afghanistan, 2005–2007

Dan McNeill, Commander, ISAF, 2007–2008

David McKiernan, Commander, ISAF, 2008–2009

Stan McChrystal, Commander, ISAF, 2009–2010

David Petraeus, Commander, ISAF, 2010–2011

John Allen, Commander, ISAF, 2011–2013

Joe Dunford, Commander, ISAF, 2013–2014

John Campbell, Commander, ISAF and Resolute Support, 2014–2016

John Nicholson, Commander, Resolute Support, 2016–2018

Austin "Scott" Miller, Commander, Resolute Support, 2018–2021

COMMANDERS, CENTRAL COMMAND

Tommy Franks, 2000–2003
John Abizaid, 2003–2007
William Fallon, 2007–2008
David Petraeus, 2008–2010
Jim Mattis, 2010–2013
Lloyd Austin, 2013–2016
Joseph Votel, 2016–2019
Ken McKenzie, 2019–2022

US AMBASSADORS TO AFGHANISTAN

Ryan Crocker, 2002 (Chargé d'Affaires)
Robert Finn, 2002–2004
Zalmay Khalilzad, 2004–2005
Ronald Neumann, 2005–2007
Bill Wood, 2007–2009
Karl Eikenberry, 2009–2011
Ryan Crocker, 2011–2012
James Cunningham, 2012–2014
Michael McKinley, 2015–2016
Hugo Lorens, 2016–2017
John Bass, 2017–2020
Ross Wilson, 2020–2021 (Chargé d'Affaires)

US SPECIAL REPRESENTATIVES FOR AFGHANISTAN AND PAKISTAN

Richard Holbrooke, 2009–2010
Marc Grossman, 2011–2012
Jim Dobbins, 2013–2014
Dan Feldman, 2014–2015
Rick Olson, 2015–2016
Laurel Miller, 2016–2017 (Acting)
Zalmay Khalilzad, 2018–2021 (Special Representative for Afghanistan Reconciliation)

Abbreviations

ANSF	Afghan National Security Forces
ARTF	Afghanistan Reconstruction Trust Fund
ANDS	Afghan National Development Strategy
AUMF	Authorization for the Use of Military Force
BSA	bilateral security agreement
CDP	Capacity Development Program
CENTCOM	Central Command
CERP	Commander's Emergency Response Program
CIA	Central Intelligence Agency (US)
CJSOTF-A	Combined Joint Special Operations Task Force–Afghanistan
CJTF	Combined Joint Task Force
CN	counternarcotics
CNAS	Center for a New American Security
COIN	counterinsurgency
CSF	Coalition Support Funds
CSTC-A	Combined Security Transition Command–Afghanistan
CT	counterterrorism
DDR	disarmament, demobilization, and reintegration
DEA	Drug Enforcement Administration (US)
DoD	Department of Defense (US)
DoS	Department of State (US)
EUCOM	European Command
FATA	Federally Administered Tribal Areas (Pakistan)
FID	foreign internal defense
GDP	gross domestic product
GoA	Government of Afghanistan
HVT	High-Value Target
IDLG	Independent Directorate of Local Governance
IDP	Internally-displaced persons
IMF	International Monetary Fund

INL	Bureau of International Narcotics and Law Enforcement Affairs (US)
ISAF	International Security Assistance Force
ISI	Inter-Services Intelligence (Pakistan)
ISIS	Islamic State in Iraq and Syria
JSOC	Joint Special Operations Command
KTD	Key Terrain District
LOTFA	Law and Order Trust Fund for Afghanistan
MEDEVAC	medical evacuation
MNNA	Major Non-NATO Ally
NATO	North Atlantic Treaty Organization
NEO	noncombatant evacuation operation
NGO	nongovernmental organization
NIE	National Intelligence Estimate
NSA	National Security Agency (US)
NSC	National Security Council (US)
NTM-A	NATO Training Mission–Afghanistan
NUG	National Unity Government (Afghanistan)
OEF	Operation Enduring Freedom
OMB	Office of Management and Budget (US)
PRT	Provincial Reconstruction Team (Afghanistan)
PTS	*Program Tahkim-e Sulh* (Strengthening Peace Program)
RC	Regional Command
SIV	Special Immigrant Visa
SOCOM	Special Operations Command
SOF	special operations forces
SPA	Strategic Partnership Agreement
SRAP	Special Representative for Afghanistan and Pakistan (US)
TTP	*Tehrik-e Taliban Pakistan* (Pakistani Taliban)
UN	United Nations
UNAMA	United Nations Assistance Mission in Afghanistan
UNODC	United Nations Office on Drugs and Crime
US	United States of America
USAID	US Agency for International Development
USFOR-A	US Forces–Afghanistan

1

MYTHS AND MYSTERIES OF WAR IN AFGHANISTAN

Why did the United States lose the war in Afghanistan? In one sense, there is no mystery: the United States lost because every president who oversaw the war made major strategic errors. President George W. Bush underinvested in peace building and invaded Iraq. President Barack Obama announced a surge but also a timetable for the withdrawal of troops; dumped too much money too quickly into reconstruction; and failed to synergize his surge with a negotiating strategy. President Donald Trump negotiated a deal with the Taliban while declaring his intent to withdraw, giving the enemy everything they demanded for virtually nothing in return. President Joe Biden withdrew US forces and deprived the Afghan army of the support they needed to survive. And no president was able to solve the problems of Afghan corruption or Pakistani perfidy.

Each decision shrank the range of possible outcomes, each stage progressively limiting what could be achieved in the next. The progress of the war was like a network of tunnels in which American policymakers continued to choose narrower and narrower branches that went more and more steeply downhill until they ended abruptly in a collapsed mineshaft. It is tempting to say that American policymakers never missed an opportunity to make a mistake in Afghanistan – in which case, the question is not why America lost, but why it took so long.

But that record of missteps and failure is not a full accounting of the war – and dwelling exclusively on the failures implies a false sense of inevitability, as if the United States was doomed from the outset to get everything wrong. A full accounting of the war should note islands of success amid a larger sea of failure. The United States executed a remarkable military campaign in 2001 that overthrew the Taliban government and destroyed al-Qaida's most important strategic asset. The United States sponsored a successful political process for creating a new Afghan government under a new constitution which remained popular with Afghans to the very end. The Afghan economy grew, sometimes very strongly, and a generation of Afghans came of age in a more open society.

The United States eventually mustered the will and resources to mount an ambitious, if incomplete, counterinsurgency campaign against a resurgent Taliban that achieved success in some places, at certain times. The United States created a new Afghan army and Afghan police force virtually from scratch, who fought off the Taliban for over a decade. These successes did not add up to strategic victory, but they are an important part of the story. If we are to understand why we lost, we must understand why we were able to get some things right, some of the time, and why we were unable to sustain or expand those successes. Understanding success also highlights American policymakers' agency: getting some things right proves that getting the rest wrong was not inevitable, and policymakers are accountable for their poor choices.

This book recounts American policymakers' choices about the war in Afghanistan. It is not a history of the war in Afghanistan, but a history of American decision-making about the war. It is a history of four presidential administrations' deliberations and debates over the primary strategic issues they faced, including the beliefs they expressed and how those beliefs were translated into policy and strategy. It is also an assessment: Were their beliefs warranted? Were their decisions sound? Was their strategy effective? The final answer to the last question is, of course, no. This book seeks to account for how and why that came about. Why did American policymakers misjudge the war in Afghanistan? What explains how four presidential administrations from both political parties across twenty years who share little in common nonetheless came to share in a common legacy: losing America's longest war? How and why did they choose defeat?

MY STORY

I lived and breathed the war in Afghanistan for almost a decade. I was in the US Army on September 11, 2001, attending class at the Army's intelligence training center in Fort Huachuca, Arizona, having just completed my master's in public policy at Harvard. The instructors canceled class and told us to report back to our barracks because of an unspecified emergency. We went to the common room and turned on the news just in time to see the North Tower of the World Trade Center collapse on live television. I remember the palpable pulse of anger and the audible wave of profanity that vibrated around the room. I spent the summer of 2002 at Bagram Airbase in Afghanistan, an analyst in the intelligence support element of Combined Joint Task Force 180. I sat at a keyboard in a tent, pounding out summaries of political and military upheaval around the country. We thought it was wartime. It turned out my brief tour – after the battle of Shahi-kot in March 2002, but before the emergence of the Taliban insurgency in late 2005 – was the safest time in Afghanistan since 1979.

I subsequently worked as an analyst at the Central Intelligence Agency (CIA) in the office of South Asian Analysis. When I first joined the Agency, I expected to find a salty veteran who had been sitting on the Afghanistan desk for twenty or thirty years, a man who spoke six languages and could tell stories of dining with the king in the early 1970s, training mujahedin in the 1980s, and doing shots with Northern Alliance warlords in the 1990s. He didn't exist, at least not in the Directorate of Intelligence. I had been reading every book I could find on Afghanistan for two years, since the day after 9/11, but I could hardly count myself a real expert. The team grew substantially, but the salty veteran never showed up.

When President Bush appointed a "war czar" in May 2007 – officially, the deputy national security advisor for Iraq and Afghanistan – the move came with an expansion of the National Security Council (NSC) staff. The CIA seconded me to the NSC, where I worked for Lieutenant General Doug Lute from September 2007 to September 2009 as director for Afghanistan (along-side three or four other directors and under a senior director; I was very much one member of a hardworking team). Soon after his appointment, the satirical newspaper *The Onion* ran a piece joking that Lute would be "living high off the sweat and labor of the war serfs." Ever since, I've wanted to include "war serf" on my LinkedIn profile. Because I was a civil servant, not a political appointee, I worked through the presidential transition from Bush to Obama. On the Friday before Obama's inauguration, we handed over our files and hard drives to the National Archives for preservation by the George W. Bush Presidential Library. The day after the inauguration, we reported back to empty offices and new computers. On the NSC staff, I supported Lute, Bush, Obama, and national security advisors Steve Hadley and Jim Jones for their meetings and phone calls related to Afghanistan and Pakistan. I supported Bush's strategy review on Afghanistan and Pakistan in late 2008 and Obama's first strategy review in March 2009.[1]

Over the course of my nearly ten years of public service, I traveled to Bagram, Kabul, Kandahar, Herat, and Jalalabad. I met with many senior members of the Afghan government, including Nangarhar Governor Gul Agha Shirzai, Herat Governor Ismail Khan, Kandahar Provincial Council Chairman Ahmed Wali Karzai (President Hamid Karzai's brother),

---

[1] "Bush's New 'War Czar,'" *The Onion*, May 23, 2007.

Vice President Amrullah Saleh, Vice President Yunis Qanuni, Foreign Minister Rangin Dadfar Spanta, and Speaker of the House of Elders Sibghatullah Mojaddedi, among many others. Shirzai entertained me in his palace over dinner one evening, asserting loudly that Afghanistan's problems would be solved if it handed the country back to the Barakzai tribe (conveniently, his own). Wali Karzai – widely rumored to be among the chief drug traffickers in his region at the time – gave me one of the most impassioned anti-drug tirades I ever heard. While waiting with Mojaddedi in the West Wing before a meeting with the president, I began explaining the artwork, including the famous painting of George Washington crossing the Delaware. "Yes, I know," Mojaddedi interrupted, "I remember from my last visit, with President Reagan."

I am not the foremost American expert on Afghan history and culture. That distinction belongs to Boston University anthropologist Thomas Barfield, New York University political scientist Barney Rubin, and Army War College strategist Larry Goodson, who have collectively studied Afghanistan for more decades than I have been alive. They really are the salty veterans of Afghanistan studies (along with Carter Malkasian, foremost among the next generation of Afghan historians), who know the country and its languages better than most non-Afghans ever have. While I cannot rival their depth of expertise on Afghan history and culture, I had the good sense to read their books, and I've had a chance to meet and learn from them. I also have some claim to knowing the American side better than most. Since leaving government service, I've continued to follow events in Afghanistan and study and write about it in my academic work, and I have spent years seeking out and talking with former US policymakers about their experience working on the war effort. While most Americans paid far more attention to the war in Iraq – or, frankly, to the ups and downs of the Kardashians – I kept an eye on my war.

AFGHANISTAN IN THE AMERICAN IMAGINATION

It is hard to write about Afghanistan. Americans do not know very much about it. In our ignorance – where knowledge is absent or reality too complex – we tell stories to make sense of things. These stories, true or not, are shortcuts through the messiness. They stick in the brain because messy reality does not fit. It is difficult to cut through the made-up stories with anything that might contradict them. Given a choice between the story and the messiness, we choose the story every time. Unfortunately, this book is about the messiness.

The stories we told ourselves about Afghanistan started in the 1980s. Afghanistan was nonexistent in American pop culture and mainstream consciousness before the Soviet–Afghan War briefly brought it to the forefront. That war provided the setting for the most popular Hollywood movies set in Afghanistan before 2001: Sylvester Stallone's *Rambo III* (1988) and the slapstick comedy *Spies Like Us* (1985), starring Dan Aykroyd and Chevy Chase. In these stories, the Afghans are noble warriors and occasionally reliable allies, little else. The movies were not famous for anthropological accuracy.

After the Afghans dutifully helped America win the Cold War, their country receded in our consciousness for the next decade. Attention soared after 2001, peaking during the surge years. During that brief window when the Hindu Kush again held our attention, we learned about the war in Afghanistan through our movies, literature, and newspapers. But at first, it was mostly about ourselves. As a wave of war memoirs hit bookshelves, we read about our soldiers' courage and ingenuity. Our fighting men became *Horse Soldiers* in bands *Twelve Strong* who fought like *Lions of Kandahar* because fighting for one's comrade-in-arms is *The Only Thing Worth Dying For*. We learned that the CIA was *First In*, that the campaign only took *88 Days to Kandahar*, and that a secret team code-named *Jawbreaker* led *The Attack on Bin Laden and al-Qaida*. From these memoirs, a picture emerges: the war was noble though harsh; America was fighting for a just cause to avenge 9/11; and the Taliban were Central Asian Nazis while the average Afghan was a decent enough fellow who needed a helping hand.[2]

Public opinion supported the war in these years. In 2001, 93 percent of Americans believed it was the right choice to send troops to Afghanistan; the *New York Times* said Bush made the "right choice" to go to war and said of the American soldier that "the nation supports their cause and yearns for their success." In 2003, it criticized Bush for letting Iraq overshadow Afghanistan and called on his administration "to augment its efforts to bring security and development to Afghanistan." In 2004, the *Times* called for more troops and money "to keep Afghanistan from disintegrating back into a collection of local fiefs in which groups like al-Qaida and the Taliban can again take root." In 2005, it endorsed "nation building" in Afghanistan and in 2008

---

[2] Stanton, *Horse Soldiers*, later retitled *Twelve Strong*. Bradley and Maurer, *Lions of Kandahar.* Blehm, *The Only Thing Worth Dying For.* Schroen, *First In.* Grenier, *88 Days to Kandahar.* Berntsen and Pezzullo, *Jawbreaker.*

called on Bush to "develop a comprehensive military and political strategy to address the Taliban-Qaida threat." In March 2009, the *Times* praised Obama because "with his new comprehensive plan for Afghanistan and Pakistan, President Obama has asserted leadership over the war that matters most to America's security." As late as 2008, 68 percent of Americans believed the war was not a mistake.[3]

War was the major theme of books that focused on Afghanistan itself, not just the American intervention, and here the first notes of pessimism sounded out. In the American imagination, Afghanistan was a place of unceasing war, the setting for *Charlie Wilson's War* and *Ghost Wars*. The Soviets fought there, but so had everyone else, from the ancient Greeks and Genghis Khan to the British Empire. Books told the story of Afghanistan as *A Military History from Alexander the Great to the Fall of the Taliban*, presenting a narrative of continuous battle and, inevitably, imperial defeat. Afghan wars were secretive, wild, and adventurous, but also futile. To drive the point home, we got up-close, authentic glimpses of the eternal truth that war is hell from the Oscar-nominated documentary *Restrepo*, its sequel *Korengal*, an accompanying book titled simply *War*, and the Danish equivalent, *Armadillo*.[4]

The history-as-cautionary-tale trope got a name shortly after 9/11 when Milton Bearden, the CIA Station Chief in Pakistan from 1986 to 1989, warned in the pages of *Foreign Affairs* that Afghanistan was a legendary "Graveyard of Empires." Afghanistan "has witnessed the traverse of the world's great armies on campaigns of conquest to and from South and Central Asia," Bearden wrote. "All eventually ran into trouble in their encounters with the unruly Afghan tribals." He recapped the history of the three Anglo-Afghan wars, narrated in greater depth the Soviet–Afghan war, and used that history to caution against offending Afghan sensibilities with a large invading ground force.[5] The phrase "graveyard of empires" was so catchy it inspired thousands of headlines and editorials over the next twenty years, appeared in almost every memoir by an American policymaker who worked on the war, and graces the cover of at least three books about

---

3 "A Job Half Done in Afghanistan," *New York Times*, May 15, 2003. "NATO Falls Short in Afghanistan," June 26, 2004. "Building on Afghanistan's Elections," October 28, 2005. "Unfinished Business in Afghanistan," June 20, 2008. "The Remembered War," March 28, 2009. Frank Newport, "Afghan War Edges Out Iraq as Most Important for US," Gallup, July 30, 2008.

4 Crile, *Charlie Wilson's War*. Coll, *Ghost Wars*. Tanner, *Afghanistan*. Junger, *War*.

5 Bearden, "Afghanistan, Graveyard of Empires," 17.

Afghanistan published after 2001. It was the first note in the mood music of pessimism that would swell throughout the war.[6]

In all this, we didn't learn much about the effect of war on the Afghans, nor about Afghanistan apart from the subject of war.[7] And, of course, Iraq always overshadowed Afghanistan anyway. The blockbuster film *American Sniper*, set in Iraq, made $330 million at the US box office – almost twice as much as the top two movies set in Afghanistan, combined: *Lone Survivor* made $125 million in 2013, and *Twelve Strong* made $45 million in 2018. Iraq even overshadowed Afghanistan at the Oscars. *Sniper* was nominated for six Academy Awards in 2014, including Best Picture, and *The Hurt Locker*, also set in Iraq, won the top prize in 2009. One might argue the point by highlighting that *Zero Dark Thirty*, about the hunt for Osama bin Laden, was nominated for five Oscars in 2012 – except that film takes place almost entirely in Washington, DC, and Pakistan, not Afghanistan. The same raid, by the way, inspired not one, but two Navy SEAL memoirs, *The Operator* and *No Easy Day*. Americans' boundless appetite for stories of our heroic vengeance helped reduce a complex twenty-year war, for many readers and viewers, to a single successful raid.[8]

For those willing to dig deeper, we could catch glimpses of Afghanistan on its own terms. The Afghan-made film *Osama* told the story of a young Afghan girl under Taliban rule forced to disguise herself as a boy to work and support her family. The film won the Golden Globe for Best Foreign Language Film in 2003 – but no one saw it. It earned just $1.2 million at the US box office and $2.6 million internationally. *The Kite Runner*, by Afghan American novelist Khaled Hosseini, published in 2003, had further reach. It became a *New York Times* bestseller and a 2007 film (earning just $16 million at the US box office), a heartfelt and aching portrayal of family, friendship, and perseverance amid ethnic tensions, war, and creeping Taliban tyranny. Hosseini's next novel, *A Thousand Splendid Suns*, continued those themes through the lens of mother–daughter relationships.

Another rare bright spot amid the overwhelming cultural output about war and misery was the 2009 British documentary *Afghan Star*, about the Afghan television show of the same name. The Afghan version

---

[6] Jones, *In the Graveyard of Empires*. Isby, *Afghanistan: Graveyard of Empires*. Tyler, *Afghanistan: Graveyard of Empires*. A search of Nexis-Uni turned up over 3,500 articles with "Afghanistan" and "Graveyard of Empires" since 2001.

[7] The one exception is Barfield, *Afghanistan*, the single best book about the country published in English since Louis Dupree's work in the 1980s.

[8] O'Neill, *The Operator*. Owen, *No Easy Day*.

of *American Idol*, the show ran for fifteen seasons and was wildly popular. The British documentary is now a time capsule, a vignette of relatively free life in republican Afghanistan, bracketed by a government that bans music, performances, and unveiled women in public. It is notable that *Osama, Afghan Star*, and Hosseini's novels are the closest most Americans got to hearing an Afghan voice, and – despite the real misery that surrounds them – the most hopeful. Afghans, better acquainted with Taliban tyranny and jihadist violence than any of us, were keenest to imagine and work for something better.

By contrast, the portrait of Afghanistan that emerges in American portrayals is violent, poor, tragic, and – as the years went on – almost certainly doomed to stay that way. As early as November 2009, the *New York Times* began to sour on the war, warning that "there will never be enough American troops on the ground to defeat the Taliban or provide security for Afghans." The following August, the editorial board confessed that "we are increasingly confused and anxious about the strategy in Afghanistan and wonder whether, at this late date, there is a chance of even minimal success." In June 2011, it was markedly more dire: "Americans are impatient – and increasingly despairing – about the war in Afghanistan." In November 2012, it criticized Obama for withdrawing troops too slowly and called for a complete withdrawal within a year. For the rest of the war, the *Times* argued it was unwinnable and that the United States should withdraw all forces. In 2019, the *Times* argued the war was "at worst . . . hopeless."[9]

Other observers and scholars followed suit: by 2014, books appeared entitled *Why We Lost* and *Why We Couldn't Win the War or the Peace in Afghanistan* and proclaiming it was *Unwinnable*. In 2014, for the first time, Americans were evenly split on whether the war had been a mistake, according to Gallup, and opinion remained closely divided for the rest of the war. The pessimism was reflected in mainstream entertainment. In 2017, Netflix produced an attempt at a satire, *War Machine*, starring Brad Pitt and loosely adapted from a book about General Stanley McChrystal and the counterinsurgency campaign in 2009 and 2010. The book and the film are startling in their cynicism. "What do you do when the war you're fighting just can't possibly be won in any meaningful sense?" the narrator asks in the film's opening. The Taliban insurgents were "just guys who just picked up

9 "Mr. Obama's Task," *New York Times*, November 18, 2009. "The State of the War in Afghanistan," August 12, 2010. "The Way Out?" June 22, 2011. "The Pace of Leaving Afghanistan," November 27, 2012. "End the War in Afghanistan," February 3, 2019.

weapons because, so would you if someone invaded your country." The narrator intones trite lessons of history. "The thing about counterinsurgency is that it doesn't really work. We tried it in Vietnam. That went well," he dryly observes. "You can't win the trust of a country by invading it. You can't build a nation at gunpoint."[10]

The American stories – fiction and nonfiction, on film and on paper – grew thick with an air of pessimism, even as they overwhelmingly focused on Americans rather than Afghans. Afghanistan became a place of American endeavor and American frustration, a stage on which we played out our debates about our role in the world and the fate of American hyperpower. The script we eventually wrote for ourselves said that Afghanistan had been a place of privation and bloodshed for so long – it was an invincible "graveyard of empires" – that it was hopeless to try to make it otherwise. Even if it was a noble effort, it was a tragic nobility. That this portrayal had little to do with Afghanistan on its own terms, that it says more about its American audience and mostly American creators than about Afghanistan, was irrelevant. It was the cultural mood music playing as policymakers made their decisions about war in Afghanistan.

The punctuation mark on the story – one that a historian would not dare invent if it were not true – is that Afghanistan had, in fact, never been known as the "graveyard of empires," not until Milt Bearden's *Foreign Affairs* article in 2001. Prior to 2001, the phrase "graveyard of empires" referred to Mesopotamia, not Afghanistan, with occasional references to the Balkans and elsewhere. Afghans do not have a reputation of legendary xenophobia, but of hospitality. Afghans are not unique in resisting foreign invaders: the French partisans against Nazi occupation would be surprised to hear so. I emailed Milt in 2014 to ask where he got the phrase "graveyard of empires." He confirmed that he was not knowingly following an older tradition of calling Afghanistan by that epitaph and, for all he knew, invented it: "I think I just came up with the name for my piece for *Foreign Affairs* in 2001." It was a convenient myth for policymakers eager for an excuse not to invest in Afghanistan, and it was an irresistible headline for a generation of pundits and editorialists who were too busy to be bothered

---

[10] Megan Brenan, "A Year After Withdrawal, 50% Call Afghanistan War a Mistake," Gallup, August 29, 2022. Bolger, *Why We Lost.* Fairweather, *The Good War: Why We Couldn't Win.* Farrell, *Unwinnable.* *War Machine,* directed by David Michôd and released by Netflix in 2017, was inspired by Michael Hastings, *The Operators.*

with its accuracy. Such was the power of the idea that it became an unquestioned truth for twenty years.[11]

THE "AFGHANISTAN PAPERS"

The mood music affected scholars and especially journalists, who wove their own strands into the tapestry of myth. Among the prevailing explanations for America's defeat in Afghanistan, probably the most well known to American readers is the *Washington Post*'s "Afghanistan Papers," first serialized in the *Post* in 2019 and later published as a book. Deliberately echoing the leak of the "Pentagon Papers" about the Vietnam War in 1971, the *Post*'s reporting was based on declassified interviews with US policymakers (including me) conducted by the Special Inspector General for Afghanistan Reconstruction (SIGAR). The "Afghanistan Papers" purport to uncover a hidden scandal of American incompetence, deceit, and waste.[12]

The *Post*'s most dramatic claim was that US officials were "at war with the truth" and "misled" the American people about how the war was going. "Senior US officials failed to tell the truth about the war in Afghanistan throughout the 18-year campaign, making rosy pronouncements they knew to be false." The *Post* references one interviewee who "said it was common at military headquarters in Kabul – and at the White House – to distort statistics to make it appear the United States was winning the war when that was not the case."

The *Post*'s second accusation is that the United States bumbled into a "nation-building" campaign that was unnecessary and doomed to fail. The

---

[11] Bearden, email to author, October 7, 2014. The phrase as applied to Afghanistan is sometimes attributed to Mahmud Beg Tarzi, a turn-of-the-century Afghan nationalist intellectual and Foreign Minister, but there is no confirmed citation of Tarzi's usage of the phrase. New York University's Middle Eastern and Islamic Studies Librarian, who helps oversee the Afghanistan Digital Library there, confirmed that the phrase as applied to Afghanistan is sometimes attributed to Tarzi but was unable to provide a specific citation (email, October 1, 2014). Amin Tarzi, a descendent of Mahmud Beg Tarzi, denied that Mahmud Beg coined the phrase in an email to me (October 3, 2014).

[12] Craig Whitlock, "At War with the Truth," *The Washington Post*, December 9, 2019. Craig Whitlock, *The Afghanistan Papers*. As with many interviewees, my name was redacted in the published transcript. I am the unnamed NSC official here: www.washingtonpost.com/graphics/2019/investigations/afghanistan-papers/documents-database/share/pdf.htm l?document=background_ll_01_xx_phone_07142015.

war, it claims, should have been limited to killing the Taliban and al-Qaida, and that anything aside from limited military strikes was counterproductive, wasteful, and foolish. "Within six months, the United States had largely accomplished what it set out to do. The leaders of al-Qaida and the Taliban were dead, captured or in hiding."

Third, the *Post* portrays US nation-building efforts as doomed to fail because Afghanistan was unsuited to democracy. "Washington foolishly tried to reinvent Afghanistan in its own image by imposing a centralized democracy and a free-market economy on an ancient, tribal society that was unsuited for either," the *Post* reported. "US officials tried to create – from scratch – a democratic government in Kabul modeled after their own in Washington. It was a foreign concept to the Afghans, who were accustomed to tribalism, monarchism, communism and Islamic law."

Fourth, the *Post* rightly catalogues enormous amounts of waste, fraud, and abuse with the money allocated to rebuild Afghanistan. But, in doing so, it characterizes the nation-building effort as historically large and implies that the United States erred by investing too much in Afghanistan. "Since 2001, Washington has spent more on nation-building in Afghanistan than in any country ever."

And fifth, the *Post* claims that Bush and Obama alike failed "to devise a clear strategy with concise, attainable objectives." More: "The goals and mission kept changing and a lack of faith in the US strategy took root inside the Pentagon, the White House and the State Department."

The *Post*'s myths are dramatic, attention-getting, and have a surface plausibility. Many readers likely find them intuitively persuasive because they read well and are pithy and dramatic: we lost the war; something clearly went wrong; surely failure was a combination of stupidity and deceit. The same had been true of Vietnam, after all, so why shouldn't there be a presumption of its truth for Afghanistan? The simple explanation resonates with the pessimistic cultural mood music.

But that does not mean it is true. Some of the *Post*'s investigative reports lack context, perspective, or depth; some are simply false. James Cunningham, who served as US ambassador to Afghanistan during the Obama administration, characterized the *Post*'s project as one of the "worst examples" of shallow, hot-take analysis because it took "a lot of really unsubstantiated allegations and portrayed them as fact," in part by "interviewing a lot of people who have had axes to grind."[13] Reality is messier, and harder to summarize.

---

[13] Cunningham, interview by author. The following is drawn from Miller, "What Really Went Wrong in Afghanistan," *The Dispatch*, January 29, 2020.

Responding to the *Post*'s accusation that policymakers consistently lied about the war, Michael O'Hanlon, a left-of-center scholar at the Brookings Institution with nothing to gain from defending the government, explained, "The *Washington Post* did a disservice with this report . . . there has not been a campaign of disinformation, intentional or subliminal." He catalogued many times US officials publicly admitted the war was going poorly, including in the 2009 strategy review that concluded the United States was losing the war. Senior officials, especially in the military, often couched their public comments in the cadence of official optimism and a relentless can-do attitude, but that hardly amounted to a campaign of deceit.[14]

Second, the *Post* also mischaracterized American goals in the war. The US set out to deny safe haven to terrorists in Afghanistan, to defeat al-Qaida worldwide, and to deter other terrorist groups and state sponsors of terrorism. The goal required killing and capturing militant and terrorist leaders. It also required building Afghan capacity to continue denying safe haven after US forces left. Training Afghan security forces and rebuilding the Afghan government was, at least rhetorically, part of the mission from day one. As early as December 6, 2001, before the Taliban had even fallen from power in Kandahar, Richard Haass, the State Department's director of policy planning, sketched out reconstruction plans to the Senate Foreign Relations Committee. "The effort will be comprehensive, ranging from so-called quick impact projects (demining, local road rehabilitation, provision of seeds, renovation of water supplies, reopening schools, etc.)," he said, "to longer term and larger undertakings in the areas of agriculture, household and light industry, infrastructure modernization, education, and health." Nation building was not the result of "mission creep."[15]

Third, the *Post*'s claim that nation-building efforts were doomed to fail because they involved the United States "imposing" democracy on an "ancient, tribal society," supposedly opposed to "Western" values, is surprising for how overtly racist it is. Such a view treats Afghans as a mysterious and exotic "other," ignores the popularity of their democratic constitution, and is appallingly ignorant of Afghan history and culture, the realities of global democracy, and what nation building involves. There is nothing uniquely "Western" about roads, schools, and hospitals, nor about bureaucracy, political institutionalization, the rule of law, or even consultative forms of

---

[14] Michael O'Hanlon, "What the *Washington Post* Gets Wrong about the US and Afghanistan," The Brookings Institution, December 10, 2019.

[15] Senate Foreign Relations Committee, "The Political Future of Afghanistan," December 6, 2001, 14.

governance, all of which are prevalent across wide swaths of Africa and Asia. The 2004 Afghan Constitution, including its democratic elements, was based not on the United States Constitution, but on Afghanistan's own 1964 constitution. That earlier document established a constitutional monarchy with an elected parliament under which Afghanistan held relatively free and fair elections in 1965 and 1969.

The only truly "Western" innovation in Afghanistan's constitution was arguably the Article on human rights – though even that is debatable. "I have heard some say that openness and democracy conflict with our Middle Eastern culture and tradition," Ishaq Shahryar, the Afghan ambassador to the United States, told the Senate Foreign Relations Committee in February 2003. "Nonsense. It was Cyrus the Great of Persia who issued the world's first declaration of human rights," he said, referring to Cyrus' decree in 539 BC freeing slaves and announcing a form of religious tolerance. Afghans strongly supported human rights, including women's rights, throughout the war, and even grew more supportive as the years went on. "Surprisingly, more males (89.6%) than females (88.9%) say women should be allowed to vote," in 2019, according to the Asia Foundation's annual *Survey of the Afghan People*. "The figure for males is the highest ever recorded."[16]

Fourth, the *Post*'s claims about the size and scale of American state-building efforts in Afghanistan lack context. Between 2002 and 2021, the United States spent between $130 and $146 billion on Afghanistan reconstruction – but the *Post* does not mention that very little of that money (only 5 to 8 percent) flowed for the first five years of the American intervention. In complex reconstruction operations, timing matters. Earlier money matters far more than later money – an ounce of prevention is worth a pound of cure. But from 2001 to 2006, the United States did virtually no nation building at all – despite what Bush said in various speeches in 2002 and despite what Haass told the Senate Foreign Relations Committee – and tried to outsource the job to the United Nations and to European allies, who proved not up to the task.

Then, from 2007 to 2012, the United States pivoted to a rushed, almost panicked counterinsurgency and nation-building campaign – over 40 percent of all aid was delivered in those years – under unrealistic deadlines that guaranteed waste, fraud, and abuse. With billions wasted and little to show for it, Obama lost faith in the effort. As the Obama administration began drawing down US military forces in 2011 and 2012, it gave up on nation

---

[16] Senate Foreign Relations Committee, "The Reconstruction of Afghanistan: An Update," 50. The Asia Foundation, "Survey of the Afghan People, 2019," 170.

building. The US reverted to a counterterrorism operation with little regard for Afghan reconstruction for the final decade of the war. And in any case, for the duration, nearly two-thirds of all American aid went toward the Afghan army and police, not to roads, schools, and hospitals.

Simply put, there was no twenty-year nation-building campaign in Afghanistan. Nation building was a meaningful part of US strategy in Afghanistan for, at most, four or five years. Nation-building efforts did not go well, clearly, but the problem was not that the United States tried and failed. The problem was that, initially, the United States hardly tried at all, and once it finally started to put out a serious effort, the delay, the sense of urgency, and the artificial deadlines made the situation dramatically worse.[17]

Lastly, regarding the *Post*'s claims that the Bush and Obama administrations lacked both a clear goal and a clear strategy to achieve it: the *Post* is right that the US approach to Afghanistan was marked by ambiguity. But the problem was not that the United States simply lacked either a goal or a strategy altogether. Rather, there was a sharp disconnect between the United States' declared goals and its actual strategic choices. The United States' publicly declared goals were often far-reaching and ambitious – a stable, prospering, democratic Afghanistan – but policymakers consistently chose to do only what was minimally required to stave off immediate or catastrophic defeat. The result was a constant sense of failure and a persistent lack of progress toward long-term goals. Despite Bush and Obama's aspirational rhetoric about rebuilding Afghanistan, their budgetary and deployment decisions – what might be called a de facto strategy – prioritized killing and capturing jihadist militants while investing just enough in counterinsurgency and stability operations to preserve operational freedom for American counterterrorism forces.

This was a clear strategy, despite what the *Post* reports, though Bush and Obama can be faulted for not admitting it publicly, and it is not the strategy I recommended. It was a strategy of "forever war." Though often rightly criticized, "forever war" was not a sign of failure: it is what US policymakers deliberately chose because they would neither pay the price of a more ambitious campaign to resolve the conflict nor, until Biden took office, accept defeat. It was a feature, not a bug, of American strategy. It also meant that many of the United States' declared goals and subordinate objectives – those related to reconstruction and democracy – were there for rhetorical

---

[17] Figures derived from "US Foreign Assistance, Fiscal years 1946–2019" dataset available on www.foreignassistance.gov and from SIGAR, "Quarterly Report," October 2021. USAID and SIGAR report different sets of numbers, but the general trends are consistent.

effect only. The US did not defeat the Taliban, win the war, rebuild Afghanistan, or establish conditions for long-term stability because, for most of the twenty years it was there, it was not trying to accomplish those things.

THE TALIBAN'S THEORY OF VICTORY

Another prominent myth about America's defeat came shortly after the *Afghanistan Papers*. Carter Malkasian, a historian with a PhD in military history from Oxford University, attempted the first full history of the war with *America's War in Afghanistan*, first published in July 2021, weeks before the fall of Kabul. Malkasian knows the war from the ground up: he served as a civilian on a Provincial Reconstruction Team in Kunar, spent two years with the State Department in Helmand, speaks Pashto, and was a political advisor to the US commander in Afghanistan in 2013 and 2014. Malkasian knows the war far better than the *Washington Post*.[18]

The greatest strength of Malkasian's work is his ability to craft a comprehensible narrative out of a sprawling conflict that crossed four presidential administrations and saw a dozen or more commanding generals lead the fight. Besides its breadth, one of the book's selling points is Malkasian's deep familiarity with and access to Pashtun and Taliban sources. He quotes Taliban poetry, histories, and biographies, many presumably from his own translations. Given how few historians share Malkasian's fluency in Pashto, it is unlikely we will see a historian of the conflict with better access to the Taliban's perspective for a generation.

Unfortunately, he not only records the Taliban perspective: he essentially adopts it. Malkasian's myth is that the Taliban were fighting to defend Afghan national identity against an illegitimate foreign invasion. "The Taliban exemplified something that inspired, something that made them powerful in battle, something closely tied to what it meant to be Afghan," Malkasian argues. "They fought for Islam and resistance to occupation, values enshrined in Afghan identity." He judges that their truer embodiment of Afghan identity compared to Afghan government forces gave them superior morale and better staying power and was a necessary ingredient in their victory.[19]

---

[18] This section is drawn from Miller, "Review" in H-Diplo Roundtable XXIII-44 on Malkasian, *The American War in Afghanistan*, January 27, 2023.

[19] Malkasian, *The American War in Afghanistan*, 5.

Throughout the book, Malkasian presents the Taliban in their best light. "Islam blossomed under the Taliban," he writes of the Taliban government during the 1990s, "adherence to its fundamental tenets had never before been so strong" – which is an odd way to characterize religious observance when a Ministry for the Propagation of Virtue and the Prevention of Vice would harass, beat, arrest, or execute nonconformists. He calls the Taliban's form of Islam "traditional" even though their Deobandi practice was widely viewed as a foreign import from Pakistani madrassas when it first arrived in the 1990s compared to Afghans' historic practice of Hanafi Islam. He writes admiringly of the Taliban's form of order, suggesting there is "a beauty in how that order grew out of Islam and its message of oneness and justice." The victims of public beheadings likely did not see the beauty in it, nor did the Islamic clerics around the world who have condemned the Taliban's inter- pretation of their faith.[20]

Malkasian claims that in 2009 "56 percent of Afghans admitted sym- pathy for the Taliban," citing a poll by the Asia Foundation. Malkasian's claim is false; that is not what the poll asked. The poll asked about sympathy "with the motivations of armed opposition groups," and the use of violence by "anti-government groups." Considering that 60 percent of Uzbeks and 51 percent of Tajiks expressed some degree of sympathy, it is almost certain that they interpreted the question to refer to their own armed militias – that is, to warlords' illegal private armies, who fought *against* the Taliban – not to the Taliban, who were an overwhelmingly Pashtun movement. By 2019, on the eve of Taliban victory, the same poll changed its wording and asked specifically about the Taliban: the number who admitted sympathy plum- meted to 13 percent, and just 4 percent who expressed "a lot" of sympathy. How could the Taliban's victory be chalked up to popular support when they won at the nadir of their popularity?[21]

The idea that Afghans supported the Taliban underscores Malkasian's thesis that the Taliban won because they embodied the true spirit of Afghan identity, that "the Taliban stood for what it meant to be Afghan." It is likely many Pashtun men in southern provinces agreed with Malkasian and the Taliban. But it strains credulity to assume that all Afghans view Afghan identity that way. Malkasian's thesis depends on essentializing Afghan iden- tity, adopting the Taliban's perspective on it, and ascribing causal agency to it. But Afghan identity – like American identity – is contested, and that

[20] Malkasian, *The American War in Afghanistan*, 45, 50, 51, 167, 175.
[21] Malkasian, *The American War in Afghanistan*, 160. Asia Foundation, "Survey of the Afghan People," 2009, 65, and compare the 2019 report, 70.

contest was precisely what was at issue in the Afghan war. There is good evidence that the Taliban's view was the minority view compared to the 87 percent of Afghans who told pollsters they had no sympathy at all for the Taliban; to the hundreds of thousands of Afghans who served in the army and police fighting against the Taliban; to the 66,000 who died in combat against them; to millions of Tajiks, Hazaras, Uzbeks, who are excluded from Taliban governance; and to 20 million Afghan women and Shia whom the Taliban treat as enemies. They, too, embody something of the Afghan spirit.[22]

In the final pages of the book, Malkasian ruminates: "The moral question for Afghanistan boils down to whether intervention is just, how our presence harms a people, how innocents pay for our security." Malkasian concludes, "the United States exposed Afghans to prolonged harm in order to defend Americans from another terrorist attack." I agree with this verdict – the United States fought a selfish war with little regard for the Afghans – but my conclusion is that the United States should have fought a different war with much greater emphasis on reconstruction, stabilization, and state building from the beginning. Malkasian argues something closer to the opposite: that the United States should never have intervened in the first place. "Without [US] intervention, Afghans would have been deprived and oppressed, but alive," he writes in his opening pages. "We should stand back and ask: In the name of stopping terrorism for our own sake, did we liberate, or oppress, the Afghan people?"[23]

With these rhetorical questions, Malkasian suggests that the United States was an illegitimate, occupying power, and he implies a moral equivalence between the mistakes of the American war and the tyranny of Taliban rule. His notion that, without the United States, the Afghans would be "deprived and oppressed, but alive" suggests that the American war involved killing on such a mass scale as to make the Taliban's rule preferable. Yet as Malkasian himself acknowledges in more sober passages, the Afghan war was small – barely a war for Americans, and for the Afghans hardly comparable to the Soviet–Afghan War, which truly did involve mass killing and national destruction.[24]

That does not excuse American mistakes or Kabul's corruption. It is to insist on some perspective. One does not have to be an American military

---

[22] Malkasian, *The American War in Afghanistan*, 454.

[23] Malkasian, *The American War in Afghanistan*, 8, 460.

[24] Malkasian, "Response by Carter Malkasian," in H-DIPLO Roundtable. In responding to my review of his book, Malkasian wrote that I am "absolutely correct" to interpret him this way.

enthusiast to recognize that millions of Afghans rejected the false choice to be "deprived and oppressed, but alive" when they resisted the Taliban, fought against them, cast votes in elections, or otherwise put their hopes in a new and different Afghan future. They understood that without the United States and allied intervention, al-Qaida and their jihadist emulators would have continued their campaign of terror – a campaign that has killed tens of thousands of Muslims across the Middle East and South Asia. Without US intervention, a generation of Afghans would not have grown up under a regime of relatively greater freedom and opportunity. Most of all, Afghan women would never have known a brief, twenty-year respite from the world's worst gender apartheid, an existence for which Malkasian's description – "deprived and oppressed, but alive" – might lead them to ask, "but what kind of life?"

The moral question of the Afghan war was whether it was just for the United States to fight al-Qaida – which it plainly was, in which case it was just and necessary to ally with the Afghan people in their fight against al-Qaida's allies, the Taliban. That second fight – with the Afghan people against the Taliban – held out hope to create a better peace for America, Afghanistan, and the world, and to achieve lasting success (which continues to elude the United States) against international terrorist groups that threaten the United States. But since the United States rarely took that second fight seriously, it is unsurprising that we lost it. Knowing we lost makes it attractive to conclude that it was an illegitimate war in the first place; it is easier to accept defeat if we believe our side did not stand for anything admirable. It is far harder to accept the truth: the war was just and necessary – and we lost anyway.

THEORIES OF DEFEAT

We did not lose the war in Afghanistan because of a campaign of deceit by senior policymakers. We did not lose because of mission creep, Afghan culture, the unsuitability of democracy, or the intrinsically impossible nature of nation building or counterinsurgency. We certainly did not lose because the Taliban embodied Islam or Afghan identity nor because we provoked a nationalist uprising against an intrusive and illegitimate foreign occupation. There is no predetermined script that made our defeat an inevitability. What then?

There are scores of books about the war offering various explanations. Journalists' accounts focus on warlordism, corruption, and American arrogance or incompetence. Sarah Chayes, a former NPR journalist who moved to Afghanistan to run a civil society organization in Kandahar, concluded in 2006 that American support for warlords undermined Afghan democracy while American money fueled corruption. Anand Gopal, another journalist, argued that the United States' arrogant and overbearing intervention created more problems than it solved. Aid programs and warlord alliances distorted Afghan society while counterterrorism operations killed innocent Afghans and spread fear. Pakistani journalist Ahmed Rashid blames "the international community's lukewarm commitment to Afghanistan," which "has been matched only by its incompetence, incoherence, and conflicting strategies – all led by the United States."[25]

Rajiv Chandrasekaran of the *Washington Post* argued that failure "wasn't an issue of grand strategy," but rather, "the American bureaucracy has become America's worst enemy." He believed "our uniformed and civilian bureaucracies were rife with international rivalries and go-it-alone agendas. Our development experts were inept. Our leaders were distracted." In 2014, Carlotta Gall, the Afghanistan and Pakistan correspondent for the *New York Times*, struck a different emphasis when she blamed the United States' inability or unwillingness to confront Pakistan, arguing that the American war in Afghanistan was fighting "the wrong enemy." The journalists' accounts are persuasive but piecemeal; the problems they identify are real, but they focus more on description than explanation.[26]

Some veterans, especially those with experience in either Vietnam or Afghanistan, find fault with American leadership for ordering the military to do the impossible. Bing West – a Marine, Vietnam War veteran, and former assistant secretary of defense in the Reagan administration – wrote in 2011 that the United States fought "the wrong war" by attempting to rebuild Afghanistan. "Mistakenly, the generals agreed that defeating an insurgency required our soldiers to be nation builders as well as war fighters." Daniel Bolger, a retired US Army Lieutenant General and veteran of the wars in Iraq and Afghanistan, made the same argument in 2014 about counterinsurgency. US policymakers were guilty of "misusing the US Armed Forces, which are designed, manned, and equipped for short, decisive, conventional conflict," not for "long, indecisive, counterinsurgent struggles ill-suited to the nature of our forces."[27]

---

[25] Chayes, *The Punishment of Virtue*. Gopal, *No Good Men among the Living*. Rashid, *Descent into Chaos*, xxxix.

[26] Chandrasekaran, *Little America*, 329, 331–332. Gall, *The Wrong Enemy*.

[27] West, *The Wrong War*, xiii. Bolger, *Why We Lost*.

Karl Eikenberry, who headed American efforts in Afghanistan first as commanding general of US forces and later as US ambassador to Afghanistan, made a similar argument in 2013. Eikenberry, using the acronym for counterinsurgency, argued that "COIN failed in Afghanistan." Counterinsurgency is an unworkable theory: "'Protect the population' is a vague and open-ended guide to action, with increased effort alone regarded as an end in itself," he argued. "Deploying highly trained US soldiers to Afghanistan to serve as social workers or to manage development projects comes at a high price."[28]

I am unconvinced that the war was inherently unwinnable. There are examples of successful state building and counterinsurgency elsewhere in the world, including in geographically challenging places, and – despite what some US policymakers later claimed – Afghan culture and history are not a constant record of insurgency, terrorism, or drug trafficking. There was nothing inevitable about the war turning out the way it did. It is true that many things made the intervention in Afghanistan more difficult and less likely to succeed, but claiming the war was unwinnable by its very nature is an overly simplistic explanation that conveniently exonerates all but the most senior policymakers for the United States' failure. It also leaves unanswered why policymakers made such choices. Why did we not recognize the challenging nature of those missions and adjust accordingly? Why did we not make better choices to either change those parameters, if possible, or more effectively maneuver within them, if not? Within the range of possible outcomes, why did we choose the worst one?

A third group, the community of defense and foreign policy intellectuals – Americans who work in think tanks and public policy schools, some of them with policy experience – tend not to blame American arrogance, nor do they believe the war was an impossible mission. They tend to focus on specific strategic decisions that, they believe, set the war on a failing course. Jim Dobbins, a diplomat with experience in Afghanistan who later led research at the RAND Corporation, points to the low levels of aid the United States gave to Afghanistan in the early years of the intervention. He argues that Afghanistan was a failed state, and weak or nonexistent governance was the enabling condition that allowed the Taliban to return. Michael O'Hanlon of the Brookings Institution sees flaws at each stage of the war. He blames the Bush administration for not doing more to help build the Afghan state earlier on, but he also blames the Obama administration for subsequently trying to do

---

[28] Eikenberry, "The Limits of Counterinsurgency Doctrine."

too much, too quickly during the surge. He also argued that the United States changed strategy too often.[29]

Steve Biddle of Columbia University pointed to the centralized democratic model of governance established by the Afghan constitution, arguing it was incompatible with Afghanistan's needs. Separately, he found fault with the United States' inability to enter serious negotiations with the Taliban. Joe Collins, who served as assistant secretary of defense for stability operations and later taught at the National Defense University, highlighted the United States' poor track record in capacity building. "The United States has for a decade argued in its advisory and development activities that 'teaching people how to fish is better than giving them fish,'" he wrote in 2011. "The truth of the matter is, however, that the United States is superb at providing fish and not very good at teaching people how to fish."[30]

Anthony Cordesman, though solidly a member of the defense intellectual community at the Center for Strategic and International Studies, blends arguments from all three communities. He agrees with O'Hanlon that the US never settled on a coherent strategy, echoes the journalists that the war was never worth the investment of resources the United States put into it in the first place, and shares with the veterans the view that "the US might have done better by avoiding any effort to rapidly transform Afghan politics, governance, security forces, and its economy." Similarly, Ben Barry, a veteran of the British military and fellow at the London-based International Institute for Strategic Studies, argued that the US and Britain were distracted by Iraq, overstretched in their military resources, with an unrealistic expectation of succeeding in both – and that they suffered from a lack of clear military strategy and poor implementation.[31]

A THEORY OF VICTORY

I have more sympathy for these kinds of explanations because the only two laws of history are that nothing is impossible, and nothing is inevitable. Any

---

[29] Dobbins et al., *The UN's Role in Nation-Building* and *America's Role in Nation-Building*. Michael O'Hanlon, "A Preliminary Verdict on Afghanistan Strategy," The Brookings Institution, October 5, 2021. www.brookings.edu/articles/a-preliminary-verdict-on-afgh anistan-strategy/.

[30] Biddle et al., "Defining Success in Afghanistan," and Biddle, "Ending the War in Afghanistan." Collins, *Understanding War in Afghanistan*, 114.

[31] Cordesman, *Learning the Right Lessons*, 15. Barry, *Blood, Metal, and Dust.*

historical explanation that begins with an assertion that something as complex as America's defeat in Afghanistan was inevitable is not very insightful, nor are arguments that start from the premise that nation building or counterinsurgency are intrinsically impossible. Such claims ignore that the *way* we failed was unique and could have happened differently. They overlook the occasional successes that suggest failure was an option, not an inevitability. It is clear to me that specific decisions by US policymakers caused direct, avoidable harm to the war effort, and that they could have been decided differently. We did not have to lose – certainly, not in the time and manner we did in August 2021 – which suggests our defeat was a choice.

In military terms, strategy is the proper linkage of *ends, ways,* and *means,* or between ultimate goals, courses of action, and tools and resources.[32] Defeating al-Qaida, shutting down their safe haven, and preventing and deterring future attacks was the *end* or goal of the overall War on Terror. Because of the tie between al-Qaida and the Taliban, defeating the Taliban and rebuilding Afghanistan were necessary, though subordinate, objectives (or ends of the war in Afghanistan, distinct from the war against al-Qaida). Counterinsurgency and nation building were thus the required *ways*; and reconstruction money and counterinsurgency troops were the *means.* In light of that linkage, the lack of counterinsurgency and reconstruction assistance for the first five years was disastrous. Afghanistan remained a failed state, the Taliban were able to regroup and launch an insurgency, and al-Qaida regained safe haven. Earlier aid, sustained for longer, could have changed the trajectory of the war.

Put another way, winning the counterinsurgency war against the Taliban was a necessary precondition to winning the counterterrorism war against al-Qaida. It sounds counterintuitive, but the way to defeat al-Qaida was not simply to kill individual terrorists day after day until they were all dead. Winning meant *permanently* defeating al-Qaida, *permanently* denying safe haven, which meant, in turn, building something in Afghanistan capable of fighting terrorists and denying safe haven so that US troops could go home. So long as jihadist ideas survive (likely forever), we can only defeat them by killing as many as we can (through counterterrorism) while also constraining their movement, starving them of resources, and depriving them of recruits (through counterinsurgency), and building up alternatives to their vision (through nation building). Counterterrorism operations are necessary but insufficient by themselves; counterinsurgency and nation building – of some kind, at

---

[32] Lykke, Jr., "Defining Military Strategy."

some scale – should have been essential components of our long-term strategy. But in practice, we continuously traded short-term progress killing terrorists for long-term setbacks and delays building Afghan capacity until, after twenty years, we had a pile of dead terrorists yet no Afghan state or army strong enough to stand on its own.

The Bush and Obama administrations rightly, if belatedly, shifted to a counterinsurgency strategy, though still overshadowed by Iraq. But a new problem arose. Where the effort had previously been starved of troops and money, now the effort was starved of time. Obama's withdrawal timetable undercut his entire strategy and made the halting progress of the surge and counterinsurgency era fragile and easily reversible. The timetable also created an extraordinarily damaging sense of hurry, converting billions of dollars needed for reconstruction and stabilization into a massive exercise in waste, fraud, abuse, and corruption, leading to the administration's disillusionment and premature abandonment of nation-building efforts. And Obama failed to synchronize his military escalation with diplomatic efforts. Without the timetable, the United States might have had the time to do reconstruction and counterinsurgency more slowly, on a longer time-frame, with more sustainable results. Without the timetable, Obama's surge might have driven the Taliban to a favorable negotiated settlement at the point of maximum US military leverage.

Instead, by the end of Obama's presidency, the war had ground down to a simmering stalemate. The US was making no progress toward long-term victory, but it could indefinitely hold the Taliban at bay and keep an eye on al-Qaida. It was sustainable, though morally questionable and costly for the Afghans. Unfortunately, by the time the Trump administration took office, there was little opportunity to reinvest in stabilization and reconstruction even if Trump had been inclined to do so. Instead, after an eighteen-month delay, he gave up even on a sustainable, minimal presence. He pursued a negotiated settlement while, at the same time, unilaterally withdrawing US troops, the worst possible conditions under which to negotiate with an enemy in wartime. The 2020 Doha agreement paved the way for the Taliban's victory, making all the more inexplicable Biden's choice to adhere to the agreement and complete the withdrawal in 2021.

THE PROBLEM OF "REALISM"

Why did we make these choices? The answer, I believe, lies in a combination of how we think, the strategic trade-offs we accepted, and the nature of bureaucracy. Certain features of American strategic culture made us blind to the unique demands of the war in Afghanistan and the war against al-Qaida, leading us to persistent short-term strategies at the expense of long-term victory; but even after we recognized and tried to adapt, the bureaucracy proved largely inflexible and unable to match policymakers' growing strategic awareness. We lost because we defined our interests and goals in narrow, truncated, self-oriented ways, which affected the strategies we chose, which became institutionalized in bureaucratic pathologies.

We lost, first, because of specific strategic missteps and poor decisions. The foreign policy intellectuals are right: the seeds of our defeat were sown by our own choices. But not just one: there was a series of bad choices all along the way. There is a very long list of decisions, small and large, that critics contend were made poorly, including the pace of troop rotations, the failure to train enough linguists, designing a confused military chain of command, adopting a light footprint, under-resourcing the effort, waging two wars simultaneously, ordering a surge and withdrawal under deadline, and negotiating with the Taliban at the nadir of our leverage.

However, I am not convinced that any of the thousand small mistakes, if reversed, would have led to success. Nor am I convinced that any one large single decision could explain the twenty-year failure. If the war was lost by a decision in December 2001 (the light footprint), or March 2003 (the invasion of Iraq), or December 2009 (the withdrawal timetable), why did the United States stay until 2021? That itself was another decision that needs explanation and that contributed to the *specific* defeat we suffered. I want an explanation for why we lost in the particular time and manner that we did. Only a unique path could have led us there.

We cannot argue that "if we had made *every* decision differently, we would have succeeded," because that is a little like arguing that if we waged a different war with different decision-makers and if we were a different nation, we would achieve a different outcome. That may be true, but it is not very insightful. It leaves unanswered one large question: Why did the United States make a thousand small mistakes? Why did we wage the war we did? Why are we the kind of nation we are? Only a repeated habit of decision-making or a way of thinking about the war and about America's role in it explains consistent strategic miscalculation that led to defeat. I argue that we were predisposed to thinking about this war in an unhelpful way. We framed the war, defined its purpose, and prioritized tasks within it in ways that had to do more with our cultural and characterological preferences than with what strategic logic would have demanded. We fought the war we wanted to fight rather than the war we needed to fight.

Policymakers (including me) consistently exhibit a collection of cognitive biases, like hyperbolic discounting (valuing smaller short-term rewards more than larger long term ones), the Delmore effect (the tendency to specify more concrete goals for lesser priorities), the law of triviality (organizations spend more time on trivial but simple tasks than complex, important ones), and ambiguity bias (we favor options that are articulated more clearly because we dislike uncertainty and ambiguity). The common thread is that policymakers favor the appearance of simplicity and comprehensibility, which proves self-defeating when faced with a complex and ambiguous challenge, like war, counterinsurgency, and nation building. While these are universal cognitive biases, they may be especially true of Americans because of our known tendency to be present-oriented, ahistorical, and pragmatic. Americans are uncomfortable with the vagaries of history and strategy.

These biases are reinforced and worsened by the academic discipline of international relations and its dominant school of "realism," in which many policymakers are steeped. This may sound counterintuitive to readers who have only heard of "realism" when presidential candidates invoke it to sound tough, hawkish, and hard-nosed. That sort of realism bears no relation to academic "realism," which is best understood as ideological opposition to moral aspiration in politics. A variety of twentieth-century thinkers such as Hans Morgenthau, E. H. Carr, Kenneth Waltz, and John Mearsheimer argued that naive idealists like Woodrow Wilson and his vision of making the world safe for democracy were to blame for the failure of the peace after World War I, planting the seeds for its sequel. To avoid such catastrophe in the future, policymakers had to be "realistic," that is, they had to stop chasing large moralistic dreams and instead accept and work within the constraints of the world as it is. This kind of "realism" is opposed, in principle, to nation building and democracy promotion, arguing they are too aspirational, moralistic, and utopian: they are the problem of, not the solution to, American foreign policy.[33]

This proved disastrous when faced with an enormously complex challenge after the terrorist attacks of 2001. I am not arguing, as some have done, that the mysteries of Afghan culture proved too formidable for naive American analysts. Rather, the vagary I have in mind is the relationship between the various kinds of intervention the United States attempted in

---

[33] By contrast, I am making a "constructivist" argument insofar as I argue the United States should have aspired to alter the social reality of Afghanistan through counterinsurgency and nation building.

Afghanistan. Over twenty years, the United States undertook counterterror-ism, counterinsurgency, counternarcotics, reconstruction, stabilization, economic development, democracy promotion, state building, and more. The relationship among them should have been governed by the strategic logic of the war: defeating al-Qaida (the goal) required defeating the Taliban and rebuilding Afghanistan to a level of self-sufficiency (subordin-ate goals), which in turn required counterinsurgency and nation building (ways and means). Counterinsurgency and nation building should have been the main effort of the American intervention, the conceptual focus that tied together and coordinated all the other vast and diffuse efforts.

Instead, policymakers in every administration prioritized counterterrorism – a comparatively simple, easily defined, immediate, "realistic," concrete mis-sion with specific, easily countable metrics of success (dead terrorists). They subordinated broader, more ambiguous, harder-to-define, morally aspir-ational, long-term efforts, such as counterinsurgency and nation building. They told themselves they were being "realistic," which was the conscious justification for a host of unconscious cognitive biases.

Policymakers did so even though – as repeated strategy reviews showed – the Taliban and al-Qaida were linked; success in the war against either depended on success against both; and counterinsurgency and nation build-ing were necessary, alongside counterterrorism operations, to achieve the larger goal of al-Qaida's defeat. Every president understood that building Afghan capacity was the American exit strategy: we deny safe haven to al-Qaida long enough for the Afghans to do it on their own, then we can leave. The war was not – or should not have been – only a war to kill a single terrorist or destroy a single group, but also to deny safe haven and deter future attacks. That required a longer-term, broader, and, yes, aspirational approach.

When children first learn chess, they immediately attack the oppos-ing king because that is the goal of the game. Seasoned players under-stand the principles of material, position, and initiative: getting control of the board, controlling the pace of play, establishing strong positions, recognizing the enemy's patterns, and denying him space for maneuver before the final assault. Counterinsurgency and nation building were about controlling the board, denying the enemy space, establishing a strong position, creating an environment favorable for our movement and hostile to his. Our policymakers and strategists played childish chess: mounting a frontal assault on the enemy king over and over, killing terrorists year after year, telling themselves that was the "realis-tic" strategy – while ignoring the state of play, the shape of the board, and the future of Afghanistan.

In coming to this answer, I have been deeply influenced by an argument from the mid twentieth-century theologian Reinhold Niebuhr about how nations define their interests. As I discussed in one of my earlier books, Niebuhr warned against the self-defeating "'realism' of those who are myopically realistic by seeing only their own interests and failing thereby to do justice to their interests where they are involved with the interests of others." Such realists "counsel the nation to consult only its own interests." But, he warns:

> a consistent self-interest on the part of a nation will work *against* its interests, because it will fail to do justice to the broader and longer interests, which are involved with the interests of other nations. A narrow national loyalty on our part, for instance, will obscure our long range interests where they are involved with those of a whole alliance of free nations.[34]

Niebuhr called himself a Christian Realist. He *agreed* with the "realist" critique of Wilson and the naivete of liberal internationalism. But Niebuhr could not agree with the cynical alternative of secular, academic "realism" because he believed that it did not actually understand the nature of reality. Niebuhr understood that nations could defeat themselves by defining their self-interest so narrowly they ignored and even undermined the broader community of nations and the culture of world order in which they existed. The best understanding of the "national interest" considers the broader world in which the nation is situated. We live in a community of nations; if we keep our head down and pursue our gain without thinking about how it affects others, we're bound to knock about and alienate others, making it harder, not easier, on ourselves.

In Afghanistan, the US treated Afghans' interests as only instrumentally important, important insofar as they could help us kill a few more terrorists; but that very approach is what ensured the United States did very little to advance Afghans' interests, which guaranteed that the broader social and political environment remained hostile, empowered the Taliban, and made it impossible to defeat al-Qaida permanently. The US defeated itself by trying to solve one problem – terrorism – without appreciation for how that problem grew from a complex political, social, cultural, and economic environment. Often US efforts ignored those aspects of the problem; sometimes our efforts actively made them worse. But even when the United States recognized the broader aspects of the problem, it addressed them in short-term, truncated ways that were shallow and sought only to make them "good

---

[34] Niebuhr, "Augustine's Political Realism," 134 in *The Essential Reinhold Niebuhr.*

enough" from the US perspective, rarely sustainable for the long term on their own merits, like building an Afghan army that could hold off the Taliban but which Afghanistan could not sustain. By prioritizing counter-terrorism, the United States ensured it would fail in counterinsurgency and state building – which in turn undermined any long-term counterterrorism success. The United States approached the war in Afghanistan like riot-control police who congratulate themselves on arresting looters to save the neighborhood – while it burns down around them.

Statesmanship requires a broader and longer-term perspective, an appreciation for the national interest broadly defined, one informed by historical understanding and unapologetic moral aspiration. American pol-icymakers from both parties in four administrations adopted the opposite, consistently choosing a narrow, short-term, "realistic" definition of the national interest that prioritized immediate US safety from terrorists and subordinated other aspects of its intervention. US policymakers' thinking about the war in Afghanistan was consistently short-term, truncated, and narrow, often with only secondary or peripheral regard for the interests of the Afghan people, the nations of South Asia, or the world – and sometimes at the expense of them. Even more remarkably, repeated strategy reviews continued to stress the need to reframe the war to account for the broader, long-term context, yet each president was unable or unwilling to fully commit to what his own strategy reviews called for. Because of that short-termism, US efforts did not improve and sometimes actively hurt the broader environment in which the American intervention took place – which, in turn, ended up redounding to the United States' disadvantage. We killed an invasive species of fish while ignoring the poison in the water.

Such "realism" defeated the United States. In Afghanistan, the United States was self-absorbed, myopic, and provincial. The "realism" of post-Cold War American strategic culture predisposes US policymakers to define American national interests narrowly, so narrowly that it becomes self-defeating. A generation of policymakers was so besotted with the urgent need to be ruthlessly pragmatic that they ended up pragmatically choosing defeat.

BUREAUCRACY DOES ITS THING

Habits of thinking only explain so much. At some points, three of the four presidential administrations – all but Biden's – hit on components of the right strategic approach. Bush's 2006 and 2008 strategy reviews got the outline basically right, as did Obama's first 2009 review. The surge, counter-insurgency, and more reconstruction assistance were all necessary and appropriate efforts. Trump's 2017 South Asia Strategy was about the best that could be envisioned at the time. Though he forswore nation building and invested nothing in Afghan capacity, he did much better than Obama's post-surge strategy in treating the war as a war. Many policymakers at various points correctly understood the nature of the war and endorsed compo-nents of the right strategy: they got the right words on paper.

Getting the words right means nothing if you cannot implement them, and this brings us to the second major reason why America lost Afghanistan: the nature of bureaucracy. Policymakers make decisions; those decisions get translated into programs, budgets, troop deployments, and personnel assign-ments. They become embedded in the bureaucratic machinery of the US government's executive branch. Sometimes policymakers made bad choices, and the bureaucracy became institutionally vested in perpetuating them. When policymakers chose bad strategy, the bureaucracy kept implementing bad strategy on autopilot and resisted change when policymakers and repeated strategy reviews highlighted the problem. Sometimes policymakers recognized their bad choices through repeated strategy reviews, yet the intellectual task of coming up with better ideas was the easy part: it proved extraordinarily difficult to force change through the system into new budgets, programs, deployments, and assignments. And sometimes policymakers had good ideas yet could not make the bureaucracy do the thing they wanted to get done because the bureaucracy captured and reinterpreted their ideas to accommodate bureaucratic preference.

"It was never difficult to decide what should be done," General Maxwell Taylor, commander of the Military Assistance Command in Vietnam (MACV), once reflected, "but it was almost impossible to get it done, at least in an acceptable period of time." Taylor's comment is captured in a report by Robert Komer in 1972. Komer was head of Civil Operations and Revolutionary Development Support in the Vietnam War. He was the chief civilian charged with coordinating the civilian component of counterinsur-gency. Komer's report, *Bureaucracy Does Its Thing*, is required reading in my class on strategy and should be required reading for every student of public policy and international affairs. "The policymaker must take fully into account the ability of institutions carrying out the policy to execute it as intended. Adequate follow-through machinery at all levels is also needed, to force adap-tation if necessary," Komer argued. The parallels fifty years later are striking.[35]

---

[35] Komer, *Bureaucracy Does Its Thing*, xii, 7–8.

A bureaucracy is a collection of humans hired to perform specific, discrete tasks, according to a set of rules and procedures laid down in the bureaucracy's charter. But it is also a public concentration of political power, vested with authority to do things and spend money. As such, it behaves the way every person and institution with power has ever behaved: it protects and expands its own power. A bureaucracy's main purpose – the goal of its own strategy, so to speak – is its own perpetuation and the increase of its power, wealth, and jurisdiction. I'm not being cynical or judgmental; I'm describing what decades of social science has consistently catalogued. Bureaucracies can be made to do useful things if they perceive that doing so will enhance their power. And so most bureaucracies at least make a show of doing the thing they were commissioned to do. The post office delivers the mail, the military kills people, and your local power company provides electricity. But given a conflict between protecting their power and undertaking a new mission, they will choose power every time. Bureaucracies are not set up to ask big questions or reevaluate their purpose. They're like robot vacuum cleaners. You turn them on and set them loose. They take dumb, meandering paths through the house, ram into walls, and take twice as long as you would if you just did it yourself, but eventually about half the carpet is a little cleaner.

Once a bureaucracy is ensconced and performing a function, it will go on doing that function on autopilot forever whether it is achieving anything, because doing something means it can keep getting money from Congress. And then it can ask Congress for even more money to do its thing a little better, or to do more of it, or to expand. What it will never do is tell Congress that its function is unnecessary or ineffective. "It is difficult to alter course," Komer wrote. "Instead, programs tend to acquire a built-in momentum of their own. And if obstacles are encountered, the natural tendency is to do more of the same – to pour on more coal – rather than to rethink the problem and try to adjust response patterns." Fast-forward to Afghanistan: "A project that completed required tasks would be considered 'successful,' whether or not it had achieved or contributed to broader, more important goals," wrote the Special Inspector General for Afghanistan Reconstruction.[36]

Komer thought that this "institutional inertia" was one of the fundamental dynamics of his war. The "built-in reluctance of organizations to change preferred ways of functioning except slowly and incrementally" affected every issue. The complex and changing dynamic of a war like

---

[36] Komer, *Bureaucracy Does Its Thing*, 66. SIGAR, "What We Need to Learn," XI.

Vietnam – with overlapping challenges of combat, training, reconstruction, economic development, and more – required adaptability, creativity, and flexibility. While it took policymakers and military officials years to understand the challenge, once they did, they still could not make headway against it because their tools for doing so were inadequate. Their tools – the bureaucracy – "preferred doing more of what it was already used to doing, rather than change accepted patterns of organization or operation."[37]

Compare Bob Komer's observations about Vietnam to General Stan McChrystal's about Afghanistan. "[The army] was unwilling to go to war," McChrystal told me. "All of the institutional processes and habits and whatnot that we had, we were loath to change those. We were very reluctant to say, we're at war, therefore, we're going to do some things differently." McChrystal, commander of the International Security Assistance Force (ISAF) in 2009 and 2010 and architect of the surge, was frustrated at the military bureaucracy's inflexibility. "Instead, the US Army very much wanted to continue business as usual," he said. "Unit rotations, assignments, all those kinds of things, were resistant to change, even if sometimes it was freaking obvious that you should do it." Marin Strmecki shared a similar observation about the Office of Management and Budget. "So OMB comes along and is essentially operating within the lines," he said. "It wasn't willing to help us think outside the lines . . . . or color outside the lines . . . or re-draw the lines." Wartime demands creativity and flexibility, neither of which are hallmarks of bureaucracy.[38]

Worse, the bureaucracy actively undermined and reshaped Washington's articulated policy and strategy. "Each organization inevitably tended to make policy conform in practice to that with which it was most familiar – to play out its standard organizational repertoire," Komer wrote. This is what policymakers in DC find most maddening. Policymakers make a decision, give it to the implementers, and the implementers reshape the decision to suit what they are already doing, what they are most comfortable with, and what will be most advantageous for their next budget request. The implementers effectively freelance their own foreign policy. It is the perfect way to undermine strategy. The means come to define the end, rather than the other way around; the bureaucracy dictates the goal rather than the goal directing the bureaucracy. The bureaucracy "did the thing that we had the most readily available capacity to do whether or not it was the most relevant," Komer wrote.

---

[37] Komer, *Bureaucracy Does Its Thing*, ix.

[38] McChrystal, interview by author. Strmecki, SIGAR interview.

"Whatever overall policy called for, the means available tended to dictate what we actually did."[39]

Peter Lavoy, who served in a variety of roles in the intelligence community, the NSC, and the Department of Defense throughout the war in Afghanistan, saw the same dynamic. The president could become a victim of his own success. "Ironically, the more effective you are, the more you disrupt attacks against the homeland . . . it means the president has to spend less time [on it], and so he spends time on other things," Lavoy said. "The organizations themselves have delegated authority, so they start going back to their own muscle movements, their muscle memory of how they like to operate." That's when integrated strategy starts to unravel. "Then you get these incoherent inconsistencies that diverge from that clear focused strategy from the beginning."[40]

Andrew Erdman, the NSC director for Iran, Iraq, and strategic planning, expanded on the theme of bureaucratic pathologies at length. "Afghanistan became a means to an end, a way for bureaucracies to enhance their prominence or relevance, or a new way to justify old programs," he said. It was a classic case of a self-licking ice-cream cone: a self-perpetuating activity with no purpose other than itself. "Bureaucratic needs drove strategy, rather than the other way around," he said. Once bureaucracies understood that "Afghanistan" was a justification that could be used to perpetuate themselves, they had a "vested interest in being involved in Afghanistan," not for the sake of making a difference in Afghanistan, but for Afghanistan to make a difference for them. Ambassador Marc Grossman believed that "our reconstruction efforts and, God bless them, our aid efforts and all of that enormous money and time and talent and everything else that we put into it . . . It was about the projects and about us rather than about [Afghans'] employment."[41]

Bureaucratic pathologies account for a host of problems that critics observed about the war in Afghanistan (and Vietnam and elsewhere). "One consequence of [South Vietnamese] and US attempts to deal with the unusual requirements of insurgency war through the existing bureaucratic structure was a plethora of programs conducted by different agencies," Komer wrote, "each jealously guarding its prerogatives and insistent on its own procedures."[42] I heard a chorus of similar observations about bureaucratic reduplication and poor coordination throughout the Afghan war. Each

---

[39] Komer, *Bureaucracy Does Its Thing*, 14.   [40] Lavoy, interview by author.
[41] Erdmann and Grossman, interviews by author.
[42] Komer, *Bureaucracy Does Its Thing*, 77.

agency – and coalition partner and NGO and multilateral organization – wanted a piece of the action, so there were scores upon scores of offices, programs, organization, and actors involved in Afghanistan, making cohesion nearly impossible.

The problem with bureaucracy and implementation is not simple incompetence, though the Special Inspector General for Afghanistan Reconstruction found plenty of that. Bureaucracy institutionalizes the intellectual habit of seeking clarity, prioritizing what is measurable, and focusing on the immediate and short term at the expense of the long term. Policymakers started out in that mindset, which accounts for why the intervention in Afghanistan drifted for the first few years. But even when some policymakers understood that the challenge required a different approach – as they did in repeated strategy reviews – they faced enormous obstacles to imposing change on the bureaucracy. It can be done, as this book shows, but – to return to policymakers' strategic decisions – key strategic errors at crucial points undermined their ability to do so.

DEFEAT IN THEIR OWN WORDS

In writing this book, I have not simply recapitulated the views I came to as they took shape during the war. Rather, I have gone back to reexamine the war, including my small part in it, in light of new information, new scholarship, and the perspective that comes with some time and distance from the subject, especially now that the war has reached its conclusion. I've changed some of my views – for example, about reconstruction at the height of Obama's surge, recognizing that too much, too fast was actively harmful; and about the necessity of opening a dialogue with the Taliban in conjunction with the surge. I've reviewed policymakers' memoirs, government documents, and scholars' first efforts at writing a complete history of the war.

But more than that, this book benefits from interviews with scores of former US policymakers in the aftermath of the war's ending. In 2021–2023, I sat down and talked with dozens of key decision-makers in the Bush, Obama, and Trump administrations, including six national security advisors, four secretaries of defense, one secretary of state, seven ISAF or Coalition commanders, and over a dozen US ambassadors to Afghanistan and special representatives for Afghanistan and Pakistan. With few exceptions, these interviews were on the record, and I quote from them extensively throughout this book. (Officials in the Biden administration, still in office while I wrote this book, were unwilling to talk on the record.) I found almost all my interviewees were willing and eager to talk – no doubt, in part, to protect their legacies, settle old scores, or get their preferred narrative into the history books. (Anecdotally, I detected more finger-pointing among the Trump officials I spoke to.)

But I also got a strong sense from most interviewees that they wanted to talk because they knew the questions I was asking were important, and that if we failed to learn anything after twenty years' effort and frustration, then it will truly have been in vain. The officials I spoke to cooperated with this project even though they knew their own role would come under scrutiny. Even the most cynical observer must recognize that policymakers tell themselves that they are working in good faith and full sincerity to serve the public good (and, having been in their shoes, I tend to believe most of them, most of the time, except for Trump). That self-understanding leads them naturally to cooperate with efforts at a full historical accounting, even if they also bring their own agenda to the table. I found the more junior officials I spoke to tended to be freer with their comments and critique, while more senior officials, who may have felt they had more to lose, tended to keep their comments in more predictable bounds. Even so, as I hope the reader finds, some of the interviews were startling for their frankness.

I benefited from the accidental timing of this project. I did not plan to start my interviews and research immediately after the fall of Kabul, but that is how the funding and timing lined up. As a result, the policymakers I spoke to were freshly aware of how the war had ended, and many were especially reflective, even confessional. Some – the ones who spent multiple tours over a decade or more on the war – were emotional. Because I have told this story through the words of its participants, it is close to being an oral history of policymaking about the Afghan war. Critics may accuse me of writing the US government's official version of events, of being the court stenographer faithfully recounting exactly what those in power want remembered. If so, it is, in places, a remarkably self-critical stenography. It is often said that history is written by the victors. This book is the opposite: a history of defeat, told by its architects.

It is more than stenography, of course. I not only describe and explain how and why policymakers made their decisions; I assess and critique them. That might invite another criticism: that I am partisan or unfair, or that I am hopelessly subjective because of my own involvement. Whether I am unfair or not is up to the reader to decide: I have serious criticisms of all four administrations who oversaw the war, though not in equal measure. As for partisanship, I lay my cards on the table: I was a Republican until 2016, when Trump drove people like me out of the party, and have been contentedly independent since. And I freely admit that my judgments are subjective because I do not believe there are any other kind. In the few places where my own small role merits comment (in Chapters 6–7), this book mixes history with memoir.

In one respect, some readers may come away unsatisfied. My goal is not personal recrimination or finger-pointing. For the most part, I have left unreported the gossip, slander, and innuendo I occasionally heard in my interviews. We already know the individuals who are most directly responsible for losing Afghanistan: George W. Bush, Barack Obama, Donald Trump, and Joe Biden. As commanders-in-chief, they bear ultimate responsibility for the war they led. The buck stops with them; that is enough for me. (All four declined to be interviewed for this book.) I critique the debate surrounding some of the largest decisions each administration made, including the lines of argument some individual policymakers advanced. But, by and large, while subordinates sometimes gave bad advice or did not implement decisions as competently as could be expected, I see little to be gained by assembling a comprehensive ledger of merits and demerits for every policymaker who touched the war over twenty years. I have no personal axes to grind.

My focus is elsewhere. This is a study of foreign policy decision-making, but not from a typical angle. I am trying to convey what it feels like, from the inside, to have responsibility at any level for any part of a major foreign policy issue, to be a cog in the vast and lumbering machine that is the US government and the interagency process. I teach courses on strategy and decision-making, and I know of few books that convey the humanity of it. Most are works that analyze – drily, impersonally, and from the outside – how the process is supposed to work, and they do almost nothing to prepare my students for what it is really like to be the proverbial "man in the arena" (who is soon more likely to be a woman, judging from the gender balance in my classrooms). It seems to me that there is a visceral, experiential dimension to the process that needs attention. I hope the human dimension shows through the policymakers' words. In that sense, this book aspires to be a unique contribution to the literature on strategy, decision-making, US foreign policy, bureaucracy, and the psychology of the foreign policy process.

I am specifically interested in tracing what we think, *how* we think, how we debate with colleagues, and how our beliefs translated into decisions, decisions into action, and action into defeat. That is why this book recounts policymakers' beliefs in their own words. I want to capture what they believed and how those beliefs became strategy before I critique the strategy – not because the sincerity of belief makes for better strategy (every misadventure is honestly begun), but in the hopes of making even bad strategy more explicable. Understanding the *how* and *why* helps convey the humanity of the policymakers, which might help the reader recognize themselves and judge more fairly. More, I want my students and future policymakers to recognize themselves, to understand that regular people can make mistakes and to know that even if a mistake is honest, it can have large consequences. You don't need to be a cackling villain to bring ruin to yourself and others. If there is any lesson, it is humility: "Lean not on your own understanding."

This is very much an American story – not because other voices are unimportant, but because other voices merit books of their own. The voice I most regret leaving out is the Afghans' voice – so I stress again, this is not a comprehensive history of the war, but of American decision-making about the war. Indeed, one of the main lessons of this narrative is that American decision-making too often did not include the Afghan perspective and that the war effort needed more local ownership. But every story needs boundary lines to remain coherent. I chose these boundaries because the conversation among American policymakers was the most consequential in setting the course of the international project in Afghanistan.

Neither policymakers' recollections nor their memoirs are fully reliable, nor are they complete. The story I tell in what follows is also drawn from other historians and contemporary journalistic accounts, all of which serve to balance and inform one another. The one missing piece is the documentary record, buried in still-classified archives, which will not be available for another decade or two for the Bush and Obama administrations, and another generation for the Trump and Biden administrations. This, then, is a first draft, an effort to tell the story of how and why American policymakers made the decisions they did, and how we chose defeat in Afghanistan.

2

2001

Victory

"We will make no distinction between the terrorists who committed these acts and those who harbor them," President George W. Bush said in a televised address to the nation on the evening of September 11, 2001. "We stand together to win the war against terrorism." In this first speech, hours after al-Qaida's terrorist attacks in New York, Washington, DC, and Shanksville, Pennsylvania, Bush called the conflict a "war" and said that the enemy was not just the group that the hijackers affiliated with, but their government sponsors, "those who harbor them." The United States Congress swiftly passed an Authorization for the Use of Military Force (AUMF), giving the president authority to carry out operations against anyone found to be behind the attacks and anyone who had "harbored such organizations or persons." As the world discovered in coming days, that meant the United States was going to war against the Taliban.[1]

The United States lost – but not right away. In fact, within months it appeared as if the reverse were true. The Bush administration improvised an impressive campaign to overthrow the Taliban regime, destroy al-Qaida's safe haven in Afghanistan, and, seemingly, put the country on the road to stability. What happened to unravel that early success? The Bush administration faced three major strategic choices between September 11 and October 7, when the military campaign started: how to define the war, what to do about the Taliban, and what kind of military footprint to deploy. The administration chose to frame the conflict as a War on Terror, to treat the Taliban as of secondary importance, and to adopt a light footprint. The first choice – to declare a War on Terror – has been the subject of ample and justified criticism, then and now. The latter two choices made more sense at the time, and the Taliban's fall from power two months later, on December 7,

---

[1] "Statement by the President in His Address to the Nation," September 11, 2001. https://georgewbush-whitehouse.archives.gov/news/releases/2001/09/20010911-16.html. "Authorization for the Use of Military Force," Public Law 107–40 (September 18, 2001).

seemed to vindicate the administration's impressive improvisation. But the sense of vindication also numbed the administration to the need to adapt as circumstances changed.

"WAR ON TERROR"

The United States was at war – but with whom, and to what end? The Bush administration faced a decision about how to frame the war, how to define its goals, and how to identify the enemy. From the beginning, the president pushed to define the war expansively. "Our war on terror begins with al-Qaida, but it does not end there," Bush told Congress on September 20. "It will not end until every terrorist group of global reach has been found, stopped and defeated." He repeatedly identified the enemy as "terrorists" or "terrorism." He used the word "terror" and its derivatives over thirty times in the speech, but "al-Qaida" just six times and "Taliban" only five times.[2]

The administration's desire to define the war expansively was understandable. The attack on the United States was brutal, public, and humiliating. Thousands were dead – more Americans were killed on 9/11 than during the attack on Pearl Harbor in 1941 – and Lower Manhattan looked and felt like a war zone. It took three and a half months to put the fires out beneath the rubble of the World Trade Center. Smoke from the Pentagon could be seen from Capitol Hill and the White House. To say that the American public was angry and fearful does not communicate the unified rage and the demand to *do something* that gripped the nation in the days and months after the attack.

Eric Edelman, then advising Vice President Dick Cheney on national security affairs, visited Ground Zero in New York with Cheney in October. He recalls "surveying a five-block square area of devastation, with the ground still smoking, the fumes still coming up from the ground, the smell of death everywhere because you had decaying bodies buried throughout the whole area. There was no choice but for the president to do something that would attempt to root out the terrorist threat." The administration knew it had not only to respond, but to respond in a big, demonstrative way – something that Bush was temperamentally suited to do anyway. "My first reaction was outrage," Bush later wrote. "Someone had dared attack America. They were going to pay." Within hours of the attacks,

---

[2] "Address to a Joint Session," September 20, 2001. https://georgewbush-whitehouse.arch ives.gov/news/releases/2001/09/20010920-8.html.

Bush told Cheney: "We're going to find out who did this, and we're going to kick their asses."[3]

But whose asses needed kicking? CIA Director George Tenet briefed Bush and the National Security Council that al-Qaida, a terrorist group headquartered in Afghanistan, was responsible. Bush and his advisors debated the point in an NSC meeting on September 12. "Do we focus on bin Laden and al-Qaida or terrorism more broadly?" Donald Rumsfeld, the secretary of defense, asked. Colin Powell, the secretary of state, favored terrorism more broadly, and Cheney spelled out the implication: "To the extent we define our task broadly, including those who support terrorism, then we get at states." A consensus emerged quickly that the war should not be limited to al-Qaida. As discussions evolved, they debated sequential targets, broadening in scope: al-Qaida first, other terrorist groups next, and finally state sponsors of terrorism. Rumsfeld continued to stress the need to look for targets outside of Afghanistan to convey the breadth of the War on Terror. Some wanted to avoid singling out bin Laden personally, fearing it would elevate his status. They also worried that focusing too narrowly on al-Qaida might set the United States up for failure if the group proved elusive or melted away without a definitive battlefield defeat.[4]

Most importantly, they believed the war's main purpose was to set a precedent, to alter the world's calculations about the acceptability of terrorism. "The primary purpose of America's reaction to 9/11 should be prevention of attacks and the defense of the American people, not punishment or retaliation," Rumsfeld later wrote. At an NSC meeting at Camp David on September 15, "Bush said the ideal result from this campaign would be to kick terrorists out of some places like Afghanistan and through that action persuade other countries that had supported terrorism in the past, such as Iran, to change their behavior." Rumsfeld summarized the administration's war aims: to ensure that "harboring terrorists carried a price" as well as to gather intelligence against al-Qaida and the Taliban; "to develop relationships with key groups in Afghanistan that opposed the Taliban and al-Qaida"; to shut down al-Qaida's safe haven; and humanitarian operations.[5]

Doug Feith, the bespectacled and wonkish undersecretary of defense for planning, later reflected that for him and for Rumsfeld, "9/11 did not

---

[3] Edelman, interview by author. Bush, *Decision Points*, 127. Woodward, *Bush at War*, 18.

[4] Woodward, *Bush at War*, 43, 48.

[5] Rumsfeld, *Known and Unknown*, 355, 386–387. See also 403. Rice, *No Higher Honor*, 90. Woodward, *Bush at War*, 81.

mean simply that the United States had an al-Qaida problem. We had a terrorism problem. A strategic response to 9/11 would have to take account of the threat from other terrorist groups." To wage a War on Terror meant that the United States must confront "the entire network of states, non-state entities, and organizations that engage in or support terrorism against the United States and our interests, including the states that harbor terrorists. All those organizations and states constitute a threat, jointly and severally."[6]

In short, the Bush administration aspired to alter the social reality of international politics to make terrorism unthinkable. It was a breathtakingly ambitious undertaking, especially striking because of Rumsfeld's insistence, in other debates, on setting realistic, achievable goals. He and others squared the circle through the administration's belief in the United States' unmatched power. Coming at the end of a decade of talk about America as a unipolar hegemon and a "hyperpower," American policymakers saw almost limitless possibilities and few constraints on what the United States could achieve, given sufficient will, time, and resources.

Bush's sequential targets – al-Qaida first; any other terrorist group "of global reach" next; and finally state sponsors of terrorism – taken literally might imply military operations against any of the twenty-eight groups on the State Department's list of Foreign Terrorist Organizations at the time, though it is unclear how Bush intended to measure "global reach." It could also imply declarations of war against Iran, Iraq, Syria, Libya, Sudan, Cuba, and North Korea, all of which were on the State Department's list of state sponsors of terrorism in 2001. (Afghanistan was not on the list because the United States never formally recognized the Taliban as the government of Afghanistan and thus not a "state" sponsor of terrorism, one of those technicalities that perfectly illustrates how bureaucratic rationality results in irrational policy.) Of course, the administration did not intend the War on Terror to be quite that expansive. But it is instructive that some fuzziness was built into the war's purpose from the outset, and that, to the extent there was a singular focus to the overlapping conceptions of the enemy, the focus was terrorism. "The enemy was extremely hard to define and conceive of," Feith told me, and that difficulty "is part of the reason that it's called the War on Terrorism rather than the typical thing, which is calling it the war against the enemy." The Pentagon "said the enemy is essentially a network, you could even say, since the key elements of the network, like al-Qaida, were themselves networks, that it was a network of networks."[7]

[6] Feith, *War and Decision*, 50, 125.   [7] Feith, interview by author.

Critics then and now seized on the administration's decision to call the conflict a "War on Terror" as a category mistake. Even some members of the administration were wary. Richard Boucher, who served in the administration as assistant secretary of state for public affairs and, subsequently, for South and Central Asian Affairs said that Bush's inclusion of "all those who harbor them" as a target in the war "is a pretty expansive definition" and that the goal to "eliminate" terrorism "is a dramatic and absolutist sort of word. You ended up with this sort of constantly expanding mission. It was defined from the beginning as a mission that was going to creep."[8]

Interestingly, there seems to have been little discussion on the point at the time. Bush used the phrase "war on terrorism" on September 11, and the phrase immediately caught on. Rumsfeld raised concerns about the "War on Terror" framing in internal memos in 2004 and 2006, but there is no available record of him raising the point in 2001. Richard Armitage, the deputy secretary of state, recalls some discussion of the merits of that framing in later years, but not in 2001. He also noted that the Bush administration's thinking about counterterrorism grew from Ronald Reagan's secretary of state, George Schultz, who called for military action against terrorists in 1984, and from the precedent of Reagan's bombing of Libya in 1986. Larry Wilkerson, Colin Powell's chief of staff, believed that Powell was not happy with calling the administration's response to 9/11 a "war," or using the military as the primary tool, and "certainly ... not very happy about using it the massive way we did and the length of time we did." Powell envisioned, at most, a "limited action." But Powell ultimately did not object because "he understood that with this President and with this Vice President, you probably couldn't avoid it. And so, he was going along with it."[9]

Powell had other difficulties. As a retired general and former national security advisor and chairman of the joint chiefs, he obviously had significant expertise to share on military affairs – but those issues lay outside his role as secretary of state. Cheney, who had previously served as secretary of defense under George H. W. Bush, helped Rumsfeld jealously guard the Pentagon's bureaucratic turf. Additionally, Powell's mode of thinking differed from the other principals. "I'm different from most people in senior foreign policy circles, both in the United States and among my colleagues

---

[8] Boucher, interview by author.
[9] Rumsfeld, "What Are We Fighting?" memo to the president, June 18, 2004, and "Nature of the Long Struggle," memo to Steve Hadley, August 4, 2006. Boucher, Armitage, and Wilkerson, interviews by author.

overseas, in that I'm not an academic and was not raised to be a foreign policy intellectual," Powell told an interviewer in 2004. "It's not as if I was at the John F. Kennedy School at Harvard. Most of my foreign policy senior level education came from the National War College. Till then, I was just another infantry officer."[10] As a result, "there was a ships-passing-in-the-dark quality to disagreements between Powell and the others," Feith said.[11]

The counterargument to the "War on Terror" framing is obvious: terrorism is a tactic, not an enemy. After Pearl Harbor, Congress did not declare war on "Surprise Attacks" or on "Combined Sea–Air Operations," but on Imperial Japan, the political entity behind the attack. The analogy is imperfect in that terrorism in intrinsically immoral, involving the intentional murder of civilians, and every government claims to oppose terrorism as a matter of principle and policy. But to respond to a terrorist attack by declaring war, not against the group responsible or the ideology that inspired it, but against the tactic of terrorism, is counterintuitive. As critics have often noted, it is impossible to measure progress against a concept like terrorism, much less win a definitive victory – as "wars" on drugs and poverty have demonstrated.[12]

I sympathize with the criticism, but, in a way, I think it does not go far enough. It misses a more important downside to framing the conflict as a "War on Terror," one less commented on but which eventually had far-reaching implications for the war against the Taliban. The war was both too expansive, including targets outside of Afghanistan unrelated to al-Qaida, and not expansive enough, prioritizing terrorism as a tactic and not the movement that used it and the political-military ideology behind it – the ideology of jihadism. By focusing on "terrorists," the administration chose an enemy that was easily defined and targetable but, in doing so, chose a framing that was shallow and would ultimately prove ineffective because it overlooked the broader (but harder to define) ideological context. It both grew out of, and reinforced, a narrow way of thinking about war.

A decade later, Rumsfeld publicly said it was a mistake to call it a "War on Terror." "What we're really engaged in is a competition of ideas with

---

[10] O'Rourke, "A Conversation with Colin Powell," *The Atlantic*, September 2004. www.thea tlantic.com/magazine/archive/2004/09/a-conversation-with-colin-powell/303436/.

[11] Feith, *War and Decision*, 62. That may explain why Powell is relatively absent from most accounts of the administration's deliberations. Powell also left no memoir of his time in the Bush administration, the only principal not to do so, which may artificially reduce his profile in history until the archives are declassified.

[12] Boucher and Armitage, interviews by author. Rumsfeld, *Known and Unknown*, 352–353.

violent extremists, with radical Islamists." Rumsfeld was right. Noticeably absent in the administration's early debates about how to define the enemy was another option: a war against *jihadism* as a political, cultural, and military movement that encompassed al-Qaida and some, but not all, other terrorist groups and one clear state sponsor in the form of the Taliban. Bush's decision to think of 9/11 as more than an al-Qaida problem made sense; but the choice to see it as a *terrorism* problem rather than a *jihadism* problem did not.[13]

The administration was reluctant to talk about the enemy this way because it carried religious overtones and could be easily misunderstood. Bush was at pains to stress that "the face of terror is not the true faith of Islam," as he said at the Islamic Center of Washington, DC, on September 17. "That's not what Islam is all about. Islam is peace," a message he made central to his public remarks about the war. Bush wanted to avoid a popular backlash against Muslims or against Islam generally – in this respect, far outshining President Franklin Roosevelt and his response to Pearl Harbor, when he rounded up and imprisoned over 120,000 Japanese and Japanese Americans in internment camps – and he was also aware that the United States' most important allies in the war would be individuals and governments in the Islamic world.[14]

Bush occasionally tried to describe the ideology. "The terrorists practice a fringe form of Islamic extremism that has been rejected by Muslim scholars and the vast majority of Muslim clerics – a fringe movement that perverts the peaceful teachings of Islam," he told the nation in his September 20 address to Congress. "The terrorists are traitors to their own faith, trying, in effect, to hijack Islam itself." But his administration generally walked gingerly around the issue, aware of its sensitivities in part because of reactions to Bush's occasional missteps. Allies across the Middle East strongly criticized Bush when, on September 16, he answered a reporter's question by saying, "This crusade, this war on terrorism is going to take a while," offending Muslim sensibilities about the medieval crusades. It was a difficult needle to thread, and Bush chose to err on the side of under-emphasizing the religious ideology behind the attacks.[15]

---

[13] CNN Official Interview: "Donald Rumsfeld: War on terror label a mistake," March 8, 2011. www.youtube.com/watch?v=VVK-Qj6FWd8.

[14] Bush, "'Islam Is Peace' Says President," September 17, 2001. https://georgewbush-white house.archives.gov/news/releases/2001/09/20010917-11.html.

[15] Bush, "Remarks by the President upon Arrival," September 16, 2001. https://georgew bush-whitehouse.archives.gov/news/releases/2001/09/20010916-2.html.

It may be unfair to expect the administration to fully, immediately grasp the complex nature of the challenge it faced and communicate it to the public – but on the other hand, Bush clearly intuited that the war needed to be understood as more than a brief one-off reprisal against al-Qaida, and he knew that public communication was key to the war's long-term success. He repeatedly stressed that the war was going to be broad and long-lasting, suggesting he could have been receptive to a different framing. Different framing was conceptually available to the foreign policy establishment at the time. Two former US officials published *The Age of Sacred Terror* in 2002, recounting the rise of Islamic extremism and violent Islamist movements, for example, and the pages of *Foreign Affairs* were filled with essays on the history of the Middle East and violent forms of political Islam in the months after 9/11.[16]

Instead, the "War on Terror" implied that a war against a group as far-flung as Abu Sayyaf in the Philippines, where the United States deployed hundreds of troops for years after 9/11, was of first importance, while the Taliban – the group most closely tied to al-Qaida – was only instrumentally important, through the deterrent effect their overthrow would have on other governments. The Taliban earned their peripheral status on a technicality, because they were not a "terrorist" group, important only insofar as their defeat enabled the United States to get al-Qaida and set a precedent, not intrinsically important, as they would be in a war on jihadism. By broadening the war so much, the United States would focus *less* on the Taliban.

Feith argued that "the fundamental strategic goal of our attack ... was never to punish the Taliban, but to pressure state supporters of terrorism globally and thereby disrupt terrorist planning and operations," which is an odd distinction to draw considering the Taliban were, at the time, the primary state supporter of terrorism. Feith acknowledged that "if you look at Afghanistan through a soda straw, so that you see Afghanistan and only Afghanistan, and you view the war out of its broader context of the War on Terrorism, I think certain things that we did are not comprehensible." There is a flip side to that observation: viewing Afghanistan through the soda straw of the War on Terror outside the broader Afghan context eventually made some aspects of the war in Afghanistan incoherent.[17]

The distinction made no difference during the first phase of the war because in 2001 the two groups were indistinguishable on the battlefield.

---

[16] Benjamin and Simon, *The Age of Sacred Terror.*

[17] Feith, *War and Decision*, 50, 125. Feith, interview by author.

The administration came to believe, rightly, that it had to overthrow the Taliban to get at al-Qaida and deter other state sponsors of terrorism. In later years, it became apparent that there were two wars: the worldwide "War on Terror" against al-Qaida and a counterinsurgency in Afghanistan against the Taliban, and American policymakers lost sight of the relationship between them. But in the early days, there was no distinction, which also meant the Bush administration gave little thought to a strategy for Afghanistan separate from its strategy in the War on Terror in these early months (aside from the Bonn Process; see Chapter 3).

But the administration's "War on Terror" framing would eventually undermine America's main goal in going to war – defeating al-Qaida, preventing further attacks, and shutting down their safe haven – by under-emphasizing the Taliban, adopting an uncritical hard line against them after their fall from power, and giving insufficient attention to an Afghanistan strategy. Again, the effect of the administration's strategic concept was not immediately evident because the Taliban chose to stick by al-Qaida and forced the United States to go to war against both groups – and early success seemed to vindicate the administration's theory of the war. But after the initial phase, when it became evident that the Taliban would be a long-term political-military challenge, the strategic concept the administration settled on in the first weeks after 9/11 became increasingly unfit for changing circumstances. It would take five years for the president and his team to revisit their assumptions about the nature of the war in Afghanistan.

TALKING TO THE TALIBAN

The flaw lurking within the Bush administration's framing was dormant during the first phase of the conflict. Initially, the concept seemed sound because the fates of the Taliban and al-Qaida were bound together, and there was no need to think carefully about how the fight against one might impact the other, or how campaigns against the different groups might require different strategies. Al-Qaida had carried out the terrorist attacks, al-Qaida was in Afghanistan at the invitation of the Taliban regime then in power, and Bush had told the nation that he would "make no distinction between the terrorists who committed these acts and those who harbor them." On September 13, Wendy Chamberlain, US ambassador to Pakistan, privately told Pakistani President Pervez

Musharraf that "there was no inclination in Washington to engage in a dialog with the Taliban."[18]

Chamberlain was wrong. Over the next month, the administration briefly, and sensibly, put out peace feelers toward the Taliban, though few expected the overture to bear fruit. Bush addressed the Taliban directly in his speech to the US Congress on September 20. He detailed their crimes against the Afghan people and their relationship with al-Qaida. Importantly, he tied the Taliban directly to the 9/11 attacks: "By aiding and abetting murder, the Taliban regime is committing murder," he said. Bush then made five specific demands of the Taliban, including releasing American prisoners, protecting journalists and aid workers, turning over al-Qaida to the United States, closing terrorist training camps, and allowing American authorities to verify the camps were closed. "These demands are not open to negotiation or discussion," he said. "The Taliban must act, and act immediately. They will hand over the terrorists, or they will share in their fate." Bush's speech was direct and confrontational, but, at least rhetorically, gave the Taliban a way out if they wanted it. "I laid out an ultimatum to the Taliban," Bush later wrote. "We had little hope that Afghanistan's leaders would heed it. But exposing their defiance to the world would firm up our justification for a military strike."[19]

The speech was an accurate reflection of the Bush administration's thinking about the Taliban in September and October. Contrary to later critics who believed the administration rushed to war against the Taliban too quickly, the Bush administration made at least four separate attempts to reach out to the Taliban in the days and weeks after 9/11 and give them an opportunity to avoid war. In fact, one of the administration's critics – Richard Clarke, who served as the director for counterterrorism on the National Security Council staff in 2001 – criticized the administration for being too *lenient* toward the Taliban immediately after 9/11. The administration was damned if it did, and damned if it did not attempt peace with the Taliban. Bush and his team tried diplomacy, did not expect the Taliban to take the opportunity for peace, and continued planning for war while the formalities of diplomacy played out. Their war-planning does not mean their peace overtures were insincere; it means they were planning for different contingencies, a sensible approach in a fast-moving crisis amid uncertainty. My criticism that the administration's "War on Terror" underemphasized the Taliban's importance to American war aims does not mean the United States should have adopted an immediate and unrelenting hard line against them;

---

[18] Embassy Islamabad, 005087. Available through the National Security Archive.
[19] Bush, *Decision Points*, 192–193.

that is not what taking the Taliban seriously means. It means using all tools of American power – including diplomacy – to address the threat.[20]

Bush's speech was the public version of his administration's outreach to the Taliban. Second, in private and at the same time, Bush administration officials reached out to Pakistan and asked for its help to pressure the Taliban. CIA Director George Tenet met with his Pakistani counterpart, Lieutenant General Mahmud Ahmed, director-general of Inter-Services Intelligence (ISI), and asked that he meet with Taliban leader Mullah Omar "and make it crystal clear to him that the Taliban was going to pay a terrible price if it insisted on continuing to protect al-Qaida and Bin Ladin." Tenet asked Mahmud to pass to the Taliban the American offer: that they could avoid war if they turned against al-Qaida. Secretary of State Colin Powell and his deputy, Richard Armitage, had similar meetings with Mahmud and a phone conversation with Pakistani President Pervez Musharraf. Armitage – bullish, barrel-chested, and famously gruff – told Mahmud, "we don't want to fight the Taliban," and asked Mahmud to convey to the Taliban "if you walk away from [al-Qaida], no harm, no foul to you."

Mahmud agreed and met with Omar, who in turn held a two-day council with advisors and religious leaders to deliberate what to do. The council decreed that bin Laden was free to leave on his own. After the council's decree, Omar rebuffed the American demands and chose to stick with bin Laden and al-Qaida. "If war comes, it is the will of God," Omar reportedly told Mahmud, and Mahmud relayed the message to Armitage. "Mahmud got back and called me up and said, now, because of Pashtunwali, they're not going to do it," Armitage said, referring to the Pashtun tribal code of honor. "They have to give hospitality to their Arab guests. And all I said was, well ... you'll be in the soup too." Tenet's, Armitage's, and Powell's meetings show that Chamberlain was premature when she told Musharraf that Washington had "no inclination" to talk to the Taliban.[21]

---

[20]   Clarke, *Against All Enemies*, 245. An internal State Department memo on September 14 reflects this line of thinking, laying out a proposed ultimatum to the Taliban while outlining diplomatic preparations for war. State Department, "Gameplan for Polmil Strategy for Pakistan and Afghanistan," https://nsarchive2.gwu.edu/NSAEBB/NSAEBB358a/doc06.pdf.

[21]   Tenet and Harlow, *At the Center of the Storm*, 180–181. Coll, *Directorate S*, 61. Grenier, *88 Days to Kandahar*, 89, 113. Armitage, interview by author. The National Security Archive has published declassified State Department cables detailing several of these meetings. In one version of events, Omar offered to hand over bin Laden to a third party, not to the United States. If true, in light of the preponderant evidence of the Taliban's refusal to turn against al-Qaida, the offer was almost certainly a stalling tactic. See Malkasian, *The American War in Afghanistan*, 55.

Third, the CIA made a more direct approach. Bob Grenier, the station chief in Islamabad, met with Mullah Osmani, commander of the Taliban's Kandahar corps and the second-most powerful Taliban leader. Grenier laid out a number of possibilities: "The Taliban could turn Bin Ladin over to the United States for prosecution," according to Tenet. "If that violated their religious obligation to be good hosts, they could administer justice themselves, in a way that clearly took him off the table. Or if they wanted to save face altogether, they could stand aside and let the Americans find Bin Ladin and extricate him on their own." Grenier also proposed that Osmani overthrow Omar and replace him. Osmani was tempted but rejected Grenier's proposals.[22]

Fourth, Tenet also recounted how individual CIA officers in the field attempted to reach out to their Taliban counterparts during the war in October and November, trying to persuade them to defect, surrender, or turn against al-Qaida. During the military campaign, "Agency officers in Afghanistan also secretly contacted Taliban officials to try to get them to turn over Bin Ladin. In one case, an agency team traveled to a virtual no-man's-land outside of Kabul for what they hoped would be a meeting with a very senior Taliban intelligence official," Tenet recalled. "The Taliban official failed to show up, however, but did send his deputy. The stand-in made it clear that they had no intention of being helpful to us." The military made similar efforts. "Rumsfeld directed his commanders to look for ways to divide the Taliban and al-Qaida and to aggravate fissures between the Taliban and the Afghan people," according to Feith. Some of these efforts bore fruit: hundreds of foot soldiers and scores of lesser Taliban commanders switched sides in October and November as it became increasingly clear that the Taliban was collapsing.[23]

The administration did not expect the Taliban to accept its overtures. Condoleezza Rice wrote, "we all knew that the outcome would be a declaration of war against the Taliban and an invasion of Afghanistan." Immediately after the terrorist attacks, Tenet told the administration that "the Taliban and al-Qaida were really the same," according to Woodward's account. Tenet and Cofer Black, director of the CIA's Counterterrorism

---

[22] Tenet and Harlow, *At the Center of the Storm*, 182–183. Coll, *Directorate S*, 58–59. Grenier, *88 Days to Kandahar*, chapters 9 and 13.

[23] Tenet and Harlow, *At the Center of the Storm*, 210. Feith, *War and Decision*, 56. Woodward, *Bush at War*, 214. Bush reaffirmed his commitment to leaving the door open for a diplomatic solution with the Taliban at a meeting of the NSC on September 26. Woodward, *Bush at War*, 149–150.

Center, briefed the administration on September 13 on options to strike back. "Cofer made it clear that we would be taking on not just al-Qaida but the Taliban as well," Tenet wrote. "The two were inseparable unless the Taliban chose to make the separation itself, and that seemed unlikely, despite our best efforts to drive a wedge between them." On September 12, General Tommy Franks, commanding general of Central Command, understood his mission included planning to "remove the Taliban regime," because "they coexist ideologically and physically" with al-Qaida.[24]

At the September 15 Camp David meeting, Bush and his advisors understood that they were "going to apply pressure [to the Taliban] in the hope that it would break with al-Qaida and give up bin Laden. They didn't think this was likely but they agreed they had to make the effort." Grenier sent a field assessment before the 22nd that judged Mullah Omar "would throw in his lot with bin Laden and the Taliban would 'fatalistically' join in that support." Feith later recounted that "if the United States wanted to persuade terrorist-supporting regimes around the world to change their policies, we knew we would have to oust the Taliban regime, not just hit al-Qaida." Larry Wilkerson believed that Cheney "was adamantly opposed to any settlement other than war" from the outset. "You do not resurrect your presidency from an attack on the country worse than Pearl Harbor unless you are seen as being a warrior and you go out and kill some people. That was Cheney's evaluation of it."[25]

Their expectations were fully vindicated, particularly given the Taliban's responses to meetings with Mahmud and Grenier. That Mullah Omar went to the trouble of convening a two-day assembly to debate the issue before announcing his decision to reject the American offers is the most telling evidence that peace with the Taliban was impossible in the fall of 2001. The Taliban and al-Qaida did have differences, and some Taliban leaders had reservations about al-Qaida, but when forced to the point after 9/11, none of their concerns were great enough to prevent them from joining al-Qaida as cobelligerents against the United States. Grenier recounts Osmani telling him that "the Taliban can't hand [bin Laden] over publicly any more than they can publicly reject Islam ... Omar has made a public commitment to bin Laden; he can't simply renounce it now." The two groups were bound together by shared religious ideology, by years

[24] Rice, *No Higher Honor*, 83. Woodward, *Bush at War*, 33, 52. Franks and McConnell, *American Soldier*, 251, 255. Tenet and Harlow, *At the Center of the Storm*, 175.

[25] Woodward, *Bush at War*, 82, 121. Feith, *War and Decision*, 80.

of fighting together against the Northern Alliance, and by intermarriage. The Taliban included the 055 Brigade, sometimes called the "Arab Brigade," a force of some 1,000 al-Qaida fighters, fighting alongside its regular army. Bin Laden had publicly sworn an oath of loyalty to Omar before 2001, pledging his group's allegiance to the Taliban's cause in exchange for their protection. "As for bin Laden, 'only his death or mine' relieved Mullah Omar of the obligation to protect a Muslim guest," Omar reportedly told Mahmud.[26]

Even in the face of the two groups' extremely close ties, the administration still debated ways to turn other Taliban leaders against Omar and al-Qaida and tried to sequence military operations to target the Taliban last to give them maximum time to change sides – all without success. The administration finally gave up on the possibility of peace with the Taliban leadership at a Principals Committee meeting on October 3, four days before the military campaign began. Cheney commented that the administration should continue to be "obscure on the future of the Taliban" in public in case any Taliban leaders wanted to defect. "But [in] the long term – we need the Taliban to be gone." In Woodward's account, this is when the Bush administration finally "embarked on regime change in Afghanistan," almost a full month after 9/11. On October 7, Bush announced the start of military operations in Afghanistan. He reminded the world that he had laid out a series of demands for the Taliban. "None of these demands were met," he said. "And now the Taliban will pay a price." In November, he told the United Nations (UN) that the Taliban and al-Qaida "are now virtually indistinguishable."[27]

The evidence of the Bush administration's outreach to the Taliban in the early days after 9/11 is at odds with the popular perception of what happened, a perception other scholars and historians have echoed. American officials "did not try to reach a political settlement with the Taliban in 2001," according to counterinsurgency expert David Kilcullen,

---

[26] Grenier, *88 Days to Kandahar*, 118. Grenier sent another field assessment on October 11 that again judged that the Taliban was unified around Omar and al-Qaida and unlikely to either fragment or defect. Woodward, *Bush at War*, 234. Coll, *Directorate S*, 61. See Strick van Linschoten and Kuehn, *An Enemy We Created*, for the view that the two groups were not inextricably entwined and could have been pried apart after 9/11.

[27] Woodward, *Bush at War*, 127–128, 187. Rice was still questioning whether or not the United States had to defeat the Taliban on October 11 (Woodward, *Bush at War*, 226). Woodward, *Bush at War*, 192. George W. Bush, "Presidential Address to the Nation," October 7, 2001. ht tps://georgewbush-whitehouse.archives.gov/news/releases/2001/10/20011007-8.html. Bush, "President Bush Speaks to United Nations," November 10, 2001. https://georgewbush-whitehouse.archives.gov/news/releases/2001/11/20011110-3.html.

who later advised the American war effort in Afghanistan, "and had they done so then at a time of maximum leverage, the current debacle might have been avoided." Jack Fairweather argued that "the Americans – from their political leaders down to their soldiers – had dangerously conflated al-Qa'eda and the Taliban. The two groups had similarities, of course, but they differed in vital ways." Carter Malkasian, similarly, blames the Bush administration for its "inflexible approach" toward the Taliban, accuses the United States of having "misunderstood the Taliban movement as inseparable from al-Qa'eda," claims that "with more time and diplomatic effort, Taliban who were against war might have found a way to get Mullah Omar to give up bin Laden," and concludes that "one of the tragedies of 2001 is that Bush and his team could not find a way to give compassion a little more time."[28]

These historians have gotten the story wrong, and Malkasian's accusation is especially odd because his own narrative convincingly shows that the Taliban chose to be inseparable from al-Qaida and that they repeatedly rejected US overtures. Malkasian acknowledges as much, recounting how "one university-educated member of the [Taliban's] political commission lectured me that the Taliban were right not to turn over bin Laden in 2001." The Taliban official asked a series of rhetorical questions, which to Malkasian "hinted at just how close the Taliban and its leadership were to al-Qa'eda." Malkasian rightly notes that, in 2001, "Omar's own obstinacy" contributed to the American belief that the two groups were inseparable. Hillary Clinton, hardly George W. Bush's strongest defender, told the Senate Foreign Relations Committee as much in 2011 when serving as secretary of state. "I remember when President George W. Bush basically said to Mullah Omar and the Taliban: Look, turn over bin Laden and al-Qaida and we're done; we're not going to come after you. And they would not do it, and they never have agreed to do it."[29] There was no opportunity for peace with the Taliban in September and October of 2001.

A LIGHT FOOTPRINT IN THE "GRAVEYARD OF EMPIRES"

Once Bush decided to frame the response to 9/11 as a War on Terror, and to begin the war by attacking al-Qaida and its Taliban hosts in Afghanistan,

---

[28] Kilcullen and Mills, *The Ledger*, 12. Fairweather, *The Good War*, xix. Malkasian, *The American War in Afghanistan*, 76, 59, 58, 79.

[29] Malkasian, *The American War in Afghanistan*, 437. Senate Foreign Relations Committee, "Evaluating Goals," June 23, 2011, 37.

he and his advisors had to decide what that would look like. America's most recent conflict had been an air campaign to oust Serbian leader Slobodan Milosevic in 1999, a campaign that lasted seventy-eight days, involved no ground troops, and saw no combat casualties. Bush clearly had in mind something more involved: he regularly cited former President Bill Clinton's antiseptic and risk-averse warfare as an example to avoid, and Bush officials criticized the Kosovo campaign as "war by committee." General Hugh Shelton, the Chairman of the Joint Chiefs, briefed Bush on airstrike options on September 15. "President Bush told him to go back and come back with more options," according to Steve Hadley, the deputy national security advisor, "and he wanted options that involved some boots on the ground because he thought it would show a seriousness about the War on Terror."[30]

But at the other end of the spectrum was the 1991 Gulf War, a war that had involved over a half-million American troops. Such an operation in Afghanistan – mountainous, and with no infrastructure to support a huge and heavy conventional army – was daunting. "We're going to wish this was the Balkans," Rice said. "The problems of Afghanistan and the surrounding region were so complicated," Woodward commented. "[Rice] looked at a map and just thought 'Afghanistan.' It evoked every negative image: far away, mountainous, landlocked, hard."[31]

Over the course of debates between September 11 and October 7, the administration quickly gravitated to a light footprint – but a footprint that did involve boots on the ground. One reason was Rumsfeld's belief in defense transformation. Rumsfeld and a cabal of defense intellectuals spent the 1990s arguing that the advent of high technology and telecommunications would enable militaries to accomplish more with less manpower. They envisioned a transformed military of networked, pared-down, lean but tech-powered joint units of soldiers, sailors, airmen, and Marines responding in real time to changes on the battlefield, digital technology finally conquering the notorious fog and friction of war that had bedeviled commanders since the age of Thucydides. Famous videos of precision-guided munitions flying through windowpanes during the Gulf War convinced a generation that a digitized battalion would accomplish tomorrow what an analog division did yesterday.[32]

Rumsfeld's vision meshed seamlessly with another set of beliefs circulating in Washington: that Afghans were legendarily xenophobic and had a strong track record of successful irregular warfare against invading

---

[30] Hadley, interview by author.   [31] Woodward, *Bush at War*, 80.
[32] Rumsfeld, "Transforming the Military." Feith, interview by author.

superpowers. Milt Bearden's article, "Afghanistan: Graveyard of Empires," appeared in early October and immediately found an audience. "Afghanistan's history nagged at the president's advisers," according to Woodward, because they saw it as "the nemesis of the British in the 19th century and the Soviets in the 20th. Rice was wondering whether it might be the same for the United States in the 21st. Her fears were shared by others." Bearden's headline instantly crystallized an image for Americans of Afghanistan that would persist for twenty years. The concern to avoid the British and Soviet mistakes and references to the "graveyard" trope litter the Bush administration's memoirs and interviews. It appears in virtually every memoir from the administration.[33]

For example, Bush recounts in his memoir learning about Afghanistan in conversations with his advisors and with General Tommy Franks, who would lead the initial military campaign there: "The people of Afghanistan have a way of banding together against foreigners. They drove out the British in the nineteenth century. They drove out the Soviets in the twentieth century. Even Alexander the Great failed to conquer the country. Afghanistan had earned a foreboding nickname: Graveyard of Empires." Cheney recounts an identical concern in his memoir:

> As we had begun the planning for our military operations in Afghanistan, many worried that we were taking on too formidable a task. As the Soviets could testify, Afghanistan was known as the graveyard of empires for good reason. Any power that would prevail there had to take into account not only the rugged, inhospitable terrain, but the fact that the Afghans were among the toughest, most ruthless fighters in the world.[34]

The administration, fearing a potential Afghan uprising against US forces – especially a Pashtun uprising – keenly wanted to avoid American forces looking like an invasion or occupation force. "We would be making a mistake if our military effort appeared to the Afghans as an American invasion aimed at taking control of their country," Rumsfeld wrote. "I concluded it would be far better to position ourselves as the allies of indigenous Afghan forces. I saw this as the best way to avoid the heavy-handed errors of Afghanistan's past invaders and occupiers." George Tenet

---

[33] Woodward, *Bush at War*, 82.

[34] Bush, *Decision Points*, 194. Cheney and Cheney, *In My Time*, 346. See also Rumsfeld, *Known and Unknown*, 408. Steve Hadley said in an interview, "we did have the understanding of the problem that the Russians and the British had in Afghanistan, and the last thing we wanted to be was occupiers." Paul Wolfowitz invoked the British and Soviet experience in Congressional testimony in June 2002.

insisted "We have to avoid looking like a US invasion." When the CIA developed its plan to embed its officers with Northern Alliance units, it was keen to minimize the US footprint because "if the US repeated the mistakes of the Soviets by invading with a large land force, they would be doomed." Rice concurred: "The President rejected any strategy based on a large US ground presence, deciding instead to have the Afghans take the lead in the ground campaign."[35]

The administration's aversion to nation building, its belief in defense transformation, and the "graveyard" trope dovetailed to make the administration overwhelmingly in favor of a small, surgical military operation, albeit one that involved some kind of ground force and took more risks than the Clinton-era operations. Practical considerations were the *coup de grâce*. Bush, reflecting the mood of the nation, was eager to act, and the administration believed it had to strike back quickly to deter future attacks, but Rumsfeld told the president that the military had no on-the-shelf plans for an invasion of Afghanistan and that it could take months to send a large force. Tenet, meanwhile, told the president that the CIA could send small teams from its Special Activities Division to link up with the Northern Alliance within weeks. The president approved the CIA's plan shortly after the September 15 Camp David meeting. Joining forces with the Northern Alliance – locked in a life-or-death struggle with the Taliban – meshed with the administration's emerging belief that the Taliban would have to be destroyed.

That is how the administration came to improvise one of the most celebrated aspects of the entire war in Afghanistan. Instead of deploying a large US military force, Bush sent small teams of CIA personnel and special operations forces to link up with Afghan militias – the Northern Alliance plus a few Pashtun groups in the south – to be the connective tissue between Afghan ground forces and American air power. Powell and Armitage had reservations – the eponymous Powell Doctrine emphasized the need to use overwhelming force to achieve decisive victory – but they were in the minority. The nation was overwhelmingly supportive – 88 percent of Americans favored the use of military force in Afghanistan. The *New York Times* said Bush made the "right choice" and told American soldiers deploying to war that "as they go, they should know that the nation supports their cause and yearns for their success." Because it was an improvisation, there was some blurriness in the bureaucratic turf between the CIA

---

[35] Rumsfeld, *Known and Unknown*, 372–373; see also 367. Feith, *War and Decision* 101, 140; see also 76–77, 89. Woodward, *Bush at War*, 182, 193. Rice, *No Higher Honor*, 91–92.

and the military that needed sorting out in Washington. But on the battle-field, the combination proved devastating. The campaign started on October 7; Kabul fell on November 14; and the Taliban's last stronghold in Kandahar fell on December 7.[36]

In late October, there were worries within the administration and criticism in the press that the campaign had stalled. Admiral William Fallon, the vice chief of naval operations, thought the operation was "knee-jerk" and "pretty sketchy" because "we're throwing bits and pieces of what-ever we can pull together." He felt the operation was close to collapse, that "we're flailing around," and most people were not aware "how close we came to failure in 2001." On October 31, the *New York Times* editorialized that Afghanistan was deteriorating into a "quagmire," analogizing the effort to Vietnam. The administration briefly debated Americanizing the war and sending a force of some 55,000 US troops, but Bush rejected the proposals and stuck with the initial strategy. A week later, Mazar-e Sharif fell, catalyzing a bandwagon effect among Taliban commanders who quickly defected to join the winning side.[37]

Some critics blamed the light footprint for the US's failure to kill or capture bin Laden in 2001. They argued that if Bush used more troops and got bin Laden right away, America's involvement in Afghanistan might have ended as quickly as it had started. US forces fought a two-week battle against al-Qaida at Tora Bora, a cave complex in the mountainous border region of Nangarhar Province, in early December, where bin Laden was widely believed to be hiding. Gary Berntsen, the CIA officer working with Afghan militias in the area, asked for US troops to block bin Laden's escape route, but never got them. "The biggest and most important failure of CENTCOM leadership came at Tora Bora when they turned down my request for a battalion of US Rangers to block bin Laden's escape," he wrote. General Tommy Franks later defended his decision to rely on local Afghans. "I was very mindful of the Soviet experience," he explained, which to him argued that Afghan leadership and a minimal US footprint was the safer course.[38]

It is possible that more US troops would have meant bin Laden's death ten years sooner than it happened – but it almost certainly would not have

[36] Schroen, *First In*. Berntsen and Pezzullo, *Jawbreaker*. "The Ground War Begins," *The New York Times*, October 20, 2001. AEI Studies in Public Opinion, "America and the War on Terrorism," June 24, 2008, 58–59.

[37] Fallon, interview by author. R. W. Apple, "A Military Quagmire Remembered: Afghanistan as Vietnam," *New York Times*, October 31, 2001.

[38] Berntsen and Pezzullo, *Jawbreaker*, 314. See 277, 290–291, 307–308.

affected the course of the war very much. The rest of al-Qaida's leadership was still at large. Khalid Sheikh Mohammad, the architect of 9/11, was not captured until 2003. It took years to track down other al-Qaida leaders: Abu Hamza Rabia was not killed until 2005; Muhsin Musa Matwalli Atwah, in 2006; Abu Laith al-Libi, in 2008; and Ayman al-Zawahiri, bin Laden's successor, in 2022. Bush repeatedly stressed that the war was not against a single terrorist or even a single terrorist group, but against terrorist groups of global reach and even against the concept of terrorism itself. He was hardly going to declare victory and bring US forces home if bin Laden were killed at Tora Bora. "I've said all along that if you walked in and said 'Here is Mr. Bin Laden,' the problem would not go away," Rumsfeld told reporters in December 2001. "There are any number of people in the al-Qaida network who could continue to operate that network." And despite the Bush team's aversion to nation building, they did not want to let Afghanistan collapse and knew US troops were a stabilizing presence, which is part of why they did not leave in 2002. After US intelligence and special operations forces eventually found and killed bin Laden in 2011, the United States stayed in Afghanistan for ten more years, suggesting bin Laden's death in 2001 would not have ended the American presence then either.[39]

The US, international allies, and Afghan militias had achieved a stunning victory, accomplishing regime change in two months. Talk of the "graveyard of empires" abated until 2009. Scholars immediately began celebrating, then debating, the "Afghan model" of warfare, arguing how much was new and how much old-style fire-and-maneuver warfare wrapped in a shiny package of precision weapons and Special Forces' élan. What did not seem in doubt was that the United States had won a major victory in its War on Terror. Al-Qaida's safe haven in Afghanistan was over. The Arab Brigade was destroyed or scattered. Al-Qaida's senior leadership was dead, captured, or on the run. Its Taliban hosts were driven from power. A state sponsor of terrorism had been overthrown, setting an important precedent for other governments around the world. In the flush of victory, it did not seem necessary to ask was how appropriate a "light footprint" was for the next stage of America's involvement in Afghanistan, or whether the myth of the "graveyard" was a useful guide for a long-term state-building intervention.[40]

---

[39] Defense Department Briefing, December 27, 2001. www.c-span.org/video/?168014-1/ defense-department-briefing.

[40] Biddle, "Allies, Airpower, and Modern Warfare." Andres, Wills, and Griffith, "Winning with Allies." Andres, "The Afghan Model in Northern Iraq."

PAKISTAN

In devising its strategy toward Afghanistan, the Bush administration had to deal with Pakistan. The history was complicated. Pakistani military and intelligence personnel had given the Taliban training, advice, and equipment to help their rise to power in the 1990s, and Pakistan was one of just three states that formally recognized the Taliban government before 9/11. The US declaring war on the Taliban came perilously close to declaring war on Pakistan – a nation with five or six times the population and armed with nuclear weapons. But the United States and Pakistan were, ostensibly, allies, having signed a pair of mutual defense treaties in the 1950s and having counted each other vital partners against the Soviet Union, especially during the Soviet–Afghan war. There was also bad blood: the Pakistanis were resentful that the Americans had abandoned the region after the Cold War and sanctioned Pakistan for its nuclear weapons programs.

On September 13, 2001, Colin Powell and Richard Armitage met with ISI Director Mahmud Ahmed and presented him with an ultimatum and a list of demands: join the United States in its war against al-Qaida; condemn the terrorist attacks; give the American military overflight and landing rights and access to naval and air bases; break ties with the Taliban and stop all logistical support to them. Musharraf later claimed that Armitage threatened the United States would "bomb you back to the Stone Age," if Pakistan did not cooperate (Armitage denies having said that). Ambassador Chamberlain presented the same list to Musharraf in Islamabad, minus the bluster. The message was clear: there is no middle ground, and Pakistan must choose a side.[41]

Initially, Pakistan appeared to be a strong, irreplaceable partner in the War on Terror. Musharraf agreed to every item on the American list of demands. Even as thousands of Pakistanis streamed across the border to join the Taliban and fight against American forces in the opening months of the war, Musharraf denounced the terrorist attacks, broke ties with the Taliban (temporarily), gave logistical and intelligence support to the war, and mobilized a small number of troops along the border. He gave a dramatic and politically risky speech on January 12, 2002, strongly condemning political and religious extremism and the perversion of Islam. Perhaps chastened after Pakistani terrorists attacked the Indian parliament the previous month and brought the two nuclear-armed nations to the brink

---

[41] Woodward, *Bush at War,* 58–59. Coll, *Directorate S,* 51–53. Block, "Armitage Denies Making 'Stone Age' Threat," NPR, September 22, 2006.

of war, Musharraf recounted his efforts over the previous two years to ban Islamist terrorist groups and rein in the Taliban; banned several extremist groups; condemned the 9/11 attacks; and vowed action against any Pakistani group or individual "found involved in terrorism within or outside the country." He even challenged the terrorists' notion of *jihad.* "Have we ever thought of waging *jihad* against illiteracy, poverty, backwardness and hunger?" he asked. "This is the larger *jihad.*"[42]

Pakistani law enforcement and parts of the ISI worked alongside their US counterparts to hunt, capture, or kill al-Qaida leaders and operatives, including Abu Zubaydah, a senior al-Qaida leader, captured in 2002; Ramzi bin al-Shibh, among the 9/11 planners, in 2002; and Khalid Sheikh Mohammad, the mastermind of the 9/11 attacks, in 2003. "CIA may have captured more terrorists with ISI cooperation than with any other service," Mike Hayden, CIA director from 2006 to 2009, wrote. "In those first years we didn't have many complaints about the Pakistanis," recalled Steve Hadley. "We did have concerns about their capabilities, and we went out of our way to try to strengthen their capabilities." Musharraf fired Mahmud Ahmed, the head of ISI, who clearly sympathized with the Taliban, and several of his deputies. To all appearances, he had gone all-in as an ally in the War on Terror. "The United States was able to develop an increasingly constructive partnership with Pakistan," Rumsfeld wrote. "When he saw that America intended to act forcefully after 9/11, Musharraf chose the United States." Pakistan's cooperation against al-Qaida was so well known and so effective that the terrorist group tried to assassinate Musharraf twice in 2003.[43]

In these early months, Pakistan appeared to be a strong and reliable ally in the War on Terror, and the Bush administration felt it had safely navigated the tricky waters and troubled history that might have derailed the relationship. "Afghanistan's fate was not its own to determine. Pakistan held more than a few keys to its neighbor's stability," Condoleezza Rice wrote in her memoir, but ultimately, "that was not a good thing." The first half of that sentiment – that Pakistan was instrumental in Afghanistan's future – was obvious. It took years for the second half to sink in. Musharraf eventually managed to create a middle ground for himself, exploiting the ambiguity in American war aims and the US stance toward the Taliban. In the war between the United States and al-Qaida, he chose the United States; but

---

[42] "In Musharraf's Words: 'A Day of Reckoning,'" *New York Times,* January 12, 2002. www .proquest.com/central/docview/2231338543/873C300E723141CFPQ/.

[43] Hayden, *Playing to the Edge,* 205. Coll, *Directorate S,* 47. Rumsfeld, *Known and Unknown,* 397. Hadley, interview by author.

in the war between the United States and the Taliban, he eventually chose the Taliban. It took four or five years for some in the Bush administration to grasp the double game; some never did.[44]

MISSED CHANCES FOR PEACE?

Some historians and critics have suggested that the Bush administration missed two opportunities to achieve lasting peace in early December as the Taliban was collapsing. First, some believe the administration blundered by not inviting the Taliban to participate in the Bonn conference, a UN-moderated meeting of prominent Afghan factions to agree on a process of political reconstruction in post-Taliban Afghanistan. The suggestion is odd: the conference convened on November 27, while the Taliban were still fighting in and around Kandahar. Lakhdar Brahimi, the UN special representative for Afghanistan and the UN's face at Bonn, believed at the time that "the Taliban had gone and were not a possible partner." Brahimi later changed his view, calling the omission of the Taliban from Bonn the "original sin" of the Afghanistan mission, but nothing Brahimi said later suggests that it was *possible* to include the Taliban, no matter how desirable he later felt it might have been.[45]

US diplomats and Bush administration officials have universally argued – persuasively – that there was no meaningful opportunity to include the Taliban at Bonn. Ambassador Jim Dobbins, the US representative at Bonn, told me that "if the Taliban were invited to Bonn, no one would've come," because they were still trying to win the war – and if they had come, the Northern Alliance would have stayed home for the same reason. Zalmay Khalilzad, the US official with the greatest familiarity with Afghan politics, later wrote that "Kandahar had not yet fallen, and even at this late stage, the Taliban leadership had not broken with al-Qaida. I am skeptical that the international community could have lured the Taliban to the table at Bonn." Khalilzad was later accused of being too favorable to

---

[44] Rice, *No Higher Honor*, 344.

[45] See, for example, Kilcullen and Mills, *The Ledger* and Giustozzi, *Koran, Kalashnikov, and Laptop.* Frontline, "Behind the Scenes at Bonn," www.pbs.org/wgbh/pages/frontline/s hows/campaign/withus/cbonntheme.html. Mary Sack and Cyrus Samii, "From the Archives: An Interview with Lakhdar Brahimi," October 23, 2018. https://jia.sipa.colum bia.edu/online-articles/archives-interview-lakhdar-brahimi.

the Taliban; if even he believed the Taliban were not a viable negotiating partner in 2001, there is no compelling reason to doubt his judgment.[46]

Condoleezza Rice offered a visceral reminder of the obstacles to including the Taliban. "You have to remember what the Taliban had represented at the time; this was a group that executed women in a stadium given to them by the UN," she said. "I don't think it would have been acceptable to the Afghan people. I don't think it would've been acceptable to people like Hamid Karzai. I don't think it would've been acceptable to the Northern Alliance." The nascent Afghan government would have rejected any deal with the Taliban or fallen apart if any faction or warlord accepted one. Hadley, similarly, recalls that by late November and early December, "there wasn't much Taliban left. It had been routed," making negotiations with them impractical. "I don't recall much discussion about whether the Taliban should be in the negotiations or out because the Taliban was kind of gone."[47]

Political reality limited what the administration could realistically do. Eric Edelman spoke at length on the point:

> I don't remember too many people actually saying "negotiate with the Taliban" at the time ... In the wake of what had just happened, the sting of the attack, the refusal of Taliban to divorce itself from al-Qaida, what appeared to be the complete and utter rout of the Taliban and al-Qaida ... I think it would've been very difficult for any administration to actually negotiate with the Taliban and put the Taliban back into some seat of power given what had just happened. So to me, the idea that this was a big lost opportunity is wrong.[48]

Suggesting that the Taliban could have been at Bonn is a mix of wishful thinking with Monday-morning quarterbacking. It would have been preferable if such an opportunity existed, and we can easily imagine how subsequent history would have unfolded far better for everyone if it had. We *want* it to be true, it *should* have been true, and so many believe it was, in fact, true, despite the clear evidence that it was not. The Taliban made their choice before the war started, and neither they nor the international coalition were inclined to revisit the question before Bonn. Bonn was a meeting to discuss the future of *post*-Taliban Afghanistan; the Taliban were still fighting to prevent that future from happening. Historical precedent was on the administration's side: the Allies did not invite Hitler to Yalta.

---

[46] Dobbins, interview by author. Khalilzad, *The Envoy*, Kindle location 2300.
[47] Rice and Hadley, interviews by author.   [48] Edelman, interview by author.

Simultaneously with Bonn, one specific incident has stood out for those who accuse the administration of missing an opportunity for peace. On December 6, several senior Taliban figures, including Mullah Obaidullah, the Minister of Defense, and Abdur Razzaq Akhundzada, the Interior Minister, met with Hamid Karzai outside Kandahar to offer some form of concession. What exactly they offered is unclear, and at least eleven separate primary accounts have emerged about the meeting in subsequent years from interviews with participants and their writings. Broadly, there are two distinct narratives: that the Taliban offered to lay down arms, end the war, and recognize Karzai's government; or that they offered to evacuate Kandahar in exchange for safe passage. The first would have marked the strategic defeat of the Taliban; the second would have been no more than a tactical retreat, an effort to spare Kandahar the destruction of urban warfare while the Taliban regrouped elsewhere.[49]

Each side told the version most useful to themselves. Accounts from Karzai's side support the narrative of comprehensive surrender – a story Karzai used to shore up his authority and legitimacy with Pashtun audiences. Most accounts from the Taliban side do the opposite, minimizing what they allegedly offered to protect their reputation and bolster the justification for their later insurgency. It is possible the participants themselves confused the two: an offer to evacuate Kandahar – the Taliban's

---

[49] Malkasian, *The American War in Afghanistan*, 73–74. Accounts that reflect Karzai's version of events include (1) Blehm, *The Only Thing Worth Dying For*, 413 (see also 90, 107, 208, 322, 327); (2) Grenier, *88 Days to Kandahar*, 279–281; (3) Kolenda, *Zero Sum Victory*, 70–72; and (4) Gopal, "The Battle for Afghanistan," 8. Kolenda repeated the claim in an interview with the author. These accounts are drawn from interviews with Karzai and his supporters, including Haji Ibrahim and other unnamed officials. This version has made its way into official US government accounts: see Special Inspector General for Afghanistan Reconstruction, *Reintegration of Ex-Combatants*, September 2019, 17–19. Accounts that reflect the Taliban's perspective include (5) Wakil Ahmed Mutawakil (former Taliban foreign minister), *Afghanistan and Taliban* (as reflected in Malkasian's narrative); (6) Abdul Salam Zaeef (former Taliban ambassador to Pakistan), *Taliban: From Kandahar until Mazar*, and (7) Gall, *The Wrong Enemy*, 34. Gall's account is sourced to an interview with Taliban general Abdul Waheed Baghrani (called Raees Baghrani in other accounts). An anomalous source is (8) Jack Fairweather's *The Good War*, 40–45, also sourced to an interview with Baghrani that nonetheless disagrees with Gall's account. Two more balanced views include (9) Dam, *A Man and a Motorcycle*, 181–185 and (10) Chayes, *The Punishment of Virtue*, 45–47, both discussed in what follows. Finally, there is (11) an interview with Lt. Col. David Fox, the Special Forces officer assigned to Karzai, by the PBS show Frontline, that tracks closely with Grenier's account and conclusions: www.pbs.org/wgbh/pages/frontline/shows/campaign/interviews/fox.html.

cultural and spiritual capital and their last major stronghold – could be interpreted as a final surrender, whether the Taliban intended it that way or not. On the other hand, the Taliban's request for safe passage and amnesty could be seen, not as an offer to lay down their arms, but as a wait-and-see stratagem, a ploy to buy time and see if the Americans would leave and give the Taliban an opportunity to return.

Two accounts reflect a more balanced view: Bette Dam's *A Man and a Motorcycle*, which is sourced to interviews with both sides; and Sarah Chayes' *The Punishment of Virtue*, based on an interview with Mullah Naqib, the intermediary between the two sides in the negotiation. Dam's account includes Karzai's claim that the Taliban offered to recognize his government, but Dam also cites two of Karzai's own supporters who dispute Karzai's story. Chayes' account, which was the earliest published and is the only account drawn from the mediator in the negotiation, supports the more limited version of events: the Taliban offered to hand over Kandahar city but made no mention of a strategic surrender or an offer to recognize Karzai's government. At the time, the *New York Times* reported that the Taliban "agreed to surrender its last remaining stronghold, the southern city of Kandahar," which would "reduce their control of the country to a few pockets in the north, and to still unsettled mountainous areas in the east," which suggests the more limited interpretation.[50]

Bob Grenier, the CIA Station Chief in Islamabad, was in touch with his field agents, with Karzai, and with Mullah Jalil, the Taliban's Deputy Foreign Minister, that week. His book recounts Karzai's narrative of comprehensive surrender, but Grenier nonetheless concludes more elliptically: "In their many confused interactions with Hamid Karzai as he made his way south from Uruzgan, [the Taliban] were not so much seeking a political settlement as assurances of personal safety for themselves." He does not believe the December 6 meeting was a singular missed opportunity (though he believes the US government did prove too inflexible toward the Taliban later). Jalil told Grenier that Mullah Omar "was not going to surrender, he was not going to recognize Karzai," though Omar "would not hold it against anyone else if they did." It was a "fluid situation," Grenier told me. Karzai wanted a comprehensive peace agreement, and the Taliban representatives said just enough to let him hear what he wanted to hear, which wasn't hard because Karzai was "prone to wishful thinking." In any case, Karzai "didn't

---

[50] Dam, *A Man and a Motorcycle*, 181–185. Chayes, *The Punishment of Virtue*, 45–47. Brian Knowlton, "Rumsfeld Rejects Plan to Allow Mullah Omar 'To Live in Dignity,'" *New York Times*, December 7, 2001.

have the forces to enforce whatever agreement he reached," which, to Grenier, made the Taliban's supposed surrender "nominal" and "highly dubious." Karzai was a bit like the Wizard of Oz, holding power through bluff and showmanship; the Taliban, for their part, made a show of treating with him just long enough to slip away. "Their main concern was to secure their ability to leave Kandahar safely," Grenier said. Lieutenant Colonel David Fox, the US Special Forces officer assigned to Karzai, concluded similarly: "The Taliban believed if they kept Karzai at bay in the north and Sherzai at bay in the south, [with these] negotiations and a set date to surrender, this gave them the time to pick up, get in their vehicles and drive off."[51]

Considering the Taliban's record of refusing American overtures of peace prior to December 6, this seems the more likely interpretation. Karzai's belief that the Taliban were offering to end the war and recognize his government is almost certainly an *ex post facto* construction. Mullah Omar had first reached out to him weeks before December 6, well before Karzai was elected chairman and thus before Omar could have conceivably wanted to recognize any new government. News of Karzai's election came on the same day, just hours before the Taliban delegation arrived to talk. The coincidence of timing conflated the events in Karzai's mind such that the offer to evacuate Kandahar became the symbolic beginning of his presidency. The Taliban had reportedly agreed to hand in their weapons as part of the deal but fled still armed. A final data point: after the Taliban left Kandahar and Karzai's forces moved into the governor's palace, the US military found the building had been rigged with massive explosives, an enormous booby trap designed to wipe out the leadership of the new government – hardly a magnanimous gesture of reconciliation by a movement keen on recognizing the new regime (a fact conveniently omitted by critics who accuse the United States of missing a chance for peace). There was no comprehensive Taliban surrender left on the table in early December 2001.[52]

RUMSFELD'S PRESS CONFERENCES

Complicating the picture yet further, Secretary of Defense Donald Rumsfeld was asked at press conferences in November and December

---

[51] Grenier, *88 Days to Kandahar*, 360. Grenier, interview by author. PBS Frontline, "Interview: Lt. Col. David Fox," September 8, 2002. www.pbs.org/wgbh/pages/front line/shows/campaign/interviews/fox.html.

[52] Grenier, *88 Days to Kandahar*, 314–315. Blehm, *The Only Thing Worth Dying For*, 416.

about the possibility of accepting a Taliban surrender, opening negotiation with them, or offering amnesty to senior leaders. Rumsfeld's answers have been widely misreported and fed the narrative that the United States missed, or deliberately rejected, an opportunity for peace with the Taliban.

Rumsfeld is a fascinating character, clearly one of the most intelligent and tenacious people to hold high office in recent American history. Yet – this will be a recurring theme – he could not see past his own blind spots. Rumsfeld had previously served as a member of Congress, ambassador to NATO, White House chief of staff, and secretary of defense in the 1960s and 1970s. He was already something of an elder statesman before 2001, and he was widely regarded for his intelligence, depth of knowledge, work ethic, bureaucratic savvy, and personal stamina. He was also infamously arrogant, prickly, and brusque with subordinates.

On November 19, Rumsfeld told the press that "the United States is not inclined to negotiate surrenders" – but the reason he gave was because the United States lacked enough troops on the ground to enforce any agreement or take prisoners. He acknowledged that the Northern Alliance and other anti-Taliban groups were striking local deals with Taliban groups to avoid fighting. He opposed negotiations that allowed al-Qaida members to escape or senior Taliban leaders to receive amnesty but left the door open for other terms. In reference to the battle for Kunduz then raging against al-Qaida (not the Taliban), Rumsfeld rejected negotiations but welcomed the idea of surrender. Similarly, on November 30, Rumsfeld and General Peter Pace noted reports about the possible surrender of Kandahar city but expressed opposition only to giving amnesty to Mullah Omar.[53]

Even if they had been open to the idea, the Bush administration would have faced a major obstacle to negotiations or, especially, amnesty: the Taliban were still under international sanctions that predated 9/11. The UN had listed 143 individuals associated with the Taliban on its sanctions list in 1999, after the African Embassy bombings, and the US Treasury Department designated them a terrorist group the same year (though they were never designated on the State Department's separate list). UN officials had spent two years meeting with Taliban leaders demanding they hand over bin Laden in compliance with various UN Security Council Resolutions, to no avail.

---

[53] "Pentagon Briefing with Secretary Rumsfeld," November 19, 2001. "Rumsfeld Briefs Press on War Effort," November 30, 2001. www.washingtonpost.com/wp-srv/nation/specials/attacked/transcripts/rumsfeldtext_111901.html and www.washingtonpost.com/wp-srv/nation/specials/attacked/transcripts/rumsfeld_text113001.html.

At virtually every meeting that [UN Special Representative] Mr. Vendrell held with Taliban representatives, he urged them to accept the need to surrender Bin Laden and cease support for terrorism, warning them of the serious consequences that their lack of cooperation could entail, particularly if there were to be another terrorist incident that could be attributed to Bin Laden's network.[54]

The Taliban's tie to al-Qaida, the UN sanctions, and the terrorist designations made it politically risky and legally complicated to talk to the Taliban, and it was unclear what kind of deals the United States or the United Nations could offer them. This is a small but important detail commonly overlooked by critics who insist the United States should have immediately included the Taliban in the new Afghan government. Lifting sanctions and crafting a negotiating strategy are painstaking, laborious, time-consuming efforts that require outreach and coordination with the legal and diplomatic representatives of every nation that had a stake in the sanctions regime. It took months, even years, to do that kind of work in later years.

On December 6, hours after Karzai's meeting with the Taliban, the press asked Rumsfeld about a possible deal that left Mullah Omar "in control of the opposition." Whatever the Taliban and Karzai had discussed had not been passed up the chain to Bush, Rumsfeld, or any of the principals through official channels. Rumsfeld's answers, then, were in response to rumors conveyed to him by the press, not to any verified report. Rumsfeld replied somewhat positively that he had seen various reports about a possible surrender offer and that, "at least at this moment I have not seen or heard anything that would suggest that anyone is negotiating something that would be contrary to what our interests are," emphasizing that American interests were combating al-Qaida and shutting down their safe haven. He qualified his answer, saying that he hadn't had a chance to think through whether conditions could be found that squared American interests with the possible deal with Omar: "I don't know, and I haven't thought of what it might be."[55]

---

[54] United Nations, A/56/681, S/2001/1157, 2–3.

[55] I asked several Bush officials, and none could recall being informed about Karzai's meeting that day. There was no US embassy operating in Afghanistan at the time, which would have been the normal channel through which such an offer would usually be conveyed. Reports may have filtered up through military and intelligence channels, but Rumsfeld's comments make clear that nothing confirmed had reached his desk by the time of his press conference. Defense Department Briefing, December 6, 2001. www .c-span.org/video/?167684-1/defense-department-briefing.

Moments later, Rumsfeld hardened his position when journalists pressed him further, asking if Omar would be allowed to "live in dignity," to which Rumsfeld replied, "No, that would not be consistent with what I said," reflecting an openness to talks with the Taliban as a group coupled with a harder line toward individual senior Taliban leaders. When a journalist suggested he sounded supportive of the talks, he replied, "Well I'm not, I just don't know where these talks are going. And I think there has been a lot of speculation in the press ... I like to deal with a little more factual material than speculation and press reports. Therefore, I am without an opinion and will remain without one until we get something substantively." Rumsfeld clearly did not have details of whatever Karzai and the Taliban had discussed and just as clearly was not rejecting talks out of hand. Asked again, a few minutes later, if there was any kind of surrender deal the United States would find acceptable, Rumsfeld replied, "That's what we've been trying to get them to do. Stop fighting, surrender." Pressed yet again to explain "what would be acceptable to the US in the Kandahar situation?" Rumsfeld said, "Surrender."

Rumsfeld was open to a Taliban surrender and to some form of negotiations between Afghan factions and the Taliban, but not to amnesty for senior leaders and certainly not for al-Qaida. That nuance, and his efforts to hedge and qualify his statements, were lost on the press and later historians. Carter Malkasian's assertion that "in a press conference on December 6, US Secretary of Defense Donald Rumsfeld vetoed any peace talks with the Taliban" is clearly false. David Kilcullen referenced Rumsfeld's press conferences and condemned "the Bush administration's failure even to bother negotiating a semblance of a peace deal with the defeated Taliban," which again is false. Steve Coll misreports that, at the December 6 press conference, "Rumsfeld announced that any negotiated end to the war against the Taliban was 'unacceptable to the United States.'" What Rumsfeld said was "I do not think there will be a negotiated end to the situation that will be unacceptable to the United States." Rumsfeld was commenting on the likelihood of negotiations compromising American interests, not announcing his opposition to them, and referring to negotiations over Kandahar, not the war as a whole. Negotiations would not yield a result "unacceptable to the United States" because the United States would shape their outcome, not stop them from happening. The headline in the *New York Times* the next day read "Rumsfeld Rejects Plan to Allow Mullah Omar 'to Live in Dignity,'" which is true but not characteristic of his comments as a whole.[56]

---

[56] Kilcullen and Mills, *The Ledger*, 77. Brian Knowlton, "Rumsfeld Rejects Plan to Allow Mullah Omar 'To Live in Dignity," *New York Times*, December 7, 2001.

Reporters were not always clear if they were asking about surrender, negotiations, or amnesty – three very different things – nor about the difference between al-Qaida and the Taliban, nor the difference between foot soldiers and senior leaders. The Bush administration clearly favored surrender, opposed amnesty, and was ambivalent about negotiations. It was still debating its policies toward different groups in different scenarios, leaning softer toward the Taliban than al-Qaida and toward foot soldier than leaders, in line with the sanctions and terrorist designations from 1999. Previously, the Bush administration was aware of the possibility that the Taliban might want to negotiate or surrender and had been actively debating how to respond. Powell had raised the possibility of negotiating with the Taliban amid hostilities as early as September 15,[57] and Feith recounts how the Deputies had discussed the possibility of a Taliban surrender while military operations were ongoing in October and November:

> [Deputy National Security Advisor] Stephen Hadley raised the question of how the United States should respond if Taliban leaders offered to surrender and we came under pressure to halt US military operations. [Deputy Secretary of Defense Paul] Wolfowitz noted that we hadn't yet completed our military mission against the Taliban and al-Qaida, so a cease-fire would be premature. Who, he asked, would be in a position to accept a Taliban surrender? ... Hadley asked if we wanted a provisional government to come into being that could accept surrenders.[58]

In that context, if the Taliban had tendered a formal offer of surrender on December 5–6 – which they almost certainly had not – and the offer had made it up the chain to the Bush administration (which it had not), the administration would certainly have debated it, and likely accepted it, depending on its specific conditions (they would not have accepted amnesty for senior leaders). That Rumsfeld's comments are so clearly improvised and speculative reinforces that there was no formal Taliban proposal before US policymakers. Rumsfeld's main sticking point in the press conferences was not about negotiations or surrender – toward which he was clearly open – but about amnesty for senior leaders and about Mullah Omar's individual status, which was complicated by US and UN sanctions. Rumsfeld was responding, off the cuff, to reporters' questions about an unconfirmed, rumored deal, trying to leave the door open while also

---

https://www.nytimes.com/2001/12/07/news/rumsfeld-rejects-planto-allow-mullah-omar-to-live-in-dignity-taliban.html

[57] Woodward, *Bush at War*, 87.   [58] Feith, *War and Decision*, 133.

reiterating the administration's existing policy and sanctions on the Taliban's senior leadership.

The Bush administration did eventually prove inflexible toward the Taliban and missed opportunities to open meaningful dialogue with them, but critics have read that later failing backward into the earliest days of the war, letting their knowledge of subsequent events color their analysis of the past, blurring the distinction between the situation in late 2001, while the war was ongoing, and the situation in 2002, after the Taliban's fall from power. In light of how the war turned out, some critics seem eager to go back and find the root of all failure at the earliest possible point, to find a single decision when it all went wrong, or the one chance for peace that a villainous and overbearing secretary of defense snubbed. If the war was really lost on December 6, 2001, later mistakes do not matter as much. The outcome comes to look as if it were foreordained; a sort of fatalism takes over the telling of history, and the rest of the war is narrated as a tragic but inevitable outcome. It makes for an emotionally satisfying, dramatic narrative that conveniently minimizes every subsequent mistake and exonerates later pol- icymakers of their share of blame, but it is bad history. Though Rumsfeld shares a large amount of blame for what went wrong in Afghanistan, his missteps come later and mostly relate to the administration's underinvest- ment in nation building. Critics' antipathy toward Rumsfeld's overall legacy – justified in other respects – has colored their ability to hear the evidence of what he said in December 2001.

There are plenty of faults in the Bush administration's record on Afghanistan; its late 2001 diplomacy toward the Taliban is not one of them. In September and October of 2001, the Bush administration reached out to the Taliban, and the Taliban rejected the opportunity for peace. Despite what later historians have claimed, the Taliban did not try to end the war on December 5–6, and Rumsfeld did not preemptively shut the door to peace talks. Through negotiations with the Obama administration from 2010 to 2014 and the Trump administration from 2018 to 2020, and in the aftermath of their victory in 2021, the Taliban never denounced al-Qaida, acknowledged its responsibility for 9/11, or broke ties with the group. Preserving its relationship with al-Qaida is among the longest-lasting and most deeply entrenched of the Taliban's policies, dating to 1996, almost to the Taliban's founding. In 2001, the Taliban were demonstrably committed to fighting the United States and rejecting peace.

The Bush administration got many things right in the months after 9/11. Over three weeks of deliberation, the administration sensibly sent out peace feelers to the Taliban but just as sensibly prepared for the war it expected was unavoidable. Forced to respond to an unanticipated crisis with no time for planning, the administration improvised an impressive military campaign that achieved surprisingly quick results. Bush's own verdict that "there had been no famine, no outbreak of civil war, no collapse of the government in Pakistan, no global uprising by Muslims, and no retaliatory attack on our homeland" is a fair reminder of all that could have gone wrong but didn't. The early victory vindicated the administration's theory of the war – a War on Terror best waged with a light footprint to avoid a quagmire in the "graveyard of empires" – because the theory had, for the moment, worked.[59]

Success always raises the risk of overconfidence. The administration's vindication meant that they did not feel any need to reexamine their strategic assumptions. But the world continues to change, even after victory, and policymakers always need to reexamine their beliefs and assumptions – constantly, continuously, relentlessly – to see if they still match reality. In Afghanistan, circumstances changed faster than the administration's theory of the war. The Taliban were not defeated; they changed from a government to a movement-in-exile and eventually into an insurgency. The security problem in Afghanistan changed from state sponsorship of terrorism to state failure and collapse. The American mission should have changed as well. The mission started as regime change in service of counterterrorism; it should have become state building and peacekeeping in service of counterterrorism – something which the Bush administration was ideologically committed to avoiding.

[59] Bush, *Decision Points*, 202.

3

2002–2003

Neglect

The war in Afghanistan was over, and the United States had won. That, at least, is what the Bush administration – and much of the world – believed in December 2001, a belief that persisted through mid 2005. The Taliban had fallen from power and al-Qaida was on the run. A new government took power, a political process began, refugees began streaming back, life bustled in the streets of Afghanistan's cities. The War on Terror could move on to other battlefields. There was one more major engagement – the Battle of Shah-i-Kot, or Operation Anaconda, in Paktia Province, in March 2002 – after which Afghanistan settled into its most peaceful era since 1978. The sense of victory was reinforced by Afghanistan's slow but successful process of political reconstruction, called the Bonn Process.

But there were still broader questions. Since it had accomplished its immediate objectives, the spring of 2002 was an ideal moment for the administration to pause and reassess its strategy, goals, and purpose in Afghanistan. What were the United States' interests in Afghanistan, if any, apart from its counterterrorism mission? Or perhaps the more relevant question was: What else was required to ensure the counterterrorism mission succeeded over the long term? With the Taliban gone and a new, friendly government in power, what should the United States' strategy be with respect to that government? What was the relationship between an *Afghanistan* strategy and a *counterterrorism* strategy? There was no question about what the Bush administration wanted: everyone wanted Afghanistan to succeed. But aspirational goals are not a strategy. The question was whether and how much the United States would help it succeed, how much it would spend, and whether it would use American troops for that purpose, which in turn rested on the question of how necessary a successful Afghanistan was to defeating al-Qaida.

The problem is not that the Bush administration got the answers wrong. The problem is that it failed to ask the questions in the first place. Rather than grapple with the newfound complexity, a sense of inertia, drift, and inattention took over. The most obvious course of action led directly toward the administration's *bête noire*: nation building. The Bush administration had no interest in that, as it had made clear throughout the presidential campaign. Some officials recognized the logic that long-term success against al-Qaida required Afghan stability, but Afghanistan's apparent success in early 2002 seemed to suggest that the United States could leave it to the UN and others and avoid getting enmeshed in a messy, protracted nation-building effort. The situation was amorphous, and there was no sense of urgency.

There was, of course, a sense of urgency and a serious debate starting in the spring of 2002, but it was not about Afghanistan. As the year wore on, the administration became almost wholly consumed with preparations for the war in Iraq. Whether or not that entailed material resources being diverted from one theater to the other – a point still hotly debated – it certainly diverted time and attention, the most valuable resources of all. Policymakers have limited bandwidth, and the competition for their time is necessarily zero-sum: As they spend more time on one issue, they spend less on another. As time spent on Iraq rose, time spent on Afghanistan diminished.

Counterintuitively, the drift and inattention could occasionally work to Afghanistan's benefit. The Bonn Process unfolded as planned and was widely seen as a success, with only loose oversight by policymakers in DC and more leadership from the UN. Unfortunately, Bonn would prove to be the easy part. While the political process unfolded, the international community tried and, absent American leadership, failed to mount the most ambitious reconstruction and stabilization operation since World War II. The depth of Afghanistan's need was too great, the international community too fragmented, the expertise on state building too shallow – and the United States too distracted, its attention increasingly monopolized by its second post-9/11 war. Meanwhile, despite increasing warnings from experts and leaders in the field, senior US policymakers largely failed to recognize that reconstruction efforts in Afghanistan were stagnating and security was slowly deteriorating. The Taliban did not.

THE BONN PROCESS

Some critics suggest that, in early 2002, the administration could have declared victory and come home. There was no realistic option of leaving, and no serious discussion within the administration of doing so: al-Qaida's senior leaders were still at large in the region. Afghanistan's warlords might easily have fallen to fighting among themselves – as they did, at a low level, throughout 2002 and 2003 – and an Afghan civil war would hardly be a congenial environment for the American war on al-Qaida. Keeping American troops around helped keep the lid on warlords' ambitions and thus sustained a permissive operating environment against al-Qaida. The Bush administration "didn't want to repeat the mistakes of the early 1990s where they then just left it and it turned into chaos," recalled Ambassador Tony Wayne, the assistant secretary of state for economic and business affairs. There was little question that the United States would stay in Afghanistan to hunt remnants of al-Qaida and to train Afghan partners. That led the administration to increase the US military presence, slowly, in 2002 and 2003.[1]

"With all that would occur later, it's hard to remember that in 2005 we thought that the Afghan project was in relatively good shape," Rice wrote in 2011, reflecting the attitude of the administration and much of the world. After March 2002, political violence in Afghanistan receded. Occasional rocket attacks or ambushes by anonymous militants were sporadic, random, and without strategic effect. "In the opening years, it was pretty calm," recalled Steve Hadley. "In 2004 and 2005, we actually think things are going pretty well in Afghanistan." "We thought we had won the war," Khalilzad recalled, "that the Taliban had been defeated, that they disappeared or disintegrated." Afghanistan was not yet called the "good war," because few people thought of it as a war at all. Political scientists sometimes use an arbitrary figure of 1,000 combat deaths per year to measure when something counts as a "war." By that capricious measure, from April 2002 to April 2005, Afghanistan was not at "war."[2]

It was also the era in which I first went to Afghanistan. I arrived in May 2002 and spent most of my time in a dusty tent at Bagram Airbase only interacting with Afghans hired for construction projects on base. I traveled to Kabul for a brief trip, crossing the Shomali Plain in an armored SUV past UN demining teams through Northern Alliance checkpoints. I was struck by the freewheeling happy chaos of the city. Traffic circles were jammed with people, donkey-drawn carts, and shop sellers hawking wares while traffic lights hung useless and broken. I ambled down Chicken Street two blocks from the presidential palace, in uniform and by myself – an unheard-of risk years later – and bought scarves and pakol caps and a small carved camel

---

[1] Wayne, interview by author.

[2] Rice, *No Higher Honor*, 345. Hadley and Khalilzad, interviews by author. The Uppsala Conflict Data Program records 60 combat fatalities in Afghanistan in 2002, 660 in 2003, 711 in 2004, and 1,628 in 2005. https://ucdp.uu.se/conflict/333.

figurine as souvenirs and gifts for my family. The shopkeepers were warm and welcoming. Older men looked hesitant, but young Afghan children flocked to me in the street asking for treats and posing for photos. I handed out gum and felt like we were staging a World War II-era propaganda photo – but it was entirely genuine. There was a sense of relief and celebration in the air. Afghanistan had been liberated.

The challenge in Afghanistan was no longer fighting the Taliban or al-Qaida; it was finding someone to put in charge after the Taliban government fell. The issue first arose in early and mid October of 2001 when the administration debated whether to allow the Northern Alliance – mostly made up of the Tajik, Uzbek, and Hazara minorities – to march on Kabul. Some intelligence officers and Bush officials – including Powell and Armitage – were concerned that the Alliance occupying the capital city would provoke a Pashtun uprising and an Afghan civil war. Pakistani officials encouraged that belief in their meetings with American counterparts because they wanted a pliant, Pashtun-dominated government in Kabul. The Bush administration was more concerned with attacking al-Qaida and had no desire to risk a civil war. In mid and late October, it asked the Northern Alliance to hold off in hopes more Pashtuns would join the fight against the Taliban. In the event, the Northern Alliance took Kabul on November 14 without incident, but the discussions laid the groundwork for Afghanistan's political future. The Bush team quickly realized a new government needed to be put in place, and the government would have to include the Northern Alliance but not be limited to them.[3]

Bush instinctively knew that meant democracy for Afghanistan. "I felt strongly that the Afghan people should be able to select their new leader," he wrote. "They had suffered too much – and the American people were risking too much – to let the country slide back into tyranny. I asked Colin [Powell] to work on a plan for a transition to democracy." Bush's instinct for democracy was matched by the Afghans', who never contemplated anything else in the months ahead (though there was some debate about whether democracy should fall under a constitutional monarchy, as it had in the 1960s). Powell turned to veteran diplomat Ambassador Jim Dobbins. Dobbins felt the urgency of the moment. "Powell was reflecting the wider administration concern that the diplomatic aspects of the Afghan campaign were not keeping pace with the military," he wrote. "Specifically he was worried the Taliban regime would fall before a successor government was

---

[3] Woodward, *Bush at War*, 215, 223, 230–233, 236–237, 241, 275, 280, 304ff. Coll, *Directorate S*, 89–91.

ready to take its place. My assignment was to produce such a successor regime, thereby forestalling the necessity for an American military occupation."[4]

Beyond that, however, when it came time to flesh out the plan, the administration was happy to defer to the international community while the United States focused on counterterrorism. Bush told a press conference on October 11, 2001, that "my focus is on bringing al-Qaida to justice," and that "it would be a useful function for the United Nations to take over the so-called 'nation-building' – I would call it the stabilization of a future government – after our military mission is complete." He pledged that "we'll participate" in rebuilding Afghanistan but invited the UN to "provide the framework." In his January 2002 State of the Union address, Bush briefly pledged that "we'll be partners in rebuilding" Afghanistan, but the speech overwhelmingly focused on terrorism, weapons of mass destruction, and the "axis of evil."[5]

The United Nations was more than willing to take the lead. The day after the Taliban evacuated Kabul, the United Nations Security Council outlined its vision for the next Afghan government. It should be "broad-based, multi-ethnic and fully representative" and "respect the human rights of all Afghan people." The United Nations envisioned a strong position for itself. "The United Nations should play a central role in supporting the efforts of the Afghan people to establish urgently such a new and transitional administration." The UN, with US help, convened a conference among Afghan factions in Bonn, Germany, to broker agreement on an interim administration and a process for reconstruction. Talks lasted from November 27 to December 5.[6]

The US and UN representatives at Bonn played a crucial role brokering compromises and putting together the interim administration. Although they did not participate or vote in the official sessions, their presence at the conference allowed them to engage in side discussions. Dobbins, the head of the American delegation, said that Lakhdar Brahimi, the UN special representative for Afghanistan, "took the lead in moving the Afghans towards our [US and UN] desired goals." Brahimi and Dobbins, backed by

[4] Bush, *Decision Points*, 197. Dobbins, *Foreign Service*, 233.
[5] "President Holds Prime Time News Conference," October 11, 2001. https://georgewbush-whitehouse.archives.gov/news/releases/2001/10/20011011-7.html. "President Delivers State of the Union," January 29, 2002. https://georgewbush-whitehouse.archives.gov/news/releas es/2002/01/20020129-11.html.
[6] United Nations, S/RES/1378, November 14, 2001.

coordinated pressure from several capitals, helped break the biggest logjam surrounding the naming of the transitional cabinet and chairman, with Brahimi drawing up the list of names, compiled from different factions' nominations.[7]

But Dobbins' presence at Bonn does not mean the Bush administration was keenly following events or dictating the outcome. "There was little interagency process behind the decisions made at the Bonn conference," Dobbins told me. "I had no instructions except that we don't want to govern Afghanistan. We want a government that can be put in place that's broadly representative, that's acceptable to the elements of the opposition, and can exercise responsibility from the day the Taliban leave Kabul." Dobbins added that the Bush administration "didn't care who was in the government, what kind of government it was, nothing of that sort. I was really under no restrictions other than to get it done."[8]

The resulting agreement reflected the UN's agenda. The Bonn Agreement copied the UN's language, envisioning a "broad-based, gender-sensitive, multi-ethnic and fully representative government." The Afghans requested that the UN authorize a military force to secure Kabul, monitor the implementation of the agreement, advise the interim government on how to create a politically neutral environment, train new Afghan security forces, compile a voter registry, take a census, investigate human rights abuses, and be an honest broker throughout the process. Most importantly, the Afghans agreed to the formation of an interim government headed by Hamid Karzai, a noted Pashtun tribal leader, and a cabinet of some thirty ministers, carefully allotted to include, appease, and balance among various factions. They agreed to operate under Afghanistan's 1964 constitution until a new one could be drafted. Contrary to critics who accuse the United States or United Nations of having forced or pressured the Afghans into a democratic system, there was hardly any debate and almost immediate consensus among the Afghans that they would adopt some form of electoral and representative system, the only system feasible for a pluralistic nation barely emerging from civil war.[9]

The success of the Bonn conference, almost simultaneous with the fall of Kandahar and the Taliban's defeat, added momentum to the sense of victory and the atmosphere of optimism. The United Nations and the World Bank established an alphabet soup of policy architecture for the

---

[7] Dobbins, *After the Taliban*, 80.

[8] Dobbins, interview by author. Dobbins, *Foreign Service*, 233, 246.

[9] United Nations, S/2001/1154, December 5, 2001, 2. Dobbins, *After the Taliban*.

reconstruction of Afghanistan: the International Security Assistance Force (ISAF) to keep the peace in Kabul; the United Nations Assistance Mission in Afghanistan (UNAMA) to coordinate international assistance; an Afghanistan Reconstruction Trust Fund (ARTF) and a Law and Order Trust Fund for Afghanistan (LOTFA) to pool donor money. The Afghan interim government took power in late December. In coming years, UNAMA would try to advise the interim government, train new Afghan security forces, compile a voter registry, and take a census. (Despite twenty years of discussion and planning, no census was ever taken.)

The first major milestone in the Bonn Process was an emergency *loya jirga* or grand council of elders, in May 2002. The Bush administration's only goal for the jirga was to support Karzai and oppose the restoration of the Afghan monarchy, according to Richard Armitage, but they were broad aspirations without the sort of detailed staff work typical for foreign policy decisions. "Do we have a goal? Yeah. But was it specific and laid out? No," Armitage recalled. On the monarchy, "there was a discussion of this and we decided that [the royal family] was too far out of it, too long gone." Some delegates, particularly Pashtuns, wanted to see the restoration of a constitutional monarchy as a symbol of national unity over a democratically elected government, but the Northern Alliance and the Bush administration objected. Armitage argued that postwar nations are best led by those who stayed and endured the hardships of war with their people, which made Karzai a better pick than the former king and the royal family, who had lived in Rome for the previous three decades. The king renounced the throne and was designated "Father of the Nation" instead.[10]

THE TALIBAN

Some critics have suggested the United Nations, the United States, and the Afghans again missed an opportunity by not including the Taliban in the jirga. "Formally involving the Taliban," however, "would have provoked the Northern Alliance's ire, jeopardizing the Loya Jirga's broader success," Khalilzad judged. "The United Nations and the Afghans made the right call," he believed. "They did not invite the Taliban to participate, but the permissive rules of the Loya Jirga elections provided ample opportunity for former members of the Taliban to join the political process." Khalilzad is probably right that the Taliban's participation would have risked the

[10] Armitage, interview by author.

collapse of the jirga, but the idea that the Taliban would openly run for public office six months after their military defeat is naive: other Taliban who came forward around the same time were arrested by American forces. The Taliban were likely uninterested anyway: "It is doubtful that the more committed Taliban would have been cooperative," Khalilzad argued. "The very concept of a Loya Jirga was anathema to them, representing the democratic and national values they despised."[11]

But the jirga raised an important question: what was the place of the Taliban in postwar Afghanistan? The difficulty of what to do with the Taliban, navigating the tension between holding them accountable for the past and co-opting them into a new future, would bedevil the American and Afghan governments for the next twenty years. After 9/11, the Bush administration had sensibly tried to reach out to the Taliban, to no avail, forcing the United States to conflate the Taliban and al-Qaida during the first phase of the war. But after the Taliban's fall, starting in the spring of 2002, the Bush administration might be expected to see the value in trying again to co-opt the Taliban into the political process, dividing it from al-Qaida and broadening the Afghan government's base of support. That would have required reevaluating the conceptual framework of the "War on Terror," and the wartime strategy of treating the Taliban as indistinguishable from al-Qaida, which would have been challenging both legally and politically. The Taliban were still under international sanctions and, as a group, refused to denounce al-Qaida or acknowledge its responsibility for the 9/11 attacks.

It was a difficult problem – but rather than grappling with it and trying to come up with a solution, the administration proved to be inflexible. For example, the Taliban Foreign Minister, Wakil Ahmed Muttawakil, surrendered to Karzai in early 2002, hoping to join the new government. When American forces learned of his surrender, they took him into custody as an enemy combatant – a perfect example of bureaucracy doing its thing. While he was in detention, parts of the intelligence community saw the potential and worked with him on pitching a new group – "Taliban for Karzai" – according to Steve Coll's account. They "worked up a presentation about Taliban defectors and the future of Afghan politics" and briefed the idea in Washington, a rare example of bureaucratic creativity. While it would have been a politically and legally difficult undertaking, the Bush administration did not even try. "We're not doing that," Cheney reportedly said when he heard the briefing, vetoing creativity and reinforcing bureaucratic inertia.

---

[11] Khalilzad, *The Envoy*, Kindle location 2800.

(Muttawakil was later released and ran for a seat in the new Afghan parliament. Far from bringing the Taliban into the fold, he was disowned by the Taliban for his moderation, suggesting his defection may not have been a great lost opportunity.)[12]

Cheney's response captured the administration's stance toward the Taliban in 2002 and 2003. "You'll have to keep in mind what was coming out of the White House," General Dan McNeill, commander of US forces in 2002–2003, recalled. "The Taliban had been considered and deemed a terrorist organization. We do not negotiate with terrorists." "This goes a little bit back to the mood of the country and the mood of the president. 'Eliminate,' you know?" recalled Richard Boucher, then serving as assistant secretary of state for public affairs. "It goes back to, 'we don't need to hear about the complications, we don't need to hear about history.' It's just, 'get these guys, we got to get these guys before they get us.' It was a pretty absolutist kind of feeling at the time."[13]

Because the Taliban had rejected American overtures in late 2001 and continued to maintain ties to al-Qaida, the Bush administration saw little reason to revisit its approach – especially regarding the senior Taliban leadership, the top dozen or two leaders around Mullah Omar who were under UN sanctions. The strategy "didn't have any space for opponents of the government. It wasn't designed to make them settle in and become political opponents," Boucher said. "I never saw a strategy that was designed to split the Taliban, bring in regional ethnic groups and leaders, and expand the political base." Bob Grenier, the former CIA station chief in Islamabad, agreed that the United States missed an opportunity for a "magnanimous approach" to the Taliban in 2002 and 2003. Wilkerson, Powell's chief of staff, did not believe the administration wanted to reach out to the Taliban in the early years. They acted as if "you never want to show anybody that your enemy, as you're bashing [them] about the head and ears, might actually be human," he said. "So I don't think there was any attitude in the West Wing" to reach out.[14]

"There was definitely a missed opportunity, at a minimum, of co-opting some of these people into the new regime, and perhaps more than that," Jim Dobbins believed, noting that both Karzai and the UN "would've welcomed such an opportunity." But the Bush administration was not interested,

---

[12] Coll, *Directorate S*, 411. Grenier notes that Muttawakil "had no influence with Omar or the rest of the senior leadership … He had no independent political power base, and commanded no troops." See *88 Days to Kandahar*, 123.

[13] Boucher, interview by author.   [14] Boucher and Wilkerson, interviews by author.

rejecting the opportunities "without any debate, without any discussion, as far as I know. It was never raised at the White House, it was never raised with the State Department, not a single discussion in the first six months after 9/11." Dobbins insists there were no meaningful opportunities to include the Taliban in 2001, "but co-opting them afterwards piecemeal ... was in retrospect a real possibility which we missed. It was one of the critical early errors, unforced errors on our part."[15]

Cheney's response reflected a decision the administration made in 2001. The main goal of the "War on Terror" – and there was no distinction yet between that war and the war in Afghanistan for the Bush administration – was to defeat terrorist groups, deter future terrorism, and set a precedent that state sponsors of terrorism would pay a price. That decision became embedded in the bureaucracy. "Now, that became a key concept for the Defense Department," Feith recalled, "but what that meant was we really had to hit the Taliban hard. It was a crucial part of our strategy because hitting the Taliban could send signals to the Libyas, and the Syrias, and the Sudans, and the Iraqs, and the Irans that if they support terrorism, pursue weapons of mass destruction, and do things that make us nervous, then they would pay a price, the way the Taliban paid a price." That strategic concept led the administration to maintain its hard line against the Taliban long after 2001, after the situation had changed.

Feith complained about people in the intelligence community who would

> come in and say, you should attack al-Qaida targets, but *not* Taliban targets. And we kind of slapped our foreheads and said, why don't you get it? The whole point of this is to attack the Taliban because that's a crucial way of getting the message to other people who have contacts with terrorist groups that they better pull the reins in on them and have them not attack the United States.

Feith said, "If we gave a pass to the Taliban after they had given safe haven to al-Qaida to attack us, what's the message that we're sending to other state sponsors around the world? So, we were surprised, not to say flabbergasted, that [they] would be completely missing the strategic concept behind attacking the Taliban." Feith's reasoning, forged in the earliest days of the war, made sense in 2001 but lingered long after the situation on the ground had changed. I specifically asked how his reasoning influenced the

---

[15] Dobbins, interview by author.

administration's thinking *after* the Taliban's fall from power. "We didn't want to reach out to the Taliban. What we wanted to do was to make an example of the Taliban," he replied.[16]

NATION BUILDING

As successful and important as the Bonn Process was, it amounted to an agreement to have a state while doing little to make that state a reality. With tragic irony, the Bush administration came into office famously opposed to nation building. "Are we going to have a nation-building corps from America? Absolutely not. Our military is meant to fight and win war," Bush said during the 2000 campaign. "We need to convince the people who live in the lands they live in to build their nations." Bush was responding to the American peacekeeping operations in Bosnia and Kosovo, which were unpopular among Republicans and, at the time, considered to be faltering efforts that fostered a culture of dependency on American largesse (decades later, they are generally seen as imperfect but broadly successful). Bush was worried nation-building operations would overstretch the military, but he was also concerned about their effect on America's reputation abroad. "I just don't think it's the role of the United States to walk into a country and say, 'We do it this way, so should you,'" he said.[17]

Weeks after 9/11, Powell first raised the question of the post-Taliban government of Afghanistan. "The president won't want to use troops to rebuild Afghanistan," White House Chief of Staff Andy Card replied. Bush's view was initially shared by most of his administration. Rumsfeld and Feith argued at length and repeatedly – one suspects, defensively – about the dangers of nation building in their memoirs. "I recommended reassuring the Pashtuns that 'nation-building is *not* our key strategic goal,'" Feith wrote, to allay Pashtuns' fears that they might become ensnared in dependency as the Balkans appeared to have been. "We did not want the Afghans to think we intended to take the same approach to their country," one that would have involved "the kind of 'nation-building' arrangement that would have put Afghanistan under UN or multinational control."[18]

---

[16] Feith, interview by author.

[17] "George W. Bush 'US Should Not Nation Build' 2000 Campaign Debate," www.youtube.com/watch?v=P6nW2Uow-zk from the October 11, 2000 presidential debate.

[18] Woodward, *Bush at War*, 191–193, 195. Feith, *War and Decision*, 101–102, 134.

Rumsfeld shared the concern. "We ought not to make a career out of transforming Afghanistan," Rumsfeld advised the president. He believed deeply that the United States could not, and therefore should not try to, alter other societies, and that such a mission was peripheral to American interests anyway. "The Iraqis and Afghans would have to govern themselves in ways that worked for them," he later wrote. "I believed that political institutions should grow naturally out of local soil: not every successful principle or mechanism from one country could be transplanted in another . . . We were not in Afghanistan to transform a deeply conservative Islamic culture into a model of liberal modernity," which hardly seems a relevant concern when the Afghans had already readopted their own democratic constitution from 1964.

Rumsfeld was echoing concerns originating in the Vietnam War. He approvingly cited a fellow policymaker's belief that "American heavy-handedness had been a mistake in Vietnam." That is also why Rumsfeld was passionate about not encouraging dependency and ensuring the Afghans would take the lead in their own reconstruction. "Though we would do what we could to assist, we ultimately couldn't do it for them," he said. "We were not there to take ownership of Afghanistan's problems, tempting though it was for many Americans of goodwill. Instead, Afghans would need to take charge of their own fate." Rumsfeld had raised identical concerns about Vietnam in 1966 when serving in the US House of Representatives – local ownership was "one of the lessons of Vietnam for me," alongside the importance of American credibility, he later wrote – and he claimed that the success of the initial military campaign against the Taliban in 2001 and the Bonn Process proved his concept of deferring to local leadership. He made his views explicit in orders to the military: "We're not going to do any nation building," he told General Dan McNeill. (McNeill, for his part, thought avoiding nation building was "nigh to impossible," given the realities on the ground.)[19]

Rumsfeld usually gets most of the blame for resisting nation building, but he was hardly alone. The military "is not a civilian police force. It is not a political referee. And it is most certainly not designed to build a civilian society," Condoleezza Rice had written as the Bush campaign's foreign policy advisor in 2000. "Using the American armed forces as the world's '911' will degrade capabilities, bog soldiers down in peacekeeping roles, and fuel concern among other great powers that the United States has decided

---

[19] Rumsfeld, *Known and Unknown*, 398, 483, 682. On dependency in Vietnam and the need for local leadership there, see 99, 209, 373, 488, 666. McNeill, interview by author.

to enforce notions of 'limited sovereignty' worldwide in the name of humanitarianism." Rice's view was shared by the State Department after 9/11. Powell initially did not envision a long-term American presence in Afghanistan, according to his chief of staff. "Powell probably became a reluctant partner in [reconstruction]," Wilkerson recalled, knowing that "this is going to be an extremely difficult thing to do because this is the graveyard of empires." Powell shared Rumsfeld's concerns about the lessons of Vietnam and ordered his staff to draft a paper for Bush on the subject (which Wilkerson believed Bush never read).[20]

Powell's attitude was reflected in the department's public statements. "We do not want to get involved in the sort of intrusive nation-building which would be resented by Afghans," Richard Haass, the State Department's director of policy planning, told the Senate Foreign Relations Committee in December 2001, despite saying in the same briefing that the United States was committed to "comprehensive" reconstruction, including "demining, local road rehabilitation, provision of seeds, renovation of water supplies, reopening schools" and more. Haass' testimony reflected a tension that would recur again and again: officials knew they had to do some kind of rebuilding but insisted they were not interested in "nation building" – and they never defined the difference.[21]

The administration had another reason to resist nation building. They were concerned such an underdeveloped country could not absorb much aid. "We were worried about putting too many resources into the economy because it was so primitive," Steve Hadley explained. "And we were worried about corruption and inflation – and, surprise surprise, when in 2006 we started to really pump resources into that country, we got corruption and we got inflation."[22]

The administration's concerns conflated two different issues – cultural imperialism and aid dependency – neither of which addressed the United States' strategic interest, which was to deny safe haven to al-Qaida indefinitely, without a permanent American military presence. The logic was straightforward: the United States had successfully ejected al-Qaida from Afghanistan, but they would easily regroup upon the departure of the American military unless the new Afghan government could deny safe haven on their own. Rebuilding something in Afghanistan was the essential

---

[20] Rice, "Campaign 2000: Promoting the National Interest." Wilkerson, interview by author.
[21] Senate Foreign Relations Committee, "The Political Future of Afghanistan," December 6, 2001.
[22] Hadley, interview by author.

precondition to long-term success against al-Qaida. Nation building was strategy, not charity.

Rumsfeld understood the logic. He worried in an internal memo in April 2002 that "we are never going to get the US military out of Afghanistan unless we take care to see that there is something going on that will provide the stability that will be necessary for us to leave." Rumsfeld never squared that concern with his long-standing objection to nation building; "nation building" seemed to stand for something utopian and unrealistic, which he opposed, but Rumsfeld still wanted to do some degree of limited and achievable reconstruction. It was a distinction without a difference, but Rumsfeld's (and others') inflated concerns about the boogeyman of nation building hamstrung his ability to recognize and embrace fully the necessity of rebuilding Afghanistan. Paul Wolfowitz, the deputy secretary of defense, told the Senate Foreign Relations Committee in June 2002 that, "while our primary mission in that country has been to kill or capture terrorists who threaten the United States, or those who have harbored them, it is also important to help the Afghans establish long-term stability in that country, so that it does not once again become an outlaw country that provides sanctuary for terrorists," which, again, implied a much greater commitment to nation building than the administration wanted to admit.[23]

Rumsfeld's recognition of the need to do *something* conflicted with his instinct to avoid dependency and imperialism – but neither he nor anyone else asked which impulse was more urgent, nor which was more warranted. If Rumsfeld had asked, he might have realized that his concerns about cultural imperialism were baseless. State-building programs are often criticized as a form of cultural imperialism, yet the Afghans asked for more, not less, international involvement. Few state institutions are uniquely "Western." Countries across Africa and Asia have law codes, courts, police departments, central banks, departments of public works, power and water utilities, tax-collection agencies, post offices, census bureaus – the reconstruction of which is the focus of most state- or nation-building efforts. As for aid dependency, Rumsfeld apparently did not grasp the extent of Afghanistan's brokenness. Afghanistan was not at risk of *becoming* dependent on foreign aid; it was *already* dependent on outside

---

[23] Rumsfeld, memo to Feith, April 17, 2002, available at National Security Archive, https://nsarchive2.gwu.edu/NSAEBB/NSAEBB358a/doc23.pdf. Senate Foreign Relations Committee, "Afghanistan: Building Stability, Avoiding Chaos," June 26, 2002, 11–12.

help, and almost always had been. It had been a client of the British Empire from the 1840s and of the Soviet Union during the Cold War.[24]

Zalmay Khalilzad argued the point with Bush and Rumsfeld. Khalilzad occupies a special place in the saga of America's war in Afghanistan. He had started in the Bush administration as a senior director on the NSC staff, but that hardly conveyed the reality of what he brought to the table. Born in Mazar-i Sharif, in northern Afghanistan, Khalilzad participated in an exchange program to attend an American high school in the 1960s. He attended the American University in Beirut before getting a PhD at the University of Chicago, thereafter making his home in the United States as a naturalized citizen. He taught at Columbia before serving in the Reagan and first Bush administrations in the State Department and the NSC, now a card-carrying member of the American national security establishment. With far greater knowledge, language ability, and cultural awareness than most American diplomats – he speaks Arabic, Farsi, and Pashto – Khalilzad's life was an American immigrant success story, like Henry Kissinger or Zbigniew Brzezinski, though how much of it is true is an open question: Khalilzad's memoir, *The Envoy*, is a well-written, fascinating, and enjoyable trip through his life and career that one colleague described to me as "a work of fiction."

Within months of 9/11, Bush named Khalilzad his special presidential envoy for Afghanistan. Khalilzad used the position to argue for more attention to Afghanistan reconstruction:

> I argued that we would need to help Afghans stabilize their country to prevent terrorist attacks down the road. President Bush interjected, "Zal, we're not there to fix their problems!"
>
> "We can't fix our problems without helping them fix their problems," I countered . . .
>
> Rumsfeld, trying to cut off my argument, replied, "Zal, you have to take your hand off the bicycle seat!" Rumsfeld was suggesting that we had to allow the Afghans to succeed or fail on their own. Having heard Rumsfeld's bicycle analogy one too many times, I was exasperated. I had seen actual conditions on the ground in Afghanistan – the complete devastation produced by a quarter century of war. I recounted the abysmal conditions in Afghanistan point by point. "Mr. Secretary," I concluded, "there is no bicycle!"[25]

---

[24] For the opposite view, see Chandler, *Empire in Denial.*
[25] Khalilzad, *The Envoy*, Kindle location 2659–2688.

Rumsfeld loved the bicycle metaphor. One chapter of his memoir is entitled "Hands Off the Bicycle Seat." In the metaphor, the United States is a loving parent, and Afghanistan is a toddler learning how to ride a bike. The Afghans' inability is simply because of their immaturity and inexperience; they need encouragement, instruction, and support, but ultimately it is up to them to grow up. It is ironic that Rumsfeld, professing that he wanted to avoid cultural imperialism, evoked the same condescending paternalism character-istic of real imperialists. Condescension aside, the other main problem with the analogy, as Khalilzad rightly pointed out, was its ignorance. I recall a colleague in the intelligence community, sometime in 2004 or 2005, giving a summary of a meeting with Rumsfeld in which Rumsfeld used the bicycle analogy. We were incredulous and joked to each other that if there was a bicycle, it had a flat tire, no handlebars, and a broken chain. Perhaps the analogy was simply wrong altogether: Afghanistan was not a happy, healthy toddler with a shiny new bike; Afghanistan was a seasoned but wounded warrior in need of an ambulance.[26]

Feith defends their stance as a posture of humility. "Part of [Rumsfeld's] approach to the particular style of nation building was that the much more aggressive, can-do nation building is inherently arrogant," he said. Rumsfeld clearly disliked the idea of a complex reconstruction and stabilization operation, owing in large part to his experience in Congress, the White House, and the Pentagon during and after the Vietnam War. But the bicycle metaphor and the claim of humility look in retrospect like fig leaves, or a classic case of motivated reasoning, or the product of "realism": they believed nation building was arrogant, unnecessary, and impractical because they *wanted* to believe it was bad, no matter what the evidence said.[27]

"If some later contended that we never had a plan for full-fledged nation building or that we under-resourced such a plan, they were certainly correct," Rumsfeld wrote in his memoir. "We did not go there to try to bring prosperity to every corner of Afghanistan. I believed – and continue to believe – that such a goal would have amounted to a fool's errand," a utopian attempt "to remake Afghanistan into a prosperous American-style nation-state." Of course, nation building in Afghanistan was never an effort to bring prosperity "to every corner," or "remake Afghanistan," or export the "American style" to Afghanistan. Rumsfeld turned "nation

[26] Rumsfeld, *Known and Unknown*, chapter 45; see also page 667. Feith invokes the bicycle analogy too; see *War and Decision*, 148.
[27] Feith, interview by author.

building" into a boogeyman and spent more time warning against it than answering his own legitimate concern to put something in place so that US troops could go home. Nation building was, or should have been, the effort to provide enough assistance to help jump-start Afghanistan's political and economic life, to return it to a normal trajectory of development, nothing more. In Rumsfeld's argument with history, he defeated an army of straw men.[28]

In an interview with Doug Feith, I played devil's advocate and presented Khalilzad's perspective that Afghanistan was so broken that aid dependency was unavoidable. Feith has a professorial air and a thoughtful inquisitiveness, and I found his memoir, a 700-page rumination on national security decision-making, extremely insightful. But I wanted to challenge him: if Khalilzad was right, Feith's and Rumsfeld's hesitance to embrace nation building was not just mistaken; it was counterproductive. I asked Feith if he still thought the administration was right to be concerned about dependency and to avoid nation building. "I think there's some merit to what you're saying," he replied. But "I'm not sure that we actually disagree." He claimed the administration fully recognized "that Afghanistan was a thoroughly failed state" and that "if anything substantial was going to be done, we were going to have to play a substantial role." The difference is that "with the frame of mind that Rumsfeld insisted on ... at least when you're doing your work, do it with an understanding of the merit of not aggravating the problem of dependence."

In other words, state building was necessary, but every program and initiative had to include avoiding dependency as part of its design. Feith offered examples of how and when he believed the United States adopted the right posture: the initial military campaign, which relied on local militias; and the Bonn Process and the immediate creation of a new Afghan government rather than an American occupation. Feith suggested that the way the war ended in 2021 – the Afghan army collapsing once American support was withdrawn – partially vindicated his and Rumsfeld's view. American failure in 2021 was at least partly because the United States created an Afghan military that could not survive without American help, something Rumsfeld explicitly warned against in 2002. "And I really think Rumsfeld deserves credit for understanding that." In light of how the war ended, Feith's argument is powerful and not easily dismissed.[29]

---

[28] Rumsfeld, *Known and Unknown*, 683.   [29] Feith, interview by author.

But we do disagree. I believe his view sidesteps the issue of timing, sequencing, and starting points. The early military campaign worked because the United States could work with the Northern Alliance, a preexisting resource. When it came to the rest of the state-building agenda, there were no existing Afghan institutions or resources, which made deference to local leadership devastatingly counterproductive. "Resources matter. We had a lot more [local] resources to work with in Iraq and Colombia Hadley recalled. "You couldn't have had fewer resources to work with, both human and infrastructure, in Afghanistan than we did." Second, Feith is simply wrong about the Bonn Process being an example of local leadership; while the Afghan government was superficially in charge, the UN led, directed, and funded the Bonn Process far more than Feith seems to recognize. Bonn was a success, but that demonstrates the usefulness, not of local leadership, but international engagement.[30]

The Bush administration's dislike of nation building was an almost perfectly designed mismatch to the needs of the moment. Afghanistan was not at risk of *becoming* dependent on foreign aid; it had already been dependent on foreign aid for most of its existence and was incapable of being otherwise for the foreseeable future. The main risk to American security in 2002 to 2005 was not Afghan free-riding; it was the potential collapse of the new Afghan government and the return of the Taliban. The administration's hand-wringing over nation building looks like a case of mistaking molehills for mountains, of focusing on a small but definable problem (dependency) at the expense of the larger, more diffuse, harder-to-quantify challenge (stability). Previously formed beliefs about nation building – taking their cue from the Balkans – were imported into the new and wholly different challenge of Afghanistan without much effort to revise or update those beliefs in line with changing realities. Afghanistan was in desperate need of a new bike, not paternalistic advice to pedal harder.

DRIFT

The question of whether or not to engage in nation building was a serious issue with strong arguments on both sides. In later years, when faced with consequential issues, every administration would come to hold periodic strategy reviews to debate the grand questions of the war. They became something of a Washington tradition, including nine reviews over twenty

---

[30] Hadley, interview by author.

years by my count. In that context, the absence of a strategy review in 2002 is remarkable; it is the dog that did not bark of the Afghan war. The administration was facing serious, complex, consequential questions: What would be the relationship between the United States and other international efforts in Afghanistan? Should it participate in stabilization and reconstruction or leave it to a multinational coalition? What should the priorities and sequencing be in a nation-building campaign? Instead of debating these questions, laying out courses of action, and choosing between them, the administration's Afghanistan strategy was set by inertia and preexisting judgments about nation building.

Because of the Bush administration's initial aversion to state building and the priority it put on counterterrorism, American aid to Afghanistan in 2002 and 2003 was anemic. The UN drew up a "preliminary needs assessment" for a donor conference in Tokyo in January 2002 that estimated Afghanistan would need $15 billion over the next decade and specifically requested that aid be front-loaded, given early in the decade to have the greatest impact. The US pledged $500 million to Afghanistan at the conference, but it was repackaged aid that had already been planned as humanitarian assistance prior to 9/11, according to Jim Dobbins. (The Bush administration gave significant humanitarian aid to help avert famine in the winter of 2001–2002.) The United States eventually disbursed about $700 million in aid to Afghanistan that year – but most was for humanitarian relief, not reconstruction, and thus not a contribution to the UN's $15 billion total. Dobbins argued to Powell that aid to Afghanistan was disproportionately low compared to what the United States was giving to reconstruction efforts in the Balkans. Powell "responded with a pained grimace," in Dobbins' recollection, and Dobbins believed Powell never raised the point to the president. "It wasn't that we had a conscious meeting and said, let's not do this. It was everybody's assumption," Dobbins said. To the Bush administration, the Balkans were cautionary tale, not a precedent to follow.[31]

Afghanistan was simply not a priority for American aid compared to the $3.9 billion the United States gave to Israel, $3.3 billion to Egypt, and $1.1 billion to Pakistan in 2002. The following year, the disparity grew: aid to Afghanistan increased modestly, to $1.3 billion – and more of it was dedicated to reconstruction – but aid to newly occupied Iraq ballooned to $5.3 billion; Israel, to $5.1 billion; and Poland, which had been supportive of

---

[31] Dobbins, interview by author. Dobbins, *Foreign Service*, 255. See Rice, *No Higher Honor*, 109, for a more positive spin on the Tokyo conference and early reconstruction efforts.

the war in Iraq, to $5.3 billion. The Bush administration had the means and political will to give billions in aid when it chose to. For Afghanistan, in 2002 and 2003, it did not. The lack of money was matched with a lack of attention. "The US government did not engage, anywhere in any of its various departments and agencies, in extensive planning for a post-Taliban Afghanistan," according to Dov Zakheim, the comptroller of the Pentagon. "There was no time, and not much incentive, to do so. Policy was focused on obviating the threat of another attack on the American homeland from al-Qaida's sanctuary in Afghanistan." Zakheim felt the inattention undermined implementation. "What Afghanistan required was that the highest levels of the US government focus on implementing their policy objectives," he said. "But because the government's top policymakers were now turned elsewhere, that did not happen."[32]

Dobbins, similarly, was "disturbed by the lack of attention being paid by top levels of the administration to developments in a country we had just overrun and liberated," he wrote. He felt that "there was no prodding to get things moving or to show results," compared to previous efforts he had been involved in in Kosovo, Bosnia, and Haiti. Ambassador Ryan Crocker was sent to reopen the US embassy in Kabul and served briefly as chargé d'affaires in early 2002. "My strong sense, based on my experience there, was that there wasn't a great deal of high-level interest anywhere in Washington as to what happened next in Afghanistan," he said. "We had gotten rid of the Taliban. We had answered 9/11. DoD in particular absolutely did not want to see us get involved in nation building, hence the total economy-of-force effort. We had knocked off the bad guys. We had paid back for 9/11. Our work there basically was done."[33]

The Bush administration also opted not to participate in the International Security Assistance Force (ISAF), the UN-mandated force to keep the peace in Kabul. American military forces operated independently of ISAF and focused on counterterrorism, not peacekeeping (see Chapter 6). Rumsfeld opposed using US forces for peacekeeping and wanted to avoid entanglements that might compromise American forces' operational independence, though he recognized the United States needed to be involved at some level. In October 2001, Feith wrote in an internal memo that "the US should not commit to any post-Taliban military

---

[32] UN Press Release, "Donors Meet in Tokyo," January 18, 2002, www.un.org/press/en/20 02/afg181.doc.htm. Interview with Dobbins. Data from USAID's online database of historical aid figures: https://foreignassistance.gov/aid-trends. Zakheim, *A Vulcan's Tale*, 3, 171.

[33] Dobbins, *Foreign Service*, 258. Crocker, "Bush Oral History."

involvement, since the US will be heavily engaged in the anti-terrorism effort worldwide." Rumsfeld responded that "the US needs to be involved" to "assure that our Coalition partners are not disaffected" but clearly favored keeping US involvement to a minimum. He believed ISAF was an ideal way for allies to contribute to Afghanistan without interfering with American priorities.[34]

General David Barno, commander of US forces in Afghanistan from 2003 to 2005, though more willing to use US forces in a peacekeeping role, nonetheless agreed that keeping the US military footprint small and non-invasive was important. "Having a relatively light footprint was extremely important, because of the cultural sensitivities that the Afghans had," Barno said. "The goodwill of the Afghan people to have these international forces there is a very finite bag of capital and we wanted to spend that capital very slowly because we're going to be here for a long time and we didn't want to aggravate the Afghan population and their culture by having a lot of troops there." Rumsfeld agreed, writing in an internal memo in July 2003 that, "unlike the Soviets, the US, as a liberating power, will avoid having a presence that triggers a hostile response from the Afghan people."[35]

The Bush administration's paltry aid and peacebuilding effort in Afghanistan was a source of lasting frustration for some officials and diplomats, particularly given that Bush gave what proved to be false hope with soaring rhetoric. "We know that true peace will only be achieved when we give the Afghan people the means to achieve their own aspirations," Bush said in an April 2002 speech. "Peace will be achieved by helping Afghanistan develop its own stable government. Peace will be achieved by helping Afghanistan train and develop its own national army. And peace will be achieved through an education system for boys and girls." Bush spoke of building roads and clinics and investing in economic development. He invoked the legacy of the Marshall Plan, which had helped rebuild Europe after World War II, and promised a new Marshall Plan for Afghanistan when

---

[34] OSD Policy Memo, "US Strategy in Afghanistan," October 16, 2001, https://nsarchive2 .gwu.edu/NSAEBB/NSAEBB358a/doc18.pdf. Barno, interview by author. Critics sometimes claim Rumsfeld opposed ISAF itself or its expansion. Feith disagrees. "Rumsfeld resented that the Pentagon was blamed for opposing ISAF expansion," Feith claimed in his memoir, "when the Pentagon – meaning Rumsfeld – would have been delighted if other countries contributed enough new resources to ISAF to allow it to operate outside Kabul." On the other hand, Dobbins claims Rumsfeld and the other principals did make a conscious decision at an NSC meeting in early 2002 to oppose ISAF's expansion. Compare Feith, *War and Decision*, 156–157 with Dobbins, *Foreign Service*, 256.

[35] OSD, "Principles for Afghanistan," July 7, 2003, 2.

he praised George Marshall's vision as "a beacon to light the path that we, too, must follow." It was a hopeful vision and would have been an effective strategy of using American power to solve our problems by helping others solve their problems.[36]

"But nothing [happened]," Dobbins said. "Bush said it, and there was no follow through," there was "no increase in US assistance, and no effort to galvanize a broader international effort." US aid to Afghanistan did not significantly increase for almost two years after Bush's speech. This became the first instance of a problem that would bedevil the American effort in Afghanistan for years – and a source of confusion for journalists, historians, and pundits trying to understand American strategy. The Bush administration and, to a lesser degree, the Obama administration had a habit of saying one thing and doing another. Scholars can find documents that say, on paper, that the United States was committed to bringing freedom, democracy, and development to Afghanistan, as if the United States had mounted a massive and ambitious nation-building campaign immediately after overthrowing the Taliban (which is why the Bush administration is typically criticized for being *too* ambitious and *too* grandiose in its aspirations). For most of its tenure, the administration claimed in various documents that its goal in Afghanistan was to help establish "an Afghan Government that is moderate and democratic; respects the rights of its citizens, is characterized by a legal private sector economy, and is a dedicated partner on the global War on Terrorism." General Tommy Franks claims in his memoir that he understood immediately after 9/11 the need to plan a three-to-five-year operation to stabilize and rebuild Afghanistan and adopt a counterinsurgency strategy to forestall a Taliban insurgency.[37]

But no such nation-building campaign existed in 2002 and 2003. The budget and deployment patterns, where strategy is implemented, tell a different story, one that prioritized counterterrorism and expended virtually no resources on roads, schools, and hospitals – let alone law courts, ministries, or police forces – for the first two years of the American intervention, and very little for the first five years. There is no evidence that Franks' planning, if it took place, had any impact. One of the *Washington Post's* critiques in the "Afghanistan Papers" is that the United States did too much

---

[36] Bush, "President Outlines War Effort," April 17, 2002. https://georgewbush-whitehouse .archives.gov/news/releases/2002/04/20020417-1.html.

[37] Dobbins, interview by author. Dobbins, *Foreign Service*, 259. "United States Policy in Afghanistan," U.S. House of Representatives, Committee on International Relations, September 22, 2005, 19. Franks, *American Soldier*, 271.

nation building – a surprising critique when, between 2002 and 2005, it did almost no nation building at all. "If your strategist doesn't control the money or the troops, he doesn't have much of a strategy," Barney Rubin later quipped. If you want to understand a nation's strategy, do not read its official documents; watch how it spends money and deploys troops. By that metric, the Bush administration had a clear strategy: kill terrorists, and leave the rest to others.[38]

LEAD NATIONS

The others were incapable of picking up the slack. At a January 2002 Tokyo donors' conference, Dobbins invited donors and allies to sign up as "lead nations" for rebuilding different parts of the Afghan state: Germany for the police force, the United Kingdom for counternarcotics programs, Italy for the justice sector, Japan for a disarmament, demobilization, and reintegration (DDR) effort, and the United States for the Afghan army. The "lead nation" model of state building, which guided international reconstruction efforts through 2005, failed. It led to "conflict and incoherence, and no one wanted to repeat that approach," Rice later wrote. Japan's effort was the most successful, Italy's the least, but overall the different pieces failed to cohere, programs conflicted, gaps went unaddressed, and the level of effort was a fraction of what Afghanistan needed.

"This was an example of leaving important tasks to the 'international community' and not a lot happened," Feith said. John Gastright, deputy assistant secretary of state for Afghanistan and Pakistan, recalled that "lead nation was the Bush administration's attempt to divvy up the level of effort. Nobody was really over the top with that. It was a pretty light effort." Gastright believed part of the problem was that policymakers tended to believe that Afghanistan historically had gotten by with a weak government. They believed the Afghan government "didn't provide a tremendous amount of support and services to its population," and so "if we provided the minimum, then they should be okay." The Bush administration eventually came to recognize that the lead nation model was "too slow and . . . too disorganized," in Rice's words. "This distribution of responsibility has been justly criticized," Dobbins later admitted. "Over the next several years none of these lead nations, with the exception of Japan, delivered on their promises." But Dobbins also argued that "at the time there was no real

---

[38] Rubin, SIGAR interview.

alternative" because neither the US nor the UN were willing or able to lead the reconstruction of Afghanistan: "I introduced the lead nation arrangement not because it would work well, but because it was better than nothing."[39]

The United States signed up to create a new Afghan National Army, an effort led by General Karl Eikenberry in 2002 and 2003. He felt from Washington "a nervousness about staying too long in Afghanistan, committing too many resources," a sense that "we'll do nation building on the cheap," which was challenging because, in 2002, Afghanistan did not have an army. The Taliban army was defeated, the police did not exist, and the Northern Alliance militias were undisciplined, poorly trained, and ill-equipped groups with questionable loyalties. Starting from scratch and rebuilding on the cheap was essentially impossible. "When I arrived, it was a pretty disjointed, anemic effort," Eikenberry recalled, because of the "lack of resources, and direction, and authority." Eikenberry moved slowly but deliberately to put in place a sustainable foundation. "We truly believed that the Taliban had been vanquished and was scattered, so time was on our side," meaning the United States did not have to move with urgency. As a result, Eikenberry focused on building a small but sustainable force with local leadership. "One thing I think I got reasonably right, was that the effort had to be sustainable," he said, though he also recognized that some critics felt the training effort "needed to up the game, professionalize the force more," and that he had erred on the side of "going a little bit too Spartan."[40]

He and the allies and donors also believed that the main purpose of the Afghan army was to counteract warlords' militias – for which it was successful – not to wage counterinsurgency against the Taliban. "I think we were complacent, not because we were lazy, but because we just didn't see the Taliban threat emerging as it did." The effort was also hampered by a years-long battle between the Afghan government and the US Department of Defense over how large an army Afghanistan needed (Karzai wanted a larger army than Rumsfeld wanted to pay for). And because everyone believed the war was over, there was, again, little urgency to the effort. The upshot was that the Afghan army grew slowly, numbering just 26,000 soldiers by 2005, and it was not prepared for a resurgent Taliban.[41]

---

[39] Rice, *No Higher Honor*, 191. Feith "Bush Oral History." Gastright, interview by author. Dobbins, *Foreign Service*, 255. See also Cheney, *In My Time*, 499.

[40] Eikenberry, interview by author.   [41] Eikenberry, interview by author.

Similarly, the German effort to rebuild the police had only produced 40,000 trained police officers by 2005 – their effort "was about an inch wide and a mile deep," Eikenberry recalled, focused exclusively on building an elite national police academy in Kabul, not a "comprehensive and holistic" approach. "They wanted to train Sherlock Holmes," McNeill recalled. "It was a three-year program. It makes no sense." It focused on advanced skills and elite sleuthing rather than getting local cops walking beats; it lacked urgency and breadth. But when the United States took over years later, State and Defense fell to fighting over who had the authority and funding to lead the effort – and, in any case, "to build a competent police force on the ruins of a destroyed country and in the middle of an escalating insurgency was new to all of us," Ambassador Ronald Neumann wrote. Training Afghan security forces in the early years "was a fairly slow build and that was a very minimally resourced effort," according to Barno. Even though Barno and others were using the language of counterinsurgency as early as 2003, the rhetoric was belied by the lack of an urgent training effort for Afghan security forces, who are the key players in counterinsurgency doctrine.[42]

The level of aid to Afghanistan mattered because in 2001 Afghanistan was the most failed state in the world. "The devastation in Afghanistan at the end of '01, beginning of '02, was almost absolute," Ambassador Ryan Crocker recalled. "Just driving in from Bagram to Kabul, not a building standing, bridges out, we had to ford a river, whole city blocks of Kabul were gone. It looked like pictures of Berlin in 1945." Afghanistan regularly appeared at or near the bottom of world rankings in almost every indicator of social, political, economic, and human development; the parade of statistics paints a picture that is both shocking and depressing. Afghans were the world's seventh-poorest people, comparable to the poorest of sub-Saharan Africa. The International Monetary Fund was unable even to estimate unemployment. There was no national currency. Little more than a tenth of the roads were paved. Less than a third of Afghans had access to sanitation, and only a fifth to clean water. A third or fewer of Afghans could read and write, and only 1.1 million were enrolled in the nearly defunct educational system.[43]

Larry Goodson estimated that 50 percent of Afghans had been killed, wounded, or displaced by the Soviet war, a human toll of near-genocidal proportions – *before* the civil war of the 1990s. There were at least 3.8 million

---

[42] Eikenberry and Barno, interviews by author. Neumann, *The Other War*, 76.
[43] Crocker, "Bush Oral History."

Afghan refugees and another 1.2 million internally displaced persons (IDPs) in Afghanistan in 2001. Within a year, almost 2 million refugees and more than three-quarters of a million IDPs had returned, overwhelming urban areas and creating massive, overcrowded slums at risk of disease and exposure. Seventy percent of Afghans were undernourished, only a third of Afghans survived to age sixty-five, and Afghans had the sixth-shortest life expectancy and twelfth-highest infant mortality in the world. The government collected less than 1 percent of GDP in revenue, compared to an average of 11 percent across South Asia and 26 percent worldwide. The country lacked an educated elite to run public institutions. By 2001, most ministries had effectively ceased to function because they lacked the basic levels of people, money, and equipment required to do anything. For most practical purposes – like obtaining an education, clean water, or protection for one's property – there was no government. Larry Goodson judged that "every economic and political element in Afghanistan would have to be rebuilt."[44]

In the face of Afghanistan's bottomless need, the Bush administration was unwilling to invest much, and the international community was too disorganized to make up the difference. The result was a drastically underfunded, uncoordinated aid effort. "The administration squandered an opportunity to manage a postconflict environment properly," according to Dov Zakheim. "Instead, the country became the world's largest producer of illicit drugs and, more ominously, the Taliban and al-Qaida were able to regroup and, in the case of the Taliban, once again seek control of the country." Jim Dobbins later led a team of researchers in an exhaustive study of US- and UN-led nation-building interventions over the previous several decades. He concluded that the intervention in Afghanistan was one of the least-funded reconstruction efforts in the world on a per capita basis during its first two years. Aid to Iraq was almost quadruple that to Afghanistan. The world's most failed state was entrusted to the hands of the world's least interested state builders[45]

---

[44] Central Statistics Organization, *Afghanistan Statistical Yearbook 2003*. International Monetary Fund, *Afghanistan: Selected Issues and Statistical Appendix*. International Monetary Fund, *Islamic Republic of Afghanistan: Fifth Review*. Cramer and Goodhand, *Try Again, Fail Again, Fail Better?* 131–156; Larry P. Goodson, *Afghanistan's Endless War*. UNHCR, *Statistical Yearbook, 2001* and *2002*. World Bank, *World Development Indicators Database*. Goodson, "The Lessons of Nation-Building in Afghanistan."

[45] Zakheim, *A Vulcan's Tale*, 170–171. Dobbins et al., *The UN's Role in Nation-Building*, 239.

PAKISTAN

The administration's neglect of Afghanistan also made it blind to increasing signs of Pakistan's duplicity. Pakistan was plainly an ally in the war against al-Qaida, which satisfied the Bush administration's top priority. In 2001, that also meant, temporarily, that it was an ally against the Taliban. But after the Taliban regime fell and its leaders fled to Pakistan, the United States remained focused on al-Qaida and, increasingly, Iraq. Pakistani President Pervez Musharraf faced a choice. Should he pursue the Taliban with the same vigor as he pursued al-Qaida or turn a blind eye toward them, passively allowing Pakistan's former client to hide and regroup while he prioritized the fight against the enemy who had brought the American military to his neighborhood? Especially when the Taliban might be a valuable asset again in the future? In retrospect, it seems an easy choice. Even after agreeing to all the Americans' demands, Musharraf tried to impress on Bush the difference between the Taliban and al-Qaida and defend the possibility that some moderate Taliban could defect and become important partners.

Pakistani journalist Ahmed Rashid reports that Musharraf held a series of meetings with his top advisors immediately after 9/11. After hours of debate, they decided they would respond to American demands with a "yes, but ... " They would initially agree to support the United States and do what they needed in the short term but later express "private reservations" and refuse compliance "with all the details," according to Rashid. As "high-ranking Taliban officeholders melted into Quetta, the I.S.I. ignored them or claimed they could not be located," according to Steve Coll. "Even though I.S.I.'s counterterrorism directorate found it agreeable to operate with the Americans against al-Qaida, other I.S.I. directorates might simultaneously monitor and support Pakistan's indigenous jihadi clients, including the Taliban. The Bush administration and the C.I.A. accepted this arrangement as necessary, if chronically frustrating, during 2002 and 2003." Hadley claims the administration knew about ISI ties to the Taliban, "but we thought Musharraf was doing what he needed to do."[46]

That Taliban leaders were in Pakistan, and that Pakistan could not or would not act against them, was apparent early on. Where else would they have gone? Western Pakistan – the Federally Administered Tribal Areas (FATA) and much of Baluchistan and Khyber Pakhtunkhwa Provinces – was nearly ungoverned and populated by fellow Pashtuns, many of whom lived in decades-old Afghan refugee camps and went to Pakistani madrassas

---

[46] Rashid, *Descent into Chaos*, 27–30. Coll, *Directorate S*, 152, 153. Hadley, interview by author.

that had been among the Taliban's first recruiting grounds. Many ISI officers remained sympathetic to the Taliban and kept ties to them, even after Musharraf's public disavowal. The long Afghan–Pakistani border was impossible to monitor or control, and militants had ample experience exploiting it during the Soviet–Afghan war. In 2003, Mullah Omar reformed the Taliban's senior leaders in a group everyone called the "Quetta Shura," a name that did not try to hide where the leaders were. Western Pakistan was the Taliban's second home. "It was clear by 2006 that the Taliban sanctuaries in Pakistan were directly contributing to an insurgency and the destabilization of neighboring Afghanistan," Rumsfeld wrote.[47]

More difficult for the Bush administration was the question of the Pakistani government's stance toward the group. Was Pakistan unable, or unwilling, to confront the Taliban, and what could the Bush administration do about it? Were Pakistan's leaders merely incompetent, or duplicitous? Some Bush administration officials never made up their minds. "Over time, it became clear that Musharraf either would not or could not fulfill all his promises," Bush wrote in his memoir, without taking a side in the debate. I asked Condoleezza Rice about Pakistan and its relationship to the Taliban. "Some of the rogue elements of the – well, I never really actually knew whether they were rogue or not," Rice answered, interrupting herself, "let me say, the ISI, some elements of the military ... continued to harbor the Haqqani network and others in the high mountains. That's how the Taliban reconstituted." Rice understood that at least some elements of the Pakistani state were supporting the Taliban; but she remained uncertain how far up the duplicity went (or unwilling to say). But then she concluded, "I mean, come on, we found Osama bin Laden in Pakistan."[48]

Ryan Crocker, who served as US ambassador to Pakistan from 2004 to 2007, related one anecdote that suggested the problem was capacity, not will. "We prodded the Pakistanis into an operation," against the Taliban senior leadership in Quetta. "ISI led with some Special Forces against a location in which we were confident senior Taliban leadership were present," he said. "They ran into a firefight in which they were hopelessly outgunned. They did not have the firepower, and they did not have the intelligence to operate in that environment." Crocker's anecdote is an interesting anomaly; I have found no other reference to ISI operations

---

[47] Rumsfeld, *Known and Unknown*, 689. Khyber Pakhtunkhwa Province was called the North West Frontier Province until 2010.

[48] Bush, *Decision Points*, 213. Rice, interview by author. See also Hayden, *Playing to the Edge*, 204–205, 344.

against the Taliban in Quetta. And the ISI was, by all accounts, extremely capable in carrying out operations against al-Qaida, which makes the story of their operational incompetence in Quetta hard to credit. It may be that the Pakistanis simply fabricated the story for Crocker's benefit or deliberately sent unqualified operators on the Quetta mission to make a show of going after the Taliban. It is even possible that one part of the ISI worked at cross-purposes to another.[49]

Regardless, other US officials felt the problem was will, not capacity. "From March of 2003, we were getting a whole lot of intel showing that the ISI was back in the business of replenishing and rearming the Taliban," recalled Ashley Tellis, who worked in the US Embassy in New Delhi before serving on the NSC staff as director for Afghanistan in 2003. But the intelligence was unpopular. "In Washington, nobody wanted to see this," because Pakistan had been so helpful against al-Qaida. "And you get a bizarre debate that goes on for almost about three or four years about whether the ISI is doing this on the margins," by rogue agents acting on their own "or whether this is a conscious Pakistani state policy." In late 2003, Tellis asked the US ambassadors in Kabul and Islamabad to write separate assessments on the question. "And both memos essentially had the same headline story that the ISI is back in the business of supporting the Taliban."[50]

"I took a couple of trips out there and I sat across the table from Pervez Musharraf," Gastright recalled, "and he wanted to completely deny that Pakistan was behind it, of course." The Bush administration gave Musharraf the benefit of the doubt because of his cooperation against al-Qaida. "And so, we were acknowledging that insurgency was happening from safe havens across the border without acknowledging that the government of Pakistan was behind those, and continuing to believe that the government of Pakistan was our partner. We obviously held onto that way too long," he concluded. Eric Edelman had a similar line of thinking. "One of the things that we clearly underestimated was the malign duplicity of Pakistan and the ISI," he said. "We should have probably come down harder on the Pakistanis." Edelman concedes it was hard because "they were cooperating to some degree with us on counterterrorism" but recognizes "it was meant to propitiate us and keep us off the scent." Pakistani officials

---

[49] Crocker, "Bush Oral History." Directorate S of the ISI was in charge of external operations, including the relationship with the Taliban, while Directorate C was in charge of counterterrorism and regularly worked with the United States against al-Qaida. The two directorates sometimes were at odds with each other, a major theme of Coll, *Directorate S.*

[50] Tellis, interview by author.

would tell their American counterparts that the "War on Terror" only applied to terrorist groups "of global reach," which meant al-Qaida, not the Taliban.[51]

Some felt more certainty about Pakistan's duplicity. By early 2003, "the Pakistanis relaxed the restrictions that had been placed on the activities of the Taliban's leadership in Quetta in southwestern Pakistan," according to Mike Vickers, who served in the intelligence community and later in the Pentagon, and by 2005 "Pakistan ended all restrictions on the Taliban and increased its support for the group substantially." In August 2006, Marin Strmecki briefed Rumsfeld that "Pakistan's ISI provides some operational support to the Taliban, though the level at which this assistance is author-ized within the Pakistani government remains unclear" but also concluded that "Musharraf has not made a strategic choice to cooperate fully with the United States and Afghanistan to suppress the Taliban."[52]

Khalilzad became known for his hawkish, anti-Pakistan stance. He believed "Pakistan's double game was undeniable," as early as the spring of 2003; he characterized the safe haven as "our biggest problem" and argued strongly it was a matter of will, not capability. "Colin Powell and I used to argue a lot about it. Colin would tell me, 'Why are you saying this, that there is a sanctuary?' Because he valued Musharraf a lot. And I was saying, 'Well, because I read this in the intelligence, I get that in my briefings.' And he said, 'I haven't seen anything like that.'" Khalilzad believed that the intelligence reporting was clear, but that the principals would "pick on things," like whether or not it could be proven that Musharraf was in a particular meeting or gave a specific order. Khalilzad felt their obsession with minutiae meant they were missing the forest for the trees. "Karzai became crazy in my view because of this, in part," Khalilzad said. "From being a very good partner, to being a very bad partner," because of the American unwillingness to confront Pakistan.[53]

Lower-level officials appeared readier to believe in Pakistan's duplicity – or, at least, they later claimed that was the case. I was a junior analyst in the CIA at the time, and from the weight of evidence I had come to believe by late 2004 or so that the Pakistani government had a conscious policy of supporting the Taliban; that the ISI was following orders, not going rogue. I wasn't the only one. "Now, at my level, there was an acknowledgement that something was wrong, but it certainly had not cracked the most senior

[51] Edelman, Gastright, Barno, interviews by author.
[52] Vickers, *By All Means Available*, 299. Strmecki, "Afghanistan at a Crossroads," 11.
[53] Khalilzad, interview by author. Khalilzad, *The Envoy*, Kindle loc. 3533, 3387.

level," Gastright claims, adding that Ambassador Neumann and General Eikenberry also saw the "double game." But "there was a slowness" at higher levels "to acknowledge that they were playing the double game." The US mobilized humanitarian response to earthquakes in Pakistan in 2005 and 2008, and US officials had a hard time believing Pakistan would lie to them while accepting American aid.[54]

Part of the administration's difficulty in recognizing Pakistan's deceit was because Musharraf continued to profess his innocence and had forged close ties with Bush and a few others. Cheney said he found Musharraf "straightforward," and that "I liked working with him. I thought he was a friend of the United States," even as he acknowledged Musharraf would not rein in the ISI. Powell spent time in Islamabad in January 2002 to defuse a crisis between Pakistan and India and bonded with Musharraf over their common military background. Musharraf told Powell he "didn't know what the ISI was doing," according to Powell's chief of staff, but Musharraf "was honest enough" and told Powell, "don't ever expect us to completely abandon" the Taliban. Powell did not push back, apparently.[55]

Further up the chain, the idea that Pakistan was playing a double game "certainly had not cracked the president, who believed that he and Pervez Musharraf had a real understanding," Gastright said. Tellis concurs, recalling an occasion when he wrote a memo recommending that Bush push Musharraf hard on the issue in 2003. "Bush did not push back with the zeal that we thought the problem deserved," Tellis believed. "The investment in Musharraf was so absolute that nothing that called into question Musharraf's commitment to the War on Terror was actually acceptable in the councils of power." Eventually, the message began to get through, Gastright believed. "By the time I was leaving [in 2007], I think Eikenberry's double game language was beginning to really stick and make it uncomfortable, make it difficult." "We held the Pakistanis to their commitments on al-Qaida," Tellis concluded. "We did not prioritize equally holding the Pakistanis [accountable] with respect to their commitments on the Taliban."[56]

The administration was also slow to see the problem because it simply was not a high priority. "We had thought that the Taliban was completely defeated," Tellis recalled, "and that whatever the Pakistanis were doing was

---

[54] Gastright, interview by author.

[55] Rosen, *Cheney One on One*, 149, 150, 151. Wilkerson, interview by author.

[56] Gastright and Tellis, interviews by author.

completely ignorable because it was marginal crap." It was just the Pakistani bureaucracy doing its thing. Even if Pakistan was knowingly supporting the Taliban, it did not matter very much.

> That was essentially the received wisdom ... [the Taliban] are completely irrelevant to the future of Afghanistan. If the Pakistanis want to support them, we don't like it, we slap them on the wrist, but we are not going to make this a capital case because the Talibs don't matter anymore. That was pretty much the judgment that operated within the administration, I would say, until early 2006.[57]

IRAQ

The Bush administration did take time in 2002 to deliberate a major strategic initiative with urgency: not Afghanistan, but Iraq. The Iraq war would involve far more American troops, money, and attention than Afghanistan for the next six years. Critics have universally argued that the war in Iraq detracted from the war in Afghanistan, making success in the latter effort harder and less likely. What most observers have missed is that Bush initially agreed. When Rumsfeld and others pushed to target Iraq immediately after 9/11, Bush said no, Afghanistan had to come first. "If we tried to do too many things – two things, for example, or three things – militarily, then ... the lack of focus would have been a huge risk," Bush explained to Bob Woodward before the invasion of Iraq.[58]

Bush was right, but in the spring of 2002, he concluded the war in Afghanistan was over and he could safely turn to planning for war in Iraq. Doing so necessarily meant the administration focused less on Afghanistan because, as Feith noted in a different context, "the calendar was a zero-sum game." As a global superpower, the United States had money and weapons to spare, but its decision-makers still operated within the same, limited twenty-four-hour day as everyone else. Time is the rarest and most valuable resource for policymakers, and as Bush's team began spending more on Iraq, they had less to spend on Afghanistan.[59]

General Dan McNeill, who commanded US forces in Afghanistan from 2002 to 2003, was called in to brief Bush in December of 2002 about the situation in Afghanistan. "I had my say just simply walking around the

---

[57] Tellis, interview by author. [58] Woodward, *Bush at War*, 84.
[59] Feith, *War and Decision*, 148.

various sections of Afghanistan and giving anecdotes about, here's who Karzai has as a governor; or, here is my experience, this is what I think we can do there, and those kinds of things," he recalled. McNeill later realized what the purpose of the briefing was. "They wanted to be confident that I could keep a lid on Afghanistan when the attack in Iraq occurred." How damaging that proved to be remains a point of contention between the senior decision-makers and lower-level officials tasked with fleshing out plans, drawing up budgets, and implementing decisions.[60]

Rumsfeld, for example, continued to defend the administration's ability to focus on Afghanistan. "Some political opponents of the administration claimed that the war in Iraq 'distracted' the Bush administration from what was referred to as the 'good' and 'right' war in Afghanistan," he wrote. "Yet it was precisely during the toughest period in the Iraq war that Afghanistan, with coalition help, took some of its most promising steps toward a free and better future," referring to the Bonn Process and Afghanistan's elections, which took place during the first two years of the war in Iraq. Hadley, similarly, insisted that, aside from possibly diverting some intelligence assets, the invasion of Iraq did not pull away resources or attention from Afghanistan. The argument that "Iraq diverted attention, diverted resources, and diverted focus – it never looked that way to me . . . It certainly didn't divert my focus; it certainly didn't divert the president's focus." Rice, too, argued that, "aside from the fact that you're having to deal with two wars simultaneously and there's kind of a limited attention span, I never felt that I dropped Afghanistan . . . to deal with Iraq."[61]

Others disagreed. "The essence of your question is, did Iraq consume resources that could have been applied in Afghanistan?" asked McNeill. "The answer to that is just too obvious." Barno, commander of US forces from 2003 to 2005, understood "that the priority theater is Iraq and Afghanistan was going to be the economy of force effort, explicitly." Barno felt that because of Iraq's priority, the message to him was "you make the most of what resources you have, and you get the most mileage out of them, but you don't draw on additional resources." That included the resource of time and attention; Barno felt that Afghanistan was clearly not the focus of attention in Washington. The priorities "reflected the amount of attention that Afghanistan was getting in Washington . . . we were the economy of force in the policy attention domain as well." Regarding Barno's plan to secure the Afghan elections, for example, "I basically executed that

[60] McNeill, interview by author.
[61] Rumsfeld, *Known and Unknown*, 682. Hadley and Rice, interviews by author.

without any guidance or permission from CENTCOM," or from Washington.[62]

Iraq's effect on Afghanistan started well before the actual invasion. "In the six to twelve months before [the invasion] there had been a huge amount of military effort put into preparing for the invasion of Iraq ... And that took a lot of resources and priority off of Afghanistan," according to Barno. The competition for resources "wasn't just for troops, but for headquarters and capabilities. No service wanted to nominate a three-star headquarters, even a two-star headquarters, to go to Afghanistan when the big fight was in Iraq." The bureaucracy knew that Iraq would be a bigger, more prestigious undertaking with far more money and resources at stake. Staffers tasked with finding resources for Iraq referred to the exercise as "feeding the monster," and "the monster had an infinite appetite ... so there was a lot of reluctance on the services' part to provide any resources they weren't absolutely forced to provide for Afghanistan," Barno said. Rice did acknowledge "the tempo of having two wars simultaneously," and the "strain on the forces" it created. "That, to me, would've probably been the biggest issue" of how Iraq affected Afghanistan.[63]

Barno's view was amply corroborated by others. Admiral Bill Fallon said that in early 2002, "everything began to focus on Iraq, and Afghanistan went by the wayside." Richard Armitage argued that "the misadventure of Iraq" caused the administration to "take our eye off the ball in Afghanistan, put it on automatic pilot." He said the war in Iraq "saps the energy of an administration because you have to have constant meetings, constant decision memos and meetings," which he characterized as one of the "hidden difficulties" of waging simultaneous wars. I asked if he believed Powell had shared his views. "Absolutely," he replied. Wilkerson, Powell's chief of staff, concurred. Powell "knew as a military professional, you couldn't do two at once," Wilkerson recalled. "Even if you made [Afghanistan] an economy of force operation, you are really going to tax things like your air bridge, your logistical chain and so forth." But Powell felt powerless. The simultaneous wars "troubled Powell a lot towards the end of his tour, because he thought Afghanistan was headed for disaster and there was nothing he could do about it," because his influence was ebbing and his time was consumed with other priorities.[64]

---

[62] McNeill, interview by Jake Tapper, CNN Special. Barno, interview by author.

[63] Barno and Rice, interviews by author.

[64] Eikenberry, Armitage, and Wilkerson, interviews by author.

Afghanistan was regularly called the "economy of force" mission as a way of explaining why it always got fewer resources. "Economy of force" is a military doctrine that says you should dedicate the minimum force necessary to achieve a mission. Under that definition, Afghanistan never enjoyed an economy of force because it never got even the minimum required. Economy of force is not an excuse to *under*resource a mission; it is a principle of stewardship to achieve success at an acceptable cost. The coach doesn't get to the championship, leave half the positions vacant, and shrug it off as "economy of force."

Nonetheless, "after Iraq started, Afghanistan was not a focal point of anyone's attention," according to Andrew Erdmann, director for Iran, Iraq, and strategic planning on the National Security Council staff, because of their "limited bandwidth." "Iraq just sucked the oxygen out of everything," he said, noting the "the intensity of the thought and debate and discussion" on Iraq and "how Washington was just stretched so thin on every dimension because of Iraq." He compared the crisis atmosphere around Iraq with the lack of a "sense of urgency among the senior leaders of my office" about Afghanistan. "It was pretty clear that [Iraq] was the higher priority in 2003, in terms of our resources, money, personnel," judged Nicholas Burns, the US ambassador to NATO. "We had security issues that would require more troops in Afghanistan," Tony Harriman, director for Afghanistan on the NSC from 2003 to 2007, said, but we "didn't have the resources to do it. And they committed the resources to Iraq."[65]

The distraction was not limited to the military. "The whole economic part of the State Department got shifted from paying really any attention to Afghanistan to thinking through what the economic issues are going to be post-invasion of Iraq," said Ambassador Tony Wayne, the assistant secretary of state for economic and business affairs. John Gastright saw a similar dynamic. "What I got from my joint staff counterpart, who met with us every day in the Afghan Interagency Operations Group was, 'there's no more blood in the stone, guys. We got what we got,'" he recalled. "'The resources are going elsewhere, so you have to figure out how to do what we can with what we have.' So, by 2006, when we were deep in Iraq, there were no more resources to give." Ashley Tellis said that for his job, "the first problem is getting money for Afghanistan, which was proving very hard to do because Iraq was the giant sucking sound."[66]

---

[65] Erdmann and Harriman, interviews by author. SIGAR, "Interview with: Ambassador Nicholas Burns."

[66] Wayne, Tellis, and Gastright, interviews by author.

That Afghanistan would never be the top priority for the Bush administration's attention – until, perhaps, mid 2008 – would prove to be one of the most consequential facts that set the Afghan war on its course. But Bush had reason to believe his focus on Iraq was a sound decision. He made his case for war central to the 2002 midterm election campaign. Cheney gave a major address on the topic in August; Bush addressed the UN on the threat from Iraq in September; and Bush gave another major speech to the nation on Iraq in October. A majority of voters favored going to war on the eve of the November election, and Republicans expanded their majority in the House of Representatives, one of the few times in American history that the president's party did not lose seats in the midterm. By March, when the US invaded, 72 percent of Americans supported the war. Bush successfully persuaded the American people to back the war in Iraq, and he paid no immediate political cost for turning his attention away from Afghanistan.[67]

---

[67] Saad, "Top Ten Findings about Public Opinion and Iraq," Gallup, October 8, 2002. Newport, "Seventy-Two Percent of Americans Support War Against Iraq," Gallup, March 24, 2003.

4

2003–2005

Refocus

The case for more aid to Afghanistan – that "we can't fix our problems without helping them fix their problems," as Khalilzad put it – slowly gained ground from late 2002. The view seems to have been most common below the level of the principals, especially among officials who worked on Afghanistan full-time, and those with the most direct experience in the field. "[Deputy national security advisor Steve] Hadley ensured that preparations were being made to organize an international donors conference, launch key infrastructure projects, and provide basic health and educational services," according to Khalilzad. McNeill, the commander of US troops in 2002 and 2003, came to interpret his mission expansively, to include the notion that "we've got to help Karzai extend his reach," to help create stability. Bush himself did an about-face. "After 9/11, I changed my mind" about nation building, he wrote in his memoir. "Afghanistan was the ultimate nation building mission. We had liberated the country from a primitive dictatorship, and we had a moral obligation to leave behind something better. We also had a strategic interest in helping the Afghan people build a free society." His April 2002 speech calling for a Marshall Plan was not insincere; it was premature, out of step with the budgetary and strategic decisions he had already put in motion. "Helping Afghans fix their problems," became the new, albeit underdeveloped, strategic idea.[1]

The Accelerating Success initiative, coupled with the Bonn Process and a new Afghan Constitution, began to move reconstruction efforts in the right direction. A new reconciliation program recognized the need for a settlement with the Taliban. But enduring challenges from recalcitrant warlords, international donors, inflexible diplomacy, and a sclerotic bureaucracy counteracted whatever progress was achieved from 2003 to 2005.

---

[1] Khalilzad, *The Envoy*, Kindle location 2154. McNeill, interview by author. Bush, *Decision Points*, 205.

ACCELERATING SUCCESS

The administration slowly came to recognize that a hands-off approach was not working. "There was a recognition that the light footprint wasn't building the government infrastructure and the economic infrastructure required to lure the population away from the Taliban," Gastright recalled. "If we can provide the Afghan people economic opportunities, and we can provide some form of security, then the Afghan people will choose to side with the new government." But the change took time. "I think [poor historical awareness] is why we came to the idea of helping state build reluctantly," Khalilzad believes, but "Bush quickly embraced the idea, not only of bringing the bad guys to justice, but that we couldn't abandon this country again." Bush later wrote that "democracy is a journey that requires a nation to build governing institutions such as courts of law, security forces, an education system, a free press, and a vibrant civil society," reflecting his newfound embrace of nation building. Even then, efforts were sometimes naive. Some officials felt "these guys should get together like our founding fathers," according to Khalilzad. American policymakers looked at their Afghan counterparts and wondered, "Why don't they rise to the occasion?"[2]

Even Rumsfeld and Feith came to agree with the case for more reconstruction. "I am persuaded that the critical problem in Afghanistan is not really a security problem," Rumsfeld claims he told Bush in August 2002. "Rather the problem that needs to be addressed is the slow progress that is being made on the civil side." Rumsfeld made the case that "Karzai's government needed help building his country's institutions so he could show the Afghan people that a life of freedom offered more prosperity and security than life under the Taliban." Feith saw the clear logic: "If reconstruction failed, Afghanistan could once more become a safe haven for al-Qaida or other terrorists." Feith believed that success in Afghanistan would catalyze broader changes. "Such success could stimulate support for political reforms throughout the Muslim world. It could help counter the appeal of extremist ideologies."[3]

Oddly, Rumsfeld and Feith made these arguments in the same memoirs in which they expressed their opposition to nation building, yet they do not seem to have grappled with the obvious tension. The unresolved contradiction recurred in the Obama and Trump administrations, and their failure to address it is one of the chief examples of poor strategic thinking during the war. Everyone knew Afghanistan needed some degree of assistance to

[2] Gastright and Khalilzad, interviews by author. Bush, *Decision Points*, 209.
[3] Rumsfeld, *Known and Unknown*, 683. Feith, *War and Decision*, 148.

enable the United States to leave while still denying safe haven, yet nearly everyone had an allergy to "nation building," an allergy that undermined efforts to give Afghanistan the aid it needed. No administration held a strategy review that focused on civilian assistance; none gave a definitive answer as to how much and what kind of nation building to do or what the priorities and sequencing of foreign aid should look like. Civilian efforts were less guided by strategy than by a tug-of-war between those who wanted to do more and those who wanted to do less.

The administration's change of heart reflected a growing consensus outside the executive branch. In November 2002, the US Congress unanimously passed the Afghanistan Freedom Support Act to "support efforts that advance the development of democratic civil authorities and institutions in Afghanistan." The bill – cosponsored by Senator Joe Biden, among others – expressed its belief that "By promoting peace and security in Afghanistan and preventing a return to conflict, the United States and the international community can help ensure that Afghanistan does not again become a source for international terrorism." The Act was not ambitious – it only authorized $300 million in assistance per year – but reflected a growing awareness of the connection between Afghan reconstruction and American security.[4]

In late 2002, Rumsfeld tapped a contact outside of government, Marin Strmecki, to travel to Afghanistan, get a feel for the ground truth, and brief the Defense Policy Board. Strmecki had followed the Soviet–Afghan war closely while a fellow at the Center for Strategic and International Studies in the 1980s and was one of the few American defense intellectuals with a genuine working knowledge of the region. "The terrorist safe havens and the negative externalities coming out of Afghanistan [in the 1990s] were products of our not thinking about what comes next, during the Soviet–Afghan war," Strmecki later recalled. "Those of us who spent a lot of time thinking about Afghanistan in the 1980's and 1990's saw that as an enormous mistake." Strmecki wanted to avoid repeating the mistake. After his brief, Rumsfeld brought him on board as a special advisor in the Defense Department to develop a comprehensive way forward in Afghanistan with support from Feith and his staff.[5]

---

[4] Afghanistan Freedom Support Act of 2002, Public Law 107–278, December 4, 2002.

[5] Strmecki, "Lessons Learned Record of Interview." Full disclosure: Marin Strmecki later served as a Vice President at the Smith Richardson Foundation, which partially funded this project. The Foundation and its personnel do not exercise editorial control over its

Powell and Armitage were in favor but were not driving the initiative. "Strmecki developed the outline of a plan that called for greater US initiative on the state- and nation-building front," Khalilzad wrote. "He argued that a redoubled US effort was needed to help Afghans defend and police their country and to address warlordism." During the spring of 2003, Strmecki's work meshed with Khalilzad's advocacy for more aid, gaining support from Rice and others along the way. Together, they drew up a proposal they called "Accelerating Success." Their work is a good case study of the policymaking process: policy entrepreneurs – Strmecki and Khalilzad – found patrons at higher levels (Feith and Rumsfeld) and created a window through advocacy and accumulated expertise. They used the new window to recast options previously treated as infeasible (more money, confrontation with the warlords) as not only feasible, but necessary. They got buy-in from various stakeholders so that by the time it reached the president, a new consensus had formed.[6]

Accelerating Success was the first attempt at a comprehensive plan to invest in Afghan reconstruction, stabilization, and development. It was "a comprehensive strategy to work with Afghans in developing an enlightened constitution, curbing warlordism, building up the Afghan National Army and Afghan National Police, and countering the nascent insurgency in the south and east," as Khalilzad described it. "The plan also called for stepped-up economic development programs." Feith's office produced a memo in mid 2003 stating that "the Coalition is now working to help the Afghans create a stable government and society that will prevent Afghanistan from serving as a base for terrorists" and called on the US-led coalition to "defeat and eliminate" the Taliban. It envisioned completing reconstruction efforts by 2007.[7]

Under Accelerating Success, aid to Afghanistan doubled to almost $2.6 billion in 2004 (while aid to Iraq more than doubled to $11.6 billion) and to $4.8 billion the next year. While it was still overshadowed by Iraq, still mostly military aid, and still small compared to the bottomless depth of Afghanistan's needs, it was a significant increase compared to the nadir of 2002 and 2003. "At the time we were thinking that this was big money,"

funded projects, and no member of the Foundation previewed or vetted this work prior to publication.

[6] "Victory has a thousand fathers," as the old aphorism has it, and many people claim paternity for Accelerating Success. Feith, Khalilzad, and Armitage, interviews by author. Coll, *Directorate S*, 185–186. Khalilzad, *The Envoy*, Kindle location 3425.

[7] Khalilzad, *The Envoy*, Kindle location 3437. "Principles for Afghanistan – Policy Guidelines," July 7, 2003. http://library.rumsfeld.com/doclib/sp/438/2003-07-07%20r e%20Principles%20for%20Afghanistan-Policy%20Guidelines.pdf.

Gastright said. "We said, wow look at what we're doing, look at the difference we're making ... Compared to later high-water marks, it wasn't very significant, but at the time we were breaking rocks for the first time." Accelerating Success would have made Afghanistan the top recipient of American aid in 2002, exceeding even Israel. The amount of aid to Afghanistan would finally exceed aid to Iraq in 2008.[8]

The president approved Accelerating Success in June 2003, nominated Khalilzad to be ambassador in September, and sent General David Barno to take command of US forces and establish a new headquarters in October. The American presence in Afghanistan got a new sense of mission and a new infusion of resources. It also had a new tool. In late 2002, McNeill began building in Gardez an experimental hybrid civilian–military unit called a Provincial Reconstruction Team (PRT). Drawing inspiration from Vietnam-era counterinsurgency operations that blended development, reconstruction, and security into a cohesive effort, the military component of the PRT was intended to create a bubble of security within which civilian contractors would arrange for locally executed development projects. The Gardez PRT began operations in March 2003; PRTs opened in Bamian, Konduz, Mazar-e Sharif, Kandahar, and Herat over the course of the year.

PRTs enabled "the US military to flatten its force posture throughout the country while still maintaining a relatively light footprint." Rumsfeld saw them as "a decentralized way of enabling Americans to work with local Afghan (and Iraqi) leaders on reconstruction projects." Barno described them as "an 'economy of force' way to not do peacekeeping but extend security and reconstruction together," without a large commitment of troops. PRTs were intended "to further security, promote reconstruction, facilitate cooperation with NGOs and [intergovernmental organizations] in the area, and help the local authorities in governance and other issues," wrote Joe Collins, who as deputy assistant secretary of defense for stability operations helped originate the PRT concept. "Without a nationwide peacekeeping force, these teams were often the only way diplomats and government aid professionals could get out to the countryside."[9]

---

[8] Data from USAID's online database of historical aid figures: https://foreignassistance .gov/aid-trends, and from SIGAR, *Quarterly Report to the United States Congress*, October 2008, 21. Gastright, interview by author.

[9] US Army Combined Arms Center, *Afghanistan PRT Handbook*, 3. https://usacac.army.mil/ sites/default/files/publications/11-16.pdf. Collins, *Understanding War in Afghanistan*, 66–67. Rumsfeld, *Known and Unknown*, 686.

This also marks the first time the American effort started to speak the language of counterinsurgency. "General Barno and Ambassador Khalilzad recommended shifting the strategic emphasis from counterterrorism to counterinsurgency," Rumsfeld wrote. "Coalition forces would move strategically located outposts in key population centers outside of Kabul and the main base at Bagram airfield to help to defend the population from enemy infiltration and intimidation."[10] But even then, Rumsfeld was keen on a light footprint. "This approach to counterinsurgency didn't require tens of thousands of US troops. It used Afghan army and police to bolster the small American presence." Barno was content with the troop level – about 12,000 when he arrived and 20,000 when he departed, two years later – which he felt was enough to help secure the elections in an environment where "the level of Taliban resistance and the amount of combat actions were quite low." It was impressionistic counterinsurgency, gesturing toward a different approach before the US Army published a new counterinsurgency manual in late 2006. A typical operation, Operation Mountain Resolve, in November 2003, involved a few hundred troops. They swept into Nuristan province, targeted an individual militant leader, spent a few days rooting out weapons caches, and withdrew back to Bagram Airbase, a far cry from the kind of counterinsurgency the United States would attempt during the surge.[11]

Accelerating Success and the PRTs held promise. They mark, in my view, one of the few times that the United States understood that permanently denying safe haven to al-Qaida meant some level of nation building in Afghanistan. They were the right words on paper. Whether and how the United States could implement them was a separate question.

THE AFGHAN CONSTITUTION

While Accelerating Success was getting off the ground, the Afghans were preparing to take another major step toward political reconstruction: drafting and ratifying a new constitution. The Bonn Process readopted Afghanistan's 1964 constitution as an interim legal framework until a new document could be drafted. The 2002 jirga established a commission to host consultations throughout the country and draft the new document with the help of UN

---

[10] Rumsfeld, *Known and Unknown*, 686. "Principals for Afghanistan," July 7, 2003, 2. Combined Forces Command–Afghanistan, "What Has Changed," December 6, 2004.

[11] Barno, interview by author.

advisors. The constitutional loya jirga convened in December 2003 to debate the document and ratify it the following month.

The Bush administration was more attentive, recognizing the importance of the moment for Afghanistan's future stability. Feith authored a memo in 2003 that outlined American goals for the Afghan constitution to be "based on limited and representative government, the rule of law, free market principles, and universal human rights." Khalilzad, by then serving as the US ambassador to Afghanistan, attended the jirga; "shared the US 'red lines'" about human rights and other concerns; and helped broker deals about official languages, women's representation, and dual citizenship. He publicly lobbied representatives to the jirga for its ratification, and UN Special Representative Lakhdar Brahimi met with delegates behind the scenes to broker compromises. Following the jirga was one of my first assignments as a newly minted analyst at the CIA. Every day for three weeks, I went to work at 2 am, read every news, diplomatic, and clandestine report about what had happened in the previous twenty-four hours, reduced it to one paragraph, and delivered it to the briefers just before they headed to the White House for the president's daily brief.[12]

The constitution reflected the international community's concern with human rights. The document contained an entire Chapter – Articles 22 through 59 – dedicated to civil rights. The Chapter protected equal rights for men and women; individual liberty; freedom of expression and association; the right to vote and stand for office; the privacy of homes against warrantless search; and travel. Article Two allowed non-Muslims to practice their religion. It ranked among the most liberal constitutions in South Asia and in the Muslim world, and it remained popular with Afghans throughout its seventeen years as Afghanistan's governing document. Rice highlighted progress in women's rights as among the administration's strongest accomplishments in Afghanistan. "You pretty quickly get to a place where women are actually freed in Afghanistan to go to school, to become policewomen, to become members of the armed forces," she said. "When you think about how long it took for the United States to get women to that point, that's pretty remarkable what was achieved there in terms of gender equality, and women entering the parliament." It was an achievement that lasted as long as the US military presence did.[13]

---

[12] "Principles for Afghanistan – Policy Guidance," July 7, 2003. Khalilzad, *The Envoy*, Kindle location 3743.

[13] Rice, interview by author.

The international community's active role helped ensure the success of the Bonn Process. The process was completed with a pair of elections that the United States paid for (which accounted for almost all of the governance assistance the United States gave in those years) and the United Nation administered. Some 8.1 million Afghans voted in the nation's first-ever presidential election in October 2004 (electing Karzai to a five-year term), and 6.4 million elected the nation's legislature in September 2005, Afghanistan's first freely elected legislature since 1973. The Taliban tried and failed to derail the elections by attacking poll stations, election workers, and candidates. They failed, in part because the US military's focus in 2004 and 2005 was on providing a secure environment for the Afghan elections. "My military main effort that I established in writing for 2004 was to set conditions for a successful Afghan presidential election," General David Barno, commander of US forces in Afghanistan from 2003 to 2005, said. "Not because I wanted to be in politics, but my perception was that a political defeat of the Taliban on that order of magnitude would have a much greater impact on our ability to succeed in Afghanistan."[14]

After the elections, Freedom House upgraded Afghanistan from "not free" to "partly free," recognition by a credible, third-party observer that Afghanistan's government was measurably more open, freer, and more accountable. Seventy-seven percent of Afghans said they were satisfied with democracy in 2006, according to the Asia Foundation. Afghans had been at war since 1978 and were divided between north and south; Pashtuns, Tajiks, Hazaras, and Uzbeks; Sunni and Shia; Dari and Pashto speakers; ex-communists and former mujahedin; former Taliban and Northern Alliance warlords. The Bonn Process helped bring Afghans together to agree on how they would compete for and share power peacefully.[15]

It seemed to cap off a successful four-year effort to put Afghanistan on a stable trajectory of peace, prosperity, and democracy – a sense that obscured deeply rooted challenges growing under the surface. "The successful election in Afghanistan produced a sense of complacency in some quarters of Washington," Khalilzad believed. The United States signed a Strategic Partnership Agreement with Afghanistan in 2005 promising a long-term commitment to its security and prosperity. The international community followed suit with a conference in London in early 2006 that laid out an "Afghanistan Compact" to succeed the Bonn Process. They were broad documents with aspirational goals that would have been useful

---

[14] Barno, interview by author.

[15] The Asia Foundation, Afghanistan in 2006: A Survey of the Afghan People, 3.

guides for decades-long, peacetime development programs. They proved inadequate – glacially slow, with no sense of urgency – for the challenges about to unfold.[16]

One aspect of Afghanistan's new political system, and America's alleged role in designing it, has accumulated a layer of myth and criticism over the years. Some critics – the writers of the *Washington Post*'s "Afghanistan Papers," for example – contend that the new constitution created an overly centralized government on a "Western" model with little or no roots in Afghan history; that the United States had encouraged or forced the centralized, Western, democratic system on the Afghans; or that centralization was a primary reason state-building efforts faltered. Bob Gates, echoing a common criticism, believed that "strengthening the central government in Afghanistan" was a "central strategic error" because Afghanistan "had never had a strong central government."[17]

Gates was wrong. At the 2001 Bonn conference, as mentioned, the attendees adopted the 1964 constitution as their interim legal framework, including its centralization and democratic features. When the constitutional loya jirga convened in late 2003, they started with the 1964 text. Neither the centralizing nor democratic features of the Afghan constitution were created or imposed by the United States, and they were not "Western" innovations. They were long-standing features of Afghanistan's constitutional history. The constitutional features that bore the strongest stamp of American and international influence included women's rights, religious freedom, and national languages, not centralization or parliamentary elections.[18]

Critics who suggest centralization is foreign to the Afghan government, "these are people who don't know anything about Afghanistan," according to Barney Rubin, a professor of political science at New York University and one of the foremost scholars of Afghan society, culture, and history. "They think, 'Oh, Afghanistan is this tribal country with no centralized government,' which is not true. The only thing we did about the centralization of the Afghan Government was, we left it in place." Rubin believed the problem was not Afghan culture or centralization. "The problem is, Afghanistan is poorer than you can imagine," he said. "It has a lower literacy rate than you can imagine. The thing they call a state is so much weaker than anything you can imagine." Afghans' extreme poverty made American planning assumptions irrelevant. "Any model that you have won't work, not because

---

[16] Khalilzad, *The Envoy*, Kindle location 4265.   [17] Gates, interview by author.

[18] Khalilzad, *The Envoy*, Kindle locations 3750–3811.

it's Western culture and Afghans have their own ... Afghans didn't like the Taliban, but the thing about the Taliban was, they could afford it."[19]

Rubin, who advised the UN and attended the Bonn conference, does have criticisms of how the international community related to the central government. "We funded it and gave it all kinds of new functions that it never had before, that it was not designed for, that it could not carry out." While Afghanistan traditionally did have a centralized and functional government, it also decentralized the provision of public services. Gates, who wrongly said Afghanistan never had a functioning central government, more accurately said that "we didn't have a full appreciation of the complexities of the relationships between the provincial governments and the center, or even the district governments and provincial and central government." The king appointed local officials but otherwise focused on internal security and external defense, while tribes and provinces took the lead in local policing, education, or irrigation projects. That is what the international community tried to change, and the change threatened traditional channels of patronage.[20]

Whether it was a good idea for the Afghan constitution to remain so highly centralized is a separate question. I think it probably was not, and Karzai was foolish to try to use some of the powers the constitution gave him – but I am also inclined to think this is one area in which Rumsfeld's instinct to remain aloof was right. The specific design features of the Afghan constitution were not best fashioned in Washington, DC. Perhaps the Afghans erred by defaulting to 1964, but there is no guarantee that Western technocrats or UN diplomats would have designed anything better. One of the most accurate criticisms of the international role in Afghanistan over the years was foreigners' ignorance of Afghan political and cultural realities, especially its tribal nature. Given that reality, why would we think we could write a better constitution? American and UN officials, like Khalilzad and Brahimi, had to strike a delicate balance, giving advice where possible and nudging the Afghan delegates on issues of highest importance to the international community – especially human rights – but not pushing so hard as to provoke a backlash and incur accusations of neoimperialism. If the Afghans felt comfortable with an updated version of their 1964 constitution, it would not have been helpful for Western diplomats to second-guess them.

---

[19] Rubin, interview by author. Strmecki, SIGAR interview.
[20] Rubin, Interview by author. Strmecki, "Lessons Learned Record of Interview." Gates, interview by author. McKiernan, interview by Madison Lockett.

WARLORDS

A major concern shared by the participants at Bonn was how to provide security in a post-Taliban Afghanistan. In late 2003, the UN reported that "Afghanistan has experienced a deterioration in security at precisely the point where the peace process demands the opposite," noting an "increase in terrorist activity, factional fighting," the drug trade, and "unchecked criminality." Warlords were the main concern. When the communist government had fallen from power in 1992, factions headed by rival warlords fought a brutal civil war that destroyed much of Kabul and paved the way for the rise of the Taliban. Many feared a repeat. After the fall of the Taliban in 2001, 50,000–70,000 Northern Alliance militiamen were a poorly managed, largely unaccountable force deployed across the country.[21]

"We were literally fending off rival factions," Gastright said. "We would drive through the city of Kabul, and you would go past Fahim Khan's guys dressed in one uniform, and then you go to another section of town and there would be [Abdul Rashid] Dostum's guys dressed in another uniform, and then [Abdul Rassul] Sayyaf's guys dressed in a different uniform," he said, referring to some of the principal warlord leaders of the Northern Alliance. Ostensibly allied, the warlords remembered the recent civil war and remained wary; the challenge was "managing these rival groups so that we didn't go back to the civil war." In the power vacuum, the UN noted that "factional clashes are taking place between rival Afghan political and military actors seeking regional influence." Low-level mini-civil wars simmered between local strongmen in disparate regions across the country.[22]

Political violence was not the only sign of insecurity. The UN judged in early 2002 that "banditry continues as a lingering manifestation of the war economy." The drug trade, suppressed in the Taliban's last year in power, sprang back into existence (the poppy crop expanded almost tenfold, from 8,000 hectares to 74,000 hectares between 2001 and 2002), enriching a new set of elites and creating a wealthy criminal class neither loyal to Kabul nor cooperative with the Allies. The combination wove a "mosaic of security threats" of "drug smugglers, Islamic radicals, former Taliban," and warlords. On top of these threats, and unlike other fragile states in which the

---

[21] United Nations, S/2003/1212, 2. Bhatia, Lanigan and Wilkinson, *Minimal Investments, Minimal Results.*

[22] Gastright, interview by author. United Nations, A/56/875–S/2002/278, March 18, 2002, 8.

international community has sought to reform or retrain existing security forces, in Afghanistan there simply was no professional army or police.[23]

The Afghans knew they needed outside help to provide an atmosphere of neutral security while the political process played out. As part of the Bonn Agreement, the Afghan parties asked the UN to authorize a peacekeeping force, which it did two weeks later, inaugurating the International Security Assistance Force (ISAF). The Afghans also delicately asked the UN to "assist in the reintegration of the mujahidin into the new Afghan security and armed forces," a diplomatic way of asking the UN to disarm warlords and build a new army.[24]

There was some disagreement early on about how overtly the United States should try to help Karzai deal with the warlords, but by 2003 the Bush administration's warlord strategy involved disarming their militias of heavy weapons, selectively integrating them into a new national army, and co-opting the leaders into the new government as governors or ministers – while also continuing to pay them under the table for their loyalty, intelligence, and cooperation against terrorist targets. It amounted to taking warlords' guns away in exchange for political power, wealth, and help against al-Qaida. Rumsfeld's July 2003 internal memo claimed the United States would "dissociate" from "factional leaders" who fought in "the civil wars of the 1990s." Rumsfeld was describing aspiration more than reality.[25]

The administration described the warlord strategy as a short-term necessity while a long-term solution took root. "While we must continue to rely in some areas on local leaders to provide security and stability," David Johnson, the State Department's coordinator for Afghanistan assistance, told the Senate Foreign Relations Committee in February 2003, "in the longer term we have to help Afghans create national institutions with national sources of support, rather than relying indefinitely on regional leaders with independent militias. Only by doing this will we draw the center and the regions together." But the drawbacks were clear. With the long-term part of the strategy, "we were building the state, the army, and so forth," Khalilzad recalled, but progress was continually sacrificed for short-term needs as "we began to build warlordism again, because we relied on these strong men for services, for transportation, and to look after our forces, for security of facilities ... And we gave them money and they became empowered once again." The upshot was that "we did

---

[23] UNODC, Afghanistan Opium Survey – Oct 2002. Goodson, "The Lessons of Nation-Building in Afghanistan."

[24] United Nations, S/RES/1386, December 20, 2001.

[25] "Principles for Afghanistan," July 7, 2003, 3.

things that were contradictory and different elements of our policy instruments were not well integrated."[26]

Some parts of the strategy were relatively successful. The UN disarmament program, under Japanese auspices, collected and cantoned 70,000 weapons and demobilized 259 militias. The reintegration phase, which aimed at a broader and harder-to-measure goal, was less effective. Individual warlords put on suits and joined the government – Fahim Khan as minister of defense, Abdul Rashid Dostum as deputy minister of defense, Ismail Khan as the minister of water and power, Gul Agha Shirzai as governor of Kandahar, among others. Most of the warlords had been commanders in the Northern Alliance and, as victors against the Taliban, expected nothing less than the spoils of political power. By enticing them to join together under the umbrella of the newly formed government, Karzai and the United States bought their loyalty and mitigated the risk of civil war. "Getting the warlords out of power and putting in elected officials was one of the success stories of the period before 2005," Tony Harriman believed. A follow-up effort at the disarmament of illegally armed groups (DIAG) ran from 2005 to 2011 and was aimed at criminal gangs, leftover Taliban, other Islamist groups, and warlords who refused to disarm the first time around.[27]

The second half of the strategy conflicted with the first. Some warlords converted themselves into private contractors and did business with US forces for fuel, supplies, and private security – the Afghan version of Halliburton or Blackwater. Some Afghan private security forces – still equipped with small arms – became auxiliary intelligence and paramilitary forces helping US forces hunt for al-Qaida because of their knowledge of the local terrain and their ability to blend in. Steve Coll reports that the United States "trained and paid rough militias as armed reconnaissance forces" and that such operations "empower[ed] strongmen with poor human rights records." Some critics, like Sarah Chayes, argued this fundamentally undermined the entire state-building agenda. "American policy in Afghanistan was not imposing or even encouraging democracy, as the US government claimed it was," she wrote. "Instead, it was standing in the way of democracy. It was institutionalizing violence," by supporting the warlords.[28]

On the other hand, others argue the United States should have relied on warlords even more than it did because they were the only realistic

---

[26] "The Reconstruction of Afghanistan," 5. Khalilzad, interview by author. Khalilzad, *The Envoy*, Kindle location 3969.

[27] SIGAR, "Reintegration of Ex-combatants," 20.

[28] Coll, *Directorate S*, 116. Chayes, *The Punishment of Virtue*, 182.

option for authentic governance and security. For example, Abdul Raziq Achakzai, a powerful border police commander and eventually Kandahar's chief of police, was widely reputed to be an illiterate, corrupt warlord and likely a drug trafficker. "But he is definitely a warrior," recalled General David McKiernan, ISAF commander in 2008 and 2009. "He is definitely anti-Taliban, and he's a fighter." Because he was a reliable fighter, "our special operations guys leveraged Raziq" and worked with him. "Was Raziq the guy that could stand [for] election in the United States? No." But "one Raziq is worth thirty educated Afghans." In 2018, after working with the United States for nearly twenty years, Raziq was assassinated by a member of the provincial governor's security detail.[29]

It is easy to criticize the warlord strategy for its self-contradictory nature. But it could also be seen as an effort to hedge bets, or to mitigate the downside risk of one approach by adopting the other, which is a valid strategic approach. "I always say, 'okay, so what was the alternative?'" asks Rice, of the warlord strategy. "It's not as if you have a perfect set of alternatives under these circumstances ... At that point, you're left with certain choices, none of which are particularly good." Imagine a rigid strategy in either direction – either a strategy of consistent state building and institutionalization that tried to sideline or even imprison the warlords; or, in the other direction, a strategy of looking to the warlords as permanent governance structures, relying on them to keep the regional peace and not even pretending to build an Afghan government. The first sounds idealistic but would have been imperialistic; it would have risked provoking the warlords and their supporters to revolt against an overbearing American presence. The second is too cynical, giving up on any hope of a real Afghan state or any kind of lasting justice or peace there.[30]

Strategy is never a matter of crafting an optimal plan with no downsides, but of recognizing trade-offs and mitigating costs. Feith raised the same idea. "We were conscious of needing to strike a balance between empowering Karzai in Kabul, but not being unreasonable in our expectations about how much political control could be exercised throughout the country," he said. "And we weren't looking for Karzai to be so aggressive that it would trigger a civil war, warlordism, regional insurrections, and the like. But we also didn't want Karzai to be merely the Mayor of Kabul." Feith recognized that the warlords "were not necessarily model figures" but defends bringing them into the government because "I think it worked to some extent, at least for a while."[31]

---

[29] McKiernan, interview by Madison Lockett.   [30] Rice, interview by author.
[31] Rice and Feith, interviews by author.

Rice's and Feith's explanations are excellent for classroom discussion; I tell my students much the same thing. The challenge is getting the balance right in implementation. In the case of the warlords, bringing them into the government and granting them a degree of legitimacy could be squared with the long-term state-building goal; it amounted to offering amnesty for past crimes in exchange for peace and cooperation in the present, a form of transitional justice with precedent in other nations emerging from conflict. It even made sense to recruit ex-militiamen as intelligence sources, given their knowledge of the terrain and of key players.

But paying the warlords under the table to keep their militias in the field for US counterterrorism operations was plainly out of balance. Hiring them as "private security" or enablers for US counterterrorism operations directly undermined the state-building agenda and went beyond amnesty to giving them a new lease on life as warlords and de facto power brokers in Afghan society. It gave the warlords a hedge against the Afghan state, ensuring they never fully invested themselves in its success. Their participation in a peaceful, demilitarized Afghanistan was never more than a pantomime so long as they could moonlight as auxiliaries to America's counterterror war.

The problem may have been the fault of bureaucratic inertia as much as a conscious decision. The initial military operation involved US special forces and CIA teams linking up with the Northern Alliance – that is, with the warlords. The partnership was so successful it made sense to keep up the relationships after the Taliban's fall from power. Absent a clear directive from the president or department heads to *stop* working with warlords, the brilliant innovation from the fall of 2001 simply continued by inertia despite changing circumstances that made the partnership counterproductive. When a bureaucracy adopts a course of action, it takes conscious effort to stop doing it – which would have required more attention than the administration gave. Policymakers' inattention meant bureaucratic autopilot kept up a strategy long past its usefulness.

Regardless, the problem persisted well past the Bush administration. In 2010, Gates raised the issue with President Obama. "Hillary [Clinton] and I both again raised the contradiction between (not to mention the hypocrisy of) US payments to Afghan officials and our public stance on corruption," he wrote. "We ran into a stone wall named [CIA Director Leon] Panetta. The CIA had its own reasons not to change our approach." General H. R. McMaster, who served as national security advisor in 2017 and 2018, similarly wrote about intelligence officers who "prioritized close relationships with militia leaders over incentivizing the reforms necessary to counter corruption and strengthen the Afghan state." It was another example of bureaucracy pursuing its own goals irrespective of the broader national interest.[32]

RECONCILIATION

The question of the Taliban's place in Afghanistan continued to raise its head, in part because sporadic violence was slowly increasing across the country. Afghan President Hamid Karzai was far more receptive to Taliban outreach than the Bush administration. In December 2001, he offered amnesty to any Taliban foot soldiers who laid down their arms (though he could not promise them exemption from UN sanctions or US targeting). Throughout 2001 and 2002, Karzai explored ways to encourage Taliban leaders and foot soldiers to defect, surrender, lay down arms, or otherwise join the new Afghanistan.

On April 30, 2003 – the day before Rumsfeld announced the end of "major combat operations" in Afghanistan – Karzai gave a major address that included an open invitation to the Taliban. Karzai told the nation that he intended to distinguish between "good" Taliban and "bad" Taliban. "Most people in the movement, most of the Taliban were good people," he said. The movement originated in the jihad against the Soviet Union and included many fighters known for their piety and love for Afghanistan, Karzai claimed, but the movement was corrupted by foreigners. Karzai repeatedly proclaimed his love for and loyalty to the "common Taliban," by which he seemed to mean any Afghan who fought the Soviets. "No one has the right to arrest them or trouble them," he said of the "good" Taliban. He condemned unnamed foreigners, terrorists, and troublemakers, but praised several Taliban leaders by name. "The common Taliban is the son of this country, he is from this land, he is a Muslim and may God bless him and bestow on him long life. He is our brother and we will support him," Karzai said.[33]

Some in the Bush administration and the military recognized the logic. Barno, then in charge of US forces and an early advocate for counterinsurgency, believed that there should have been a push for reconciliation in the

---

[32] Gates, *Duty*, 501. McMaster, *Battlegrounds*, 128.

[33] NPR, "Interim Afghan Leader Karzai on Amnesties," December 6, 2001. www.pro quest.com/central/docview/2397061555/927D3AB3B7914B93PQ/85?accoun tid=11091. BBC Monitoring South Asia, "Afghan Leader Tells Scholars and Clerics What Is Expected of Them," May 2, 2003. www.proquest.com/central/docview/452 090264/B55FEAC0070D4DA0PQ/32?accountid=11091.

aftermath of the 2004 and 2005 elections. "By early 2005 I think there was a political opportunity there we probably missed," Barno said. "The Taliban were on the ropes, and they could see that this was not going well, and they had gotten a political knockout punch with the election." Barno was not representative of the military or the Bush administration in viewing the American intervention as a counterinsurgency campaign in 2003. But those who did recognized that a major component of counterinsurgency is political outreach to insurgents. If insurgency and counterinsurgency are, at root, a political struggle, it is essential to have a political strategy to talk to the insurgents, understand their movement, address any legitimate griev-ances, try to persuade them to defect and join the government – even offer to share power, if necessary – and otherwise sow division in the movement.[34]

Barno's view slowly gained ground. "Wars don't end on the battleship anymore. They don't end with the 11th day of the 11th hour, or the bunker in Berlin. They end with a political settlement," Boucher said. "And if you're fighting a war as a continuation of policy by other means" – the famous aphorism by the nineteenth-century Prussian strategist Carl von Clausewitz – "then the end of war is a political act," which highlighted the need for a political strategy, including outreach to the Taliban. Some critics have wrongly suggested that the Bush administration rejected opportunities to reach out to the Taliban in 2001; in fact, it was the Taliban who rejected American overtures immediately after 9/11. But after their fall from power, when it became apparent the Taliban had survived and persisted, the need to craft a political strategy and reach out to the Taliban became more apparent. "I understand the idea that after a war you have a period when you reach out to all parties," Rice recalled, which is why, eventually, "our approach was to try to demobilize Taliban fighters who might be reintegrated into the society."[35]

The demobilization and reconciliation effort took time to get off the ground. In May 2005 – two years after Karzai's speech – the Afghan govern-ment finally inaugurated a program with American backing aimed at recon-ciliation with Taliban fighters. The Bush administration had, by this point, come around to recognize the value of such outreach but remained wary and insisted on stringent conditions. It was called the "Strengthening Peace Program" (known by its Dari acronym, PTS, for *Program Tahkim-e Sulh*), and "the aim was to reopen reconciliation talks with the opposition, including the Taliban and Hizb-i-Islami," according to the Afghan Research and Evaluation Unit. "Its primary goal was to encourage and provide former enemy combatants with an opportunity to recognise the GoA as legitimate,

---

[34] Barno, interview by author.   [35] Boucher and Rice, interviews by author.

to accept the constitution, and to lead normal lives as part of wider society." PTS was the main reconciliation effort during the Bush administration's final years, in tandem with its push toward counterinsurgency.[36]

"What people probably don't realize is what an extensive effort there was to demobilize the Taliban and bring foot soldiers back into society," Rice said, responding to critics who focus only on the administration's hard line in its first few years. In Khalilzad's final months as ambassador, in mid 2005, "I traveled to outlying provinces and made direct appeals to the insurgents to join the political process," he wrote:

Several Taliban commanders contacted me to discuss reconciliation. I worked with [Sibghatullah] Mojaddedi, who headed the Afghan government's reconciliation and reintegration program, to follow up on each of these leads. Some lower- and middle-level commanders, as well as their fighters, decided to lay down their arms as a result. I put a great deal of energy into this reconciliation effort.

Gastright believed the program was trying to "peel away pieces of" the Taliban and "drive a wedge between Taliban leadership and [internal] factions, because we did acknowledge that there are lots of factions, and that would go a long way to ending the insurgency." The administration had finally, slightly, relaxed its stance toward the Taliban.[37]

It was too slight. PTS amounted to a managed surrender program, not a negotiation or open dialogue with the Taliban. The program's requirements that the Taliban lay down arms and recognize the constitution was just another way of restating what the Bush administration had demanded of the Taliban in 2001. The program officially reconciled 8,700 Taliban but never amounted to a strategically effective outreach. "We had very limited success" with outreach, according to Gastright. The program "ultimately ... proved unsuccessful," Khalilzad judged, "While there were some takers among the Taliban, the numbers were not enough to transform the situation." He blamed Pakistan, suggesting that the Taliban's backers "did not want the Taliban to make a deal on their own – they wanted negotiations to go through Islamabad." Whether true or not, there were other problems. "From the start, PTS suffered from weak management, insufficient resources, and a lack of political will," according to the Afghan Research and Evaluation Unit.[38]

[36] Afghan Research and Evaluation Unit, "Peace at All Costs?" October 2010, 7–8.
[37] Rice and Gastright, interviews by author. Khalilzad, *The Envoy*, Kindle location 4252.
[38] Khalilzad, *The Envoy*, Kindle location 4528. Afghan Research and Evaluation Unit, "Peace at All Costs?" October 2010, 7–8. SIGAR, "Reintegration of Ex-combatants," 32. Gastright, interview by author.

The PTS program turned out to be a good example of activity without progress, a classic example of bureaucracy doing its thing. The Karzai and Bush administrations knew they needed a political component to counterinsurgency. PTS fit the box. Every month, the program produced statistics about how many former insurgents had been processed, ostensibly removing them from the battlefield and creating an illusion of success. It fooled me; I thought PTS was working back in 2006 and 2007. So long as it continued reporting the numbers, the Afghan and American governments could tell themselves that they were *doing something*, there was a program, budgets were allocated, money spent, reports written, numbers compiled. All the while, nothing happened – nothing, except bureaucrats in Kabul and Washington continued reporting that progress was being made and all we needed was more time, the next budget, and a little patience. The illusion of progress obviated the need to step back and reevaluate the strategic assumptions that shaped the program in the first place.

The flaw was that the program made denouncing al-Qaida and accepting the constitution preconditions, not outcomes, of any talks, which ensured that only the most casually committed Taliban fighter would participate. PTS was, by design, not real political outreach to the Taliban. Meaningful political outreach might have looked like an open dialogue, allowing the Taliban to shape the agenda, *in exchange for which* Kabul and Washington could insist that they denounce al-Qaida and accept the constitution, which is what the Obama administration attempted in 2010. Such an approach might have turned into negotiations for the Taliban to return *en masse*, not individually, and join the political process – the sort of political counterpart to counterinsurgency that the field manuals and strategists talk about.

Real dialogue with the Taliban required incentives: "There had to be a carrot," Jim Shinn argued. "The carrot was going to be not killing them, taking them off the terrorist lists, and some prospect of a reasonably safe role economically and politically in Afghanistan." The last part was especially crucial, yet absent from PTS. The Bush administration seemed unable to "look past the kinetic activities to the prospect of some kind of a political solution" during its final years in office, according to Shinn, in part because there was little political appetite to pursue a strategy that could exact a price at the polls. "If we'd had sufficient insight and hadn't been blinded by Iraq and had a little political courage not to see it as negotiating with terrorists, but just correctly distinguished between the Taliban and al-Qaida, I think, yeah, maybe things could've gone differently."[39] The administration still saw the Taliban through the lens of the "War on Terror."

Shinn is right but tells only half the story. While it is true the Bush administration was inflexible and missed opportunities, so were the Taliban. They, too, had a choice and made a daily choice, year after year, not to participate in disarmament programs or accept the offer of reconciliation. Most importantly, they never budged on the single immovable American demand: denounce al-Qaida and sever ties with them. Had the Taliban done so, the Bush administration would have no reason not to accede to Karzai's desire for true political outreach to the Taliban. The Bush administration was wrong to make its demand the precondition, rather than the outcome, of the reconciliation program, but that failure does not excuse the Taliban's reciprocal inflexibility and refusal to distance itself from al-Qaida.

BUREAUCRACY STILL DOING ITS THING

Accelerating Success, provincial reconstruction teams, the new constitution, and the move toward reconciliation collectively represented a new direction for the American effort in Afghanistan. Rice wrote a memo for Bush in December 2004 touting the progress Accelerating Success had made. Reconstruction efforts showed results: the Kabul–Kandahar highway, for example, was repaved at enormous cost with American and Japanese help and reopened in December 2003. But the new efforts ran into major roadblocks. Just as the multilateral coalition could not coordinate action among various donor states and intergovernmental organizations, the agencies and departments of the US government could not do so either. "Reconstruction efforts were important to achieving our ultimate goal, which was to empower Afghans and assist them in acquiring the capability to help themselves," Rice wrote, but rebuilding failed states proved to be "a monumental task, one for which the United States had inadequate institutions to integrate the military and civilian capabilities as such missions required."[40]

Rice put it more delicately than most. To talk to anyone involved in Afghanistan at any point of the twenty-year war, or to read their memoirs, is to encounter a barrage of criticism that poor coordination, bureaucratic

---

[39] Shinn, interview by author.
[40] "'Accelerating Success in Afghanistan' in 2004: An Assessment," January 18, 2005. Rice, *No Higher Honor*, 109.

ineptitude, parochial turf wars, administrative bloat, red tape, and sheer incompetence riddled America's war in Afghanistan. "Everybody was doing things they didn't know how to do because nation building is something that no agency is structured to do, and only tight oversight can force them to do it," Dobbins said. "And only tight oversight can force them to coordinate … rather than doing it badly and doing it in an uncoordinated fashion, which is what happens when they're left alone. Which is what ended up happening." Khalilzad was disheartened. "I was struck by how poorly equipped the US government was for the task at hand," he wrote. "I found that no organization possessed the expertise to do serious post-conflict planning and implementation." Ronald Neumann, who took over as ambassador in June 2005, surveyed aid programs and concluded "that we had a long list of important tasks we should be doing, but no agreed sense of priorities." The *means* part of the ends–ways–means equation were sorely wanting.[41]

The Defense Department was even more critical. "Afghanistan's reconstruction proved largely to be a series of unfulfilled pledges by well-intentioned but poorly equipped coalition partners," Rumsfeld wrote. "So too the contributions of the civilian departments and agencies of our government were modest … The threads of national power – military, financial, intelligence, civic, communications – were sometimes working at cross-purposes." Feith concurred: "We now faced the challenge of reconstructing the Afghan community after regime change – a task the US government was not well organized to carry out," he wrote. "Our armed forces and civilian officials lacked the institutions, authorities, and resources needed for reconstruction work." He was even more candid in an interview, bluntly suggesting that "I think we did not handle the stabilization and reconstruction stuff in an ideal fashion."[42]

Barno, reflecting on the war as a whole, judged that "the lack of an integrated whole of government effort throughout the entire twenty years really undermined and unraveled a lot of the potential that could have been achieved." In November 2007, Bob Gates, who took over as secretary of defense, devoted a major speech to the need for better civilian–military integration and stronger tools of soft power, characterizing those ideas as among the "most important lessons of the wars in Iraq and Afghanistan."

[41] Dobbins, interview by author. Khalilzad, *The Envoy*, Kindle location 3437. Neumann, *The Other War*, 11.

[42] Rumsfeld, *Known and Unknown*, 483, 621. 690. Feith, *War and Decision*, 139, and interview with author.

The United States may have had the right theory of the war, but it discovered that it did not know how to execute it.[43]

Part of the problem was that some agencies – the State Department and the US Agency for International Development (USAID) – had the legal responsibility from Congress to do reconstruction, while the Defense Department had the money and the logistics. For example, State and Defense fought bitterly about who would assume lead for training the Afghan police. The State Department's Bureau of International Narcotics and Law Enforcement Affairs (INL, affectionately nicknamed "drugs and thugs") typically administers aid and training programs for police departments because policing is a civilian, not military, activity. But the State Department had nowhere near the money or expertise to start a new police force from scratch, operate at the scale required in Afghanistan, or operate in a war zone. State nonetheless jealously guarded its turf for years until Defense eventually took the lead on police training in 2005 – which came with its own problems because the Defense Department knows how to train militaries, not civilian police forces.[44]

The American government's personnel policies proved to be another formidable roadblock. Military units, commanders, and diplomats rotated in and out of the country too quickly to sink roots, develop expertise, or form relationships with locals, the essential ingredients for success in complex reconstruction operations. Each rotation rebooted the war. "I watched everybody who had to go through and get their ticket punched and move on," recalled Jim Shinn, who was involved in Afghanistan from a variety of positions, on and off, for much of the war. "It's war by rotation. If we were serious about it, you think they might pick a general and leave him in ISAF long enough until he figures out what the hell's going on." Shinn wondered why the Pentagon acted as if the war in Afghanistan "wasn't important enough to depart from the US military's rules of senior officer rotation, it wasn't serious enough to change the rules for deployment and operational tempo." The Special Inspector General for Afghanistan Reconstruction catalogued how "every agency experienced annual lobotomies as staff constantly rotated out, leaving successors to start from scratch and make similar mistakes all over again."[45]

"Every new commander reinvented stuff," Edelman recalled. Even if a commander proved competent, he soon rotated out and the next

---

[43] Barno, interview by author. Gates, "Landon Lecture."

[44] Zakheim, *A Vulcan's Tale*, 182. Quinn, interview by author.

[45] Shinn, interview by author. SIGAR, "What We Need to Learn," x.

commander inevitably threw out whatever initiatives had been ongoing because "that's not our project." After he rotated out of command, Barno recalls asking another commander what he would do differently if he could not go home until the war was won. "We would do everything differently," he replied. "We would be out with the Afghan National Army getting them ready to take this over so that we could get out of here." But American efforts were designed not to encourage that kind of thinking. Stan McChrystal, who took command of ISAF in 2009 and intended to serve for three years, longer than any other ISAF commander, believed it was a problem that "we don't have people own things. We rotate people and leaders out into the war, so there's not somebody who really has a sense of beginning, middle and end," and no one with "ownership" of the war. Echoing an observation made about Vietnam, critics routinely noted that the United States did not fight a twenty-year war, it fought a one-year war, twenty times. Fifty years ago, Robert Komer decried "the shocking lack of institutional memory largely because of short tours for US personnel" in Vietnam. Little has changed.[46]

Similarly, the nontraditional challenge of Afghanistan fit poorly with the conventional career path that foreign service officers typically followed. The State Department's culture and incentive structure did not encourage or reward the entrepreneurialism and initiative required for PRTs. Khalilzad noted that Afghanistan needed American diplomats who knew "how to be entrepreneurial in a real crisis situation," but that "traditional foreign service officers read talking points" and write reporting cables. Traditional diplomacy involves talking to other government officials in offices or at the proverbial cocktail party. Afghan diplomacy required drinking tea to smooth things over with a local thug in a tent with no air conditioning. "There are some foreign service officers who can handle things like that," he added. "We have had a good number. They're very few and far between, I'm sorry to say." The PRTs "proved difficult to staff with the needed non-military experts able to help Afghans in agriculture, education, civil society, and building local government institutions," Rumsfeld wrote. Khalilzad also noted that "promotion cycles among career professionals in the Foreign Service and military tend to discourage specialization."[47]

In 2006, General John Abizaid, commanding general of CENTCOM, observed the same phenomenon during a field visit to the PRT in Jalalabad.

---

[46] Shinn, Edelman, Barno, Neumann, and McChrystal, interviews by author. Komer, *Bureaucracy Does Its Thing*, viii.

[47] Khalilzad, interview by author. Khalilzad, *The Envoy*, Kindle location 2078. Rumsfeld, *Known and Unknown*, 686.

"My concern is that the Government of the United States needs to be in the field to its full capacity everywhere if we expect to win this war," he wrote after noting unfilled civilian posts in the PRT. "That we have fallen short for nearly five years is a disgrace." Neumann observed "for a country at war, only the military parts of the US government appeared to have truly been mobilized." Like Zal, I admired the dedication and diligence of the foreign service officers I met and worked with but often felt the State Department's institutional culture was too technocratic, managerial, and officious to delve into the freewheeling, messy realities of culture, identity, and religion that were essential to working in a place like Afghanistan.[48]

A final problem with Accelerating Success was its timing: it was almost two years too late. Early money makes more difference than later money: an ounce of prevention is worth a pound of cure. "You succeed or fail on whether you can do these things in a timely manner," Strmecki believed. Rumsfeld's memo of July 2003 said as much: "Spending more now will save more money later by advancing US goals and enabling the withdrawal of US forces." Getting in early, in the first months after a war during the so-called golden hour, can create a self-reinforcing virtuous cycle of confidence, success, and optimism. The Bush administration was very close to achieving that with the rapid overthrow of the Taliban regime and the inauguration of the Bonn Process. The failure to match those successes with money for reconstruction was a devastating break in the cycle. The money for Accelerating Success was included in an emergency supplemental request to Congress in mid 2003; the first money hit the ground in December 2003 with programs reaching maturity in the spring and summer of 2004 – two years after Bush's "Marshall Plan" speech. "We clearly wasted the two first two or three years that were the most permissive," Neumann judged.[49]

Hadley, reflecting on what lessons policymakers should learn from the wars in Iraq and Afghanistan, argued that "if you're going to do an intervention, you need to start with phase IV planning" – that is, planning for reconstruction and stabilization – "and work backwards ... You have to figure out what is the end state you want to leave. What does that end state look like?" The planning process would be akin to reverse-engineering a functional state. Doing so forces the decision-makers to adopt a very long-term perspective, to set priorities, to sequence efforts and recognize what has to be done first. "Back

[48] Neumann, *The Other War*, 202. Abizaid quoted in Neumann, *The Other War*, 70.
[49] Strmecki, "Lessons Learned Record of Interview." Neumann, interview by author. Rumsfeld, "Principles for Afghanistan," July 7, 2003, 5.

it up so that from the day your intervention starts, you're building towards that outcome, not moving away from it or having conflicting objectives."

"We don't do it that way," Hadley added.[50]

Bureaucratic realities are the strongest objection to my argument about nation building. Nation building may be strategically vital, as I argue, but the US government proved incompetent to execute more aid when it came. The problems with coordination, bureaucratic bloat, red tape, waste, fraud, and abuse cast doubt on the ability of the government to do anything right, even when the strategic ideas were sound. If the government's level of competence is so low, it would be foolish to pursue policies, like nation building and reconstruction, that require high levels of coordination, nuanced understanding of the environment, or carefully calibrated implementation. I often tell my students that in foreign policy, "big, dumb, and simple" is more likely to get results than artfully crafted interventions that require the nuance of a Cambridge don and orchestral levels of coordination.

This is a serious challenge. I respond, first, by returning to the issue of timing. A lower level of aid started sooner and sustained more consistently would have been easier to administer over the long run, and thus likelier to achieve results. "You can't short sheet these things," McNeill argued, and "the earlier you decide that you're not going to short sheet it, maybe the better off you are … We underestimated what we needed to do early on." Second, history shows that failure was not inevitable. Success in foreign aid isn't, by itself, impossibly complex. The United States has done it in other places, including the Marshall Plan in postwar Europe and Plan Colombia in the 1990s. As I have shown in my other work, the United States and United Nations were improving their track record of armed state building and reconstruction in hostile environments, including in the Balkans, Sierra Leone, Liberia (in 2003), and elsewhere. The interventions of the 1990s were difficult but had yielded important lessons learned and led to several institutional reforms. By 2001, the international community was better prepared for something like Afghanistan than it had been for decades.[51]

Third, I return to Rice's question about the warlords: what is the alternative? It was not viable for the United States, in 2002, to have walked away from Afghanistan and refused it any reconstruction assistance, simply handing it over to the warlords. That would almost certainly have led to a reprise of the Afghan civil war of the 1990s, inviting the Taliban back, giving safe haven back to al-Qaida – and also blackening America's name

[50] Hadley, interview by author.
[51] McNeill, interview by author. Miller, *Armed State Building*.

and reputation throughout the region and the world by abandoning the Afghans again. Critics argue we should have stuck with a "counterterrorism-only" option. That's exactly what the Bush administration did in 2002 and 2003, and the failures of that approach are what forced the administration to rethink its position in the first place. There was no realistic option other than to try, even when trying meant doing something the government was not well designed to do. There are ways to surmount the challenges of bureaucracy (see Chapter 16). But one solution is simply attitudinal. The right response to a hard but important challenge is not to give up; it is to try harder. The military used to say, "the difficult we do immediately; the impossible takes a little longer." If rebuilding Afghanistan seemed impossible, it should have called forth the best of American can-do optimism.

How much of this can be laid at the Bush administration's feet? Some in the administration saw the problem and started advocating for a change of course very early, in 2002, months after 9/11. Bush gave his Marshall Plan speech in April. But it took until late 2002 for Rumsfeld to ask for a fact-finding mission, the spring of 2003 for the bureaucracy to generate an initial proposal, the summer of 2003 to get presidential buy-in, the fall of 2003 to get a new ambassador and commanding general, the end of 2003 to get the money appropriated, and the spring of 2004 to see any results. If my experience is anything to go by, that's a typical timeline for a significant foreign policy initiative, and it is a good illustration of how the US government's sclerotic, glacial policymaking and budgetary process is incapable of responding to the needs of American national security – another common theme one hears from veterans of the Afghan and Iraq efforts.

Presidents can force things to happen faster – Bush's surge in Iraq followed a shorter timeline – but only by making it a singular focus to the exclusion of nearly everything else. Scholars and think tanks have been writing reports for decades about the dire need to reform the national security establishment and make it more responsive and accountable, but no president has an incentive to spend time and political capital on an effort that will not bear fruit until years after he has left office. Bush cannot be blamed for going to war with the bureaucracy he had, not the one he wished he had. His administration made modest efforts to leave a better bureaucracy for his successor: Bush issued a national security presidential directive in 2003 establishing a framework for interagency cooperation in postconflict stabilization operations. The State Department created an Office of the Coordinator for Reconstruction and Stabilization in 2004. The next year, Rumsfeld approved a Defense Department directive stating that stability operations were a core mission of the armed forces. None of these initiatives grew into robust, lasting reforms, in part for lack of support from the Obama administration.[52]

But institutional process and bureaucratic politics can only explain so much. Bush and his team were especially unsuited to this challenge because of their antipathy to nation building. Accelerating Success was a good idea; it would have been an even better idea if it had been incorporated into war planning in October 2001. Some understood the problem – Rice reportedly told her staff to begin thinking about postconflict reconstruction days after 9/11. But as a whole, the Bush administration did not give serious time, attention, or resources to thinking about reconstruction for almost two years. "The basic root of it was the attitude toward nation building, from the debates of the nineties," Jim Dobbins argued. "The stabilization phase takes more manpower, more money, and more time than it does to overrun and conquer a country. That's the basic lesson that they didn't absorb."[53]

The most telling rebuttal to the anti-nation-building argument is simply the evidence of what happened next. Rumsfeld got his way; the United States underinvested in peacebuilding as a result, Afghanistan remained a failed state – and the Taliban returned. Each link is clearly connected to the next in the chain of events that led to the Taliban insurgency. That the Taliban were able to return is the most damning indictment possible of the Bush administration's legacy in Afghanistan. Why and how that happened is one of the central questions of the war.

[52] For one such proposal, see the *Project on National Security Reform.*
[53] Dobbins, interview by author.

5

2006

Insurgency

Why did the Taliban insurgency happen? At one level, the answer is simple: the Taliban still existed and were religiously committed to reestablishing their Islamic Emirate. That is true, but only half an answer. When we ask, "Why did World War II happen?" to answer "because Hitler invaded Poland" is true but facile. A fuller answer makes reference to the Treaty of Versailles, the Great Depression, the rise of fascism, the Spanish Civil War, German rearmament, American isolationism, European passivity, and British appeasement. To ask, "Why did the Taliban insurgency happen?" is to ask, "What are the underlying conditions that enabled the Taliban insurgency to take place?" and "How did those enabling conditions come about?" and "Who allowed those conditions to happen and why?"

The Taliban insurgency happened because they enjoyed a permissive environment: safe haven in Pakistan, state failure in Afghanistan, and an America increasingly focused on Iraq. In turn, most of those had common roots in the Bush administration's decisions in 2001: to define the conflict as a "War on Terror" best waged with a light footprint and to conflate the Taliban and al-Qaida. Some of those decisions made sense in 2001, but none of them bore scrutiny as the situation in Afghanistan changed, and the Bush administration failed to adapt quickly enough. "After initial military successes in both countries, when the situation in both began to deteriorate, the president, his senior civilian advisers, and the senior military leaders had not recognized that most of the assumptions that underpinned early military planning had proven wrong," according to Bob Gates, who took over as secretary of defense in 2006, "and no necessary adjustments had been made."[1]

BACK TO WAR

On May 19, 2005, some 600 clerics gathered at Kandahar's famed Blue Mosque for a ceremony. The mosque houses the *kirka sharif*, a shrine in

---

[1] Gates, *Duty*, 115.

which is housed a cloak purported to have belonged to the Prophet Muhammad. Years earlier at the same site, in 1996, Mullah Omar had taken out the revered relic and wrapped himself in the cloak, proclaiming himself *Amir ul-Mu'minin*, Commander of the Faithful, a seminal moment in the Taliban's rise and a cornerstone of its claim to religious legitimacy. In 2005, the Afghan clerics, led by Malawi Abdullah Fayaz, the head of Kandahar's council of clerics, issued a religious ruling denying Omar his self-proclaimed title. The ruling, building off an earlier one declaring the Taliban's jihad illegal, attacked the bedrock of the Taliban's religious self-understanding. It was an existential threat, a declaration to the world that the Taliban had no religious legitimacy, that the Islamic authorities of Afghanistan were on the side of the new government. It was an Islamic endorsement for Afghan democracy.[2]

Ten days later, Taliban gunmen rode up to Fayaz's office on motor-cycles and shot him dead. Three days after that, a suicide bomber infiltrated the Abdul Rab Akhundzada mosque, where Fayaz's funeral was being held. He blew himself up and killed nineteen mourners, including Kabul's chief of police, and wounded over fifty others in a scene of carnage unseen in the new Afghanistan to that point. After three years of relative calm, the assassination and the suicide bombing were a shocking one–two punch, a direct retaliation against the cleric who had attacked the core of the Taliban's religious identity. It was a dramatic, unmistakable statement: the Taliban were back, and Kabul could protect no one. One month later, nineteen Americans, including eleven Navy SEALs, were killed in an ambush and a downed helicopter, the greatest single-day loss of life for the American military in Afghanistan to that point by a wide margin. (It would end up the second-most lethal day for American forces in the twenty-year war.)[3]

After Fayaz's assassination, the bombing of his funeral, and the attack on the SEALs, a sense of foreboding descended on American officials working on Afghanistan. It "is much more evident in 2005 when I arrive that Taliban being a threat is going to require more work," recalled Eikenberry, who took over as commanding general after Barno. Eric

---

[2] Tom Coghlan, "Clerics Strip Fugitive Taliban Leader of Power," *The Daily Telegraph*, May 20, 2005.

[3] Carlotta Gall, "Gunmen Kill Afghan Cleric," *New York Times*, May 30, 2005, A3. Carlotta Gall, "Suicide Bombing at Afghan Mosque Leaves 19 Dead," *New York Times*, June 2, 2005, A3. Oddly, most historians have missed the Fayaz assassination and funeral bombing as the symbolic start of the insurgency. It goes unmentioned by Malkasian, Coll, and others.

Edelman, who had moved from Cheney's staff to be undersecretary of defense for policy, visited Afghanistan in October 2005. "Karl [Eikenberry] was pretty clear that the insurgency was coming back," Edelman recalled. Eikenberry "started sending notes and PowerPoint slide decks that said there's an insurgency underway and it's being fueled by Pakistan and here they are coming across the border," Gastright said. "The level of intensity is increasing by the day, and we've got to change our strategy."[4]

In January 2006, Ambassador Ronald E. Neumann, who had replaced Khalilzad the previous year, reminded Washington, "We are still fighting a war and we need to look at the commitment of resources in terms of what is necessary to win, not as a developmental priority in competition with other needy areas of the world." Neumann had lived and traveled in Afghanistan in his twenties when his father, Ambassador Ronald G. Neumann, was the US ambassador to Afghanistan in the 1960s and 1970s. (Neumann and his father are the only father–son pair to serve in the same diplomatic post since John Adams and John Quincy Adams.) The younger Neumann served as an infantry officer in Vietnam prior to his travels and joined the foreign service afterward, eventually serving as ambassador to Bahrain and Algeria before his posting to Kabul. Neumann's memoir, *The Other War*, mixes historical narrative with extended meditations on the frustrations of working within the bureaucratic machinery of government.

Neumann was blunt: "Because it is a war, if we do not pay adequately now, we will very probably pay a stiffer price later." The warnings did not fully get across to the principals. "Before [2007], we thought they were still kind of a hit and run organization," Rice recalled. "They may have been reconstituting and we didn't really see the extent of it ... I don't think we thought they had fully reconstituted by that time. We were much more concerned about trying to deal with the drug trade." Neumann could sense the attitude from Kabul. "Washington's perceptions were stuck in an increasingly unrealistic appraisal of the situation," he wrote. In late 2006, the UN reported that "the level of insurgency in the country has risen, as has the sophistication of the insurgents' weaponry. Their tactics are more brutal and effective."[5]

The insurgency was the result of years of planning. In early 2003, Omar had called on Afghans to wage jihad against the United States, formed a new leadership council, designated two military commanders, and ordered

---

[4] Eikenberry, Edelman, and Gastright, interviews by author.
[5] Neumann, *The Other War*, 49, 52. Rice, interview by author. UN, A/60/224-S/2005/525, 14.

them to begin planning for a military offensive to retake the country. "Rather than being a '2006 surprise,' the insurgency had already started developing strong roots inside Afghanistan in 2003," according to Antonio Giustozzi, a scholar who interviewed hundreds of Taliban. The United Nations was far quicker than the United States to note what was happening, describing the residual Taliban's violence as the tactics of "insurgency" as early as December 2003. The Fayaz assassination was an opportunity for the Taliban to test the waters and demonstrate to Kabul – and to themselves – what they were capable of and what they could get away with. Their success gave them momentum throughout the second half of 2005, heading into their 2006 offensive.[6]

Militants launched around fifty to eighty attacks per month around the country during the spring, summer, and fall of 2005. An "attack" could be a single mortar round fired at an Afghan government building or a US military base, an attempted assassination of a local official, or a roadside bomb going off. Some was criminal violence and some warlord-on-warlord skirmishes – but some, undoubtedly, was the Taliban. The attacks were sporadic – it amounted to two or three small-scale violent incidents per province each month, in a country the size of Texas with the population of California – and had little strategic effect other than to perpetuate a low-level sense of unease, a feeling of insecurity, and a reminder that the Taliban were still lurking, always watching. But the attacks were also increasing, perhaps up to a third more frequent than the previous year. (There are no US military records tracking the number of attacks prior to 2004 because they were so rare no one thought they were combating an insurgency.) Just 108 US servicemen were killed in action in over three years, from the start of the war to the end of 2004; then, 82 were killed in 2005, 86 the following year, and 92 the year after.[7]

The Taliban were not only increasing the frequency of their attacks. They were also growing more sophisticated. "In 2005, you had the first appearance of the Taliban actively being able to separate and then combine for military action and disperse again," according to Neumann, "that was something which showed training and it showed a campaign plan." Ambushes, far riskier and requiring more training and discipline than mortar attacks or roadside bombs, became much more frequent. Militants

---

[6] Malkasian, *The American War in Afghanistan*, 115–116. Giustozzi, *Koran, Kalashnikov, and Laptop*, 1. United Nations, S/2003/1212, 15.

[7] Brookings Institution, *Afghanistan Index*, October 19, 2010.

launched up to 200 attacks per month at the peak of the 2006 fighting and nearly 300 the year after.[8]

Militants also continued a steady drumbeat of high-profile terrorist attacks. In February 2007, a suicide bomber killed almost two dozen people outside Bagram Airbase while Vice President Cheney was visiting. In January 2008, another suicide bomber attacked the Serena Hotel in downtown Kabul, widely known for its international clientele and for hosting the Australian Embassy. In February of that year, another bomber targeted a crowd of Afghan civilians in Kandahar, killing over 100. In July, yet another a suicide bomber killed fifty-eight people outside the Indian Embassy. The attacks gave Kandahar and Kabul a siege mentality. In 2002, I walked around downtown Kabul freely and safely; in 2007, I had to navigate a thicket of security barriers, checkpoints, blast walls, and barbed wire.

STATE FAILURE

The first major enabling condition of the Taliban insurgency was the Afghan government's enduring weakness and the American and international insistence on a light footprint. Afghanistan was the most failed state in the world in 2001. After the Taliban's fall, the Bush administration ignored state building and peacekeeping for two years, and the international community was incapable of picking up the slack. When statebuilding efforts finally got underway, they were too little, too late, and crippled by poor coordination and bureaucratic incompetence. Even after Accelerating Success, "roads, power, and agriculture were interlocking roadblocks to economic progress," Neumann reported from Kabul in late 2005. "We reviewed Washington decisions made earlier and reported that the 'comprehensive strategy approved by the Deputies cannot be implemented and sustained without additional funding.'" The Afghan government remained institutionally broken, incapable of basic functions like policing, education, or electricity. For all intents and purposes, there was no government outside of Kabul and a few provincial capitals well into 2005.[9]

Nature abhors a vacuum. Where there is no government, others will step in. In the best cases, mullahs and tribal elders tried to fill the gap. Too often, warlords, criminals, and drug traffickers were the strongest actors around. Afghanistan became a patchwork quilt of local powerbrokers and

---

[8] Neumann, interview by author.   [9] Neumann, *The Other War*, 41, 42.

opportunists vying for control of a district bazaar, lucrative poppy farmland, the local mosque, or a highway checkpoint. The Taliban were one of the factions competing for position. After spending 2002 nursing wounds and regrouping in Pakistan, Omar and the Taliban leadership decided in early 2003 to make a bid to return to power. Because of Afghanistan's state failure, they met little resistance. The Afghan government was too weak to stop them, and there were too few US or ISAF military forces to notice them. "The critical task is not the military confrontation with the Taliban, important as that is," Neumann hypothesized, "but the establishment of governmental authority." Writing in 2009, he mused, "it seems strange to look back at how tentative our understanding of this problem was in mid-2005."[10]

Theo Farrell and Antonio Giustozzi provided one of the few pictures of the Taliban insurgency drawn from interviews with the Taliban themselves, focusing their research on a single province (Helmand). They concluded that "the Taliban crept back into Helmand, with small vanguards secretly preparing the way from 2004–2005 for large groups to follow" – a deliberate effort that would not have borne fruit or been sustainable if the province had had a functioning government and either Afghan or international security forces. In the vacuum of governance and security that was present in Helmand in 2004, however, the Taliban were able to set the stage for their breakout in ensuing years. Once they did, the international community responded by expanding ISAF, but in a counterproductive way. "By arriving with insufficient force, aligning themselves with local corrupt power-holders, relying on firepower to keep insurgents at bay and targeting the poppy crop, the British made matters worse." The insurgency was made possible by poor governance, insecurity, and insufficient security forces.[11]

Some scholars characterize insurgency and counterinsurgency as a contest in competitive state building, which means state building is not a luxury indulgence, but a strategic necessity. "An insurgency is an organized, protracted politico-military struggle designed to weaken the control and legitimacy of an established government, occupying power, or other political authority while increasing insurgent control," according to the US Army's Counterinsurgency Manual. At root, an insurgency is a contest for political power: "Each side aims to get the people to accept its governance or authority as legitimate." In Afghanistan, the state's institutional capacity

---

[10] Neumann, *The Other War*, 9.

[11] Farrell and Giustozzi, "The Taliban at War: Inside the Helmand Insurgency, 2004–2012," 867.

remained weak, the rule of law was nonexistent, and the security services were still embryonic.[12]

As Seth Jones has argued, "weak governance is a common precondition of insurgencies. The Afghan government was unable to provide basic services to the population; its security forces were too weak to establish law and order; and too few international forces were available to fill the gap. Afghan insurgent groups took advantage of this anarchic situation." The Taliban, recognizing the vacuum of power in Afghanistan, began to reassert itself from its safe haven in Pakistan and went virtually uncontested. "Simply put, the Taliban would not have been resurgent if the United States had looked to Afghanistan's reconstruction and economic development needs after the Taliban were routed in 2001," wrote Zakheim. Eikenberry faulted himself and his superiors for "not understanding the tactical situation on the ground because we didn't have enough forces ... that we didn't see the problem growing."[13]

The weakness of the Afghan government also meant that abuses, criminality, and grievances went unanswered – including criminality from the government itself. While Kabul and its international backers retained a strong amount of goodwill from most Afghans in the early years, that goodwill slipped away by inches when local warlords ran villages like criminal fiefdoms with impunity, when drug traffickers extorted farmers into growing poppy, or when banditry on highways and in bazaars went unanswered. It slipped away more quickly when officials in the nascent Afghan government used their privileged position to siphon off international aid or demand bribes for services. "The Afghan government was its own worst enemy with the corruption game," Gastright said. "We have an Afghan government that almost felt predatory and in a lot of cases that was not necessarily bringing everybody aboard but was alienating people." And Afghan goodwill took its hardest hit when the United States bombed the wrong vehicle convoy or allowed itself to be manipulated into tribal feuds under the guise of counterterrorism. "We didn't appreciate the grievance culture, the winners and losers on the ground," Gastright said. "By siding with one group, we made them the top dog in this eons-long Hatfield and McCoy thing that was going on." As the years ticked by,

---

[12] United States Department of the Army and United States Marine Corps, *Field Manual no. 3–24: Counterinsurgency* (Washington, DC, 2006). Vaishnav, "Afghanistan: The Chimera of the 'Light Footprint.'"

[13] Jones, "The Rise of Afghanistan's Insurgency," 8. Zakheim, *A Vulcan's Tale*, 277. Eikenberry, interview by author.

legitimate grievances against the government and against the United States accumulated.[14]

Some scholars have emphasized Afghan grievance as a predominant cause for the insurgency. "Tribal rivalries and misguided US military operations generated a degree of popular support for the Taliban," according to Carter Malkasian. Astri Suhrke argues the insurgency was, in large part, a reaction against Kabul's abuses and criminality and against an overbearing, invasive international presence. If true, it turns the moral dimension of the war on its head. Kabul and its Washington backers were the bad guys all along; the Taliban were leading an understandable national resistance movement against corruption, criminality, and international heavy-handedness. That is certainly what the Taliban claimed, and their foot soldiers undoubtedly believed it. Such beliefs, then, did contribute to the insurgency, whether they were well founded or not.[15]

However, Malkasian and Suhrke overstate the case. The Taliban's jihadist ideology, which called for the reestablishment of their Islamic Emirate, had motivated the Taliban's rise to power, their civil war against the Northern Alliance, and their totalitarian rule for almost a decade prior to the international intervention. It was the primary motivation for the insurgency, especially for the senior leadership. Additionally, the Taliban were hardly models of honest and clean government. The Taliban could only persuade their followers and international academics that they were fighting corruption by glossing over their own behavior. While they built a reputation by combating warlordism in the 1990s, their increasing complicity with the drug trade made their anticorruption posturing absurd.

Additionally, Afghans' grievances about corruption and civilian casualties do not correlate with the timing of the insurgency. The high point of Kabul's corruption came later, during the peak of counterinsurgency and reconstruction projects – after 2009, three to four years after the insurgency had started. Similarly, US military operations were relatively few and far between before 2006. There were only 10,000 to 20,000 US troops in Afghanistan from 2002 to 2005, far too few to interact with most Afghans or give them an opportunity to form an impression, either positive or negative. In 2004, an overwhelming majority of Afghans – 75 percent – viewed the Taliban unfavorably, compared to just 13 percent who viewed

---

[14] Gastright, interview by author.
[15] Malkasian, *The American War in Afghanistan*, 103. Suhrke, *When More Is Less*.

them favorably, according to the Asia Foundation. Afghan grievance was not strong enough to explain an insurgency that started in 2005.[16]

More to the point, the solution to Afghan grievance was a stronger Afghan government – which required more international aid and more state building, not less. Warlords, drug traffickers, and corrupt officials got away with criminality because there were no police, no functioning courts, and no trained lawyers and prosecutors, all of which called for more international aid. Suhrke and other critics argue that the international community should have given up on state building because formal state institutions and bureaucracy were somehow unfit for Afghanistan's culture or history or because the international effort backfired and undermined the Afghan state by fostering dependency and distorting incentives. The only Afghans who made that argument were the warlords and the Taliban.

Most Afghans were frustrated with their government, but they generally wanted it to work better, not to hand the reins to the Taliban. In the 2004 poll, Afghans expressed support for their new government (57 percent favorable) and for the idea of democracy. "Roughly 90% accepted the principle of equal rights for all, irrespective of gender, tribe, or religion, and of the public accountability of officials," according to the Asia Foundation. Almost two-thirds of Afghans believed the country was on the right track, and the top three reasons they cited were peace, reconstruction, and freedom; while among those who thought the country was on the wrong track, most were dissatisfied with the performance of the government and the pace of reconstruction. Afghans wanted more reconstruction and better governance, not less.[17]

As for errant or abusive American military operations, those, too, might have been mitigated with more, not less. That probably sounds counterintuitive for scholars with no familiarity with how militaries function, but consider: a light footprint means fewer eyes and ears on the ground. That means US forces were sometimes operating with bad intelligence, unable to distinguish legitimate targets from tribal feuds or, worse, from civilians. A light footprint also meant many American forces were operating with loose oversight. General Stan McChrystal, then serving as chief of staff in the lead US headquarters, commented on the "Wild-West feel" and the "atmosphere of adventure and confusion," in Afghanistan in early 2002. The military environment, especially in 2001 and 2002, was shockingly lax, as trigger-pullers were given a long leash to find and kill terrorists without the

---

[16] *Voter Education Planning Survey*, The Asia Foundation, 2004, 9.
[17] *Voter Education Planning Survey*, The Asia Foundation, 2004, 8, 15–16.

normal checks usually in place from commanders, headquarters, inspectors general, targeting specialists, and Judge Advocate General (JAG) officers. A heavier footprint would mean more oversight and better intelligence. The light footprint was a brilliant innovation in 2001 but had become a liability by 2003. The conditions of state failure needed more foreign aid and more international military forces, not less.[18]

In this context, one particular belief still prevalent within the Bush administration was especially unhelpful: that Afghanistan was a legendary "graveyard of empires." Policymakers believed the British and Soviet experiences in Afghanistan taught them they should be cautious and not intervene in Afghanistan with too large of an international presence lest they provoke a backlash. "We wanted this to be a narrative about the triumph of the Afghan people," Hadley recalled. "And if we had started shipping tens of thousands of US troops after the Taliban had been routed, it would've converted a liberation into an occupation. And the antibodies in the Afghan system, that we knew well from history, would've come to the fore. So, we were not anxious to rush in with lots of troops." Hadley argued that the "lessons of Afghanistan" – the initial success in 2001 with a light footprint – made it seem that more troops were unnecessary and possibly counterproductive. While the administration had other reasons to minimize foreign aid, state-building programs, and peacekeeping forces, the "graveyard" myth reinforced their existing inclinations to minimize their footprint.[19]

But the evidence suggests that Afghans overwhelmingly welcomed the international intervention. In 2004, Afghans expressed a welcoming attitude toward foreign workers (80 percent favorable), the UN (84 percent), and US military personnel in Afghanistan (67 percent). Among the small minority (11 percent) who felt the country was on the wrong track, the top concern was governance and reconstruction: "it is noteworthy that they did not say that they want the Taliban back or foreign aid workers out," the Foundation observed. Afghans continued to register strong support for foreign assistance from the United States, the United Nations, and coalition partners for years. "Afghanistan's legendary xenophobia had convinced the administration to pursue a light footprint strategy," Khalilzad wrote, but in fact "Afghans wanted to see a much larger foreign role in stabilizing their country."[20]

[18] McChrystal, *My Share of the Task*, 77.

[19] Hadley, interview by author, Hadley, "Bush Oral History."

[20] The Asia Foundation, *Survey of the Afghan Electorate*, 2004, 8ff. Khalilzad, *The Envoy*, Kindle location 2489.

US policymakers dramatically misread the political situation in Afghanistan from 2001 to 2005 and thereby missed an opportunity to secure greater gains toward stability early on. The United States failed to recognize its own popularity in Afghanistan because its policymakers were consulting the wrong era of Afghan history. By focusing on the 1840s, 1880s, and 1980s, looking for evidence that the Afghans were about to rise in rebellion, they were overlooking the 1990s – the era of history most relevant to the US intervention. By the time the Taliban government fell, Afghanistan was the most failed state on the planet. Amid such misery and chaos, the popularity of foreign aid workers and peacekeepers should not have surprised outsiders. Even foreign troops would be welcomed because virtually anything was preferable to the Taliban. By obsessing about Afghanistan's mythological reputation as an imperial graveyard, the United States missed an opportunity to invest far greater resources in the country when Afghans were most receptive to it.

The Bush administration believed that deploying too many troops or intervening with too invasive of a state-building effort would spark an insurgency; by adopting such a light footprint, they achieved the very result they most hoped to avoid. The insurgency did not occur because of the presence of too many foreigners, but, in part, too few. By relying on a light footprint and ignoring state building, the United States inadvertently contributed to the circumstances that enabled the rise of the Taliban insurgency: poor governance and insecurity. The United States invaded with enough force to make an enemy out of the Taliban, but not enough to decisively defeat them. It intervened with enough diplomatic engagement to set up a new government in Kabul, but not enough foreign aid to establish it on a firm institutional foundation. The Afghan government could not, and the international community did not, improve Afghan governance, establish the Afghan government's authority, or enforce security throughout the country while the Taliban regrouped. "We could have been helping their society in a much better way and made it a lot less likely that the places are going to turn into shit city again," Admiral Fallon lamented, "which is what it did."[21]

PAKISTAN

The second major enabling condition of the Taliban insurgency was the Taliban's safe haven in Pakistan. The Taliban had fled to Pakistan,

[21] Fallon, interview by author.

regrouped, and launched their insurgency from bases in Pakistani territory – all with the Pakistani government's benign neglect or, more likely, with its active support. What could the Bush administration do about the Taliban's safe haven in Pakistan? The president and the principals wanted to believe the problem was capacity, not will, which meant the solution was aid and support, not pressure and crackdown. Aid had been almost nonexistent in the 1990s. After 9/11, Bush waived sanctions – in place since 1990 and tightened in 1998 in response to Pakistan's nuclear weapons program – and turned the aid spigot back on. Aid grew from $92 million in 2001 to $800 million the next year, most of it emergency economic and humanitarian assistance. In subsequent years, the Bush administration increased foreign military financing for Pakistan – allowing it to buy more American weapons – and forgave chunks of Pakistani debt.

Even as many in the administration increasingly believed Pakistan was lying and deliberately aiding the Taliban, the administration disbursed about $4.6 billion in foreign aid to Pakistan between 2001 and 2008. It also inaugurated Coalition Support Funds (CSF), a pool of money from which the United States reimbursed Pakistan for military operations that supported the War on Terror (ostensibly – CSF was not always disbursed or accounted for carefully) amounting to another $6 billion. "We put a lot of money into Pakistan as well for getting those young boys out of madrassas and into normal schooling," Rice recalled. "We put a lot of money into Pakistan to help them with intelligence against the organizations that were operating in the borders between Pakistan and Afghanistan." The administration's thinking was, "all we needed to do was to help [Musharraf] develop additional tools and resources so that he could ultimately address what was happening in the tribal areas," according to Gastright.[22]

Bush also designated Pakistan a Major Non-NATO Ally (MNNA) in 2004. MNNA status is a designation a president can unilaterally bestow on other countries, like Israel and Japan, whom he deems vital to American security. It does not carry a mutual defense obligation and does not require a Senate-ratified treaty, but it does grant the designee expedited access to American weapons and defense and technical cooperation. It also implies a certain sense of closeness or affiliation, a commonality of purpose between the two countries. "I thought it was a terrible decision," recalled Khalilzad,

---

[22] US Foreign Assistance, https://foreignassistance.gov/data and "Oversight of US Coalition Support Funds to Pakistan," Subcommittee on National Security and Foreign Affairs, US House of Representatives, June 24, 2008. Rice and Gastright, interviews by author.

among the strongest voices critical of Pakistan in the administration. He felt it was a concession with no gain for the United States. "It was an exchange for what?" he wondered.[23]

Another carrot the administration tried was to target Pakistan's enemies. Musharraf complained that the United States was asking for Pakistani cooperation against America's enemies but did not reciprocate. "We had a list of high-value targets," according to Hadley. "We updated that list of targets and added names that Pakistanis gave us," including militants associated with the Pakistani Taliban. "So, it wasn't just them helping us against threats to the United States ... We were going to work together against threats to both us and you. But," he concluded, "it never really took."[24]

Suspicion toward Pakistan grew within the administration slowly between 2004 and 2006. Hadley thinks it was around 2004 and 2005 "where the relationship started to go a cropper." Problems with drone strikes in Pakistan started to raise alarms. "We would identify [a target], we would inform the Pakistanis that we were going after them, somebody would clearly tip off the terrorists, and they would go to ground" and evade the strike, he said. "That began to raise real questions about intent," rather than capability. "Particularly once I became national security advisor [in 2005] I became more aware of it. It may have been a problem sooner."[25]

The Bush administration grew even more frustrated with Pakistan after Musharraf struck peace deals with some tribes and militant groups. The Pakistani military had conducted limited operations in the tribal regions after 9/11, searching for al-Qaida and its tribal sympathizers. The army had limited success, and militants grew bolder, launching attacks against Pakistani targets. The Bush administration hoped the growing violence would catalyze a change of heart for any Pakistani officials who still sympathized with the Taliban. "We had been saying to them throughout this period, 'there aren't good terrorists and bad terrorists, there aren't your terrorists and the other guy's terrorists, they're all terrorists,'" Hadley recalled. "One day they may be coming for your neighbor, but rest assured at some point they will come for you."[26]

Instead, the Pakistani government tried a different tactic. It signed a series of agreements in April 2004, February 2005, September 2006, and

---

[23] Khalilzad, interview by author.   [24] Hadley, interview by author.

[25] Hadley, interview by author. Woodward, *Obama's Wars*, 5. Bush, *Decision Points*, 217. New America Foundation, "The Drone War in Pakistan."

[26] Hadley, interview by author.

May 2008 with different tribal groups and militias, agreeing to halt operations and withdraw the regular Pakistani army in exchange for promises
from the tribes to turn over foreigners and disallow terrorist safe haven. "But
it didn't work, and those tribal leaders basically let their areas become safe
havens for al-Qaida and Taliban," recalled Hadley. It was like "having a six,
eight lane highway across the border from Pakistan into Afghanistan," for
militants, and "the whole thing really fell apart at that point in 2006–
2007."[27] The deals uniformly failed, and they finally persuaded the administration that Pakistan was hopelessly unreliable and uncommitted to the
fight against the Taliban. "The truth is that the Pakistanis had no stomach
for fighting in the rugged border region between Pakistan and
Afghanistan," Rice later wrote:

> Musharraf decided to cut a deal with the tribal leaders – a kind of live and
> let live. In exchange for a stand-down of the Pakistani military the tribes
> agreed to control their "guests." Only the first half of that deal was realized
> and the region became a safe haven for several terrorist groups: fighters
> commanded by Baitullah Mehsud; the Haqqani network, still active after
> we left office; and remnants of al-Qaida.[28]

It is noteworthy that Rice wrote the region "became" a safe haven
after the tribal agreements, implying that it had not been a safe haven
prior to them; in another passage, she said the agreements created
a "new safe haven" for the Taliban. Perhaps she meant that the peace
deals expanded the safe havens or made them even more permissive –
except Bush, Gates, and Hayden also wrote similar passages in their
memoirs, arguing that the Taliban's safe haven was a function of
Pakistan's deals with the tribes.[29] But the Taliban's safe haven in
Pakistan predated the tribal deals and had been amply demonstrated as
early as 2003, suggesting again how slowly some in the Bush administration came to recognize the problem. That the tribal deals play such
a prominent role in the administration's memoirs suggests that they
saw them as a convenient explanation for why they did not recognize
or act against the safe haven earlier. It took time to overcome the
cognitive dissonance of Pakistan acting like an ally and an enemy simultaneously. Pakistan had been consistent and reliable in the fight against

---

[27] Hadley, interview by author. [28] Rice, *No Higher Honor*, 444.
[29] Rice, *No Higher Honor*, 345. Bush, *Decision Points*, 213–214, 216. Gates, *Duty*, 3601. Hayden,
Playing to the Edge, 345–346.

al-Qaida. "And to walk away from that, to say to the Pakistanis, you're lying to us – that was a big moment," Gastright said.[30]

Up to that point, the administration's approach toward Pakistan had been all carrot and no stick. But if the problem was will, not capacity, was there an alternative? By the time the Bush administration was ready to contemplate sticks, Pakistan was caught in a chaotic spiral of violence. Jihadist militants occupied the Red Mosque in downtown Islamabad in July 2007, forcing a week-long standoff and a violent conclusion that left scores dead. Former Prime Minister Benazir Bhutto was assassinated in December 2007 by a suicide bomber when she returned to Pakistan to campaign for office. The same month, militant groups came together and proclaimed the formation of a new umbrella organization: the Pakistani Taliban. Violence throughout the tribal regions surged. The Bush administration believed if the United States pressed Pakistan too hard, it might backfire, enflame Pakistani opinion against America, empower militants, and endanger the stability of the Pakistani state and the security of its nuclear weapons.

"One of our real anxieties about Pakistan was that the disruption in Afghanistan and the increasing Taliban presence would . . . encourage the extremists and the Pakistani Taliban," Hadley said. "Our nightmare was that the Pakistani Taliban would take over the government in Islamabad. Then you would have an extremist, terrorist-supporting government in Islamabad with access to nuclear weapons." Rumsfeld echoed the concern. "The thought of Pakistan's nuclear arsenal falling under the control of Islamist extremists or their terrorist allies was nightmarish." Hadley ordered his staff to review options, to see if there were any viable sticks: "We did some analysis about what it would look like to really crack down on Pakistan, and how would Pakistan respond." Hadley did not share what possibilities they came up with, but "we concluded that it would not get us to where we needed them to be . . . It would have just the opposite [effect]."[31]

One option was the drone program: using armed, unmanned aerial vehicles to surveil and strike targets where manned fighters and bombers could not go. The program had started in the earliest days of the war but was small, involving just one or two strikes per year. In 2007, Bush, frustrated with the lack of progress against al-Qaida, asked for more options. Peter

---

[30] Gastright, interview by author.

[31] Rumsfeld, *Known and Unknown*, 687. Hadley, interview by author. Though I was working on the NSC at the time, I was focused solely on Afghanistan. The Afghanistan and Pakistan directorates were merged later, under the Obama administration.

Lavoy, then serving as the national intelligence officer for South Asia, traveled to Pakistan and spoke with senior Pakistani officials. He wrote up his assessment that "we were overly self-constrained, we were overly self-deterred from taking more unilateral action" against al-Qaida in Pakistan. The US had room to push Pakistan harder. Bush pushed the intelligence agencies and the military to draw up plans for a more aggressive approach, which led to "decisions to ramp up drone production, ramp up pilot recruitment, ramp up strikes, ramp up. Everything changed at that meeting," Lavoy said.[32]

The plan involved "far more intense and essentially unilateral Predator strikes," according to Vickers, who worked on the plan. Previously the United States had asked Pakistan for permission before each drone strike; now it would only provide "concurrent notification" when a strike was already underway, telling the Pakistanis about the strikes only as they were happening, after it was too late for them to warn targets. The plan also increased the number of "orbits" – more drones covering more terrain – from three to eight and eventually to fourteen. There were just ten drone strikes in Pakistan between 2001 and 2007, according to the New America Foundation's database; then, in 2008, the number jumped to thirty-six in a single year.[33]

Drones might have become an effective tool against the Taliban's safe haven in Pakistan. But drone strikes were reported exclusively in Pakistan's Federally Administered Tribal Areas (FATA) in northwestern Pakistan, against al-Qaida, the Haqqani Network, and the Pakistani Taliban – apparently all the Pakistani government would allow. The Afghan Taliban leadership, by contrast, was widely believed to be in Quetta, nearly 400 miles to the south, apparently well outside the drones' authorized orbits, even after their expansion. "We didn't have the permissions and airspace clearance from the Pakistanis that we would need to get at the Quetta Shura and its sanctuary in the south," Vickers wrote. Drones were a vital and effective part of the counterterrorism campaign against al-Qaida and other militants in the FATA; they were never employed in the counterinsurgency campaign against the Afghan Taliban (with one exception much later in the war). Drone strikes in the densely populated city of Quetta would have been more difficult than

---

[32] Lavoy, interview by author.

[33] Woodward, *Obama's Wars*, 25–26. Vickers, *By All Means Available*, 229–232, 236. New America Foundation, "The Drone War in Pakistan." The New America Foundation estimated that 32 percent of strikes under the Obama administration targeted the Taliban, but the data does not distinguish between Afghan Taliban and Pakistani Taliban.

in the rural areas of the FATA, but the Bush administration apparently never even tried.[34]

A far riskier option was unilateral cross-border ground operations without Pakistani permission, like the Abbottabad raid years later, but against Taliban targets. "There were geographic limitations to where we were allowed to take actions," General David Petraeus later recalled. "We were never allowed to go after the Taliban headquarters in particular, with one reported exception." Bush authorized special operations raids inside Pakistan in 2008. US forces launched one raid at Angur Ada, inside Pakistan, in September 2008, originally envisioned as the first of many. But the raid was "too much to bear for the Pakistanis who viewed it as a violation of their sovereignty ... Predator strikes were acceptable; cross-border raids were not," Vickers wrote. Petraeus inherited the result: "We were never allowed to do another [raid], not on the ground," against the Taliban, he said. Three years later, the bin Laden raid would be the last time the United States launched a unilateral ground operation in Pakistan. "The notion of cross-border operations that would have gone after Taliban safe havens and so on, I think just wasn't in the cards because the Pakistanis wouldn't tolerate it and wouldn't cooperate with us," Gates added.[35]

The Bush administration – and, to be fair, its successors – never solved the problem of Pakistan. Trump perhaps came closest when he finally suspended aid to Pakistan in 2018, but by then it was far too late to make a difference. With hindsight, Rice believes "the inability to have a political solution for Pakistan turns out to have been maybe the death knell for the whole thing." So long as the Taliban had safe haven there, it made progress against the insurgency extremely difficult. "I think we kind of knew it ... But ultimately we really failed in getting the Pakistani government to accept responsibility, but also to see that their interests were best served by a stable Afghanistan" she said. "So I would say on that one, we probably get a failing grade. We just weren't able to do anything about that." The notion that "we kind of knew it," is intriguing, suggesting that the Bush administration kept going despite knowing structural conditions made success unlikely – presumably in the hopes that, at some point, those conditions would evolve or

---

[34] Vickers, *By All Means Available*, 303.
[35] Vickers, *By All Means Available*, 236. Petraeus and Gates, interviews by author. "American Forces Attack Militants on Pakistani Soil," *New York Times*, September 3, 2008. Woodward, *Obama's Wars*, 8.

change on their own, which calls to mind an aphorism about the relationship of hope to strategy.[36]

Hadley found a small silver lining. "Pakistan was a safe haven, but our operations could prevent it from being a safe haven from which attacks could be mounted against the homeland or against our friends and allies," he said, likely referring to the drones. Even though "we couldn't eliminate it as a base of support for the Taliban and the Haqqanis in Afghanistan," the United States could ensure "it wasn't a base of terrorist operations" against the American homeland. It was a safe haven for the Taliban, but not for al-Qaida. That was good enough.[37]

IRAQ

The third major enabling condition of the Taliban insurgency was the American war in Iraq, which started in March 2003. As discussed earlier, Iraq was a major factor in the administration's neglect of Afghanistan in 2002 and 2003. The Bush team is sensitive, even today, to the criticism that Iraq distracted from Afghanistan – it was a major line of attack from Senator John Kerry during his campaign against Bush for the presidency in 2004 – but the problem worsened each year. As Iraq deteriorated in 2005 and 2006, the administration became almost wholly consumed trying to manage the crisis and develop the surge. "That is one area where maybe we were distracted by Iraq because Iraq is really falling apart in 2006 and we have to gin up the surge," recalled Eric Edelman, then serving as undersecretary of defense for policy. "My priority number one as undersecretary was clearly Iraq and Afghanistan was second, but it was second by some measure."[38]

The senior ranks of the military frankly recognized Iraq's priority. General Karl Eikenberry took command of US forces in Afghanistan in 2005. "So as the coalition commander I'm now starting to ask for more resources," he said, "but those resources, ISR [intelligence, surveillance, and reconnaissance], troops, special forces, they're moving over to Iraq." Secretary of Defense Bob Gates, who took over from Rumsfeld in late 2006, recognized that with the surge in Iraq, more troops for Afghanistan would put a huge strain on the force. "My intent upon becoming secretary had been to give our commanders in Iraq and Afghanistan everything they needed to be successful," he later wrote, but "I realized on this initial visit

---

[36] Rice, interview by author.   [37] Hadley, interview by author.
[38] Edelman, interview by author.

to Afghanistan I couldn't deliver in both places at once." Admiral Fallon, who took over as commander of Central Command in 2007, was blunt. "Once things turned to shit in Iraq, believe me, nobody cared" about Afghanistan.[39]

A dramatic and public statement of the problem came in December 2007. "Our main focus, militarily, in the region and in the world right now is rightly and firmly in Iraq. It is simply a matter of resources, of capacity," Admiral Mike Mullen, the chairman of the joint chiefs of staff, testified to the House Armed Services Committee, summarizing it with a pithy saying that perfectly captured the reality: "In Afghanistan, we do what we can. In Iraq, we do what we must." I was newly arrived at the White House as director for Afghanistan on the NSC staff at the time. Mullen's testimony reverberated around the community of policymakers and analysts who focused on Afghanistan. We were unsurprised – we knew it was true – but shocked and demoralized that a senior official was so blunt and public about it, that the administration accepted it as reality and apparently could or would do nothing about it.[40]

Mullen's frank aphorism was a case of saying the quiet part out loud, being too explicit in public about something that the administration did not want to acknowledge so clearly. "Mike got into trouble for saying that with the President," Gates recalled, because "it raised the uncomfortable reality that we were unable to properly resource our efforts in Afghanistan because of the invasion of Iraq." Steve Hadley, the national security advisor, objected to Mullen's pithy synopsis and called him. "I really take offense at that," he recalls telling him, "because that's not how I saw it." If Mullen really believed Afghanistan needed more troops, "why did you not come to the president of the United States and tell him?" If he would have asked, Bush would have found the troops, Hadley believed. "The President thought that he had in Afghanistan what he needed to succeed in Afghanistan." Hadley believed the military leadership was hesitant to ask because they feared putting too much stress on the force. In effect, it was Mullen – not Bush – who made the decision "that Iraq was going to be a war of 'do what we must' and Afghanistan was a war of 'do what we can.' That shouldn't have been his decision, that should have been a decision for the president of the United States," Hadley said. Gates, however, thought Mullen was simply "describing reality, however politically uncomfortable."[41]

---

[39] Eikenberry, interview by author. Gates, *Duty*, 200. Fallon, interview by author.

[40] House Armed Services Committee, "Security and Stability in Afghanistan," December 11, 2007, 7.

[41] Hadley, interview by author. Hadley, "Bush Oral History." Gates, *Duty*, 202.

Whose fault is it that Iraq trumped Afghanistan? This turns out to be a fascinating case study in how decisions are made and by whom. Bush never explicitly told anyone "do less in Afghanistan," and we are unlikely to find a signed memo in the archives to that effect – but he didn't have to. Gastright recalls that as he generated budget requests and sent them up the chain

> it felt like we were just being ground down. We're ground down with "there's no more there, don't ask." … The guys in OMB [the Office of Management and Budget] were saying, no, there's no more there. And it's possible that Steve Hadley was saying, "if I would have requested, [the president would have approved]," but it's also very likely that before our request could go from my level to the deputies, they were being ground to sand.[42]

Others had a similar experience. "By September of 2005, I had reported in front channel cables that I believe the war was going to get worse," recalls Ambassador Ronald Neumann. "It was certainly part of my belief that we were underfunding on the development side." Neumann repeatedly and energetically requested more money for development and reconstruction during his years as ambassador in Kabul. "It was hell on wheels to find the money in the bureaucracy … We have the battle I waged for $600 million in economic supplemental for 2006, and after a lot of back and forth, I got $43 [million] … Nobody ever said to me that we weren't going to give you the money because of Iraq," but Neumann felt it was obviously because of Iraq: "So, I actually felt somewhat lied to." He felt that OMB "seemed to lack a sense that we were at war" in Afghanistan.[43]

"I am absolutely convinced that the United States would have realized its objectives of permanently ridding Afghanistan of al-Qaida and the Taliban and laying a solid foundation for a functioning pro-Western Afghan government far more quickly and successfully had the US government's preoccupation with Iraq not led it to ignore Afghanistan," wrote Dov Zakheim, who, as comptroller of the Pentagon, was charged with leading the Department of Defense's reconstruction efforts in Afghanistan:

> Senior US policymakers simply bit off more than they could chew when they opted for nearly simultaneous military action to overthrow Iraq's Saddam Hussein … The policy planners seemed unaware of any opportunity cost in starting a second war in Iraq, that is, the impact that

---

[42] Gastright, interview by author.
[43] Neumann, interview by author. Neumann, *The Other War*, 45.

massive wartime expenditures might have on the baseline budget, let alone the unfinished effort in Afghanistan.[44]

The bureaucracy enforced a priority which everyone believed was there, a belief that was reinforced by public statements like Mullen's. The priority became embedded in everyday operations, in bureaucratic processes, in baseline assumptions, all of which went into budget discussions and deployment plans. Those who focused exclusively on Afghanistan, like Gastright, Neumann, Zakheim, and others, were banging on drums warning that Afghanistan needed more attention and resources, but as their requests filtered upward, they were put through a bureaucratic machine that subordinated their views to the needs of the Iraq war. By the time the larger package of requests reached the president, he didn't have to make an explicit decision to do less in Afghanistan or more in Iraq. It was already embedded in what the bureaucracy had put on his desk, programmed into the bureaucracy's autopilot.

That does not absolve Bush, who was, after all, the chief executive officer of the federal bureaucracy. Bureaucrats – including 4,000 political appointees across scores of agencies and departments – take their cues from the next rung up the managerial ladder, who in turn take their cues from the next, and so on until the buck stops at the Resolute Desk. In that fashion, each president nudges the steering wheel of the bloated supertanker that is the US federal bureaucracy. The supertanker can resist, the rudder can move slowly, and it often takes months, even years, for a turn in the steering wheel to translate into a new direction for the ship – but the president is still at the helm.

That presidential leadership matters, and that an active, engaged president can make the bureaucracy respond to his priorities is best demonstrated by Bush's decision to surge in Iraq. The joint chiefs of staff, the secretary of defense, and much of the professional national security establishment opposed the surge in 2006, and the normal interagency process did not develop the surge option on its own. The initiative came from outside channels, and Bush worked for six months to pressure and cajole his administration and the military leadership to back the idea. He fired the secretary of defense, replaced the commanding general, and committed himself and his administration singularly to the goal of bringing the war in Iraq back from the brink.

---

[44] Zakheim *A Vulcan's Tale*, 1, 187. See also 189, 211, 213, 267, 275.

Whatever the merits of the surge in Iraq – I think it was clearly necessary – it demonstrates that the president can impose his priorities on the bureaucracy, that the bureaucracy's priorities could be forced to reflect his agenda. Bush did not impose that kind of priority for Afghanistan. Bush's defenders argued then and now that he was right to prioritize Iraq because the stakes were higher and the war was going much worse than Afghanistan in 2005 and 2006. But in defending Bush's decision to prioritize Iraq, they concede the larger argument about the war in the first place: because the administration decided to go to war in Iraq, it put another item on their agenda that eventually became all-consuming and crowded out attention for Afghanistan.

Hadley argues that the president and his administration were capable of prioritizing both wars, if only they had been told what was truly needed in Afghanistan. The administration did focus on Afghanistan: Bush approved Accelerating Success in 2003, the US military helped secure Afghan elections in 2004 and 2005, and Hadley oversaw a strategic review on the NSC staff in 2006 that yielded more money and more troops for Afghanistan in the administration's final two years (see Chapter 6). "If everyone is right that our attention was diverted, that shouldn't have happened, but it did," he offers. In 2007, Bush asked Congress for authority to increase the size of the Army and Marine Corps by 92,000 troops to alleviate the strain on the force from prolonged deployments in two wars. Bush recalls in his memoir that in late 2006, "I decided that America had to take on more of the responsibility [in Afghanistan], even though we were about to undertake a major new commitment in Iraq as well. 'Damn it, we can do more than one thing at a time,' I told the national security team. 'We cannot lose in Afghanistan.'"[45]

Bush had a point: the United States is materially capable of waging more than one war at a time, as it did on a much larger scale in World War II. The problem is not that the United States lacked the population, money, or industrial capability to wage two wars. The problem is that none of the four presidents who oversaw the wars ever came close to mobilizing the resources required for that level of effort, even for the war in Iraq, let alone for Iraq and Afghanistan combined. As for Afghanistan, Hadley concedes that the strategy review was "certainly not as intensive an effort as it was in Iraq, but there's a reason for that. Our investment in Iraq at that point is much greater, and the situation in Iraq was much graver, we are losing that war in Iraq." Hadley also recognizes that "it turns out we were losing the war in Afghanistan, but it didn't look like that to us at the time." Peter Feaver, who

---

[45] Hadley, interview by author. Bush, *Decision Points*, 211.

worked for Hadley on the NSC staff as a special advisor for strategic planning and institutional reform, reflected on the simultaneous strategy reviews for Iraq and Afghanistan. "Our conclusion was, yes, [Afghanistan is] not going well, it is going to need more resources," he said, "but we've got to do Iraq first because that's the higher urgent priority – we can do a holding action in Afghanistan, we have to turn around Iraq." Even when Bush was determined not to ignore Afghanistan, he still settled for a "holding action" and subordinated it to Iraq. Bush is right that we *could have* done more than one thing at a time, which means it was a conscious choice not to.[46]

The bureaucratic dynamic meshed with the administration's view (before 2006) that the war in Afghanistan was over and the peacebuilding operation had been successfully handed off to others. "People got comfortable with the idea that Afghanistan was the war that was going well, Iraq was the war that was going poorly, so Afghanistan was neglected," according to Eliot Cohen, who served as Counselor to the State Department in 2007 and 2008. It was a marriage of wishful thinking, administrative passivity, and crisis-driven policymaking. If Bush never told anyone to do less in Afghanistan, he also did not exert active and engaged leadership to keep Afghanistan a top priority amid the war in Iraq and was naive to believe others would or could balance the two without his holding them accountable. Presidents are the ones who program bureaucratic autopilot in the first place, and who can override it when it goes awry. Bush allowed an incentive structure to take root which encouraged the bureaucracy to enforce the priority for Iraq without being told. "The planning for the next war created fresh incentives for officers and intelligence analysts in Afghanistan to downplay signs of trouble in that theater," according to Coll. "If you wanted promotion and frontline battlefield assignments, you went on to the next war."[47]

Gates believed that Bush "saw Iraq as central to his legacy, but less so Afghanistan, and he resented any suggestion that the war in Iraq had deprived our effort in Afghanistan of adequate resources." Bush's and Hadley's defense is an important reminder that the administration did not *ignore* Afghanistan, as their harshest critics claim, but it is clear that Iraq and Afghanistan competed for attention, time, and resources – and Iraq consistently won. One can imagine the counterfactual: if the United States had not invaded Iraq, policymakers might have had the time and

---

[46] Hadley, interview by author. Feaver, "Oral History."

[47] Cohen, Eliot. Interview by author. Coll, *Directorate S*, 135.

attention to recognize earlier what was happening in Afghanistan and to respond sooner. (Though it is possible that if Bush had not invaded Iraq, the administration's bandwidth would have been taken up with something else – Iran or North Korea, for example – not Afghanistan.) The timeframe in which the Bush administration planned for Iraq, invaded Iraq, managed the aftermath, and then began planning for and implementing the surge – 2002 through 2007 – overlaps perfectly with the same timeframe in which the Taliban regrouped, state failure in Afghanistan became apparent, the golden hour for state building closed, and the insurgency began. The one thing Afghanistan needed the most – time and attention – was what was most lacking because of Iraq.[48]

COUNTERTERRORISM

The Taliban launched their insurgency because they had the motive (their ideology), means (safe haven in Pakistan), and opportunity (state failure in Afghanistan, the light international footprint, and an America focused on Iraq). Would the insurgency have happened without these strategic missteps?

The Bush administration is not at fault for the Taliban's ideology and had few tools to influence it. The main blame for the Taliban's insurgency must always lie with the Taliban itself for preaching, propagating, and following a theocratic and totalitarian religious ideology that rejects democracy, excuses terrorism, and justifies oppression. It sounds trite to belabor the point, but historians and critics often leave it unsaid, which robs the enemy of their agency and implies that the United States is the only actor that matters. But the enemy gets a vote: no matter what the Bush administration did after 9/11, the Taliban were jihadists and were going to do jihadist things. It is highly likely that the senior Taliban leadership would have tried to reconstitute their movement and sponsor political violence after their fall from power regardless of what the Bush administration did, as demonstrated by their refusal to engage in talks with the United States, denounce al-Qaida, or participate in the reconciliation process.

But the Bush administration is culpable for its choices. It did not create the safe haven in Pakistan, but it was too slow – perhaps two or three years too slow – to admit what was going on. Bush and his team *wanted* to believe that Pakistan was an ally because the converse was too difficult – maybe too

---

[48] Gates, *Duty*, 94.

embarrassing – and invited too much cognitive dissonance. Hadley is right that, even if they had recognized Pakistan's duplicity, there were few good options for how to respond. But if they had recognized earlier, they might have at least had time to try before the downward spiral of violence in Pakistan in 2007. In the event, all the administration could do was wait out the clock. In the early years, the Bush administration did not force the point, create a red team to challenge their assumptions, play a game of "what if?" to think through the possibility that the United States was being played the fool in an epic geopolitical con. Rice was right to give the administration a failing grade on Pakistan. Bush, the play-from-the-gut Texan, was snookered.

As for Iraq: it is obvious that Iraq hurt the war in Afghanistan by monopolizing policymakers' attention and competing for money and troops – as most Bush administration officials now admit. But I supported the war, narrowly, in 2003. In my book on the just war tradition, I reexamined the case closely and concluded it was morally permissible, though clearly imprudent, to invade. The merits of the war in Iraq are not solely about how it affected Afghanistan; there are broader considerations. It is easy to forget that the situation in Iraq was not sustainable. The sanctions regime was collapsing, Saddam Hussein had ejected weapons inspectors, and most of the world believed he was developing weapons of mass destruction. Bush's error was not the invasion, but impatience. The attacks of 9/11 had created a sense of urgency to do things and do them quickly, to move fast and break stuff, an impulse which crowded out the deliberation and reflection required for sound strategy. Iraq likely could have waited a year or two, while Afghanistan clearly needed focused attention in its fragile early post-Taliban months and years. While the case for war in Iraq was stronger than most critics now admit, the administration was grossly premature to conclude their duty in Afghanistan was done in early 2002.[49]

Because the job was not done in Afghanistan. The Bush administration did not create state failure in Afghanistan – but it is squarely at fault for doing almost nothing about it for two years and very little for several years after that. Of all Bush's mistakes, this one I find least explicable. The administration's initial hostility to nation building was small-minded, historically ignorant, and morally callous – an attitude that, to his credit, Bush eventually repudiated. Coming from a team that talked a big game about restoring American leadership on the world stage, they exercised little of it when it came time to rebuild the most failed state on the planet and help the

---

[49] Miller, *Just War and Ordered Liberty*, chapter 8.

world's neediest people. It was fair for Rumsfeld to warn against moral hazard and dependency and to expect allies to do their part – but that requires that we also do our part, which we did not do in 2002 and 2003. Global leadership should be magnanimous, known for its broad-minded concern for the common good. In the early years, the Bush team – especially Rumsfeld and the OMB – instead came off as stingy, narrow-minded techno-crats obsessed with the balance sheet more than as statesmen wielding American hegemony to invest in a just and lasting peace. This is the worst legacy of the Bush administration's war in Afghanistan.

There is a common thread tying these failures together: the Bush administration prioritized counterterrorism above every other consider-ation. Pakistan was an ally against al-Qaida – the administration's top concern – which made its complicity with the Taliban harder to notice or even care about. Iraq was described as part of the War on Terror and, after the rise of al-Qaida in Iraq, really was a major battlefield in that conflict. And nation building seemed to have only a tangential connection to killing terrorists. Because the administration defined the war as a war on terrorism, not a war on jihadism, it made key strategic mistakes which in turn enabled the rise of the Taliban insurgency – which, in turn, eventually undermined America's war against al-Qaida.

In 2002, Rumsfeld told McNeill that his priority was to get al-Qaida and train Afghan security forces. "We're not going to do any nation building," Rumsfeld said. Reconstruction got off to a slow start because "we had not made a number of decisions, and had not done much of anything at all, because we went in there with counterterrorism aims," according to Tony Harriman. Similarly, the intelligence community "prioritized pursuit of the Arab, Chechen, and Uzbek volunteers who had followed bin Laden," almost to the exclusion of other intelligence missions, according to Steve Coll. "What I found was that counterterrorism, the global war on terrorism imperative, dominated everything else," recalled Ambassador Bill Wood. "Our intelligence assets were overwhelmingly oriented to counterterrorism. We didn't know very much about Afghanistan, and we didn't try to find out." Neumann observed that "Washington's original focus on hunting terrorists and avoiding entanglement in nation building also resulted initially in resistance to large assistance commitments."[50]

---

[50] Harriman and Wood, interviews by author. McNeill, interview by Jake Tapper, quoted in CNN Special. Coll, *Directorate S*, 134, 117. Neumann, *The Other War*, 38. The anecdote about Rumsfeld's instruction to McNeill was corroborated by Neumann.

Even after 2006, Mike Hayden, the CIA director, was "struck by how much [his briefings with the president] focused on terrorism, and within terrorism how much they were about South Asia – Pakistan and Afghanistan. And during the last six months of the administration, I was struck that we covered the hunt for HVT-1 (High-Value-Target-1, i.e., bin Laden) and HVT-2 (Zawahiri) in practically every session. We were certainly focused." Hayden worried about the "obsession" with counterterrorism. General David McKiernan, ISAF commander in 2008 and 2009, judged that America's national security interest in Afghanistan was "exacting revenge on al-Qaida."[51]

Eric Edelman recounted his visits to Afghanistan as undersecretary of defense for policy. "Whenever I got briefed by the SOF [special operations forces] guys I was really worried," because of the exclusive emphasis on counterterrorism. "You'd meet with the white [overt] SOF guys and they would give you a briefing on all these hunter-killer missions that they were doing. And my sense was, well, isn't your job FID [foreign internal defense]?" he asked. "Why aren't you guys training the Afghans in foreign internal defense instead of going out and killing people, which is the black [clandestine] SOF's job to do?" Edelman was concerned that the overt special operations forces were simply not suited to counterterrorism. "These white SOF guys didn't necessarily know what they were doing, which made it worse," he worried. "We did a lot of damage to ourselves by alienating a lot of Afghans in rural areas with the counterterrorism operations we ran ... The counterterrorism strategy that was operating was without real good oversight and ended up doing more harm than good." "Green Berets among the Army's Special Forces, trained to influence local populations through engagement and small development projects, traveled patiently and for the most part peaceably, but theirs was not the predominant mission. Terrorist hunting was," according to Coll.[52]

Karl Eikenberry, similarly, saw "contradictions" among the United States' various goals. Eikenberry characterized the counterterrorism bureaucracy as saying, "I'm okay with the idea of passing bags of cash out to unsavory people if they can help me get Bin Laden," even though that undermined the peacebuilding and state-building agenda. "Don't talk to me about building governance out in the provinces," they implied. Of course, development and reconstruction were supposed to be tied to the counterterrorism mission: building Afghan capacity meant helping the

---

[51] Hayden, *Playing to the Edge*, 329. McKiernan, interview by author.
[52] Edelman, interview with author. Coll, *Directorate S*, 142.

Afghans deny safe haven to al-Qaida. But Eikenberry felt no one took that idea seriously. "Regardless of what the doctrinal manual says about COIN [counterinsurgency], there's a triage and a priority," he said, "What's really gripping the decision makers around the table is, we still don't have bin Laden."[53]

The problem was that the Bush administration did not recognize the difference between "the two probably quite distinct wars, between the one against al-Qaida and the one against the Taliban," according to Jim Shinn, who worried about "how they got conflated." The Bush administration did not have a Taliban strategy distinct from its al-Qaida strategy. Al-Qaida always took priority – understandably, considering 9/11 – but the administration misunderstood the relationship between the two wars. To defeat al-Qaida, it needed a Taliban strategy, which meant it needed to treat counterinsurgency and nation building with the same urgency and attention as it treated counterterrorism. Instead, insofar as the Bush administration paid attention to the Taliban, it treated them as an extension of al-Qaida – a group that could not be negotiated with and had to be killed. That proved ineffective: because the Taliban were an insurgency, not a terrorist group, combating them required a different kind of approach. "The cycle time of effectiveness of a counterinsurgency strategy is rather longer and more attenuated than the cycle time of a counterterrorism strategy," Shinn commented, which made it difficult to contemplate.[54]

From 2002 to 2005, the Bush administration underinvested in peace building, invaded Iraq, was blind to Pakistan's complicity in the Taliban's safe haven, and was preoccupied with counterterrorism. The Bush administration cannot be blamed for the senior Taliban leadership's ideological commitment to rebuilding their movement and launching an insurgency – but they can be blamed for decisions that made it much easier for Taliban leaders to act on their beliefs and to find recruits for their cause. The insurgency almost certainly would not have happened in the time, place, scale, and manner that it did without the Bush administration's missteps. The Bush administration is sometimes accused of having waged a needless war in Iraq. But in retrospect, it seems clear the war that erupted in Afghanistan in 2005 was, even more than the one in Iraq, a conflict that did not need to happen

---

[53] Eikenberry, interview by author.
[54] Shinn, interview with author. Barney Rubin made a similar point to SIGAR.

6

2007–2008

Counterinsurgency

In late 2006 and early 2007, the Bush administration recognized that Afghanistan was deteriorating sharply and undertook a series of strategy reviews. Successful elections in 2004 and 2005 marked the end of the Bonn Process, warlords appeared to be disarmed and co-opted, and economic life sprang back after the Taliban's fall. But those successes were overshadowed by the exploding drug trade, growing corruption in the Afghan government, and, above all, the Taliban insurgency. Ambassador Ronald Neumann warned about the deteriorating situation repeatedly in his cables from Kabul, including one in August 2006 that starkly opened, "We are not winning in Afghanistan."[1]

The reviews led to more troops and a new counterinsurgency strategy with attention to training Afghan security forces and improving governance, reconstruction, and counternarcotics. As in 2003, the new approach ran into the buzz saw of bureaucracy, the fog and friction of war, unanticipated challenges, and, now, a far stronger and more resilient enemy. The Bush administration did succeed in beginning to move the supertanker of the US government toward a more coherent counterinsurgency posture and, by the end of Bush's second term, could point to signs of progress. The problems with the American war effort in 2007 and 2008 were less problems of strategy than of implementation. Having blundered badly in the early years and created huge problems for itself, the American effort was now playing catch-up, trying to adjust rapidly to a deteriorating situation. Bureaucracies resist both rapidity and change. The tools and programs available for the new counterinsurgency campaign had not been designed for counterinsurgency. Trying to change them, scale them up with massive funding, use them in a new way, and use them in a coordinated fashion on a compressed timeline was more than most policymakers could manage.

---

[1] State, KABUL 003863. https://nsarchive2.gwu.edu/NSAEBB/NSAEBB358a/doc26.pdf. Neumann, *The Other War*, 109.

THE 2006 STRATEGY REVIEWS

"My CIA and military briefings included increasingly dire reports about Taliban influence," Bush wrote, and by November 2006, "it was clear we needed to adjust our strategy." Rumsfeld sent Marin Strmecki – whose 2002 trip and subsequent report had been the catalyst for the Accelerating Success initiative – back out to Afghanistan for another fact-finding trip and urged Cheney and Steve Hadley to hear his report. Condoleezza Rice, now secretary of state, hired Eliot Cohen, a professor of strategic studies at Johns Hopkins University's renowned School of Advanced International Studies, as Counselor to the State Department and sent him on a similar trip. And Hadley, Rice's successor as national security advisor, oversaw a review by the NSC staff. "It's 2006 when it really starts deteriorating. That's what provokes the 2006 strategy review," Hadley recalled.[2]

Stephen Hadley graduated from Cornell University in 1969, went to Yale Law School – where he was a classmate of Hillary Clinton – and alternated between practicing law and working for Republican administrations. After a few years in the US Navy, he served on Gerald Ford's NSC staff in the 1970s, helped investigate the Iran-Contra scandal in the late 1980s, and served in the Pentagon in the George H. W. Bush administration. He joined the George W. Bush campaign as a foreign policy advisor and served as Rice's deputy in Bush's first term. Among national security advisors who oversaw the Afghan war, Hadley adhered closest to the Brent Scowcroft model (a quiet process manager) rather than the Henry Kissinger model (a high-profile advocate). Like Gates, he seems to pride himself on a quiet, understated persistence. He questions a problem like a prosecutor, yet he has an almost-gentle demeanor, which succeeds in commanding a room because of how rare it is in Washington, DC. Bush liked to tease him for it – but if anyone is responsible for the course corrections of Bush's second term (after Bush himself), it is Hadley.

In late 2006, the military and the intelligence community disagreed on what was happening in Afghanistan (a familiar story for historians of the Vietnam War). "I remember a couple of times the intelligence community would do this assessment of government control, Taliban control, and contested areas by district throughout the country," Hadley said, but "the military would contest [their analysis]," believing the intelligence community was too pessimistic. The gap persisted, but by late 2006 the Bush

---

[2] Bush, *Decision Points*, 210–211. Rumsfeld, *Known and Unknown*, 688. Cheney and Cheney, *In My Time*, 497–98. Hadley, interview by author.

administration "began to put more weight on what the intelligence community was telling us." As a result, "we made a judgment that we were not
winning." "We all knew that the effort in Afghanistan was floundering, but
Eliot [Cohen] thought it was nearing catastrophic failure," Rice wrote. Not
all the principals saw it that way. Rumsfeld wrote of the situation in late 2006
with comparative equanimity that, "after four years of relative dormancy, the
Taliban was poised to mount a serious offensive," which overstates their
dormancy and misses that the Taliban had already mounted a serious
offensive earlier that year.[3]

The parallel efforts from State, Defense, and the NSC came to broadly
similar conclusions. Strmecki argued "the deteriorating security situation in
2006" came from the Taliban's decision to escalate and from "weak or bad
governance ... that created a vacuum of power into which the enemy moved."
He concluded that the Taliban was "mounting steady year-on-year improve-
ments in its capabilities," and that "left unchecked, the Taliban threat is likely
to grow in 2007 and beyond, further undermining security and eventually
imperiling the legitimacy of the Afghan government." He recommended that
the administration focus on "hardening Afghanistan against insurgent activities," by accelerating training and governance programs, while "inducing
Pakistan's leaders to deprive the Taliban of sanctuary and support." Above all,
the administration needed to stop thinking of Afghanistan as a "post-conflict"
environment and should design and fund its programs "with an urgency
appropriate to war."

Strmecki recommended a "multi-year COIN plan," arguing that US
forces had "steadily improved its counterinsurgency operations since the
shift from a counter-terrorist strategy in late 2003," because of its "engage,
clear, hold, and build" strategy. The administration had not, in fact, shifted
from a counterterrorism to a counterinsurgency strategy in 2003, at least not
fully. It was a bureaucratic I-told-you-so. Strmecki's 2006 review was saying,
as diplomatically as possible, that the administration had never fully implemented the vision behind his 2003 Accelerating Success initiative.[4]

Hadley's NSC review echoed Strmecki's brief, recommending that the
administration "follow through on post-conflict stabilization and development," "resolve the crisis of weak and bad governance," accelerate training
of the Afghan army and police, change Pakistan's behavior, and more.

[3] Hadley, interview by author. Rice, *No Higher Honor*, 636. Rumsfeld, *Known and Unknown*,
688.

[4] Strmecki, "Afghanistan at a Crossroads," 2, 5, 7, 10, 24. Rumsfeld, *Known and Unknown*,
687–688.

Interestingly, the review characterized reconstruction efforts as "counter-insurgency infrastructure building and economic development," which sounds like a rhetorical effort to force civilian activities into military usefulness, or perhaps force the military to recognize the military value of civilian efforts.[5]

Few of the ideas were new, but the overall package was. It amounted to restating and fitting together a clutch of ideas that had been floating around since 2003 – in Accelerating Success, in Barno's nascent counterinsurgency plans, in the PRTs, and in Neumann's and Eikenberry's warnings, among other places – but gave them a new cohesiveness and an urgency to match the ideas with more troops and money. "I don't think we felt like we needed a complete strategy change, which is of course what we did need in Iraq, but I don't think we felt we needed that in Afghanistan in 2006," Hadley said. "We concluded that given the resources we were putting in, we weren't winning, we were losing ... [So] we decided to put in more resources." New resources and a new sense of urgency enabled a newly coherent counterinsurgency strategy, a new cohesiveness to the *ways* part of the ends–ways–means equation.[6]

Barno and Khalilzad had used the language of counterinsurgency as early as 2003, but it was COIN-lite, a sort of impressionistic counterinsurgency waged with relatively few resources in a handful of districts and without the attention from Washington, DC, that would give it the "urgency appropriate to war." "The commanders we had in Afghanistan – Eliot Cohen likes to say they spoke pidgin COIN," Edelman reflected. "They could throw around some of the COIN phrases, like unity of effort and this and that, population centric, blah, blah, blah. But they didn't actually operate that way." That is unfair to Barno and Eikenberry, the commanders from 2003 to 2007: they implemented as much of a counterinsurgency strategy as they were able given the resources, mission, and authorities they had at the time. The quip might have been true of some of their subordinate commanders. But Edelman is right that the campaign in Afghanistan to that point could not be called a full-blooded counterinsurgency campaign. It lacked cohesion, clarity, and resources. Even in late 2006, "we don't have a counterinsurgency strategy. We're fighting an insurgency. What the hell do we think is going to happen? Why do we think it's not going well? Because we're not fighting the right war," Edelman recalled.

[5] Miller, Lute, O'Sullivan, "Chapter 5: Afghanistan," in Hadley et al., *Hand-Off*. Rice, *No Higher Honor*, 636.

[6] Boucher and Hadley, interviews by author.

"The effort ought to be 80–90 percent civilian and 10–20 percent military, and we were way out of whack. We had it exactly backwards."[7]

Counterinsurgency requires close coordination and integration between the civilian and military components of the government. "The counterinsurgent uses all of the instruments of national power to support the government in restoring and enforcing the rule of law," according to the US Army's new counterinsurgency manual that was published in late 2006. "Counterinsurgency thus involves the controlled application of national power in political, information, economic, social, military, and diplomatic fields and disciplines." Counterinsurgency is not just a military operation; it is an act of the full government to exert its power and establish its authority. Diplomats, aid workers, police officers, judges, public utilities, educators – every public servant is part of the counterinsurgency effort, both for the host nation and its international backers.[8]

But the reviews revealed, and perhaps worsened, bad blood between the civilian and military agencies. "All three – security, diplomacy, and the economy – had to be closely linked," Rumsfeld wrote. "If progress was absent in one, the others would be hindered." Naturally, he deflected blame away from his department. "But from the Defense Department's standpoint, we knew that while our military would not lose a battle, it was also true that we could not win strategic success by military means alone, particularly in irregular warfare and counterinsurgency," he wrote. "Our non-military institutions were bound by outdated regulations and statutes, slowed by bureaucratic inertia, and in large measure kept away from the action by a government culture that did not promote and reward individuals willing to deploy abroad."[9]

Rice, now serving as Secretary of State, returned the criticism. From the beginning of the war, she tried to emphasize to Bush the need for better integration and better political oversight of military operations. "'Mr. President,' I said, 'you need *political*-military plans, not just military plans, and that requires all of the expertise of the NSC,'" she wrote in her memoir. "The President nodded in agreement and did insist on full vetting for issues such as collateral damage. But Don [Rumsfeld] was resistant to a review of the actual battle plan with the NSC Principals, relying instead on briefings with the President that were sometimes short

---

[7] Edelman and Fallon, interviews by author.

[8] United States Department of the Army and United States Marine Corps, *Field Manual no. 3–24: Counterinsurgency* (Washington, DC: 2006), 1–1.

[9] Rumsfeld, *Known and Unknown*, 691. Edelman echoed the point in an interview.

on operational detail." Rice's and Rumsfeld's critiques of each other's departments were not mutually exclusive: the State Department was incapable of coordination at the tactical and operational level, while the Defense Department was unwilling to coordinate at the strategic level.[10]

To enforce greater coordination at the strategic level, Bush made a change on the National Security Council staff. Meghan O'Sullivan had previously served as the deputy national security advisor for Iraq and Afghanistan – ostensibly in charge of coordinating interagency action on both wars – but only held the rank of a special assistant to the president. In White House rankings, a "special assistant" is junior in rank to a "deputy assistant" and "assistant" to the president. Bush elevated O'Sullivan's office to the rank of "assistant" – making the office equal in rank to the national security advisor – and sought a senior military figure to fill it. This is the figure whom the media reported as Bush's "war czar." When I read the news, I thought it was a good idea but immediately knew there should be two czars, one for each war: any figure charged with overseeing both would inevitably focus on Iraq. After several candidates passed on the opportunity, Bush appointed Lieutenant General Doug Lute to fill the role in May 2007.

Lute, a 1975 West Point graduate, had a master's in public policy from Harvard and taught at West Point's prestigious Department of Social Sciences. His career alternated command assignments in armored and cavalry regiments with a series of staff jobs, including with the Army Chief of Staff, on the Joint Staff's J-5 directorate (in charge of strategic plans and policy), as the J-3 (director of operations) at Central Command, and the J-3 on the Joint Staff – key preparation for his czardom. Lute's staff experience gave him an expert's familiarity with the machinery of military bureaucracy, one of his chief strengths in the role. He also has the affable demeanor essential for successful staff officers, like Eisenhower: they are diplomats negotiating delicate agreements between the sovereign realms of different military commands and services. Lute recalled that he expected to spend "about 85 percent on Iraq and 15 percent on Afghanistan, or maybe even 90 percent attention on Iraq and 10 percent on Afghanistan." The CIA seconded me to his staff in September 2007, joining several others from various agencies.[11]

---

[10] Rice, *No Higher Honor*, 96.

[11] Lute, "Lessons Learned Record of Interview." Jim Jones told Bob Gates that Doug Lute had twenty-five people on his staff working on Afghanistan. I have no idea where he got that number, but he was off by a factor of five. We had no more than five to six people working on Afghanistan and a slightly larger team working on Iraq. During my time on

Bush made other changes. Hastened along by the 2006 midterm election in which voters dealt Bush and the Republican Party a strong rebuke for the deterioration in Iraq, he fired Rumsfeld and replaced him with Bob Gates. ISAF completed its expansion, assumed responsibility for security nation-wide in October, and deployed more PRTs. For the first time, ISAF would be commanded by an American: General Dan K. McNeill, who assumed command in February 2007 (McNeill had previously commanded US forces in Afghanistan in 2002–2003). Bush nominated a new ambassador, William Wood, who arrived in April 2007. And General David Petraeus' new counterinsurgency manual had just been completed.

Bush increased the troop presence in Afghanistan from 21,000 to 31,000 and quadrupled aid to the Afghan army and police. He had come to recognize that the light footprint was a mistake. Initially, "I agreed with our military leaders that we did not need a larger presence," he wrote. "But in retrospect, our rapid success with low troop levels created false comfort, and our desire to maintain a light military footprint left us short of the resources we needed. It would take several years for these shortcomings to become clear."[12] Though Hadley's NSC had charted the way forward, he had some reservations. "We probably had to do it," he said, "but we lost the lessons of the first four years in Afghanistan, which were keep a light footprint and empower the Afghans so that they could do it." Regardless, for the second time, the American war in Afghanistan got a new sense of mission, more resources, and the appearance, at least, of better coordination and cohesiveness.[13]

ISAF AND OEF

The Bush administration wanted to wage a cohesive counterinsurgency campaign, which required a military force with the posture, training, and mission for counterinsurgency. But the American and international military presence in Afghanistan was, from the beginning, fraught with a convoluted

the NSC, the Afghanistan directors included me, Christa Skerry from USAID, Marie Richards from the State Department, and another official from the Defense Department; reporting through senior director John Wood (Col., US Army). Others rotated in for shorter tours, including John Gallagher, a White House Fellow and Army Lt. Col., and later John Tien, another Army Colonel.

[12] Bush, *Decision Points*, 207.

[13] Bush, *Decision Points*, 211–212. Hadley, "Bush Oral History."

chain of command, poor coordination, and unclear missions. The organizational mess became infamous among everyone involved in the war.

American forces were initially deployed under the auspices of Operation Enduring Freedom (OEF), a US-led multinational coalition to overthrow the Taliban regime and hunt al-Qaida, not to wage counterinsurgency or keep the peace. In December 2001, as the new Afghan government took power, the UN authorized a peacekeeping force – the International Security Assistance Force (ISAF) – to stabilize Kabul and create a neutral security environment for political reconstruction. But ISAF was limited to Kabul and had no mandate for counterinsurgency or counterterrorism. The two international military forces – ISAF (for peacekeeping) and the OEF coalition (for counterterrorism) – both operated in Afghanistan but neither had a counterinsurgency mission and had only a loose connection with each other.

That would be unusual enough, but the situation grew more complex. American forces were split. Most were under the command of a joint task force that reported to Central Command (CENTCOM), the combatant command with geographic responsibility for the Middle East and South and Central Asia. But most Special Operations Forces (SOF) fell under Special Operations Command (SOCOM) and were further split between overt SOF (the Green Berets), who fell under the Combined Joint Special Operations Task Force–Afghanistan (CJSOTF-A), and another task force comprised of a small number of clandestine forces who remained under Joint Special Operations Command (JSOC). They both had counterterrorism missions, but CJSOTF-A operations were overt while JSOC's were clandestine. JSOC had a global mandate, and its task force (designated TF-714 when General Stan McChrystal commanded it) operated across the entire CENTCOM theater, meaning they mostly focused on Iraq, and they were not integrated with other forces in Afghanistan.[14]

---

[14] McChrystal, *My Share of the Task.* The US task force had its own drama of organizational complexity. It was initially named Combined Joint Task Force-180 (CJTF-180) in 2002 and 2003 (the unit in which I served). It was replaced by Combined Forces Command–Afghanistan (CFC-A) from 2003 to 2007. In 2007 and 2008, the senior US headquarters was simultaneously ISAF's headquarters for Regional Command-East and was designated, in turn, CJTF-76, CJTF-82, and CJTF-101. Finally, in October 2008, the US headquarters was reseparated from RC-East and designated US Forces–Afghanistan (USFOR-A) for the rest of the war. Sometimes any US forces operating outside ISAF were simply referred to as "OEF" forces, that is, forces operating under the mandate of Operation Enduring Freedom.

"The black [clandestine] special operators refused to brief me in the same room as the white [overt] special operators," Ambassador Wood recalled. "The white special operators were in theory counterinsurgent. The black special operators were in theory counterterror," but in practice they both did counterterrorism. Wood asked the senior commander in Afghanistan if all special forces reported to him, and he said yes. He asked the operators the same question, and they said no, they reported to JSOC. General Karl Eikenberry, who commanded US forces from 2005 to 2007, noted that as coalition commander, when it came to a raid being conducted in the country, "I didn't have operational control" because of the separate chains of command. It was "extraordinarily dysfunctional."[15]

Meanwhile, NATO took command of ISAF in 2003, which gradually expanded to the rest of the country between October 2004 and October 2006. NATO, having invoked Article V for the first time after 9/11, wanted to play a bigger role in Afghanistan, which Rumsfeld had initially resisted. "When the war first broke out, he was reluctant to give NATO any kind of responsibilities outside of stability operations for Kabul," Eikenberry recalled, "because he thought that they would slow us down with rules of engagement and all kinds of requirements that would satisfy their political capitals." Even when NATO did get involved, "the US didn't pay much attention to what was going on in the NATO section of Afghanistan until 2006," according to General Jim Jones, the Supreme Allied Commander in Europe.[16]

Later, Rumsfeld was eager to turn over as much as possible to NATO to free up US forces, but his initial concerns were vindicated. Ostensibly, all NATO forces were supposed to operate cohesively through a single command reporting to NATO headquarters in Brussels, Belgium. In reality, NATO's involvement meant that, at the beginning of the war, eighteen other NATO allies became chefs in the kitchen, bringing eighteen chains-of-command, eighteen national priorities, and, often, eighteen distinct sets of national caveats limiting what their forces were legally allowed to do. Some allies simply were not capable of making a meaningful contribution. "So, you can get a country to contribute 200 soldiers to ISAF," recalled McKiernan, "but when they get there, they have caveats, they have lack of capabilities, lack of training, lack of leadership, and so you can only fit them into guarding the [forward operating base] or some mission like that. The

[15] Wood and Eikenberry, interviews by author.
[16] Eikenberry and Jones, interviews by author.

question is, is that worth the effort of building a coalition? The answer is usually no."[17]

Allied military forces "don't go to the latrine without a vote of their Parliament," Peter Rodman, the assistant secretary of defense for international security affairs, told the House International Relations Committee in 2005. "This is not helping." The number of NATO allies grew to twenty-nine as the Alliance expanded over the course of the war, strengthening European unity in the face of a resurgent Russia but bogging down decision-making in Afghanistan. "NATO was not helpful," Admiral Bill Fallon, who commanded Central Command in 2007 and 2008, argued. Despite "all the great things that NATO brought, it sure made the decision making more complicated," Rice agreed. "In retrospect, we all would've tried to drive a stronger sense of what the mission actually required," she said, "rather than having the participants define the mission in whatever way was consistent with their own capabilities." The needs of the bureaucracy – in this case, alliance management – trumped the needs of the mission; the means came to dictate the end, rather than the other way around.[18]

The European allies had signed up for peacekeeping, not counterinsurgency. As the Taliban insurgency grew, some allies resisted changing their mission. "It was a clash of military culture between the countries that were more accustomed to fighting, like the United States and Britain," and countries that "didn't want to be seen as war fighters," according to Nick Burns, the US ambassador to NATO. "This was a real problem for us," which eventually led to some "bitterness" from the countries with higher casualty rates, including the Canadians and the Dutch, also deployed to southern Afghanistan. "Of the forty-two nations that were under my command in 2008–2009, less than a handful would actually fight," McKiernan said. "That's not going to win a war."[19]

NATO's involvement meant that alliance management became part of the American military's task. When General Dan McNeill was named commander of ISAF, Jones implored him "don't fracture the alliance." Barno thought that noteworthy: "that's different than 'destroy al-Qaida', or 'keep the Taliban suppressed,' or 'keep the Afghan Government in position.'"

[17] McKiernan, interview by author.

[18] Rice and Fallon, interviews by author. Cheney and Cheney, *In My Time*, 499–500. House International Relations Committee, "United States Policy in Afghanistan," September 22, 2005, 22.

[19] McKiernan, interview by author. SIGAR, "Interview of: Ambassador Nicholas Burns," January 14, 2016.

Barno believed the allies were there for "a presence mission," that is, they were there to be seen by the Afghans and to make Afghans feel safe, but otherwise they did not have "a mission to actually accomplish anything ... they did not embrace counterinsurgency. They couldn't even say counterinsurgency." At its 2008 summit, NATO embraced a "comprehensive approach" in Afghanistan, the closest it could come to saying "counterinsurgency."[20]

Things got worse on the American side: as ISAF expanded, the United States contributed some American forces to it, forces that were not part of the OEF counterterrorism force. Because ISAF was commanded by NATO, headquartered in Europe, those American forces fell under European Command (EUCOM), the third combatant command involved in Afghanistan after CENTCOM and SOCOM. In 2006, the United States formed the Combined Security Transition Command–Afghanistan (CSTC-A, "sea-STICK-uh"), to train the new Afghan army and police forces; it operated semi-independently from both OEF and ISAF. Naturally, NATO had to follow suit with the NATO Training Mission–Afghanistan (NTM-A) in 2009. Finally, the CIA and Afghan partners continued to support JSOC and still focused almost entirely on counterterrorism, according to Steve Coll. And the United States' drone operations constituted yet another aspect of the war.[21]

"When we talk about the Afghanistan war, it wasn't really one war. We fought like five or six different wars," Edelman recalled. Lute often tallied seven or eight different wars, and Wood counted nine separate chains of command. It was an alphabet soup – ISAF, OEF, NATO, CJSOTF, CSTC-A, NTM-A, JSOC, CENTCOM, SOCOM, EUCOM, the CIA, the State Department, USAID, and the PRTs – and each was fighting its own battles. The arrangement made a mockery of the military's doctrine of the unity of command. In wartime, a single commander is supposed to be in charge to ensure a cohesive effort following a single campaign plan. The haphazard, crazy-quilt military structure in Afghanistan had a surreal, fly-by-night quality to it; no one could believe that someone had allowed this to happen.[22]

Barno and I talked about a related issue, the rapid rotation of commanders in and out of Afghanistan: "When I arrived in Afghanistan on temporary duty, with no orders, and no authority as a two star in October of 2003, [CJTF-180 Commanding General] John Vines and I passed in the

---

[20] Barno and McNeill, interviews by author.   [21] Coll, *Directorate S.*
[22] Edelman, interview by author.

night at the airport in Germany and had a cup of coffee," Barno said. "It was our transition. And then we went our separate ways."

"Is any of this normal?" I asked. He replied, "No, this is not at all, this is not even slightly normal."

"Not even slightly normal" is a good epitaph for the military bureaucracy – if not for the entire war – in Afghanistan. It captures the *Catch-22* absurdity of the convoluted and redundant chains of command. I remember in 2008 standing in Doug Lute's office in the basement of the West Wing with Lute (a three-star general) and another senior military officer staring at a handful of organizational charts taped to the wall. We debated who reported to whom, who was in charge, and who had which mission. With decades of accumulated policymaking, military, and intelligence experience between us, we couldn't figure it out. "The command design was a prescription for error," Coll assessed.[23]

Shinn believed that the Pentagon "wasn't serious enough" about the war in Afghanistan "to actually integrate the special ops and black ops people with the conventional war fighters, with the train-and-equip people," and make them operate under a unified command toward a common strategy, something that "common sense" should dictate. The conflicting chains of command "produced in my view a fundamental tension between our counterterror effort and our counterinsurgency effort," according to Wood. The counterterrorism bureaucracy, freed of oversight from ISAF or CENTCOM, went on autopilot toward its counterterrorism goals, whether they contributed to the counterinsurgency or nation-building operations or not.[24]

"I was slow to appreciate how screwed up the command structure was when I became Secretary," Gates admitted. Lute campaigned relentlessly against the convoluted chain of command until allied capitals agreed on a partial solution. Some of the mess was partly straightened out in October 2008 when General David McKiernan was dual-hatted as commanding general of both ISAF and US forces in Afghanistan, an arrangement that would persist for the rest of the war. Dual-hatting helped, "but what it didn't fix was the inherent inefficiency of ISAF headquarters," McKiernan said. It just meant that a single commander had to juggle input and oversight from NATO headquarters in Brussels, EUCOM headquarters in Stuttgart, CENTCOM and SOCOM headquarters in Tampa,

---

[23] Coll, *Directorate S*, 126. The mess was so complicated I am not fully confident that my summary of it here is accurate in every detail.

[24] Shinn and Wood, interviews by author.

twenty-nine allied capitals from London to Riga, and the Pentagon and White House in Washington, DC. "I had a German chief of staff. Typically, they'd call back to Berlin before they'd do anything," McNeill (McKiernan's predecessor) recalled, "and then when they did it, they often didn't do what I asked them to do." McKiernan had a similar problem. "At one point I had an Italian chief of staff who was not fluent in English," he recalled. "How are you going to run a warfighting headquarters like that?"[25]

But McKiernan resisted further reforms that Gates and Petraeus were pushing, such as creating a subordinate operational-level ISAF headquarters, one of the reasons Gates eventually fired him. As a result, many of the same problems persisted when General Stanley McChrystal took command in June 2009. "When I went to Afghanistan, I was told that . . . the air forces don't work for me," McChrystal recalled. "They support me, but they don't work for me." Then he found that the Marines deployed to Helmand also did not report to him. "The Marines were determined to keep operational control of their forces away from the senior US commander in Kabul and in the hands of a Marine lieutenant general at Central Command in Tampa," Gates wrote, criticizing the Corps' leadership for "put[ting] their own parochial service concerns above the requirements of the overall Afghan mission." McChrystal thought that was a sign of unseriousness about the war. "We let services make these doctrinally based arguments, let egos get involved, and we don't think it's serious enough to make those decisions because we're not really thinking we're going to lose," he said. "If everybody thought we were going to lose, maybe they'd get serious, but they don't."[26]

Bureaucratic parochialism reached absurd heights. McChrystal, who was a legend within the military for his long leadership of covert special operations forces, found that not even the special forces thought they had to report to him.

> I was told by special forces "Hey, we don't work for you, we support you, et cetera." And I said, "Okay, well, why don't you work for me?" And they go, "Well, because we've learned historically that we can't have generals who don't understand Special Forces Command." And I said, "Look at who you're fucking talking to."[27]

It makes for a funny anecdote, like something written for a *M*A*S*H** remake, but it had real consequences. McChrystal recounted how, before his command, "there was a friendly fire incident where a bunch of people were killed,"

---

[25] Gates, McKiernan, McNeill, interviews by author. McChrystal, *My Share of the Task*, 343.

[26] McChrystal, interview by author. Gates, *Duty*, 340.   [27] McChrystal, interview by author.

caused in part by confusion because "there were four different American forces operating all under different command and control, and that was just laughable," in a tragic, infuriating way. "I did not get this and other command problems in Afghanistan fully fixed until 2010," Gates confessed in his memoir. "I should have seized control of the matter well before that. It was my biggest mistake in overseeing the wars in Iraq and Afghanistan."[28]

Counterinsurgency is challenging in the best of circumstances, with unified command and seamless coordination between civilian and military agencies. Waging counterinsurgency by coalition with a divided command structure made an already-difficult mission needlessly harder. A bigger question is why the Bush administration allowed such an arrangement to take root in the first place and why they and the Obama administration tolerated it for so long – and the answer is, again, that the arrangement served the counterterrorism bureaucracy. The administration kept US forces separate from ISAF to maintain operational independence and to focus exclusively on counterterrorism, the root from which other organizational aberrations grew. "We obviously have to work out questions of command arrangements," Richard Haass, the State Department's director of policy planning, testified to Congress in December 2001, days before ISAF was created by the UN. "One thing, though, is critical. Such a force must do nothing that would in any way inhibit the coalition from carrying out the primary objectives of ridding Afghanistan of terror."[29]

That made sense in late 2001, when the United States was engaged in daily ground combat against al-Qaida and Taliban forces, but it was immediately counterproductive after the Taliban's fall from power. Unfortunately, institutional arrangements, once set, persist by inertia; they are much harder to change after the fact than to design at the outset. The military bureaucracy in Afghanistan was designed to protect the autonomy of counterterrorism operations, and the bureaucracy faithfully continued to do that with almost-irreversible force. If it was understandable that the administration wanted to protect the independence of its counterterrorism operations in 2001, it was also shortsighted to design a long-lasting arrangement around that goal. Ironically, the Bush administration's desire to protect its operational autonomy was in reaction to the "war by committee" that had characterized the war in Kosovo in 1999 – yet in allowing a convoluted military bureaucracy to take root in Afghanistan, they ended up with the very situation they hoped to avoid.

---

[28] Gates, *Duty*, 340.

[29] Senate Foreign Relations Committee, "The Political Future of Afghanistan," December 6, 2001, 15.

In retrospect, it seems clear that the UN should have held off deploying ISAF until the United States was done with the initial phase of the war, and then OEF should have been wound down and US forces rolled into the new UN force with a nationwide deployment and expansive peace enforcement mandate, ensuring cohesion from the outset. Instead, peacekeeping and counterinsurgency suffered for the sake of counterterrorism, even though the former were the precondition for long-term victory in the latter.

Could it have been fixed earlier? Gates' description of how he solved the problem with the Marines is revealing. "After deferring for too long to multiple senior military voices supportive of or resigned to the status quo, I simply directed the command change." After years of organizational absurdity, all it took was an order from the secretary of defense. Some readers may be surprised to hear how rare it is for senior executives to simply issue orders. In practice, leadership is usually consultative and consensus-driven, even inside the military, because that is what most books and classes on leadership recommend. But sometimes consultation means delay when the answer is obvious, in which case leadership requires assertiveness in the face of bureaucratic parochialism. "It had taken far too long to get there, and that was my fault," Gates wrote. It was also Rumsfeld's fault, and Bush's and Obama's and the NATO Secretary General's, who collectively built and tolerated a bureaucratic morass so absurd it became its own parody. But for nine years, none of them issued the orders. McChrystal was scathing. "I damn everybody involved," he said, including the vast and uncoordinated civilian and intelligence agencies. "Sometimes you have got to get somebody in charge." It was the stupidest, most avoidable mistake of the war.[30]

THE AFGHAN ARMY AND POLICE

One of the biggest effects of the 2006 strategy reviews was an enormous increase in the training effort for Afghan security forces. Funding for "peace and security" programs – support for the army and police – jumped from $2.4 billion to $8.2 billion in a single year. The change was welcome but introduced its own problems. "We just had $7 billion dumped on us, with daily screams from Washington about our burn rate," Ambassador Wood recalled. "And nobody was spending that money well, even halfway." The burn rate is a measure of how quickly the field is spending its money. In DC,

---

[30] McChrystal, interview by author. Gates, *Duty*, 478.

we saw large amounts of money piling up in various accounts, appropriated by Congress but unspent and useless. We asked for a regular report on how much money they were spending, pressuring them to spend more quickly – which created an incentive for the field to loosen standards and spend without full accountability. With a huge increase in funding and pressure to spend quickly, the result – waste, fraud, and abuse – was predictable. It was another trade-off: act with urgency, or with efficiency? "Afghanistan almost from the get-go has been a place where there are no good choices," recalled Neumann. "Over time you had a choice of maybe worse choices, but there weren't good ones."[31]

Corruption was especially pronounced in the police. "Every time we give any money to any layer of the police, a percentage of it disappears before it reaches the next layer," Wood recalls being told by one of the US officials involved in the training effort. "So the cop on the beat, the cop in the station who is illiterate ... is getting a fraction of what we want to pay him." The official came up with an idea. "So, what we're going to do is, we're going to give everybody ATM cards and we're going to establish ATM posts. And so that they can all go collect their money." Wood was incredulous. "My immediate thought was, if you can't trust the chain of command, getting the cop on the beat paid through an ATM doesn't solve your problem." The ATM idea was a way of circumventing the main problem – pervasive corruption – to solve a smaller one. "We never beat that problem," Wood said. Corruption would plague the police training effort for the duration of the war.[32]

The accelerated training ran into other problems. Most of the Afghan population was illiterate, making recruits ineligible for any but the most rudimentary kind of policing or soldiering. "So, we had to start with functional literacy training," to go beyond the basics of patrol duty and infantry tactics, according to Edelman. But "they don't teach our guys how to do that." The US military does not teach its soldiers how to teach Afghans reading and writing. Any third-grade public school teacher can tell you that literacy training is an enormously time-consuming, labor-intensive process that requires one-on-one attention and careful relationship skills. But few American soldiers spoke Dari or Pashto, the Afghan recruits did not speak English, and the Americans' annual rotations ensured they never formed deep relationships with their Afghan counterparts.[33]

---

[31] Aid numbers derived from www.foreignassistance.gov dataset. Wood and Neumann, interviews by author.

[32] Wood, interview by author.   [33] Edelman, interview by author.

In fact, the US military has a unit specially designed to train foreign militaries and to specialize in local languages: the Army's Special Forces (the Green Berets) – who, in Afghanistan, were too busy hunting al-Qaida to train the Afghan army. Eliot Cohen quipped that Special Forces were preoccupied with the "direct-action mission," because it was "their qualifying test for Delta" – clandestine special mission units, or black operations – where they really wanted to be. "The Green Berets mostly wanted to be in JSOC, because they were kicking down the doors and fighting terrorism," Lute said. "They dismissed, or placed at a lower priority, the task we really needed them to do." Why? Because, according to Eikenberry, "their war was to get bin Laden, right? Their war was not to build an Afghan army." Fallon, the commander of Central Command, wanted more Special Forces for training but couldn't get any. "I had to settle for Marines," he said. "God love them … they were not the right people for that task." Army Special Forces' very reason for existing was to train local partners, which is exactly what Afghanistan needed, but they preferred to spend their time shooting terrorists: the single best vignette that captures, in miniature, why America lost Afghanistan.[34]

The accelerated training effort bore some fruit. In two years, the Afghan army increased from 36,000 in 2006 to just over 100,000 in 2009, and the police added another 45,000 patrol officers. Fallon believed the Afghan army was progressing faster than the Iraqi one and was impressed with their initiative. But the increase in numbers obscured a deeper problem: the *kind* of army the United States was building. "We turned them into a force that relied on high-tech intelligence, surveillance, and reconnaissance," Edelman recalled, the kind that required "exquisite mission planning capabilities that our military brings to each mission set, combat air power to call in airstrikes whenever you get in trouble, and contract logistics support to keep vehicles running and rotary and fixed wing in the air." The US military was building an Afghan counterpart in its image, a flaw that posed no difficulty so long as the US military stuck around to support the Afghan army. Edelman saw a precedent in the Vietnam War. He cited Bob Komer's study of the Vietnam War "about all the mistakes we made training the [South Vietnamese Army], which we tried to turn into a little US army," he recalled. "And then we go out in Afghanistan and do exactly the same thing." Edelman claims he sensed the problem at the time, but not clearly enough to solve it. "I constantly had the concern that's what we were doing, but it was very hard to get your hands around it when you were getting

---

[34] Cohen, Eikenberry, and Fallon, interviews by author. Lute, "Bush Oral History."

briefed because you'd get hit with all these PowerPoints about how many people we'd trained." Activity without progress. It proved catastrophic in 2021.[35]

There were never enough national police for a full counterinsurgency campaign – and policing is most effective at the local level anyway. The police needed help: in June 2008, the Taliban mounted a sophisticated attack on Sarposa Prison in Kandahar, quickly overwhelming the small Afghan police presence and freeing up to 1,000 prisoners, including captured insurgents. The US and Afghan governments went through several programs designed to rapidly improve local police forces, including the Afghan National Auxiliary Police from 2006 to 2008 and the Afghan Local Police after 2010. The programs recruited young men from local villages, gave them a few weeks of training, and sent them back to their villages for static duties – to man checkpoints or pull guard duty at district government offices – freeing up the army and the national police. There were predictable problems: too little oversight or vetting from Kabul, and they became little more than the militia for a new local warlord; too much, and they lost their local character, got caught up in Kabul's bureaucratic morass, and became an extension of the corruption of the Ministry of Interior Affairs. On balance, the programs were among the more cost-effective investments the United States made in Afghan security. In 2008, the Afghan government and the US training mission started a new effort to target high-priority districts called the Focused District Development program. They withdrew all local police from a village or district, temporarily backfilling them with national police, while the local force underwent several months of intensive immersion training.

Training the Afghan army and police illustrated broader problems with counterinsurgency and state-building efforts. We did not have an alternative: we had to try. The Afghan army and police were our exit strategy. But the hurdles were so massive as to make the effort maddening and progress glacial. Any solution that addressed one problem – more funding, more urgency – usually caused more problems in another area – corruption, waste, or the pressure to count metrics. General McKiernan, ISAF commander in 2008 and 2009, felt that "we want immediacy, we want to see immediate effects, we want something to happen this year," but that was unrealistic because "that's not the operational environment." Domestic opinion and Americans' traditional can-do optimism were not prepared for the massive challenges of operating in Afghanistan with almost-universal

---

[35] Edelman, interview by author.

illiteracy, no infrastructure, and a legacy of war. It was intensely frustrating, at a personal level, to participate in or monitor any of these programs, knowing how important they were, believing in the mission, looking for any sign of hope or progress. I spent half of 2008 attending interagency meetings talking about efforts to reform the Afghan Justice and Interior Ministries, something that never bore much fruit. Our desire to see progress may have led us to see it when it was illusory. Lacking any easier way to track success, we counted the amount of money spent and the number of recruits and graduates, which gave a deceptive sense of forward momentum.[36]

I am not suggesting that the effort was impossible. McKiernan highlights one success story: the Afghan Army's special forces. "US Special forces helped select the leaders. They trained them to the right level of capability," McKiernan explained. "They partnered with them on operations, and over time, after I left, most of those operations were Afghan commando-led, just enabled by US air power or intelligence." The Afghan commando units were small, sustainable, and fit Afghanistan's "operational environment," in McKiernan's view, as opposed to the large, conventional Afghan army. Training conventional army units was "form over function," teaching Afghan soldiers things that "had absolutely no bearing on providing security for Afghanistan," but that ticked a box for the US trainers and created an unwieldy, unsustainable military bureaucracy.[37]

Many critics look at the litany of problems I've highlighted and conclude it was hopeless all along and that we should never try something like this again. I think it highlights a different lesson: how damaging it was to have thrown away the first two to five years. Imagine the same police and army training programs, but started earlier, carried out more slowly, with the same ultimate level of resourcing but spread out over a longer period. Such programs would have had fewer problems with waste and corruption and more time to design the right kind of security forces. If we had had a different personnel rotation policy and invested more in language training, genuine relationships between Americans and Afghans could have grown. These solutions are relatively small, realistic, and achievable changes: changes to the timing and pacing of programs, to personnel rotations and language training. They do not require months-long strategy reviews or billion-dollar budget increases. They are not the sexy, headline-grabbing focus of major presidential addresses. On the other hand, they might work.

---

[36] McKiernan, interview by author.   [37] McKiernan, interview by author.

Or rather, they might have worked if implemented in 2002. The administration faced a separate question in 2006: With past mistakes already made and the situation rapidly deteriorating, what do we do now? How do we staunch the bleeding and pull back from the brink of catastrophe? Talk of long-term solutions was pointless if there was no long term. The administration needed to reverse the downward trajectory to *create* a long-term time horizon – which was the point of the 2006 reviews and ensuing changes – after which we could step back and take in the big picture. That urgency explains the many trade-offs the Bush administration accepted in its last two years.

COUNTERNARCOTICS

As the Bush administration turned the supertanker slowly toward counterinsurgency, a related problem became unignorable: drugs. Afghanistan had long been the world's leading source of opium poppy, the botanical precursor for heroin. The drug trade was a major source of income for warlords, criminal gangs, and, eventually, the Taliban. Drug-related corruption constantly sapped efforts to rebuild the justice sector, field an honest police force, and foster the rule of law. In 2002, Afghan farmers cultivated around 74,000 hectares of poppy, a figure that soared to 193,000 by 2007. That year, the illicit economy was worth some $4 billion, accounting for 53 percent of the entire Afghan economy.[38]

The problem worsened in the early years because of the lack of attention to nation building. "The lack of sufficient reconstruction assistance, including agricultural training and support, as well as road building, meant that Afghan farmers had little alternative to high-paying poppy production for the heroin trade," Zakheim wrote. "Cities could not expand their economies sufficiently to absorb farmers who might seek a better life away from their fields. It meant that the country was ripe for a Taliban revival." Neumann agreed. "Nothing less than the building of an entire Afghan rural economy would work," he wrote. "This would take years, even if we were not deprived of the proper funding." The United Kingdom was initially in the lead for counternarcotics efforts but, as with most "lead nation" efforts, showed little progress. The US spent just $3 million on counternarcotics programs in 2003.[39]

---

[38] UNODC, "Opium Cultivation in Afghanistan," November 2022, 12. UNODC, "Opium Survey 2007," October 2007, iii.

[39] Zakheim, *A Vulcan's Tale*, 268. Neumann, *The Other War*, 60. SIGAR, Quarterly Report, October 30, 2008, 21.

The Taliban benefited from the drug trade, though to what extent was unclear and likely changed over time. The Taliban probably did not get much money from the drug trade before 2005 because they did not control territory on which they could levy taxes or extort money from farmers. But after the insurgency gathered momentum, the Taliban and the drug trade became symbionts. The more territory the Taliban controlled, the more money they could extract from farmers and traffickers and, in turn, the more protection they could offer them from eradication and interdiction. Around 2006, the United States came to believe "that [the Taliban] were being robustly funded through the drug trade," Gastright recalled, "which very well may be true. I never got a hundred percent assurance on that, but the interagency made the decision that we were going to attack the drug trade a lot more." General David McKiernan told an audience in 2008 that the drug trade "funds the insurgency. It is the single largest financial contribution to the Taliban." He described how simple opium processing was. "There are literally hundreds, if not thousands, of those drug labs dotted around the countryside." By 2008, we believed the drug trade provided the Taliban with between $53 and $80 million per year.[40]

The new US ambassador, Bill Wood, had previously served as ambassador to Colombia another country in which the United States had worked with a local partner to fight the drug trade and an insurgency. "Plan Colombia" had been a relatively successful blend of foreign aid and military assistance dating from the Clinton administration. Bush hoped for something similar in Afghanistan. "So, 2007 was a year in which we were trying to come to terms with what the previous six years had produced," Wood recalled. "That's largely thanks to my predecessor, Ron Neumann's campaign, while he was ambassador, to urge increased assistance and increased attention." Neumann's call for more attention to Afghanistan created space for a new effort against the drug trade. "We moved from Neumann to Wood and our focus changed," Gastright recalled. "Part of what we wanted to do was end the financial support to the insurgency" from the drug trade. Funding for counternarcotics rose to $737 million in 2007. On paper, the counternarcotics strategy had five pillars: a public information campaign to persuade Afghans of the evils of the drug trade; providing farmers alternatives to growing poppy; eradicating poppy fields; interdicting poppy and

---

[40] Miller, Lute, O'Sullivan, "Chapter 5: Afghanistan," in Hadley et al., *Hand-Off.* Gastright, interview by author. "Transcript: General David McKiernan Speaks at Council's Commanders Series," The Atlantic Council, November 19, 2008.

drugs shipments; and reforming the justice sector. "The problem was that most of these elements take years to bear fruit," Neumann later wrote.[41]

As in all areas of the American war in Afghanistan, programs met reality. "We committed to the strategy, but not to the implementation," said Maureen Quinn, the State Department's Coordinator for Afghanistan from 2004 to 2006, about the counternarcotics strategy. For example, "we needed helicopters to make anything work, to get anywhere, to transport people, to eradicate the poppy," recalled Quinn, but that raised a host of problems. "For example, what kind of helicopters are you buying? INL [the Bureau of International Narcotics and Law Enforcement] had ... second-hand helicopters from somewhere, but appropriators in Congress wanted new ones made in America." But even if we could find or buy the right helicopters, "Where do you put the helicopters?" Were they a military asset or a civilian asset? Who owned them and flew them, where do they park and get fuel, who protects them and provides maintenance and logistics? "We didn't pull it off as a government. We committed to it, but we didn't follow through. You meet the reality of it and you can't accomplish it because you have disagreements between Congress, between DoS and DoD."[42] The American government had become so cumbersome it could no longer do something as simple as buy helicopters.

A much bigger problem emerged. "A highly sensitive point was how to handle eradication," according to Quinn. The Afghans, Americans, and British disagreed about the best method to eradicate poppy. Aerial eradication – spraying fields with herbicide from helicopters – was the most efficient method and had been used in Colombia. Karzai adamantly refused. Afghans widely believed, probably rightly, that the Soviet Union had used chemical weapons on them in the 1980s; Karzai feared the image of international forces spraying chemicals from helicopters would immediately turn Afghans against the coalition. Wood "pushed hard on the Afghan government" to accept aerial eradication, according to Gastright – earning him the moniker, "Chemical Bill" – but "Karzai said no," apparently sticking to his refusal even when Condoleezza Rice made a personal phone call. "The recriminations coming out of that phone call were pretty nasty," said Gastright. And if the coalition could not eradicate from the sky, "then okay, we would use ground cutting," Quinn said, "so now we had to train teams, and have people in the field cutting it down, cutting down the poppy – but you have to hide them, and then get them into

---

[41] Gastright and Wood, interviews by author. Neumann, *The Other War*, 59.
[42] Quinn, interview by author.

the field," and protect them from the farmers and the Taliban. Every solution raised new problems, new headaches of implementation.[43]

Any method of eradication risked an even bigger problem. Spraying, cutting, or burning the poppy crop impoverished farmers and could drive them into the arms of the Taliban. Far from harmonizing counternarcotics with counterinsurgency, the two were at odds. "The strategy didn't work, it wasn't accepted," Quinn recalled. "The military was really worried about this because of the effect of eradication on the people." Gates shared the concern. "The day we go in and eradicate somebody's crops, we had better be there with alternative seeds, some money and a way to get that product to market, or we will have just recruited somebody else for the Taliban," he told Congress in December 2007. "I think too often there has been a desire to go after the eradication without the rest of the package being there right then." But the United States never did get its programs coordinated enough to ensure eradication would not alienate locals. That is why, "in spite of our rhetoric, we absolutely decided to allow opium cultivation and trafficking to continue," Wood said. "It would've been too disruptive to take it on directly." Wood recalled "pictures of NATO troops walking through opium poppy fields," doing nothing to stop the cultivation, "and all of the statistics on opium poppy" increasing. In 2007, every metric – hectares under cultivation, opium yields per hectare, total opium production, export value of opium – was rising. Afghanistan accounted for 93 percent of the global opiate market.[44]

It was, yet again, a question of trade-offs. How do you balance counterinsurgency against counternarcotics? Progress on one threatened the other. Which one should take precedence? Is it safe to ignore either one? Wood recognized the administration faced a tough call but believed the decision to effectively give up on eradication was the "wrong one." Wood argued that "it's very hard to have an anti-corruption agenda when the largest single source of indigenous income in the country is opium trafficking." Wood's judgment is understandable but, I think, incomplete. With the warlords, for example, the Bush administration managed to pursue a contradictory strategy that showed some success: the inherent tensions between state building and co-opting the warlords into the government served to hedge and balance rather than undermine one another (except for continuing to pay them under the table). It wasn't out of the realm of possibility to look for something similar

---

[43] Gastright and Quinn, interviews by author.

[44] Quinn and Wood, interviews by author. House Armed Services Committee, "Stability and Security in Afghanistan," December 11, 2007, 31. UNODC, *Afghanistan: Opium Survey 2007*, iii.

with counterinsurgency and counternarcotics. Attack the drug trade to fight corruption and the insurgency while simultaneously improving security, governance, and development to provide farmers with alternative livelihoods: achieve enough success along both lines to reinforce the other.[45]

But the dynamic never took hold. Even with the additional resources afforded by the 2006 reviews, there simply wasn't enough to pursue both simultaneously in the face of bureaucratic obstacles and Afghan resistance. "I think it is patently obvious that we have not been successful in the counternarcotics effort in Afghanistan," Gates told Congress in December 2007. And most of this happened when the war in Iraq was approaching its culminating moment, fully occupying the attention of the Bush administration. "I think this was a key moment on CN [counternarcotics] that led to the US failure in Afghanistan," Quinn said.[46]

The failure of counternarcotics efforts reverberated into other areas of the war and state-building efforts. The Taliban continued to make money off the drug trade, corruption ate away at the justice sector and the police, and the illicit economy pulled Afghans away from development and reconstruction efforts. It also poisoned relations between the Afghan government and the coalition. Gastright believed it was a mistake to allow Karzai to shut down eradication. "We just trained him to say 'no,' and he just learned that it's okay," he said. "So that felt like a moment where our partnership with Karzai really took a different turn. From that he became much more open to criticize [us]." Wood concurs: "Washington was getting increasingly impatient with Karzai." Karzai's assertiveness could be seen as a sign of progress, of course, though it was regrettable he decided to assert himself on this issue. But the ultimate casualty may have been the sense of forward momentum and optimism that had prevailed in Afghanistan through 2005. "When I went to Afghanistan, I thought that the job was very doable," said Wood. "When I got there, I found out I was wrong."[47]

GOVERNANCE

A final aspect of the Bush administration's counterinsurgency strategy was an effort to improve Afghan governance. Improving "governance" is a vague

---

[45] Wood, interview by author.

[46] House Armed Services Committee, "Stability and Security in Afghanistan," December 11, 2007, 31. Quinn, interview by author.

[47] Gastright and Wood, interviews by author.

aspiration that, when defined, can become almost impossibly broad. It includes technical competence, such as is required in the finance ministry to balance accounts, disburse spending, and deliver reports in line with international standards; or in the ministry of energy and water to build, operate, and maintain dams, power plants, and irrigation canals. Good governance can also mean character traits in public officials, like honesty and integrity to resist bribes and favoritism and put the public good above private gain. Good governance can also mean clear rules, transparency, and accountability in the government's internal processes. Most abstractly but perhaps most importantly, good governance can mean the rule of law, fairly and impartially applied through a competent and functional justice system.

Trying to improve governance in a failed state thus presents another trade-off: do nothing, and the state is guaranteed to stay failed; try anything, and your efforts are guaranteed to be piecemeal and insufficient. The Bush administration tried doing nothing in 2002 and 2003, after which it became persuaded that continued state failure threatened American security. It did something with Accelerating Success and the Bonn Process, paying for a few big infrastructure projects and the Afghan elections in 2004 and 2005. Those were piecemeal and insufficient. "To us in Afghanistan it was clear that force and development were the two major tools at our disposal," Neumann wrote about the situation in 2006. "Both needed attention, but only the military side seemed to have much resonance in Washington." Eikenberry, similarly, ended his tour as commander of US forces in 2007 concerned that the war was "stalemated" primarily because of the state of Afghan governance. Fallon felt the US military was doing all the work: "The rest of the government was not at war."[48]

The administration decided its governance programs, conceived in what they thought was peacetime, were insufficient for wartime counterinsurgency. Funding for governance and development, which had decreased in 2006, ticked back upward, slightly, in 2007 and 2008 – but now with a different emphasis. Gates believed that "there was too much emphasis on building a strong central government . . . and too little emphasis on improving governance, security, and services at the provincial and district levels, including making better use of local Afghan tribal leaders and councils." Boucher characterized state-building efforts to that point as "a government in Kabul extending itself in the countryside, as opposed to building a government in the countryside that was connected to the people." After 2006, instead of paying for the ring road and a few elections, the Bush and Karzai administrations

---

[48] Neumann, *The Other War*, 124. Eikenberry, interview by author.

inaugurated programs to improve bureaucratic capacity and local governance. Here, finally, five years after 9/11, were some of the first real "nation-building" programs.[49]

The US Agency for International Development (USAID), for example, ran a Capacity Development Program (CDP) from 2007 to 2012. "CDP provides technical assistance in the areas of financial management, program management, and monitoring and evaluation," according to USAID, "ultimately building the capacity of the Afghan Government to serve its people and guide its own development." The program sent advisors, trainers, and consultants to train Afghan bureaucrats how to implement more effectively. The irony of Americans teaching Afghans about bureaucratic efficiency was not lost on me. "We had to set up a government and every bureaucracy in Washington eventually got out there and started telling Afghans how to run a bureaucracy," Boucher recalled, "how to run a DEA, just like ours, how to run an Afghan agriculture ministry, just like ours." Another trade-off: train quickly but rely on American methods, or train more slowly but with greater local leadership. Bad as it was, the American bureaucratic model was nonetheless a real improvement for the Afghans, whose bureaucracy had been set up by the Soviet Union and broken by the Taliban.[50]

With more local leadership, the Afghan government initiated the National Solidarity Program, which ran from 2004 to 2012. The NSP held village elections to form community development councils, then gave the councils small block grants of up to $60,000 to spend on a local development project of their choosing, such as a well, road, or school. The NSP spent over $1 billion on some 65,000 local projects over a decade. A later study found that the NSP made an appreciable difference to Afghans' access to clean water and electricity and, perhaps more importantly, gave villagers a greater sense of optimism, increased female participation in civic life, and encouraged villagers to participate in national elections. The NSP was a bright spot, relatively speaking, among the many programs and initiatives launched in the counterinsurgency era.[51]

---

[49] Gates, *Duty*, 197. Boucher, interview by author.

[50] USAID, "Capacity Development Program," www.usaid.gov/basic-page/capacity-develop ment-program-cdp. Boucher, interview by author.

[51] SIGAR, *Quarterly Report*, October 30, 2009, 132–133. USAID, "Capacity Development Program," www.usaid.gov/node/52036. Beath, Christia, and Enikolopov, "Randomized Impact Evaluation of Afghanistan's National Solidarity Program," https://openknow ledge.worldbank.org/handle/10986/16637.

The emphasis on local governance got a central hub when, in 2007, the Afghan government created, with American encouragement, the Independent Directorate of Local Governance (IDLG). The IDLG was a new agency to manage relations between Kabul and the provinces, removing that responsibility from the corrupt and unreliable Interior Ministry and putting it directly within the presidential palace. "We had great hopes that it would empower governors and provide for the kind of localized response to local, to very different local situations that could strengthen the central government's hand in a decentralized way," Wood recalled. Under strong American pressure, Karzai shuffled governors around, fired some of the most corrupt and incompetent, and appointed a few more professional and educated candidates.[52]

As with efforts to train the Afghan army, activity could be a seductive substitute for progress, particularly when our efforts were diffuse and uncoordinated. "You build a school," said Tony Harriman, "but is anybody going?" Some activity could make progress more difficult. With more programs and more money came more demands to collect data to measure progress, but "metrics – collecting statistics to measure how programs are performing – often actually retards real work," Neumann later wrote. "I cannot recall an instance in which the data reported in this process told us of a problem of which we were unaware by other means."[53]

The international community tried to create an overarching concept for rebuilding Afghanistan with the "Afghanistan Compact" in January 2006 and the Afghan National Development Strategy (ANDS) in 2008. The ANDS was supposed to be the common sheet of music that got everyone singing the same tune; in reality, it ended up codifying the discordance. It became a wish list of everything that needed to be done. That Afghanistan's needs were bottomless and that everything needed to be done right away was true enough, but, as was true with US efforts, a UN document could not impose a sense of priorities, cohesion, or triage on the vast community of donors and NGOs tripping over their good intentions. They were managed (poorly) by an unwieldy Joint Coordination and Monitoring Board cochaired by the UN and the Afghan government, which moved at a glacial pace more appropriate to long-term, peacetime development.

In mid 2008, I sensed that the whole of our efforts was less than the sum of its parts; all our frenetic activity was not amounting to much. Success in fostering good governance is not the result of any one program so much as an emergent property from all of them: the programs have to catalyze

---

[52] Wood, interview by author.

[53] Harriman and Wayne, interviews by author. Neumann, *The Other War*, 199, 200.

a tipping point, achieve a critical mass, to change the culture of governance so that it becomes normal for civil servants to take initiative, assume responsibility, strive for excellence, accept accountability, and take pride in their work. I spearheaded an effort to draft a "governance strategy," a document that would bring coherence to various programs. I chaired countless meetings with my counterparts at USAID and the Departments of State, Treasury, Commerce, Justice, and more. The document died on the vine – not because Lute or Hadley or Bush ever considered the strategy and rejected it, but because it never made it to the deputies' agenda, much less the principals'. The governance strategy was crowded out by other, more urgent issues – after we had gone through twenty-two drafts.

Did anything work? The quality of government changes very slowly, and it is very hard to measure for the same reason that it is hard to define. The Bush administration's post-2006 governance initiatives did not have time to mature and show meaningful results by the end of his term. The World Bank publishes data on "governance indicators" which it claims measure the "traditions and institutions by which authority in a country is exercised." Its data showed a small improvement in "government effectiveness" in Afghanistan from 2002 to 2004, followed by a decline for the rest of the Bush administration. The same dataset showed essentially no change in the rule of law or regulatory quality – and a *decline* in the control of corruption. Transparency International publishes an annual Corruption Perceptions Index that ranks countries by how honest or corrupt their governments are. Afghanistan fell from 117th place in 2005 to 172nd place in 2007. With only 179 states ranked, Afghanistan's was among the most corrupt governments in the world. On the other hand, clear majorities of Afghans expressed satisfaction with the government's performance throughout the war, according to the Asia Foundation, including 80 percent who were satisfied with their provincial governments in 2012. Municipal government was consistently the least well liked.[54]

Why did governance programs not show more progress? First, the overall level of resourcing remained low. The 2006 strategy reviews led to a massive increase in assistance for the Afghan army and police, not for civilian reconstruction and governance. Funding for governance and reconstruction peaked during Accelerating Success in 2004 and 2005, declined in 2006, and modestly rose in 2007 and 2008. The Bush administration's

---

[54] Transparency International, *Corruption Perceptions Index*, 2005 and 2007 data sets www.transparency.org/en/cpi/2021. World Bank, Governance Indicators dataset http://info.worldbank.org/governance/wgi/. Asia Foundation, "Survey of the Afghan People, 2019," 137.

counterinsurgency effort remained heavily military. Despite some critics' complaints that the Bush administration mounted a massive and foolish nation-building campaign, the actual level of resourcing belied their accusation. I could only wish that our nation-building efforts were half as large as what the critics believed they were.

Second, many of the same problems with training the Afghan army were replicated in governance programs: having delayed too long, we rushed to catch up and tried to show results too fast, which loosened standards and fueled corruption and waste. Governance does not change or grow in two years; institutions grow in timeframes measured in decades, not months. "We rushed the creation of Afghan's self-governance so rapidly," Wood recalled. As with the army and police programs, if we had the same amount of money (or more, in the case of governance) and the same programs but started them earlier and sustained them longer, there would have been a very different outcome. Wood also cited the rapid rotation of diplomats and aid workers as another difficulty. "The State Department managed to spectacularly not step up to the challenge," he said, noting that within six months he had more time in country than anyone in the embassy.[55]

We also ran into another version of the problem that had bedeviled the police training effort: one agency had the authority, while another had the money. In the case of governance and reconstruction, USAID officially had the responsibility to lead American efforts. "Since the 1990s, however, Congress has drastically reduced the agency's size," according to Zakheim. "As a result, USAID personnel rarely carry out their own projects; instead they are put in the hands of contractors, whose overhead and other charges can absorb as much as half a project's value." Not only did that decrease USAID's contact with their own projects, but it also put pressure on other agencies to pick up the slack. "USAID's limitations resulted in greater pressure on the military to take on more reconstruction work," he wrote, "but the Department of Defense simply did not have the legislative authority to do so." The military tried to plug gaps with the commander's emergency response program (CERP), a slush fund of cash for American commanders to fund one-off local projects, like a well, road, or courthouse.[56]

A final part of the problem was Hamid Karzai. It is hard to remember that in 2001 he seemed almost providentially designed as the man for the moment: a respected Pashtun tribal elder with a college education, fluent in a half-dozen languages, appreciative of Afghanistan's sartorial diversity. Karzai was a unifying symbol when Afghans badly needed one. His mere

---

[55] Wood, interview by author.   [56] Zakheim, *A Vulcan's Tale*, 181–182. See also 278.

presence probably helped avoid a civil war in 2002. Karzai was also a canny politician (tactically, not strategically) with an instinctive feel for how to maneuver through the daily minefield of warlords, tribal elders, ex-communists, and former Taliban. But "Karzai was not an institutional leader," Wood said. He presided over a government that, officially, was committed to an ambitious and expansive international state-building effort – and he undermined it at every turn. "Karzai himself ran the country as an Oriental tribal leader," Wood said, also likening him to Boss Tweed, the head of New York City's nineteenth-century Tammany Hall political machine. Karzai governed through personal ties to individuals, whether they had any formal role in the government. "His well-known operating style made it difficult to maintain a disciplined Afghan chain of command," Neumann wrote. He circumvented or simply ignored institutional processes and even legal rules regulating his powers and his relationship to other parts of the government; he acted more like a king than a president, but without kingly power.[57]

Karzai also grew alienated from the United States. After Khalilzad left, "he didn't have a confidant, somebody that I think he really felt he could sit down and talk with to connect back to what the hell was going on in DC," Admiral Fallon, then serving as commander of Central Command, argued. "I think that's important. Again, the human dimension of this stuff is what really drives a lot of reality in history. We kind of just overlook that."[58]

Some critics of nation building argue that Karzai was not to blame; we were, for trying to force him into a "Western" mold of governance. We should have deferred to his way of doing things, they say, because it was locally legitimate and more functional than anything we would try to build. But there is scant evidence that Karzai's governing style was effective at anything other than protecting Karzai's and his tribe's privileges. The point of institutional norms and processes is to regularize governance, to differentiate it from simple nepotism and tribal favoritism. The only Afghans who agreed with the nation-building critique were rich Pashtun men; they were in favor of informal, personalistic rule because they were its beneficiaries. More relevant to American security, personalistic rule by a single leader would not have defeated the Taliban insurgency or denied safe haven to al-Qaida.

Was there an alternative? There is another model of international reconstruction that the UN and others have tried in places like East

---

[57] Wood, interview by author. Neumann, *The Other War*, 102.
[58] Fallon, interview by author.

Timor, Bosnia, and Cambodia: international receivership or trusteeship. In those cases, international bureaucrats took over the sovereign functions of government for a limited time, overriding national sovereignty in exchange for efficiency and technical competence, a sort of last-ditch effort to reboot a nation's government and economic life. "You know, when you conquer a country, people expect to take orders from you, right?" Wood commented. "We never actually took advantage of that. We were too busy chasing terrorists and arresting tribal leaders without explaining why." It is an extreme solution, and it is the one the Bush administration attempted in Iraq with the Coalition Provisional Authority. It did not work in Iraq, and almost certainly would not have worked in Afghanistan – not because of any nonsense about imperial graveyards, but because the Afghans were unanimous at the 2001 Bonn conference about their intention to form an interim government. The UN did take over Afghanistan's electoral bodies in 2004 and 2005, but otherwise overriding Afghan sovereignty with a UN or NATO trusteeship would likely have alienated even more Afghans. The Bush administration had no alternative to international assistance with local leadership, despite its many problems.[59]

THE 2008 STRATEGY REVIEW

The Bush administration made some genuine progress in its final two years. "I arrived in Kabul on December 4 [2007] and helicoptered to Khowst province in eastern Afghanistan," Bob Gates recalled. "The 82nd Airborne had, in fact, done a superb job there of fighting an effective counterinsurgency, and despite the increase in violence, it was clear . . . that we still had the initiative." Gates was hardly a Pollyanna about the war; he had come into office warning Bush that it was a losing effort and clearly saw the steep challenges it faced. He felt that even in 2007 and 2008 the "aspirations were too ambitious," but at least within the administration "there was recognition of the military problem." In Khowst, he saw an example of what could be achieved if all the right pieces fell together. "I came away from Khowst impressed with the effective partnering of military efforts with civilian experts from State, AID, and the Department of Agriculture. It was a genuinely comprehensive counterinsurgency, combining military operations with robust reconstruction efforts, with Afghans fully integrated."[60]

---

[59] Wood, interview by author.   [60] Gates, *Duty*, 211. Gates, interview by author.

Yet significant challenges remained. McKiernan felt even in 2008 that the mission was only "loosely defined," that Iraq still commanded the priority of attention, and that there were not enough troops in Afghanistan. After he took command in June 2008, he did an initial assessment. "I knew there weren't enough boots on the ground to influence security, especially in South," he said. "I say we immediately need about 30,000 more [troops]" in the South, and 10,000 more in the East. But Bush "was not going to act on that because he was in lame duck status." After the flurry of activity and change since 2006, the US presidential election came to overshadow the war. Washington began to tread water while we awaited the election, and McKiernan's troop request sat unaddressed.[61]

Bush understood the dynamic but wanted to spur one more bout of creative thinking on the war. In September 2008, he ordered a final strategy review, an effort to account for the changes of the previous two years and chart a possible way ahead for his successor. "One of my national security team's last projects was a review of our strategy in Afghanistan," Bush wrote. "It was led by Doug Lute, a brainy three-star general who coordinated day-to-day execution of our operations in Afghanistan and Iraq." I interpreted it as an effort to institutionalize the changes of the past two years, explain their intent and coherence to the next president, and thereby give them longer life and more time to show results. I had not participated in the 2006 review – I was still at the CIA at the time – so the 2008 review would prove to be my most direct participation in policy development. CENTCOM, the Joint Staff, and ISAF also carried out parallel reviews at the same time.[62]

The 2008 review was preceded by a new National Intelligence Estimate (NIE) on Afghanistan. An NIE is "the most authoritative level of analysis," according to Gates, and represents the consensus view among the sixteen agencies of the US intelligence community. The NIE "portray[ed] the situation in Afghanistan as very bleak." Gates thought it might be too bleak. "Even before publication of the estimate, the view was becoming commonplace in Washington that Afghanistan had a 'feckless, incompetent, corrupt government'; the coalition was treading water; Taliban assaults on towns, even when beaten back, were undermining a sense of security and confidence in the coalition and the government; and the insurgents were

---

[61] McKiernan, interview by Madison Lockett.

[62] Hadley, "Bush Oral History." Bush, *Decision Points*, 218. See also Woodward, *Obama's Wars*, 40–44. Eric Schmitt and Thom Shanker, "Bush Administration Reviews Its Afghanistan Policy, Exposing Points of Contention," *New York Times*, September 22, 2008. www.nytim es.com/2008/09/23/washington/23policy.html.

getting closer to Kabul." Gates agreed the situation was grim but worried about "the bandwagon effect of pessimism." What Gates worried was pessimism I felt was simply realism. "We are at war in Afghanistan," General McKiernan told an audience that November. "It's not peacekeeping. It's not stability operations, it's not humanitarian assistance. It's war." It was refreshing to hear.[63]

I knew the situation was dire. In late 2007, as the surge in Iraq was showing results, I bet a colleague that the violence in Afghanistan would surpass violence in Iraq by the end of 2008. I won the bet – in October, months ahead of the deadline. As Iraq progressed, Afghanistan cratered. The Battle of Wanat in July 2008, in which hundreds of Taliban assaulted and nearly overran an American outpost in Nuristan Province, killing nine US troops, seemed a portent of the war's trajectory. We worried about a "Taliban Tet," a nationwide version of Wanat.

The 2008 review took place over the course of sixteen to nineteen meetings involving some two dozen policymakers from agencies and departments across the government, each meeting three to four hours long, sometimes twice a day. In addition to the normal attendees at deputies committee meetings, we involved outside experts, academics, Afghan officials, CIA analysts, and current and former US military and diplomatic personnel who had served in Afghanistan. Ambassador Wood, General McKiernan, and General David Petraeus (then the commander of CENTCOM) participated in some sessions, sometimes through secure video teleconference.

We started with basics, refreshing everyone on Afghan demography, geography, and culture. Intelligence analysts presented the NIE and gave their current assessment of every aspect of the war. The military briefed us about their posture and force strength, their capabilities, and their view of the war. (The gap between the military and the intelligence community had narrowed some.) We debated America's core interests, how they were implicated in Afghanistan, and what our goals should be. We argued – at length – what was truly, realistically achievable. I and the other NSC directors wrote memos for Lute, Hadley, and Bush summarizing aspects of the debate, advocating for positions, and shaping the agenda. Because I was one of the few experts in or out of government who had focused on the war as my exclusive, full-time job almost every day since 9/11, I was able to provide some institutional memory of what had happened over the previous seven

---

[63] Gates, *Duty*, 222. McKiernan, "Transcript: General David McKiernan Speaks at Council's Commanders Series," The Atlantic Council, November 19, 2008.

years, knowledge of which I discovered was a surprising rarity. Already in 2008, the rotation of people in and out of the war had fragmented the government's understanding of its own past decisions.

In 1953, President Dwight Eisenhower ordered his NSC staff to fundamentally reexamine US strategy toward the Soviet Union. The result was the famous Solarium exercise. The NSC and participants from across the government spent six months and developed three different scenarios which served as the basis for Eisenhower's Cold War strategy. Solarium is often held up as the gold standard of strategic thinking in American foreign policy. The 2008 Afghanistan review was less intensive – three weeks of discussion followed by a month of writing and revising – but it felt, to me, like a step in the right direction, a mini-Solarium, a genuine effort to strip our assumptions to the beams. For the first time, we could ask what strategy in Afghanistan should be, unencumbered by Iraq.

After weeks of debate, Lute began to distill an argument into a forty-page document, a process that took several more weeks. The final document is Lute's work, though he actively involved me and the other directors in shaping it, each of us pitching in on the parts that touched on our expertise. The document opened with a blunt warning that the United States was not winning the war. Lute emphasized that "the vital national interest was defeating al-Qaida." But to defeat al-Qaida, we had to "stabilize Afghanistan." Lute was always more skeptical of governance and reconstruction efforts than I was, and he chose his language carefully to reflect his skepticism. For him, "stabilize" meant bringing Afghanistan to a minimal threshold of public order. Lute felt that anything more was unrealistic (I felt we had hardly tried and thus could not conclude it was unrealistic, and good governance was a goal most Afghans shared anyway, so there was no reason to abandon it). Regardless, security was the more pressing concern. Finally, "we made explicit that Afghanistan and Pakistan should be viewed as one theater," Lute recalled, which the Obama administration would fully embrace. Like the Accelerating Success initiative in 2003 and the strategy review in 2006, "the report called for a more robust counterinsurgency effort, including more troops and civilian resources in Afghanistan," Bush wrote in his memoir.[64]

As Lute was finishing the review, Hadley directed each NSC office to produce a memorandum for the record summarizing the state of play for the incoming Obama administration. I took the lead writing the transition

---

[64] Lute, interview by author. Bush, *Decision Points*, 218. See also Cheney and Cheney, *In My Time*, 500–501; Gates, *Duty*, 221. Lute's report is still classified.

memo. I summarized and assessed what the Bush administration had tried to accomplish with its final two years, surveyed the findings of the 2008 strategy review, and reviewed some evidence of progress. Then, contrary to the *Washington Post*'s accusation that American officials consistently delivered "rosy pronouncements they knew to be false," I warned bluntly that the situation was dire. "Violence has risen more than five-fold over the last five years. The quality of governance has declined because of rampant corruption. Afghan public support for the Afghan Government and international military forces has steadily declined over the last few years. Borders remain porous. The Taliban continue to enjoy safe haven in Pakistan." What was the solution? I quoted from Lute's strategy review: "Put counterinsurgency first. We should organize US efforts around counterinsurgency, aligning all other efforts in support." We described the goal: "Defeat the insurgency in Afghanistan by improving security in order to enable democratic governance and development." We were clear: A counterinsurgency campaign to defeat the Taliban and restore order to Afghanistan was the essential precondition to defeating al-Qaida. That was our best understanding of the right strategy in 2008. Fifteen years later, I think we got it right.[65]

Bush could not do much with our recommendations in his remaining weeks in office. He had ordered the review to create a record of his administration's efforts and give Obama a running start. "We debated whether to announce our findings publicly in the final weeks of my presidency," Bush wrote. "Steve Hadley checked with his counterpart in the incoming administration" – General Jim Jones, the incoming national security advisor – "who preferred that we pass along our report quietly." Bush was pragmatic: "I decided the new strategy would have a better chance of success if we gave the new team an opportunity to revise it as they saw fit and then adopt it as their own." Bush's restraint was an admirable and gracious gesture to give his successor smooth political waters on a difficult and sensitive issue. At that point, we had no idea if we would be asked to stay and work for the Obama team or if we would be sent back to our home agencies. We passed along the strategy review and the transition memo and waited.[66]

Bush declined to be interviewed for this book, assuring me through his spokesman that what he has already said and written, and the memories of

---

[65] Whitlock, "At War with the Truth," *The Washington Post*, December 9, 2019. Miller, Lute, O'Sullivan, "Chapter 5: Afghanistan," in Hadley et al., *Hand-Off*.

[66] Bush, *Decision Points*, 218.

those I had interviewed, were more reliable than anything he could now recall. His final word on Afghanistan, then, is the retrospective he left in his memoir. "I knew it would take time to help the Afghan people build a functioning democracy consistent with its culture and traditions," he wrote. "The task turned out to be even more daunting than I anticipated." That Afghanistan's challenges would prove "even more daunting" than anticipated is probably true for most of the people who worked on the effort over the years, and it is not as if the Bush administration could have pulled a nation-building plan for Afghanistan off the shelf. The administration was thrust into a set of challenges for which it had no preparation or planning. Bush is entirely correct that "our government was not prepared for nation building."

Still, the administration might have gotten a grip on the scale of challenges more quickly if they had not wasted years wringing their hands about the supposed dangers of nation building, divided their attention with Iraq, or deluded themselves about Pakistan. And the administration's choice to frame the war first and foremost as a counterterrorism mission – as a "War on Terror" – hovered above and behind every other decision. As he left office, Bush knew there was work yet to be done. "I also knew I was leaving behind unfinished business," he wrote. But the passage was revealing. The work he was referring to was not Afghanistan: "I wanted badly to bring bin Laden to justice."[67]

---

[67] Bush, *Decision Points*, 220.

7

2009

False Start

In 2008, Senator Barack Obama promised to win the war in Afghanistan. He strongly opposed the war in Iraq but argued Afghanistan was a just and necessary war vital to American interests. He projected confidence and optimism; the most enduring image from his 2008 presidential campaign is the faded red, blue, and off-white stencil of his face cast upward, looking afar, captioned by the lone word: "Hope." Yet the story of 2009 is the story of his administration losing hope in Afghanistan. While Obama approved a new strategy in the early months of his presidency, over the course of the year it became apparent he was unwilling to pay the price his new strategy required in the face of mounting challenges. Obama then faced the need to develop an Afghanistan strategy he was prepared to execute, which turned out to be different from the vision he initially promised.

THE 2008 CAMPAIGN

Obama argued in *Foreign Affairs* in 2007 that "we must refocus our efforts on Afghanistan and Pakistan – the central front in our war against al-Qaida – so that we are confronting terrorists where their roots run deepest." In his signature foreign policy speech while campaigning for president, in July 2008, his main theme was the folly of the war in Iraq and the need to do more in Afghanistan. When he turned to Afghanistan, despite his unrelenting criticism of Bush, he accepted Bush's framing of the "War on Terror." "The central front in the war on terror is not Iraq, and it never was," he said. "That's why the second goal of my new strategy will be taking the fight to al-Qaida in Afghanistan and Pakistan." There was a difference: the Bush administration had focused on prevention and deterrence. The war's purpose was to stop the next attack, though they were also keen to kill or capture bin Laden. Obama, however, seemed focused almost exclusively on retribution. "It is unacceptable that almost seven years after nearly 3,000 Americans were killed on our soil, the terrorists who attacked us on 9/11 are still at large," he said. Regardless, he promised to "make the fight against al-Qaida and the Taliban the top priority that it should be."[1]

Obama, a constitutional law professor and community organizer, had served in the Illinois state senate for eight years and the US Senate for two. Tall, cerebral, and Black, Obama broke through the normal noise of politics and seemed to represent something new: for Democrats, a new promise of postpartisan and even postracial politics; for Republicans, a new threat of progressive dominance. I met him only once; I was struck by his poise, height, and – like most politicians – sense of self-assurance. His memoir is unusually observant, well written, and long.

Obama went on: "This is a war that we have to win." Remarkably, it turned out to be one of the few times in the twenty-year war that an American president – or presidential candidate – would vow to "win" the war against the Taliban. Obama only did so on one other occasion. Ben Rhodes, Obama's chief speechwriter, noted that Obama "consistently took out of the speech any language that spoke of winning or victory," because, Obama said, "we should not glorify war."[2] Every administration was wary of using the language of victory because they could not guarantee a clear end point. But while the form of victory in an unconventional war like Afghanistan would, of course, look different than for a conflict like World War II, it was a rhetorical blunder not to use the language of victory. The American people – and the American soldier – need to know that the commander in chief is committed to the cause. To speak of "victory" is not to glorify war; it is to affirm that winning is important and just. The way that Obama (and Biden) talked about Afghanistan was bloodless and technocratic, as if it were a problem to be managed rather than a moral struggle that must be won.

I do not mean, as some do who make a similar critique, that we lost the war because we held ourselves back and never fought with the full might of the US military, as if more bombing and more killing could have achieved a victory that counterinsurgency and state building could not. Rather, I mean that how we talk about war matters; that every war – even unconventional war – is a moral contest; that our leaders need to speak a moral language when they are sending men and women to fight, kill, or die; and that language must include the moral necessity of victory in a just cause.

[1] Obama, "Renewing American Leadership," 9. "Full Text: Obama's Foreign Policy Speech," July 16, 2008. www.theguardian.com/world/2008/jul/16/uselections2008.barackobama.

[2] Rhodes, *The World as It Is*, 79.

Some policymakers and scholars may be uncomfortable talking about the moral imperative of victory because it can sound like self-righteous crusading. But consider the alternative: if there is no moral dimension to war, it is indistinguishable from murder, and we should all be pacifists. Only if we are fighting for a just cause can we justify killing other human beings – and if it is a just cause, it is just and necessary to win. None of the four presidents who oversaw the war in Afghanistan spoke like this. Bush did, but mostly about the wars against al-Qaida and in Iraq, not the post-2001 Taliban.

I was not the only one who felt this way. Gates noted Obama's "lack of passion" about the war in Afghanistan. "When soldiers put their lives on the line, they need to know that the commander in chief who sent them in harm's way believes in their mission," Gates wrote in his memoir. "They need him to talk often to them and to the country, not just to express gratitude for their service and sacrifice but also to explain and affirm why that sacrifice is necessary, why their fight is noble, why their cause is just, and why they must prevail. President Obama never did that." In the summer of 2009, Gates urged Obama to talk more directly and with moral clarity about the war. Obama responded once, with an August 2009 speech that stands out as the only other time he ever spoke of "defeating" the Taliban. After that, it was painfully clear as the years went by that the only time Obama ever spoke about Afghanistan, it was to talk about withdrawing from Afghanistan. "He rarely spoke about the war in Afghanistan except when he was making an announcement about troop increases or troop drawdowns or announcing a change in strategy," Gates wrote.[3]

In the 2008 speech, Obama promised to send more troops – two brigades – and to focus on training the Afghan army and supporting the Afghan judiciary. He promised "more resources and incentives for American officers who perform these missions," seemingly in response to the rapid rotations of personnel in and out of the combat zone. Like Bush in 2002, he invoked the Marshall Plan and promised "an additional $1 billion in non-military assistance each year" (a promise he kept – once, from 2009 to 2010) and highlighted the need to invest in provincial and local governance. He promised to crack down on the Taliban's sanctuary in Pakistan but, like the Bush administration in the early years, believed the problem was capacity, not will. He promised to continue military aid and endorsed what became the Enhanced Partnership with Pakistan Act "to triple non-military aid to the Pakistani people and to sustain it for a decade."

---

[3] Gates, *Duty*, 298–299.

Obama summarized his theory of the war and its relevance to the United States. "The Afghan people must know that our commitment to their future is enduring," he said, "because the security of Afghanistan and the United States is shared." This was exactly correct – echoing Khalilzad's comment years earlier that to solve our problems we had to help the Afghans solve their problems – and should have been the cornerstone of American strategy from the beginning. Obama had an opportunity to make it the foundation for his war in Afghanistan. Despite his campaign rhetoric, he never did. It is naive, of course, to interpret a campaign speech as a statement of national security strategy. Obama's intent in his 2008 speech was to capitalize on his opposition to the war in Iraq while protecting himself from accusations that he was soft on national security by backing the war in Afghanistan. On the other hand, in January his transition team wrote an internal memo in which they argued that "the president and his top advisers will need to signal firmly that the United States is in this war to win and have the patience and determination to do so," suggesting Obama's language about winning the war was not mere campaign rhetoric.[4]

Remarkably, nothing that Obama said was controversial at the time. His opponent in the election, Senator John McCain, agreed with his Afghanistan strategy; their major difference was over Iraq. There was a strong bipartisan consensus that the war in Afghanistan was important but had been neglected, and it was time to refocus. In the final month of the presidential campaign, Doug Lute reached out to the McCain and Obama campaign teams to offer a meeting. We were deeply concerned that a presidential transition midwar could be dangerously disruptive. We hoped meeting early would facilitate a smooth transition. Lute was technically an appointee in the Bush administration, but he was also a respected three-star Army general with no partisan credentials. Rumors had circulated in Washington for a year suggesting that Obama might ask Gates to stay as secretary of defense; if so, Lute had a reasonable expectation that he might also be asked to stay if Obama won. As for the staff, many NSC directors used a presidential transition as a natural point to rotate back to their agencies. But in our office, every director and senior director wanted to stay. We had diverse partisan preferences, but all felt a duty to ensure a solid handoff, to give the commander in chief – whoever he was – the best support possible in wartime.

Lute hosted the meeting with campaign representatives at The Army and Navy Club two blocks north of the White House, across Lafayette

---

[4] Gates, *Duty*, 281.

Square, in October. Lute gave an early readout of the strategy review we were working on; I sat on the sidelines taking notes. The campaigns listened, but the meeting did not come to a point. I suspect they were too concerned about saying something in front of the other campaign that could be used against them. But "it was an early signal that Bush was going to be committed to a smooth transition," Lute said, "so I think that was important." The meeting went unreported in the press, to our relief. We had no more contact for another month or two.

Then, "I went over to the transition headquarters in late November or December of '08, and briefed [Thomas] Donilon, [James L.] Jones, the team that was then forming in the Obama administration," Lute recalled. "Not long after that, partly because I had served with Jones a number of times . . . he asked my team and me to stay on." Lute's continued presence – and, by extension, ours – in the White House was not a foregone conclusion. "Obama's aides wanted to get rid of him as an unreliable holdover," according to George Packer, a journalist and biographer, "but the new national security advisor, James Jones, persuaded the president that Lute was a loyal soldier." It helped that Jones and Lute were members of the same elite club: the club of those whose first name is "General." Lute hoped that meant our 2008 review would feed into the Obama administration's thinking on Afghanistan. "One of the cornerstones of that agreement was that we needed to do something about this review, and then it went from there," he said.[5]

THE RIEDEL REVIEW AND THE MCKIERNAN REQUEST

On Obama's second day in office, he held an NSC meeting on Afghanistan. Earlier, in his inaugural address, he had promised his administration would begin to "forge a hard-earned peace in Afghanistan," the war's only mention on the historic occasion. Once in office, Obama faced an immediate decision on troop levels. General McKiernan had requested 30,000 more troops in August 2008, which would almost double the number of troops then in Afghanistan. But "General McKiernan's request for forces arrived at an inconvenient time," General Stan McChrystal, then serving as the director of the joint staff, later wrote. The looming US presidential election made it a politically awkward time for a major troop increase – "they didn't want to present whoever the new president was with

---

[5] Lute, interview by author. Lute, "Bush Oral History." Packer, *Our Man*, 463.

a *fait accompli* of escalation" – and so McKiernan's troop request sat. After the election, Hadley asked Jones if Obama preferred Bush to make the decision or leave it for the new president. Please wait, came back the reply, which delayed action on the troop request for another two months. Obama's team "understood the value of what President Bush had done," Lute recalled, "which was to give Obama an opportunity early on to do what he had said that he would do, which was refocus on Afghanistan and al-Qaida."[6]

McKiernan – and probably Gates – had a reasonable expectation that the troop request would be quickly approved by the new president. "[Chairman of the Joint Chiefs of Staff Mike] Mullen had explained that the Taliban were likely to mount a summer offensive and we'd want additional brigades on the ground in time to try to blunt it," Obama later wrote. "McKiernan was also worried about providing adequate security for the [Afghan] presidential election" coming up in August, and "if we wanted to get troops there in time to achieve those missions, Mullen told me, we needed to put things in motion immediately." But at the first NSC meeting, Vice President Joe Biden pushed back on the troop request, insisting that a new strategy precede any decisions about troops. Biden "saw Afghanistan as a dangerous quagmire and urged me to delay a deployment," Obama wrote, "suggesting it would be easier to put troops in once we had a clear strategy as opposed to trying to pull troops out after we'd made a mess with a bad one."[7]

Hillary Clinton, though she would otherwise be a consistent supporter of the military's recommendations, saw the logic of delaying a decision on troops: "It was reasonable to ask whether it made sense to deploy more troops before we had time to decide on a new strategy," she wrote. Newly appointed secretary of state after two terms in the US Senate, eight years as the punching bag of the 1990s Republican Party, and six months in a hard-fought loss to Obama in the Democratic primary campaign, Clinton was diligent, guarded, and keenly focused on 2016. Her memoir, published in 2014, is more substantive than a typical campaign biography, less detailed and more evasive than a historical record.[8]

---

[6] Lute, "Bush Oral History." Woodward, *Obama's Wars*, 80–81. Obama, *Promised Land*, 317. McChrystal, *My Share of the Task*, 283. McChrystal, interview by author. Gates, interview by author. Woodward omits the fact that Bush deferred to Obama on the troop request, implying instead that Bush had simply ignored the troop request out of neglect, a small act of journalistic malpractice.

[7] Woodward, *Obama's Wars*, 80–81. Obama, *Promised Land*, 317, 318.

[8] Clinton, *Hard Choices*, 132.

Obama and Biden disliked the pressure for an immediate decision. Obama recounts how Biden pulled him aside after the first NSC meeting on Afghanistan in January. "'Listen to me, boss,' he said. 'Maybe I've been around this town for too long, but one thing I know is when these generals are trying to box in a new president.' He brought his face a few inches from mine and stage-whispered, 'Don't let them jam you.'" He probably used a more colorful word than "jam." The next month, Biden publicly "told the press that he wasn't going to let the military 'bully' the White House into making decisions about more troops for Afghanistan." Biden's suspicion of the military was misplaced, if not bizarre. The military was not saying anything Obama hadn't said himself on the campaign trail, or that Biden hadn't said in the Senate. As a Senator, Biden spent eight years warning of Afghanistan's deterioration and calling for more troops, and just months earlier Obama had warned the war was going poorly and promised to send more troops. McKiernan was repeating Obama's campaign rhetoric back to him, telling him he was exactly right and providing detail about how many troops were required.[9]

But Biden, having pivoted from senatorial gadfly to commander-in-chief-in-waiting, saw the war with new eyes, jaundiced by a recent meeting with Karzai. He turned swiftly against it and, in the process, planted seeds of doubt against his administration's own strategy. "It was perhaps natural that the military leadership wanted more," Obama later wrote of the initial troop request, "it was probably inevitable that the debate over 'how much more' would become a recurring source of strife between the Pentagon and my White House." But again, Obama himself had called for more before he became president, suggesting there was nothing inevitable about the strife that arose. Obama could have taken McKiernan's request as vindication of his campaign's message rather than listening to Biden's warnings against being "jammed." But the damage was done: wrangling over McKiernan's request set the Pentagon and White House off on awkward footing.[10]

Obama later wrote that "the lack of a coherent US strategy didn't help matters." He was concerned that there was no clear goal. "Depending on who you talked to, our mission in Afghanistan was either narrow (wiping out al-Qaida) or broad (transforming the country into a modern, democratic state that would be aligned with the West)." This was an artificial debate between rival caricatures, a common rhetorical trope Obama relied on throughout his public life. It is striking that Obama invoked the same caricature – the supposed goal to "transform" Afghanistan – as had

[9] Obama, *Promised Land*, 319.   [10] Obama, *Promised Land*, 320.

Rumsfeld in his memoirs. More to the point, Obama's comment misunderstands the relationship between the two efforts: nation building was not an alternative to counterterrorism, but a complement to it; it was not an end by itself, but one of the *ways* in the ends–ways–means formula. Regardless, like Rumsfeld, Obama invoked the trope to make lowering his ambitions seem more reasonable. Gates reinforced Obama's tendency, having concluded as early as the previous December that American goals in Afghanistan were "too ambitious for us to achieve," and counseling Obama to adopt "limited and realistic objectives."[11]

Instead of ordering more troops right away, Obama opted to direct another strategy review. He brought on board Bruce Riedel, a former CIA analyst and a campaign advisor, to lead the effort. Riedel's review replicated the process and much of the content of Lute's review, and the latter flowed into the former. "The NSC review that my team and I had done served as one start point" for Riedel's process, in Lute's recollection. I had not previously met Riedel but respected his expertise – thirty years in the CIA, much of it focused on South Asia, with tours on the NSC and in the DoD. He was close to being the salty veteran of Afghanistan studies I had always hoped was lurking somewhere in the bowels of Langley but had never met. Riedel held meetings with representatives from across the interagency, as we had done; indeed, except for the new political appointees, some of the participants were the same. I, and most of my colleagues on Lute's staff, sat in on Riedel's review sessions and contributed where we could.[12]

But the Riedel review felt, to me and others, perfunctory and predetermined. Lute recalls on the first day, after the first session of the review, "Bruce says, 'thank you very much. I'll have a draft of the report to you by Friday,'" suggesting Riedel already knew the outcome of the process; he came into it with the conclusion drawn from a report he had written for the Brookings Institution the previous year. Riedel did not consult with McKiernan, then commanding US forces and ISAF. Peter Lavoy, the national intelligence officer for South Asia, felt the review was really a transition document forced through the interagency process "without sufficient transparency," in a sort of "process foul," which led to "resentment and a feeling of inadequate participation and buy-in … by interagency officials." Riedel's position on the NSC was ambiguous – he was adamant that he would only work in government for sixty days – and so he had no permanent office or staff. Lute naturally offered to help, but Riedel did not make use of our offer of staff support, perhaps a concession to optics: it

[11] Gates, *Duty*, 278. Obama, *Promised Land*, 316.   [12] Lute, "Bush Oral History."

would have reflected poorly on Obama if the *Washington Post* reported that his signature strategy review on Afghanistan was directed behind the scenes by "Bush holdovers," as we were sometimes called.[13]

A parallel debate about McKiernan's troop request was ongoing – but it was separate from the Riedel review, a fact most in the administration later seemed to forget. McKiernan warned the incoming White House team that more troops were necessary to ensure a stable environment for the August 2009 Afghan presidential election. His urgency did not sit well with the White House. "The President had to make a decision well before the conclusion of the Riedel review," Gates recalled. "This made everybody very uncomfortable, and I think logically so. They were being asked to make a big commitment before the assessment of the strategy was complete." The "pressure for an early decision on a troop increase in Afghanistan had the unfortunate effect of creating suspicion in the White House that Obama was getting the 'bum's rush' from senior military officers," though Gates denied any "ulterior motives" on the military's part, highlighting that *not* approving the troops would constrain the president's future options as much as approving them would. Obama tasked Tom Donilon, the deputy national security advisor, to get more clarity on why the troops were needed and what justified the exact number McKiernan had requested. With Lute playing intermediary, the White House and the Pentagon haggled back and forth for a few weeks. The number came down to 21,000, which Obama approved on February 17 – more than a month before the Riedel review was done and unconnected to the new strategy.[14]

Later in 2009, the administration would retrospectively but wrongly link the troop request to the Riedel review. The timing – debating troop levels at the same time they were formulating a new strategy – led some to believe they were tied, that McKiernan's troops were somehow meant to implement the new strategy, despite that the original troop request predated Riedel's review by six months. "The decision [on McKiernan's troop request] was detached from any strategic consideration" related to the Riedel review, Gates said. McKiernan's troop request was meant as an emergency stopgap to prevent catastrophic failure, not to resource a new strategic approach. Compounding future misunderstandings, Gates also told the president that he did not anticipate asking for more troops for the rest of the year. "I may

---

[13] Lute, "Bush Oral History." Lute and Lavoy, interviews by author. Woodward, *Obama's Wars*, 90. Clinton, *Hard Choices*, 132–133. Riedel, *The Search for Al-Qaida*, see especially 148–152.

[14] Gates, interview by author. Gates, *Duty*, 338.

come to you with small requests for enablers or for specific needs," he said, "but in terms of another significant troop commitment, I don't see any reason for me to come back to you before early 2010." Jones and probably Obama interpreted Gates' comment more strongly than Gates intended, taking Gates' "statement of intent" as a promise. These were the first dominos in a cascading series of misperceptions and misunderstandings that eventually unwound the promise of Obama's early moves in Afghanistan.[15]

THE MARCH 2009 STRATEGY

The Riedel review came to similar conclusions as the 2008 Lute review – and, indeed, the 2006 strategy reviews and the 2003 Accelerating Success initiative. Gates saw the similarity. The report was "breathtaking in its ambition," and "just as ambitious as the aspirations of the Bush administration," which Gates meant as a criticism. A more positive interpretation is that every review saw the clear strategic logic: permanently denying safe haven to al-Qaida required some degree of stabilization and reconstruction in Afghanistan. Riedel emphasized the need to go after al-Qaida. "The core goal of the US must be to disrupt, dismantle, and defeat al-Qaida and its safe havens in Pakistan, and to prevent their return to Pakistan or Afghanistan," he wrote. He clearly articulated the tie between the policy goal (defeating al-Qaida and deterring future attacks) and the necessary counterinsurgency means. "The growing size of the space in which they [al-Qaida] are operating is a direct result of the terrorist/insurgent activities of the Taliban and related organizations." That is why counterinsurgency and nation building came front and center in his recommendations. His first two recommendations were "Executing and resourcing an integrated civilian-military counterinsurgency strategy in Afghanistan," and "Resourcing and prioritizing civilian assistance in Afghanistan."[16]

---

[15]   McChrystal, *My Share of the Task*, 283. Woodward, *Obama's Wars*, 94–98. Obama, *Promised Land*, 320. Gates, interview by author.

[16]   Gates, interview by author. Gates, *Duty*, 342. All quotes from the Riedel review are taken from "White House White Paper on US Policy to Afghanistan and Pakistan," *Foreign Policy*, March 27, 2009. https://foreignpolicy.com/2009/03/27/white-house-white-paper-on-u-s-policy-to-afghanistan-and-pakistan/.

Riedel's emphasis on counterinsurgency and civilian assistance was repeated, explicit, and detailed. "Our counter-insurgency strategy must integrate population security with building effective local governance and economic development," he wrote. "We will establish the security needed to provide space and time for stabilization and reconstruction activities." He went on, calling on the United States to promote "a more capable, accountable, and effective government in Afghanistan that serves the Afghan people and can eventually function, especially regarding internal security, with limited international support." He drew a direct tie between civilian assistance and defeating al-Qaida. "Agricultural sector job creation is an essential first step to undercutting the appeal of al-Qaida and its allies."

Riedel also emphasized the need for some form of reconciliation with elements of the Taliban. Like the Bush administration, he discounted the possibility of reconciling with senior leaders. "While Mullah Omar and the Taliban's hard core that have aligned themselves with al-Qaida are not reconcilable and we cannot make a deal that includes them," he wrote, "the war in Afghanistan cannot be won without convincing non-ideologically committed insurgents to lay down their arms, reject al-Qaida, and accept the Afghan Constitution." There was nothing new here: Riedel's criteria were identical to the Bush administration's and simply replicated the outline of the PTS reconciliation program that had started in 2005 and was still going in 2009, but he emphasized that the war "cannot be won" without meaningful political dialogue.

Obama endorsed Riedel's review in a speech on March 27. Obama was clear on the connection between Afghanistan's stability, the Taliban insurgency, and al-Qaida's threat to America. "If the Afghan government falls to the Taliban – or allows al-Qaida to go unchallenged – that country will again be a base for terrorists who want to kill as many of our people as they possibly can." That required an enduring American presence and commitment to Afghanistan. "We are in Afghanistan to confront a common enemy that threatens the United States, our friends and our allies, and the people of Afghanistan and Pakistan who have suffered the most at the hands of violent extremists." Staying in Afghanistan meant investing in its institutions and its stability. "To succeed, we and our friends and allies must reverse the Taliban's gains, and promote a more capable and accountable Afghan government."[17]

---

[17] Obama, "Remarks by the President on a New Strategy for Afghanistan and Pakistan," March 27, 2009. https://obamawhitehouse.archives.gov/the-press-office/remarks-president-a-new-strategy-afghanistan-and-pakistan.

Obama emphasized this point to distinguish his administration from what he believed was the overly militarized approach of the Bush administration. "This push must be joined by a dramatic increase in our civilian effort," he said. "We need agricultural specialists and educators, engineers and lawyers" to help rebuild. Obama anticipated the criticism that civilian efforts were peripheral to the main goal of defeating al-Qaida. "These investments relieve the burden on our troops. They contribute directly to security. They make the American people safer." Obama also endorsed Riedel's conclusion on reconciliation. "There will also be no peace without reconciliation among former enemies," he said. Like Riedel and Bush, he recognized that "there is an uncompromising core of the Taliban. They must be met with force, and they must be defeated." But he saw – correctly – no conflict between winning a war and talking with the enemy. Done right, the two should reinforce one another.

Between Riedel's paper and Obama's speech, the administration had said all the right things. I was elated. More than seven years on, Afghanistan had emerged from Iraq's shadow and seemed to have the full attention and support of a commander-in-chief who would make it central to his presidency, was willing to give it the resources it needed, had endorsed the right strategy, and had time to see it through. The days of "in Iraq we do what we must, in Afghanistan we do what we can" were over. I was troubled that Obama never actually said "counterinsurgency" in his speech, but, since Riedel had foregrounded counterinsurgency in his paper so strongly, I was certain Obama had bought into the idea.[18]

As in 2003 and 2006, a new strategy came with a change in personalities. In January, Clinton created the position of special representative for Afghanistan and Pakistan (SRAP) and appointed Richard Holbrooke to the role. In May, Obama appointed General Karl Eikenberry, who had commanded US forces from 2005 to 2007, as US ambassador to Afghanistan. The same month, on Gates' recommendation, Obama fired General David McKiernan and appointed General Stanley McChrystal to command ISAF and US forces. The three new faces would prove to be consequential additions.

Clinton intended for Holbrooke to coordinate strategy toward Afghanistan and Pakistan from across the interagency – which seemed to replicate Lute's responsibilities within the White House. (In 2009, his office shed Iraq and gained Pakistan.) "Their offices were bound to be a point of friction if the lines of authority weren't clear," according to Packer. "Lute

---

[18] Lute, interview by author.

repeatedly asked Jones for Holbrooke's terms of reference, but Jones blew him off – they would figure it out as they went along . . . As a result, no one in the White House understood Holbrooke's job." For his part, Jones later complained about Holbrooke's "huge staff over at the State Department that rivals the NSC staff," which he blamed for "a disjointed effort." Holbrooke attracted hard-charging high achievers from the State Department. "Some were rising stars from around the government who jumped at the chance to work for a living link to [George] Kennan and [Averell] Harriman," according to Packer. At the staff level, my colleagues and I had a few moments of awkwardness with our counterparts on Holbrooke's staff, who came to their new roles believing they were in charge and starting from scratch, only to find us working our second strategy review in six months. To their credit, despite the ambiguity and some early tension, Lute and Holbrooke worked hard to establish a productive rapport and eventually became allies in their effort to open negotiations with the Taliban in 2010. In a town notorious for big egos, Lute accepted a demotion – one that was eventually rewarded by his appointment as ambassador to NATO in 2013.[19]

As for McKiernan's firing, "Relieving McKiernan of command was one of the hardest decisions I ever made," Gates claimed. "He had made no egregious mistake and was deeply respected throughout the Army." Gates believed McKiernan was not supportive of some changes Gates thought important, including more action to reduce civilian casualties and to create a new ISAF operational-level headquarters. He "seemed to lack the flexibility and understanding of the battlespace required for a situation as complex as Afghanistan." McKiernan was given the opportunity to retire but refused. He had made a commitment, and "if you are going to replace me, you've got to fire me," McKiernan said. He believed "I wasn't the face that Washington wanted," because "I wasn't optimistic enough maybe."[20]

Some of McKiernan's fellow generals were critical of the firing. Lute complained it was "done in a less than fully consultative manner." George Casey, the army chief of staff, strongly objected and sent a letter to Obama. Jones believed "there was no real reason offered to replace McKiernan except that they thought that they needed some new energy, some new blood." But Petraeus, Mullen, and Michèle Flournoy, the undersecretary of defense for policy, backed the move. In public, Gates simply said "that a new strategy required a new commander." In twenty years, McKiernan would be

---

[19] Packer, *Our Man*, 464, 463, 459. Jones, interview by author.
[20] Gates, *Duty*, 344–345. McKiernan, interview by author.

the only commanding general fired over the war in Afghanistan. It may have been necessary, but it was certainly unfair to leave him with the singular distinction as the only senior official held accountable for the failing war effort. General Stanley McChrystal, who had spent years commanding the secret counterterrorism JSOC task force, replaced him. Though McChrystal would himself be fired a year later, it was not because of the war.[21]

THE AFGHAN PRESIDENTIAL ELECTION

Several events during 2009 sowed serious doubts within the Obama administration about the feasibility of its new strategy. The UN continued to warn of deteriorating security, and violence worsened dramatically: insurgent-initiated attacks in the summer of 2009 increased by 65 percent compared to the previous summer, including a suicide bombing of NATO headquarters in Kabul in August, a dramatic attack on the UN compound in October, and another attack on the Indian Embassy the same month. In December, a suicide bomber posing as an intelligence asset infiltrated Camp Chapman, in Khowst Province, and blew himself up, killing seven CIA officers and contractors, one of the deadliest days in the CIA's history. Three hundred fifty-five US soldiers were killed in action in Afghanistan in 2009, more than double the previous year.[22]

The American public was increasingly pessimistic. In July 2009, 54 percent of Americans believed things were going well, compared to 43 percent who thought they were going badly. Five months later, even that tenuous optimism had collapsed: 32 percent thought it was going well, compared to 66 percent who thought it was going badly. In November, the US ambassador to Afghanistan, Karl Eikenberry, reportedly wrote that Karzai was "not an adequate strategic partner" in a cable that was quickly leaked and made public, further souring diplomatic relations. The crises of 2009 led Obama to a "reassessment of whether the war was as necessary as he first believed," according to New York Times reporter David Sanger. Obama came to believe that "progress was possible – but not on the kind of timeline that [he] thought economically or politically affordable."[23]

---

21 Gates, *Duty*, 344–345. Lute, interview by author. Jones, interview by author. Clinton, *Hard Choices*, 133.

22 DoD "Report on Progress," October 2009.

23 Jones, "In US, New High of 43% Call Afghanistan War a 'Mistake,'" Gallup, August 3, 20101. Schmitt, "US Envoy's Cables Show Worries on Afghan Plans," *New York Times*,

The largest reasons for the collapse of faith in the war were the administration's openly antagonistic relationship with Afghan president Hamid Karzai and the disastrous presidential election in August. The Bush administration had recognized Karzai's weakness but tended to believe his heart was in the right place. In 2007, on our recommendation, Bush initiated a monthly (not weekly, as is sometimes reported) video teleconference with Karzai to raise Afghanistan's profile and create a channel for communicating our top concerns directly to Karzai. Obama's team believed Bush's approach enabled Karzai's dependence. The monthly conferences were too much hand-holding, they thought, and were discontinued.

Instead, the Obama administration took a confrontational approach. Biden visited Kabul in January, before he was sworn in as vice president. "Talking to US diplomats, commanders, and soldiers in Kabul, Biden found confusion at all levels about our strategy and objectives," Gates later reported, leading him to be "deeply disturbed about what he had found in Afghanistan." Over dinner and in front of Karzai's cabinet, Biden lectured Karzai on the need to address corruption, improve governance, and avoid sectarianism. He accused Karzai's brother, Ahmed Wali, of drug trafficking and corruption. Karzai pushed back, complaining about the continued drumbeat of civilian casualties from American military operations. Biden and Senator Lindsey Graham, who accompanied Biden on the trip, acknowledged the problem but turned the attention back to Karzai. Karzai habitually denounced reports of civilian casualties in public and without waiting for an investigation; Biden demanded that Karzai wait and address such incidents in private. Karzai, a politician up for reelection in a few months, was hardly going to stay silent on such a sensitive issue and said so.[24]

The meeting grew heated, the recriminations bitter. Biden threatened that the United States might leave Afghanistan. Biden and Karzai began shouting at one another. Bill Wood, then in his final months as US ambassador to Afghanistan, intervened. "I can only tell you that the ambassador found himself in the position of getting between the Vice President-elect and his host head of state," he told me. "No ambassador in the world ever wants to be in that position." He worked to defuse the meeting with some

---

January 25, 2010. http://www.nytimes.com/2010/01/26/world/asia/26strategy.html. Sanger, *Confront and Conceal,* 29, 56, 128. See Sanger's chapters 2, 5, and 10 for the broader narrative of Afghan policy. Also www.nytimes.com/2012/05/20/us/obamas-journey-to-reshape-afghanistan-war.html. Mark Landler, *Alter Egos,* chapter 4, and James Mann, *The Obamians,* chapters 9–10 and 16, cover similar territory.

[24] Gates, *Duty,* 336, 337.

diplomat-speak – "we've both determined how important these issues are to each of us, now let's see if we can make some progress on coming together" – which was necessary because, Wood recalled, "they were yelling at each other."[25]

The meeting set a bad tone for the Obama administration's relationship with Karzai. Biden had acted like a neoimperial viceroy, lecturing Karzai about how to govern in front of his cabinet, insulting him as the "mayor of Kabul," and raising questions about his family's integrity. He had no authority to threaten to withdraw American troops – neither as a Senator nor as Vice President-elect. It was a stunning mix of condescension, political deafness, and incompetent diplomacy. But Biden left the meeting convinced Karzai, rather than Biden himself, was in the wrong, and that the United States lacked a partner in the Afghan government capable or willing to do its part. Karzai might have been forgiven for feeling the same of the United States. It was an extraordinary about-face for Biden, who had been among the foremost champions of nation building and increased resources for Afghanistan in the Senate until that point.

Holbrooke agreed with Biden's estimation of Karzai. He also visited Kabul before assuming his new role as special representative. "He criticized Karzai to his face," according to Packer's biography of Holbrooke, telling him "you are responsible for some of the failures of the past few years." Holbrooke's estimate of Karzai was so low that he "believed that the war would be lost if Karzai remained in the Arg [the presidential palace] for another five years." As such, "Holbrooke's first priority as SRAP was to prevent [Karzai] from winning re-election in August," an astonishingly overt exercise of imperial power. "He didn't try to hide the fact – he was extraordinarily indiscreet about it." Holbrooke explored every means available to leverage his office against Karzai. "He convinced President Karzai that the US was really out to replace him as President of the country," according to Jones, because Holbrooke "was trying to do that." "Karzai knows that the United States is conspiring against him in the election," Gates recalled. "So this wasn't exactly conducive to a productive working relationship." Predictably, "Holbrooke's maneuvers enraged Karzai," Packer wrote. "The effect of Holbrooke's anti-Karzai campaign was to offend Afghan sensibilities and rally Pashtun support around the president. If Karzai won in August, some Afghan politicians thought, it would be partly Holbrooke's fault."[26]

---

[25] Woodward, *Obama's Wars*, 66–73. Wood, interview by author.

[26] Packer, *Our Man*, 442, 475, 477, 480. Jones, interview by author. Gates, interview by author.

The election was a disaster. Widespread reports of fraud cast doubt on the election's legitimacy among international observers. After hundreds of thousands of fraudulent ballots were disqualified, Karzai failed to secure 50 percent of the vote, triggering a runoff election between Karzai and his chief challenger, former foreign minister Abdullah Abdullah. Karzai refused to acknowledge his failure to secure a majority, and the international community did not want to pay for and secure another election. But after his attempts to interfere in the election, "Holbrooke was now persona non grata in Kabul," according to Packer. The man who was supposed to coordinate US strategy toward Afghanistan was not welcome in the country and utterly incapable of playing a constructive role negotiating a solution to the electoral crisis. "The White House view was that Holbrooke, who waved a gun in Karzai's face and failed to shoot, had gone rogue and then screwed up the election."[27]

"We lost Karzai's trust at that point because it came so early in the Obama administration," Lute recalled. "And because it was indisputable, frankly, even in Washington, that Holbrooke had misstepped." Two years later, Obama nominated Ryan Crocker to replace Eikenberry as ambassador in Kabul. "When President Obama told me to reset the relationship [with Karzai], he didn't have to spell it out, and I didn't need to say it back to him," Crocker recalled. "A lot of that had to do with the damage Holbrooke had done. If you're going to rig an election, boy, better be sure it works." Clinton clearly should have fired Holbrooke after the election, who had become a liability precisely where he should have been an asset. Obama tried, but not until January of the following year, and Clinton successfully protected him. Instead of Holbrooke, Senator John Kerry flew to Kabul and mediated between Karzai and Abdullah. After days of wrangling, Karzai agreed to accept, in principle, that he had not won 50 percent of the vote, while Abdullah withdrew from the runoff, granting Karzai his reelection without the expense or risk of another election. Kerry would pick up where he left off when he was named secretary of state in Obama's second term three years later.[28]

THE GRAVEYARD, VALHALLA, AND VIETNAM

As a result of spiking violence, the election debacle, and the rupture in relations with Karzai, a sense of pessimism descended on the Obama

---

[27] Packer, *Our Man*, 488, 489, 501–504.
[28] Lute, Crocker, interviews by author. Kerry, *Every Day Is Extra*, 372.

administration's view of Afghanistan in the late summer of 2009, much like the sense of foreboding that overcame the Bush administration in late 2005. What had recently been called the "good war" and been the focus of one of the administration's first major decisions was starting to feel out of control. "I think there's an evolution in [Obama's] thinking. He became President believing he could fix this and that it required more resources," Gates told me. "But I think pretty steadily over the course of 2009, he probably became more and more skeptical whether our objectives could be achieved." The administration was concerned about "the ability of the Afghan government ever to be able to hold up its end of the bargain" because of pervasive corruption and incompetence. In his memoir, Gates mused that Obama's "political and philosophical preferences" were against escalating the war, but that "conflicted with his own pro-war public rhetoric" during the campaign. General McKiernan, who commanded ISAF until June 2009, felt that even in the early months of the year the emphasis was on "how do we get ourselves out of Afghanistan?"[29]

As in the Bush administration, old tropes and myths resurfaced to give words to the administration's worries. Afghanistan "has been called the 'Graveyard of Empires' because so many invading armies and would-be occupiers have foundered in its unforgiving terrain," Clinton wrote in her memoir. Senator John Kerry, who assumed the chairmanship of the Senate Foreign Relations Committee in January, agreed. "As I took on the chairmanship, I remained especially anxious about Afghanistan for a number of reasons," he wrote. "Its history as the 'graveyard of empires' was instructive. Afghanistan was the country where Great Britain and Russia had suffered enormous losses." The historical analogy served to excuse America's difficulties: if the British and Soviets couldn't win in 200 years, it's not much of a loss if we can't manage either.[30]

In his memoir and interview, Gates focused attention on Obama's growing pessimism, but Gates himself was probably the most influential voice cautioning against too much involvement in Afghanistan. Gates – a Kansan, Eagle Scout, and Air Force intelligence officer – was the quintessential national security professional. He spent a career as a CIA analyst and NSC director in the 1970s and 1980s, earning a PhD from Georgetown University along the way. He served as the deputy national security advisor and the director of the CIA in the George H. W. Bush administration. He then lectured widely and served as president of Texas A&M before Bush

---

[29] Gates, interview by author. Gates, *Duty*, 569. McKiernan, interview by author.
[30] Clinton, *Hard Choices*, 130. Kerry, *Every Day Is Extra*, 370.

tapped him as secretary of defense. The blend of military, intelligence, academic, and policymaking experience coupled with bipartisan credentials and respect made him ideal to lead the Pentagon during the divisive and failing effort in Iraq. Unlike Rumsfeld, Gates carried himself with an understated professionalism, even humility, with an intelligence analyst's skepticism of everything, including himself. The flip side is that Gates sometimes waffled; he saw, and occasionally agreed with, every side to every debate.

On Afghanistan, Gates wanted to up the level of effort, but even during the Bush administration, he worried that the effort was unfocused and too ambitious. He told Bush, "we need to narrow our ambitions and our objective here," and he consistently advocated with both presidents for "narrowing the mission." In January 2009, shortly after Obama's inauguration, he cautioned Obama against "grandiose aspirations" in Afghanistan, and he testified to Congress that "if we set ourselves the objective of creating some sort of Central Asian Valhalla over there, we will lose, because nobody in the world has that kind of time, patience or money," invoking the hall of the heroic dead in Norse mythology. In December, he told the House Foreign Affairs Committee that he was concerned that Obama's March speech endorsing the Riedel review had been "interpreted by many as saying, well, we are going into full-scale nation building, and we are going to try and reestablish or establish a strong central government in Kabul," in response to which Gates and Obama had worked to "narrow the mission." In his memoir, Gates recounted his experience as deputy director of the CIA during the Soviet–Afghan war. The experience led him to believe that "the idea of creating a strong, democratic (as we would define it), more or less honest and effective central government in Afghanistan, to change the culture, to build the economy and transform agriculture, was a fantasy."[31]

Gates argued that the mission in Afghanistan should have been limited to building "the capacity of the Afghan government to maintain control of the country and keep al-Qaida at bay," he told me. "That's all we're here for and all the other things that you want to do are not military missions." Gates is right that Bush had articulated ambitious goals – his Marshall Plan speech was an example – but the actual priorities were, as Mullen had said, "in Iraq we do what we must, in Afghanistan we do what we can," which was hardly ambitious. Gates' emphasis on narrowing the mission is another

---

[31] Gates, *Duty*, 336–337, 374. Gates, interview by author. House Foreign Affairs Committee, "Afghanistan Strategy," December 2 and 10, 2009, 31.

example of "realism" undermining long-term strategic coherence. Because Gates emphasized repeatedly that he believed our goals were too ambitious, I pressed him to give specific examples of things we were doing that we should have stopped doing. He replied by shifting his critique slightly. The problem wasn't ambition per se, it was a lack of strategic clarity and focus:

> Which was more important? The counternarcotics or counterterrorism or counterinsurgency [mission], or getting rid of corruption, or making the Ministry of Health more effective, or the Ministry of Education, or the Ministry of Finance? ... My position from the very beginning and from my interview with President Bush was that the effort needed to be much more focused and particularly concentrate on a handful of ministries that actually were critical to being able to keep the Taliban at bay.[32]

Gates is right, but that is not a problem of ambition. It could be described as a problem of cohesion, priorities, or coordination. We recognized the problem in the 2008 Lute review and recommended organizing everything around counterinsurgency. But the problem in Afghanistan, the war where "we do what we can," was never excessive zeal. Gates concluded his memoir with a reflection that the Afghan mission was "embarrassingly ambitious," but he adds an important qualifier: it was ambitious "when compared to the meager human and financial resources committed to the task, especially before 2009." That is a crucial point: the problem was not the strategy, but the gap between strategy and resources (including time). By saying, elsewhere, that it was a problem of ambition only – rather than a problem of inadequate resources and poor coordination – Gates fed the misapprehension that we had been engaged in a hopelessly naive, massive, and expensive nation-building campaign for almost a decade driven by dreamers and utopians. No such campaign existed, but by implying it did, Gates fed the growing sense of defeatism: if we had been doing big things yet failing for a decade, it proved the impossibility of such undertakings, pre-emptively prejudicing the debate over counterinsurgency and reconstruction about to unfold.[33]

Nonetheless, Gates cautioned against excessive ambition and argued against investing too much or too heavily in Afghanistan. "By midsummer 2008, even before McKiernan's request for a significant increase in troops, I began to have misgivings about whether the foreign military presence in Afghanistan was growing to the point where most Afghans would begin to

---

[32] Gates, interview by author.   [33] Gates, *Duty*, 569.

see us as 'occupiers' rather than allies," he wrote. "I had been involved with Afghanistan and Pakistan during the 1980s and had watched the Soviets fail despite having nearly 120,000 troops there: their large presence (and brutal tactics) turned Afghans against them." Gates belatedly came to back more troops and to see the flaw in his historical analogy. McChrystal argued to him that "the size of the force (or footprint) was less important than what you did with it. In and of itself, this wasn't an earthshaking insight," Gates recalled. "But I had viewed Afghanistan for so long through the lens of the Soviets' experience that his comments had a serious impact on me." McChrystal's insight was not "earthshaking"; indeed, it was obvious, yet it was one that most officials in the Bush and Obama administrations did not see.[34]

Other Obama administration officials invoked a different historical analogy, one the Bush team had largely eschewed: the Vietnam War. Holbrooke and Jones had served in Vietnam, the former in the foreign service and the latter in the Marines. Biden, who had advocated for withdrawal from Vietnam during his first campaign for the US Senate in 1972, was decisively shaped by his engagement with that earlier conflict (see Chapter 15). Rumsfeld had also been shaped by Vietnam, but in a different direction. Everyone agreed that Vietnam illustrated the vital importance of local leadership, but Rumsfeld also felt Vietnam taught the vital necessity of American credibility and willpower – "weakness is provocative," he wrote – the absence of which had led to America's defeat. To the Obama team, by contrast, Vietnam was not about the need for willpower and credibility. It was a cautionary tale, a warning not to engage in foreign counterinsurgency and nation building in the first place. It was historical proof of the impossibility of such utopian aspirations. (Colin Powell's view on Vietnam and its relevance to Afghanistan and Iraq was closer to the Obama team's, but his voice was consistently drowned out.)[35]

Jones invoked Vietnam at length in my conversation with him. He started his career as a second lieutenant, serving as a platoon and then a company commander. "It was clear to me," he recalled, "that the South Vietnamese army was – regardless of what we were giving them and doing – not prepared to fight . . . As we pulled out of South Vietnam and the North Vietnamese invaded with very little resistance, we all know what the result of that was." That's not entirely fair to the South Vietnamese, who fought for two years after the American withdrawal before the North's victory. Regardless, Jones continued: "Ask yourself why that happened. And

[34] Gates, *Duty*, 217, 335.   [35] Rumsfeld, *Known and Unknown*, 695.

I think it happened because the South Vietnamese army was very happy to let the US carry the whole load." Jones made the analogy explicit. "Then you fast forward to Afghanistan and then the war in Iraq in 2003, and you have the same thing." Biden echoed Jones' critique in 2021 when justifying the withdrawal of American forces, despite that the Afghan army had fought for ten years, including the last seven in the lead.[36]

Holbrooke, who spent six years in Vietnam as a foreign service officer, was the most outspoken about it. "Bringing up Vietnam came naturally. There was no way to avoid it," according to his biographer. "Holbrooke carried that war around with him like a book he had committed to memory when he was young, and now whole passages were coming back to him." He "brought it up all the time. He couldn't resist." For Holbrooke, the Vietnam analogy was complex. Though it was a story of failure and defeat, Holbrooke seems to have felt that it was a worthy fight, and that Afghanistan was a chance to vindicate America's integrity and competence. "Here was the paradox: he knew from Vietnam that what we were doing in Afghanistan wouldn't work – but he thought he could do it anyway." Later, a fellow diplomat noticed that Holbrooke had arranged the physical layout of his State Department suite like the US embassy in Saigon. He "had the sense that Holbrooke was consciously re-creating the old Saigon embassy and trying to make the story come out differently." For Holbrooke, Vietnam taught the importance of negotiations, the dangers of military escalation, the difficulties of counterinsurgency, the need for a regional approach, and the folly of promising progress on a fixed timetable.[37]

Holbrooke brought Vietnam up so often it started to grate on others. "Obama actually didn't want to hear about Vietnam. He told his young aides that it wasn't relevant, and they agreed: Vietnam was ancient history," according to Packer. "So Obama told Jones, and Jones told Clinton, and Clinton told Holbrooke: stop it with Vietnam. 'They don't think they have anything to learn from Vietnam,' she said. 'They're going to make the same mistakes!'" he replied. Clinton recalled in her memoir how "younger White House aides rolled their eyes when he invoked lessons learned in Vietnam." But Obama's ban on discussions about Vietnam did not mean the analogy played no role in the administration's decision-making. Quite the opposite: Biden's thinking about Afghanistan was decisively shaped by the analogy, and he played a major role in the outcome of the next strategy review.[38]

[36] Jones, interview by author.
[37] Packer, *Our Man*, 454, 472, 474, 486. See also 449, 468, and 496.
[38] Packer, *Our Man*, 427, 473. Clinton, *Hard Choices*, 141.

THE MCCHRYSTAL ASSESSMENT

The administration's rapidly growing pessimism was the mood music playing when General Stanley McChrystal's stark assessment of the war landed on August 31 and helps explain the administration's extraordinary reaction to it. McChrystal replaced McKiernan and assumed command in June (joining Generals McNeill, McColl, McKenzie, and McMaster to guarantee confusion for students of the war). McChrystal had spent years commanding US Special Operations Forces and had a reputation for a lean, spartan lifestyle. His exploits were the stuff of legend: his troops killed Abu-Musab al-Zarqawi, head of al-Qaida in Iraq, during his command there. Unlike many flag officers who spend their final years in uniform behind a desk, McChrystal exudes "warrior" more than "bureaucrat." That came with a cost. McChrystal was largely insulated from the administration's rapidly shifting view of the war and was politically tone-deaf compared to other senior military officers, like Petraeus or Mullen. McChrystal, to his credit, had sensed the need to connect with the president before he took command. He told the White House staff, "I need a session with the president. I need him to tell me what he wants," but he was told "no, you don't need that," and instead they met "for about two minutes [with] no discussion of the war."[39]

As is normal for new commanders, he began work on an assessment that captured the state of the war and the state of the coalition's warfighting posture, something Gates had tasked him to do anyway. "This is a very typical US Army way to assume command. You go around, you watch around your command. You go to the motor pool, you go to the rifle range" and assess the state of things, Lute said, "so, Stan did just what was both natural to him and what the Secretary of Defense had asked him to do." Gates noted how "reasonable, indeed innocuous" it was to ask for a new commander's assessment. In McChrystal's telling, his assessment was more formal and detailed than a normal commander's assessment because it was in response to orders from Gates and from the NATO Secretary General and, presumably, because he was aware of the stakes. "I got some outsiders to be part of it, some civilian experts and all that, because I wanted to get as balanced a look as I could," he told me. Despite its routine nature, it proved controversial.[40]

---

[39] McChrystal, interview by author. McChrystal and I served together in Combined Joint Task Force 180 in 2002, though as he was the chief of staff and I was a lowly intelligence analyst, I have no specific memory of interacting with him.

[40] McChrystal, interview by author. Lute, interview by author. Gates, *Duty*, 349. Obama, *Promised Land*, 323.

McChrystal's sixty-six-page review is an unusually well written, blunt piece of writing for a government document. He opened by acknowledging the link between Afghan stability and American security, echoing the same language Obama had used in March. "If the Afghan government falls to the Taliban ... Afghanistan could again become a base for terrorism, with obvious implications for regional stability." But he warned in more striking language just how dire the situation was. "The situation in Afghanistan is serious; neither success nor failure can be taken for granted," he wrote. "Many indicators suggest the overall situation is deteriorating." He characterized the insurgency as "resilient and growing" and warned of "a crisis of confidence" that "undermines our credibility and emboldens the insurgents."[41]

McChrystal repeated Riedel's recommendation that the new strategy be "properly resourced and executed through an integrated civilian-military counterinsurgency campaign." He bluntly repeated the need for counterinsurgency over and over throughout the document: "Success demands a comprehensive counterinsurgency (COIN) campaign." The overarching goal was to defeat al-Qaida, which, McChrystal stated clearly, required "defeating the insurgency," though he also recognized that "the Afghans must ultimately defeat the insurgency," which meant far more attention to training Afghan security forces. He was also clear that "defeat" did not mean "seizing terrain or destroying insurgent forces," because "security may not come from the barrel of a gun," but only through a combined effort to provide Afghans with a "secure environment." The coalition needed to "prioritize responsive and accountable governance." He emphatically did not suggest the United States had to eradicate the Taliban or win the war solely through military means. Defeating the insurgency meant achieving "a condition where the insurgency no longer threatens the viability of the state," which was just as likely to come about by strengthening the Afghan state as it was by weakening the insurgency. The overarching message was the need to protect the population.[42]

McChrystal criticized ISAF's risk aversion, tolerance for civilian casualties, and organizational structure. He called on the military to change its culture, reduce its fixation on force protection, decentralize decision-making, and draw closer to the Afghan people whom it was supposedly

---

[41] Commander's Assessment, 1–1. Available on the National Security Archive: https://nsarchive.gwu.edu/document/24560-headquarters-international-security-assistance-force-kabul-afghanistan-gen-stanley.

[42] Commander's Assessment, 1–1, 1–2, 1–3, 2–2.

trying to protect. He was keenly aware of the dynamics of bureaucracy. His first recommendation was for ISAF to "change its operating culture," to prioritize counterinsurgency, and to clean up its internal command-and-control arrangements. He wanted to turn ISAF into a COIN bureaucracy, to align its procedures and internal goals with the mission requirements: a custom-tailored bureaucracy fitted to the task at hand. He called for longer tours, knowledge of local languages, and respect for local culture. He also emphasized the psychological aspect of the war. He warned that the "perception that our resolve is uncertain makes Afghans reluctant to align with us against the insurgents" and emphasized the need to "signal unwavering commitment" to reassure them. The psychological element was especially important because the insurgency succeeded in part by intimidation and fear: the more international forces telegraphed hesitance or lack of commitment, the easier it was for the insurgents to persuade the population that they would win. A month later, McChrystal told *60 Minutes* his plan amounted to "an awful lot of bad habits we've got to deprogram." McChrystal was going to war against the bureaucracy.[43]

Only after emphasizing the new approach centered on protecting the population did McChrystal broach the subject of more troops and money – which, he claims, was not his original intent. At the outset of his review, "I did not expect to ask for more troops," he told me, but the review process convinced him that counterinsurgency would require more than even what McKiernan had requested. "Additional resources are required, but focusing on force or resource requirements misses the point entirely," he wrote, as if to blunt the edge of his troop request. "The key take away from this assessment is the urgent need for a significant change to our strategy and the way that we think and operate." But he did argue for more resources. "Our campaign in Afghanistan has been historically under-resourced and remains so today," he wrote, echoing not just Obama, but the universal consensus of the American and allied national security establishments. "Almost every aspect of our collective effort and associated resourcing has lagged a growing insurgency . . . Resources will not win this war, but under-resourcing could lose it." The purpose of more American and NATO troops, McChrystal argued, was to train the Afghans and be a bridge to when they could take over. "This 'properly resourced' requirement will define the minimum force levels to accomplish the mission with

---

[43] Commander's Assessment, 2–11, 1–1. *60 Minutes*, "McChrystal's Frank Talk on Afghanistan," September 24, 2009. www.cbsnews.com/news/mcchrystals-frank-talk-on-a fghanistan/.

an acceptable level of risk." Crucially, McChrystal was also clear that "resources" included more than troops. "A 'properly-resourced' strategy places enough things, in enough places, *for enough time.* All three are mandatory."[44] The final requirement – "for enough time" – would be the missing ingredient in Obama's war.

"THE ROOM EXPLODED"

National Security Advisor Jim Jones traveled to Afghanistan in the summer to hear McChrystal's views before the formal assessment was done. Jones strongly opposed new troops and told McChrystal not to ask for more. Jones felt that McChrystal's draft implied there had been a dramatic deterioration in just the short time since he took command, which Jones found implausible. Jones warned McChrystal that if he asked for more troops after Obama had already approved 21,000, the president would react badly. Jones was transparently trying to politicize the military's assessment, telling McChrystal to shape his report and troop request to accommodate political realities in Washington.[45]

There were two problems with Jones' reaction. First, Gates had changed commanders precisely because the administration believed it needed to get fresh eyes – eyes through which Afghanistan would likely look worse than before. The assessment of the previous commander, David McKiernan, was out of step with the emerging consensus in the intelligence community and elsewhere (and echoed in Obama's campaign rhetoric), and Gates felt he was not moving with the urgency the situation required. McChrystal's new perspective was a feature, not a bug, of his new command. The deteriorating situation in mid 2009 was proof, not that McChrystal was overreacting, but that Obama had been right.

Second, this is when the administration's misunderstanding – or misrepresentation – about the nature of David McKiernan's 2008 troop request became apparent. Jones argued that, before any further troops could be justified, McChrystal needed to use the 21,000 troops Obama had ordered back in February to implement the Riedel review, show a proof of concept that counterinsurgency could work, and reverse the war's momentum. Jones told Mullen, "It's not fair to the president to take the decision that

---

[44] McChrystal, interview by author. Commander's assessment, 1–1, 1–3, 1–4. Emphasis added.

[45] Woodward, *Obama's Wars*, 128–134, 141.

he took in March, decide before you ever even got the 21,000 troops there that things are going so bad you need another 40,000." But that is not what the 21,000 troops were for. The 21,000 troops – originally requested by David McKiernan in August 2008 and not approved until February 2009 – were to staunch the bleeding, secure the elections, and prevent failure. Stan McChrystal's 40,000 were to begin healing the patient and to implement counterinsurgency. McChrystal was not asking for more troops because things were going badly (though he was alarmed by how quickly things were deteriorating); he needed them to implement the president's new strategy. Gates told the president that the McChrystal assessment "did not represent a new strategy but focused on implementing what the president had approved in March." Jones conflated the two, which made it seem as if the military was double-dipping, going back to the well for more troops to accomplish the same purpose.[46]

The misunderstanding bled over into perceptions of the Riedel review. Obama reportedly believed that "they had just started to implement the Riedel review and talk of more troops was premature," according to Woodward. He felt that five months was not enough time to gauge progress, and thus McChrystal couldn't make the case that he needed more. But again, that misstated the situation. They had not begun to implement the Riedel review and thus could not assess its progress; McChrystal's assignment was not a progress report on Riedel's strategy, but a plan to implement it. "I based [the commander's assessment] on the mission statement and intent as I understood it and as it had been articulated in the Riedel report," McChrystal said. Gates agreed: "McChrystal's request was in fact a statement of the resources required to implement the Riedel report."[47]

The Riedel review was a high-level strategic concept, not an operational plan, and it had not been accompanied by any new troops. The Riedel review (and a parallel review on Iraq) "weren't really strategies," Lute recalled. "They were conceptual policy documents that didn't really drive strategy to its end point, which is resources." Flournoy characterized the report as focusing on "what should be done, but the how was missing." McChrystal observed that the Riedel review lacked "a really hard set of recommendations," that is, recommendations with specificity to them. When McChrystal tried to provide those specifics, Obama, instead of

---

[46] Woodward, *Obama's Wars*, 132, 141. Commander's Assessment, 2–20. Jones, interview by author. Gates, *Duty*, 362.

[47] Woodward, *Obama's Wars*, 141, 164. McChrystal and Gates, interviews by author.

embracing the newly fleshed-out strategy, faulted the entire concept for being too expensive.[48]

Obama's misunderstanding – or evasion – is evident in his memoir. "The US commitment the Riedel report was calling for went well beyond a bare-bones counterterrorism strategy," he wrote, "and toward a form of nation-building that probably would have made sense – had we started seven years earlier, the moment we drove the Taliban out of Kabul." But going beyond bare-boned counterterrorism is exactly what Obama had called for in March, emphasizing the need for "agricultural specialists and educators, engineers and lawyers" to invest in Afghan governance, as he said at the time. Riedel was doing no more than fulfilling the mandate given him by the president as reflected in his campaign rhetoric, using counterinsurgency (against the Taliban) as the means for a counterterrorism goal (against al-Qaida). Obama is right about the issue of timing – everything would have been easier if started earlier – but he is otherwise reading his later doubts back into the earliest days of his administration.[49]

Now, in September, Obama reinterpreted McChrystal's report the same way. "Not only was McChrystal proposing a more ambitious approach than what I'd envisioned when I'd adopted the Riedel report recommendations in the spring," Obama wrote, "he was also requesting at least forty thousand troops." But McChrystal was describing what he thought was necessary to implement Riedel's recommendations, not go beyond them. In Obama's telling, Riedel was more ambitious than Obama, and McChrystal more ambitious than Riedel – but Riedel and McChrystal both believed they were doing no more than translating the president's goal, outlined in his campaign, into a strategic concept (the Riedel report) and then into an operational plan (the McChrystal assessment).[50]

In retrospect, it seems clear that Obama embraced the Riedel review without fully grasping its implications. Obama told Woodward he did not, in fact, fully buy into a counterinsurgency strategy, despite having endorsed the Riedel review, because that implied "responsibility for Afghanistan over the long term," which he wanted to avoid. Though he devoted one of his first major presidential addresses to endorsing Riedel's recommendations, he quickly abandoned them when it became evident how much it would cost in troops, money, and time.[51]

---

[48] Gates, *Duty*, 341. Lute, McChrystal, interviews by author.
[49] Obama, *Promised Land*, 320–321.   [50] Obama, *Promised Land*, 432.
[51] Woodward, *Obama's Wars*, 183–184.

Obama's misunderstanding about the purpose of the 21,000 troops, and the background of growing pessimism, helps explain why the administration reacted so badly to McChrystal's assessment and troop request. When Gates heard of the coming request, "I nearly fell off my chair," he wrote. "It didn't take a clairvoyant to see a train wreck coming." When Gates previewed the possibility of a new troop request with the president and his senior advisors, "the room exploded," and "the president said testily there would be no political support for any further troop increase." Biden pushed back hard. McChrystal's troop request "really jolted the whole system," Jones recalled. McChrystal's report "was not what the White House wanted to hear," according to Clinton. Gates was discouraged by the administration's "total focus on the politics" of another troop request. "Not a word was mentioned about doing whatever it took to achieve the goals the president had so recently set or to protect the troops," he wrote.[52]

The McChrystal review could only catch the administration off guard if they were not paying attention. McChrystal's assessment was a vindication of what Obama had said on the campaign trail and in his speech in March. McChrystal was saying to Obama, in effect: you're right, the war is going badly, it has been dramatically underresourced, your new strategy will work, but we need more troops, and we need much more attention to reconstruction and stabilization. Every element of McChrystal's report had been foreshadowed by either Obama's campaign, the Riedel review, or Obama's March 27 speech. Obama could have embraced the McChrystal assessment as a validation of his previous warnings. The political cost, coming early in his first term, would not have been prohibitive. But "people were tired of Afghanistan," McChrystal recalled. "To say we're going to get serious now, people go, 'Holy shit, we've been at this for nine years, what are you talking about?' It was hard to convince people."[53]

McChrystal's assessment and troop request was so unwelcome it triggered a wholesale reevaluation of the entire war and America's goals in fighting it. Obama felt McChrystal's proposed strategy – which McChrystal believed was simply Obama's strategy, given more detail – rested on impossible assumptions. "Given the resilience of the Taliban and the dysfunction of Karzai's government, there was no guarantee of success," Obama wrote. "In their written endorsement of [McChrystal's] plan, Gates and the generals acknowledged that no amount of US military power could stabilize Afghanistan 'as long as pervasive corruption and preying upon the people

---

[52] Gates, *Duty*, 349, 353. Jones interview by author. Clinton, *Hard Choices*, 133.

[53] McChrystal, interview by author.

continue to characterize governance,'" which Obama thought unlikely. "I saw no possibility of *that* condition being met anytime soon."[54]

Obama was caught in a bind. Faced with the reality of what his campaign promise and his March speech would cost in troops, time, and money, he balked. But he also recognized the national security interests at stake. "We couldn't afford to let the Taliban return to power, and we needed more time to train more capable Afghan security forces and to root out al-Qaida and its leadership," he later wrote. Oddly, considering his comfort that fall in overriding his generals on most of the important decisions in the upcoming strategy review, he claimed that "as confident as I felt in my own judgment, I couldn't ignore the unanimous recommendation of experienced generals who'd managed to salvage some measure of stability in Iraq and were already in the thick of the fight in Afghanistan."[55]

Obama was also aware of the political dynamics. More troops would be unpopular with his base, but ignoring the military's advice would be risky for a first-term president with no military experience. To square the circle and gain political cover for whatever decision he came to, Obama launched another strategy review, "a series of NSC meetings where – away from congressional politics and media grousing – we could methodically work through the details of McChrystal's proposal, see how they matched up with our previously articulated objectives, and settle on the best way forward." In a change from last time – and from Bush's 2008 review – Obama attended and chaired each of the nine NSC sessions himself. The fall 2009 strategy review would prove to be the hinge on which the entire war turned.[56]

---

[54] Obama, *Promised Land*, 433.   [55] Obama, *Promised Land*, 433.
[56] Obama, *Promised Land*, 433, 437. Clinton, *Hard Choices*, 133.

8

2009

The Hinge

Why launch another strategy review? Obama read the McChrystal report and concluded, as he later told Woodward, "we've got to get everybody in a room and make sure that everybody is singing from the same hymnal." That had been the purpose of the Riedel review, of course. But "I think the Riedel report retained ambiguity about what our central mission was," Obama said. Obama was using Woodward to rewrite history: the Riedel report was unambiguous that "the core goal of the US must be to disrupt, dismantle, and defeat al-Qaida and its safe havens in Pakistan, and to prevent their return to Pakistan or Afghanistan," and Obama repeated the sentence, virtually word for word, in his speech in March. In his discussion with Woodward, he claimed some in his administration interpreted Riedel as a mandate for a beefed-up counterterrorism strategy, while others saw it as an endorsement for a counterinsurgency strategy – again, an odd claim considering Riedel had written as his first recommendation, "Executing and resourcing an integrated civilian-military counterinsurgency strategy in Afghanistan," seemingly leaving little room for debate.[1] The problem was not that the Riedel review was ambiguous. The problem was that the president had endorsed a strategy but not the resources required to implement it.

Obama launched the second strategy review on September 13, less than six months after the conclusion of the previous one. The review unfolded over the next two-and-a-half months and again replicated the process of the previous two reviews, but at a higher level, involving the principals and the

---

[1] Woodward, *Obama's Wars*, 183–184. Much of the narrative that follows is drawn from Woodward's book. Peter Lavoy, who attended every session of the strategy review but did not speak to Woodward for his book, described Woodward's book to me as "very accurate." None of the administration's memoirs or my interviews contradict Woodward's narrative except on the issue of the withdrawal timetable. After its publication, White House press secretary Robert Gibbs encouraged the public to read the book and, when repeatedly asked, did not dispute its accuracy. See "Press Gaggle," September 22, 2010, https://oba mawhitehouse.archives.gov/the-press-office/2010/09/22/press-gaggle-press-secretary-ro bert-gibbs-aboard-air-force-one-en-route-.

president, and at greater depth. Lute believed that the fall 2009 review was the deepest and most substantive of the three, likening it to a "graduate seminar." In Obama's recollection, most of his team immediately voiced support for McChrystal's assessment and endorsed his request for 40,000 more troops. "Mike Mullen, the Joint Chiefs, and David Petraeus all endorsed McChrystal's COIN strategy in its entirety; anything less, they argued, was likely to fail and would signal a dangerous lack of American resolve to friends and foes alike," he wrote. "Hillary and Panetta quickly followed suit." Gates did too, overcoming earlier doubts about the wisdom of a large troop presence. "Meanwhile, Joe [Biden] and a sizable number of NSC staffers viewed McChrystal's proposal as just the latest attempt by an unrestrained military to drag the country deeper into a futile, wildly expensive nation-building exercise." (I had left the NSC staff by then.) There was nothing pro forma about the discussions. The Obama administration had awakened to the fact that the war required real attention rather than a ticket-punching campaign exercise – which is what the Riedel review turns out to have been.[2]

The 2009 strategy review resulted in the most consequential decisions of the war. While scholars and historians have typically focused on the surge of 30,000 additional troops, the administration's strategy was not simply to add more troops. Obama rejected the logic that to defeat al-Qaida required defeating the Taliban and made an explicit decision not to seek the Taliban's defeat – but he also chose to escalate the war against them anyway. Instead, Obama adopted a vague goal of "reversing their momentum," while training Afghan security forces. That was muddled enough, but he undermined even those goals by adopting a public withdrawal timetable for US troops and failing to coordinate the surge with reconstruction and diplomatic efforts. Coupled with internal miscommunications, tensions with the military, and a growing attitude of pessimism, the changes introduced in the December 2009 strategy hamstrung the surge and set the course for the rest of Obama's presidency.

DEFEAT THE TALIBAN?

The debate revolved around the central questions of the war: "Do we really need to get to the Taliban to degrade al-Qaida?" Obama asked. Was it necessary to defeat the Taliban to defeat al-Qaida? Was counterinsurgency

---

[2] Lute, interview by author. Obama, *Promised Land*, 433.

against the Taliban the necessary precondition for successful counterterror-ism against al-Qaida? The Obama administration was revisiting questions the Bush administration had first asked in the weeks after 9/11. John Brennan, then serving as Homeland Security Advisor, noted the lack of consensus on "how to define the mission." "How far beyond destroying al-Qaida and terrorist safe havens should that mission go?" he recalled. "It's this issue of nation building. How much the US should invest in really trying to build up an Afghan government ... as opposed to ensuring that those terrorists' hideouts were destroyed, and that al-Qaida couldn't carry out another 9/11-type attack."[3]

Mullen, Petraeus, Gates, and Clinton all believed the answer was yes to each of those questions, to varying degrees, and supported McChrystal's troop request. McChrystal's assessment described the goal as "defeating" the insurgency. "We used the term defeat because that's the word that [Obama] had used," he told me, referring to Obama's speech in 2008 and another in August in which the president had spoken of the insurgency's "defeat." Petraeus had argued back in January, during the first NSC meeting, "you can't just do counterterrorism with drone strikes and infantry raids, you have to do counterinsurgency to stabilize the country," an argument Petraeus repeated throughout the fall review. McChrystal echoed the same line in September. Counterterrorism "doesn't work unless it is enabled by effective counterinsurgency ... they complement each other." Clinton simply stated, "the Taliban are linked to al-Qaida," endorsed the Riedel review's conclu-sions, and argued that no troops guaranteed no progress on either security or governance. Gates agreed that "the Afghan Taliban and al-Qaida had become symbiotic," and thus fighting the Taliban was an essential part of America's war on al-Qaida. Anne Patterson, the US ambassador to Pakistan, argued the groups were "mutually reinforcing." Obama saw the logic. "One of the chief arguments for adopting McChrystal's plan was its similarities to the COIN strategy Petraeus had used during the US surge in Iraq," he wrote. "As a general matter, Petraeus's emphasis on training local forces, improving local governance, and protecting local populations – rather than seizing territory and piling up insurgent body counts – made sense."[4]

Vice President Joe Biden led the other side of the debate. Biden repeat-edly asked what more troops could accomplish if the Afghan government could not or would not improve, and if the Taliban's safe haven in Pakistan

---

[3] Woodward, *Obama's Wars*, 164. Brennan, interview by author.

[4] Woodward, *Obama's Wars*, 80, 190, 191, 202, 203. Obama, *Promised Land*, 437. Gates, *Duty*, 373. See also Panetta and Newton, *Worthy Fights*, 251. McChrystal, interview by author.

remained. For Biden, "the idea of a surge was a nonstarter," Clinton later wrote, because he believed "a large-scale effort at 'nation-building' in a place with little infrastructure or governance was doomed to fail." Brennan noted the military was more optimistic, arguing "I just needed more time, effort, and resources," but "Biden was a strong proponent of reducing the US military presence there and finding an exit ramp out," Brennan recalled, because he was "quite skeptical that the United States was going to be able to really redefine or reshape the Afghan landscape politically, militarily. And [he] was quite skeptical of a lot of the US military assessments that were done." Holbrooke, similarly, highlighted problems with corruption and policing, arguing that no success was possible without progress there. Obama was increasingly persuaded by Biden's skepticism. "With each Sit Room session, it became clearer that the expansive view of COIN that McChrystal imagined for Afghanistan not only went beyond what was needed to destroy al-Qaida," he wrote, "it went beyond what was likely achievable within my term of office, if it was achievable at all."[5]

Biden and his allies chipped away at the other side's insistence that the United States had to "defeat" the Taliban, in part by playing a word game about what "defeat" meant. Back in April, Lute began to draft a strategic implementation plan to turn the Riedel review into actionable steps. As it took shape, Gates argued the plan should say that the goal was to "defeat" the insurgency, but Lute believed that was a broad, ambitious goal that might go beyond what Obama intended, and he sought clarification. To me, it seemed obvious: waging a war and *not* seeking to defeat the enemy made no strategic or moral sense. I wrote a memo for Lute arguing for "defeat" to be kept in. "Troops risking their lives need to be told that their goal is to 'defeat' those trying to kill them," Gates later wrote in his memoir, though he ended up arguing the opposite case in the fall of 2009.[6]

But some in the Obama administration had a cartoonish idea of what "defeat" meant. I got tired of hearing, year after year, that the war in Afghanistan would not end in a surrender ceremony on the deck of a battleship, as if that were a new or particularly insightful observation (Japan formally surrendered to the United States in a ceremony aboard the USS *Missouri* in September 1945, ending World War II). Of course, that was true – it is true for most wars – but that is not the only form that defeat can take. "Defeat is to render a force incapable of achieving its objectives,"

---

[5] Woodward, *Obama's Wars*, 220–221, 226. Brennan, interview by author. Clinton, *Hard Choices*, 138. Obama, *Promised Land*, 437.

[6] Gates, *Duty*, 475.

according to Army doctrine. Defeat "does not mean you wipe out the enemy," McChrystal said. "It means you just prevent them from achieving their mission. If we don't kill any Taliban, but we stop them, all right, we won." His commander's assessment clearly defined defeating the insurgency as "a condition where the insurgency no longer threatens the viability of the state." We might have defeated the Taliban by negotiating an end to their insurgency, or by building the capacity of the Afghan state to the point that the Taliban could no longer compete. There were several possible pathways to rendering the Taliban "incapable of achieving its objective" – its objective being the violent overthrow of the Afghan government. In July, Jones cleared on the language in Lute's document, and McChrystal understood his mission was to "defeat" the Taliban insurgency.[7]

But Biden and his allies raised questions about the United States' ability to defeat the insurgency during the strategy review in September and October. Biden "didn't think that the Taliban could be defeated, and he believed that sending more US troops was a recipe for another bloody quagmire," according to Clinton. Holbrooke pressed McChrystal on what defeat meant. McChrystal replied that it meant to degrade them to the point that they could not take over the country. Some in the room believed that was a significant change, a climb-down from McChrystal's previous stance that they had to defeat the Taliban. It wasn't: McChrystal was simply restating the goal using the Army's definition of "defeat." But those who opposed McChrystal's troop request now used his new language – "degrade" – to argue that he had lowered the goal posts without changing his troop request, casting doubt on how necessary the 40,000 troops really were. Gates, seemingly reversing his position from the summer, furthered the word game, saying the Taliban would continue to be part of Afghan life regardless, that the United States could not "destroy" the Taliban, and that therefore "we need to redefine the goal." He wrote a memo for the president arguing that "the notion of defeating them is probably unrealistic. They're going to be a part of the political fabric going forward." But McChrystal had never argued that the United States should completely wipe out the Taliban or remove them from the fabric of Afghan life, and his troop request was not premised on such an understanding of the mission.[8]

The two sides were talking past each other. When Biden and his allies argued that the US could not "defeat" the Taliban, they were saying, effectively,

---

[7] Army Doctrine Publication 3–0, *Operations*, section 2–10. McChrystal, interview by author. Commander's Assessment, 2–2.

[8] Clinton, *Hard Choices*, 138. Woodward, *Obama's Wars*, 145, 203, 213, 219, 224, 253, 259, 260. Gates, interview by author. Gates, *Duty*, 381.

we cannot kill every last Talib and achieve peace in Afghanistan exclusively through military means. The "Taliban are Afghans from that social fabric," Lavoy argued, and once they regrouped after 2001, "you can't put the genie back in the bottle. I think you could no longer have defeated them." The problem, in his view, is that "the military did not come to grips with that" and did not recognize that the Taliban were "just part of Afghan culture, and you can't expunge that." This was unfair to McChrystal, but it also had no bearing on the debate because it refuted an argument no one made. In Obama's recollection, "John Brennan, the Homeland Security Advisor and future CIA director, reemphasized that unlike al-Qaida in Iraq, the Taliban was too deeply woven into the fabric of Afghan society to be eradicated," as if the military had ever proposed "eradication" as the goal. It's unclear how many had actually read McChrystal's assessment, which had stated quite plainly that "seizing terrain or destroying insurgent forces" was not the point of counterinsurgency; the point was protecting the population.[9]

Nonetheless, Obama used the same language again in summing up the debate, claiming that "the generals conceded that eradicating the Taliban from Afghanistan was unrealistic." It was not a concession so much as a clarification. When McChrystal and his allies said they were going to defeat the Taliban, they meant the United States would render the insurgency incapable of victory by applying the resources of a whole-of-government counterinsurgency. McChrystal and his allies did a poor job explaining that vision, likely in part because they felt it was not their job to speak for the State Department about its role in a counterinsurgency campaign.[10]

COIN VS. CT

There were real stakes to the debate; it was not just a word game. The debate about whether to seek the defeat of the Taliban was also a debate about the relative merits of counterinsurgency versus counterterrorism. The president faced a basic strategic choice between a lean, pared-down counterterrorism mission focused on al-Qaida, or a larger and more ambitious counterinsurgency strategy to beat back the Taliban while improving Afghan governance. If the administration gave up on "defeating" the Taliban, it also undermined a key argument in favor of counterinsurgency. Biden championed counterterrorism, or what he termed "counterterrorism-plus," an option that involved deploying 10,000 special forces for raids on terrorist targets and 10,000 troops

---

[9] Lavoy, interview by author. Obama, 437. [10] Obama, *Promised Land*, 442.

to accelerate training for Afghan forces. Biden's strongest argument was that counterinsurgency depended on having a credible partner in the host nation's government, which he and others believed was not the case in Kabul because of rampant corruption and widespread fraud in the August presidential election.

"Biden seized on a couple substantive points, which frankly he never let go of to this day," Lute recalled, including the lack of "a capable and reliable Afghan government partner," the Taliban's continued safe haven in Pakistan, and "the lack of physical and human capital in the country itself, and institutional capacity." Lute, who agreed with Biden's view and joined him and Eikenberry for discussions on the sidelines of the strategy review, argued that "even if we give McChrystal everything he wants, you're going to have to contend with these underlying factors. And those are going to make this a long shot. Even if you go all in." But Gates felt that Biden's plan had "all the disadvantages of a counterterrorism strategy and not enough capability to reap any of the advantages of a counterinsurgency strategy."[11]

The military largely opposed Biden's option because they believed effective counterterrorism depended on a background of increasing stability and local capacity that counterinsurgency created. McChrystal characterized Biden's proposal as a reprise of the "butcher and bolt strategy that the British had used" along the frontier in the nineteenth century, "I did not believe that would be durable," because al-Qaida and the Taliban would return after the US Army bolted. McChrystal felt the COIN versus CT argument was "squishy" in that it did not recognize the central point. "You're either going to have Afghanistan survive as a nation, or you are not. To me, that was the central point," he explained. "If you're going to have Afghanistan survive as a nation, it's going to need certain stuff," which implied some level of reconstruction and development, "and if you're not, then that's a different proposition entirely." McChrystal argued that counterterrorism operations could disrupt terrorist groups, but "they are not scalable in the absence of underlying infrastructure, intelligence, and physical presence." Gates, despite arguing against "defeating" the Taliban, nonetheless recognized the importance of something broader than just counterterrorism (in this, as in many other debates, trying to have it both ways). Earlier in the summer, he had agreed with McChrystal that "stability in Afghanistan is an imperative," and that "if the Afghan government falls to the Taliban – or has insufficient capability to counter transnational terrorists – Afghanistan could again become a base for terrorism."[12]

---

[11] Lute, interview by author. Gates, *Duty*, 365.
[12] McChrystal, interview by author. Gates, *Duty*, 355.

Clinton sided with the Pentagon in favor of counterinsurgency. "The problem with [Biden's] argument was that if the Taliban continued to seize more of the country, it would be that much harder to conduct effective counterterrorism operations," she wrote. "We wouldn't have the same intelligence networks necessary to locate the terrorists or the bases from which to launch strikes inside or outside Afghanistan. Al-Qaida already had safe havens in Pakistan. If we abandoned large parts of Afghanistan to the Taliban, they would again have safe havens there as well." Two years later, she echoed a similar message to Congress. "I think this debate between COIN and counterterrorism is to some extent unfortunate, because there is no real contradiction between the two insomuch as there is a phasing from one to the other," she told the Senate Foreign Relations Committee. "If we didn't have a significant enough presence we would have one-off CT victories, but we would not change the momentum of the Taliban."[13]

Holbrooke disagreed with his boss. "The parameters of the debate have been defined almost entirely by the military," he wrote in a memo to her in early October. "I do not believe the full political, regional, and global implications of McChrystal's requests have been adequately discussed." Though Holbrooke did not share his doubts more broadly – he did not want to disagree with Clinton in front of others and knew his influence with Obama was low – he was pessimistic. "Holbrooke believed that counterinsurgency would never succeed in Afghanistan," according to his biographer.[14]

Eikenberry gave Biden's argument a major boost on November 6 with a cable from the Embassy in which he outlined his "reservations about a counterinsurgency strategy." Eikenberry had expressed his reservations in a prior session; Biden and others urged him to commit his thoughts to paper to give them more weight. Eikenberry, Deputy Ambassador Frank Ricciardone, "and two aides pulled an all-nighter at the embassy, eating pizza and drinking beer, and constructed a powerful argument against the surge," according to Packer. Eikenberry worried that more US forces would increase Afghan dependency and deepen US involvement in a war "that most agree cannot be won solely by military means" (again refuting an argument no one had made). Counterinsurgency requires an effective host government, but "President Karzai is not an adequate strategic partner," because he "continues to shun responsibility for any sovereign

---

[13] Clinton, *Hard Choices*, 138. Senate Foreign Relations Committee, "Evaluating Progress towards Goals," June 23, 2011, 34.

[14] Packer, *Our Man*, 496.

burden." Beyond Karzai, Eikenberry saw "little to no political will or capacity to carry out basic tasks of governance" elsewhere in the country.[15]

Poor governance, of course, is what Khalilzad, Neumann, and a host of others had been warning about since 2002. Eikenberry took the absence of governance as proof, not of Afghanistan's brokenness, but of the futility of counterinsurgency – an odd argument considering how little aid had been dedicated to improving Afghan governance to that point (though overall aid levels had increased in 2007 and 2008). The Obama administration was under the misapprehension that the Bush administration had launched an ambitious nation-building campaign in 2002 and, after nearly eight years, had nothing to show for it. In fact, they had nothing to show for it because they never launched it in the first place, at least not until 2007.

Somewhat paradoxically, Eikenberry then called for more reconstruction assistance. "Accelerating our work on signature projects to deliver greater access to electricity, water, and education could have a higher payoff in stability over the long term." Eikenberry objected to counterinsurgency but called for more reconstruction, not recognizing that the latter was, properly understood, the civilian component of the former. Eikenberry's cable, which he had not shown McChrystal beforehand, was surprisingly confrontational: the ambassador and the commanding general were openly at odds with each other in official channels. Eikenberry was also at odds with the State Department. Clinton "considered Eikenberry's end runs around official State Department channels as verging on insubordination and wanted him replaced," according to Obama.[16]

Unfortunately, Biden won the debate. The short-term goals of counterterrorism won out over the long-term vision of counterinsurgency. "We've recognized that we're not going to completely defeat the Taliban, which we all agree on," Obama summarized at the October 9 meeting. At the end of the month, he attributed the view to McChrystal. He told Army Chief of Staff George Casey, "What Stan [McChrystal] concluded is in terms of the Taliban, using the word 'defeat' is probably overambitious," which was not an accurate representation of McChrystal's view. Regardless, Gates codified the change in

---

[15] Packer, *Our Man*, 495. Lute, interview by author. KABUL 03572, November 6, 2009, available on the National Security Archive at: https://nsarchive.gwu.edu/document/24 561-u-s-embassy-kabul-cable-3572-subject-coin-strategy-civilian-concerns-november-6-2009.

[16] Obama, *Promised Land*, 437. KABUL 03572, November 6, 2009. McChrystal agreed with the diagnosis of Afghanistan's challenges, but not with the characterization of Karzai nor with Eikenberry's estimation of counterinsurgency. Compare *My Share of the Task*, 355.

a memo on October 30, and Jones repeated it again at an NSC meeting on November 11. "Our goal is to deny the Taliban the ability to threaten to overthrow the Afghan state ... It is not to defeat or destroy the Taliban," he said, and Obama reiterated his agreement. It was a fundamental change in the entire purpose of the war.[17]

Donilon summarized the emerging consensus on November 23. "We are not accepting the argument in this discussion that to defeat al-Qaida means we would have to do a long-term counterinsurgency strategy to defeat the Taliban," he said, arguing that counterinsurgency would take "a trillion dollars and six to eight years." When describing his final decision to his closest advisors on November 29, Obama specified, "this is neither counterinsurgency nor nation building," and that "this represents a strategic modification of what Stan [McChrystal] drew from the Riedel report and the Strategic Implementation Plan." Changing the ends had downstream implications for the ways and means as well, affecting how the administration thought of counterinsurgency and nation building. Despite his first strategy review's recommendations to adopt a counterinsurgency strategy, the conclusion of the second review was "not fully resourced counterinsurgency or nation building, but a narrower approach tied more tightly to the core goal of disrupting, dismantling, and eventually defeating al-Qaida and preventing al-Qaida's return to safe haven in Afghanistan or Pakistan," according to the internal NSC memo codifying the result of the review. Counterterrorism seemed practical, affordable, realistic, and quantifiable, compared to the vague and undefined nature of counterinsurgency.[18]

THE TIMETABLE

Alongside the debate over defeating the Taliban and the merits of counter-insurgency, another issue loomed large: Obama wanted an end point to the war. He disliked the open-ended nature of McChrystal's proposal. "As far as I could tell, there was no clear exit strategy; under McChrystal's plan, it would take five to six years just to get US troop numbers back down to what they were now," he later wrote. Obama felt the war in Afghanistan needed a timeline to reassure Americans, limit American investment, and pressure the Afghans to take responsibility, though he recognized the downsides. "I'm always wrestling with this issue," he said during an October 9 NSC

---

[17] Woodward, *Obama's Wars*, 228, 259, 260, 269–270, 297, 325, 326.

[18] Woodward, *Obama's Wars*, 387.

meeting, according to Woodward. "We don't want our enemy to wait us out, but we also need to show some light at the end of the tunnel."

Obama worried he would lose support at home. "We can't sustain a commitment at home and with allies without having some explanation that involves timelines," he claimed. "How could we ramp up as recommended and have an exit strategy within a reasonable time?" At one point, Obama claimed "I'm not an advocate of the timetable" but said Congress was forcing him into it because "a Democratic Congress would insist on a timetable," a claim for which there is little evidence. "I need an exit strategy," he said on October 26. "I'm not doing 10 years. I'm not doing a long-term nation-building effort. I'm not spending a trillion dollars." On November 11 he insisted, "I'm not going to leave this to my successor . . . A six-to-eight-year war at $50 billion a year is not in the national interest of the United States." Derek Chollet, the assistant secretary of defense of international security affairs, later credited the president for insisting on the withdrawal timetable as "necessary to disciplining the process."[19]

How did Obama's general interest in an end point turn into a specific, public timetable? Because the timetable became one of the most heavily criticized aspects of Obama's strategy, no one has volunteered authorship, and memories differ as to its provenance. Most of the principals opposed an explicit timetable at the time, and most of the Obama administration officials I interviewed later criticized it. Interestingly, despite Biden being the widely recognized leader of the opposition to counterinsurgency, no one points to him as the origin of the timetable. It likely came from Obama himself.

In Woodward's version of events, on November 11, in response to the president's pressure, Gates suggested "we should have a plan that says [in] 18 to 24 months we will begin reducing our forces, thinning them out." Obama records a slightly different version, that "Gates also agreed that we treat any infusion of new troops more as a surge than an open-ended commitment, both by accelerating the pace of their arrival and by setting a timetable of eighteen months for them to start coming home." Obama does not quite claim that Gates proposed the timetable, but that he "agreed" to it. "For me, Gates's acceptance of a timetable was particularly significant. In the past, he'd joined the Joint Chiefs and Petraeus in resisting the idea,

[19] Obama, *Promised Land*, 433. Woodward, *Obama's Wars*, 230, 232, 253, 251, 278, 280. Chollet, *Long Game*, 81. *New York Times* reporter Mark Landler also credits Obama in *Alter Egos*, 68.

claiming that timetables signaled to the enemy that they could wait us out."[20]

Lute also emphasized Gates' responsibility for the timeline. "Gates, and many others who were in that room, including Petraeus and Stan [McChrystal] and others, critiqued the timeline, but never attributed it back to Gates," he said, which he found odd because "it came from Bob Gates." In Lute's recollection, "Obama asked, 'so how will we know this is working?' He was trying to attach a timeline to clear, hold, build, transfer. Gates . . . said, well, for me, Mr. President, if we're not able to do this model in a district center within 18 to 24 months, I will know that we can't do it."[21]

Obama used Gates' comments to claim that the military recommended the timeline. The timeline "was actually on the chart [the Pentagon] briefed to us," Obama claimed. "They identified it as the point when Afghans would be able to take the lead and responsibility in certain areas."[22]

But "I don't think I was the one who suggested it," Gates told me, noting his opposition to the timetable in Iraq. "I always thought timetables just told the enemy how long you had to wait." Gates and the military originally opposed the timetable and did not propose the idea on their own initiative. In his memoir, he implies it was a mix of the president's initiative and the military's response. "The military had been saying that areas cleared of the Taliban would be ready to transition to Afghan government security responsibility within two years," he wrote. "I had opposed any kind of deadlines in Iraq but was supportive of the president's timeline in Afghanistan because I felt some kind of dramatic action was required to get Karzai and the Afghan government to accept ownership of their country's security. I also accepted the military's two-year forecast." To Gates, it was "the president's timeline" and "the military's two-year forecast."[23]

The most likely interpretation is that the timetable came about as an evolution, the product of a negotiation, between Obama and the military, with Gates playing intermediary. Obama asked for some kind of timeline. Gates responded with a timeline for when they should know if the surge was succeeding or not, which Obama then latched onto as a timetable for withdrawal – which is not what the military or Gates intended, but did serve Obama's purposes. Gates recognized political reality. He told the military, "this is just a plain fact of life. If we don't agree to a plan that

---

[20] Woodward, *Obama's Wars*, 271. Obama, *Promised Land*, 442. Jones more or less supported Obama's version in an interview.

[21] Lute, interview by author.   [22] Woodward, *Obama's Wars*, 312.

[23] Gates, interview by author. Gates, *Duty*, 379.

involves [the timetable], we're not going to get any new troops. Obama made that very clear to me." Obama ordered the surge in exchange for the military's support for the timetable, with Gates brokering the compromise. "I think that the timeline was an evolving, an evolutionary process that began with Obama's taking the military statement about two years," he said.[24]

Ben Rhodes, the deputy national security advisor for strategic communications and Obama's chief foreign policy speechwriter, characterized Gates' support of the timetable as "a concession to Obama's view," suggesting that Obama was the chief proponent of the timetable, and Gates only the first and most important convert. The timeline may have been on a slide that Gates and the military eventually briefed, but only after the president spent a month insisting on an option that included some kind of exit strategy or timeline; it was hardly their first choice. The Pentagon supplied the details when asked, but all available evidence suggests the initiative for a timetable came from the president. Obama was skilled at planting ideas and then, when others expressed them, using their words to either claim an emerging consensus or deflect blame from himself.[25]

Regardless, Obama successfully used Gates' comment to fundamentally change the debate. Gates' concession was the first time the Pentagon had attached itself to any kind of timeline. To that point, the debate had been about how much and how quickly to surge; now, for the first time, it was about how long to surge and how quickly to come home. Throughout November, the conversation returned to that theme. On November 23, Gates repeated the idea of beginning to thin out the troop presence in July 2011. Mullen echoed the idea, suggesting "I'll know whether the strategy is working by July 2011," which gave more room for the idea of a timeline. Petraeus argued for a conditions-based drawdown, but his view was losing steam with Obama as Gates was now going along with some kind of time limit.[26]

To that point, however, the discussion was imprecise. Obama had not made explicit his intent to announce in public a timetable with specific dates. Obama held a video teleconference with McChrystal and Eikenberry on November 29 to share his decision. "Among other things, the president seemed to be eliciting my reaction to an announced withdrawal date," McChrystal recalled in his memoir. "Earlier, Secretary Gates had asked what I thought about the idea. I cited concerns that it would give the Taliban a sense that if they survived until that date, they could prevail, and that it might decrease

---

[24] Gates, interview by author.

[25] Lute, interview by author. Rhodes, *The World As It Is*, 76.

[26] Woodward, *Obama's Wars*, 292–293, 299, 294.

confidence in the strategic partnership we were trying to build on so many levels with the Afghans," concerns many others had raised. "But," McChrystal continued, diplomatically repeating the president's arguments, "I also knew it would provide a clear impetus for Afghans to speed up efforts to assume full responsibility for their future." He judged the downsides were an "acceptable risk" and concluded, "if I'd felt like the decision to set a withdrawal date would have been fatal to the success of our mission, I'd have said so." The next week, he told Congress that he was "comfortable with the [president's] entire plan." In hindsight, this seems a good example of when the military's inveterate optimism proved self-defeating.[27]

Petraeus claimed that when Obama communicated his final decision in an Oval Office meeting on November 30, the inclusion of a specific and public withdrawal timetable was "a stunner." "The truth is that it was such a surprise that it caught me, and I think Mullen and maybe Gates as well, completely off balance," he said. "Otherwise, we would've said: 'Wait a sec, time out.' But it was essentially a take it or leave it moment. And we took it." It probably did not take Gates off guard, given the repeated conversations about an end point during the strategy review. That Petraeus was surprised during the Oval Office meeting shows that Obama had not made clear that his repeated insistence on an end point would translate into an operation-ally specific limitation committed to paper, included in the president's orders, and announced in public as part of the surge decision. Petraeus not only disagreed that the military came up with the timeline; he denies it was ever discussed during the strategy review at all. The timetable "was never discussed in any of the nine or so actual NSC meetings, neither the ones that chaired by President Obama, nor in any of the Principals Committee meetings," he told me. Lavoy agreed that the timetable was "done behind closed doors" and believed it came from either Obama or Tom Donilon.[28] Other staffers involved in the review confirmed that the specific timetable and its public nature were not organic to the process but were introduced at the very end and announced as a *fait accompli*.[29]

Obama publicly defended the timetable as a necessary concession to reality and a tactic to compel the Afghan government to take responsibility

---

[27] McChrystal, *My Share of the Task*, 357. Senate Armed Services Committee, "Afghanistan," December 2 and 8, 2009, 118.

[28] Petraeus and Lavoy, interviews by author. Petraeus made the same claim in his SIGAR interview.

[29] Petraeus, interview by author and SIGAR interview. Woodward claims that Biden had called Petraeus days before the Oval Office meeting and asked if he'd support a timeline

for security and tackle corruption. In his speech announcing the surge and withdrawal, Obama claimed that the alternative to a timetable was an "open-ended escalation of our war effort – one that would commit us to a nation-building project of up to a decade," which was not a fair characterization of McChrystal's original proposal. "I reject this course," Obama said, "because it sets goals that are beyond what can be achieved at a reasonable cost, and what we need to achieve to secure our interests."

Obama also claimed the timetable would make it "clear to the Afghan government – and, more importantly, to the Afghan people – that they will ultimately be responsible for their own country." He acknowledged that some critics opposed setting a deadline but countered, "the absence of a timeframe for transition would deny us any sense of urgency in working with the Afghan government ... America has no interest in fighting an endless war in Afghanistan." Gates later wrote that he "was supportive of the president's timeline in Afghanistan because I felt some kind of dramatic action was required to get Karzai and the Afghan government to accept ownership of their country's security ... The deadline put the Afghan government and security forces on notice that they had to step up their game, for their own survival if nothing else."[30]

Despite agreeing that he could live with the timetable, McChrystal was torn. Days after Obama's announcement, in testimony to Congress, after dutifully repeating the administration's talking points, he told them that the timetable was an "information operations challenge," because the Taliban "will try to paint this in a particular picture" and "use it for propaganda purposes." Years later, he said it was "another one of those things that signaled the lack of resolve, the tentative nature [of the US presence] and a complete misunderstanding of our opponent." He felt the decision was "tragically wrong," though not the single factor that led inevitably to failure in Afghanistan. McChrystal stressed that failure was the result of "a combination of factors," of which the timetable was one.[31]

McChrystal's skepticism was widely shared in the administration. "Everyone around the table recognized that there were real pros and cons

to begin a drawdown, to which Petraeus reluctantly agreed. But Petraeus does not recall the conversation and disputes that such a call would have taken place. "Frankly, I cannot imagine the VPOTUS calling me directly," rather than going through the chairman of the joint chiefs or the secretary of defense.

[30] Obama, "The New Way Forward," December 1, 2009. Gates, *Duty*, 379.

[31] McChrystal, interview by author. "Afghanistan," Senate Armed Services Committee, December 2 and 8, 2009, 118. House Foreign Affairs Committee, "US Strategy in Afghanistan," 104.

to putting out any specific dates for reduction in forces," Brennan said. In addition to the effect it would have on the Afghans, "it was also intended to send a strong signal to the Pentagon that [they can't] keep coming back to the well. That there is going to be a sunset on this operation," Brennan said. "[Obama] wanted to set some timelines to really instill in them a seriousness of purpose that he thought was lacking." Clinton, similarly, saw some logic to it. "I shared the President's reluctance about an open-ended commitment without any conditions and expectations," she wrote. "Planning for that transition, and getting the buy-in of the international community, would have to be a priority going forward."[32]

Domestic political considerations also played a part. Obama felt compelled to begin talking about withdrawal because he was worried about the political sustainability of the war. Derek Chollet wrote that the president understood the risks of the withdrawal timetable "yet believed that such clarity was needed to sustain public support for the mission." Obama worried in meetings that "I can't let this be a war without end, and I can't lose all the Democratic Party," according to Woodward's account. "And people at home don't want to hear we're going to be there for ten years." Gates believed that "the American people aren't going to tolerate being there more than five years" and later argued in his memoir that "with the deadlines Obama politically bought our military – and civilians – five more years to achieve our mission in Afghanistan." Jones told me that the timetable "was probably inserted for political reasons to make sure that the Congress didn't react too adversely, because the President's own party was not really happy." One senior military officer thought it was obvious. "Now I'm not a domestic political expert, but even a blind man on a dark night can see that that is because of domestic political reasons," he said. "He's taking a decision that will be unpopular with his base. He's going to run for reelection in 2012, so he wants to be sure the base understands his sensitivity to their desire not to do this forever."[33]

Other officials worried that the withdrawal would risk undermining the United States' political and military gains in the war. Clinton, though she supported the idea of a timetable in principle, later wrote that "this was a starker deadline than I had hoped for, and I worried that it might send the wrong signal to friend and foe alike." She also disliked its public nature: "I

---

[32] Brennan, interview by author. Clinton, *Hard Choices*, 147.

[33] Chollet, *Long Game*, 73. Woodward, *Obama's Wars*, 336, 230. See also Mann, *Obamians*, 127 for Vice President Biden's concerns about the Democratic Party. Jones, interview by author.

thought there was benefit in playing our cards closer to our chests." Vikram Singh, an advisor in the Defense Department who later served as deputy special representative for Afghanistan and Pakistan, thought the surge and timetable were "the worst of all worlds. You're surging, but you're announcing that: 'All you guys have to do is to chill out for 18 months until the surge is over.'" Brennan agreed. "Obviously the cons were quite notable. I don't like giving timelines," he said. "I much prefer to have it based on conditions on the ground, but I think that Obama and Biden and others felt that the military was not giving them a fair rendering of the conditions on the ground."[34]

The timetable was controversial. Senator John McCain, who had lost the presidential election to Obama the year before, strongly supported the surge in Afghanistan. But he added:

> What I don't support and what concerns me greatly is the President's decision to set an arbitrary date to begin withdrawing US forces from Afghanistan. A date for withdrawal sends exactly the wrong message to both our friends and our enemies in Afghanistan, Pakistan, and the entire region, all of whom currently doubt whether America is committed to winning this war. A withdrawal date only emboldens al-Qaida and the Taliban, while dispiriting our Afghan partners and making it less likely that they will risk their lives to take our side in this fight.[35]

Policymakers and military officials struggled to explain or defend the timetable in public, torn between publicly supporting the president's decision and voicing their own doubts. Congress grilled Gates, Clinton, and Mullen immediately after Obama's speech. Gates emphasized the timetable was the beginning of a transition. "But, is that date conditions-based, or not?" Senator Carl Levin, chairman of the Senate Foreign Relations Committee, asked. "No, sir," Gates replied. Gates and Mullen tried to soften the line, insisting that the process of transferring responsibility to the Afghans after July 2011 would be "based on conditions on the ground," a distinction likely lost on the Senate, the Afghans, and the Taliban. Senator David Vitter, a Republican from Louisiana, asked Gates the obvious question: "Do you believe that a timetable for withdrawal is consistent with a commitment to victory in Afghanistan?" Gates dodged, reciting the administration's reasoning that the timetable was necessary to signal that "the US military is not going to be there forever."[36]

---

[34] Hillary Clinton, *Hard Choices*, 148. Brennan, Singh, interviews by author.

[35] Senate Armed Services Committee, "Afghanistan," December 2 and 8, 2009, 4.

[36] Senate Armed Services Committee, "Afghanistan," December 2 and 8, 2009, 21, 97.

The following June, Petraeus told the House Armed Services Committee that both the start date and the rate of withdrawal should be based on "conditions on the ground," which is not exactly what Gates had said, and that the timetable should be flexible. "It's important that July 2011 be seen for what it is, the date when a process begins based on conditions, not the date when the US heads for the exits," he said, which reflected Petraeus' views more than Obama's. He told the Senate, "I support the policy of the president," including the "message of urgency" that the July timetable communicated, but added that it was the "beginning of a process" that would be "conditions-based," which again bordered on freelancing his own foreign policy. The collective worries about the possible downsides to the timetable would prove prescient. It was among the most consequential decisions of the entire war.[37]

WHITE HOUSE VS. PENTAGON

There was a consistent undercurrent of tension between the White House and the Pentagon during the fall 2009 strategy review. On each issue – whether to "defeat" the Taliban, on the merits of counterinsurgency versus counterterrorism, and on the merits of a timetable – the civilian leadership was at odds with the military, and the civilian leadership consistently imposed its view. But the tension predated the strategy review, having built steadily from the first days of the administration, and created an atmosphere of mistrust, even acrimony. Sometimes the clash of rival views can clarify options, sharpen the debate, and result in a clearer decision. "Having at least one contrarian in the room made us all think harder about the issues," Obama wrote, referring to Biden's role as the designated skeptic. But it is also possible that a clash of views can be too fundamental, that it can poison relationships that hadn't yet had time to form. Too much disagreement can ultimately undermine, rather than support, a clear debate and a sound decision.[38]

The mistrust started within a day of the Obama administration taking office when Biden pushed back on McKiernan's long-delayed troop request. But the strife worsened dramatically over the summer. The Obama

---

[37] House Armed Services Committee, "Developments in Afghanistan," June 16, 2010, 15. Senate Armed Services Committee, "The Situation in Afghanistan," June 15 and 16, 2010, 22–23.

[38] Obama, *Promised Land*, 319.

administration viewed its approval of the Riedel review and McKiernan's troop request as fulfilling its pledge to refocus on Afghanistan. But as word came back from the field that McChrystal would likely ask for more troops, Obama felt betrayed. "It was tough not to feel as if I'd been subjected to a bait and switch," he wrote, suggesting that "that the Pentagon's acquiescence to my more modest initial increase of seventeen thousand troops and four thousand military trainers had been merely a temporary, tactical retreat on the path to getting more." It was another unfair accusation: McKiernan, Mullen, and the other supporters of the initial troop request had never sold it as the final resource package for Obama's new strategy – the troop request predated Riedel's strategy by at least six months – but only as an emergency stopgap to prevent catastrophic failure during the 2009 fighting season and to secure the Afghan presidential election. Gates' assurance to the president earlier in the year that he would not ask for more troops had been a misjudgment unfounded in any strategic assessment that now fed acrimony and mistrust between the White House and the Pentagon. "The potshotting and rumormongering by late summer created a volatile atmosphere for considering McChrystal's report," Gates wrote.[39]

Ideally, the president might have called in McChrystal, Gates, and his top advisors to try to clear the air – which is what the fall strategy review should have done. Unfortunately, the McChrystal report leaked to the press in late September. The White House immediately concluded the Pentagon leaked the report to create public pressure on the president to approve McChrystal's strategy. "With the leaking of that assessment, there really was a change in atmosphere or a change in tone at the White House," Lute recalled, "because there was this impression that the military was trying to box the President in by leaking this report." The assumption came naturally to the White House, Lute felt, because "they reverted to their experience base and their experience base was the campaign world," in which leaks and counterleaks are a normal part of the fight. The leak of McChrystal's assessment seemed to confirm the White House's worst suspicions of the military, which had been building since the first debates over McKiernan's troop request in January. It "flavored the rest of the Obama administration in terms of doubt and skepticism and suspicions" between the White House and the Pentagon, and the White House "felt jammed, or boxed in," Lute said. As for the military leadership, Obama felt that "despite their patience and good manners, they had trouble hiding their frustration at having their

---

[39] Obama, *Promised Land*, 433. Gates, *Duty*, 350.

professional judgments challenged, especially by those who'd never put on a uniform."[40]

Just as the White House was absorbing the shock from both McChrystal's request and its subsequent leak, McChrystal gave a public speech at the International Institute of Strategic Studies in London on October 1 describing and defending his recommended strategy. In response to a reporter's question about whether a limited, counterterrorism-only mission would be sufficient – the option Biden had been championing – McChrystal flatly said no. Petraeus made similar comments to the *Washington Post*, and Mullen testified to the same effect before Congress around the same time. The White House interpreted the public remarks, together with the leaked report, as a deliberate effort by the military to weigh in on the public debate over the administration's war plans – which, if true, would be tantamount to insubordination, a dangerous politicization of the military, and a threat to civilian control of the armed forces.

"Rahm [Emanuel, White House Chief of Staff,] remarked that in all his years in Washington, he'd never seen such an orchestrated, public campaign by the Pentagon to box in a president," Obama wrote. He shared Emanuel's suspicion. "I agreed ... I felt as if an entire agency under my charge was working its own agenda." Gates felt that "a wall was going up between the military and the White House," and the atmosphere was growing "poisonous." Woodward captured the feeling inside the White House in October. "Facing an unexpected and stunning strategic request was not where Obama had planned to be in the fall of the first year of his presidency," he wrote. "On top of that, the military was out campaigning, closing off his choices, and the White House was losing control of the public narrative." In Obama's recollection, "Biden was more succinct: 'It's fucking outrageous.'"[41]

Obama demanded that Gates rein in the military and voiced his suspicions about their motives. "Is it a lack of respect for me?" he asked, in Gates' recollection. "Do they resent that I never served in the military? Do they think because I'm young that I don't see what they're doing?" Interestingly, none of the participants in their interviews or memoirs mentions another dynamic that surely added a shade of tension, though Obama's questions hint at it. Gates, Mullen, Petraeus, and McChrystal were all experienced, credentialed, older white men confronting the nation's first African American president, who was much younger and had no experience in

[40] Lute, interview by author. Obama, *Promised Land*, 437.
[41] Woodward, *Obama's Wars*, 195. Gates, *Duty*, 369. Obama, *Promised Land*, 434.

national security affairs. The military risked coming off as an old white boys' club closing ranks to exclude the outsider. For his part, if Obama allowed the perceived challenge to go unchecked, he risked being seen as overly subservient and unwilling to stand up for himself, a proverbial Uncle Tom. The racial dynamics, though never openly acknowledged, almost certainly affected how each party calculated the public perception of their actions.[42]

Obama later acknowledged that his White House overreacted. "Looking back, I'm inclined to believe Gates when he said there was no coordinated plan by Mullen, Petraeus, or McChrystal to force my hand," he wrote. "They considered it to be part of their code as military officers to provide their honest assessment in public testimony or press statements without regard to political consequences." That is how McChrystal defended his speech and his remarks to the press. "I was a commander focused on explaining the mission I understood I'd been given and the strategy currently being prosecuted," he said, acknowledging that he "could have said it better" and that he had not fully realized that the strategy review was not just reviewing his assessment but was "reevaluating the mission itself." Mullen, for his part, was giving sworn testimony to Congress and was legally and ethically bound to answer truthfully when asked for his assessment. Lute exonerated most of the military leadership. "I don't think there's a conspiratorial or political bone in Stan McChrystal's body," he said. As for leaking the assessment: "That's not Mike Mullen. That's not really Bob Gates" – that is, not their way of doing business, he believed.[43]

But again, the damage had been done. After almost a year of repeated stumbles and cross talk between the White House and the Pentagon, the strategy review was bound to become a focal point of tension. "As much as any specific differences over strategy or tactics, such fundamental issues – the civilian control of policy making, the respective roles of the president and his military advisors in our constitutional system, and the considerations each brought to bear in deciding about war – became the subtext of the Afghan debate," Obama wrote. His decisions about counterinsurgency, the timetable, and whether or not to seek the defeat of the Taliban were driven by his political concerns and his and Biden's suspicion and mistrust of the military – a suspicion that was founded on a series of misunderstandings, miscommunications, and distortions that came from their lack of military

---

[42] Gates, *Duty*, 368. See Obama, *Promised Land*, 319, for his observation about the racial makeup of the senior military leadership.

[43] Obama, *Promised Land*, 435, 442. McChrystal, *My Share of the Task*, 349, 350. Lute, interview by author.

experience and Biden's jaundiced, Vietnam-era view of the war – concerns which Obama allowed to trump the strategy he had approved just months previously. Obama openly told Gates that "my poll numbers will be stronger if I take issue with the military over Afghanistan policy."[44]

Lavoy recalled a later comment from Obama that he felt captured Obama's mindset toward the military during the review. In 2015, Obama reversed course and decided not to complete the withdrawal from Afghanistan (see Chapter 12). He felt comfortable doing so because, Lavoy recalls Obama saying, "I feel that we finally cured the fever." The "fever" was the military's desire to "keep the war machine going unabated," which Obama had cured by insisting on constraints in 2009. Lavoy thought the comment "revealed [Obama's] thinking all along, [which] was that 'I've got to constrain the military machine, otherwise it's just going to be out of control. It's going to be Vietnam, it's just going to run forever.'" Obama "didn't want to enable the war machine to go on in perpetuity unconstrained." Lavoy shared Obama's view. "The military to this day would still be trying to defeat the Taliban if they could," he believed. "I do think those constraints were important because I don't think that a war of attrition would've been possible to be successful. I think it was doomed to failure."[45]

Obama's eagerness to assert control over the military was one more buttress in his arguments against counterinsurgency and in favor of the timetable and a more limited mission. Contrary to later critics who suggested the president got "rolled" by the military, Obama used the Afghanistan review as an opportunity to demonstrate his authority. The military had asked for 40,000 troops with no deadline to wage counterinsurgency and defeat the Taliban. Obama gave them 30,000 under a tight deadline to wage a partial counterinsurgency not to defeat the Taliban, but to reverse their momentum. Doing so required Obama to reject all options that were on the table and craft a new one for himself. "He personally had to help design a new option," Woodward reported. Each feature of Obama's new strategy that departed from the military's recommendation bore his personal stamp and prevailed against the advice of most of the military leadership and even strained against Clinton's and Gates' inclinations. "I was more involved in that process than it was probably typical," he told Woodward.[46]

Obama, as commander in chief, was well within his rights to do so. As strategists and scholars of civil–military relations never tire of reminding us,

[44] Obama, *Promised Land*, 436, 437. Gates, *Duty*, 378.   [45] Lavoy, interview by author.
[46] Woodward, *Obama's Wars*, 279. See also 280–281.

the president's control of the military is essential to preserving a democratic, civilian government accountable to the people. George Washington's resignation as commander of the Continental Army in 1783 and Harry Truman's firing of General Douglas MacArthur in 1951 are among the most celebrated milestones solidifying this crucial democratic norm in American history. Obama describes his assertion of authority in the same vein: he claimed in his memoir that the review process and his decision to override the military's advice put "an end to Pentagon freelancing for the duration of my presidency" and "helped reaffirm the larger principle of civilian control over America's national security policy making."[47]

Obama's claim is odd considering that, in the same memoir, he concluded that the military was not, in fact, challenging his control of foreign policy – there was no "coordinated plan" to "force his hand." Nonetheless, Obama invoked the specter of military insubordination to justify overruling their recommendations. The president's right to override the military is not the same as the wisdom of doing so, especially if the military was not actually challenging the president's authority. In critiquing the Bush administration, Obama had commented on how the public "*rightly* saw the military as more competent and trustworthy than the civilians who were supposed to make policy." Obama recognized that the military was often better trained and educated to think strategically, to understand how the levers of foreign policy and national security move and operate. Yet when it came to his own administration, he saw no reason to defer to their expertise, instead inflating a nonexistent threat to civilian–military relations to justify his decision to ignore their counsel. Obama dismissed as an illusion the notion that the military was scheming to control his foreign policy, then claimed credit for having vanquished it anyway. He ignored the military's advice and put in place a flawed strategy to defend the principle of civilian control – which had never been endangered in the first place.[48]

THE DECISION

Obama came to a decision and announced it in a speech at West Point on December 1. He rehearsed the *casus belli* of the war, defending its importance and legitimacy. "The Taliban has maintained common cause with al-Qaida, as they both seek an overthrow of the Afghan government," he said, echoing the same language he and Bush had consistently used for the past

---

[47] Obama, *Promised Land*, 444. [48] Obama, *Promised Land*, 436. Emphasis added.

eight years. "I am convinced that our security is at stake in Afghanistan and Pakistan." He defended his initial strategy and described the surge as an extension or continuation of it because "the Taliban has gained momentum" and "our forces lack the full support they need to effectively train and partner with Afghan security forces and better secure the population."[49]

Obama avoided acknowledging too explicitly the key differences between the Riedel review and the new strategy that underlay the surge – that the United States would no longer seek the defeat of the Taliban nor mount a full counterinsurgency campaign. Instead, Obama focused on troop numbers and the timetable – 30,000 more troops and an 18-month timeframe. He came close to acknowledging the difference by how he characterized the purpose of the surge: "We must reverse the Taliban's momentum and deny it the ability to overthrow the government." The climbdown from his July 2008 speech – "This is a war that we have to win" – was remarkable, but only to those few who remembered it. Obama also promised a "more effective civilian strategy" to hold the Afghan government accountable for honesty and good performance and emphasized the regional nature of the threat, crossing the border into Pakistan. Neither the strategy review nor the speech addressed negotiations or reconciliation with the Taliban.

"We landed on a set of achievable objectives," he later wrote, which included "reducing the level of Taliban activity," pushing Karzai to reform key ministries rather than "revamp the entire government," and accelerating training of Afghan security forces. He claimed that "the hours of debate had made for a better plan" because "it forced us to refine America's strategic objectives in Afghanistan in a way that prevented mission creep," avoiding the danger, apparently, that the mission might creep to include the defeat of the enemy. He also claimed that the process "established the utility of timetables for troop deployments in certain circumstances" – which it had not done – "something that had been long contested by the Washington national security establishment." The process had established, not the utility of a timetable, but the president's insistence on adopting one anyway.[50]

Ultimately, the president settled on a strange strategy. He attempted to forge a compromise between counterinsurgency and counterterrorism, between McChrystal's request for 40,000 troops and Biden's option of 20,000. Obama ordered a surge of 30,000 troops – more than required for

49 Obama, "Remarks by the President in Address to the Nation on the Way Forward in Afghanistan and Pakistan," December 1, 2009.
50 Obama, *Promised Land*, 442, 444.

a narrow counterterrorism operation, but fewer than required for a counterinsurgency campaign – and a diplomatic push to ask NATO to contribute another 10,000. He changed the mission from defeating the Taliban to reversing their momentum. Against the counsel of most of his advisors, he put a timetable on the troop deployment and publicly announced it in advance. "I have determined that it is in our vital national interest to send an additional 30,000 US troops to Afghanistan," he announced in his speech. "After 18 months, our troops will begin to come home."

In effect, he personally designed a version of counterinsurgency-lite, underresourced in both troops and time. And because Obama decided against fully resourced counterinsurgency, he also backed off his commitment to promoting accountable and effective government in Afghanistan. While he continued publicly to argue that improved governance was important to the overall mission, privately the administration settled for investing only in the ministries of defense and interior and a few others, a move with major long-term consequences. Civilian aid to Afghanistan decreased every year after 2010. By eschewing investments in Afghan governance and reducing civilian aid while still deploying 100,000 troops, Obama abandoned any vision of a political end state that would allow the United States to disengage with its interests intact or that would yield peace or justice in Afghanistan.

Obama faced a classic conundrum, juggling the demands of politics against strategy. "Compromise between opposing preferences is the key to success in politics but to failure in military strategy," according to Columbia University political scientist Richard Betts. "Political leaders have the last word on strategy in a democracy, so they tend to resolve political debates about whether to use force massively or not at all by choosing military half-measures, which serve no strategic objectives at all." Betts wrote those words in 2000, almost a decade before Obama's strategy review, but they were strikingly prescient as a description of the Obama administration's deliberations in the fall of 2009. There was a clear logic to both McChrystal's proposal for counterinsurgency and Biden's proposal for counterterrorism. Both could describe how to harness specific ways and means to achieve given ends, and both could defend their whole package as a worthwhile investment given their understanding of America's interests. Obama's compromise, by contrast, in trying to capture the logic of each, vitiated both. Vikram Singh quipped that the strategy was "the 'reverse Goldilocks' – not cold enough, not hot enough, just wrong."

Obama ended up with a Frankenstein strategy pieced together from different options that had little inner logic of its own.[51]

Obama denied that was the case. "There was a logic to it that went beyond simply splitting the difference between McChrystal's plan and the option Biden had worked up," he wrote in his memoir. He justified the compromise as a balance between short-term and long-term views. "In the short term, [the decision] gave McChrystal the firepower he needed to reverse the Taliban's momentum, protect population centers, and train up Afghan forces. But it set clear limits to COIN and put us firmly on the path of a narrower CT approach two years out." That has the clarity and reasonableness of an *ex post facto* rationalization. The logic of counterinsurgency demanded time, which Obama's timetable denied; the logic of counterterrorism demanded efficiency, which Obama's surge undid. The short-term–long-term framing Obama adopted did not account for how time and cost affected the logic of each approach. Obama ended up with the most expensive and unwieldy version of a counterterrorism strategy possible – or, from another angle, the most anemic and poorly conceived counterinsurgency strategy imaginable.[52]

Ironically, several participants looked back on the strategy review as an exceptionally good process. Jones, in charge of the process as national security advisor, described how "we spent a lot of time bringing everybody up to speed so that everybody had a good sight picture of what was going on." His deputy, Tom Donilon, "thought it was one of the rare examples in recent American history where a president had fully understood the contours of a national security decision," and that it was a "model for presidential decision making." Brennan praised the "exceptionally thorough, detailed, extensive" process that involved "endless meetings where there was a really rigorous discussion." Panetta, similarly, felt there was "a real discipline about the process" in Obama's White House. Gates recalled, "in my entire career, I cannot think of any single issue or problem that absorbed so much of the president's and the principals' time and effort in such a compressed period."[53]

The process was exhausting, but it was not exhaustive. It focused almost exclusively on military options and troop levels and – as became apparent the following year – included no discussion about reconciliation or negotiations with the Taliban and only a vague, underdeveloped idea for a civilian

---

[51] Betts, "Is Strategy an Illusion?" 43. Singh, interview by author.

[52] Obama, *Promised Land*, 442.

[53] Woodward, *Obama's Wars*, 343, 344. Jones, interview by author. Brennan, interview by author. Gates, *Duty*, 370.

surge, both of which should have been crucial diplomatic and political counterparts to the military surge. "The only variable in the courses of action considered in the fall of 2009 were all military variables," Lute recalled. "And I think one course of action that we should have developed and tabled and debated seriously was one that put much more reliance on the politics of the situation." Gates, too, noted that the review paid inadequate attention to "the broad challenge of getting the political and civilian part of the equation right" and felt that "all of us at the senior-most level did not serve the president well in this process." Worse, the strategy review had not been driven by strategic considerations. "I felt this major national security debate had been driven more by the White House staff and by domestic politics than any other in my entire experience," Gates later wrote. "The president's political operatives wanted to make sure that everyone knew the Pentagon wouldn't get its way."[54]

The fall 2009 strategy review did not help (and may have actively hurt) the tension between the White House and the Pentagon; it obscured more than clarified the debate over whether to "defeat" the Taliban; it enabled a muddled compromise between counterterrorism and counterinsurgency with no consistent strategic logic; and it gave political cover for the president's insistence on a timetable about which virtually everyone had misgivings.

DEFEATISM

There is a consistent theme to the Obama administration's decisions coming out of the strategy review: the United States should do less and lower its ambitions. Obama and his team believed that the United States had been too ambitious, too aspirational in what it was trying to achieve in Afghanistan; that its lofty goals were impractical, too expensive, and unnecessary. A year earlier, Gates had been worried that American goals were "too ambitious for us to achieve," a message he repeated throughout 2009. Instead of its lofty goals, the United States needed to focus on "creating an Afghan government that could prevent al-Qaida and others from once again attacking us from a safe haven in Afghanistan and leave more ambitious governance and development goals for the long term." During the fall strategy review, Gates argued that the United States should "quietly shelve trying to develop a strong, effective central government." He felt that

---

[54] Lute, interview by author. Gates, *Duty*, 370, 384.

"one positive result" of the strategy review was that it led to "a steady narrowing of our objectives."[55]

Gates persuaded Obama. The new strategy "is not as much as it takes for as long as it takes," Obama reportedly said of his decision in late 2009. "We are going to have a turning point here and it's going to be July of 2011." Obama felt it was important to set limits, to guard against a spirit of crusading, and to balance the needs of the war against domestic priorities. "To insist that our safety and our standing in the world required us to do all that we could for as long as we could in every single instance, was an abdication of moral responsibility," he reflected in his memoir, and "the certainty it offered [was] a comforting lie." Obama was articulating an important, if obvious, truth: that some battles are unnecessary, some victories Pyrrhic. But it was a strange critique of a war that Obama himself had routinely, and rightly, criticized for being ignored and underresourced. It is hard to understand how the war in Afghanistan was an example of excessive ambition when, as recently as December 2007, it had been the war of "do what we can" while Iraq commanded the priority of attention and resources. If there was a small window during which hope rose for Afghanistan in late 2008 and early 2009, it was due largely to Obama's justified critique that Afghanistan had been overshadowed and to his promise to refocus attention there, which hardly amounted to utopian aspirations.[56]

That aside, Obama was again refuting an argument no one had made – that the United States should "do all that we could for as long as we could in every single instance." Obama (like Rumsfeld) seemed incapable of engaging with the best version of his critics' arguments. The opposing argument was not that the United States should do everything, but that we should do counterinsurgency; not in every instance, but in this one. It was the argument that five consecutive strategy reviews and assessments from two different administrations had made – Accelerating Success in 2003, the 2006 review, the 2008 Lute review, the 2009 Riedel review, and the 2009 McChrystal assessment – and which both administrations managed to not fully implement. Obama defended the limits he put on the mission as cost-conscious prudence. "Our mission had to be defined not only by the need to defeat an enemy, but by the need to make sure the country wasn't bled dry in the process," he wrote. It was another odd warning: Afghanistan was one of the smaller wars in American history. Afghanistan at the height of the surge took up less than 3 percent of the federal budget, less than one-tenth

[55] Gates, *Duty*, 278, 374, 569.
[56] Woodward, *Obama's Wars*, 321. Obama, *Promised Land*, 439.

of 1 percent of US GDP. As many US troops died in twenty years in Afghanistan as died in four or five months in Vietnam at its height, which is not to make light of the loss of life but to insist on historical perspective. The war never came close to "bleeding America dry," nor would it have with the larger investment the military had called for.[57]

Obama's expectations were so low, in fact, that he may not have even believed the surge would work. "There was so much buyer's remorse, I thought, in the White House," McChrystal felt, "so much hesitancy about the mission." In his assessment, McChrystal had described the "crisis of confidence" surrounding the war; now, he felt, the administration was "unintentionally [making] it worse." Obama's hesitancy was widely understood within the administration. Obama "did not really believe the strategy he had approved would work," Gates later wrote. "I think he was willing to give this a try," Lute said, "but he suspected that it was gonna be a heavy lift." "President Obama was not convinced that the surge was going to produce the results that were hoped for," Brennan believed, "but I think he was convinced that in light of what had already occurred in Afghanistan, and the commitment that we made, it was worth the effort to see whether or not it was going to produce desired results." Eikenberry believed that for Obama, "there was always a big skepticism there" toward counterinsurgency, as if Obama were communicating "You've got until June 2011 to prove that your counterinsurgency strategy works. I'll give you the resources and a bit of time, but I'm skeptical . . . What I remain really interested in is counterterrorism."[58]

There is a more cynical version of this critique: Obama knew the strategy would fail but ordered it anyway out of political convenience. In Woodward's version, "Obama had to do this 18-month surge just to demonstrate, in effect, that it couldn't be done." George Packer, Holbrooke's biographer, concurred. "The uncharitable view was that his objective was to demonstrate failure and get Afghanistan behind him." If they are right, Obama ordered the surge and sent troops to fight and die in a war he did not believe in. He believed in Biden's counterterrorism strategy and only accepted a time-limited version of counterinsurgency that he could reframe as a temporary bridge to get to his actual preference.[59]

McChrystal and Gates, for their part, do not buy the more cynical version. While McChrystal understood Obama had doubts, "I don't accuse

---

57 Obama, *Promised Land*, 437.

58 McChrystal, interview by author. Gates, *Duty*, 483. Lute, interview by author. Brennan, interview by author. Eikenberry, interview by author.

59 Woodward, *Obama's Wars*, 338. Brennan, interview by author. Packer, *Our Man*, 499.

him of being duplicitous or being intentional that way," he said, "I think he reluctantly did it, but I think he sort of in the back of his mind thought it wouldn't work." Gates, similarly, credits Obama's good faith. "I totally do not believe that he agreed to the surge to prove failure. He's not that cynical," he said. "I do think that he lacked confidence that the strategy would actually work, but he was willing to give it a shot." McChrystal reserved his cynicism for Obama's political advisors. "I think that there were people around him who were more cynical about it and wanted to give the military just enough rope to hang themselves."[60]

Just over a week later, on December 10, Obama mused at length on the "imperatives of a just peace" while accepting the Nobel Peace Prize in Oslo, Norway. "Peace is not merely the absence of visible conflict," he argued. "Only a just peace based on the inherent rights and dignity of every individual can truly be lasting." Obama rightly recognized the close connection between peace and justice: either one without the other was only a partial version of itself. True peace and true justice are components of each other and must point toward a broader vision of flourishing. "A just peace includes not only civil and political rights – it must encompass economic security and opportunity. For true peace is not just freedom from fear, but freedom from want." Obama called on the world never to lose sight of that vision of flourishing, even in the face of the most intractable difficulties. "Let us reach for the world that ought to be," he said. Even as we cultivate a realistic appreciation of the world's perennial ills, we never stop working for something better. "We can acknowledge that oppression will always be with us, and still strive for justice," he concluded. "Clear-eyed, we can understand that there will be war, and still strive for peace."[61]

It remains one of the finest, most hopeful speeches I have ever heard an American president deliver – and it rang hollow in the shadow of the defeatism that underlay Obama's strategic compromises in Afghanistan, compromises that ensured America would no longer try to achieve lasting peace or justice there. The Obama administration's decision not to seek the defeat of the Taliban insurgency, to time-limit America's involvement and opt against full counterinsurgency, was to abandon any hope for peace or justice in Afghanistan. The contrast between his Nobel speech, calling on the world to "reach for the world that ought to be," and his decision in

---

[60] McChrystal, interview by author. Gates, interview by author.

[61] Obama, "Remarks by the President at the Acceptance of the Nobel Peace Prize," December 10, 2009. https://obamawhitehouse.archives.gov/the-press-office/remarks-president-acceptance-nobel-peace-prize.

Afghanistan, in which he accepted the war, privation, and misery that was, is striking. He spoke of a "just peace based on the inherent rights and dignity of every individual" and adopted a strategy that explicitly rejected any such aspiration. Collectively, those decisions are a major milestone on the Taliban's path to victory. The United States stayed in Afghanistan for another twelve years, and critics complained that it had become a "forever war." It became a forever war because the Obama administration decided to continue fighting it without trying to win it.

In 2021, Biden defended his decision to withdraw American forces by arguing that if we had not won the war by then, we never would. The argument was disingenuous: the United States had not won because it was not trying to – dating back to a decision in 2009 that Biden had championed. Obama's doubts about the war led to key strategic compromises which made failure more likely and thus retrospectively seemed to justify his doubts. But that retrospective justification is illusory. Obama did not prove the impossibility of counterinsurgency, but the folly of time-limited, resource-compromised counterinsurgency – which is an option no one had recommended in the first place, but one he personally designed because of his distrust of the military and disinterest in anything more resource-intensive. Obama's decision to adopt a strategy he doubted, and then to hamstring that strategy by depriving it of the resources it needed to succeed, was a clever way to win an argument. It was not an effective way to win a war, nor a wise use of the nation's resources, nor a responsible risk to run with soldiers' lives.

9

2010–2011

Surge

Thirty thousand additional American troops deployed to Afghanistan over the next nine months after the president's speech. The war reached its fever pitch in 2010 and 2011. They were the two deadliest years for American forces, accounting for almost 40 percent of all US fatalities in the entire war. Military operations were supposed to synergize with a civilian surge to invest in Afghan governance. Improving governance and security together would, in theory, catalyze a psychological change as allied Afghans and the Taliban alike would come to believe the government was winning and the Taliban was losing. With renewed momentum and confidence, the Afghans could take the lead, and American forces could begin to safely draw down – all within eighteen months.

Did it work? Did the surge bring the United States closer to, or further from, an acceptable end state? When strategists and students look back, will they see a model to emulate, or a cautionary tale? It is a simple question, yet fascinatingly difficult to answer, depending on how we measure success. The surge had a major impact on the military situation, reversing the Taliban's momentum and rapidly growing the Afghan army. Yet it seems equally clear that, by the beginning of the withdrawal in July 2011 – or even by the transition in 2014 – Afghan governance had not improved enough, and there was no self-sustaining psychological dynamic of growing optimism and confidence.

Importantly, the military surge cannot be evaluated apart from either the civilian surge or the withdrawal timetable because they were components of a single strategy. The civilian surge largely failed, replicating many of the same problems the Bush administration had seen when it tried to ramp up assistance for governance and reconstruction. But even more consequentially, the time-table – the most distinctive aspect of the Obama administration's war – drove so much of the implementation and the decision-making as to become the controlling dynamic of the war. Together, the timetable and the civilian failure squandered whatever military gains the surge accomplished. By 2011, the insurgency had lost momentum, but the Afghan government was no closer to victory.

DID THE SURGE WORK?

Simply getting the troops to Afghanistan was a formidable logistical challenge, made more so because the American military was also drawing down from Iraq. The additional troops, along with 6,000–7,000 more NATO troops, brought the total international military presence to some 140,000 by late 2010. General McChrystal used the additional troops to mount a major offensive in Helmand Province, reinforce existing efforts in the east along the Afghan–Pakistani border, and inaugurate a new program called "village stability operations." He focused efforts on seventy to eighty "key terrain districts," mostly in the south and east where increased stability would have the greatest impact, covering population centers, crucial infrastructure, and strategic farmland. The key districts would be the "inkblots" that would gradually spread stability to surrounding areas.[1]

McChrystal was trying to implement a classic counterinsurgency campaign. Remarkably, despite months of debate and discussion, there was still no consensus about counterinsurgency, no shared understanding within the administration about what the mission was. "Biden, Donilon, Lute, and others bridled when McChrystal referred to his strategy as 'counterinsurgency,' accusing him of expanding the mission the president had given him," Gates later wrote, but in his view, "the core of that mission was, in fact, counterinsurgency, albeit with fairly tight geographical and time limits." Mullen testified to Congress in December that the mission "is principally counterinsurgency . . . focused on key population centers," not "throughout the country." Biden and his allies interpreted those limits as fundamental changes to the mission; McChrystal, Gates, and others as nothing more than new conditions within which the mission as previously defined should be carried out. The ongoing wrangling made it harder for the administration to measure progress later in the year.[2]

Was it working? "I'm obviously really biased here," McChrystal told me, but "yes," he judged the surge was working. "I thought we were building Afghan confidence." For McChrystal, the psychological dynamic was "the essential thing." "You have to create that perception in people's minds, the enemy, you have to convince him, you cannot win, you will never win, so cut a deal," he said. "You have to convince the Afghans, you will not lose."

---

[1] Gates, *Duty*, 354.
[2] Gates, *Duty*, 475. House Foreign Affairs Committee, "US Strategy in Afghanistan," December 2 and 10, 2009, 52.

McChrystal deliberately did not pay attention to developments in Afghanistan after his command and so could not comment on the surge's success after mid 2010, but he felt that things were moving in the right direction to that point.[3]

McChrystal was right about his bias, of course, and a macabre joke routinely made the rounds among Afghan hands about generals who rotated in and out after brief tours and insisted "we were winning when I left." In McChrystal's defense, he originally planned on a three-year tour – longer than any general served as commander of ISAF or US forces. More importantly, his judgment about the surge was widely corroborated by other policymakers and outside observers. "After the surge, CIA's district assessments" – which had always been more pessimistic than the military's – "showed a marked improvement in the areas under government control and a reduction of those under Taliban control," Mike Vickers wrote. Jones, who had been more skeptical of the surge, judged that "the amount of troops that we put in managed to stem the flow of fighters coming to and from Pakistan and the havens in Pakistan." Gates concurred. "I think that the surge worked in a military sense and that it significantly improved the security situation in the country as a whole," he said, "especially in the south and in the east, where the Taliban were the most active." Ryan Crocker, who served as US ambassador to Afghanistan in 2011 and 2012, agreed. "Yeah, it was working," he said. "Conditions were definitely improving in Afghanistan, casualties were down, and movement was easier."[4]

General David Petraeus, commander of CENTCOM at the beginning of the surge and commander of ISAF after McChrystal, argued strongly that the surge was succeeding. He listed five tasks: halting the Taliban's momentum, rolling its presence back in key locations, accelerating the development of Afghan security forces and security ministries, "develop[ing] a transition concept," and counterterrorism. He claimed ISAF made progress in all five areas. "The Taliban were on the march when Stan McChrystal took over," but, through the surge, "we halted the momentum of the Taliban and retook control of the vast majority of Helmand of Kandahar." Afghan security forces grew significantly, and "we did drive violence down notably about six months into the surge," compared to the previous year, he argued, and "it stayed down for the subsequent seven months of my command and for at least four to six months after I left."

---

[3] McChrystal, interview by author.

[4] Vickers, *By All Means Available*, 321. Gates, Jones, Crocker, interviews by author.

The transition concept was developed and some districts transitioned to Afghan forces. And he cited the Abbottabad raid as indicative of broader success against al-Qaida.[5]

In October 2011, the Department of Defense reported: "After five consecutive years where enemy-initiated attacks and overall violence increased sharply each year (e.g., up 94 percent in 2010 over 2009), such attacks began to decrease in May 2011 compared to the previous year and continue to decline." It was the first time since 2002 that Afghanistan was *less* violent than the year before. More troops meant less violence, a direct rebuttal to those who claimed a light footprint was the safer course. DoD estimated that enemy-initiated attacks decreased by 17 percent in 2011.[6]

The administration's judgment about the military surge was echoed by nonpartisan and nongovernmental sources. In 2011, the *New York Times* reported, "the Taliban have been under stress since American forces doubled their presence in southern Afghanistan last year and greatly increased the number of special forces raids aimed at hunting down Taliban commanders." Seth Jones, the foremost scholar of the Taliban insurgency, wrote in May 2011, "after years of gains, the Taliban's progress has stalled – and even reversed – in southern Afghanistan this year." Even the UN noted progress. "The number of districts under insurgent control has decreased," it reported in March 2011. "An increasing number of anti-Government elements are seeking to join local reintegration programmes . . . In Kabul, the increasingly effective Afghan national security forces continue to limit insurgent attacks." The following year there was even more progress. "The first eight months of 2012 saw a 30 per cent reduction in incidents compared with the same period in 2011," according to the United Nations. Steve Biddle later examined the record of US operations in Afghanistan at the height of the surge and concluded, "the Afghan experience shows that current US methods *can* return threatened districts to government control, when conducted with the necessary time and resources."[7]

---

[5] Petraeus, interview by author.

[6] DoD, "Report on Progress towards Stability," October 2011, 1. See also the December 2012 report.

[7] Carlotta Gall, "Losses in Pakistan Haven Strain Afghan Taliban," *New York Times*, March 31, 2011. www.nytimes.com/2011/04/01/world/asia/01taliban.html?_r=3&hp. Seth Jones, "Beating Back the Taliban," *Foreign Policy*, March 15, 2011. https://foreignpolicy.com/2011/03/15/beating-back-the-taliban-2/. United Nations, A/65/783-S/2011/120, 9 March 2011. UN, A/67/778-S/2013/133, 5. Stephen Biddle, "Afghanistan's Legacy." See also Daniel L. Byman, "Friends Like These."

The surge could also be judged by its effects on other aspects of the war. Many surge troops were trainers or mentors for Afghan soldiers and policemen. The size of Afghan security forces grew rapidly from 195,000 in December 2009 to 323,000 two years later. It came with a cost: the rise of "insider attacks" by Afghan soldiers and policemen against their American advisors. Such attacks rose in 2010 and 2011 and peaked at forty-eight attacks in 2012 before declining as American forces withdrew. The attacks, whether by Taliban infiltrators or by Afghan soldiers genuinely angry at the Americans, were crippling to the trust that was essential for the US–Afghan partnership to survive.[8]

The surge was primarily "a surge of American combat power," according to Ash Carter, who served as deputy secretary of defense and secretary of defense from 2011 to the end of Obama's second term, but that was "not at all what anybody wanted in the long run." The long-term solution was Afghan security forces. The surge "was simply necessary to buy the time to build the Afghan security forces and, I think, it did buy enough time." Before 2009, he believed, the Bush administration "had not put in the effort that would be required to make the Afghan security force capable enough," he said. "The strategy before that was just being there and not doing anything of any lasting consequence." Carter's criticism is unfair to the Bush administration's new strategy in 2007 and 2008: one complaint from the field was that the Bush administration ramped up aid to Afghan security forces so fast that the money could not be spent quickly enough to keep up. Regardless, Obama continued and accelerated aid to the Afghan army even more. By that measure, Carter believed, the surge was both necessary and successful.[9]

The new campaign in 2010 and 2011 was not just about adding troops. McChrystal had emphasized the overriding importance of protecting the Afghan population – including from ISAF's own operations. Civilian casualties from coalition operations ran counter to the very purpose of ISAF's mission; Gates said that "every incident was a strategic defeat." Reducing such casualties was thus among McChrystal's top priorities. "To reduce civilian casualties, McChrystal had issued restrictive guidelines about when troops could fire and when air strikes could be called in for support," Gates wrote. The new guidelines worked, accelerating an existing trend; civilian casualties caused by Afghan and ISAF operations peaked in 2008 and started to decline in 2009, before McChrystal took command, and continued to

---

[8] DoD, "Report on Progress," April 2014, 15. Brookings, "Afghanistan Index," May 25, 2017, 6.
[9] Carter, interview by author.

decline through 2013. More troops came with greater restraint (another demonstration of the argument against the light footprint). The surge led to progress in other areas: fatalities of US troops began to decline in 2011. Poppy cultivation appeared to be holding steady and was well below its 2007 peak, while opium production plummeted in 2012. Afghanistan's rank in Reporters Without Borders' index of press freedom markedly improved after 2012. Afghans even registered optimism in public opinion polls. The percentage who said the country was on the right track rose steadily throughout the surge years and peaked in 2013 at 57 percent.[10]

Peter Lavoy had a more mixed view of the surge because he also judged its impact on the Afghan government (which he thought was negative) and on US counterterrorism operations (which he thought was positive). "I don't dispute that it was showing tangible benefits," he said. "Were they strategic? I'm not sure." Real impact required improving Afghan governance. "How can you win if the Afghan government is never able or willing to do things it takes to govern the country and to gain legitimacy?" But, he believed, the surge hurt more than it helped. "The more effective we were at a military campaign and achieving a military operation, the less legitimate and effective the Afghan government was," he argued. "They were less able and willing to control events on the ground of their own country because the US military was [controlling things], and that fundamentally reduced their legitimacy . . . I think that dysfunction was built into our strategy early on."[11]

That said, Lavoy did see benefits to the surge. "I think the surge did create the ability for us to have a much more decisive impact on al-Qaida." Echoing arguments that McChrystal, Petraeus, Clinton, and others had made during the strategy review, Lavoy believed that more robust counterinsurgency operations enabled more effective counterterrorism – so much so that, "we, for all intents and purposes, defeated al-Qaida." US intelligence tracked Osama bin Laden to a compound in Abbottabad, Pakistan. American Special Operations Forces raided the compound, killed bin Laden, and found a trove of al-Qaida documents – an intelligence windfall – in May 2011, near the height of the surge.[12]

Whether the surge led directly to the Abbottabad raid or not, the link between counterinsurgency and counterterrorism seems clear: more

---

[10] Gates, *Duty*, 359, 492. Brookings, "Afghanistan Index," August 2020, 10, 23. UNODC, *Afghanistan Opium Survey 2013*, 18, 44. Asia Foundation, *Survey of the Afghan People*, 2014, 16.

[11] Lavoy, interview by author.   [12] Lavoy, interview by author.

American eyes and ears meant better intelligence. More American trainers meant more capable Afghan partners, which meant more stability, a less permissive operating environment for the Taliban and al-Qaida, and more bandwidth freed up for Americans to focus on al-Qaida. More troops meant a higher operational tempo, which kept the Taliban and al-Qaida on the back foot and gave them less room for error. Lavoy acknowledged that "remnants and offshoots remain, they'll always remain, but from an operational point of view, the ability for al-Qaida to conduct external operations was terminated." That, for Lavoy, justified the surge and Obama's broader approach to war in Afghanistan. "I think that was successful, so I think the surge, yes, was a good decision." Obama and Biden would make similar claims when campaigning for reelection in 2012.[13]

THE CIVILIAN SURGE

But the surge clearly did not live up to Obama's highest hopes. "We did achieve some military results on the ground, but they were not to be lasting," Eikenberry said. "There's clearly a missing ingredient," McChrystal agreed. "I'd say the biggest missing ingredient was our inability to produce legitimate government below the national level." McChrystal likened insurgency to a sickness and counterinsurgency to medical treatment. Violence is the symptom; poor governance is the disease. For lasting success, you don't treat the symptoms, you treat the underlying disease and you approach the body's health holistically. "COIN is equivalent to strengthening the health of a human body," he said. "It is by definition, trying to change the conditions of weakness that allow an insurgency to get a foothold."[14]

Those conditions of weakness are rooted in bad governance and economic problems. "An insurgency gets a foothold when things are shitty," he said. "If a country's doing well and the politics are legitimate and the economy's good, there's not a lot of insurgents." The military side of counterinsurgency can only kill the bad guys; the civilian side is about shoveling out the shit. "The most effective long-term tactic against terrorism is governance," he told Congress in December 2009. "Where you establish effective governance with rule of law in an area, it is very difficult for terrorist groups to operate." It briefs well. "Theoretically, it's an elegant strategy," he later reflected. "You're going to make the body healthy and you're going to reject the infection and you're going to be good." But when theory meets reality, it gets ugly. "When

---

[13] Lavoy, interview by author. [14] Eikenberry and McChrystal, interviews by author.

you get close to it, and you deal with corrupt officials ... If you get up close and you see all the shit show that's involved in a place like that, it's easy to become overwhelmed."[15]

To address governance and reconstruction, the military surge was supposed to be complemented by a civilian surge, "the State Department's plan to recruit more than a thousand American experts and deploy them to Afghanistan's cities and districts," as Holbrooke's biographer described it. It was a daunting task. "Based on our experience in Iraq, I harbored deep doubt that the required number of civilian advisers ... could be found and deployed," Gates wrote. "My doubts would prove justified." McChrystal, too, felt the civilians largely failed to show up. "There were some really good operators out there, civilian operators who do great work, but there was no civilian surge," McChrystal said. "We didn't get the numbers of people. We didn't get the commitment of people. We never got anywhere close to creating the kind of parallel capacity in the civilian side ... as we did in the military." Gates and McChrystal were not alone in seeing the looming problem. "If you're going to build your whole strategy on a two-year surge and try to make a military difference," Tony Wayne, one of the deputy ambassadors in Kabul, judged, "if you don't have a whole system behind that to take advantage of the military victories," through improved governance, "you're going to have problems."[16]

It is not quite true, as McChrystal claims, that there was no civilian surge. "As part of the surge, in 2009–2010, we ended up getting 600 or 700 more civilians into Kabul," Gates said. The embassy in Kabul ballooned; it became one of the largest US embassies in the world, with over 1,000 people. There were five ambassadors – four deputies reporting to Eikenberry – because, as Wayne recalled, "there were so many three-star generals and others that you actually needed civilians with titles to get them to talk to you." Frank Ruggiero, who served as the senior civilian in Kandahar in 2009 and 2010 before joining Holbrooke's staff, recalled that "when I arrived in Afghanistan, I think there were ten US civilians in all RC-South. By the time I left, I think it was close to 200."[17]

The Obama administration increased civilian aid to Afghanistan, by one measure, from $2.8 billion in 2009 to $4.3 billion in 2010 (the only year in

---

[15] McChrystal, interview by author. House Armed Services Committee, "Afghanistan: The Results of the Strategic Review: Part II," December 8, 2009, 27. www.govinfo.gov/content/pkg/CHRG-111hhrg57832/html/CHRG-111hhrg57832.htm.

[16] Packer, *Our Man*, 481. McChrystal, Wayne, interviews by author. Gates, *Duty*, 343.

[17] Gates, Waye, Ruggiero, interviews by author.

which he would keep his campaign promise for increased aid to Afghanistan). Almost half of all civilian aid was delivered between 2007 and 2012; about 40 percent of all US aid, civilian and military together, was delivered between 2009 and 2012. It was the high point of nation-building ambition in Afghanistan. The State Department produced a spreadsheet tracking the deployment of civilians to Afghanistan. Vikram Singh felt the pressure to show that the State Department could get the job done became a parody of micromanagement. "The Deputy Secretary of State is asking about individual USAID personnel being deployed to villages in central Afghanistan," he recalled, calling it an example of "competitive bureaucracy."[18]

But the extra bodies and dollars did not add up to a coherent civilian strategy for reconstruction and stabilization – which is perhaps what McChrystal meant. "I'm not sure influence matched the size of the embassy," recalled McKiernan, who saw the beginning of the civilian surge before his departure in June 2009. "The president of Afghanistan really didn't want to see [the US ambassador], he wanted to see the guy with the money – and that's the military." The civilian surge failed to beef up the ambassador's clout. "The problem was, [the civilians] were mostly in Kabul," Gates said, "they weren't out in the provinces," which wasn't entirely true. Civilians had a hard time getting around the country because of security restrictions, though the military tried to help. Most of them worked in Kabul or in large provincial centers near or on international military bases. "Of all the civilians who were sent in 2009–2010, I think something like 85 percent of them ended up working from within the walls of the embassy," Gates estimated. The civilian surge was mostly a surge of office workers to the capital. They never materialized in the countryside in large numbers, among Afghans where they were meant to make the most difference. "The numbers and location of civilian experts would remain a source of frustration among our commanders and the rest of us at Defense," Gates wrote, and he later added "I think the civilian part of our surge was basically a wash. I'm not sure it accomplished very much."[19]

At root was the administration's unwillingness to admit what it had signed up for. During the strategy review, Gates asked: "How do we change the subject from 'nation-building' with all that implies to a more minimalist objective of capacity-building?" It was an empty question, a distinction without a difference. The civilian surge was a nation-building campaign,

---

[18] Singh, interview by author. Aid figures derived from USAID Green Book, www.foreign assistance.gov.

[19] McKiernan, interview by author. Gates, interview by author. Gates, *Duty*, 348.

no matter what Gates tried to call it. "'Nation building' was just as dirty a word for Obama as for Bush, but that's what this was, even by the latest euphemism: 'fully integrated civil–military effort,'" according to Packer. Like Rumsfeld and Feith, most of the Obama administration hated the idea of nation building but also knew that there had to be some sort of civilian component of the campaign. In December 2009, Gates repeatedly told Congress the new strategy was not nation building and then turned around and admitted that "you cannot do pure counterterrorism unless you have a government, or provincial and local governments, that create a hostile environment for the Taliban." Rebuilding the Afghan government was an essential precondition for successful counterterrorism, and Gates knew it, no matter what label it went by.[20]

In June 2010, Congress grilled Petraeus on the question. Representative Carol Shea-Porter asked: "General Petraeus, are we nation-building?" Petraeus was clearer than Gates and more honest than most anyone. "We are indeed," he replied. "You can't keep extremists from re-establishing sanctuaries if you don't carry out a comprehensive campaign, one component of which clearly can be described as nation-building. I mean, I am just not going to evade it and play rhetorical games." Shea-Porter expressed surprise because "I have heard over and over again that we are not nation-building." Petraeus responded that nation building was not the "principal mission," but that it was a key to enable long-term success in counterterrorism. Petraeus' comments mark one of the few times in the entire war any US official clearly articulated the right relationship, in my view, between nation building and counterterrorism.[21]

Laurel Miller, who served as the deputy and acting special representative for Afghanistan and Pakistan from 2013, recognized there was no real difference between civilian reconstruction, which the administration embraced, and "nation building," which it rejected. Nation building is "not really anything different than what you do in different places where you're doing development," she said. The difference was in the size and speed of the programs: "It's just at a scale that was sort of on steroids ... You're just trying to do more of it faster." That led to a conflicted attitude: the administration wanted to do enough civilian reconstruction to demonstrate activity, but not so much as to be accused of nation building. It was a never-ending psychological yo-yo: *We're not doing enough reconstruction, we must immediately do far*

---

[20] Gates, *Duty*, 365. Packer, *Our Man*, 480. Senate Foreign Relations Committee, "US Strategy in Afghanistan," December 3, 2009, 34.

[21] House Armed Services Committee, "Developments in Afghanistan," June 16, 2010, 35.

more – but then they do a double take and think, *This isn't reconstruction, this is nation building, we must immediately pull back and do less.*[22]

One year after Petraeus testified to Congress in favor of nation building, Clinton gave a different answer that was a more accurate reflection of the administration's ambivalence. Regarding "so-called nation-building," "that's not what we think we're doing," Clinton told the Senate Foreign Relations Committee, before explaining that US soldiers and diplomats are "helping these people know what it means to actually run a government, make decisions," which sounds a lot like nation building, and that doing so "is in our interests, because it gives them a stake then in the kind of future we're building with our military efforts." And two years later, Petraeus' successor as ISAF commander, General Joe Dunford, was asked the same question. "We do not have a comprehensive nation-building plan in Afghanistan," he told the House Armed Services Committee. "It is far more limited than nation-building. What we are doing is supporting a counterinsurgency effort with projects that will assist in economic development and political transition."[23]

At least some in the Obama administration and the military were true believers in what the civilian surge was supposed to accomplish. If anything, the civilian side was more important than the military side because it was supposed to cure the disease. McKiernan thought a mission like Afghanistan required "not just combat power." To him, it was clear we needed civilian resources. "We needed engineering, we needed medical, we needed governmental, we needed intelligence agencies, we needed to harness the power of NGOs and other organizations like USAID." He went on:

> The reality is you are doing nation building on day one. The first time you start treating wounded Afghan civilians or you start to try to provide clean water or take away some checkpoints that are extorting bribes as people move around, you're doing nation building, and that's a phrase that somehow we've got to come to grips with in our policymaking so that it's not a dirty word.[24]

"I think it was necessary," Ash Carter said of civilian reconstruction efforts, "You can't go into an international situation with allies and in the country and not pay any attention to the wellbeing of the people there." Carter, a physicist by training and later professor of international affairs, spoke and thought with

---

[22] Miller, interview by author.

[23] Senate Foreign Relations Committee, "Evaluating Goals and Progress," June 23, 2011, 18. House Armed Services Committee, "Recent Developments in Afghanistan," April 17, 2013, 14.

[24] McKiernan, interview by author.

a scientist's precision and a scholar's nuance, which carried him through various appointments in the Pentagon in the Clinton and Obama administrations. Investing in stability and prosperity was the precondition that allowed counterterrorism operations to continue. Carter also recognized, and embraced, the simple humanitarian good that the civilian surge would accomplish. "I don't apologize at all for anything the United States did in the way of improving the economy of Afghanistan, in the way of increasing opportunities for women and girls, and promoting democratic values."

But Carter was insistent on the strategic necessity of such efforts, apart from their intrinsic worth. "If you could get all the security value for the United States without doing anything for anybody else, I suppose you would say that that was a better strategy for America. But that's not the way the world works," he argued.

> You have to be attentive to the political and economic context and make a contribution to it, not because that by itself protects America, but because it is necessary in order to create the conditions for you to do the things that are necessary for protecting America ... All that comes with a counterinsurgency package and you can't just do the military part.

I think Carter is exactly right about this, but he also recognized that the civilian component "was less effective because it's more difficult."[25]

BUREAUCRACY NEVER STOPS DOING ITS THING

The Obama administration ran into the same buzz saw of bureaucracy, ineptitude, red tape, and infighting that had paralyzed the Bush administration's reconstruction efforts. Like Bill Murray in *Groundhog Day*, the US effort in Afghanistan seemed damned to repeat the same mistakes, day after day, year after year – not in an epic tragedy, but a mundane routine of comic stupidity. "Honestly, you're asking these bureaucracies to do the wrong things," Singh felt, because the State Department "couldn't, and it shouldn't" try to do nation building. "Most American civilians that went to Afghanistan spoke not a lick of the language," said Ruggiero, the senior civilian in Kandahar. "There was no training program to create civilian capacity that could operate in a combat zone." Because of that, Ruggiero thought it was "just a fundamentally flawed strategy." Ambassador Wayne agreed. "The civilian surge was overestimating the capacity of the civilian

---

[25] Carter, interview by author.

parts of the US government to surge," he said. "I mean, we just did not have built into USAID or the State Department the extra people to go there." The State Department aggressively recruited new hires to go to Afghanistan – and the rapid hiring and deployment of new and inexperienced people predictably led to its own problems.[26]

But one new element in the Obama administration's bureaucratic morass was Richard Holbrooke. Holbrooke championed the civilian surge in part because it "gave Holbrooke a place at the table and credibility with the generals, who were always complaining that the civilian effort lagged behind," according to his biographer. But precisely because the civilian surge was the foundation of his bureaucratic clout, he maneuvered to control it tightly. Congress authorized hundreds of millions of dollars of reconstruction money which had to be parceled out to contractors for implementation. "Holbrooke took over all the contracts," inserting himself into the process for approving, managing, and overseeing implementation, "which created huge bottlenecks at his office."[27]

Peter Lavoy saw the same problem – bureaucratic provincialism – writ large across the entire federal bureaucracy. "The military had its own goal in Afghanistan, CIA had its own goal in Afghanistan, the State Department, who the hell knows what their goal was," he said. Lavoy also listed the White House-led negotiations and USAID pursuing development: five distinct lines of effort that, he thought, were never coordinated. Michèle Flournoy, the undersecretary of defense for policy, agreed. She wrote a memo to Gates in mid 2009 expressing her concern that US efforts did not have "a comprehensive interagency plan or concept of operations." Like Lavoy and Gates, she noted that "many competing – and often conflicting – campaigns are ongoing in Afghanistan: counterinsurgency, counterterrorism, counternarcotics, and efforts at nation building." As Bob Komer had written about Vietnam, there were "a plethora of programs conducted by different agencies, each jealously guarding its prerogatives and insistent on its own procedures."[28]

"We really treated it like there was a military mission, an aid mission, a counternarcotics mission, a ministerial capacity building mission, all separately," according to Vikram Singh. "And they were all their own things, generally with their own logic, their own leadership, their own resource streams, reporting up to their own committees on the Hill about their own activities." To Lavoy, the inability of any of the four administrations that oversaw the war to "align them into a common strategy," was key to

---

[26] Singh, Wayne, Ruggiero, interviews by author.   [27] Packer, *Our Man*, 480, 494.
[28] Lavoy, interview by author. Gates, *Duty*, 341. Komer, *Bureaucracy Does Its Thing*, 77.

understanding the war's outcome. It is remarkable how closely their comments echo observations by officials in the Bush administration who also complained about poor coordination.[29]

Ambassador Marc Grossman, who took over as special representative for Afghanistan and Pakistan in 2011, agreed the civilian efforts were lacking. "We were missing a really important thing in Afghanistan," he said. "When I went to Afghanistan, and I went a lot, I used to come back with the idea that what Afghans needed more than anything else was a job." But aid efforts were not aimed at Afghan employment. "Our reconstruction efforts, and, God bless them, our aid efforts and all of that enormous money and time and talent and everything else that we put into it . . . It was about the projects and about us rather than about [Afghans'] employment."[30]

I heard versions of Grossman's critique repeated over and over: American efforts seemed designed to fulfill bureaucratic requirements, to check a box, to demonstrate activity rather than serve Afghans' needs. "We and our coalition partners, as well as nongovernmental organizations, far too routinely decided what development projects to undertake without consulting the Afghans, much less working with or through them on what they wanted and needed," Gates wrote. The American aid bureaucracy became a self-licking ice-cream cone, a bureaucracy that came to exist for no other purpose than its own perpetuation. The means became their own end, sidelining the intended goal of winning the war. Karzai often leveled this very criticism against American officials. "I thought he was right about that," Grossman recalled, "so I really wanted to focus the effort on a sustainable economic development that benefited Afghans through their jobs. I was never very successful at this."[31]

One reason for the mismatched priorities was the differing needs of counterinsurgency versus economic development. Reconstruction and development in wartime are made "to fit the military's short time horizons, when development really needs long-term horizons," said Lute. "There was always great pressure to make what we were doing relevant to counterinsurgency," Ambassador Rick Olson recalled, but "when you do stabilization operations there tends to be resistance from the development side of the house, from USAID, because you do a lot of things that from a development perspective are kind of wasteful."[32]

Development professionals try to take a long-term and top-down perspective, looking for investments that would improve a nation's fundamental

---

[29] Lavoy, Jones, Singh interviews by author.   [30] Grossman, interview by author.

[31] Grossman, interview by author. Gates, *Duty*, 359.

[32] Olson, interview by author. Lute, SIGAR interview.

economic potential – like roads, power, water, and education. But those kinds of projects took too long to make a difference on the battlefield. The military was interested in quick-impact projects that would create jobs and win hearts and minds. "You hire people to sweep the streets and clear the canals and things like that don't really do much for development," Olson said. It could become perverse: "You hire them to sweep the junk to one side of the street, and then you hire them to sweep it back to the other side of the street, you know?" Though counterinsurgency was long-term compared to counter-terrorism, even it was infected with a persistent short-term mindset relative to the even longer perspective of development and nation building.[33]

"We certainly could have done better," Ryan Crocker agreed. "I mean, let's face it, the reconstruction effort, if you will, was a mess." Crocker took over from Eikenberry as ambassador in mid 2011. He felt one of the main lessons was that "softer" projects, focusing on education and healthcare, were far more effective and worthwhile than "brick-and-mortar" programs, like buildings roads and other infrastructure, because the latter never came with budgetary assistance and training for operations and maintenance. The US would build roads that the Afghan Ministry of Transportation could not maintain or repair, for example. By contrast, simply reopening schools led to 7 million students returning to school in short order and required little more than money to help pay teachers' salaries.[34]

The biggest exception to Crocker's rule, and one of the largest recon-struction projects of the entire war, was the refurbishment of the Kajaki Dam. Built along the Helmand River with American support in 1952, the dam provides irrigation for some of the most fertile farmland in Afghanistan (including some of the most productive poppy fields). "Folks in the south in that area in Helmand remembered with great affection and nostalgia the good work that the US had done back in the 50's on irrigation schemes," Crocker said. USAID helped rehabilitate the dam in stages early in the war – including, in 2008, the transportation of a turbine across insurgent-held territory in one of the largest British military operations in decades.

But the turbine sat unassembled and uninstalled for years because of the difficulty of lining up the funding, the right engineers, and consistent security and keeping them in place for long enough. Karzai "thought it important that we see that one through" and finish the project for symbolic reasons as much as for its practical effect. Crocker and his military counterpart, General John Allen "spent hours" looking at the project, trying to figure out how to get it done. "And it was the only project out there where we had that kind of focus."

[33] Olson, interview by author.   [34] Crocker, interview by author.

For other projects, the attitude, by that time, was "turning the page on a not entirely successful chapter" of reconstruction. The turbine finally came online in October 2016, eight years after the British military delivered it to the dam – a bit late to win hearts and minds at the height of the surge.[35]

The desire to "turn the page" was evident from early on. Civilian efforts at reconstruction and development never got the same attention, scrutiny, planning, or oversight as military operations. "While the military's every move in Afghanistan was examined through a microscope, and we were under great pressure to speed the surge, no comparable attention was paid to the civilian side," Gates recalled. "We spent most of our time dissecting the one part of the strategy that actually was working pretty well – the military operations and training of Afghan security forces – while neglecting the same kind of searching examination of those elements that weren't working," namely, the civilian side. One might accuse Gates of deflecting blame from his department – except Gates' criticisms about reconstruction efforts are corroborated by an essentially unanimous chorus of other observers in and out of government before and after the surge, in every administration. No one thinks we got the civilian side right.[36]

Part of the problem was that no one "owned" the civilian side. Ostensibly, the State Department is supposed to oversee any US government civilian activities abroad. In practice, the other departments and agencies – USAID, the Departments of Treasury, Justice, Agriculture, and others – operated semi-independently. The State Department lacks the people, experience, or culture, let alone the legal authority, to play the same coordinating role that the Department of Defense plays with the Army, Navy, Marine Corps, and Air Force. Most of the State Department is a reporting agency – meeting with foreign nationals and writing cables about their conversations – not an operational agency designed to execute programs.

More to the point: no one *wanted* to own it. While everyone paid lip service to the importance of civilian efforts, no one was willing to step forward and volunteer to be on the blame line. As Jim Dobbins observed earlier in the war, no one is organized or trained for nation building. We lack a doctrine for it, in the absence of which no one is going to risk their career by taking charge and attempting to mold a coherent campaign out of a thousand disparate programs. The one person in the Obama administration who wanted to own it, Richard Holbrooke, died suddenly in December 2010. "Dick Holbrooke was a trying person to work for, but he was a *force majeure* and he was a big champion of keeping the development

---

[35] Crocker, interview by author.   [36] Gates, *Duty*, 476, 483. Gates, interview by author.

and economic side going," Wayne recalled. "Working on governance, economic development, trade, everything else." Whatever energy the civilian surge had dissipated after it lost its champion.[37]

PAKISTAN

Obama's war in Afghanistan was also undermined by the same issue that had bedeviled Bush: the Taliban's safe haven in Pakistan and the Pakistani government's duplicity. Both 2009 strategy reviews emphasized the need to address Afghanistan and Pakistan as a single geopolitical theater. Obama understood the basic problem: "Unless Pakistan stopped sheltering the Taliban, our efforts at long-term stability in Afghanistan were bound to fail." Ambassador McKinley reflected that "the Taliban felt comfortable playing it long because they did have not just the sanctuary – that's almost too limiting a term." Pakistan was their home. "Millions of Afghans lived in Pakistan, so they could afford to wait this out, not just militarily but politically and economically, in terms of their family's wellbeing." The leadership of the insurgency, and foot soldiers' families, could live safely in Pakistan, which gave them confidence to carry on the fight.[38]

But Obama did not fully appreciate the extent of Pakistan's duplicity. He and his team came into office believing that the problem was the Pakistani military, not the civilian government. Musharraf had been driven from power by protests in 2008 and succeeded by a civilian prime minister from the Pakistan People's Party. With a new civilian government in charge for the first time in a decade, there was a sense of hope that the two governments were entering a new chapter in their relationship. "Although Pakistan's government cooperated with us on a host of counterterrorism operations and provided a vital supply path for our forces in Afghanistan," Obama wrote, "it was an open secret that certain elements inside the country's military, and especially its intelligence services, maintained links to the Taliban and perhaps even al-Qaida." By pointing the finger at "certain elements" rather than the Pakistani government as a whole, the Obama administration could justify continuing support to Pakistan. The solution was to help build up the civilians.[39]

With Obama's support, Congress passed the Enhanced Partnership with Pakistan Act in October 2009, authorizing $1.5 billion in civilian aid

---

[37] Wayne, interview by author.   [38] Obama, 320. McKinley, interview by author.
[39] Obama, *Promised Land*, 680.

to Pakistan annually. Previously, US assistance to Pakistan was mostly military aid. The new civilian aid was part of a larger vision. Obama's approach to Pakistan "required a series of complicated and improbable moves," according to Holbrooke's biographer. It aimed to "reassure the Pakistanis that American support was not just short-term and transactional; strengthen the civilian government with huge increases in aid; reduce the military's suspicion of India; bring the neighbors into a regional negotiation; and reorient Pakistan's strategy away from supporting the Taliban." The 2009 strategy review had called for the United States to "change Pakistan's strategic calculus," which Vikram Singh thought was highly unrealistic. "Changing strategic calculus is not like a thing that you really can easily do, if at all," he said. The package required a startling amount of faith in the efficacy of diplomacy and aid to change the way a foreign country thought about itself and its place in the world. It was all carrots and no sticks. If there was ever an American effort at maximalist "nation building," not in dollars spent but in lofty ambition to craft a new national identity, it was in Pakistan, not Afghanistan.[40]

The Obama administration had hoped for a new chapter of cooperation. It was a new chapter, but it proved to be among the worst in the history of US–Pakistani relations. In January 2011, a US contractor shot and killed two Pakistanis in what he claimed was self-defense. Pakistani police arrested and charged him with murder; the United States claimed he was covered by diplomatic immunity. Pakistanis took to the streets to protest American hostility and impunity. Weeks after the incident was finally resolved – the US paid *diyya*, or blood money, to the Pakistani families, in exchange for the contractor's release – US Special Operations Forces raided a compound in Abbottabad and killed Osama bin Laden. The American public was incensed to learn that bin Laden had been found hiding blocks away from the Pakistan Military Academy. Then, in November, NATO and Pakistani forces exchanged fire at two border checkpoints. Twenty-eight Pakistani soldiers were killed, and each side blamed the other for starting the fight. Coming on the heels of a full year of acrimony and finger-pointing, Pakistan immediately revoked permission for NATO to send its supply trucks through Pakistan, the main route by which international military forces in Afghanistan were resupplied. In doing so, Pakistani leaders openly repudiated the commitments they had made to Colin Powell and Rich Armitage in the days after 9/11.

Amid the diplomatic bottoming-out, the Pakistani Taliban gained momentum. The group launched brazen attacks on Pakistani Army

---

[40] Packer, *Our Man*, 457. Singh, interview by author.

General Headquarters in October 2009 and on a major naval base in May 2011. The Pakistani military responded to the growing insurgency with operations in the tribal areas (not against the Afghan Taliban). The US joined the fight, reportedly killing Pakistani Taliban leader Baitullah Mehsud in a drone strike in August 2009 and his successor, Hakimullah Mehsud, in 2013 – goodwill gestures to signal American commitment to fight jihadists of any group in hopes of persuading Pakistan to do the same.

Petraeus – as commander of Central Command, then commander of ISAF, then director of the CIA – was enthusiastic about the Pakistani campaign and offered to help. "It was a counterinsurgency campaign to clear, hold and then build" in western Pakistan. He praised the Pakistani military's progress in Swat, Mohmand, Bajaur, Khyber, and South Waziristan but noted the operations taxed the Pakistani military's resources. "They didn't have the close air support, they didn't have the precision strikes," so the United States stepped in to help in limited ways. "We were flying drones to support that operation, we started flying probably in the Khyber region, and maybe some of the other areas where we were allowed to fly," to help with reconnaissance and targeting, though, "we weren't shooting for them," Petraeus noted. US officials envisioned a hammer-and-anvil strategy, crushing the Pakistani Taliban – and, hopefully, other jihadists, including the Afghan Taliban – between the Pakistani and American militaries on either side of the Afghan–Pakistani border.[41]

Despite pockets of success, it never happened. The Pakistanis were less interested in a coordinated campaign for long-term victory than with their own immediate need to staunch the violence in Pakistani cities. They deeply mistrusted the American military and after 2011 came close to viewing the United States as an enemy. Pakistan even began to cool toward cooperation with the United States against al-Qaida, despite the earlier record of strong cooperation. "Because of where al-Qaida and other high value targets were hanging out, in FATA, they were intermingled with the tribes that were critical to the ecosystem Pakistan was trying to maintain in that area," Peter Lavoy said. It was not easy to distinguish between militants of different groups. Al-Qaida, which Pakistan opposed, intermingled with the Haqqani Network, which it supported. Petraeus saw the result. "The Pakistanis never were willing subsequently to take action against the Haqqani or the Taliban headquarters and bases in Baluchistan Province," Petraeus said, arguing it "was the single biggest factor in the inability to achieve enduring success against the Taliban, Haqqani, and other insurgent and extremist elements."

[41] Petraeus, interview by author.

It became a wedge between the United States and Pakistan. "Pakistan became very apprehensive about our continued op tempo and CT operations, and the intel sharing began to slow down. Approvals for strikes were hesitant, delayed, and often never coming," Lavoy said.[42]

Years later, in 2013, when the Pakistani Taliban was again making trouble, Ambassador Dobbins encouraged the prime minister, Nawaz Sharif, to order the military into action. Sharif kicked the can down the road. "For an entire year he forbade any military action against the [Pakistani Taliban] while he sought to engage them in negotiations," Dobbins recalled. Sharif did eventually order a military operation, which "proved broadly successful, leading eventually to a significant decrease in militant violence throughout Pakistan." But "delay came at some cost," because "American and NATO troops had been drawn down substantially over that same year, and Afghan forces were severely stretched as a result." There was no anvil for the hammer to strike against. "Thousands of the militants forced out of Pakistan by the army offensive simply moved into neighboring Afghanistan and continued operating from there. Had the offensive been launched a year earlier, these militants would have been caught between American and Pakistani forces. Instead, they found unimpeded sanctuary on the Afghan side of the border," which accounts for some of the surge in violence that started as American forces withdrew.[43]

The Pakistani military's record of combat against the Pakistani Taliban showed a flaw in the Obama administration's thinking. The military was indeed ready to fight against militants – of the right kind. The dividing line was not between the civilian and military leaders of Pakistan, as the Obama administration thought, but between the Afghan and Pakistani Taliban. Pakistani leaders – both civilian and military – were consistently eager and willing to fight the Pakistani group, and both just as consistently refused to fight the Afghan group. Pakistani support to the Taliban started in the mid 1990s when Pakistan was led by civilian prime ministers, Benazir Bhutto and Nawaz Sharif, not by Pervez Musharraf's military government.

THE TIMETABLE

The surge was also hamstrung from the beginning by an extraordinary sense of hurry. "Unrelievedly, the president's strategy in Afghanistan – and the

---

[42] Lavoy and Petraeus, interviews by author.   [43] Dobbins, *Five Decades*, 281–282.

performance of the US military commander there – was under heavy pressure both from his staff and Biden in the White House and from the news media," Gates wrote. Obama announced the surge in December 2009. The new forces "were just beginning to arrive in Afghanistan in May and June" of 2010 and did not fully arrive until September. However, already by June, "the pessimists were in full cry," and "Biden and others in the White House were already pushing us to rethink the strategy," in Gates' recollection. The president had directed, as part of the new strategy, a review of progress to take place in December of 2010, just three months after the last of the surge forces had arrived. McChrystal and Petraeus were under pressure to demonstrate progress almost immediately.[44]

Why the rush? The drawdown timetable hovered over everything. It was the one immovable aspect of Obama's war in Afghanistan. "It dominated the other lines of effort," Ambassador Marc Grossman said, "the other lines of effort were subordinate to that." Very few officials thought the timetable was a good idea; at best, they defended it as a necessary evil, or a least-bad compromise. "I think in our private discussions there were considerable reservations about the idea that the entire surge had been done on a timeline," said Rick Olson, who served as US ambassador to Pakistan and later special representative to Afghanistan and Pakistan. "I think everyone privately felt that this was a strange way to do business. It was clear that what you were doing was incentivizing the Taliban to wait it out." Ambassador Tony Wayne, similarly, noted problems with the timetable. "The military knew that they had a short period of time. So they were trying to cram as much in as quickly as they could, and they wanted the civilians to be able to deliver as much as they could," he said, "but all the aid people and others knew from their previous experience that this is not going to work because it takes a long time to change societies . . . we kept trying to do it so fast that you couldn't even measure success well." I asked General Ken McKenzie, who served in ISAF and CENTCOM during the surge, how the timetable affected the surge. "It destroyed it," he replied.[45]

One of Gates' successors as secretary of defense, Ash Carter, was pointed in his critique. "Withdrawal timetables were always, in my judgment, a bad idea," he told me. "I understand that they can become a political necessity, but they are a strategic mistake because they signal to your enemy that there's a time in which you're going to forsake the battle with them." He understood the argument that "unless the Afghans thought we were leaving, they would never pull up their socks" and take the lead. Nonetheless, he insisted, "it's

---

[44] Gates, *Duty*, 485–486.   [45] Grossman, Olson, Wayne, and McKenzie, interviews by author.

strategically unwise . . . I always believed and said that timetables were unwise." Ambassador Crocker felt the same. The withdrawal timetable "was precisely the kind of thing that Generals Petraeus and Odierno and I resisted in Iraq. We would not put an end date on it. It was going to be conditions based, not based on the calendar." Crocker echoed the criticism every other observer raised: "If you do a calendar, obviously you're telling your enemy how long he has to hold out. Just absolutely contrary to the whole purpose of the surge."[46]

A few officials were supportive of the timetable. Eikenberry opposed the surge but came around to support the strategy when Obama included the timetable because he hoped it would be "a catalytic effect on getting the Afghans to step up and start to take more political and military owner-ship," though he acknowledged "that did not play out," and he had "grossly underestimated the incapacity and the political dysfunctionality of the [Afghan] regime." Lavoy acknowledged that "the surge showed positive signs of improvement," and that others could argue "if we just stayed the course a little longer," we could have achieved stability, "but I disagree. I think there were structural challenges that would prevent that," such as the corruption and incompetence of the Afghan government or domestic political support for the war, which made the timetable necessary.[47]

Jones felt that "the theory behind [the timetable] was not bad," because the administration expected that "the Afghan army would be up and run-ning more effectively," and the Taliban would be "under control" by the end of the withdrawal period, all of which amounted to "pretty sound logic." It was not sound: the timetable itself is what prevented US forces from training enough Afghans long enough and making enough progress against the Taliban to leave behind a stable situation. The administration's expectation otherwise was more hope than strategy. General John Allen, who took command of ISAF after Petraeus, told the House Armed Services Committee in March 2012 that the deadline "has helped us to focus on the mission" and helped "the Afghans to focus on their need to become proficient," echoing Obama's hope. But the special inspector general for Afghanistan reconstruction later concluded that the timelines were prem-ised on "the mistaken belief that a decision in Washington could transform the calculus of complex Afghan institutions, powerbrokers, and communi-ties contested by the Taliban."[48]

[46] Carter and Crocker, interviews by author.

[47] Eikenberry, interview by author. Lavoy, interview by author.

[48] Jones, interview by author. Allen quoted in House Armed Services Committee, "Recent Developments in Afghanistan," March 20, 2012, 36. SIGAR, "What We Need to Learn," IX.

Many officials seemed torn over the deadline. "If your goal is just to leave, then of course you put a timetable [on it], right?" Colonel Chris Kolenda, then serving as an advisor on McChrystal's staff, reflected. "If your [goal] is just to stop the war, then that's what you do. If you believe success is getting out of Afghanistan, then, you know, [the] timetable drives everything." If Obama's goal was to end the war in Afghanistan on any terms, then simply setting a deadline made sense. But Obama had campaigned in 2008 on a promise to win the war, not end it. "If you believe that negotiated outcome is your best way to become successful," Kolenda continued, "then you don't announce a troop withdrawal because troops are part of your leverage." Kolenda saw the military presence as part of a negotiating strategy. "When you announce a withdrawal in negotiations, in wartime negotiations, then your adversary knows that they just wait you out. And in the meantime, our partner on the ground – in this case, the Afghan government – is going to do everything they can to try to sabotage that timeline. So, you're creating all sorts of perverse incentives."[49]

Gates, similarly, seemed conflicted by the timetable. "Although these deadlines grated on the military, that was the deal we had made with the president," Gates wrote in his memoir. "If we couldn't get the job done in two years, how many years would it take? Down that path lay an open-ended conflict with potentially many more years of fighting." He argued that "Obama was right in each of these decisions," about timetables and with-drawals. "After eight years of war in Afghanistan, Congress, the American people, and the troops could not abide the idea of a conflict there stretch-ing into the indefinite future." Gates had come to believe that "the 'war of necessity' to punish and root out those responsible for 9/11 had become an albatross around the nation's neck," but that "with the deadlines Obama politically bought our military – and civilians – five more years to achieve our mission in Afghanistan."[50]

But that was not Gates' final word on the surge and timetable. "The only way we could sustain the gains [of the surge] was to have kept those forces there," he later told me, "because the Afghans had not been able to increase their own capabilities, both militarily and in terms of credibility of the govern-ment." That the Afghans had not improved enough was an implicit criticism of the timetable, or perhaps of the surge altogether because it was not successfully building Afghan capacity fast enough. "The July 2011 drawdown date was hotly debated, with all of us saying that drawdowns would begin on that date, the pace to be determined by 'conditions on the ground,'" he wrote, a clear criticism of a fixed timetable. And while the surge was working militarily,

[49] Kolenda, interview by author.   [50] Gates, *Duty*, 498, 571–572.

pushing the Taliban back, the looming withdrawal made those gains ephemeral. Without Afghans to take the lead, Americans would have to stay longer. But, Gates believed, "that was a political impossibility, domestically. I guess I would say that the surge was a mix of success and failure."[51]

Gates tied himself in knots. When the House Foreign Affairs Committee asked him about the timetable, he responded: "Are the Taliban going to be more emboldened than they already are because of this announcement? I don't think so." Years later, I asked him the same question, and he gave a different answer. "I think it's hard to argue that anytime you give the enemy a timeline ... " he started, then tried again: "The famous, old statement about 'you have the watches, but we have the time,' [that] kind of thing." Perhaps he came to change his mind with the passage of years and the benefit of hindsight, but it's clear from other comments he was ambivalent, at best, about the timetable, even at the time. The tension illustrates a feature of Gates' thinking that is admirable and maddening at the same time. He is smart enough to see both sides of every debate – which is more than can be said of most policymakers in Washington – but not always consistent or decisive on where he came down.[52]

Others shared Gates' concern about sustaining domestic political support for the war. James Cunningham, who served as US ambassador to Afghanistan from 2012 to 2014, generally opposed the timetable. "I was always opposed to the idea of withdrawing from Afghanistan or establishing a timetable for doing so, which was the *leitmotif* for most of our discussions during the Obama administration." He felt the timetable was strategically counterproductive. "We didn't have any hope of success unless we made clear that we were prepared to remain there over the long term." But that ran counter to political realities. "The surge itself, having more than a hundred thousand US troops in the country, along with some 50,000 coalition troops, wasn't a sustainable proposition." The solution, he thought, should have been a conditions-based drawdown of the surge followed by a smaller but sustained presence without any timetable attached. "It was the right thing to lower the presence of the US and foreign military forces in Afghanistan and to put the Afghans in the lead, that was the right strategy. The flaw was in not linking that to the kind of conditions and performances that were needed."[53]

---

[51] Gates, *Duty*, 486. Gates, interview by author.
[52] House Foreign Affairs Committee, "US Strategy in Afghanistan," December 2 and 10, 2009, 50. Gates, interview by author.
[53] Cunningham, interview by author.

Critics of the timetable understood how it introduced a new strategic logic to the war, what scholars call the "shadow of the future." Expectations about how events will unfold affect how people act in the present; alter those expectations, and people change their behavior accordingly. Once Obama began talking about the withdrawal of American troops, everyone – the Taliban, allied Afghans, NATO partners, and even US troops in the field – altered their behavior, adjusting for the new expectation that US troops would begin to leave Afghanistan relatively soon. "Obama's announcement that the United States would begin withdrawing our forces in July 2011 was widely interpreted as an end date," Gates wrote, "so many Afghans just hunkered down to wait for our departure."[54]

"The big news for the people in the region was not the surge, the big news was the US was leaving Afghanistan," according to Barney Rubin. The timetable incentivized hedging behavior by America's Afghan allies concerned for their long-term prospects. Afghan officials who worried about the shape of a post-withdrawal Afghanistan were less likely to trust their American counterparts or invest in the slow work of institution building and norm setting so crucial for reconstruction and development. The withdrawal deprived the Afghan army and police of American trainers they needed. Throughout 2013 and 2014, the US Department of Defense warned that Afghan security forces, though improving, faced capability gaps in logistics, intelligence, air support, and more, limiting their ability to undertake independent operations without US support and training.[55]

Just as importantly, the withdrawal announcements altered the Taliban's strategic calculus. Critics universally warned at the time that the Taliban would take the withdrawal announcement as assurance it could simply wait out the United States, warnings that were thoroughly vindicated. In 2010, General James Conway shared that the United States had intercepted communications of Taliban fighters explaining that this was their plan – and it is exactly what the Taliban subsequently accomplished. Even while the United States stayed in Afghanistan year after year and invested lives and money into the effort, most of it was wasted because of the participants' expectations of an imminent American withdrawal.[56]

---

[54] Gates, *Duty*, 485.   [55] Rubin, interview by author.

[56] "US General Warns Afghan Deadline Encouraging Taliban," Radio Free Europe/Radio Liberty, August 24, 2010. www.rferl.org/a/US_Marines_Likely_To_Stay_In_Afghanista n_For_Years/2136690.html.

MUSICAL CHAIRS

In addition to the timetable, corruption, and the failure of the civilian strategy, the surge was interrupted when Obama fired Stan McChrystal. In late June 2010, *Rolling Stone* ran a profile of McChrystal that quoted his staff insulting senior officials in Washington. McChrystal had given the reporter access in hopes it would "provide transparency into how my command team operated," he wrote, but was alarmed that the resulting article "attributed a number of unacceptable comments to my command team." Gates knew the article endangered McChrystal's job and the war. "Deeply fearful of its impact on the war, for once I couldn't contain my anger: 'What the fuck were you thinking?'" Gates asked him, "McChrystal offered no explanation, didn't say his staff had been misquoted or that the article was distorted in any way." McChrystal's silence came from his sense of honor. "Regardless of how I judged the story for fairness or accuracy, responsibility was mine," he wrote.[57]

Knowing McChrystal's job was in jeopardy, Gates went to bat for him, telling Obama that "if we lose McChrystal, we lose the war." McChrystal offered his resignation – "I knew only one decision was right for the moment and for the mission" – but Gates wanted Obama to "be generous" and turn it down. Obama replied that "he had to think about the institution of the presidency." He also expressed skepticism about McChrystal's strategy. "I don't have the sense it's going well in Afghanistan," he said. "[McChrystal] doesn't seem to be making progress. Maybe his strategy is not really working," which was the substantive argument of the *Rolling Stone* article. Gates was dispirited. "Hearing the president express doubt about the strategy he had approved six months earlier, just as many of the surge troops were arriving in Afghanistan, and his lack of confidence in his commander and the strategy floored me," Gates wrote. "These feelings did not spring from a magazine article but had been there all along."[58]

Obama thought the article "made McChrystal and his crew sound like a bunch of cocky frat boys," which, in my observation, is true of most soldiers, all Marines, and more than a few policymakers but is hardly a fireable offense. With more seriousness, Obama worried the article risked "reopening divisions within the Afghan team that I'd hoped were behind us." He felt that the principle of civilian control over the military was still at

---

[57] Gates, *Duty*, 487 McChrystal, *My Share of the Task*, 387–388. Hastings, "Runaway General," *Rolling Stone*, June 22, 2010. www.rollingstone.com/politics/politics-news/the-runaway-g eneral-the-profile-that-brought-down-mcchrystal-192609/.

[58] Gates, *Duty*, 487–488. McChrystal, *My Share of the Task*, 387–388.

stake. "In that *Rolling Stone* article, I'd heard in [McChrystal] and his aides the same air of impunity that seemed to have taken hold among some in the military's top ranks during the Bush years," Obama wrote, "a sense that once war began, those who fought it shouldn't be questioned, that politicians should just give them what they ask for and get out of the way." Obama's suspicion of the generals is puzzling. Bush had hardly given the military free rein to design their own war strategy in Iraq; they had largely opposed the surge, and he had to force them to accept it. Obama had clashed with the senior military leadership in 2009 but later concluded that there had been no actual insubordination. Obama's narrative of military impunity is false – but that was the narrative he invoked to justify firing McChrystal.[59]

Obama may have been upset less at the frat boy comments than the article's portrayal of a president maneuvered into a strategy he didn't want, facing a "quagmire he knowingly walked into" because he lacked the forti- tude to say no to the generals. "It was Obama versus the Pentagon, and the Pentagon was determined to kick the president's ass," the journalist wrote, even quoting one anonymous military official suggesting they might ask for another surge the following year. The accusation was inaccurate, overlook- ing how much Obama had forced changes to the mission and its parameters over the military's objections, but none of that mattered to the White House worried about the article's political fallout. Gates felt the article gave the president the excuse he wanted "to demonstrate vividly – to the public and to the Pentagon – that he was commander in chief and fully in control of the military."[60]

Obama noted that McChrystal "made no excuses for his remarks. He didn't suggest that he'd been misquoted or taken out of context," and Gates felt that "McChrystal's refusal to defend himself ... made it impossible for me to save his job." McChrystal's sense of honor was noble but, in this case, self-defeating. McChrystal saved his defense for his memoir, in which he simply noted that a later investigation "could not substantiate any violations of Defense Department standards and found that 'not all of the events occurred as portrayed in the article.'" Obama didn't wait to find out but also managed to claim he "didn't really have a choice" but to fire him.[61]

As with McKiernan's firing, McChrystal's sticks out as uniquely punitive. During World War II, when commanders were routinely relieved of duty for command failures and incompetence, General George Patton, one of the most qualified and most aggressive generals in the army, had been

---

[59] Obama, *Promised Land*, 578–579. [60] Gates, *Duty*, 491. Hastings, "Runaway General."
[61] Gates, *Duty*, 491. Obama, *Promised Land*, 579. McChrystal, *My Share of the Task*, 390.

reprimanded for slapping two subordinates in August 1943 and was passed over for prominent assignments – but was eventually returned to command. By contrast, during the Korean War, President Harry Truman fired General Douglas MacArthur, but it was for blatant insubordination over a central matter of wartime strategy. McChrystal could rightly be seen as the Patton of the war against al-Qaida. His offense – juvenile and snarky comments that were not even attributed to him, but to his staff – was even milder than Patton's, yet his punishment – he lost his command and his military career – as severe as MacArthur's.

By contrast, Obama did not fire Eikenberry. Either Eikenberry or McChrystal, or both, should have gone when Eikenberry vocally disputed McChrystal's strategy in November 2009. Though they presented a united front in testimony before Congress, Eikenberry clearly did not believe in the strategy, and the administration knew it. "Eikenberry seemed convinced the strategy Obama had approved would fail," Gates wrote, cautioning the president that "Eikenberry's pervasive negativity radiated throughout the embassy and was like a general telling troops going into a fight that the campaign would fail." Clinton wanted Eikenberry gone, arriving at one meeting ready with "a number of specific examples of Eikenberry's insubordination."[62]

Eikenberry had burned his bridges with the cables he sent in November. The *Rolling Stone* article on McChrystal claimed that Eikenberry, who had commanded US forces in Afghanistan from 2005 to 2007, "can't stand that his former subordinate is now calling the shots." More importantly, Eikenberry's cables had leaked, and Karzai read what Eikenberry wrote about him. "Unfortunately, it became difficult for me to take Ambassador Eikenberry – an old friend from our time in the Army – with me to my meetings with President Karzai," Petraeus recalled, "because Karzai would be enraged and say to the Ambassador: 'Well, you're the one who said I was an unsuitable partner.'" Petraeus took over from McChrystal in mid 2010. "I didn't realize it until I got back [to Kabul] how difficult the relationship had become between Karzai and Eikenberry," he said. Oddly, Obama notes in his memoir Clinton's desire to fire Eikenberry, yet he never explains why he kept him on. It was a consequential decision: at the peak of its counterinsurgency campaign in which everyone recognized the vital necessity of civilian–military coordination and the importance of diplomatic efforts, the United States had no effective diplomatic representation in Kabul.[63]

---

[62] Gates, *Duty*, 481.

[63] Obama, *Promised Land*, 438. Hastings, "Runaway General." Petraeus, interview by author.

Within the White House, Obama replaced Jim Jones with his deputy, Tom Donilon, in late 2010. Jones had never clicked with the rest of the Obama team and had not been the driving force behind the 2009 strategy reviews as might be expected of a national security advisor. Donilon, a lawyer and Democratic Party operative, had worked for Secretary of State Warren Christopher as chief of staff and subsequently assistant secretary of state for public affairs in the Clinton administration. His party credentials gave him the insider access Jones lacked. With his background in law and as a chief of staff, he was methodical and knew how the levers of government operated. He also had a lawyer's instinct for working tirelessly on behalf of his client, the president, without foregrounding himself. The flip side is that he seemed not to challenge the president's thinking or force the team to confront difficult or inconvenient questions about the strategy they had adopted in 2009.

THE DECEMBER 2010 ASSESSMENT

As part of his surge decision, Obama had insisted that his team evaluate progress after one year. He did not want a replay of the previous year's public scrutiny. "The president had insisted all along that he wanted the December review of progress in Afghanistan to be low-key," Gates wrote. For Obama, the clock started when he gave his speech in December 2009, despite that it took the better part of the year – nine months – for all the surge forces to arrive in Afghanistan, let alone demonstrate progress. But "by early June [2010], Biden and others in the White House were already pushing us to rethink the strategy," according to Gates. The review process started in late October, just a month after the surge forces fully arrived.[64]

The assessment replicated the disagreements of the previous year. It deteriorated into a bitter argument between Gates – who, along with Clinton and the military, believed the strategy was showing progress but needed patience – and Biden, who along with Lute and the NSC staff, largely disagreed. The stakes were the pace and timing of the drawdown. If Gates was right and the strategy was working, they could continue as planned, give the strategy the time it needed, and aim for a slower, more deliberate drawdown. If Biden was right and the strategy was failing, the situation called for a faster drawdown to cut losses and make room for other options.

[64] Gates, *Duty*, 497, 486.

Gates felt that the administration owed a duty to the president to faithfully execute his strategy as best as possible. "Unfortunately, Biden and his staff, the White House staff, and the [NSC] apparently had not taken the same oath of support," he wrote. "From the moment the president left West Point, they worked to show he had been wrong, that the Pentagon was not following his direction, and that the war on the ground was going from bad to worse." Gates believed that Biden and his allies "would gather every negative bit of information about developments in Afghanistan and use them to try to convince the president that they had been right and the military wrong." They "questioned whether any progress had been made at all" and "attempted to relitigate the president's decisions of a year earlier." He accused them of trying to "hijack" Obama's strategy by ignoring input from other departments and agencies. Worst of all, "that began before the first surge soldier set foot in Afghanistan."[65]

"I was very angry during most of that period," Gates told me. Gates felt that Biden and Lute used the assessment as an excuse to "reopen the whole argument about the whole strategy." Gates believed the exercise was supposed to be a narrow and simple assessment. "It was supposed to be, how are we [doing] now? Now that we're getting the troops in there, how are things going? And are we being successful?" Gates recalled, "Instead, the [NSC] was basically trying to prove they'd been right all along, that we shouldn't have done the big increase, that we should have done counterterrorism, and that the campaign was failing." Gates felt that "those on the ground in Afghanistan thought they were actually making pretty good headway" even if "more slowly than they had originally anticipated." The president seemed to agree with at least some of Gates' argument. "He was particularly enthusiastic about the 'Afghan Local Police' initiative, in which young men were recruited in villages, trained and equipped, and returned to those same villages."

It wasn't a strict replay of the Vietnam-era split between the field versus DC, the military versus civilians, because "the State and Defense Department were pretty much on the same wavelength," Gates said. "Panetta disagreed with the [NSC] assessment of the al-Qaida effort," he wrote, "as did Hillary on the civilian component of the strategy." The Department of Defense reported that "counterinsurgency operations are having localized positive effects" and judged that "momentum is shifting in favor of Afghan Forces and ISAF."[66]

---

[65] Gates, *Duty*, 474, 385, 499, 500, 501.

[66] Gates, interview by author. Gates, *Duty*, 499, 500, 501. DoD, "Reported on Progress," December 2010, 8, 41.

Gates accused Lute of overstepping his bounds and trying to micro-manage the Pentagon and the interagency process. Lute was certainly an irritant to Gates, but he was not freelancing. If the NSC staff is not asking pointed questions of the bureaucracy, it is not doing its job. Lute was almost certainly following cues from Biden and possibly Obama to make the opposite case and counterbalance the Defense Department grading its own paper. In Lute's retelling, the review process focused on a key data point: how many key terrain districts (KTDs) the counterinsurgency campaign was trying to clear, and how much progress McChrystal and Petraeus could show in each one. In 2009, in line with Obama's guidance, McChrystal agreed to focus his campaign on 72 KTDs (out of some 400 districts across Afghanistan). In theory, McChrystal's strategy would clear the district of insurgents, hold it while governance and development took hold, and then transfer to the Afghan government and security forces. Lute keenly tracked the KTDs (likely the source of Gates' complaint about his micromanagement).

Lute traveled to Afghanistan in late 2010 as the review was ramping up and met with the ISAF joint command. "And I said, look, one of the things we're here to do is to probe this model. How's it going, the clear, hold, build, transfer process? What can you report?" Lute was dismayed by the answer. The US military could easily clear any district and could hold so long as there were sufficient forces, but "we haven't gotten to 'transfer' on any one of them." The military was supposed to hand off responsibility for the cleared district to a newly appointed Afghan district government sent in from Kabul, a "government in a box." But this "build and transfer phase proved seriously flawed, if not fatally flawed." There was no Afghan government capable of taking over in short order. In 2010, McChrystal and Petraeus tried to turn the town of Marja, in Helmand Province, into a model of counterinsurgency. Fifteen thousand Afghan and coalition troops retook the town in one of the biggest operations of the war, showing success in "clear" and "hold." It was touted as a success – until the Afghan government failed to show up for the "build" and "transfer" phases. "There was no Afghan capacity to go along with US military forces," said Frank Ruggiero, Holbrooke's deputy. McChrystal called Marja the "bleeding ulcer" of his campaign.[67]

That was bad enough. But when Lute asked, "We're like 0 for 72 at this point?" the staff responded, "Oh no, it's now 96." ISAF had added two dozen additional key districts. Lute was incredulous. "You have a memo from the president saying focus on these 72 and you may not expand beyond those.

---

[67] Lute and Ruggiero, interviews by author.

But now you're telling me you're working 96 without the ability to show one completed case?" The expansion of KTDs at the same time that ISAF had not successfully transferred in any of them, plus an ongoing dispute about why the Marines had been sent to Helmand, added to Lute's growing skepticism about the entire surge and counterinsurgency strategy. "These points were just fuel for those . . . like Biden who were even more suspicious than Obama of COIN," Lute thought. To Lute, this was a key moment. "When the review process at the end of 2010 came back with that data, Obama decided there's no way to cap this ambition," no way to ever meet the escalating "demands of COIN." Lute believed "that was another important step that caused [Obama] to lose confidence in the project."[68]

Petraeus thought the White House's focus on KTDs that had been developed during McChrystal's command was unusual. Within ISAF headquarters, identifying key districts was done by the staff rather than by the commander, and not something on which Petraeus would place particular focus. For the White House or the NSC staff to be interested in the nuts and bolts of which districts were designated as "key," or how many to focus on, was an example of the micromanagement that Gates complained about. Petraeus doubted that Obama was as fixated on the issue as Lute believed he was (Obama omits the December 2010 review from his memoir entirely) – and, in any case, Petraeus disagreed with Biden's and Lute's pessimistic conclusions. "We had just gotten the final additional forces and resources," by late 2010, Petraeus recalled. "We had just gotten the inputs right in Afghanistan for the first time," including "the right overarching strategy, nearly the right force levels, the right organizational architecture," and given that timeline, "I don't see how one could possibly conclude in December 2010 . . . that a comprehensive civil–military counterinsurgency campaign plan would or would not achieve the objectives set out for us," he said. "It would have been extremely premature to make such a judgment at that time." Ambassador Tony Wayne, one of the deputy ambassadors in Kabul, argued that it was unrealistic to expect the so-called government-in-a-box to succeed on such a short timeline given the tensions between Afghanistan's traditional tribalism and the demands of wartime bureaucratic management.[69]

Gates and Lute were measuring different things. Gates, looking at the military component, truthfully reported progress and, on that judgment, had a strong case for continuing the strategy. Lute, from his position on the NSC, argued that the failures of the civilian component and the Afghan government had undermined the promise of the surge. "I'm not sure in the

---

[68] Lute, interview by author.   [69] Petraeus and Wayne, interviews by author.

history of COIN in Afghanistan there's a single example of where we got all the way to transfer," Lute concluded. Gates was at least partly to blame for the mismatched perspectives. "My definition of success was much narrower than Riedel's or the president's at that point," he wrote. To him, success meant "degrad[ing] the Taliban's capabilities to the point where larger and better trained Afghan security forces could maintain control of the country and prevent the return of al-Qaida." Gates' definition of success made no mention of building an Afghan government; he had moved the goalposts, which made it easier to claim progress. Despite his earlier insistence that the team give the president's strategy its full support, Gates was improvising his own foreign policy.[70]

Lute and Biden, for their part, correctly saw that it was impossible to create and transfer to a nonexistent "government in a box" within eighteen to twenty-four months. But they drew the wrong conclusion. They assumed that if it could not be done immediately, it could never be done, or at least never done at an acceptable timeline and cost. But that proposition was never tested because of the drawdown timetable. They rushed to judgment – they reached their conclusion when the surge forces had been in place for only been three months – because the timetable forced the issue well before any progress could reasonably be expected. "I was skeptical because I didn't think [the strategy] could work," Lute said. "I thought the concept was plausible. But I didn't see anything that suggested that in twenty-four months, that the Afghan national security forces would be sufficiently independent enough [for us] to actually transfer . . . I didn't think it fit the conditions in Afghanistan."[71]

Lute isn't wrong about the infeasibility of the twenty-four-month timeline, but blaming failure entirely on "conditions in Afghanistan" conveniently exonerates conditions in Washington. Obama's timetable dictated everything, creating the artificial expectation that McChrystal and Petraeus could show progress within months of surge forces arriving and the wildly unrealistic expectation that the Afghan government – the most failed in the world – could be recreated and given responsibility in wartime like a quick-fix engineering project. The civilian component of Obama's war was premised on heroic assumptions about how quickly counterinsurgency could be made to work. The timetable undermined the entire strategy by depriving it of enough time, and Biden and Lute then used the strategy's predictable shortcomings to argue it was doomed from the outset. But the

---

[70] Lute, interview by author. Gates, *Duty*, 344.   [71] Lute, interview by author.

surge did not prove the impossibility of counterinsurgency; it proved the impossibility of counterinsurgency on schedule.

The 2010 assessment was a wash, two sides talking past each other and neither with a truly complete picture of the war. Gates' view was incomplete because he overlooked the civilian side of the equation; Biden's and Lute's view was incomplete because they overlooked the all-consuming pressure of the withdrawal timetable. Petraeus was right: it was simply too early to make a call. Amidst the debate, Obama visited Bagram in early December 2010. Speaking in a spartan hangar in front of a raucous crowd of US servicemen, Obama touted "important progress," promised the troops that "you will succeed in your mission," and gave his own progress report: "We said we were going to break the Taliban's momentum, and that's what you're doing." He connected the troops' service to their predecessors across American history. Petraeus, who knows the value of theater and morale, called it a "phenomenal speech" praised its "aggressive rhetoric," and felt it conveyed the president's commitment to the strategy.[72]

Two weeks later, back in Washington, Obama spoke about the assessment – but, in line with his desire for a low-key, under-the-radar process, his remarks were rhetorical pabulum. "We are on track to achieve our goals," he said, touting "significant progress" and "considerable gains." Obama reaffirmed his team's self-contradictions, highlighting the "urgent need for political and economic progress" and "continued focus on the delivery of basic services," while adding the obligatory, almost ritualistic denunciation of "nation-building." In a fit of Orwellian double-speak, he attributed progress to the very thing most responsible for its lack: the timetable. "Much of this progress ... is the result of us having sent a clear signal that we will begin the transition of responsibility to Afghans and start reducing American forces next July," he claimed.[73]

The speech was so entirely devoted to boilerplate that it was unclear to the public what the assessment had concluded, what the president had taken from it, or who had won the debate, Gates or Biden. The answer only emerged over the next six months as the administration began to debate the pace and timing of the troop drawdown.

---

[72] Obama. "Remarks by the President to the Troops at Bagram," December 3, 2010. Petraeus, interview by author and emails to author.

[73] Obama, "Statement by the President on the Afghanistan–Pakistan Annual Review," December 16, 2010.

2011: ENDING THE SURGE

The drawdown was scheduled to begin in July 2011. Over the next six months, the Obama administration debated how many troops to withdraw and how quickly. The debate fell along predictable lines. Biden, arguing the surge had failed and progress was impossible, argued for a faster and steeper drawdown; the military leadership argued they had made slow but genuine progress and argued for a slower, steadier drawdown. Critics often complained, then and now, that the military persistently asked for more time, always insisting that *just one more year* would make the crucial difference. It is true that Generals Petraeus and John Allen, commanders during the peak of the surge and the initial drawdown, thought the drawdown was too fast. But it is also true that Biden and his allies just as persistently – and even more dogmatically – made the opposite case, insisting before the surge forces were even in place that the strategy had already failed and the drawdown should be fast and steep. The administration would rehash the same debate for the next four years.

The rehash started in January 2011. Obama asked his team for views on "the troop drawdowns in July and determining what our presence should be in Afghanistan after 2014." Biden didn't wait. "The vice president jumped in aggressively," Gates recalled, "saying the strategy in Afghanistan could never succeed, there was no government, corruption was rampant, and Pakistan was still providing sanctuaries." Gates disagreed. But in March, "Biden convened a meeting at his residence to push for a dramatic troop drawdown," highlighting that public support for the war was ebbing. Gates observed that "virtually no effort had been made by the White House to change that attitude during the fifteen months since the president's decisions on the Afghan surge." Obama conveyed clearly at a March 3 NSC meeting that "my intention is to begin the security transition in July 2011 and complete it by the end of 2014," contradicting Petraeus, who had earlier suggested that the transition would "commence" in 2014.[74]

By March, Gates had come to believe that "the president doesn't trust his commander, can't stand Karzai, doesn't believe in his own strategy, and doesn't consider the war to be his. For him, it's all about getting out." He told Tom Donilon that Biden was "poisoning the well" with his pervasive pessimism. Gates asked Obama and the team "whether the strategy was to get out of Afghanistan at all costs or to achieve some level of success for the president and the country." He accused Biden of "never accept[ing] the

---

[74] Gates, *Duty*, 555, 556.

2009 decision" and of failing to think "about the consequences if his approach failed." Nonetheless, "Biden was relentless during those few days in pushing his view and in attacking the integrity of the senior military leadership." Clinton sided with Gates and the military, arguing that "withdrawing the surge by April or July 2012 [as Biden wanted] would signal we were abandoning Afghanistan."[75]

Petraeus argued strongly in favor of a conditions-based drawdown rather than a strict timetable and pushed hard to keep the surge in place until the end of 2012, past the end of the following year's fighting season. "Just preparing to withdraw forces, you have to start filling in sandbags, bulldozing bases, retrograding massive quantities of vehicles, weapons systems, life support facilities, etc. The preparation consumes you and you shouldn't do that during the fighting season," he explained. "You should get through the fighting season and then do that in the two months or so before the snow really starts to fly." Obama pushed back against Petraeus' plan. "No, that's too small upfront and too long for the full drawdown," he said, in Petraeus' retelling. The election calendar was the unspoken subtext to Obama's pushback.[76]

Petraeus was sensitive to the fact that he would shortly testify under oath before the US Senate for his confirmation hearing as CIA director. Petraeus knew the committee would ask his views on the drawdown, and he told Obama he would be bound to answer senators' questions with his "best professional military advice." He would have to tell Congress, "this is a more aggressive formulation of the drawdown than what I recommended." It didn't go over well with Obama and his advisors, who expected consensus and public support in return for their effort at compromise. It was an uncomfortable moment, but Petraeus noted, "there's nothing changed in the facts on the ground" since he last shared his assessment, "so my recommendation is unchanged." True to his word, Petraeus reiterated his assessment to Congress on June 23, warning that the pace of the drawdown meant "there is a greater risk to the accomplishment of the various objectives of the campaign plan." It was "the only way to maintain integrity as a military commander," he later said. He had hoped for a slower drawdown but "the President not only imposed the deadline to begin the drawdown of the forces, but he also dictated the pace of the drawdown."[77]

---

[75] Gates, *Duty*, 557, 562, 563, 564.   [76] Petraeus, interview by author.

[77] Petraeus, interview by author and SIGAR interview. Senate Committee on Intelligence, "Nomination of General David H. Petraeus," June 23, 2011, 37–38, 41.

Obama's team haggled about whether to withdraw 5,000 or 10,000 troops that year, and whether to withdraw the remaining surge forces by July or September of 2012. Obama tried to split the difference – he chose to withdraw 10,000 surge troops in 2011 and the rest by September of 2012, a steeper up-front number but a slightly longer timeline for the rest. As during the 2009 strategy review, Obama's political instinct overrode the military's best advice. But what is evident with perspective is how little difference there was between the options and how little the team discussed the other fundamental aspects of the war: the effects of the timetable, the need for a negotiating strategy, the problems with the civilian surge, the Afghan government's enduring weakness, or the Taliban's safe haven in Pakistan. The team had failed to explore those issues in full during the 2009 strategy reviews, focusing almost exclusively on the size and purpose of the military surge; now, at the other end of the surge, the discussion remained stuck in that narrow channel. The most intensive period of fighting in the entire twenty-year war was also marked by some of the narrowest thinking about it.

Obama announced the end of the surge and the beginning of the drawdown in late June 2011. "We are meeting our goals," he claimed, which meant "we're starting this drawdown from a position of strength." The surge had pushed back the Taliban and "put al-Qaida on a path to defeat." US Special Operations Forces had killed Osama bin Laden in Pakistan weeks previously, bolstering Obama's case and giving him political room to argue for withdrawal. He announced the initial withdrawal of 10,000 troops that year. "After this initial reduction, our troops will continue coming home at a steady pace," he said, unconsciously echoing how Nixon spoke of withdrawals from Vietnam. He announced that US forces would hand over responsibility to Afghan forces by 2014. "In some provinces and municipalities we've already begun to transition responsibility for security to the Afghan people," he claimed, though it is unclear, from Lute's comments, to what Obama was referring.[78]

In keeping with his tone throughout almost his entire presidency, he spoke of "our effort to wind down this war," not of "winning," as he had during the campaign. Seeking to reassure the war-weary American people, he claimed that "the tide of war is receding," a phrase he would repeat in his coming reelection campaign. It is an odd phrase, implying that war is a force of nature beyond human control, like ocean tides, but one that has natural and predictable rhythms to which we can adjust. The image exonerates

[78] Obama, "Remarks by the President on the Way Forward in Afghanistan," June 22, 2011.

policymakers of their wartime choices while comforting the audience that the inevitable tide is going out. War is not an ocean tide, of course, but a violent contest for power governed by human judgment and human decisions, decisions for which policymakers are accountable – including the decision to leave.

The verdict on the surge was split, then and now. In 2013, Eikenberry argued in the pages of *Foreign Affairs* that counterinsurgency had failed in Afghanistan. He criticized counterinsurgency doctrine as a "vague and open-ended guide to action, with increased effort alone regarded as an end in itself." His most trenchant criticisms focused on the failure to rebuild an Afghan government. "It was sheer hubris to think that American military personnel without the appropriate language skills and with only a superficial understanding of Afghan culture could, on six- or 12-month tours, somehow deliver to Afghan villages everything asked of them by the COIN manual," he wrote. "The US military has overly optimistic expectations about the timelines required to build healthy local civilian institutions, such as a competent civil service or a functioning justice system."[79]

Eikenberry is right – except that the timelines were not the military's idea, the military consistently opposed them, and counterinsurgency doctrine does not call for them. "We didn't get the inputs right until late 2010," Petraeus reiterated, "and then we only kept them for seven months," until the beginning of the drawdown. The timetable created a certain mindset among the implementers in the field. "[We] threw money at problems. Because we knew we only had [the inputs] for a period of time, we did everything we could in that period of time." The limited time fed a sense of urgency – "We have it *right now*, so let's do everything we can with it" – that undermined long-term thinking. "That leads to a degree of short-term focus that can be unhelpful when what you should be trying to achieve is a sustainable long-term approach." Petraeus felt that, given the situation as it was in 2010 and 2011, "you had no alternative," given the looming drawdown. Regarding Eikenberry's criticism of counterinsurgency, "I find that puzzling, because he was a big supporter of it," Petraeus responded. "Beyond that, what you always want to ask is: 'okay, so then what would you propose?' I mean, what is the alternative to a comprehensive civil–military counterinsurgency campaign, whether fully resourced or not? What is the alternative?"[80]

[79] Eikenberry, "The Limits of Counterinsurgency Doctrine in Afghanistan."
[80] Petraeus, interview by author.

The military surge was working, showing demonstrable progress against the Taliban and rapidly creating a large, lightly trained Afghan security force. But that was only one aspect of a larger strategy. That strategy included a civilian surge to rebuild the Afghan government and a timetable for drawing down the US presence. Taken as a whole, the package failed – and it failed in large part because the timetable worked at cross-purposes with the rest of it. The surge, though showing progress, had not created conditions of lasting stability. The military consistently advised the president to give it more time, the one thing he consistently refused. Weeks after Obama's announcement, Clinton presented the administration's case to the Senate Foreign Relations Committee. Though she had sided with the military in most of the administration's debates, she knew how to present a united front in public. "This is the right pace of withdrawal," she said.[81]

---

[81] Senate Foreign Relations Committee, "Evaluating Goals and Progress," June 23, 2011, 17.

10

2010–2014

Negotiations

As the surge petered out, the Obama administration had to decide what came next. On paper, Afghan security forces were supposed to take the lead for security throughout Afghanistan by 2014. But as the military surged and withdrew, a faction within the administration began to push for another option. Those who doubted that military progress could be sustained argued that the only plausible route to ending the war was through negotiations with the Taliban. "The military surge will be effective for as long as the troops are there, and then the moment they leave that effect will be gone," argued Barney Rubin. "So you need a political settlement." Rubin was right about the need for political outreach to the Taliban. Unfortunately, the Obama administration's negotiations with the Taliban were undermined by battlefield realities, bureaucratic pathologies, and, above all, the withdrawal of US forces from Afghanistan.[1]

SEARCHING FOR AN EXIT

Richard Holbrooke was the strongest advocate for negotiations because he knew firsthand they could work. Holbrooke was famous for having achieved what diplomats dream of: he had brokered a peace agreement and ended a war. As the assistant secretary of state for European affairs, he cajoled the warring parties in the former Yugoslavia to sign the Dayton Accords in 1995, ending the first round of Balkan wars. The only thing that outstripped his justly famous achievement was his estimation of it. He spent the rest of his life trying to surpass the moment, alienating colleagues and diminishing his influence along the way.

Holbrooke spent the first six years of his career as a foreign service officer in Vietnam, overseeing aid and development projects during the war. Vietnam became his touchstone as he developed his thoughts about

---

[1] Rubin, interview by author.

Afghanistan, counterinsurgency, and the importance of negotiations. "He knew that the Taliban could not be defeated on the battlefield," according to George Packer's biography, "that nation building would be long and inconclusive." Holbrooke believed the war was important, but Washington was fighting it the wrong way. "He was critical of the war on terror and skeptical of the habitual American conflation of the Taliban with al-Qaida."[2]

Despite Holbrooke's fame and his large and active staff, his influence was limited. He was at odds with Clinton over the merits of more troops, more enthusiastic about negotiations than almost anyone else in government, and in poor standing with Obama because of his grandstanding. "Obama told Jones that he would tolerate Holbrooke in the Situation Room only if he kept his remarks short," according to Packer, "and that he wanted to be in Holbrooke's presence as little as possible." Jones seemed especially antipathetic to him. "There was clearly a faction over at the State Department led by Richard Holbrook that embarked on what I thought was a rogue type of policy," he told me. Holbrooke was "embarked on his own vision."[3]

But Holbrooke had a surprising ally: Doug Lute, whose office at the NSC so closely replicated Holbrooke's at State that the two had started out as natural rivals for influence. Nonetheless, by early 2010, they came to see eye to eye on the need for negotiations with the Taliban and became "unlikely partners." Lute was skeptical of the surge and came to believe "we should at least explore the potential for talks" as "the only way out of this," he said. Lute "recognized that there was really no way to win," Lavoy recalled, and so "the way out was cutting a peace deal with the Taliban."[4]

Lavoy moved from the National Intelligence Council to the Pentagon, joining the administration as principal deputy assistant secretary of defense for Asian and Pacific security affairs, in 2011. Negotiations "had to be the way you went," he recalled, "and it's interesting, most of the Afghan leaders that I knew understood that." As the years wore on, especially after the surge, "we saw pretty much everything through the lens of setting conditions for a negotiated settlement of the war." But, in addition to the challenges in Afghanistan and with the Taliban, "the most challenging [part] of all was getting the interagency to support this, not just on paper, but getting its actions on the ground to be supportive of a peace process."[5]

---

[2] Packer, *Our Man*, 456, 461. [3] Packer, *Our Man*, 469. Jones, interview by author.

[4] Lute, interview by author. Lavoy, interview by author. Packer, *Our Man*, 518.

[5] Lavoy, interview by author.

Holbrooke, Lute, Lavoy, and other supporters of negotiations were right about the need to open talks with the Taliban. But Lavoy's characterization – that there was no way to win, and therefore negotiations were necessary – misunderstands the relationship between negotiations and winning, or misstates what "winning" entails. Rightly understood, negotiations should be seen as a pathway to victory, not an alternative to it. Just as the Obama administration misunderstood what it meant to "defeat" the Taliban during its 2009 strategy review, so too they seemed to miss that if negotiations led to an outcome in which the Taliban stopped fighting and severed ties to al-Qaida, that was a victory for American interests. The framing was important: it was harder to sell negotiations within the administration and to the broader public than it should have been because talks were widely seen as a second-best outcome, a concession, or a sign of military and moral failure. If, however, negotiations were understood as a main effort to achieve America's core goals in conjunction with the military surge, they might have earned earlier and stronger support.

It was the same misunderstanding that led policymakers and critics over the years to repeat, *ad nauseam,* that there was "no military solution" to the problem in Afghanistan, and that therefore we had to concede to political realities and negotiate. The phrase was as vacuous and irrelevant as the observation that there would be no surrender ceremony on the deck of a battleship. Such observations are not wrong, but neither are they saying anything profound. Every war ends with a political settlement. Military success only opens the door to political settlement; it does not accomplish political change by itself. As the famous strategist Thomas Schelling argued in 1966, winning a war does not accomplish much by itself. "By force alone we cannot even lead a horse to water – we have to drag him – much less make him drink." Winning simply gives the victor the opportunity to inflict unlimited harm on the enemy unless the enemy makes the political change the victor demands. "Military victory is often the prelude to violence, not the end of it," Schelling wrote. The threat of future violence gets unreconciled enemies to start talking. Every war involves a mix of military operations and diplomacy to achieve a nation's objectives; the fact that there was a political component to the war against the Taliban was not a sign of failure, it was a sign of reality. In the ends–ways–means framework, if diplomacy helps secure the end, it should be a vital, even preferred, means of getting there. Talking to the enemy is a feature, not a bug, of sound strategy.[6]

---

[6] Schelling, *Arms and Influence,* quoted in Art, Crawford, and Jervis (eds.), *International Politics,* 217, 218.

What the critics were really saying is that there would be no unconditional surrender – which, again, is true but superficial. In this respect,
American thinking about war has been profoundly misshapen by the experience of World War II and the Civil War. Those wars were total wars fought
for unconditional surrender against moral evils with which there could be
no compromise. Unconditional surrender was appropriate in those cases, as
it was and still is in the war against al-Qaida. Unfortunately, most Americans
have wrongly taken the lesson that all war must follow the same template,
and that anything less than unconditional surrender is a sign of military
weakness and moral compromise. But World War II was the most unusual
war in history, not a template for how wars usually play out. "We want
unconditional surrender," because it is tidy and complete, thought
Ruggiero, but "I think the key lesson the United States has to learn from
Afghanistan is, how do you use force to achieve a political objective ... in
wars that are messy?" Most wars are not total wars; unconditional surrender
is very rarely the best or most effective strategy for victory.

2010: NEGOTIATING A PATH TO NEGOTIATIONS

After the Taliban rebuffed the Bush administration's outreach in the weeks
after 9/11, the US military lumped them together with al-Qaida, and
American diplomats had no leeway for talks or negotiations. Karzai pushed
for a softer approach in his April 2003 speech. A formal reconciliation
program finally got up and running in 2005, but it was little more than
a surrender program for foot soldiers. The Obama administration inherited
Bush's policy that any Taliban who wanted to stop fighting had to first
denounce al-Qaida, lay down arms, and accept the Afghan constitution.

Obama's team was initially wary of talking to the Taliban. Holbrooke
believed that, in 2009, "talking to the enemy was an unwelcome idea almost
everywhere in the US government," according to Packer. "Clinton didn't
want to hear of peace talks, and neither did the military, and neither did the
White House." The administration was "uneasy about any contacts with
a group that had not renounced its ties to al-Qaida." It was politically risky,
legally complicated, and could imply lack of confidence in the military.
"Obama and his advisors were unwilling to consider any approach except
the military one that they clearly doubted would work – as if talking with the
enemy would cost the president too much of his limited capital." That is why
"talking to the enemy – the only way to end the war – was never part of the
[2009] strategy review." In any case, "the CIA believed that Taliban leaders

didn't want a settlement because they thought they were winning." On the other hand, Holbrooke believed, "it would be irresponsible of us not to try" negotiations, especially "given the fact that there's no military solution to the war." That was true "even though the chances of success in any kind of dialogue with the Taliban are very small."[7]

Policymakers most skeptical of the surge became most supportive of negotiations, seeing the two options as alternatives rather than complements to one another. They turned to negotiations "because of deep seated skepticism that COIN alone would work," Lute said. "So it wasn't that [we believed] diplomacy would work, it's just that we better have a plan B, because we didn't." Lute recalled, "COIN was losing speed, and it was becoming more and more clear to more people, especially in the White House that we needed an alternative." Counterinsurgency was not losing speed in 2010 – surge forces were still arriving – but the perception that it was not proving itself fast enough grew over the course of 2010 and 2011, giving more strength to advocates of negotiations.[8]

In April 2010, months after the surge announcement, Lute convened a Conflict Resolution Cell in the White House, "a group of officials from different agencies who met weekly in a small, secure conference room just off the Situation Room." As Lute described it, while the surge was ongoing "we ought to take advantage of any of the military effects on the Taliban to see if we could open diplomatic channels." They reexamined the Bush-era negotiating guidance and quickly saw that it was less a negotiating strategy than a list of surrender terms. By demanding that the Taliban lay down arms, denounce al-Qaida, and accept the constitution as a *precondition* for talks – something the Taliban had to do before negotiations would even commence – the guidance demanded everything from the Taliban without offering anything in return. If the Taliban met those demands, what else was there to talk about? There had been no negotiation with the Taliban since their fall from power, and the reconciliation program had shown no real success because the Taliban had no incentive to talk. With Obama's blessing, Lute's Conflict Resolution Cell turned the preconditions into goals. They would still demand the Taliban lay down arms, denounce al-Qaida, and accept the constitution – but those would be the hoped-for *outcomes* of a successful negotiation, not the preconditions for starting them.[9]

Timing was critical. "If Obama waited to talk until the surge troops began to leave in mid-2011," Holbrooke's biographer wrote, "then he would repeat

---

[7] Packer, *Our Man*, 498, 514, 518, 531.   [8] Lute, interview by author.

[9] Packer, *Our Man*, 518. Lute, interview by author.

Nixon's and Kissinger's mistake." Nixon and Kissinger negotiated with the North Vietnamese throughout 1969–1973 while unilaterally withdrawing US forces. Negotiating while withdrawing deprived them of leverage, ultimately yielding the toothless Paris Peace Accords of 1973, the full withdrawal of US forces, and the North's victory two years later. The North Vietnamese stretched negotiations out deliberately, knowing that domestic political pressure in the United States would accomplish the chief aim of the North Vietnamese – the withdrawal of all US forces – without having to concede anything meaningful in exchange. Holbrooke and others worried – rightly, it turned out – that a similar dynamic would play out in Afghanistan.[10]

To get any traction, Holbrooke needed the military's support. "The military had opposed talking with the Taliban in the middle of the surge," so Holbrooke sent briefers to talk to McChrystal. "The three-hour briefing in the Pentagon basement convinced the general that a political strategy had the best chance of success at the point of greatest troop strength, when military pressure could reward cooperative elements of the Taliban and punish the irreconcilables." In fact, Holbrooke's briefers did not convince McChrystal; he was already on board. McChrystal had written in his 2009 assessment that "insurgencies of this nature typically conclude through military operations and political efforts driving some degree of host-nation reconciliation with elements of the insurgency," suggesting Holbrooke's briefers had a receptive audience.[11] As McChrystal later argued to me:

> The Taliban were Afghans ... they don't have anywhere to go. You look at the Taliban and say, okay, end the war, come into society. What are they going to do? They don't have land. They don't have jobs. They don't have these things, so you've got this opposition that doesn't have a credible alternative ... You've got to create this reconciliation that isn't just handshaking, it's a very thought-through program of economic reintegration, political reintegration, land reform, all these things. For us, reconciliation was going to be a much deeper program. I thought it was going to be essential ... You had to give them an option, you had to give them somewhere to go.[12]

Lute's cell found a dozen possible leads in various intelligence reports and whittled them down one by one. They pursued one lead that turned out to be a fraudster looking to turn a profit by promising to introduce the US to Taliban interlocutors for a fee. More promisingly, Holbrooke's counterpart

[10] Packer, *Our Man*, 518.

[11] Packer, *Our Man*, 518. McChrystal, Commander's Assessment, 2–13.

[12] McChrystal, interview by author.

in the German government believed he had a possible diplomatic contact with the Taliban, a former aide to Mullah Omar named Tayeb Agha. Lute and his cell tracked the contact down. Frank Ruggiero, then serving as Holbrooke's deputy, and another official from DoD met with Agha in Munich in late 2010. "That was the first substantive US government connection" between the United States and the Taliban in a decade, according to Lute. The timing was almost perfect, if accidental, "because it happened at the peak of the surge ... we were applying maximum military leverage and exploring the potential for gains in the diplomatic arena." Almost, but not quite: the surge would stay in place for a few months while the negotiations were only just beginning.[13]

The US team communicated to the Taliban that there were no longer preconditions to negotiations. With the first prospect of real negotiations in a decade, each side had to figure out what they could realistically ask for. The Taliban asked for the release of five senior leaders detained at Guantanamo Bay. Second, they wanted sanctions – some dating back to 1999 – lifted on senior leaders. Third, they demanded the ability to open a political office in Doha, Qatar, safe from US military targeting, through which to conduct diplomacy, "a public 'address' for the Taliban to facilitate talks." Fourth, they demanded to negotiate directly with the United States, not with the Afghan government. At least some sanctions relief would be a prerequisite to allow any talks to go forward; Tayeb Agha himself had been sanctioned, and "the Americans would have to take him off their sanctions list before they could talk to him."[14]

On the American side, the Obama and Trump administrations insisted that their goal in talking with the Taliban was not to end the war but to bring the Taliban to the table and open direct talks with Kabul. "Our objective was to set up a series of confidence-building measures in steps that would lead to a negotiation between the Taliban and the government of Afghanistan," according to Ambassador Marc Grossman, who took over as special representative after Holbrooke died. "We were not there to negotiate peace between the Taliban and the government of Afghanistan ... That was for them to do. Our job was to see if we could get that negotiation going." Some of the confidence-building measures the United States sought included a public statement denouncing terrorism and the release of Sergeant Bowe Bergdahl (an American soldier in Taliban captivity).[15]

---

[13] Lute, interview by author. Accounts differ as to when the first meeting with Agha occurred, August or November 2010.

[14] Packer, *Our Man*, 514, 518.   [15] Grossman, interview by author.

"Looking back on it in hindsight, that was pretty low bar," Kolenda, who would become directly involved in the negotiation, thought. "At the end of that sequence, they would start talks with the Afghan government." In parallel with American efforts, the Afghan government formed a High Peace Council in September 2010, a body of Afghan elites and powerbrokers commissioned to open talks with the Taliban. Karzai was wary of the United States negotiating a separate peace with the Taliban, leaving Kabul sidelined and unprotected. The Peace Council intended to take the baton from American negotiators once a process had been successfully started.[16]

Unfortunately, the path to negotiations suffered a setback when Ambassador Richard Holbrooke suffered an aortic dissection on December 10 while meeting with Secretary Clinton at the State Department; he died three days later. Obama paid tribute to the veteran diplomat later that week. "The progress that we have made in Afghanistan and Pakistan is due in no small measure to Richard's relentless focus on America's national interest," he said. It was appropriate, gracious, and almost true. The civilian surge was failing, and negotiations had barely started.[17]

2011: GOING PUBLIC

Throughout 2010 the Obama administration kept its internal discussions about negotiations and initial feelers toward the Taliban secret. The first meeting with the Taliban late that year had (remarkably) gone unreported in the press. The administration still felt that negotiations would be politically risky, they had already been fooled by one fraudster who posed as an intermediary to the Taliban, and publicity would bring criticism that could sink negotiations before they began. Obama started to crack open the door to more publicity in December, saying that the United States would "fully support an Afghan political process that includes reconciliation with those Taliban who break ties with al-Qaida, renounce violence, and accept the Afghan constitution."[18]

Two months after Holbrooke died, Clinton went public with the administration's new approach to negotiations. She had supported the surge, but "as we began to talk with her in the fall of '10, it was very clear that she

[16] Kolenda, interview by author.
[17] Obama, "Statement from the President on Richard Holbrooke," December 13, 2010.
[18] Obama, "Statement by the President," December 16, 2010.

supported a political settlement and she came to believe in that very strongly," said Frank Ruggiero.[19] In a speech to the Asia Society in New York in February 2011, she claimed the administration had undertaken three surges – military, civilian, and diplomatic – and that the first two "set the table for success" in the third. It briefed well and indeed should have been the strategy all along: military progress and improving governance would force the Taliban to negotiate while US and Afghan negotiators would be in a strong position. But Clinton's description belied what had happened in the administration's deliberations, which had only gradually warmed to negotiations as faith in the surge waned. It was a classic example of creating an *ex post facto* cohesiveness to policies that were, at the time, disconnected from and even competing against each other. In the same vein of wishing strategy into existence, Clinton claimed that the "escalating pressure of our military campaign" was forcing the Taliban to choose between negotiations and defeat. But by the time of Clinton's speech, US military pressure had peaked and was already starting to decline, not escalate. "They cannot wait us out," she said, which they could and did. Obama's timetable told the Taliban otherwise, and everyone knew it.[20]

Clinton's diplomatic initiative had a sound basis to it. She rightly noted that "we will never kill enough insurgents to end this war outright," which is why the United States needed "a diplomatic surge to move this conflict toward a political outcome that shatters the alliance between the Taliban and al-Qaida." That was true enough – it had been true since 2002. Clinton used the same language as the old reconciliation program. The Taliban "must renounce violence; they must abandon their alliance with al-Qaida; and they must abide by the constitution of Afghanistan." Then she slipped in the administration's major departure from its predecessor: "Those are necessary outcomes of any negotiation" – "outcomes," not "preconditions."

"The decision to have no preconditions was a recognition on the part of the United States government that if you had preconditions, you were never going to talk to the Taliban," Ambassador Grossman later told me. "One of those things that we weren't going to do was set up preconditions in order to make sure we didn't ever have a negotiation." Grossman felt starting negotiations was important enough to justify the change. He felt it was a major step "to finally say out loud that there was no military solution to this problem and that there had to be some negotiation with the Taliban." He was right,

---

[19]   Ruggiero, interview by author.
[20]   Clinton, "Remarks at the Launch of the Asia Society's Series of Richard C. Holbrooke Memorial Addresses," February 18, 2011.

even though his rationale (or at least his rhetoric) reflected the same faulty understanding others in the administration voiced. If we understand Grossman to mean there would be no "unconditional surrender," and thus negotiations were necessary, he was right. Grossman emphasized this was a major change in the mindset of American policymakers. He had previously served as the undersecretary of state for political affairs in the Bush administration's first term and was familiar with their inflexible attitude toward the Taliban after 2001. A decade later, "it was important at that time to speak the truth … that we were not in any position to force the Taliban to a negotiation in which we could set the conditions," and that the United States needed to begin the process "just to see what was possible."[21]

Major obstacles limited what was possible. In public, Clinton continued to repeat that "the Afghan Government must be prepared to be more inclusive and more accountable," which meant that it would have to accept Taliban participation in government, while simultaneously "all parties will have to commit to a pluralistic political system that respects the human rights of every Afghan," which meant the Taliban would have to accept women's rights. It was an attractive, fanciful vision: a grand coalition including Taliban, Northern Alliance warlords, former communists, Western-educated technocrats, women, Shia, and ethnic minorities. Most Afghans, especially women, disliked the idea of allowing the Taliban any share of political power, while the Taliban never budged on their position about women's rights. Negotiators faced a mission impossible so long as the Taliban remained religiously committed to theocratic totalitarianism while the United States was committed to protecting human rights.

An air of unreality attached to other aspects of the hoped-for negotiations. In his later recounting, Grossman detailed a series of international meetings and conferences in 2011 and 2012. At each meeting, Grossman and his colleague successfully secured from the international community repeated statements of support for the new Afghanistan, including its commitment to human rights. "We wanted the Taliban to receive a series of clear messages from the meetings in Istanbul, Bonn, Chicago, and Tokyo," that the international community was united behind the new Afghanistan. Grossman was successful in presenting the united front – but it was premised on the notion that the Taliban cared what the international community thought. They did not.[22]

This is the paradox of the Obama administration's effort to negotiate with the Taliban. They were right that negotiations were a necessary pathway to ending the war but seem not to have been able to admit to themselves who

---

[21] Grossman, interview by author.   [22] Grossman, "Talking to the Taliban," 25.

the Taliban really were and what real negotiations would look like. The Taliban were not interested in an "inclusive" or "pluralistic" Afghanistan, and they had no track record of caring about what the international community said or demanded. "I never developed any kind of trust that the Taliban would be serious about really trying to embrace a kind of democratic approach to governing in Afghanistan," reflected Leon Panetta, director of the CIA from 2009 to 2011 and secretary of defense from 2011 to 2013. "At least my experience and the intelligence that we had indicated that that's not where the Taliban were coming from."[23]

US officials persuaded themselves that the Taliban wanted to become responsible partners in a new Afghanistan, one voice among many. The US floated proposals for "power sharing" that were "premised on the Taliban in some ways recognizing the changes in Afghanistan that have taken place, so, recognizing the rights of minorities, freedoms for women, some elements of representative government and so on," according to Mike McKinley, US ambassador to Afghanistan in 2015 and 2016. McKinley thought it was naive to think that "the Taliban were prepared to do this." Even if the Taliban signed a piece of paper accepting the Afghan constitution, McKinley thought it was "a little bit of a stretch" to believe that the Taliban would "actually honor whatever they signed."[24]

The Taliban were, and remain to this day, a thuggish gang of theocratic totalitarians. Negotiating with them would not be akin to hashing out the details of a trade agreement with the European Union, say, or the next UN-sponsored climate accord. There are no shared values, no win–win scenarios, and no common beliefs in a liberal international order. Negotiations between enemies are a pathway for each side to force their view on the other under threat of war. That requires a hard-nosed understanding of who the enemy is, close coordination between diplomatic outreach and military strategy, and a willingness to back demands with force, yet also to make real concessions for the sake of peace. Neither the Americans, the Taliban, nor, it turned out, the Afghan government proved capable and willing to doing so.

THE US MILITARY AND NEGOTIATIONS

"There were occasions when some colleagues tried to micromanage the conversation with the Taliban in ways designed to make it impossible to continue," Grossman later wrote. He did not name names, but most observers suggested

---

[23] Panetta, interview by author.   [24] McKinley, interview by author.

the US military was opposed to the negotiations and found ways to delay or slow down the process. But Bob Gates told a different story. "Contrary to some of the things that have been written, there really wasn't anybody sitting at the table in the situation room that opposed negotiating with the Taliban," he claimed. "I think there was a general recognition that the only way the conflict would end would be through a negotiation." Why did Grossman feel that "some colleagues" tried to make negotiations impossible, while Gates claimed no one opposed them?[25]

This is another case study in how bureaucracy operates. Several things bear remembering. First, "the military" is not a monolithic entity, and its various senior leaders, both military and civilian, had different views, and their views evolved over time. Second, if a champion is well liked or personally popular, their ideas gain ground; if not, then not. Third, as negotiations picked up pace in 2011, it became unprofitable to openly oppose them; once an idea gains momentum, some officials who do not favor it chose to simply get out of the way rather than expend political capital in a losing battle. Fourth, instead of openly opposing an idea, officials often suggest delay; rather than saying "no," they say, "not yet," kicking the can down the road long enough that the window closes, or they leave office.

For example, "Holbrooke was an ardent advocate of" negotiations, and "the fact that he was an advocate probably led to some of the opposition in the Obama White House," according to Gates. Holbrooke was not well liked within the administration. Without personal cachet, he lacked the power to convene or set an agenda. If he called a meeting, people wouldn't show up; if he suggested an agenda item for a meeting, it would not make the list, or it would be put last and never addressed because time ran out. (Holbrooke never had that trouble outside the White House – he successfully created a contact group of forty to fifty counterparts in governments around the world and set the agenda for regional diplomacy in South Asia – but could never create the same momentum inside Washington.) I do not mean that Obama officials adopted a deliberate, mean-spirited, and coordinated campaign to ostracize Holbrooke. I simply mean that when people like you, they are more likely to return your phone call, answer your email, and attend your meeting. Contrary to the popular perception that only the most ruthless, manipulative, and scheming operatives succeed in Washington, DC, personal likability and human decency are valuable traits because they help get your foot in the door.[26]

---

[25] Grossman, "Talking to the Taliban," 23. Gates, interview by author.
[26] Gates, interview by author.

The military, for their part, did not have a uniform view about negotiations. McChrystal had supported the idea, especially after Holbrooke's briefing. But after his firing – precisely when Lute's conflict resolution cell started making real progress finding a Taliban contact to negotiate with – "with McChrystal gone, the military command in Afghanistan lost interest in talking to the enemy," Holbrooke's biographer claimed. "The military, and above all Petraeus, thought it was much too soon to negotiate in 2009, or even 2010 – the surge needed time to punish the enemy first." Other sources paint a slightly different picture. "Petraeus talked about [negotiations] all the time, about figuring out a way to engage with them at some point," Gates said. Petraeus spoke at the Munich Security Conference alongside Holbrooke in February 2009, among other international summits and meetings, and spoke favorably of the reconciliation program. He dutifully provided logistical support to Holbrooke and Grossman for their travel and meetings in Afghanistan and Pakistan.[27]

"*At some point*" seems to be the key for Petraeus, and this was the moment of his largest influence on the Afghanistan war. General David Petraeus was already a "celebrity general" when he took command of ISAF. Near top of his class at West Point in 1974, he was the top graduate at the Command and Staff College in 1983 before getting his PhD at Princeton, where he wrote his dissertation on the lessons of the Vietnam War. He was an early advocate for counterinsurgency and put his ideas into action as commander of the 101st Airborne Division in occupied Mosul, in northern Iraq, in 2003 and 2004. He wrote the army's counterinsurgency manual in 2006 and took command of the war in Iraq at the height of the surge in 2007 and 2008, demonstrating that his ideas – coupled with extraordinarily rapid and effective special operations forces – could turn the tide. His success there won him promotion to command CENTCOM, but when Obama fired McChrystal, there was no other conceivable successor.

"Petraeus was not opposed to peace talks in principle, but preferred to establish a stronger position on the battlefield first," according to Jim Dobbins, who took over as special representative for Afghanistan and Pakistan in 2013. Counterinsurgency doctrine clearly recognizes the importance of political and diplomatic components of an overall strategy. But the question was timing. "The president was unwilling to press the debate to a timely conclusion," Dobbins wrote, "and as a result the United States missed the opportunity to launch negotiations at the peak of its combat strength in Afghanistan." Petraeus understood the importance of

---

[27] Packer, *Our Man*, 521, 514. Gates, interview by author.

negotiations but did not believe the conditions existed for them to succeed during his time as CENTCOM and ISAF commander, from late 2008 through mid 2011.[28]

Petraeus invoked Holbrooke's involvement in peace negotiations in the Balkans to highlight its difference from Afghanistan. In September 1995, Holbrooke conducted an intensive round of shuttle diplomacy among the various combatants in the Balkan Wars simultaneously with NATO's air campaign – Operation Deliberate Force – against Bosnian Serb militias. Holbrooke explicitly threatened more bombing unless the Serbs showed up to negotiate. To make the threat credible, Holbrooke included General Mike Short, the commander overseeing the bombing, in the negotiating team, and he went to NATO to "ask them for an activation order to put the planes on ready alert on the runways." The incident is famous among American diplomats and soldiers as a prime example of a well-coordinated diplomatic-military campaign.[29]

By contrast, in 2010 and 2011, "we can't bomb these guys to the negotiating table in the same the way you could in the [Bosnian Serb] Republic of Srpska," Petraeus recalls telling Holbrooke. "Afghanistan does not only not equal Iraq, it also doesn't equal the Balkans. It's just completely different." The US could not bomb the Taliban to the negotiating table "because we didn't have the authority to go to where their headquarters and bases in Pakistan were ... we never were able to put pressure on the senior leadership." ISAF's authority ended at the Pakistani border, but the Taliban leadership lived on the other side of it. Without the ability to reach them, the Taliban would never feel the sort of pressure that Holbrooke was able to put on the Serbs in 1995. "I told him: 'Richard, we can't get to the enemy, we can't put pressure on Mullah Omar. Tell me how, what do I do to put pressure on him personally?'"[30]

Petraeus invoked another historical precedent to emphasize the point. "What kind of leverage did [Nixon] have over North Vietnam?" Petraeus asked. "Well, you actually went downtown. You bombed them, you mined their harbor, you went into a neutral country." Nixon's controversial tactics, including mining Haiphong Harbor, invading Cambodia, and the Christmas Bombing of 1972, forced North Vietnam back to the negotiating table to sign the Paris Peace Accords (which ultimately proved ineffective, in any event). "We're not going to do any of that here," Petraeus said. The US was not going

[28] Dobbins, *Five Decades*, 273.
[29] PBS interview with Richard Holbrooke, www.pbs.org/wgbh/pages/frontline/shows/kos ovo/interviews/holbrooke.html.
[30] Petraeus, interview by author.

to start bombing runs over Quetta or Peshawar or mine the ports of Gwadar or Karachi. Doing so would risk the US's ground lines of communications and resupply through Pakistan, if not provoke war with nuclear-armed Pakistan. "I don't see the leverage ... And I fear that it is just going to prove impossible."[31]

In other words, Petraeus did not actively oppose negotiations – indeed, he could point to ways he had supported them – but he also believed conditions were not ripe and thus never gave them his full support. He didn't say "no," he said, "not yet." Petraeus tried to increase American leverage through battlefield success: he loosened the rules of engagement that McChrystal had tightened and increased the tempo of airstrikes and offensive operations. Some observers faulted him for making the counter-insurgency campaign too kinetic and taking the focus off population secur-ity, but Petraeus was trying to use his diminishing military power to catalyze negotiations before the window of opportunity closed – another example of the inevitable trade-offs inherent in strategy. "Stan [McChrystal] had been a bit too cautious in the tactical restraints he had imposed on operations, so Dave [Petraeus] relaxed them a bit," wrote Mike Vickers, the assistant secretary of defense for special operations and low intensity conflict. "One involved restrictions Stan had placed on the use of close air support. The other concerned rules of engagement for ground combat. The overall effect on the battlefield of both changes was positive."[32]

Petraeus had a strong point about the inability to target Taliban safe havens in Pakistan because Pakistan was not included in the US military's authorized area for combat operations. Could that have changed? US officials raised the point with their Pakistani counterparts, seeking permission for expanded operations, which Pakistani officials repeatedly refused. As a result, the United States came to rely more and more on unilateral drone strikes, without advance permission from Pakistan. In 2013, Obama publicly disclosed that the United States "has taken lethal, targeted action against al-Qaida and its associated forces, including with remotely piloted aircraft commonly referred to as drones," something the press had reported for years. The New America Foundation estimated that the US launched 48 drone strikes in Pakistan under the Bush administration, rising to a whopping 353 drone strikes under the Obama administration. The Pakistani government privately condoned the shift in the US's drone operations even as it publicly condemned it.[33]

---

[31] Petraeus, interview by author.   [32] Vickers, *By All Means Available*, 320.

[33] Woodward, *Obama's Wars*, 25–26. Vickers, *By All Means Available*, 229–232, 236. New America Foundation, "The Drone War in Pakistan" (www.newamerica.org/future-security/reports/americas-counterterrorism-wars/the-drone-war-in-pakistan/). The New America Foundation

But, just as in the Bush administration, the drone strikes were still focused exclusively in the FATA against al-Qaida and other targets, not against the Afghan Taliban; they were tools of counterterrorism, not counterinsurgency. Could the Obama administration have expanded drone operations in Pakistan to create the pressure on the Taliban leadership that Petraeus rightly saw was lacking? The idea is not outlandish: the Obama administration did precisely that in 2016 when the media reported a US drone strike killed the Taliban's supreme leader in Baluchistan, well outside the FATA (see Chapter 12). But that was five years after the surge. That the administration did not go after the Taliban leadership at the height of the surge is likely one of the great missed opportunities of the war. Their failure to do so meant that despite the surge, the United States stopped just shy of exerting maximum, direct pressure on the Taliban leadership. That is why, during the brief window when negotiations had their best chance to proceed while the United States had the most military leverage, America's most influential military officer said, "not yet."

GROSSMAN, KARZAI, AND BONN

American and Taliban representatives met periodically throughout 2011. "We met with the Taliban probably five or six times, alternating between Doha, Qatar, and in Munich, Germany," Frank Ruggiero recalled. The American side was now led by Ambassador Marc Grossman in the wake of Holbrooke's death, with Ruggiero as deputy. "Marc is a more classic, conventional diplomat and not the sort of 'break china, bulldoze through the problems' sort of guy that Holbrook was," according to Lute. Vikram Singh agreed. "He just approached things in a much more calm, methodical, patient manner," he said. Grossman tried to bring a more patient, by-the-book approach to the problem. "Marc began to assess the situation, took his time, but then established a step-by-step approach," Lute said.[34]

Grossman wrote up a memorandum of understanding with the emir of Qatar that put down on paper the emir's role as intermediary and outlined the confidence-building steps that he envisioned both sides taking. A major goal for the American side was to get proof that Tayeb Agha had contact with the Taliban senior leadership and could genuinely represent their

estimated that 32 percent of strikes under the Obama administration targeted the Taliban, but the data does not distinguish between Afghan Taliban and Pakistani Taliban.

[34] Lute, Singh, and Ruggiero, interviews by author.

views. "All through this period, the naysayers in the interagency would say, yeah, but who are these guys? You're wasting your time," recalled Lute. "This is a wild goose chase." The US negotiators needed something that demonstrated Agha's bona fides. They asked Agha to get the Taliban leadership to insert a specific, unusual phrase in Mullah Omar's annual Eid statement, Lute recalled, so "if that phrase appears verbatim in the Eid statement then, then we'll believe that the Taliban political office has meaningful connections with the Taliban leadership." Agha delivered, demonstrating he was a genuine intermediary.[35]

The fate of negotiations seesawed throughout 2011. Just as there were divisions with the Obama administration about the wisdom and feasibility of negotiations, the Taliban themselves were not unified in their approach. "While we met with a representative of the Taliban Political Commission, who seemed interested in a negotiated end to the conflict, the Taliban Military Commission appeared to want to continue the fight," Grossman wrote. "They could not understand why they should give up what they considered they had achieved at great cost in a political settlement." The Taliban hard-liners tried to sabotage the process. On September 20, 2011, a Taliban militant assassinated Burhanuddin Rabbani, the head of Afghanistan's High Peace Council and one of the foremost Afghan champions of reconciliation, with a bomb hidden in his turban. Grossman called off negotiations to signal the United States' displeasure. How could the United States take the Taliban's peace overtures seriously while they were murdering Afghan diplomats? The murder made it that much harder for Karzai to sustain political support for talks with the Taliban. The Taliban had a "diabolically accurate sense of how damaging Rabbani's murder was for the peace effort," Grossman wrote.[36]

But it was a temporary setback; sessions were back on within months in hopes of a serious breakthrough by the end of the year. International diplomats gathered for a conference in Bonn, Germany, in December, ten years after the Bonn Accords that had created the new Afghan government. Grossman hoped it would be a milestone on the pathway to a negotiated end to the war. He had the signed memorandum from the emir of Qatar, bona fides from Tayeb Agha, and buy-in from the Obama administration. Clinton flew in to attend the conference and solidify Karzai's agreement to the negotiations with the Taliban.

Now, it was Hamid Karzai's turn to tank the deal. Throughout 2011, Grossman had vigilantly kept Karzai informed every step of the way. "Every

---

[35] Lute, interview by author.   [36] Grossman, "Talking to the Taliban," 32.

time Marc [Grossman] went to see the Taliban, he went in advance to see Karzai and then bookended the back end of the engagement with the Taliban with a second visit to Karzai," Lute recalled. "Marc was very meticulous in terms of keeping Karzai informed." Grossman had understood the need to repair the diplomatic relationship with Karzai after two years of ruinous diplomacy from Biden, Holbrooke, and Eikenberry. That meant he and his team "kept the government of Afghanistan, especially President Hamid Karzai, completely and fully informed of all of our conversations with the Taliban," Grossman wrote.[37]

Despite Grossman's meticulous attention to the relationship, when he and Clinton presented Karzai with the final package at Bonn, "Karzai goes off the rails" and claimed he had never been informed, Lute recalled. "But he was lying, he had been fully informed." In Grossman's recollection, Karzai simply said, "No, you can't go" to Doha, claiming that "you've never told me about any of this," which, Grossman said, "is of course complete nonsense." Karzai fabricated excuses, claiming that the memorandum should have been between the Afghan government and the Taliban, not the United States and the emir of Qatar. "I think he had not prepared his government," Grossman believed. "He had not prepared his society. He'd bet against us. He didn't think we could accomplish this task." Karzai had not taken the American diplomatic initiative seriously in 2011, which meant he was unprepared when it turned out to be serious.[38]

In broader terms, Karzai was responding to the shifting diplomatic climate. "Karzai wanted an Afghan-centered peace process, with the Kabul government and the Taliban inside the room and everyone else out," wrote Jim Dobbins, who succeeded Grossman in 2013. "Washington said it also wanted an Afghan-led negotiation, but Karzai no longer trusted the United States." Karzai's unexpected refusal to sanction the negotiating process undermined Grossman's standing with the Taliban. "My credibility then was shot basically," Grossman recalled. "I think I saw them once more in January, February of 2012." But the Taliban pulled the plug in March, seeing no point to talking with diplomats who couldn't deliver. The Taliban would talk to the United States, but not to Karzai; the United States would talk to the Taliban, but not without Karzai; while Karzai wanted to talk to the Taliban, preferably with the United States on the sidelines. "Apprised of Karzai's condition, the Taliban broke off further contact with the United States," according to Dobbins. "And that was kind of the end of

---

[37] Grossman, "Talking to the Taliban," 26. Lute, interview by author.
[38] Lute, Grossman, Ruggiero, interviews by author.

that," Grossman said. Negotiations were dead for 2012 and the first half of 2013. "We essentially allowed our need for Karzai as a COIN partner to supersede our need for Karzai to be a partner on the diplomatic track," in Lute's estimate. "We subordinated the diplomatic track to the promise or the potential of COIN on the battlefield."[39]

Karzai recognized that the Obama administration viewed the surge and negotiations as rivals, not complements. Karzai had called for talks with the Taliban as early as 2003, yet when the Americans finally got on board they did so reluctantly, only after they had lost faith in their military strategy. Karzai could hardly accept negotiations under those circumstances. In 2003, the US military and the Afghan government were ascendent, and Karzai recognized the timing for outreach to the Taliban was ripe. By 2011, the moment had passed, and time was on the Taliban's side, thanks to the withdrawal timetable. Because the Obama administration plainly saw negotiations as a concession, a second-best approach designed to minimize the fallout from what it thought was the inevitable failure of the surge, Karzai had nothing to gain and everything to lose from them. Negotiations had become a polite way of giving to the Taliban what the United States was unable to win on the battlefield.

Negotiations did not have to be viewed that way. "I think I would have had a ready ear had I gone to [Obama] and said, look these are competing and they don't need to compete," Lute later reflected. "They could actually complement one another, so that when our military pressure was greatest, we were most ambitious in terms of exploring diplomatic outreach. Imagine the conversation with the Taliban with 150,000 Western troops in the field." Gates agreed: "The time to reach out would have been as we were sending tens of thousands of more troops in there," he told me. Lute felt partly to blame for the failure. "I wish I had more strongly made the argument that these two [surge and negotiations] need to be kept roughly in parallel and that we should not subordinate [negotiations] because we knew that Obama wasn't going to fully resource COIN." The administration's decision to prioritize the surge and pit it against negotiations "is one of the things where I wish I had fought harder," he said. But it was Obama's overall strategy that made a fight necessary in the first place.[40]

---

[39] Grossman, Lute, interviews by author. Dobbins, *Five Decades*, 273, 274.

[40] Lute, Gates, interviews by author.

2013 AND 2014: THE DOHA POLITICAL OFFICE
AND THE PRISONER SWAP

Two more episodes were yet to come in the Obama administration's attempts to negotiate with the Taliban, one in mid 2013 and another in mid 2014. Jim Dobbins – the American representative to the 2001 Bonn conference – succeeded Grossman after the post sat vacant for five months. Just as he came back to the State Department in May 2013, the Taliban let it be known they were ready to talk again. American officials were keen to seize the opportunity. "There was all this excitement that we're about to have a big breakthrough," recalled Laurel Miller, who was onboarding as the deputy special representative under Dobbins, "and the week before I started it blew up."[41]

Dobbins wanted to respond by reviving the proposal, first floated in 2010 and 2011, that the Taliban open a political office in Qatar where the two sides could negotiate a prisoner swap. He faced an obstacle: "Before putting this proposal to the Taliban, I needed to make sure [Secretary of State John] Kerry and Secretary of Defense [Chuck] Hagel, neither of whom had been in office in early 2012 when this scheme was first devised, were on board." American policymakers tend to have relatively short terms in high office, which complicates continuity. Though in this case there was no objection, Dobbins' need to check with Obama's second-term team meant more meetings and more delay in a process already in its fourth year.[42]

Karzai was, again, reluctant. He was worried the Taliban would present themselves as a government-in-exile and conduct diplomacy on the world stage as his imminent replacement. Dobbins tried to reassure him. "I responded that we had negotiated an exchange of diplomatic notes with Qatar committing that government to enforce limits to the activities of the Taliban office." The most important point was symbolic. "The Taliban representatives should present themselves only as the political office of the Taliban movement, not as the representatives of the so-called Islamic Emirate, the name under which the Taliban had once governed Afghanistan." The Taliban had ostensibly agreed to these terms. For a moment, there seemed to be agreement in Kabul, Washington, and Doha. The Taliban prepared to open their first public office since falling from power in 2001.[43]

---

[41] Miller, interview by author.   [42] Dobbins, *Five Decades*, 274–75.
[43] Dobbins, *Five Decades*, 276, 278.

"The ceremonial opening of the office took place on June 18," Dobbins wrote:

> It closed several hours later. The Taliban representatives had done exactly what Karzai had feared and what we had agreed with Qatar they should not be allowed to do. The televised opening of the office, in the presence of Qatari officials, took place beneath the flag of the Islamic Emirate in a walled compound bearing the sign "Office of the Islamic Emirate."

Barney Rubin, who had served as an advisor for Holbrooke, Grossman, and now Dobbins, was in Doha for the opening. He strongly believed that negotiations were the only plausible pathway to stability for Afghanistan, but now, as part of the United States negotiating team, "I was the guy who went there and made them take it down," he said. He drove over to the Taliban office and demanded the Qatari security forces compel the Taliban to take down their flag and signs. There had been a miscommunication between the Americans, Qataris, and the Taliban. The message from the Americans was that they didn't care what the Taliban called the office among themselves and didn't care what signage appeared inside the building but insisted that the exterior signs could not say "Islamic Emirate." Somewhere along the line the distinction between interior and exterior signage got lost.[44]

It was a major diplomatic embarrassment – or, in Rubin's artful assessment, a "huge fuckup" – for everyone involved. The Obama administration had invested substantial time into opening a diplomatic channel to the Taliban. Holbrooke's, Grossman's, and Dobbins' efforts over the past four years had been leading up to the Taliban's office. The Taliban had hoped to gain a new sense of international legitimacy. Karzai had finally come around to backing the process. The Qataris hoped to gain prestige as a peacemaker in the Islamic world. Everyone stood to gain something, but somehow everyone ended up with egg on their face. In the annals of America's war in Afghanistan, it was just another fuckup in a twenty-year line of them, and hardly the biggest one – but it was an unusually public, avoidable, and embarrassing one.

For once, though, it wasn't wholly the Americans' fault. In the months leading up to the office's opening, US officials had no direct ties to Taliban representatives. "It was all done through the Qataris," according to Laurel Miller. "The Taliban representatives insisted the Qataris had told them it was okay to present themselves as representing the Islamic Emirate,"

---

[44] Dobbins, *Five Decades*, 278–79. Rubin, interview by author.

Dobbins later wrote. "The Qataris had even procured the flag and constructed the offending sign for them. 'It wasn't our idea to have these symbols,' the Taliban representatives insisted, 'but once having raised the flag and posted the sign, we cannot now proceed without them.'"[45]

Then again, American diplomacy succeeds best when it assumes its allies are incompetent and its enemies duplicitous. Dobbins and his team were hardly naive about the Qataris or the Taliban, but they also lacked the sort of engagement and scrutiny from the principals that tends to make staffers double- and triple-check their work, including translations to and from Arabic and Pashto, and to make an extra phone call to their counterparts to check on details. Obama had not invested heavily in the diplomatic process other than a call to the Qatari emir to secure his help as an intermediary. Aside from that, as Ash Carter argued, the administration tolerated the negotiations but never gave them "oomph." Just as Bush's neglect of Afghanistan in favor of Iraq subtly communicated itself to the bureaucracy and accounted for the frustrating budgetary process, Obama's benign neglect of negotiations was the sort of enabling condition that made bureaucratic and diplomatic fuckups more likely.

The irony is that the Taliban office, though not officially open, continued to operate without open acknowledgment. Taliban representatives flew in and out of Doha and used it as a base for worldwide diplomacy, up to and including the final 2020 negotiation. "I don't think [the office] was actually conducive to achieving anything that we wanted to achieve," Ambassador Cunningham reflected. "What they really wanted was an outlet to the world that they could use to begin establishing their legitimacy as an interlocutor, which they achieved. So that was a gain for them. And we didn't gain very much from that." A Taliban office was never going to serve US interests, Cunningham thought, because "I don't think the Taliban had any intention ever of negotiating with the Afghan government."[46]

"After the blowup, there was long gap" in contact with the Taliban, according to Laurel Miller. US forces gradually drew down to 60,000 troops in 2013, while NATO and other allied forces also drew down to 27,000 from a peak just over 40,000 a few years previously, decreasing the tempo of international military operations and eroding the United States' negotiating position. Almost half a year later, "in the fall of 2013 our line to the Taliban lit up again," Dobbins wrote. "The Qataris reported that Taliban representatives were willing to resume discussions regarding a prisoner swap."[47]

---

[45] Dobbins, *Five Decades*, 279–80. [46] Cunningham, interview by author.

[47] Miller, interview by author. Dobbins, *Five Decades*, 289.

The Taliban and American representatives communicated in writing to avoid another miscommunication, passing notes through Qatari intermediaries. "Several months were required to complete negotiations by way of this laborious process," Dobbins recalled. In contrast to previous rounds to talks, the Department of Defense was in the lead. "We did that in the coordination with the State Department, the White House, CIA, everybody played a role in that," according to Secretary of Defense Chuck Hagel, "but it was a general counsel of DOD ... who actually negotiated with the Taliban for Bergdahl."[48]

The process was successful. Sergeant Bowe Bergdahl was freed from Taliban captivity in May 2014 in exchange for five Taliban prisoners held at Guantanamo Bay. The exchange was controversial; Obama's critics argued he had given away too much and incentivized the capture of US personnel (as if the Taliban didn't already have that incentive). Criticism intensified as the circumstances of Bergdahl's capture became public – years later he was court-martialed and pled guilty to deserting his post – but even apart from Bergdahl's specific story, some were uncomfortable with the negotiations. "I had a lot of experience with hostages and matters like that from my multiple tours in Lebanon," reflected Ryan Crocker, US ambassador to Afghanistan in 2011 and 2012. "I never thought it was a good idea to have a political negotiation over a hostage release, which had been the road to hell, of course, with the hostages in Lebanon, [and] Iran-Contra." He continued: "We'll talk to anybody about anything, but we're not going to negotiate the release of hostages."[49]

Under Grossman's original plan, a prisoner exchange would be the first of many confidence-building measures that would lead to a broader agenda, eventually to comprehensive peace talks. But the military, which had stepped in to lead negotiations for the prisoner swap, was not looped into Grossman's plan (despite the presence of a military liaison on Grossman's team). "I've never heard that it was a preliminary to other negotiations," Hagel said. "I never heard that. The intent was we had a soldier missing. He'd been missing for five years. We wanted to get him back." When they got Bergdahl back, the negotiation was done. "The hope had been that [the swap] could be converted into dialogue about the peace process," Laurel Miller recalled, "but in the end it was just about that exchange and it wasn't converted." "If it was a confidence-building measure, it certainly built the confidence of the Taliban, but didn't do much for the rest of us," Crocker concluded.[50]

[48] Hagel, interview by author. Dobbins, *Five Decades*, 290.   [49] Crocker, interview by author.
[50] Miller, Hagel, Crocker, interviews by author.

Why did the diplomatic channel to the Taliban dry up after 2014? One reason is that Mullah Omar died in April 2013. Though they kept his death a secret until 2015, Taliban leaders were focused on figuring out who would take over. None were willing to risk comprehensive peace talks and risk being seen as soft just as they were consolidating their position in the new leadership. Omar's death had the effect of empowering hard-liners, especially the Haqqani network and Kabul-focused groups at the expense of Kandahar-focused groups loyal to the Quetta Shura. Mullah Akhtar Mansour emerged as Omar's successor, but "when Mansour managed to retain [the] leadership post, he was highly constrained in his ability. He did not have the same credibility, legitimacy, and authority that Mullah Omar had," Lavoy said. Omar's death and the course of the war "shifted the character of the Taliban" and "constrained the peace process."[51]

More importantly, negotiations dried up because the Taliban had already achieved their most immediate goals and believed they were well on their way to long-term victory. By 2014, the Taliban had freed their most prominent prisoners and secured an ongoing (though unofficial) diplomatic presence in Doha. And they had their most important aim simply handed to them without any negotiations whatsoever: the unilateral withdrawal of most American and international military forces. By 2015, the United States and its allies had withdrawn 90 percent of their military forces. Just 13,600 remained, from a peak of 140,000, in exchange for which the Taliban had been neither asked nor compelled to give any concession. The Taliban were winning, which made diplomacy irrelevant.

WHY DID NEGOTIATIONS FAIL?

"Diplomacy must be backed by force; the use of force must back the diplomacy. Negotiations must be part of the larger campaign and must be seen to be so by everyone involved," Marc Grossman later wrote. It is easy to say on paper, but in reality, "it is hard to fight and talk at the same time." From 2010 to 2014, the Obama administration tried to open a channel to the Taliban. They were right to do so: negotiations are an essential component of any war, especially of a counterinsurgency war. But the way the administration went about it was wrong from the start. They viewed negotiations as an alternative to the surge, rather than a complementary aspect of it. They thought of negotiations as a concession that there was "no military solution"

---

[51] Lavoy, interview by author.

to the war, rather than recognizing that armed diplomacy *is* a military solution. Negotiations and the surge were "rival policies" rather than "using force to help the negotiations," said Ruggiero. The administration treated negotiations as a last-ditch bid to salvage US interests in a failing effort, rather than the main effort around which a military strategy should be formulated. And, above all, they didn't try to talk and fight at the same time: they tried to talk and *withdraw* at the same time.[52]

The point is obvious, yet it is a horse that merits posthumous beating. "It would've made much more sense to be very serious about the peace process and to put negotiations, that kind of diplomacy, at the center of American policy at the height of American power and influence, not at the nadir of American power and influence, as was done," Laurel Miller reflected. "You don't do something as hard as trying to negotiate peace in Afghanistan when your hand is growing ever weaker. You do it when your hand is the strongest and when your opponent's hand is the weakest." American military power in Afghanistan reached its zenith in late 2010, when the diplomatic outreach had hardly begun – Lute and his team were still tracking down Tayeb Agha for first contact – and then began to decline almost immediately, within six or seven months.[53]

By the time the diplomatic outreach was maturing and talks were getting more serious, US forces were leaving, depriving negotiators of their most important bargaining chip. "When we had the greatest ground position and the greatest leverage, we were less inclined to prioritize the peace process, so that was a huge frustration," Lavoy said. "When we had dwindling leverage, then we were more desperate to approve the peace process." Lute felt they almost got the timing right, approaching Agha just as the surge forces were arriving. But "obviously we didn't make fast enough, complete enough progress on the diplomatic front before the surge expired," Lute reflected.[54]

Gates' later successor, Ash Carter, defended the administration's approach because he felt it was the only one with a serious shot at succeeding. "I thought there was never a point at which it made sense to negotiate with the Taliban," he said. Negotiations would only make sense if the Taliban "did not see the possibility of improving their situation any longer by fighting." Carter, like Petraeus, never felt those conditions were met. "Counterinsurgency wars of this kind don't end until the parties are exhausted ... I never saw that the Taliban were at that point." That is why

---

[52] Grossman, "Talking to the Taliban," 30, 31. Ruggiero, interview by author.
[53] Miller, interview by author.   [54] Gates, Lavoy, Lute, interviews by author.

he felt comfortable emphasizing counterinsurgency operations to the exclusion of negotiations. "The main game, and the only one I ever remember any serious conversations in all the eight years about was the counterinsurgency campaign," not negotiations. The negotiation track "was something that I thought was kind of permitted to proceed rather pathetically because there was a constituency for it, but not because there was any rationale for it," he said. "There was just never much oomph behind the negotiations track."[55]

For those who believed there was a rationale for it, the lack of emphasis on negotiations was a frustration and a tragedy. "It was just never resourced and emphasized in the same way," Laurel Miller argued, comparing it unfavorably to how strongly Clinton had supported negotiations in the Balkans. By contrast, for Afghanistan, "we had a little team of people doing our thing, trying to make it happen," without active, engaged support from the top. "It was not the primary effort. And it suffered for not being the primary effort." Using Carter's same terminology, she felt "there just wasn't the oomph behind it to overcome what I think was really self-defeating skepticism." The level of political commitment was "tepid." She felt the implied message was that negotiations were "an additional thing people can try, but we're not putting our weight behind it," because the administration believed "it's not really going to work." In what is perhaps the best description I've heard about government work, Miller commented that "people smell when some things aren't a priority in the bureaucracy, and it gets hard to get your thing done." Negotiations smelled unimportant.[56]

Miller was incredulous. To her, the question was not whether negotiations would work, but whether they had a better chance of working than the surge. "Well, the war's not working, and you don't seem uncommitted to that," she argued. "So why is the fact that [negotiations are] probably not going to work mean you're not going to try this as hard as you've been trying the war?" There was a mismatch in how policymakers calculated risk and the likelihood of success in civilian versus military affairs. "To me, it was totally irrational to be less tolerant of the risks of trying to negotiate than of risks of continuing with the war effort."[57] Vikram Singh felt that the sentiment throughout the administration was that "diplomacy was the stuff that State Department people did, and meanwhile, the serious people were fighting the war." Ruggiero felt negotiations were treated as "a bit of a sideshow because it was never linked to what DoD was doing on the ground."[58]

---

[55] Carter, interview by author. [56] Miller, interview by author.

[57] Miller, interview by author. [58] Miller, Singh, Ruggiero interviews by author.

Ambassador Rick Olson, special representative in 2015 and 2016, concurred. Negotiations were "the only way I saw of ending the US involvement," he said, but "it certainly didn't have a prioritization over other things, and certainly there was *de facto* prioritization of counterterrorism." It mystified Miller: "I cannot explain other than that, when you have a bunch of these dudes sitting around the table with all that brass on their shoulders, it's just somehow more impressive." And the dudes with brass had a raw, visceral aversion to negotiating with their enemy. "Some in the military and even in the intelligence community had an emotional blockage about this, that people in the State Department didn't," Miller argued. For soldiers and spies, "you have that warrior mentality, and people you know have died. You're just invested in it in a different way," which made it extremely difficult to countenance talking to the Taliban.[59] For my part, at least, she is right. Having spent a decade on the war at that point, I had a knee-jerk disgust at the idea of negotiating with the Taliban. It felt gross to treat them as legitimate interlocutors; it was only years later that I came to accept that negotiations were a necessary part of warfare.

Within the military, McChrystal seemed to be among the few to understand how the pieces should have fit together. "My strategy was really based upon trying to put enough effort into the Afghan military so that they would be confident and credible, which would convince the Taliban that winning was unlikely," he said. "And at the same time, go to the Taliban and give them an option" to reconcile. His 2009 commander's assessment had said as much, and Holbrooke found him willing to support talks with the Taliban. But McChrystal's firing removed diplomacy's most supportive commander in the entire war. Petraeus, his successor, didn't oppose negotiations but consistently argued for more time to make military progress before launching talks. Additionally, the Obama administration never directed the ISAF commander – before, during, and after Petraeus' tenure – to be part of the negotiating team. The one part of negotiations that the military was involved in at a high level (the prisoner swap) ended up being cut off from the rest of the diplomatic agenda rather than setting the stage for it. That alone communicated diplomacy's place in the overall American strategy.[60]

Colonel Chris Kolenda, who helped write McChrystal's assessment and advised senior military officials on negotiations, spoke extensively on the point. He criticized officials who insisted on postponing negotiations, "saying, oh, it's not the right time yet, we need to negotiate from a position of strength." Kolenda thought that posture "was a head scratcher because

---

[59] Olson, Miller, interviews by author.   [60] McChrystal, interview by author.

President Obama had already announced that he's inclined to remove all troops and not pour more in, so you can't get higher leverage than what we had in 2011." The US would only lose leverage as time passed, "and yet we just forfeited that opportunity." Negotiations and the surge should be components of a single, overarching strategy, but the two "didn't connect and that's the problem . . . What we never did was create a theory of success in which one had priority over the other." Singh was even more critical. The two components were not simply out of synch. "We were actually working at cross-purposes because one side is killing the people you're trying to negotiate with," he said. In theory, the military could have helped by killing Taliban leaders most opposed to negotiations, but that kind of coordinated strategy and surgical targeting never happened.[61]

It isn't clear that the administration even agreed on what negotiations meant or what they wanted to get out of talks. Kolenda argued that some officials, especially US military officials, when they talked about negotiations, meant accepting a Taliban surrender after their battlefield defeat, in which case premature negotiations would legitimize and encourage the enemy. Others, including Karzai, thought negotiations should be a defection program, a venue through which moderate and reconcilable Taliban figures were co-opted piecemeal, in which case talks should start early but not engage the Taliban as a whole. Still others – the White House and the NSC – wanted negotiations as a holistic process by which the Taliban would stop fighting in exchange for amnesty and a share of power in Kabul, in which case the sooner talks began with the Taliban as a whole, the better. "There was never a discussion within the administration about what was the authoritative point of view that we all needed to get behind," Kolenda argued. Instead, there was cross talk, indecision, and no "oomph."[62]

Kolenda outlined an alternative scenario. "Let's say our theory of success was that the most reasonable way to achieve US interests was a negotiated outcome." If that's the starting point, "that's gonna take priority over everything." That becomes the rationale for the surge. "We do a troop surge in order to reverse [the Taliban's] momentum . . . to stabilize the security situation. We're going to start negotiations based on that." On that view, Obama should have announced a diplomatic outreach to the Taliban in December 2009 in the same speech in which he had announced the surge – two sides of one strategy, holding out the olive branch with one hand and the surge with the other – not waited fourteen months for Clinton to announce talks in early 2011. "And then [do] not put a withdrawal

---

[61] Kolenda, Singh, interviews by author.   [62] Kolenda, interview by author.

timeline" on the surge, but treat the negotiations as "the drivers, the main priority," rather than as a competitor or an afterthought. Barney Rubin agreed. "If you're going to announce a surge, that is the exact moment when you announce the openness to negotiation," he said, but if you wait until all the surge troops arrive, "then you're already too late. Because you have the most leverage when you are raising the number of troops."[63]

Kolenda gets at a final reason the negotiations failed: there was no oomph because – to flay the biggest decomposing equine – of the withdrawal timetable. Obama's overarching strategy was surge-and-withdraw, not surge-and-negotiate. "Think of what this told the enemy, think of how it undermines Richard Holbrooke," Petraeus said. "What you want the enemy to think is that, not only do we have the watches, but we also have the time, and we're willing to stick this out for as long as it takes." Petraeus thought the timetable was "strategically incoherent," and "nonsensical" because "you are cutting the knees off of Richard Holbrooke," and the other American negotiators. "I mean, if the Taliban know you're going to leave, why should they negotiate with you? All they need to do is just drag it out, make you frustrated."[64]

There was and is widespread consensus that the timetable undermined negotiations. "One of the cardinal mistakes in strategy, in my view, was to commit to a timeline for withdrawal and at the same time, not to engage in a full court diplomatic and political press to create a genuine negotiation," said James Cunningham, US ambassador to Afghanistan from 2012 to 2014. "We never got to do that because we didn't create the context in which the goal of the military was to set the grounds for a peace negotiation." Leon Panetta agreed. "If we were going to have effective negotiations, I think it was important for the United States to hold the line and make clear that we're going to continue to be there," he said, "and we're going to continue to provide security assistance, and we're going to continue to confront the Taliban in that process." The timetable undercut negotiating leverage, and it took precedence over everything else such that the administration could not and did not take the time to ensure its civilian, diplomatic, and military components were working together toward a common point.[65]

"Establishing and implementing very strict timetables on the US military presence certainly was something that raised the morale of the Taliban leadership and the fighters on the ground," said Ambassador Hugo Llorens, who was involved in the negotiating effort as assistant chief of mission in

---

[63] Rubin, Kolenda, Singh, interviews by author. [64] Petraeus, interview by author.
[65] Cunningham, Panetta, interviews by author.

Kabul.[66] Marc Grossman understood the need for a withdrawal plan, "and I didn't disagree with it, truly I didn't." But the timetable undermined his efforts. "The impact on my part of my job, which was to negotiate with the Taliban ... It made my life a little bit harder." He went on:

> Because I used to think about my counterpart sitting on the other side of the table, who was the head of the political committee of the Taliban. And I could imagine that when he went home or wherever he went to report, the military commissioner of the Taliban said, "This is going great, right? They have a hundred thousand [troops] and then they have 60,000 and then they're going to have 34,000. So what are we negotiating with this guy for? We're winning here."

Grossman stressed that he believed "it was the right policy to draw down, no question," but there was equally "no question that I lost some leverage."[67] The same was true for Dobbins and every subsequent diplomat clear through to Zalmay Khalilzad, who negotiated the Doha agreement with the Taliban in February 2020 at the nadir of US leverage in Afghanistan. Why did negotiations fail under the Obama administration? Gates thought the answer obvious: "Whether the Taliban would've negotiated seriously, knowing that there was a deadline for coming out, I think is a valid question," he said. "It may be that once Obama made his decision and announced that we were all coming out in 2014, the Taliban said, why should we negotiate? We'll just wait."[68]

---

[66] Llorens, interview by author.   [67] Grossman, interview by author.
[68] Gates, interview by author.

11

2012–2014

Transition

The American and allied military presence in Afghanistan peaked between late 2010 and mid 2011. For the next ten years, the major debate in Washington was how many troops to withdraw, how quickly. Obama's original timetable, announced in December 2009, was only the first of a series of deadlines, timetables, and milestones that marked the process. Earlier that year, in his second inaugural address, Hamid Karzai announced his intent for Afghanistan to assume lead responsibility for security throughout the country by 2014, the end of his presidency. NATO affirmed the goal at its summit in Lisbon the next year, as did Obama when he announced the end of the surge in 2011. The transition to Afghan lead was an important and necessary milestone, but Obama conflated it with his goal to withdraw US forces. In his 2011 speech, Obama announced that non-surge troops would start withdrawing. In 2014, marking the transition, he finally announced his intent to withdraw all US forces by the end of 2016. Through all the noise and various deadlines, the one consistent message that came through to Afghans, allies, and Taliban was simple: the United States was leaving. Obama set the tone, and the international community followed.

The announced unilateral American withdrawal was the defining fact of the war for its final decade. The debate came to a head as the 2014 transition loomed. "The big question during 2013 and 2014 policy reviews was whether we are going to fully withdraw. Is this all over by the end of 2014 or not?" recalled Laurel Miller. "Some people criticize the focus on troop levels as an excessive focus on inputs or resources as opposed to policy," she reflected – this had been one of Gates' main complaints – "but the reality is that it's a proxy for policy decisions, or at least the most concrete manifestation of your policy direction vis à vis Afghanistan." Policymakers treated the debate over troop numbers as a proxy for a debate over larger goals.[1]

Gates might have replied: that's exactly the point. There are other aspects of strategy, like reconstruction and diplomacy, that simply cannot

---

[1] Miller, interview by author.

be subsumed within a debate about troop numbers. Rick Olson agreed. "Unfortunately, the debate in the United States about Afghanistan for so much of this time was only about troop levels, and that was the only thing that was really discussed, and it was discussed *ad nauseam*. I do think that's not the way to run a war," Olson argued. "It should be about the strategic objectives and whether the strategic objectives are being met ... I think that's really a problematic aspect of the Obama administration's entire approach."[2]

Olson's point is both obvious and, somehow, novel. The United States had not achieved its objectives, yet started to withdraw anyway – which is, as Olson said, no way to run a war. It was a clear signal that for the Obama administration, many of its stated objectives – stability, reconstruction, and democracy – were there for rhetorical effect. In May 2012, Obama visited the troops in Bagram and outlined five supposed pillars of the United States' strategy in Afghanistan: transition, training the Afghan military, a long-term partnership, negotiations with the Taliban, and international support. Yet transition and training were the only pillars with weight behind them. Having killed bin Laden in May 2011, the United States could declare victory and leave. Withdrawing troops without achieving the other objectives is how the United States gradually abandoned the rest of its war aims as slowly and expensively as possible.

THE COST OF DRAWDOWN

The withdrawal undermined intelligence operations. "The CIA, the intelligence community, was wholly reliant on the US military for its ability to operate throughout the country," John Brennan, CIA director from 2013 to 2017, explained, because of "the military's capabilities for transport, MEDEVAC [medical evacuation], security. We knew that the CIA would not be able to operate in our forward operating bases the way we did without the US military." The US was gradually losing its eyes and ears, its ability to understand what was going on in Afghanistan – not only about enemy forces, but also about the Afghan military and Afghan government – as it drew down its military forces, diplomatic personnel, and intelligence assets.[3]

The withdrawal also undermined the train-and-equip effort – arguably the most important element of the United States' exit strategy. The US could go home safely when the Afghan army could take over and operate

---

[2] Olson, interview by author.   [3] Brennan, interview by author.

independently. "It was time to begin the transition to Afghan lead for their own security and to start withdrawing," Ambassador Cunningham argued. But "what undercut that was, what became clear, was President Obama's desire to basically get out." The train-and-equip mission involved tens of thousands of US troops at its peak. As the overall footprint shrank, the US military could not sustain the same breadth and depth of training for the Afghan military.[4]

US military units that were embedded with Afghan units at the tactical level withdrew. "The president, in going down to that level, had constrained his commanders from performing various types of support operations, like close air support, intelligence support, making it difficult to assist the Afghan forces," Cunningham said. The drawdown of US forces hurt Afghan forces' morale. US advisors were routinely impressed with Afghans' fighting spirit when partnered with American advisors and especially American air cover – but also noted that the same Afghan units were less willing to take initiative or run risks once the advisors and air cover were withdrawn. "When you pull the advisor teams out," Petraeus explained, "you [also] pull out the command-and-control teams and the joint tactical air controllers, who actually enable you to employ close air support and [who] can call on other enablers and support for Afghan forces." Other senior officers agreed. "I was concerned that we were going down to numbers that would impact our ability to continue to have contact with the Afghans and continue to do [joint operations]," General Joseph Votel argued. "They were counting on us, they trusted us. They made good use of the resources that we had and were enabling them with."[5]

The withdrawal also undermined the United States' diplomatic position. That was clear in negotiations with the Taliban, as we've already seen. "Once it became clear to the Taliban that we were on the way out, they didn't have any incentive to engage in any kind of meaningful discussions," Cunningham argued. "So one of the cardinal mistakes in strategy, in my view, was to commit to a timeline for withdrawal." But it was also true with regard to Pakistan. "When you say that we want to leave, it sets off alarm bells in Islamabad as well," Petraeus argued. "If you want Islamabad to really be with you, they need to know you're going to stay for as long as it takes. But if you're not going to do that, then they're going to be very careful about whether they really go after the sanctuaries."[6]

And the withdrawal undermined reconstruction and development projects. "The number of civilians and contractors that we were working with

---

[4] Cunningham, interview by author.   [5] Cunningham, Petraeus, Votel, interviews by author.
[6] Cunningham, Petraeus, interviews by author.

was also slowly decreasing," Cunningham recalled. "The only constraint was, what could we effectively do? And where could we do it?" Those were difficult questions. "We weren't going to have the PRTs anymore." PRTs, among the most successful and effective innovations of the war, closed down in 2013 and 2014. "When people started talking about drawing down the military and civilian presence, we did economic reporting on the effect it would have in the Afghan economy," Ambassador Tony Wayne said, "and we said, this is going to lead to a big recession and a lot of unemployment," because of the loss of reconstruction assistance.[7]

IMPLEMENTING THE DRAWDOWN

Petraeus and his successor, General John Allen, who together commanded ISAF from 2010 through 2013, pushed for a slower, more gradual drawdown. "We didn't even get the inputs right in Afghanistan until late 2010" when the surge forces finally arrived, Petraeus argued, "But then of course we only keep the inputs right for six or seven months." Petraeus thought Afghanistan needed more time. In 2005, he had conducted an assessment for Rumsfeld. "I was stunned by how far behind Afghanistan was compared to Iraq, even though Iraq had only started in March of 2003, and Afghanistan started in late 2001. I could see the effect of being starved for resources." He concluded that "Afghanistan was going to be the longest of the long wars." Nonetheless, the drawdown went forward on Obama's timetable. "But that meant that in June of 2012, John Allen had to start drawing down the rest of the surge forces, and the result was that he didn't have them for that fighting season," Petraeus observed. That meant throughout the summer of 2012 US forces were "pulled in two directions. They're fighting, but they're also filling in bases and sandbags or foxholes and everything else, and preparing equipment to be sent home."[8]

Allen assumed command at the peak of the surge, in mid 2011. Obama told Allen that he would be the commander that transitioned the war: from ramping up to ramping down; from a combatant command to an advisory command; from a large, nationwide footprint to a streamlined, minimal presence. To that point, ISAF and OEF had been the primary war-fighting forces while the Afghan army trained, prepared, and undertook operations only with close international assistance. Allen had the job of reversing the roles, pushing the Afghans to the front – whether they were ready or

---

[7] Cunningham, Wayne, interviews by author. [8] Petraeus, interview by author.

not – and pushing international forces back. In Washington, the argument had been whether to remove the surge by April 2012, as Biden wanted, or November, as Petraeus argued. But neither option seemed to recognize the challenges on the ground, which involved enormous logistical tasks that Washington did not seem to appreciate.

For example, the drawdown involved closing or handing over scores of military bases. Allen could not simply abandon the facilities and risk their capture by the Taliban; ISAF had to either plan an orderly handoff to Afghan forces or spend time dismantling and bulldozing them – either of which took time away from fighting the Taliban, training the Afghans, and hunting al-Qaida. Similarly, ISAF had to redesign its plan for medical evacuations. Gates had decreed that MEDEVAC helicopters would never be more than an hour away from where troops were in combat. Sustaining that during the drawdown – to move the pieces around the chessboard in a way that allowed ISAF to withdraw safely, on time, and with continuous MEDEVAC coverage – took enormous effort and creativity. It was vital to ongoing combat operations: soldiers – Afghan and international – fight with greater confidence with medical backup than without. Even so, ISAF did not have enough and had to withdraw MEDEVAC coverage from Afghan forces to keep coverage for itself during the drawdown.

Another challenge arose: in Kabul, the Afghan Ministry of Transportation sent an urgent appeal for help because the Salang Tunnel – a strategically vital roadway through the Hindu Kush between Parwan and Baghlan Provinces – was about to collapse. The tunnel was the major ground artery between Kabul and northern Afghanistan; thousands of trucks went through it daily. The tunnel was vital not just for civilian needs and ongoing combat operations, but also to keep the drawdown on schedule because the drawdown involved the movement of thousands of tons of equipment and vehicles through the tunnel. ISAF had to come up with emergency money and reconstruction assistance to repair the tunnel – a clear example of how nation building in Afghanistan was strategy, not charity – while Washington's sole concern was removing 33,000 troops by summer's end.

These challenges fed a sense within ISAF headquarters in 2012 that the drawdown was too quick and too deep. ISAF was pulled in too many directions with too few resources. "Our ability to conduct combat operations suffered across the board," General Allen told SIGAR. It wasn't just the military that felt that way. "At the end of 2012, there was a significant feeling in the government at the most senior levels that the withdrawal needed to be slower and based more on conditions on the ground than timelines," according to Ambassador Cunningham. Even NATO allies were worried the United States was pulling out too quickly. US and international forces needed the full fighting season to push back against the Taliban, and Afghan forces needed more time. DoD reported that the insurgency had "retained its capability to carry out attacks at roughly the same level as last year. The number of enemy-initiated attacks, which had shown an encouraging decrease from 2010 to 2011, rose slightly in the spring of 2012 compared to the previous spring."[9]

Over the years, critics have regularly argued that every commander asked for more time and claimed success was just around the corner. Jim Jones, who had left his job as national security advisor in October 2010, dismissed the idea that Afghanistan needed more time. "When you change out commanders frequently, the new commander always wants more time," he said. The criticism is unfair in that it treats every commander the same and overlooks how the war and American strategy changed from year to year, especially during the peak years of the surge. If Barno had asked for more troops or time in 2003 or 2004, for example, without articulating a new strategy or receiving a new mission, the criticism might be warranted (he didn't).[10]

But McChrystal received a new mission in 2009 that he argued, plausibly, required more troops and time. Petraeus and Allen inherited the same mission plus one more: getting Afghan forces ready to take the lead. Pushing for more time and a slower drawdown under those circumstances was hardly bureaucratic empire building; it was not an unthinking, knee-jerk demand for more. Jones acknowledged, "I've talked to General Petraeus and General Allen over the years. They felt like they were a little rushed into it." "One of the features of the decision-making process, again, [that] I think was flawed, was the incessant focus on timeline and numbers," Cunningham reflected, "instead of [asking] what do we actually want to achieve, and what do we need to achieve it?"[11]

Some officials tried to maintain the fiction that the drawdown was based on conditions on the ground, but it was a fiction nonetheless. "This was, in no respect, a conditions-based presence," Laurel Miller argued. "From the time in the beginning of the Obama administration that Obama announced the surge and the 'de-surge' at the same time, that was not about conditions. That was about: 'here's our timeline for trying to achieve conditions we want to achieve.'" Miller saw the clear difficulty. "Whatever you hope to achieve

---

[9] Cunningham, interview by author. Allen, SIGAR interview. DoD, "Report on Progress," December 2012, 19 and 153.

[10] Jones, interview by author.   [11] Jones, Cunningham, interviews by author.

by asserting timelines – as if this was going to be a motivating factor for the parties on either side – was undermined by the timelines."[12]

Panetta, secretary of defense from 2011 to 2013, argued there was no appetite within the administration to reconsider the pace of the drawdown, much less the logic behind it. "There were so many in the room that were just frustrated by what was going on, there wasn't a serious consideration" of slowing the drawdown, he said. Panetta was a senior statesman within the Democratic Party. Elected to Congress in 1977, he served eight terms before moving to the executive branch as Bill Clinton's director of the Office of Management and Budget and White House chief of staff, then as Obama's first CIA director. "I think the military raised some concerns about moving too fast," Panetta recalled, "but I think generally everybody sensed the same kind of frustration that the president did." The president felt trapped because neither he nor others felt there was an alternative. "There really were no other options or alternatives that were ever discussed. The options are withdraw our forces or sustain our forces," Panetta said, again focusing on troop levels rather reexamining the administration's assumptions about governance and reconstruction and their relationship to counterterrorism.[13]

Obama was keen to tout that al-Qaida was nearing defeat and the "tide of war is receding" in time for his reelection in 2012. He faced no political cost for the drawdown: his opponent in the 2012 election, Mitt Romney, endorsed the planned 2014 transition. A new bipartisan consensus was slowly forming: it was time to turn the dial down on Afghanistan. By early 2013, the die had been cast, and the military leadership no longer pushed for a slower drawdown. General Joe Dunford replaced Allen as head of ISAF, and Chuck Hagel replaced Panetta as secretary of defense. "I never heard, that I recall, from any of the military uniform leaders arguing for a longer period," Hagel recalled. "I think one of the reasons was [that] the longer it takes, the more dangerous it is." The military internalized a new mission in Afghanistan: get out. "Once the decision's made to draw down, and we did it in consultation with the generals, let's get it done as fast as we can. And that's what we did," Hagel said. "So the focus then became ... ending our combat role, withdrawing ... most of our troops."[14]

Interestingly, Hagel thought the drawdown was necessary despite recognizing that the war was not going well. "I don't think [things] were trending in the right direction," he said. Hagel, an infantry squad leader in Vietnam, was the first former enlisted soldier to serve as secretary of

---

[12] Miller, interview by author. [13] Panetta, interview by author.
[14] Hagel, interview by author.

defense. He brought a down-to-the-trenches sensibility to the job, but the shadow of Vietnam affected how he thought of Afghanistan in the same way it affected Biden. "We were losing the people of Afghanistan," alienating them with the military presence, he felt. Hagel worried that "the people were turning against us," because they believed "we were occupiers," and "weren't helping them." The Asia Foundation's annual surveys of the Afghan people showed a slow growth in general pessimism but did not support Hagel's contention that the population was turning against the international presence: what Hagel gained in the trenches, he lost in strategic perspective. Meanwhile, "the tremendous amount of money that we pushed into Afghanistan, it resulted in terrible corruption," which was true. "We made them dependent on us," he thought, echoing Rumsfeld's misconception. "They have got to stand on their own."[15]

"AFGHAN GOOD ENOUGH"

As the administration came to grips with the disappointing results of the surge and its briefly ambitious reconstruction projects, a newfound sense of pessimism – even cynicism – took hold about governance. Given its corruption and incompetence, it seemed a fool's errand even to try to make it function better. As early as 2010, following the president's guidance, a group of White House staffers started searching for an "Afghan Good Enough" solution and exit, an obvious effort to lower the goal posts and make it easier for the United States to declare victory and leave. The phrase came from Gates. "I had told Petraeus in Iraq that a key to success was recognizing the tipping point – when the Iraqis doing something barely adequately was better than us doing it excellently," he wrote. "I thought the same principle should apply in Afghanistan and, even in the Bush administration, I had called it 'Afghan good enough.'"[16]

Some policymakers interpreted the phrase as a concession to reality or an expression of humility, similar to how Rumsfeld and Feith framed their opposition to nation building. "Afghan good enough" was "the realization that the Afghans were not going to be able to do certain things ... in a way that we would have wanted," James Cunningham, US ambassador to Afghanistan from 2012 to 2014, argued. "Afghanistan was never going to be a European country. It was one of the world's poorest countries with

[15] Hagel, interview by author.   [16] Gates, *Duty*, 344.

a large amount of development assistance ... Our ability to transform Afghanistan was limited."[17]

John Kerry, secretary of state in Obama's second term, agreed. He acknowledged in his memoir that by 2013 the administration was "war-weary" and tired of the lack of progress on Afghan governance. Kerry felt the investment in Afghanistan had become disproportionate to American interests – "We were spending infinitely more than we were in countries where our interests were more urgent" – and American interests did not include "building a Jeffersonian democracy" in Afghanistan. America had to refocus on its core mission of defeating al-Qaida, which did not, in Kerry's view, include rebuilding the Afghan government.[18]

The administration was revisiting the old argument about nation building, wrestling with the reality that some level of nation building was necessary but any level of nation building was expensive, difficult, and frustratingly slow. Cunningham, after acknowledging the limitations on our ability to transform Afghanistan, then reflected, "it was transformed actually," citing US assistance to the Afghan legal sector as one example. But "it was a troubled enterprise because there were a lot of countervailing tendencies in Afghan culture," like corruption, nepotism, patronage networks, and personalistic rule. "So 'Afghan good enough' became a catchphrase for 'it's not up to our standards, but it's good, it's going to be functioning for them by their own standards.'" Cunningham wanted to see "a little bit more humility about the ability of Westerners to transform societies that we don't understand very well."[19]

But from another perspective, "it was a terrible, patronizing, disparaging phrase," Peter Lavoy felt, as if Americans were saying, "Yeah, it's a shitty country. It's going to be an imperfect effort. Horrid economy. We'll do what we need to, but it'll be suboptimal." It had racist overtones, as if the Afghans somehow didn't deserve America's full effort or were not capable of living up to international standards. It was the perfect expression of the defeatism that had infected the Obama administration's approach to Afghanistan since mid 2009. "We have to recognize that Afghanistan will not be a perfect place, and it is not America's responsibility to make it one," Obama said in his 2014 speech announcing the end of combat operations, once again refuting an argument no one had made.[20]

"Afghan good enough," became a self-fulfilling prophecy and a self-defeating strategy. By lowering expectations, the administration also

---

[17] Cunningham, interview by author.   [18] Kerry, *Every Day Extra*, 416–417.

[19] Cunningham, interview by author.

[20] Lavoy, interview by author. Obama, "Statement by the President," May 27, 2014.

lowered its own level of commitment and resources – which made frustration, if not outright failure, almost inevitable, further deepening the sense of pessimism and further lowering expectations. McChrystal had stressed in his 2009 assessment the importance of resolve, commitment, and belief in the mission – including the importance of the *perception* of resolve and commitment. "Afghan good enough," along with the withdrawal timetable, accomplished the opposite, communicating US policymakers' loss of faith in their own efforts.

The administration's tortured attitude toward nation building was rooted in a failure to distinguish between a snapshot and a trajectory. If we look at a snapshot of Afghanistan's socioeconomic indicators at one moment in time – its GDP, literacy rate, or access to electricity in any given year – the situation looked hopeless. Even after a decade of effort, Afghanistan still ranked nearly dead-last in most world rankings. In that sense, it was true that Afghanistan would never be a developed, rich-world "European country," as disparaging as that phrase was. But focusing on the snapshot overlooked the trajectory. Afghanistan, compared *with itself* from ten years previously – not with a mythical rich-world paradise – was almost unrecognizable. It had made extraordinary progress compared to where it had been at the nadir of Taliban rule. That progress could have, and should have, been the basis for a sense of momentum and confidence that McChrystal rightly saw as the crucial catalyst for a self-sustaining virtuous cycle.

Instead, the Obama administration lost faith in civilian reconstruction and pulled the rug out from under the civilian surge. "I am concerned that funding for our State Department and USAID partners will not sufficiently enable them to build on the hard-fought security achievements of our men and women in uniform," Petraeus told Congress in 2011. "Inadequate resourcing of our civilian partners could, in fact, jeopardize accomplishment of the overall mission." Petraeus' warning – that failure on the civilian side could lose the war – went unheeded. A year later, Ambassador Cunningham saw the result. "As soon as I got to Kabul [in 2012] I realized in very short order that we weren't going to complete the civilian surge." It proved impossible to mount meaningful reconstruction or governance projects without military support. "Once the military started to withdraw ... the framework in which the civilians operated was also going to withdraw." There were hundreds of American civilians in Afghanistan at the height of the surge "embedded with military units and villages and PRTs and a whole bunch of installations trying to build up the Afghan civilian infrastructure," Cunningham said, but they could only operate within bubbles of security provided by US and ISAF military units. "In 2013, 2014, we had given up on the notion of having large civilian installations around the country because it wasn't sustainable in security terms." As the military withdrew, "we couldn't complete the civilian surge."[21] The brief era of nation building was done.

"I don't think we really did enough to build up the effectiveness of the Afghan state for the delivery of services in the countryside," Olson argued. "There were some really good programs. There was the National Solidarity Program," which had started in 2004. "In retrospect, I wish we had been pouring more money into that kind of programming." Civilian aid to Afghanistan peaked in 2010 at $4.3 billion, serious money when Iraq got $2.4 billion and Israel $3.3 billion in civilian and military assistance combined. But civilian aid fell almost every year thereafter, to $2.5 billion by 2013 and $1.2 billion in 2016. (Military assistance peaked in 2011 at $12.6 billion and fell to $4.1 billion by the end of Obama's term.) Money continued to flow at reduced rates and fed the bureaucratic machine, but the air had gone out of nation building. It smelled unimportant.[22]

The reduction reflected the administration's disillusionment with nation building, but it was also because aid workers could not spend the money fast enough and effectively enough to satisfy the administration's demand to show progress on a short timeline. "It takes a long time for USAID and others to actually design, develop and implement a program," Tony Wayne recalled. "Even though they were rushing, you had money sitting around." The money that was spent was often spent too fast and fueled waste, fraud, and abuse – while the leftover, unspent money seemed to prove that Afghanistan didn't need any more civilian assistance. It was unfair to the civilians, who were given an impossible task, but it was another example of how the administration's own defeatism undercut implementation, thus seeming to validate the pessimism that led to the decisions in the first place.[23]

The military, similarly, shifted its focus. Within ISAF headquarters, the sense was that it was not time for big ideas anymore. Military-funded projects had to scale down and focus on smaller, more sustainable projects. Attempting to create a more transparent, legitimate, and competent Afghan government were shelved. As early as September 2010, when Secretary Gates visited

[21] Cunningham, interview by author. Senate Armed Services Committee, "The Situation in Afghanistan," March 15, 2011, 20.

[22] Olson, interview by author. Figures derived from USAID, Green Book, www.foreignassis tance.gov.

[23] Wayne, interview by author.

Kandahar, a general told him that "for the foreseeable future, the choice facing us was a theocracy run by the Taliban or a 'thugocracy'" in Kabul, centered on the Karzai family. The general argued that the corrupt Karzai family nonetheless "offered the best way to show results quickly against the Taliban." Gates replied that if they "helped keep our troops alive and succeed in their mission, then that's no contest." For Gates, "Afghan good enough" meant accepting a thugocracy so long as they helped kill terrorists.[24]

It was a cynicism unwarranted by the facts. As Gates' successor Leon Panetta noted, "we have to recognize that for twenty years we were able to prevent Afghanistan from collapsing and having the Taliban take over," he said. "For twenty years, we began to make inroads in terms of education, in terms of the private sector, in terms of trying to do resource development, building highways." Panetta felt "we just were not able to find that formula" to make it sustainable – but consider how little we had even tried. Serious reconstruction efforts only started in 2007 – yet the Obama administration essentially gave up by 2011. Money continued to flow, and programs limped along by inertia, but the Obama administration declared failure after four years of rushed and poorly executed programs.[25]

The decline in civilian operations was also the result of domestic politics. "The dollars [for reconstruction] went down because the enthusiasm went down," Ash Carter reflected. That was a function of shifting political attitudes at home. "For those who didn't want to be at war in Afghanistan but wanted schools for girls in Afghanistan, they'd go along with a war if they got the social building done," he said. But "as time went on, that became less and less popular," though Carter insisted that "we were championing the cause of Afghan civil society to the end of my time as secretary of defense," and it remained "an ingredient of the strategy" throughout his term. When I asked Carter's successor, Chuck Hagel, about governance and reconstruction operations during his tenure, he just shrugged: "Well, we were pretty much past a lot of that."[26]

The administration's cynicism about Afghan governance was rooted in an unrealistic assumption about how quickly governance could have improved. But giving up on Afghan governance was the logical consequence of the Obama administration's decision in 2009 not to seek the defeat of the Taliban. If the United States was not going to try to defeat the Taliban, there was no pressing need to rebuild the Afghan government. Investing in

[24] Gates, *Duty*, 493.   [25] Panetta, interview by author.
[26] Carter, Hagel, interviews by author.

governance and reconstruction was only relevant to US interests insofar as it contributed to long-term success in a counterinsurgency campaign in which Obama had little interest.

CORRUPTION

The administration's cynicism about the Afghan government was partly justified, rooted in its ineradicable corruption. Corruption was hardly new in Afghanistan – the Bush administration had grappled with the same problem. But at some point, after 2007, when more money began to flow into Afghanistan far too quickly, the Afghan government was no longer an internationally backed state struggling with corruption. It became a kleptocracy struggling to milk its international backers as much as possible without driving them away.

Some degree of corruption is normal and even, in a certain sense, necessary to get things done in an informal, personalistic system. "When you are [in] power, you are expected to take care of your own, and feather your nest for the time when you are not in power," recalled Ambassador Robert Finn, the first US ambassador to Afghanistan after 9/11. "As far as what we call corruption, yes, it is corruption." But in return, the corrupt leader owes something back. People come to the man in power "because the sister-in-law needs an operation, or [they] want a new car, or want electricity in their house ... He is also supposed to provide these things in return for their loyalty. That is part of the deal." Finn (like Ambassador Wood) saw an analogy with Tammany Hall, the nineteenth-century patronage network that ran New York City. "It's not a bad thing, but you have to be functional."[27]

That, however, was not the sort of corruption the Obama administration found during the surge. "Tens of billions of dollars were flooding into Afghanistan from the United States and our partners," Gates wrote, "and we turned a blind eye or simply were ignorant of how regularly some portion was going to payoffs, bribes, and bank accounts in Dubai." In 2009, Afghanistan ranked 179th out of 180 on Transparency International's Corruption Perceptions Index. Encouragingly, it rose in the rankings – all the way up to third-to-last in 2011. "The ministers were incompetent, they were corrupt," Gates said, which meant that US efforts during the peak of international involvement was undermined by "failure on the part of the Afghans to take advantage of the opportunity we were providing them," as

[27] Robert Finn, SIGAR interview.

well as "the fact that we didn't have enough resources." Government positions became positions from which to plunder the Afghan people and the international donors. "A number of senior positions were purchased for a price," said Colonel Kolenda, "in the expectation that you'd recoup the cost through cuts from assistance programs, selling uniforms or ammunition on the black market, drug trafficking, or kidnapping."[28]

Panetta recalled the administration's intense frustration at the Afghan government "and the degree of corruption that continued to take place there," and whether Karzai's government would ever be able to assume responsibility. "There was a feeling that while there was some progress being made, that we were not achieving the fundamental goals of an Afghanistan that could truly govern and secure itself. And I think because of that frustration, the president just sensed, in some ways, [that he was] trapped." Obama hoped the timetable was his way out.[29]

Corruption meant the Afghan government squandered the opportunity that the surge gave them to improve governance. "The Afghans did not take advantage of the surge," according to Jeff Eggers, NSC director for Afghanistan, "to work out political arrangements among themselves that would allow the government to begin to have some credibility and some unity in dealing with the Taliban." Instead, senior officials used the time and the reconstruction money to line their pockets. "A lot of that money was diverted into fraud and corruption which only fueled the sense of kleptocracy."[30] The problem was almost universally recognized. "The pervasive corruption that existed within Afghanistan really undermined not just the ability of the government and the military and security services to operate professionally and with integrity," according to John Brennan, "but also just led to a hemorrhaging of resources away from those institutions."[31]

Paradoxically, the United States was itself a main source and driver of corruption. And contrary to Obama's claim, the timetable was a cause of, not solution to, the problem. The sheer volume and speed with which the US pumped money into Afghanistan at the peak of the surge virtually guaranteed waste, fraud, and abuse. "There's no question in my mind" that "the overall scale of US presence . . . fueled corruption," Olson thought. "When you dump more potentially than the value of the GDP into a country, you're going to have corruption." There is no law of nature that says foreign aid always creates

[28] Gates, *Duty*, 360. Transparency International, Corruption Perceptions Index, 2009–2012. Gates, interview by author. Kolenda, SIGAR interview.

[29] Panetta, interview by author.   [30] Eggers, interview by author.

[31] McChrystal, Eikenberry, Brennan, interviews by author.

corruption, but huge amounts of foreign aid that must be spent quickly with loose oversight under tight deadlines is an open invitation for human greed to assert itself. Barney Rubin agreed. "What makes [the Afghan government] into a criminal syndicate is our money," he said. The Taliban spun that into a myth of their comparative honesty. But "if we had given them money, they would have been just as corrupt as anybody else."[32]

To address corruption, Petraeus created Task Force Shafafiyat ("transparency") in August 2010, headed by Brigadier General H. R. McMaster. Based in ISAF, Shafafiyat was a forty-person multinational, interagency, civilian–military task force that integrated three existing anticorruption task forces. Simply creating the task force helped raise awareness of the problem, "particularly its pervasive and interlinked nature," according to a report by the joint staff. "We identified organized crime connected to politics as the main problem," according to McMaster, who focused the task force on "organized crime networks" that threatened "the viability of the Afghan state." McMaster ran into an obstacle. "I encountered many US officials who believed that efforts to strengthen Afghan state institutions were unnecessary, impossibly hard, and even counterproductive," he later wrote. "US officials tended to view corruption as immutable and endemic to Afghanistan rather than as a product of political competition among factions and weak institutions." McMaster felt their pessimism was fatalistic and even racist. "That view sometimes seemed like bigotry masquerading as cultural sensitivity," he insisted. "Afghans were not culturally predestined to corruption and criminality."[33]

Shafafiyat helped distinguish between the normal, everyday price-of-doing-business corruption of Tammany Hall machine politics, on the one hand, and wholesale criminal kleptocracy, on the other. One major area of focus was on contracting. Shafafiyat helped identify corruption in contracting with ISAF – a major channel by which international funds were disbursed in Afghanistan and thus a magnet for bribery, self-dealing, and skimming. Another problem arose. "Not surprisingly, the people that we identified as really corrupt were very important politically and militarily," Ambassador Wayne noted. "So, you're caught in this situation." The Afghan government had created a dedicated Central Narcotics Tribunal as early as

---

[32] Olson, Rubin, interviews by author.

[33] SIGAR Information Paper, "CJIATF-Shafafiyat," June 19, 2011. https://info.publicintelli gence.net/ISAF-CJIATF.pdf. McMaster quoted in Joint and Coalition Operational Analysis, *Operationalizing Counter/Anti-Corruption*, February 28, 2014, 23. McMaster, *Battlegrounds*, 128.

2005 to try to isolate drug-related corruption cases from political pressure, with limited success.[34]

As is typically the case with bureaucratic reorganizations, the creation of Shafafiyat did not solve the problem of coordination; it brought the lack of coordination together under one roof. Task forces bring representatives together from different nations and from different agencies and departments, each with access to a computer terminal hooked up to their home agency, to sit in physical proximity to each other. What happens then is up to the relationships they form, whether they trust each other, how much information they choose to share, and what the commander does with their information. With McMaster's bullish drive, Shafafiyat and other efforts could point to progress against individual corrupt contracting firms and improved transparency in some Afghan government processes. Afghanistan rose on Transparency International's Corruptions Perception Index: from 3rd to last in 2011 to 4th to last in 2014; 8th to last in 2016; and 16th to last in 2020.[35]

The debate about good corruption versus bad corruption, and the dilemma of corrupt but powerful Afghans, was a replay of the Bush administration's rock-and-a-hard-place warlord problem: warlords and corrupt officials provided a form of governance at a basic level – the governance that patrons provide to clients, chieftains to followers, and warlords to their militia – yet they were at odds with the kind of governance envisioned by the original Bonn agreement. "Every once in a while, they'd have an election, every once in a while they'd have a parliamentary meeting," Panetta recalled, "and everybody would say, yeah, maybe they're getting it, maybe this is okay, they'll blossom in their ability to really embrace new institutions." Then, things would go back to normal. At the end of the day, "they're not giving up on the tribes. They're not giving up on their basic lifestyle," Panetta said, "I think they just did not want to break away from that pattern of how life is sustained in Afghanistan."

Another way to put it is that American officials struggled to distinguish between the thugocracy and Afghanistan's traditional tribal governance, a feature of Afghan culture that Panetta felt was a major part of the problem. Panetta's comment about tribes echoes an old distinction political scientists used to draw between "traditional" and "modern" society, and he's not wrong: the challenge of introducing formal or institutional governance to a society with entrenched personalistic rule is real. (The challenge is not

---

[34] Wayne, interview by author.

[35] Transparency International, Corruptions Perception Index, 2010–2020 editions.

unique to non-Western countries. It is a major theme of the *Godfather* novels and films, for example.) Tribal governance is personalistic, not institutional, depending on relationships, kinship, and patronage, not impersonal bureaucracies applying abstract rules regardless of tribe, language, or ethnicity. Karzai's tragedy was precisely that he had to act like both kinds of ruler at once. "He was playing a role in both the new Afghanistan and the old Afghanistan," Panetta said, "and I think the result of that was that his credibility was badly damaged." Instead of being all things to all people, he ended up alienating everyone.[36]

Panetta recognized a real challenge – how to incorporate tribes into modern governance – but gravitated toward an alarming solution. "We needed somebody who would be able to take control," he argued. "And yeah, would it have involved compromising some of our democratic values – maybe, but that kind of leadership is what Afghanistan understands." Panetta was ready to find and back a national warlord who would impose order on Afghanistan. The Obama administration did not pursue that option, of course, but the attitude illustrates how completely the administration had given up on the possibility of growing accountable governance in Afghanistan. I think the best solution would have been to help the Afghans design a unique constitutional role for tribes in local governance that gave them legitimacy within a broader institutional context – but instead of trying to solve the difficult problem, the administration gave up and aimed for "Afghan good enough."[37]

PAKISTAN

Against the backdrop of the end of the surge, the Afghan government's endemic weakness, the American withdrawal from Afghanistan, and the deteriorating US–Pakistan relationship, Pakistani officials grew more frank with their American counterparts about their strategic calculus. Pakistani officials accused the United States – with some reason – of abandoning the region after the Soviet–Afghan war, leaving Afghanistan to civil war and warlordism and slapping Pakistan with sanctions. Obama's announced withdrawal timetable convinced the Pakistanis that the United States was again going to leave the region, and Pakistan would be stuck managing the aftermath. Pakistan needed to hedge its bets. "Some of the leaders in Pakistan would say, 'We're with you on al-Qaida, but we're not

---

[36] Panetta, interview by author.   [37] Panetta, interview by author.

with you on the Afghan Taliban because we know what you're gonna do,'" Crocker recalled. "'You're gonna do what you did to us after 1989, you're gonna pull pitch. And we are not gonna be left with the Taliban as a mortal enemy.' I got it that directly from [Ashfaq] Kayani when he was the ISI commander at the end."[38]

Petraeus got a similar admission from Kayani about Pakistan's unwillingness to go after senior Taliban leaders hiding in Quetta. "Kayani confessed to me . . . he said: 'General, the only thing we do in Baluchistan province per our agreement with the Balochi leaders is run the staff college in Quetta, and maintain the border posts along the border with Afghanistan. That is it. We do no other operations for fear of a Balochi insurrection.'" The Pakistani state had a largely hands-off approach toward the entire region, letting Baluchi leaders run the province. Petraeus continued: "That meant there's no way they're ever going to go after the Taliban."[39] Nor would they go after the Haqqani Network in North Waziristan.

Dobbins found Kayani's honesty refreshing. "When pressed to do something about the Afghan Taliban and, in particular, the Haqqani network, Kayani's response had been that the army had to concentrate on the militant groups of greatest threat to Pakistan," Dobbins wrote. "It could not afford to drive the Afghan and Pakistani Taliban closer together." That was obviously a problem for the American war in Afghanistan, but at least the United States knew what it was dealing with. "Kayani's frank acknowledgment that the army was not prepared to antagonize the Afghan Taliban was preferable to [Chief of Army Staff] General [Raheel] Sharif's insincere assurances that the army would," Dobbins recalled. "It is virtually impossible to negotiate with someone who says he agrees with you but does not."[40]

Kayani was just one example; Pakistani suspicion of American intentions was endemic throughout the Pakistani military. Pakistan continued to receive military aid and buy American weapons; a small number of US military personnel were stationed in Pakistan to train Pakistani soldiers on American weapons – but their presence was a constant irritant. "Their military was deeply suspicious of US intentions in Pakistan, believing any effort to increase the number of our uniformed personnel there was part of a nefarious scheme to seize their nuclear weapons," Gates wrote. "They welcomed our cash and our equipment but not our people. And they were

---

[38] Crocker, interview by author.
[39] Petraeus, interview by author. See also Gates, *Duty*, 476–77.
[40] Dobbins, *Five Decades*, 283–284.

not particularly interested in letting us teach them how to go after targets in their own country."[41]

Pakistan's unreliability, the evidence of its actions, and Kayani's own admissions helped persuade the Obama administration that Pakistan was untrustworthy. "I think the wild card in this whole thing is Pakistan," Jones said. "Pakistan, in my view, was one of the reasons why we weren't more successful earlier because I think they were double-dealing this ... They would tell us one thing and do another, particularly along their border, which became very, very porous, and despite their claims that they were doing everything they could." The administration shifted in response to the accumulating evidence. In May 2011, when Obama approved the raid on Abbottabad to get bin Laden, "No one thought we should ask the Pakistanis for help or permission," Gates wrote. Given advance notice, Pakistani officials had tipped off other targets before, allowing them to escape. That September, Admiral Mike Mullen publicly told the Senate Armed Services Committee that the Haqqani Network was a "veritable arm" of Pakistan's ISI, a strikingly public rebuke of America's supposed ally. Years later, in 2016, Ambassador Rick Olson told Congress that while Pakistan "has taken robust action against those groups, principally the TTP, the Pakistani Taliban, that threaten Pakistanis ... Pakistan has not taken as vigorous action against groups that threaten its neighbors."[42]

"I never believed, or trusted, what I heard from Pakistani officials," John Brennan claimed:

> Whether it be the chief of the army staff or the head of ISI or others, they played all sides of the fence ... Their continued allowance of the Haqqani [Network] to operate in those areas along the border was exceptionally frustrating. We had them dead to rights, and I would frequently bring to the Pakistanis and show them exactly the evidence of how Pakistani military ISI were facilitating the flow across the borders of weapons, operatives, and other things.

That the ISI's behavior did not change even after their most senior leaders were directly confronted is strong evidence that the ISI was not a rogue agency but was following orders.[43]

---

[41] Gates, *Duty*, 372.

[42] Jones, interview by author. Gates, *Duty*, 542. Mullen quoted in Senate Armed Services Committee, "The US Strategy in Iraq and Afghanistan," September 22, 2011, 17. Olson quoted in Joint Hearing, "US Interests," April 27, 2016, 3.

[43] Brennan, interview by author.

Given the administration's distrust, it is striking how little it did to try to stop the Taliban's safe haven or confront Pakistan's duplicity. Could they have done more? Did the United States have any sticks available? "To be fair, I think the Pakistanis had an awful lot of leverage over us," Brennan said, "since we relied on it and used Pakistani airspace for resupply flights and other things. And whenever we wanted to put pressure on the Pakistanis, we looked very carefully at, well what are their options? What might they do in retaliation? How might that hurt us?" Like Hadley's NSC, they found few options. "So it was always a balancing act with the Pakistanis, how far you can push them and press them on certain issues without having them take actions against us that would be harmful."[44]

The supply lines especially weighed on American decision-makers. Pakistan shut down supply lines for six months after the crises of 2011. "The problem that we had was that our logistical supply line came through Pakistan by way of Karachi," Gates emphasized. The Pentagon tried to develop supply routes through Russia and Central Asia, a "northern distribution network," which proved slow and enormously expensive. "I don't know of any alternative that could have been pursued that would have deterred the Pakistanis from the double game they played," Gates concluded. "I think we didn't fully appreciate just how much they were playing both sides of the street."[45]

But the United States was not without options. Obama rightly criticized the Bush administration's "pretzel-like logic" of "supporting [Pakistan] with billions of dollars in military and economic aid despite its complicity with violent extremists." It was a stale pretzel, yet one he found himself serving as leftovers. He insisted that "a complete cutoff of military aid to Pakistan wasn't an option," because of Pakistan's cooperation against al-Qaida and because of the United States' reliance on "overland routes through Pakistan to supply our Afghan operations."[46] Neither Obama nor Bush considered cutting off aid to Pakistan or designating it a state sponsor of terrorism.

Obama (and Bush) never challenged the boundaries of what they believed was realistic because America had other priorities in its relationship with Pakistan. "The problem was that the United States wanted several things from Pakistan," Dobbins wrote, including help against al-Qaida, supply routes to Afghanistan, and nuclear security. "Help combating the Taliban was only one objective among several, and unfortunately not always Washington's top priority." In fact, it was never the top priority. "Afghanistan was always a second

---

[44] Brennan, interview by author.   [45] Gates, interview by author.
[46] Obama, *Promised Land*, 321.

order policy issue," Eikenberry believed, "it was deemed to be subservient to our interest in Pakistan." The US couldn't afford to pressure Pakistan for fear it would either retaliate or collapse. Jeff Eggers, NSC director for Afghanistan, frankly said "the Taliban was not as high as al-Qaida on the list of priorities for us. We had to work with Pakistan to get to al-Qaida despite Pakistan helping the Taliban. Al-Qaida was a higher strategic objective."[47] The Obama administration believed it could win against al-Qaida without winning against the Taliban, which meant it did not have to confront Pakistan. Or, more likely, they felt confronting Pakistan was impossible and thus concluded it was unnecessary.

It's easy to argue that Pakistan matters more than Afghanistan – it is far more populous, has a much larger economy, and has nuclear weapons. But those facts are less meaningful than might be apparent. Pakistan is about as populous as Indonesia or Bangladesh, yet the United States does not give the latter two pride of place in its foreign policy deliberations. The Pakistani economy is larger than the Afghan economy, but the United States has almost no meaningful trade tries or investment with either. India also has nuclear weapons, but that has not become the singular focus in America's relationship with India. The question should not have been about the two countries' relative importance as measured by population or GDP, but about the US relationship to Pakistan compared to the US war against al-Qaida and, by extension, the Taliban. If the United States was unwilling to offend Pakistan for the sake of permanently defeating al-Qaida, it was unlikely to win.

Eikenberry thought that "the institutional memory and the institutional ties" among American bureaucracies was partly to blame for the imbalance. Eikenberry was alluding to the long relationship between the United States and Pakistan, and how that relationship was embedded in the bureaucracy. Pakistan was a strong ally during the Cold War. The U2 spy plane shot down over the Soviet Union in 1960 took off from an airstrip in Pakistan. The two countries waged a successful proxy war against the Soviets in Afghanistan in the 1980s. The US and Pakistani diplomatic, military, and intelligence agencies have invested decades in relationships with each other, relationships that become an end in themselves. When you're a junior desk officer working South Asia in the State Department or the intelligence community, you have opportunities to go to Islamabad or Lahore for meetings and conferences. Until 2001, you would never have had any reason to go to Kabul or Kandahar.[48]

[47] Dobbins, *Five Decades*, 281. Eikenberry, interview by author. Eggers, SIGAR interview.
[48] Eikenberry, interview by author.

The instinct to protect relationships you've invested in can subtly turn into bureaucratic favoritism. Some US departments and agencies developed a serious case of clientitis: they come to see themselves, not as advocates for American interests in Pakistan, but for Pakistani interests in America. They help define and enforce the boundaries of what is deemed politically realistic in the US–Pakistan relationship. Given the choice between, on the one hand, maintaining the relationship with Pakistan at the cost of tolerating safe haven for the Taliban; or, on the other, cracking down on the safe haven at the cost of offending Pakistan, policymakers chose Pakistan every time, and they could console themselves that they were still fighting al-Qaida by authorizing the next drone strike.

In the face of Pakistan's leverage and its apparent importance to other US interests, the Obama administration gave up trying to crack down on the Taliban's safe haven. "Diplomatically, our high-level outreach to Pakistani officials appeared to have had no effect on their continued tolerance of Taliban safe havens inside their country," Obama later reflected, rather dryly. "I've thought a lot about a lot about it," Gates reflected years later. "I'm not sure how you could have persuaded or coerced the Pakistanis into dramatically changing their policies and not providing safe haven."[49]

Ash Carter was even more blunt.

> There was no solution [to Pakistan's duplicity] and that was going to be part of the picture. Pakistan was consistently duplicitous in its dealings with us, with respect to the Taliban. Yes, of course everybody knew it. And it wasn't like it was irrational on their part. That was how they kept their hand in Afghanistan. So, it's not an illogical thing for them to have done strategically … It was very inconvenient for us, but the idea that we were going to solve it is ridiculous. So, I never thought we'd solve it. I thought we'd have to prevail despite it, meaning that forever more, the Afghans' forces were going to be fighting a Taliban that had a safe haven in Pakistan. And that was a state of nature.[50]

McChrystal disagreed. He felt that policymakers had the directional arrow pointing the wrong way. They were so worried about how Pakistan would affect the war in Afghanistan, but never considered how the war in Afghanistan might affect Pakistan. "I think we could have been successful if the Pakistanis believed we were going to be successful," McChrystal said. "If they thought we were going to make enough progress and be resolute long enough, I think they'd have shaped their policy to live with that reality."

---

[49] Obama, *Promised Land*, 431. Gates, interview by author.   [50] Carter, interview by author.

Obama and Bush tried half-heartedly to change Pakistan's thinking through military aid, economic aid, diplomatic chastising, and drone strikes – and nothing worked. McChrystal thought that winning in Afghanistan might have worked. "They thought we were going to get tired and go home. They were always hedging their bets to try to create conditions that would benefit them when that happened," he said. "We never got what we needed from them because they never got what they thought they needed from us, which was consistency. They needed us to be consistent allies or a consistent presence and they just didn't believe it." It's an intriguing idea but would have required policymakers to prioritize the war in Afghanistan above the US–Pakistan relationship, which policymakers' beliefs and bureaucratic inertia made impossible.[51]

AGREEMENTS AND ELECTIONS

As the United States and Afghanistan moved toward the transition, they sought to codify what their post-2014 relationship would look like. They struck a pair of agreements in 2012 and 2013: a strategic partnership agreement (SPA) in 2012 (which built on a 2005 agreement) and a bilateral security agreement (BSA) in 2013 together spelled out in more detail how US forces would operate in Afghanistan in the years ahead. The SPA expressed the Afghan government's commitment to "shared democratic values" including human rights and acknowledged ongoing US military operations in Afghanistan to "combat al-Qaida and its affiliates" (it nowhere named the Taliban). The US agreed to keep funding and training the Afghan army and to give it responsibility for security nationwide by 2014. And there were pages and pages of verbiage about reconstruction, stabilization, and governance reform. The BSA formalized and spelled out in detail the United States' access to Afghan territory and facilities for its military operations.

The two agreements were paralleled by repeated international expressions of commitment to Afghanistan, including at the NATO summits in the United States in 2012 and in the UK in 2014. Bureaucrats, diplomats, and lawyers care a great deal about official statements and agreements like these. They codify expectations and norms and act as a reference point for later conversations. An enormous amount of time went into crafting the documents and getting agreement to them in both capitals. Officials in both

---

[51] McChrystal, interview by author.

governments can point to them as among the best diplomatic achievements in twenty years. But they were not legally binding treaties, and they would mean little if not backed by money, troops, and ongoing relationships, precisely the ingredients that the US proved unwilling to commit.

And, for once, Karzai was unwilling to commit to the ongoing relationship. The BSA was controversial in Kabul. Karzai, seeking to solidify his legacy as his second term was coming to an end in 2014, refused to sign the deal for fear of being portrayed as a foreign puppet in Afghan history books. "Karzai warned me: 2013 wasn't going to be an easy year," John Kerry, now secretary of state, wrote. "Negotiations were gridlocked over joint status of forces agreements to allow the United States to keep troops on Afghan soil, having become particularly volatile after some incidents where civilians had been killed." Karzai had also started to indulge in paranoid conspiracies. In 2013 and 2014, "relations with Karzai continued to deteriorate to the point that several European leaders reported to Obama that Karzai was accusing the United States of perpetuating the war and intentionally sabotaging prospects for peace," Dobbins wrote. "Incensed, the president arranged a video conference with Karzai to rebut these charges, but when confronted with what he was alleged to have said, Karzai did not back down. Rather he stoutly reaffirmed these views, and the discussion became heated."[52]

More substantively, "Karzai refused to conclude the BSA until the United States persuaded the Taliban to begin peace talks with his government," Dobbins wrote. "The Taliban, observing this public confrontation, naturally declined to come to the table." The standoff lasted throughout 2013 and much of 2014. Karzai stuck to his guns and never signed the BSA, leaving it to his successor, Ashraf Ghani, to do so. "In the end Obama was rational and responsible and Karzai was neither, which gave the latter the advantage in such a pointless game of chicken." It was indeed pointless, but also a symbol of how frayed things had become on the eve of the transition.[53]

Another major hurdle loomed: the April 2014 Afghan presidential election. With Karzai term-limited, Afghanistan would have a new chief executive. ISAF and Afghan forces made securing the election their main effort, while the UN worked with the Afghan government to plan the necessary logistics of another nationwide election. No candidate received 50 percent of the vote, triggering a runoff election between the top candidates, Ghani and Abdullah Abdullah, the former finance minister.

---

[52] Kerry, *Every Day Extra*, 417. Dobbins, *Five Decades*, 284, 285, 286, 287.

[53] Dobbins, *Five Decades*, 284, 285, 286, 287.

The election was contentious and the campaigning bitter. Ethnic and factional rivalries played out in the polls. "There was a very real concern that the Afghan state was at risk of fracturing from internal divisions if the elections didn't lead to a government capable of providing cohesion," Kerry wrote. "It didn't take a great leap of imagination to think that civil war was just around the corner." The concern about warlordism, prominent in the early years, had never fully gone away. Ghani was "a brilliant mind" but "an inexperienced politician." His weakness, paradoxically, was that he wasn't a warlord and had no connection to them, leaving him powerless if they opposed him. Abdullah was "studious and soft spoken" with an accurate "sense of the moment," and a history of ties to the Northern Alliance and its militiamen. "He was a good pol," Kerry judged.[54]

Unfortunately, "the second round of Afghanistan's presidential election in June was a debacle." Low voter turnout and widespread accusations of fraud on both sides marred "what should have been a triumphant moment for the Afghan people." The election would successfully mark the first peaceful transition between elected governments in Afghanistan's history, and the Taliban failed to derail the polling, but the moment was spoiled by recriminations. Neither side would concede defeat, and the Afghan government became paralyzed with two claimants to the presidency. There was talk that Abdullah's constituency – mostly the Tajiks and Uzbeks of the north – might secede and form a breakaway statelet.[55]

Kerry stepped in to mediate. Seeking sticks, "I asked my team what the implications would be if we cut off all assistance." Kerry found out that American aid did not actually buy leverage over Afghanistan. "The answer I got was pretty sobering: the Afghan army would disband; the police would stop being paid and attrition would grind away most of the gains we'd made ... In short, the country would go back to the turmoil of the 1990s, when the civil war flared." The US could not credibly threaten Afghanistan's leaders because it could not afford to make good on its threats – and Afghanistan's leaders knew it. Karzai had played the game well for over a decade.[56] Having ignored long-term investments in state building, the United States was forced to respond to the immediate, short-term crises of political dysfunction and state failure – thirteen years into its intervention.

Kerry spent three days in Kabul. He issued a veiled threat: "If [Afghanistan's] future was stolen because two men who wanted to be president of Afghanistan couldn't work out their differences, the responsibility of

[54] Kerry, *Every Day Extra*, 418.   [55] Kerry, *Every Day Extra*, 419.

[56] Kerry, *Every Day Extra*, 420.

what happened would be theirs." It was an empty threat (in 2014, at least), but it worked. The result was an audit of the vote count and a National Unity Government (with an unfortunate acronym, the NUG). Ghani would be president and Abdullah would be "chief executive," a position that was not in the constitution and had no defined powers. It averted the crisis but planted seeds of frustration and political gridlock for the remainder of the war. Kerry continued his shuttle diplomacy throughout the summer and fall to keep the NUG from abruptly collapsing, including by lobbying through speakerphone, "half a world away, attempting to persuade a tentful of tribal elders that their interests lay with the unity government."[57]

Ghani, the new president, was a dual US–Afghan citizen (before he had to renounce his American citizenship) and a World Bank economist and technocrat who authored a book on how to fix failed states. His résumé inspired some donors and officials to hope that he could usher in an era of competence and meritocracy in Afghan governance. Kerry was skeptical of the war and believed the United States needed to find a way out, but "it mattered to me how we transitioned, and it mattered to the United States whether we left Afghanistan as a country – or in chaos. I believed we could choose an outcome worth the sacrifice." The election was supposed to be a key milestone on the road to transition and America's way out of Afghanistan. It almost became a roadblock. Now, with Ghani at the helm, a NUG behind him, and Karzai out of the picture, Obama hoped the transition could become a reality.[58]

2014: TRANSITION

In 2014, the war in Afghanistan was over, and the United States had won – again. For the second time, policymakers began to believe that they had achieved a sustainable posture in Afghanistan with American interests intact. Paradoxically, the feeling of success was because of, not despite, the disappointing results of the surge, reconstruction, and negotiations. Those failures led the administration to lower its sights, to define success downward, to move the goalposts so dramatically that they found they were already in the endzone. By 2014, the United States had killed Osama bin Laden, built and trained a large Afghan army, handed it responsibility for security throughout Afghanistan, and withdrawn 90 percent of US forces – which, they felt, was good enough. In 2015, the American footprint had shrunk to the size it had

---

[57] Kerry, *Every Day Extra*, 421–22, 423.   [58] Kerry, *Every Day Extra*, 418.

been in 2002 and 2003. More, it had done so seemingly without the Taliban regaining momentum – though by late 2015 that would be proven wrong.

"I think we did" reach a sustainable posture, recalled General Petraeus, "I felt at the time that we had actually reached it." By reducing its footprint, the United States had minimized the number of soldiers in harm's way and the amount of money spent on military operations. "There's two metrics: blood and treasure," and both significantly decreased with the gradual withdrawal. "There was still some counterterrorism stuff going on and still some [special forces] stuff going on, but ultimately we reached a point that I felt was quite sustainable and affordable ... And the Afghans were willing to fight as long as we had their backs with close air support, drones, and other intelligence enablers and assets." Petraeus was not the only one who felt that way. "It was all looking pretty good," Crocker felt. With the security transition in 2014, "we were bilaterally and multilaterally moving to a steady state that would be affordable and that had broad international support."[59]

Ash Carter, the secretary of defense, believed that the war was on a sustainable trajectory. The US would continue training Afghan security forces "to the level that they could keep the lid on with our help, without us being involved in day-to-day combat operations." Carter felt this was what success looked like. "It was an achievable steady state," he said. Carter had little patience for critics who accused Afghanistan of becoming an "endless war." "These armchair people who write about endless wars, it's crap, nobody ever thought they were doing that." US strategy was focused narrowly on training Afghan forces and doing counterterrorism. "That's not an endless war. It is an endless *presence*, but we have enjoyed such endless presences in such places as Germany and South Korea to the great benefit of our country." The endless presence enabled the United States to deny safe haven to al-Qaida with a gradually diminishing investment. "That was the objective. It wasn't to make a perfect society out of Afghanistan – though it was certainly a better society than it would be if it were ruled by the Taliban."[60]

Obama was keen to capitalize on the moment and announce the end of the war. In May 2014, after visiting Afghanistan, he announced his intent to bring the war to a "responsible end" and to "conclude our combat mission." He defined America's enduring interest in Afghanistan as "disrupting threats posed by al-Qaida," and "supporting Afghan security forces." He made no mention of the Taliban. And he announced his intent to draw down to 9,800 troops by the beginning of 2015, half that by 2016, and withdraw all US forces by the end of 2016. "This is how wars end in the

---

[59] Petraeus and Crocker, interviews by author.   [60] Carter, interview by author.

21st century," he said, "not through signing ceremonies, but through decisive blows against our adversaries." He was right about the signing ceremony, but the United States had not dealt a decisive blow against the Taliban. In December, he claimed "the longest war in American history is coming to a responsible conclusion."[61]

"It was clear that President Obama wanted to withdraw by the end of his presidency," Cunningham said. "He wanted to have a US military presence that was basically contained in the US embassy in Kabul." Obama's withdrawal announcements "were not condition-based but simply reflected a decision to close out American involvement in the conflict by the end of the president's term in office," Dobbins agreed. "The problem is, we forget that we actually don't end an endless war by withdrawing our forces," Petraeus argued. The war was neither over nor in the process of ending, as every Afghan knew. In 2011, Obama had announced the "tide of war is receding," as if it were a force of nature outside his control. Now he swung to the opposite extreme, simply announcing the war's end, as if wars stop by presidential proclamation.[62]

In doing so, he missed an opportunity to tout genuine progress. American policymakers could rightly recognize how different the situation was compared to the early years: the Afghan economy had grown consistently; the Afghan government had held repeated rounds of elections; an Afghan army was leading the fight against the Taliban; and al-Qaida's defeat seemed "within reach," as Panetta claimed as early as 2011. "I maintained that, although we made lots of mistakes and we were inefficient and ineffective at times in those twenty years, we did transform Afghanistan in a way that ... could have been lasting," Cunningham argued. "In terms of the impact that we had on certain key sectors, like health and education, media, press freedom, and things like that." But the gains were tenuous and not yet self-sustaining. By hastening to declare the war's end, Obama gave a false sense of closure.[63]

It was indicative of the ongoing uncertainty in Afghanistan. The intelligence community was more pessimistic than the military and argued the war had settled into an eroding stalemate, not a sustainable trajectory. "I went out to Afghanistan a number of times," recalled John Brennan, CIA director from 2013 to 2017, "and I think to a person, the US military was much more positive ... than was the CIA. And they felt that those CIA analysts back in

[61] Obama, "Statement by the President," May 27, 2014. Obama, "Statement by the President," December 28, 2014.

[62] Cunningham and Petraeus, interviews by author. Dobbins, *Five Decades*, 289.

[63] Cunningham, interview by author.

Washington really were missing out on the reality there," while "the intelligence community was skeptical of what the military assessments were." Precisely because the intelligence community was more skeptical, they tended to argue for staying, not withdrawing. Brennan said there was a "very strong view" in the intelligence community "that the intelligence presence needed to continue, which required some military presence, at least a minimal US military presence" to provide security.[64]

Analysts in the intelligence community were not the only ones who felt pessimistic. Colonel Fernando Lujan had just arrived as director for Afghanistan on the NSC as Obama announced the transition. He made the rounds, meeting his counterparts at other departments and agencies. "The vibe wasn't great," he recalled. "Things were already starting to look a little rough, and it was just a very strong feeling that this is not going to end well ... looking down at the next forty-eight or twenty-four months ahead, all the projections were pretty bad." On the eve of the transition, the Department of Defense reported that the Afghan army and police still had "four key high-end capability gaps" including "air support; intelligence enterprise; special operations; and Afghan security ministry capacity." Though the Afghans would be in the lead, they still needed substantial help.[65]

That, in turn, clouded the administration's deliberations about what to do about Afghanistan in its final years. There was still an open question about what America's goals really were, how to achieve them, and what was realistic in the short time remaining in Obama's presidency. The administration couldn't decide how to land the plane. "What was the objective?" asked Chuck Hagel. "When I became Secretary of Defense [in 2013], I don't think it was any clearer, I think it was jumbled." His predecessor Leon Panetta agreed. "I really wish we had just stopped and said: 'Now what?' We had gone after al-Qaida, we got those involved with 9/11. If we have this other mission of trying to make sure Afghanistan doesn't become a safe haven for terrorism, is there a better way to try to get that done?" Panetta asked. "We never had that discussion. We just kept doing what we were doing in the hope that somehow something would change." Carter, Obama's last secretary of defense, felt there was a strategy but no clear communication about it. "I don't think, other than a few of us for whom it was an important part of our job to articulate the strategy, there wasn't a whole lot of enunciation of the strategy," he said. Carter echoed the

---

[64] Brennan, interview by author.
[65] Lujan, interview by author. DoD, "Report on Progress," April 2014, 1.

criticism Gates had leveled at Obama years earlier. "It's a president that has to say that, and President Obama didn't go out and explain and continue to champion the strategy."[66]

"The US forces were on the way out, but [we] never quite identified what the end state would be, only what the desire was," Cunningham recalled. The process continued, but there was an air of unreality about discussions of anything other than withdrawal. "We were having interminable discussions within the administration . . . between those of us who were arguing for a sustainable military presence to support the civilian effort, and others who wanted the United States out," he said. "Although the president listened to all the arguments, it was pretty clear what he wanted to do." Cunningham characterized the ongoing discussions as a repetitive "merry-go-round," a continual argument about "what number [of troops] do we want to get to by this date?" in which "the advocates of the timeline continually won out, and they even constrained the ability to present or develop options that were outside of the timeline boundaries that had been established."[67]

Vikram Singh, who served first as deputy special representative and subsequently in a similar position in the Pentagon for most of Obama's presidency, recalled the "unceasing repeated review process and ceaseless paper drills" that characterized Afghanistan deliberations. "We were going through review after review after review," he said. "I started with the Riedel review and went through all the others. And I was asking myself why? . . . There were nights I would go home and ask myself 'Why are we doing this?'" Singh felt there were no new answers, and the questions were a fruitless effort to find a new way to spin uncomfortable realities. "It's the same answers, the same questions, the same problem with corruption, the same lack of capacity," the same issues with safe haven in Pakistan and getting "funding and arms from outside," he said. "These are all the same, and we review them over and over again. And we rewrite papers that say the same thing, and because none of them result in an easy way to win, we keep choosing these suboptimal outcomes." It was both personally challenging – "an extraordinarily difficult, frustrating period" – but also strategically counterproductive. "Those reviews were the antithesis of decision-making for warfare," he argued.[68]

The Obama administration could tout that, officially, ISAF handed over responsibility for security to Afghan security forces throughout the country

---

[66] Hagel, Carter, and Panetta, interviews by author. [67] Cunningham, interview by author.
[68] Singh, interview by author.

in stages, culminating in June 2013 (a year earlier than envisioned). ISAF's UN mandate expired on December 31, 2014, replaced by a follow-on UN mission named Resolute Support. "Okay, so what happened after 2014?" Doug Lute asked, rhetorically. "And the result after 2014 is not very satisfying," he concluded, leading him to wonder, "did we really transfer in 2014? I don't think so." Lute, who by then was serving as the US ambassador to NATO, thought the transition was illusory. "We presented it as a transfer," complete with a ceremony in Kabul, but that was belied by realities on the ground. Afghan security forces still depended on American trainers, air support, and more. "When you're paying all the salaries, when you're providing all the fuel, when you're providing all the logistics, when our Air Force is doing all the precision fires, and our SOF is essentially a shadow force," it added up to "propping up this image of Afghan control." "We may not have been in the lead, but we were standing side by side. We never really, in my view, transferred." The transition – the victory parade for Obama's war – had turned out to be a Potemkin village.[69]

---

[69] Lute, interview by author.

12

2015–2016

Obama's Forever War

The war was not over. A suicide truck bomber drove into the Afghan Supreme Court in June 2013, killing and wounding dozens. Days later, militants attacked the presidential palace with a coordinated assault involving a wave of suicide bombers followed by a group of gunmen. In January 2014, another suicide bomber and a pair of gunmen killed over twenty people at a restaurant in downtown Kabul known for its international clientele; in June 2014, yet another suicide bomber hit the prestigious Serena Hotel in Kabul (the same hotel a bomber had struck in 2008).

By early 2015, "things are not going well," Lavoy recalled. "The terrorist threat was growing at that time, or it was not abating enough rapidly enough, so we needed to do something because things were not going well." It was awkward because the president had just announced that the war was over and the military was leaving, drawing down to a normal embassy presence. "It was clear that as the clock was ticking, going to a Kabul-centric presence would create enormous challenges," Lavoy said. "We needed more time for the peace process." Laurel Miller agreed. "It was all not going well, and it wasn't headed in a direction that was clearly self-sustaining and gave you any confidence to think you could get out without too much risk of it falling apart."[1] The situation led to yet another strategy review. This time, the review focused on a single question: should the United States stick to Obama's withdrawal timetable, or not?

2015: STRATEGY REVIEW

"The Taliban began gaining ground in 2013 almost immediately after the surge began to draw down," according to Ambassador McKinley. "At what point does the back of the Afghan Government break?" The prognosis was not good. "We weren't winning this war. Notwithstanding the surge, and

---

[1] Miller and Lavoy, interviews by author.

358

certainly by 2014, I was convinced we weren't winning." The intelligence community characterized the war as an "eroding stalemate," which McKinley thought was right. The percentage of Afghans who believed the country was on the wrong track rose steadily after 2012, when international forces started to withdraw. A majority – 57 percent – said so in 2015, the first time more Afghans were pessimistic than optimistic, and their satisfaction "with the way democracy works in Afghanistan," reached an all-time low in 2016, at 56 percent.[2]

The problem was that the Afghan army was not ready for the insurgent offensive, and, at first, US forces were compelled to stand back and let them fail. After the transition, "new rules limiting US operations on the battlefield had a devastating impact on the capability and morale of [Afghan] government forces," according to Jessica Donati, a journalist who covered this era of the war. "Afghan forces were fast losing ground as both sides realized that the United States was holding back its airpower and forces, leaving the Afghan government to fight on its own. The US military, prohibited from combat operations, allowed offensive strikes in a very limited set of circumstances: to protect US forces and to target known members of al-Qaida."[3]

There was an oddity to Afghanistan strategy after the surge. "You had this paradox in which it was considered a fading international issue at a time when we were still spending tens of billions of dollars a year, and when a tremendous amount of policy time went into considerations of what to do there," McKinley recalled. The world had moved on from the war in Afghanistan: Syria was mired in civil war, Russia invaded Crimea, and Edward Snowden, an NSA contractor, stole and published a trove of classified documents about US intelligence capabilities. Few media outlets, let alone voters, were focused on Afghanistan. Yet "there seemed to be an increasing number of Deputies meetings" on the war, McKinley said. There was a debate brewing "given the inclination inside the White House to look for an exit strategy," which conflicted with "the strong sense in many other departments or agencies that we needed a longer-term strategy."[4]

The deteriorating situation led to an ongoing debate – yet another strategy review – about whether the military could really leave, whether Obama's goal of getting out was realistic. "For the duration of the administration, from 2014 to 2016, we spent countless hours in the Situation Room debating the future size, goal, and disposition of the US and NATO military presence in

---

[2] McKinley, interview by author. The Asia Foundation, "Survey of the Afghan People 2019," 35, 159.

[3] Donati, *Eagle Down*, 46. [4] McKinley, interview by author.

Afghanistan," Susan Rice, Obama's second-term national security advisor, wrote. "Originally, President Obama wanted to draw down US forces to the minimum necessary in Kabul by the end of his term – enough to continue training Afghans at the ministry level, protect the US embassy, and target foreign terrorists who threatened the US." But General John Campbell, the US commander in Afghanistan, told Congress in October 2015 that the Kabul-centric presence "did not take into account the change over the last two years," especially the rise of the Islamic State, and so, "I do believe that we have to provide our senior leadership options different than the current plan." (Obama's perspective on this debate, presumably covered in the second volume of his memoir, has not been published yet.)[5]

Colonel Lujan, on the NSC, looked at troop numbers, base closures, force protection, and ongoing counterterrorism operations. From his time on the ground in Afghanistan, Lujan knew the logistics of closing and handing over bases to the Afghan army while simultaneously protecting US forces as they withdrew were complex in a way civilians rarely understood. "It felt a little bit like a Jenga game," he said. "The tower gets wobblier and wobblier as you're pulling down the last structure," withdrawing troops and closing bases. The tower might appear stable, but it was increasingly fragile. It could collapse suddenly with the wrong block pulled out – one more unit withdrawn or base closed – or with the least amount of outside pressure, like a Taliban attack. No one knew where the tipping point was, which made the military hesitant to draw down any further than 9,800, much less leave altogether. "If you're any smaller than this, you might as well just leave the country because then we can't defend ourselves."[6]

But this time, it wasn't just the military that pushed back. "It was unanimous that you needed to revisit this decision," Lavoy recalled, exaggerating only slightly. Biden and Rice wanted to stick to Obama's stated goal of getting out, but virtually everyone else saw the need to stay, and Obama paused further withdrawals on the military's advice in early 2015. Campbell "was frustrated with the White House's fixation with numbers, which hamstrung the mission," according to Donati. He "made holding off the drawdown to fifty-five hundred troops that year his main goal." The State Department "was more disposed to a longer-term strategy to stay with it and improve the strategy with the goal to achieve it," Cunningham recalled, "as was [Defense] Secretary Panetta." John Brennan, director of the CIA, agreed. "I

---

[5] Rice, *Tough Love*, 393–4. Campbell, quoted in Senate Armed Services Committee, "The Situation in Afghanistan," October 6, 2015, 120–121.

[6] Lujan, interview by author.

was quite skeptical that by the end of the Obama administration that Afghanistan would be in such a condition that the United States no longer needed an intelligence presence there," he said, and an intelligence presence required a military presence. "I didn't think that we were going to be able to pull out everybody by the end of the Obama administration," he said.[7]

Critics like Biden and Rice accused the military and other advocates of an enduring presence of arguing out of both sides of their mouths. When things seemed to be going well, the military said they needed to stay to keep it going in the right direction. When things went badly, the military said they needed to stay to keep them from getting worse: No matter how things on the ground changed, the military always found a reason to stay. It is a superficially powerful point, but it misstates what the military and others said. At no point, even during the brief burst of optimism in 2014, did anyone argue that things were going so well that the Afghan army was ready to stand on its own. The most enthusiastic optimists never said so, and while they sometimes claimed they were on the right track, they never claimed they had arrived.

Lavoy, now serving as special assistant to the president and senior director for South Asia on the NSC staff, led the review. He had briefly left government for the private sector in 2014; when he returned, "the disunity among the departments and agencies over the White House's plan to bring all US troops home surprised him," according to Donati. "He made it his goal to get everyone to agree on the way forward and began to prepare a review of the policy." Lavoy is the perfect embodiment of the *éminences grises* who populate the higher ranks of the national security establishment. Such professionals look and sound bland and speak in a bureaucratic idiom that conceals power beneath layers of verbal clutter. "When I came into the NSC, my number one priority was to regain strategic coherence and to create an approach that aligned all the different elements of national power to achieve a common objective," Lavoy told me. That's the sort of sentence I tell my students not to write because, while truthful, it obscures more than it reveals. To speak more plainly, Lavoy led a process that persuaded Obama to change his mind and throw out the one element of his Afghanistan strategy that had survived the longest – the withdrawal timetable. Lavoy's review saved the Obama administration from making the mistake Biden would make six years later.[8]

"The objective was to set conditions for a peaceful end of the war and for us to leave," Lavoy said. But it was a delicate balancing act. "At the same time,

---

[7] Lavoy, Cunningham, and Brennan, interviews by author. Donati, *Eagle Down*, 49, 50.

[8] Donati, *Eagle Down*, 45. Lavoy, interview by author.

[we had to] make sure there was no lingering terrorist threat to the United States." The two goals were incommensurable. The United States could not both get out of Afghanistan and also defeat al-Qaida. Lavoy came to recognize that squaring the circle was a mission impossible. "I recall my first meeting when I'm dealing with my different directors, people from different elements, and I said, 'Okay, how do we do this?' They looked at me and one person was in tears because, it's like, that's too hard."[9]

Lavoy felt that "it made no sense ... to cling to preset deadlines that appeared timed for the US electoral cycle without giving the president an opportunity to weigh the views of the various departments and agencies, all of which favored continuing the mission." The Pentagon was making a case "for retaining offensive authorities and holding off on the drawdown of troops on the basis that the timeline and the cap on troop numbers were arbitrary and undermined the mission," while the intelligence community was similarly arguing "for maintaining its bases along the Afghan border with Pakistan." Lujan helped the interagency do "a mechanistic relook of presence and capability and authorities and what you could accomplish if you were a little bit more creative." Lavoy saw the logic, but it would require abandoning Obama's timetable.[10]

2015: REPUDIATION

Doing so meant going against his boss, Susan Rice, who was "strongly opposed to any idea that did not constitute withdrawing all US troops before the president left office," according to Donati. In mid 2015, Lavoy's office prepared an outline of options for staying in Afghanistan to present to Rice. "The meeting with Rice did not go well," according to Donati. "She went 'ballistic' when presented with the proposal."[11]

Lavoy's telling is more colorful:

> She hit the roof ... I was introduced to a combination of vocabulary with a level of intensity that I was not prepared for. She said, "No, we made the decision, your job is to enforce this decision." And I said "I would love to. I want to be done with this war as much as anybody. I definitely want to support the president's desires, but I think he needs to hear from his cabinet officers, and from the interagency, their views on the situation."[12]

[9] Lavoy, interview by author. [10] Donati, *Eagle Down*, 47. Lujan, interview by author.
[11] Donati, *Eagle Down*, 46, 47. [12] Lavoy, interview by author.

Lavoy understood that Obama might hear the arguments and stick with his decision anyway, but Lavoy understood it was his job as an NSC staffer to alert the president to the views of the various agencies and departments. Alarmingly, Rice was not merely opposed to keeping troops in Afghanistan. She was opposed to *talking about* keeping troops in Afghanistan. "She was opposed to a discussion about how the mission was going or any strategy that did not align with President Obama's plan to draw down to zero troops," according to Donati. "I can't do this," Rice told Lavoy, "I can't condone this process." Lavoy countered that the president "needs to hear these assessments because the intelligence and the policy judgments are fundamentally at odds with that legacy decision" to complete the military withdrawal. "She was just not into it," he later reflected, but she could not "suppress the very strong intelligence judgments, and very strong political events that were coming forward," forcing the issue. Pushing the issue forward against the internal pressure was "excruciating," Lavoy felt.[13]

The national security advisor has two roles: advising the president and managing the interagency process. There is a tension between the two roles because the process, by design, generates a range of options, some of which the national security advisor will not favor. The best advisors, like Brent Scowcroft, understood that the integrity and credibility of the role depended on fairly and impartially presenting all options to the president first; only subsequently, when invited, giving their own view. Susan Rice, in seeking to obstruct the process to protect her preferred strategy, did the opposite.

Events in Iraq interjected themselves into the debate over Afghanistan. Without international accountability after the US withdrawal in 2011, the Iraqi government degenerated into a thuggish Shia autocracy. Sectarian killing revived. Without American military assistance, the Iraqi Army lost ground to insurgents, criminals, and terrorists. Jihadists regrouped, rebranding themselves as the Islamic State of Iraq and Syria (ISIS), and made rapid gains, seizing Fallujah and Ramadi in early 2014 and Mosul in June. That month they proclaimed a caliphate, weeks after Obama announced the end of the war in Afghanistan. Genocidal violence against Christians, Yazidi, Kurds, and Shia followed in their wake. Faced with an al-Qaida-like group that claimed statehood and had access to oil wealth and a conscriptable population, Obama was forced to send US troops back to Iraq and go to war against ISIS in August 2014.

The lesson was hard to miss: the US withdrawal from Iraq left a power vacuum which enabled jihadists to regroup and pose an even bigger threat

---

[13] Donati, *Eagle Down*, 49. Lavoy, interview by author.

than before. The discussion about reengaging in Iraq "was not necessarily one that I think the president ... was overly excited about engaging in," thought General Joseph Votel, then serving as commander of Special Operations Command. He was likely not excited about the implications for Afghanistan, either. "The whole tone certainly changed ... when we saw just the absolute collapse of Iraqi security forces," said Lujan. "After things blew up in Iraq," Laurel Miller recalled, "that pretty much killed any possibility of a complete withdrawal from Afghanistan ... It wasn't really about winning the war anymore. It was about an insurance policy against things getting worse than they were." Yet the withdrawal timetable was still in place.[14]

Officials in and out of government felt an urgent need to lobby Obama to change course in Afghanistan. Ambassador Cunningham thought Obama's withdrawal plan "was not realistic for a variety of reasons." He retired and promptly organized a project at the Atlantic Council with Zalmay Khalilzad to advocate for an enduring presence. They published their report in October 2015, arguing that "Afghanistan's security and stability are directly linked with international security" and calling for "continued US engagement required to protect American interests." They argued that, above all, "US and NATO force levels and presence around the country, as well as intelligence assets, should be maintained at or close to present levels, pending review by the next administration." The war was not over, and Obama's withdrawal timetable had to go.[15]

Cunningham's arguments were not new; they echoed much of what every strategy review had said since the beginning of the war. What is remarkable about Cunningham's report is that it was publicly cosigned by dozens of prominent foreign policy practitioners and scholars, including Madeleine Albright, Bill Clinton's secretary of state; Michèle Flournoy, Obama's former undersecretary of defense for policy; Steve Hadley, Bush's national security advisor; Leon Panetta and Chuck Hagel, two of Obama's former secretaries of defense; and Jim Jones, Obama's former national security advisor, along with Grossman, Dobbins, Crocker, Neumann, and others. It was a widespread, bipartisan, and public rebuke of Obama's plan to withdraw. The national security establishment, including many of Obama's own appointees, was united in opposition.

---

[14] Votel, Lujan, and Miller, interviews by author.
[15] Cunningham, interview by author. Atlantic Council, "Afghanistan and US Security," October 2015. www.atlanticcouncil.org/wp-content/uploads/2015/10/20151016_Afgh anistan_and_us_security.pdf.

The pace of terrorist attacks picked up throughout 2015. Militants attacked the Afghan Parliament in June 2015, and the Taliban carried out a series of coordinated bombings across Kabul in August. To cap it off, the Taliban overran Konduz in northern Afghanistan, holding it against Afghan forces for two weeks in September and October, and they seized sixteen district centers across northern Afghanistan, raising the specter that they would, like ISIS, sweep through the country and unleash a wave of jihadist violence. Facing the combined effect of Lavoy's review, Cunningham's report, events in Iraq, the Taliban on the march, and most of his own advisors in opposition, Obama had little choice but to reverse course. The timing led many observers to assume Obama's decision was a direct response to the Taliban's Konduz offensive, but everyone I spoke to insisted the debate had been underway for almost a year, and Obama came to his decision before the fall of Konduz, not in response to it.

"While America's combat mission in Afghanistan may be over, our commitment to Afghanistan and its people endures," Obama said in the Roosevelt Room of the West Wing on October 15, 2015. He stressed that US forces were in Afghanistan to train Afghan forces and do counterterrorism operations, nothing more. Yet, he argued, they needed to keep at it. Claiming that he was always ready to make "adjustments" when realities on the ground made them necessary, he admitted that "Afghan forces are still not as strong as they need to be," and that "the Taliban has made gains, particularly in rural areas, and can still launch deadly attacks in cities, including Kabul."[16]

Somewhat dismissively, he acknowledged that "much of this was predictable," as, indeed, it had been predicted by Obama's critics. Nonetheless, he announced his intent to "maintain our current posture" and keep troops in Afghanistan until the next president could make a fresh assessment. "I do not support the idea of endless war, and I have repeatedly argued against marching into open-ended military conflicts that do not serve our core security interests," he said, but "I am firmly convinced that we should make this extra effort." Obama's decision was echoed at the NATO summit in Warsaw the next year in which the allies affirmed a conditions-based approach to any further withdrawals and NATO's commitment to continuing its mission in Afghanistan past 2016.

---

[16]   Obama, "Statement by the President on Afghanistan," October 15, 2015. https://obama whitehouse.archives.gov/the-press-office/2015/10/15/statement-president-afghanistan.

It was a stunning reversal. Since December 2009, the most consistent element of Obama's Afghanistan strategy was his intent to get out. "I think it was very clear that President Obama wanted to try to wrap this up by the time he left office," reflected General Joseph Votel. If Bush's decision to surge in Iraq was the ultimate, and necessary, rebuke of his earlier mishandling of that war, so too was Obama's final decision to stay in Afghanistan the strongest possible critique of his earlier eagerness to leave. Both presidents deserve credit for recognizing the need to change course, which is never easy. But neither president can claim to have been unaware of the down-sides of their earlier courses of action because both had legions of advisors and critics warning them against the choices they would spend the rest of their presidencies trying to correct.[17]

President Obama spent almost his entire presidency talking about withdrawing from Afghanistan, which ended up being the one thing he managed not to accomplish. Endless and repetitive strategy reviews had all come to similar conclusions – that the United States should stay for the long haul and do more to rebuild Afghanistan – conclusions which Obama resisted until the logic of events forced his hand. Cunningham, who had criticized the president's plan because "the desired withdrawal rate was too rapid and created too much security risk," praised Obama for changing course. "To his credit he recognized" the need to change, "so he did adjust course over that period." But the damage was done. "What he and others didn't recognize is that this whole process was extremely corrosive to our ability to convince the Taliban and others in the region and elsewhere that we were committed to a peaceful outcome, a peace agreement and a solution to the conflict. So it just gave them more and more incentive to keep waiting us out."[18]

"I don't think he wanted to make a decision that would bind his successor," Ash Carter said. Hillary Clinton, widely expected to win the presidency in 2016, supported an enduring presence, and Obama did not want to constrain her foreign policy options before she took office. "In the end, time ran out," Carter said, and so "he did not leave behind a timetable. I think that's good that he didn't." Obama had finally stopped talking about withdrawing – calling to mind Churchill's adage that the United States always does the right thing, once it has exhausted the alternatives.[19]

---

[17] Votel, interview by author.   [18] Cunningham, interview by author.
[19] Carter, interview by author.

FOREVER WAR

After Obama abandoned his plans to withdraw from Afghanistan in late 2015, the American war in Afghanistan entered a new phase. The surge was long past, and the drawdown was essentially complete. Some 12,000 US troops remained in Afghanistan. Officially, the troops were there to train the Afghan army and conduct limited counterterrorism strikes. Unofficially, however, with the insurgency gaining ground and Afghan forces unready to hold the line, US Special Forces reverted to the role they had played in 2002 and 2003, the era McChrystal had characterized as "the Wild West." As Jessica Donati wrote: "Although [Obama] announced the end of combat operations and the start of a new training mission to prepare the Afghan government to take full control, what he actually did was turn the losing battle over to US Special Operations, who could operate in near-total secrecy and with virtually no accountability to the US public." And for the first time since 2009, US forces were operating without a timeline.[20]

Afghan forces needed more help. "Gen. Campbell told [Obama] that the United States needed to keep a more robust presence in Afghanistan than originally planned," Donati reported. "The Taliban's gains, along with the emergence of the local Islamic State branch, threatened the achievements the United States had made over the past decade and a half and risked allowing a resurgence of al-Qaida." After 2014, Obama had directed the military to adopt new rules of engagement limiting when and how they were allowed to use force, part of the reason the Taliban regained momentum in 2015. "The Obama administration tended to run things with a 10,000-mile screwdriver and put a lot of restrictions on the commander's authority to be able to use this very small force that he had to maximize its effect," said Hugo Llorens, US ambassador to Afghanistan in 2016 and 2017.[21]

Eventually Obama "sign[ed] off on a tranche of new authorities that would give [special forces] greater freedom to operate in Afghanistan," according to Donati. "The rules would allow a more flexible use of airpower and increase the military's ability to dispatch [special forces] on missions with the Afghan commandos. In effect, the decision to call off the US withdrawal would extend the SOF's role in the Afghan war indefinitely." It was only the first of several decisions Obama took in his final year to escalate the war. Obama also allowed the US military to begin targeting the Islamic State in Afghanistan. "The revised rules were a victory for Gen. Campbell,

---

[20] Donati, *Eagle Down*, 20. [21] Donati, *Eagle Down*, 142. Llorens, interview by author.

who was on his way out but had lobbied for months to be granted authority to target Islamic State." And Obama gave the incoming commander, General John Nicholson, "more troops and assets to help the government fight" the Taliban.[22]

The war in Afghanistan settled into a never-ending skirmish. Except for special forces, most US troops were off the front line. Ninety-one US troops were killed in action in 2014, the year of transition; just fifty-three were killed in action the following year, and forty-three the next. Most American forces focused on training the Afghans and providing logistical and intelligence support. "It wasn't an actual war going on," thought John Bolton, who would step in as Donald Trump's national security advisor in 2018. "There were very few incidents of American troops in actual combat, and that was not their mission."[23]

Instead, the Afghan army stepped up. Some elements, especially Afghan special forces, showed promise. "They were generally very courageous, very brave. When you got them to the objective, they fought well," General Joseph Votel recalled. "You had [Afghan] commanders who were beginning to pick up some of the techniques of combined arms fighting and using helicopters or Afghan close air support in some of their operations." The Afghans, however, still depended on American help for planning, intelligence, logistics, and "everything above the tactical fighting," Votel said. On the eve of the transition, General Joe Dunford told Congress "the Afghan Forces are doing the fighting" but lacked "planning, programming, budgeting, and acquisition … getting parts distributed, pay systems, fuel, overseeing contracts," and more, for which they depended on the US military. After years of investment and training, the Afghans were doing the bulk of the fighting – and dying. Some 4,400 Afghan soldiers and police officers were killed in 2014 alone, a number that rose to 9,000 in 2017. It was very much a real war for them.[24]

American observers had a harder time understanding how the Afghan war was going. In July 2013, the US Department of Defense stopped reporting the total number of enemy-initiated attacks, previously the single most-cited statistic, claiming that the metric was not a useful way to measure progress. It was also true that, with far fewer Americans on the ground to collect data, the analysts simply did not have enough information with

[22] Donati, *Eagle Down*, 143–144, 229, 230.

[23] Bolton, interview by author. Brookings, Afghanistan Index, 8, 9, 12, 15.

[24] Votel, interview by author. Dunford quoted in Senate Armed Services Committee, "The Situation in Afghanistan," 15. Brookings, Afghanistan Index, 8, 9, 12, 15.

which to draw a reliable picture. Anecdotally, the department noted that "insurgents are intentionally increasing the targeting of ANSF [Afghan National Security Forces] and Afghan officials throughout the country, and have assassinated of a number of key provincial leaders." It also noted how the withdrawal of US forces altered the security environment. "As ISAF draws down, some communities and security sector elements are adapting to the changed environment by establishing accommodations between insurgents and elements of the [Afghan army]." Absent American backing, the Afghans were striking their own deals with the Taliban. It was an early foretaste of what would unfold much more rapidly in 2021.[25]

From 2015 to 2018, the special inspector general for Afghanistan reconstruction reported the number of districts under government control versus insurgent control, and how many remained "contested." By that metric, the Afghan government was losing ground: it controlled 72 percent of districts in late 2015 but just 57 percent of districts one year later; contested districts rose from 21 percent to 33 percent. Other evidence pointed to a worsening situation. The United Nations, which kept its own database of "security incidents," reported that violence declined during the surge and its immediate aftermath but began rising again as international forces withdrew. The number of security incidents rose by 10 percent in 2014, 3 percent in 2015, and 5 percent in 2016. The number of civilian fatalities rose from 3,000 in 2013 to 3,700 in 2014 and stayed in that range for the rest of the war. The number of internally displaced Afghans fleeing violence soared after 2012, reaching 1.5 million in 2016 and 3 million in 2019. Some 50,000 Afghans applied for asylum in 2013; nearly 250,000 did so in 2015. Economic growth slowed to a crawl. General Campbell told the Senate Armed Services Committee in February 2016 that "the Taliban have been emboldened by our withdrawal," especially by "the lack of close air support the Afghans have had." In May 2017, a massive truck bomb killed and wounded nearly 600 people near the German embassy in Kabul, the largest single terrorist attack of the war. In October 2018, a member of the Kandahar governor's security detail opened fire at a meeting with General Scott Miller, the commanding general, and assassinated the Kandahar police chief (Miller survived).[26]

Lavoy still held out hope that, even this late in the day, the United States could use a combination of escalating military pressure and diplomatic

---

[25] DoD, "Report on Progress," November 2013, 13, 15, 16.

[26] Brookings, Afghanistan Index, 8, 18, 19, 25. Campbell quoted in Senate Armed Services Committee, "The Situation in Afghanistan," February 4, 2016, 15. UN violence numbers derived from its various "Reports on Afghanistan," 2010–2020.

outreach to force the Taliban to the negotiating table. Doing so would require new authorities to conduct operations in Pakistan. Years earlier, Petraeus had argued that so long as Taliban leaders had safe haven in Pakistan, they would never feel the pressure to negotiate (see Chapters 9–10). "The strategy [in 2016] was to make it too costly to Pakistan to house the Taliban leadership," Lavoy said, "which would force them to send [the Taliban] to Afghanistan where they'd have to engage in a political process. That was our logic."

It bore fruit. In May 2016, partly because of new authorities and resources, the United States killed the Taliban's supreme leader, Mullah Akhtar Mansour, in an alleged drone strike in Baluchistan, Pakistan. "That was a culmination of this effort," Lavoy said. "It was a watershed event. Everyone in the region freaked the shit out," he told Donati. "I mean, we had maximum pressure and influence." For the first time – after ten years of the Taliban's insurgency – the United States had finally killed an Afghan Taliban leader in Pakistan. Importantly, it was the first reported drone strike in Baluchistan, outside the Federally Administered Tribal Areas and much closer to the Afghan Taliban's headquarters, threatening every Taliban leader's sense of safety.[27]

Lavoy envisioned the strike as the first among many, raining down missiles on the Taliban until they came to Doha to negotiate. "It was a bold approach, and at a certain level of leadership we had strong support for that," Lavoy told me. "We would've liked to follow that up with additional strikes if need be against the next Taliban leaders. Not just indiscriminate strikes against Taliban leaders but strikes against the leaders we had pretty high confidence were opposing the peace process." But it never happened. "There were still limitations on what the US could do, and offensive strikes could only be authorized at a high level," according to Donati. "The new policy delivered some relief to US and Afghan forces on the battlefield, but it was not enough." "Not every leader was fully on board," Lavoy said, likely a reference to Biden and Rice, who wanted to keep the United States out of the business of fighting the Taliban. Some policymakers "didn't want to rock the boat so much. They weren't willing to be as bold," Lavoy said. "The one-off ultimately didn't have strategic effects. Multiple strikes would have had that effect and I think entirely changed the equation."[28]

By default, Obama adopted a version of what Biden had called for in 2009 – and, in fact, what the Bush administration had tried in 2002 and

---

[27] Lavoy, interview by author. Donati, *Eagle Down*, 241. New America Foundation, "The Drone War in Pakistan."

[28] Lavoy, interview by author. Donati, *Eagle Down*, 231, 241.

2003: a lean, light-footprint operation to kill terrorists – maybe including the Taliban, maybe not, with no intent to rebuild Afghanistan. By this route, Obama finally made his peace with an enduring presence. "I could see at the very end that he cared a lot about the issue, and I don't think he was there to abandon the Afghans," reflected Llorens. "He did not hold to the Biden view [of complete withdrawal], but he wanted to find a politically palatable way that was sustainable." The brief and rushed era of nation building started in 2007 and ended in 2011 or 2012, when the military started to draw down. Some aid programs continued to sputter along by inertia, and a decreasing amount of money flowed for a few more years, but Obama had long since decided that counterinsurgency and nation building were neither politically palatable nor sustainable. The military, freed from counterinsurgency, could focus on what it knew best: killing bad guys. The war was smaller, but it also grew more lethal – more bombs against more targets with fewer troops and looser rules of engagement – precisely when most Americans had forgotten about the war entirely, a trend that would continue through 2018.[29]

It was, in fact, Obama's primary strategy all along, distilled to its essence. During the Obama administration, as during the Bush administration, "our main kinetic mission was our own CT [counterterrorism] mission, not the security of the Afghan state mission," Vikram Singh argued. "The CT war took precedence. It was much smaller, it was a much nicer war because it had clean metrics" – easily countable dead terrorists – "And it was directly undermining the counterinsurgency war probably 50 percent of the time." Decisions about counterterrorism operations were cordoned off from decisions about the rest of the war in the interagency process in Washington, and "the decision-making structure is biased towards kinetic action," Singh felt, because "am I going to be the one to say 'don't take this strike?'" No one wanted to say no to a counterterrorism operation and then be blamed for the next 9/11. Bureaucratic inertia played its role too: the US built the most efficient terrorist-killing bureaucracy in history, and "if you create this tool, you will use it," Singh said. Like the Bush administration, the Obama team gave highest priority to counterterrorism – directly targeting al-Qaida and, now, ISIS.[30] Even as he was deciding on the surge, Obama recounts how, in May 2009, he brought his advisors into the Oval Office: "I want to make the hunt for bin Laden a top priority," he said. "I want to see a formal plan for how we're going to find him. I want a report on my desk every thirty days describing our progress."[31]

[29] Llorens, interview by author.   [30] Singh, interview by author.
[31] Obama, *Promised Land*, 677.

The argument is so intuitive it is hard to argue against. "Was the overall policy predominantly driven by military and security factors? Yes, because we were fighting a war," Laurel Miller told me. "We didn't invade the country to do development. We invaded the country because of a terrorist attack." Counterterrorism would naturally take priority. "When you're fighting a war, the priority is war fighting. So when there is a conflict between some of your other means of achieving your objectives, your political and assistance means for instance, and what the military and intelligence elements want to do, the military and intelligence are going to win out." It was the child's chess strategy: the goal is to get the king, so go get the king. The counterargument – that nation building is how you defeat terrorism in the long term – is not obvious and thus tends to get crowded out even among those sympathetic to its logic. It takes complex moves that are not obviously related to the goal and do not offer immediate results. And so Obama stopped trying to make the argument after 2009. "As a result, the public instinctively seemed to seize on bin Laden's death as the closest we'd likely ever get to a V-Day" for Afghanistan, Obama wrote.[32]

The public's readiness to declare victory, despite that bin Laden's death did not end the war or defeat al-Qaida, suggests that, after a decade and a half of Bush's and Obama's wartime leadership, the public saw the American war in Afghanistan primarily as a war of retribution, not of self-defense, deterrence, or building a more just and lasting peace. Retribution against al-Qaida was plainly both just and strategic – I am not arguing, as some do, that we should have done nation building *instead of* counterterrorism – but retribution was not the whole of what justice or good strategy required in Afghanistan. "I've said all along that if you walked in and said 'Here is Mr. Bin Laden,' the problem would not go away," Rumsfeld rightly told reporters in December 2001. Bush had known that self-defense meant permanently denying safe haven to al-Qaida and other terrorist groups of global reach, which he came to realize entailed some level of nation building. He had also emphasized the deterrent effect of the war – making an example so that other terrorists and their state sponsors would rethink their support for terrorism. Obama's Nobel speech, similarly, talked about the need to restore peace and justice in the aftermath of war. Bush and Obama were right that the war should have focused on these broader goals, but their strategies never fully aimed at them. The only consistent element of American strategy was killing al-Qaida.[33]

---

[32] Miller, interview by author. Obama, *Promised Land*, 698.
[33] Defense Department Briefing, December 27, 2001. www.c-span.org/video/?168014-1/defense-department-briefing.

John Brennan, the CIA director from 2013 to 2017, framed the issue in an intriguing way. "I would see it almost as concentric circles," he told me. "Counterterrorism at the center, counterinsurgency is the next rung out, and the nation building further out." The closer to the center, the higher the priority and the greater the scrutiny and resources. "We always had a very strong and robust counterterrorism effort, which is the reason why al-Qaida and others were degraded to the extent that they were. The counterinsurgency effort had some ups and downs. Over time, nation building was the most difficult one, the most amorphous one." Brennan is right that terrorism was the central reason why the United States was in Afghanistan – but that does not mean counterterrorism (direct-action, kinetic operations) should have been the main effort of American strategy. Defeating al-Qaida was the proper goal, but that does not mean killing individual al-Qaida leaders was the most effective means. Strategy should focus on what is required for victory, and America's prioritization of counterterrorism did not do that.[34]

General Jospeh Votel, who served as commander of Special Operations Command and Central Command, thought that, ideally, "one buys time for the other," that is, short-term counterterrorism operations should buy time for long-term counterinsurgency and nation building to take hold. But that only works if the United States was actually trying to do counterinsurgency and nation building, which it no longer was; and it only works if the different operations are carefully coordinated to avoid working at cross-purposes, which they almost never were. "The CT effort did take priority," Votel said – which, as was true during the Bush administration, often undermined the counterinsurgency and reconstruction efforts. "Some of the things [special forces] did . . . caused a lot of problems," such as night-raids, Votel acknowledged, which could become "debilitating" and "shut down momentum" for the broader mission. The short term did not buy time for the long term; it counteracted it. Votel and McChrystal worked to improve coordination and change the rules of engagement to make counterterrorism serve counterinsurgency at the height of the surge, but that marked the end, rather than the beginning, of the United States' effort to invest in the long term.[35]

By 2016, if not before, the Obama administration was only doing short-term counterterrorism operations with no thought for the long term aside from training the Afghan army: endless tactical victories with no strategic success on the horizon. Forever war was a feature, not a bug, of American strategy. America's war in Afghanistan deteriorated into a never-ending

[34] Brennan, interview by author.   [35] Votel, interview by author.

skirmish to keep the Taliban, al-Qaida, ISIS, and their allies under pressure across South Asia. The American soldier was the proverbial Dutch boy with his finger in the dike, keeping the deluge at bay at the price of his own freedom. It was an acceptable and even successful strategy for mitigating the threat of jihadist terrorism – though "success" did not mean military victory against the Taliban or an end to the war. It meant, rather, preventing the next attack on the homeland and keeping the Taliban from taking control of Afghanistan.

The strategy was not successful at defeating the Taliban, winning the war, rebuilding Afghanistan, or establishing conditions for long-term stability – because it was not trying to accomplish those objectives. Though I would have liked to have seen the United States try to defeat the Taliban and rebuild Afghanistan, the window of opportunity for those more ambitious goals seemed long closed. The finger-in-the-dike strategy had become the best available option given America's preference to enjoy relative freedom from jihadist violence without the expense of solving the root problems from which jihadism sprang. Never-ending frontier warfare was the price Afghans paid for America's strategy of counterterrorism on the cheap.

OBAMA'S WAR IN AFGHANISTAN

In 2016, Jeffrey Goldberg of *The Atlantic* published an extensive essay on Obama's foreign policy based on hours of interviews with the president. In his opening paragraphs, he laid out the premise: "Obama entered the White House bent on getting out of Iraq and Afghanistan," a noble goal thwarted time and again by the national security establishment, the "Blob," which pushed for continued engagement, more intervention, and never-ending war. Obama finally triumphed over the Blob by refusing to intervene in Syria's civil war, despite Bashar al-Assad's use of chemical weapons on his own people. Goldberg's article captured an emerging narrative: that the post-9/11 wars failed because of American hubris, while Obama, representing a new generation of Americans, knew the wisdom of humility, restraint, and realism. America could accomplish more by doing less.[36]

It is an attractive narrative because we like history as a morality play. If the problem is hubris, we can right the ship with a season of national contrition and a new, more humble, more realistic foreign policy (a promise, ironically, first made by George W. Bush in his campaign against the

---

[36] Goldberg, "The Obama Doctrine," *The Atlantic*, April 2016.

Clinton administration's supposed adventurism). The narrative promises an easy fix to the complicated and messy realities of military frustration and political disappointment. To the Obama team, the Iraq war was not just an enormous and costly mistake: it was a glaringly obvious and utterly stupid one. As another journalist reported, they came into office thinking of themselves as the responsible, level-headed, mature professionals who would be guided by a simple maxim: "Don't do stupid shit."[37]

Leave aside the question of whether hubris was to blame for our failures – I'll have more to say about that in the conclusion. The portrayal of Obama as the heroic figure standing athwart the interventionist establishment simply ignores what he said at the outset of his presidency. Obama vowed to win the war in Afghanistan, not get out. "As President, I will make the fight against al-Qaida and the Taliban the top priority that it should be. This is a war that we have to win," he said in July 2008, promising to escalate the war, not end it. But Goldberg's narrative – that Obama was intent on getting out of Afghanistan from the beginning – had become the accepted version of history. "President Obama entered the White House with a pledge to bring home US troops from two major wars," NPR falsely reported in 2015. In 2016, Bloomberg claimed that Obama "promised to withdraw all US combat troops from Afghanistan within 16 months of taking office," confusing Afghanistan with Iraq (as much of America did). "Before he took office in 2008, Barack Obama vowed to end America's grueling conflicts in Iraq and Afghanistan," wrote the *LA Times* in 2017. Journalists wove a myth, projecting onto the Obama of 2008 and 2009 the pessimism of his later years.[38]

The narrative of prudential realism is the positive spin that Obama officials put on the defeatism and cynicism that came to inform the administration's deliberations soon after they took office. "They never believed we were going to win," Peter Lavoy believed. "You never heard that language out of their lips ... The president had a more limited, more sober sense of what was possible from the beginning. Certainly, Joe Biden exhibited that from the beginning." Lavoy understood the military's need to talk about victory, but "at the senior most political level, there was no expectation of

---

[37] Mike Allen, "Don't Do Stupid Sh— (Stuff)," *Politico*, June 1, 2014.

[38] Greg Myre, "Pledging to End Two Wars, Obama Finds Himself Entangled in Three," NPR, October 15, 2015. Justin Sink and Toulouse Olorunnipa, "Obama Finds He Can't Escape Afghan War," Bloomberg, July 6, 2016. Christi Parsons and W. J. Hennigan, "President Obama, Who Hoped to Sow Peace, Instead Led the Nation in War," *LA Times*, January 17, 2017.

defeating the Taliban." The administration hoped Kabul would slowly "develop enough capacity to govern the country effectively," but even that hope "shrunk over time." Lavoy looked to yet another scenario, a negotiated solution, which also proved fruitless – because he and the rest of the administration failed to see that the best route to a successful negotiation was to talk and fight like they believed in victory.[39]

Singh, who had decried the administration's "ceaseless paper drills," recalled how in 2009 Obama was "very clear on ending the bad war and winning the good war." If Obama meant that seriously, it had major implications for how the war should be fought. "So the strategic direction was like: 'Let's get Afghanistan right,'" but the reality turned out to be different. "Nobody wanted to be so fully enough committed for long enough to be really sure that we would be decisive," Singh said. "We divorced ourselves from some basic realities of warfare, and so even though the President's intent [in 2009] was like 'let's win this war,' it was not going to come with the resources necessary." Singh felt that "the lack of commitment from the top" led to the endless interagency reviews. Afghanistan strategy was like a stripped screw turning loosely in place, never catching hold and never holding fast.[40]

In January 2014, as the administration was deliberating drawdown plans, Obama weighed in during an NSC meeting. "You know," the president said, "that Afghanistan today has become more unpopular than Vietnam ever was." Ambassador Jim Dobbins, then the special representative for Afghanistan and Pakistan, was aghast. "This was jaw-dropping stuff," he later wrote. "Seated to the president's left was former lieutenant John Kerry, USN, and to Biden's right, former sergeant Chuck Hagel, USA," both veterans of the Vietnam War, "both of whom were old enough to know from personal experience how ludicrously untrue this assertion was." Dobbins himself had been a young foreign service officer during the height of the Vietnam War. "No one said anything, however." Obama's belief about the two wars' unpopularity was historically ignorant and detached from political reality. In 1973, about 60 percent of Americans believed the Vietnam War had been a mistake, a number that rose above 70 percent in the years and decades after the war. The highest percentage of Americans who ever said the same about Afghanistan was just 49 percent (in 2014).[41]

---

[39] Lavoy, interview by author.   [40] Singh, interview by author.

[41] Dobbins, *Five Decades*, 288–289. Megan Brenan, "Americans Split on Whether Afghanistan War Was a Mistake," Gallup, July 26, 2021. Jodie Allen, "Polling Wars," Gallup, November 23, 2009.

The anecdote is revealing of how Obama came to view the war and what shaped his decisions about it. I'm reminded of Lavoy's comment that Obama believed he had to "cure the fever," to defeat the military's desire to "keep the war machine going unabated," and his belief that "I've got to constrain the military machine, otherwise it's just going to be out of control. It's going to be Vietnam, it's just going to run forever." Jeffrey Goldberg, the *Atlantic* journalist, found a similar attitude. One of the tenets of the "Obama Doctrine," Goldberg said, was that "the innate American desire to fix the sorts of problems that manifest themselves most drastically in the Middle East *inevitably* leads to warfare, to the deaths of U.S. soldiers, and to the eventual hemorrhaging of U.S. credibility and power."[42]

In this narrative, the chief danger to American national security was not the Taliban, but the US military's desire to defeat them. The "inevitable" war, death, and loss of credibility and power inherent in the effort to defeat the Taliban was a greater long-term threat to America than the theocratic totalitarians who gave safe haven to the perpetrators of 9/11. To some readers, that will sound appallingly cynical, even unpatriotic. In Obama's defense, he was right that, historically, America has sometimes been its own worst enemy, that the national security state needs close oversight and accountability, and that lax oversight had enabled unnecessary and unjust American militarism in past conflicts.

But not this one. The war in Afghanistan does not fit the mold of America's neoimperial ambitions in Latin America in the nineteenth century or its coercive Middle Eastern oil diplomacy in the twentieth. It was a clear-cut just war of self-defense to defeat a terrorist group that murdered thousands of Americans, a war that just happened to require liberating an oppressed people. Applying a critique of neoimperialism to the war in Afghanistan was as historically ignorant as it was strategically counterproductive. Obama's suspicion of the military and the national security establishment looks, in retrospect, more like dogmatic ideological prejudice than the product of considered judgment about the merits of the particular war in question. It also explains why he underperformed his promise on the world stage. In a 2017 C-SPAN survey, American historians ranked Obama overall the tenth greatest president in American history, but just twenty-fourth for his handling of foreign affairs.[43]

Obama's belief that the US military's desire to defeat the Taliban was a danger to American security explains his immediate reversals: from

---

[42] Lavoy, interview by author. Goldberg, "The Obama Doctrine," emphasis added.

[43] C-SPAN, "Presidential Historians Survey." www.c-span.org/presidentsurvey2021/.

a campaign promise to win the war to a decision not to try; and from an embrace of counterinsurgency and nation building to a rejection of them. It also explains the withdrawal timetable, the centerpiece of Obama's strategy that either caused or embodied almost every problem with Obama's war. The timetable was not the single point of failure of the Afghanistan war, nor the only driver of all the problems with Obama's handling of it. It is, however, the most potent symbol of Obama's war. The timetable was the product of the defeatism and cynicism that pervaded every aspect of Obama's handling of the war even as it undermined the surge, obviated reconstruction, and hamstrung negotiations, compounding the very failures and disappointments that Obama used to justify lowering his ambitions in the first place, made all the worse by how predictable the consequences would be. The timetable was a remarkable confluence of political cowardice, strategic myopia, and wishful thinking, and it turned President Obama's belief that the war in Afghanistan could not be won into a self-fulfilling prophecy – a tragic irony for a team guided by an otherwise-commendable motto: "don't do stupid shit."

13

2017–2018

Trump's Forever War

Obama expected to hand off the under-the-radar counterterror war to his former secretary of state, Hillary Clinton, not to a former real-estate executive and reality-TV star with no experience in foreign policy, military strategy, or public service. Clinton, who was widely expected to succeed Obama, rarely spoke about Afghanistan on the campaign trail but had carefully cultivated a reputation as a relatively hawkish Democrat. The national security establishment felt comfortable that a Clinton presidency would mean Afghanistan would continue its course toward a steady-state US military presence.

Most of the American public did not care about the war in Afghanistan, but a small and vocal handful took issue with the forever war, including Clinton's unconventional opponent. "We are wasting trillions of dollars in Iraq and Afghanistan," Donald Trump posted on Twitter in August 2011. "It is time to get out of Afghanistan. We are building roads and schools for people that hate us. It is not in our national interests," he added the following February. He proclaimed the war a "total disaster" (March 2012) and a "complete waste" (August 2012) and called for a complete withdrawal in tweet after tweet. After declaring his candidacy for president, he fell silent on the issue, at least on Twitter, but Trump had made no secret of what he thought of the war in Afghanistan.[1]

Trump gave further depth to his foreign policy vision in a campaign speech in April 2016. "America First will be the major and overriding theme of my administration," he said at the Center for the National Interest. He argued that US foreign policy since the end of the Cold War had subordinated American interests to "the false song of globalism." Promoting democracy was the keynote of that false song. "It all began with a dangerous idea that we could make western democracies out of countries that had no experience or interests in becoming a western democracy." Trump invoked Iraq and Libya, nowhere explicitly mentioning Afghanistan, but the

---

[1] For Trump's tweets, see www.thetrumparchive.com/.

implication was hard to miss. "We tore up what institutions they had and then were surprised at what we unleashed: Civil war, religious fanaticism," he said about Iraq. Investing in democracy abroad was a waste: "We're rebuilding other countries while weakening our own," which is why under the Trump administration, "we're getting out of the nation-building business" – which had, in fact, been Obama's policy since the end of the surge.[2]

Trump's vision was rooted in a specific philosophical commitment: that classical liberal ideals of liberty and equality are not universal, but culturally specific to the West. "Instead of trying to spread universal values that not everybody shares or wants," Trump explained, "we should understand that strengthening and promoting Western civilization and its accomplishments will do more to inspire positive reforms around the world than military interventions." This idea, which he would go on to flesh out more fully in a speech in Warsaw in July 2017, lies at the heart of the reemergent nationalism that Trump represented. It is a form of cultural relativism, the idea that not everyone wants or is fit for freedom and that American efforts to champion democracy are misguided and prone to backfire. Trump is wrong, of course, for the same reason that Rumsfeld was wrong in suggesting that nation building was a form of cultural imperialism. The only people around the world who claim that their nation is not ready for democracy or development are the rich men of the ruling tribe. Women, the poor, and ethnic and religious minorities are the first to advocate for democracy and rights because they understand it is their only shot at a decent government.

Like most everyone else, I did not take Trump's presidential candidacy seriously. I had signed up as a volunteer foreign policy advisor for Marco Rubio in support of his hopeful vision of American leadership. Rubio – and Hillary Clinton, for that matter – seemed to understand and support the rationale for American leadership and for an enduring American commitment to Afghanistan. By contrast, when ISIS murdered 130 people at a theater in Paris in November 2015, Trump argued that to defeat terrorists, we should "take out their families" and called for banning Muslim immigration into the United States. Alarmed, I authored a few articles warning against Trump and signed my name to an "Open Letter on Donald Trump from GOP National Security Leaders" in March 2016. It was an early statement of the much-maligned but always-vindicated #NeverTrump movement.

---

[2] "Transcript: Donald Trump's Foreign Policy Speech," *New York Times*, April 27, 2016. www
.nytimes.com/2016/04/28/us/politics/transcript-trump-foreign-policy.html.

In the letter, we warned that Trump's "vision of American influence and power in the world is wildly inconsistent and unmoored in principle." We condemned "his hateful, anti-Muslim rhetoric" and argued it was "alienating partners in the Islamic world." We expressed concern for his admiration for dictators, including Vladimir Putin, accused him of being "fundamentally dishonest," and argued that "he would use the authority of his office to act in ways that make America less safe." Trump "poses a distinct threat to civil liberty in the United States," we concluded.[3]

Enough of the electorate disagreed to elect Trump that November. I worried that his election would be profoundly consequential for the United States and the world in ways far beyond Afghanistan. The war, as important as it was and with as much time as I had poured into it, seemed to shrink compared to the broader consequences about to unfold. But as a passing thought, I took it as a given that a Trump presidency would mean that we had lost the war in Afghanistan.

2017: MCMASTER'S WAR

It took longer than I expected. For its first eighteen months, the Trump administration steered a surprisingly defensible course in Afghanistan, thanks to many of Trump's appointees who worked to preserve something of America's interests intact within the confines of Trump's desire to reduce American commitments overseas. They were squeezed from two sides: on the one hand, the frustrating results of the Obama administration's various strategies – surge, drawdown, and negotiations – seemed (wrongly) to prove their futility. On the other hand, virtually no one was convinced that Trump's demand to get out fully and immediately was a good idea. They wanted to stay, but it was unclear what kind of posture, mission, or strategy would be more effective than what Obama had tried. "By January of 2017, Afghanistan really seemed like an intractable problem," recalled Victoria Coates, who came on board as the deputy national security advisor for the Middle East and South Asia. "We had gotten into this cycle of everybody wanting to leave. Everybody saw all the polling – that 80 percent of the American people across both Republicans and Democrats wanted the war to end," she claimed, which was not true, "and nobody was articulating clearly a reason that we should stay."[4]

---

[3] "Open Letter on Donald Trump from GOP National Security Leaders," *War on the Rocks,* March 2, 2016.

[4] Coates, interview by author.

Central to the new team was the new national security advisor, General H. R. McMaster. Capping a thirty-four-year career in the army during which he served with distinction in both the 1991 Gulf War and the 2003 Iraq War, McMaster had also managed a PhD in history, an award-winning book on the United States' failures in Vietnam, and stints advising Petraeus on counterinsurgency and commanding an anticorruption task force in Kabul. Like Petraeus, he carried himself with the command of a senior military officer but wrote with the nuance of a scholar. Temperamentally, where Petraeus was diplomatic and politically attuned, McMaster was persistent, single-minded, and driven – his detractors might say bullheaded, stubborn, even domineering. McMaster was almost alone in his desire to make Afghanistan a major priority of the new administration. "I was really surprised that nobody gave a damn about Afghanistan when I got into the administration," he told me. "I had determined that I would make this a priority because I needed to give the president options in a matter of literally life and death." McMaster felt the war had become "a real danger to us and our interests because of the lack of attention and lack of a strategy" that had characterized the war to that point.[5]

McMaster launched an Afghanistan strategy review, by now an old Washington tradition. He went to Afghanistan in April 2017 with an interagency team to tour the country and get a feel for ground truth. He felt "a great deal of resistance" from the other principals and from the bureaucracy, he said. Part of the problem was that McMaster thought like a strategist, not a politician. "He wanted to do things, strategically think things through freed of any resource questions or political questions about where things were going, as if you could have a pure strategy that was divorced from political questions," Laurel Miller, then serving as the acting special representative for Afghanistan and Pakistan, recalled. The other principals thought they couldn't ignore the politics of the war. "[Secretary of State Rex] Tillerson was one of those who put the brakes on the policy. He is like, 'you are going in a direction that is not what principals are really looking at here,'" Miller said.[6]

The resistance McMaster felt was also simple bureaucratic inertia. "The resistance was to any change in policy within the US government," McMaster said. The bureaucracy had fought hard to put together something coherent in 2015–2016 after Obama finally gave up trying to withdraw. Officials like Lavoy and his counterparts across the government felt strongly that the bottom-up effort to keep a small but sustained presence in Afghanistan had been a triumph of strategy over politics and feared what might happen if

---

[5] McMaster, interview by author. [6] McMaster and Miller, interviews by author.

Trump and his team started meddling. McMaster and the bureaucracy should have recognized each other as allies: McMaster was essentially trying to get Trump to buy into a version of the strategy Lavoy had developed the previous year. In Kabul, Ambassador Llorens and General Nicholson took advantage of the hiatus between administrations to develop a joint civilian–military "country plan" proposing "a viable military, governance, economic development, and intelligence package that was sustainable for the long term," according to Llorens, more or less what McMaster was trying to do.[7]

But something else got in the way. The bureaucracy was committed to negotiations with the Taliban, which McMaster opposed. "I advocated actually for closing the Taliban political commission [in Doha] and treating those people as they should be treated," he said. "As international pariahs, rather than allowing them to travel internationally, raise funds, and live in five-star hotels." McMaster accused colleagues who advocated for negotiations of being eager to "supplicate to the Taliban political committee," falling prey to a "form of Stockholm syndrome in which members of the administration were actually sympathetic to the Taliban" in their eagerness to open talks. Some "no longer considered the Taliban the enemy," which, McMaster said "was an astonishing reversal of morality" and was "undercutting our strategy there."[8]

McMaster's view clashed with the way others viewed the war. "The fact that in 2017 McMaster could be talking about turning around the trajectory of the war ... It's like, what planet have you been on in the last few years?" wondered Laurel Miller. "I was in a meeting where he said to a colleague of mine, 'Don't you believe in winning?'" Miller was incredulous. "What the fuck? I mean, in principle, yes, but it's not happening. This is 2017." Miller believed the war was effectively lost, and negotiations were the only face-saving exit possible. McMaster "was totally opposed to the idea of the peace process," Miller complained. "He just tried to kill it and undermine it ... He thought it was wrong to be doing it." Miller thought it was obviously crucial to keep a peace process going.[9]

The disagreement between Miller and McMaster replicated the same misunderstandings in the Obama administration about what the purpose of negotiations should have been. McMaster was obviously right that the United States had to aim at victory – preventing the Taliban from violently overthrowing Kabul and reestablishing terrorist safe haven – but that should have included a diplomatic effort to bring them in from the cold, which could

---

[7] McMaster and Llorens, interviews by author.   [8] McMaster, interview by author.
[9] Miller, interview by author.

have been, hypothetically, Miller's part of the effort. But given Miller's view of the war, McMaster understandably felt that Miller's version of negotiations would not mesh with a revitalized military strategy. McMaster feared – rightly, it turned out – that negotiations under the conditions then prevailing would advance Taliban aims more than America's. (In Bob Woodward's reporting, McMaster did include "a political settlement with the insurgent Taliban," as part of his strategy review.)[10]

Regardless, Trump was a hard audience. He "was very susceptible to this framing of Afghanistan as the 'graveyard of empires,' and we were the next empire in line," McMaster said, showing the enduring power of the old trope. At an NSC meeting in July, "Trump looked bored and seemed disengaged," according to Woodward. "I've been hearing about this nonsense about Afghanistan for 17 years with no success," Trump said, conveying his frustration that "we've got a bunch of inconsistent, short-term strategies. We can't continue with the same old strategy." McMaster tried to emphasize that "we were actually fighting alongside Afghans against those who do not represent the vast majority of Afghans." McMaster's mission was "to inform [Trump] about the nature of our effort there, help explain why it was in America's interest," with "the Afghans bearing the brunt of the fight against jihadist terrorists."[11]

In making the case, McMaster made himself a target. "I'll tell you, the sessions we had with [Trump] were often painful," he said. "I was the one bearing the brunt of his anger over challenging his predisposition toward withdrawal, but I felt it was my best way to serve him and the country was to show him multiple options and to give him access to the best advice." Put another way, "McMaster was out of step with the president," Laurel Miller commented. "He kept trying to frame this and push this in a way that was going to be more than the traffic would bear." Reince Priebus, Trump's first chief of staff, believed McMaster and the others had "not spent the time working with the president on what his basic philosophy and foreign policy positions are, and why."[12]

Mike Pompeo, the new director of the CIA, agreed. "The president selected many people for service who either didn't share his foreign policy instincts or were unwilling to accept them," he wrote in his memoir, "especially in the first two years." Pompeo was referring to McMaster, of course, but also to Jim Mattis, the new secretary of defense. Mattis was a retired four-star

---

[10] McMaster and Miller, interviews by author. Woodward, *Fear*, 119.
[11] McMaster and Miller, interviews by author. Woodward, *Fear*, 120, 124.
[12] McMaster and Miller, interviews by author. Woodward, *Fear*, 120, 124.

Marine general in charge of Central Command during the surge in Afghanistan. He commanded a battalion in the Gulf War, a brigade in the early days of the Afghanistan war, and a division in the invasion of Iraq. He took pride in his call sign, "Chaos," and his reputation as a tough, no-nonsense, hard-nosed leader who knew how to get things done. Critics of Trump hoped Mattis would be one of the sober "adults in the room" who saved the president – and the country – from his own worst instincts.[13]

Mattis and McMaster agreed with each other's view of the war, though the two men were rivals for influence because of the similarity of their backgrounds. Trump liked the generals – a third, John Kelly, was his second chief of staff – and did not always care about the niceties of the chain of command, which caused problems. Just as Rumsfeld jealously guarded the Pentagon against Colin Powell, and as Bob Gates resented Doug Lute's influence in the White House, so too Mattis apparently disliked another military officer close to the president giving advice on national security. "Kelly and Mattis constantly knifed McMaster," Jared Kushner wrote. "When the president asked for a concrete plan to withdraw from Afghanistan, for example, Kelly and Mattis delayed and then blamed McMaster when the president expressed frustration about the holdup." Pentagon provincialism is bipartisan and timeless.[14]

Mattis had a smoother relationship with Trump, but, like McMaster, was out of step with Trump's views. He was "deeply and very personally invested in the 'forever war' view of Afghanistan," Pompeo wrote. He "held deeply establishment foreign policy views on an America First team." (Pompeo's memoir was written as a campaign memoir for his presidential aspirations more than a historical record.) "The great gift of the greatest generation to us," Mattis told the president, "is the rules-based, international democratic order." From that premise, "the quickest way out [of Afghanistan] is to lose," Mattis said. In a critique of Obama's handling of the war, Mattis told Trump: "We need to know if the commander in chief is fully with us or not ... We can't fight a half-assed war anymore." It was a clever way to appeal to Trump's most fundamental political goal: Trump should stay in Afghanistan to prove he was more manly than Obama.[15]

With Trump, McMaster and Mattis stuck to pragmatic arguments: the United States should stay in Afghanistan to kill terrorists and prevent them from attacking the homeland. McMaster had to work to "limit expectations"

---

[13] Pompeo, *Never Give an Inch*, 97.

[14] Pompeo, *Never Give an Inch*, 98, 99. Kushner, *Breaking History*, 169.

[15] Pompeo, *Never Give an Inch*, 98, 99. Woodward, *Fear*, 124, 125–126, 219.

and correct mischaracterizations. "We recognize that Afghanistan will be a ward of the international community for the foreseeable future," McMaster argued. "But we can achieve an outcome consistent with our interests at an acceptable price." But McMaster had to deal with what he called "Iago figures" – Steve Bannon, among others – whispering in Trump's ear. Bannon took up Joe Biden's role: he warned Trump that the military was untrustworthy, the war was lost, the United States had wasted trillions of dollars, and Trump should withdraw all US forces immediately.[16]

Pompeo sometimes agreed with McMaster and Mattis, albeit more diplomatically. He interpreted Trump's sometimes erratic and inconsistent outbursts and tweets as conveying a "three-pronged objective: get out, leave no one and nothing behind, and, if necessary, maintain a small and quiet force to reduce risk of an attack on Americans." The second and third points were contradictory, provoking disagreement and confusion within the administration, and Pompeo sometimes echoed Trump's own inconsistency. Pages earlier in the same memoir, he wrote that "I am extremely confident that [Trump's] instincts were right about getting every single uniformed soldier, sailor, airman, and marine out of the country." Regardless, McMaster, Mattis, and Kelly "consistently urged the president to stay the course," Pompeo wrote. "Over their objections, I and others urged an adaptation of our Afghanistan strategy to align with the three conditions the president had set down." White House chief of staff Reince Priebus tried to persuade Mattis, McMaster, and the others to spend more time talking to the president to understand his views; they risked coming off as presumptuous and condescending otherwise.[17]

In July, the president met with the military's leadership at the Pentagon to discuss options. Trump criticized General John Nicholson, the coalition commander in Afghanistan. "I don't think he knows how to win. I don't know if he's a winner," he said. General Joe Dunford, now the chairman of the Joint Chiefs of Staff, clarified that "there's not a mandate to win. That's not his orders," accurately characterizing the Obama administration's decision not to seek the Taliban's defeat. Mattis proposed "new rules of engagement for US troops in Afghanistan, freeing them up to be more aggressive and lethal by lifting Obama-era restrictions on the local commanders," an idea Trump warmed to. It was a productive conversation about serious strategic options.[18]

---

[16] McMaster, interview by author.

[17] McMaster, interview by author. Pompeo, *Never Give an Inch*, 361, 366–367.

[18] Woodward, *Fear*, 224, 226–227.

But then, according to Bob Woodward's account, the president "pro-
ceeded to lecture and insult the entire group about how they didn't know
anything when it came to defense or national security," and how the United
States should charge other nations for America's protection. Secretary of
State Tillerson felt "the president was speaking as if the US military was
a mercenary force for hire. If a country wouldn't pay us to be there, then we
didn't want to be there," which was the occasion for the gruff Texan oil-
man's alleged remark that Trump was "a fucking moron." Woodward
quoted a senior White House official who claimed that after the meeting,
"many of the president's senior advisers, especially those in the national
security realm, are extremely concerned with his erratic nature, his relative
ignorance, his inability to learn, as well as what they consider his dangerous
views."[19]

It was part of the unconventional nature of the Trump White House.
"You're dealing with a guy whose mood swings are just so wild," McKenzie
recalled. "It's hard to have him as a Commander in Chief in that kind of
circumstance because he's prone to fly off the handle and be angry."
Policymaking in the Trump administration was "court politics in the court
of a pretty volatile king," said Colin Jackson, the deputy assistant secretary of
defense for Afghanistan, Pakistan, and Central Asia, "and that's the way it was
played out."[20]

THE 2017 SOUTH ASIA STRATEGY

The review came to a head at an NSC meeting at Camp David in August 2017.
McMaster knew his bullheadedness had become an obstacle to his own
review. In earlier meetings, he asked Vice President Mike Pence to step in
and help mediate discussions. Pence agreed with McMaster, Mattis, and the
others. "I still believed that it was in the United States' national security
interest that Afghanistan remain out of the hands of terrorists," Pence later
wrote. "We had ample reason to stay and fight." At Camp David, McMaster
asked his deputy, Rick Waddell, to orchestrate the briefing. The tactic
worked; Trump listened to the rest of the principals, including Pence, and
turned to McMaster last to ask his view.[21]

McMaster characterized the proposed strategy as resting on four newly
clarified assumptions: first, "a counterterrorism-only strategy would be

---

[19] Woodward, *Fear*, 224, 226–227. [20] McKenzie and Jackson, interviews by author.
[21] Pence, *So Help Me God*, 253–254.

untenable if security collapsed in Afghanistan"; second, "the Taliban, al-Qaida, and other terrorist organizations were intertwined"; third, "the Taliban could not be trusted to negotiate in good faith"; and fourth, "Pakistan would not end or dramatically reduce its support for the Taliban." The first and second restored the essential elements of McChrystal's 2009 strategy, though without the resources. The third was based on McMaster's read of the war's psychological dynamic: the Taliban believed they were winning and the United States was withdrawing, in which case negotiations would be counterproductive – more or less what Petraeus had argued even at the height of the surge, though with more justification now that the United States had withdrawn most of its combat forces. The strategy was conveniently summarized with an alliterative list: reinforce the Afghan military; realign US efforts; regionalize the problem; and eventually seek a reconciliation agreement. As McKenzie understood it, the strategy focused on counterterrorism, but "if you're going to carry out an effective CT policy, you have to operate in an ecosystem. And the ecosystem is the Afghan military."[22]

Trump, despite his harangue the previous month at the Pentagon, went along with a strategy he would quickly abandon, a sign of how volatile a king he could be. Mattis and McMaster did not persuade the president, "they exhausted him," Llorens thought, and he let them have their way. Trump announced the decision on August 21 at Fort Myer, Virginia. He was remarkably forthright. "My original instinct was to pull out," he said. He acknowledged the American people's frustration with the war and said he shared "their frustration over a foreign policy that has spent too much time, energy, money, and most importantly lives, trying to rebuild countries in our own image," furthering the myth that the United States was still nation building years after it had, in fact, abandoned the effort. Yet following "a comprehensive review of all strategic options," Trump came to believe that America's veterans "deserve a plan for victory," that "the consequences of a rapid exit are both predictable and unacceptable," and that "the security threats we face in Afghanistan and the broader region are immense."[23]

Trump claimed that his approach to Afghanistan "will change dramatically" compared to his predecessors' approaches. He touted a "shift from a time-based approach to one based on conditions," which was a shift

---

[22] McMaster, *Battlegrounds*, 162–163. McKenzie, interview by author.

[23] Llorens, interview by author. "Remarks by President Trump," August 21, 2017. https://trumpwhitehouse.archives.gov/briefings-statements/remarks-president-trump-strategy-afghanistan-south-asia/.

Obama had made two years ago, in October 2015, when he finally repudiated his withdrawal timetable. A second dramatic change, Trump claimed, would be "the integration of all instruments of American power – diplomatic, economic, and military – toward a successful outcome." This was the same rhetorical pabulum that every administration recited – and, as we will see, Trump ended up making the same mistake as Obama in his failure to coordinate diplomatic with military efforts.

"We are not nation-building," Trump insisted. Trump postured like he was saying something new and daring, but denouncing nation building had been *de rigueur* on Bush's campaign trail in 2000, was commonplace in Rumsfeld's Pentagon, was officially codified in Obama's NSC memorandum ordering the surge, and was universally echoed in Obama's war cabinet after the surge. Hating on nation building is one of the most common, bipartisan pieces of conventional wisdom of the past quarter-century, and it bears substantial responsibility for the United States' failure to invest adequately in reconstruction in Afghanistan (and Iraq, Syria, and Libya). "The Trump administration tried to make it seem like this new policy was something really new and different," thought Laurel Miller, but "it wasn't really something so new."[24]

In a replay of scenes from 2010 and 2011, Congress later grilled the administration on the subject. Senator Jeanne Shaheen of New Hampshire noted Trump's disavowal of nation building. "If we are not nation-building, does this mean that we are less committed to human rights, to fighting corruption, to promoting good governance?" she asked. John Sullivan, the deputy secretary of state, replied that the administration was looking for "certain irreducible benchmarks of basic stability," which implied a minimalist investment in governance but added, somewhat paradoxically, that those benchmarks included respect for the Afghan constitution, "which includes protections for women," which tacked back toward a maximalist vision. If there was anything new, it was Trump's willingness to cut the budget even more than Obama. In 2018, civilian assistance dipped below $1 billion for the first time since 2007. When asked to explain the cuts, Alice Wells, the assistant secretary of state for South and Central Asian affairs told the House Foreign Relations Committee that "we are committed to the long-term development of Afghanistan but not over committed to the point that we are assuming an unreasonable or even a counterproductive level of nation building."[25]

---

[24] Miller, interview by author.

[25] Figures derived from USAID Green Book, www.foreignassistance.gov. Senate Foreign Relations Committee, "The Administration's South Asia Strategy on Afghanistan,"

One change Trump did manage to implement was cracking down on Pakistan for its tolerance of Taliban safe havens. The strategy "would take a tougher approach toward Pakistan, making clear that we needed to see Pakistan crack down [on militants]," Colin Jackson, the deputy assistant secretary of defense for Afghanistan, Pakistan, and Central Asia, said. "If they would not comply, we would have to re-look at the relationship." On the question of whether the Pakistanis lacked capacity or will, the administration came down firmly on the side of will. "We believe they do have the ability . . . to expel [the Taliban] from sanctuaries in their country," Sullivan told Congress.

In 2018, Trump suspended security assistance to Pakistan, the first and only time in the entire war any president would try sticks rather than carrots. The move "really unnerved" the Pakistanis, thought Llorens, especially because it was coupled with Trump's "bombastic rhetoric." It was easier for Trump than it would have been for Obama because, with a much smaller US military presence, the United States was less dependent on supply routes through Pakistan. But Trump's willingness to crack down on Pakistan proved, at least on this one occasion, that the boundaries of what is "realistic" were broader than what the Pentagon or the Obama and Bush administrations believed they were. Whether it could have changed the course of the war, coupled with the rest of Trump's strategy, is unknown because of how quickly Trump abandoned his strategy.[26]

The most significant and practical change that Trump authorized was looser rules of engagement and much wider targeting authorities. The military had been on a tight leash since the 2014 transition. Obama had begun to loosen the leash in 2016, but Trump went further. In his speech, he spoke about the need to ensure the warfighters have "the necessary tools and rules of engagement to make this strategy work." He touted that he had already "lifted restrictions the previous administration placed on our warfighters" and promised to "expand authority for American armed forces to target the terrorist and criminal networks."

In practical terms, since Trump did not want additional boots on the ground, that meant more bombs from the air. "You saw a big uptick in airstrikes" after the 2017 strategy review, recalled Laurel Miller, because of the "loosening up of rules of engagement for targeting." From 2017 to 2018,

February 6, 2018, 14. House Foreign Affairs Committee, "The Trump Administration's Afghanistan Policy," September 19, 2019, 18.

[26] Jackson and Llorens, interviews by author. Senate Foreign Relations Committee, "The Administration's South Asia Strategy on Afghanistan," February 6, 2018, 15.

the US Air Force almost doubled the number of sorties by strike aircraft and dropped seven times the number of munitions. "We bombed the shit out of the Taliban," said Ambassador Hugo Llorens. "I mean, we bombed the shit out of them," he repeated, stressing that it "got their serious attention." In April 2017, the United States used the GBU-43 Massive Ordinance Air Blast (MOAB, the so-called mother of all bombs), the largest nonnuclear bomb in the US arsenal, against an Islamic State target in Afghanistan. The war had been at a low ebb since 2014, with a small spike in 2016. The 2017–2018 airstrikes were the most significant military escalation since the surge. The heightened tempo of airstrikes continued into 2019 but declined sharply in 2020. Trump did authorize about 4,000 troops as part of the new strategy, though he wisely did not put troop numbers at the center of the debate or the strategy. The additional troops, coupled with the airstrikes, had a positive effect. "The introduction of additional advisors and enablers in 2018 stabilized the situation, slowing the momentum of a Taliban march that had capitalized on US drawdowns between 2011 and 2016," the Department of Defense reported in late 2018.[27]

A more symbolic change, but no less important, was evident in how Trump talked about the war. Trump paid fitting homage to the American soldier and properly framed the importance of the war. "Our nation must seek an honorable and enduring outcome worthy of the tremendous sacrifices that have been made, especially the sacrifices of lives," he said. "We must secure the cause for which they gave their lives." Economists wail about the folly of chasing "sunk costs," but it was Abraham Lincoln who insisted that "these dead shall not have died in vain." The meaning of soldiers' deaths depends on whether we continue their fight, which is why we put statesmen and statesmen, not economists, in charge of wars. Trump speaks in a populist register, and he instinctively understands that the American people and the American soldier need to hear basic truths spoken plainly: when you fight a war, you fight to win. "The American people are weary of war without victory," he said, and so "our troops will fight to win . . . We will push on to victory." Trump said "win" and "victory" more times in fifteen minutes than Obama did in eight years.

Despite my broader misgivings about Trump – "misgivings" is too polite a word – I was encouraged by his Afghanistan speech. Laurel Miller is right that it was less novel than Trump touted – but that was precisely its virtue. Trump

---

[27] Miller and Llorens, interviews by author. "Combined Forces Air Component Commander, 2014–2021 Airpower Statistics" www.afcent.af.mil/Portals/82/November%202021%20Airpower%20Summary_FINAL.pdf. DoD, "Enhancing Security," December 2018, 1.

allowed Lavoy's strategy from the previous year to continue and avoided most of the big mistakes I and others expected him to make (except for his repudiation of nation building). Trump set the right tone that the rest of his administration was ready to follow. "If the Taliban were to regain control of the country, we would very likely see the same platform for that global reach of terrorists that struck New York and Washington and Pennsylvania on September 11th," Sullivan told Congress a few months after Trump's speech, which had been the basic logic behind the American presence in Afghanistan since 2002. Pence compared Trump's political courage in his Afghanistan decision to Bush's decision to surge in Iraq, both examples of prioritizing the nation's interest over the more politically expedient and popular course. "It was a moment that reflected the gravitas and lived expertise of the administration's national security team and the seriousness with which Trump took the role of commander in chief," Pence wrote.[28]

Victoria Coates thought the South Asia strategy was "a strong document," which "stands the test of time for declaring some kind of a purpose in Afghanistan." "I think it was a good strategy," reflected Colin Jackson. NSC staffers thought the product reflected a sound process. "General McMaster ran the quintessential, perfect policy process," said Lisa Curtis, the NSC senior director for South and Central Asia. "He understood the role of the NSC, that it was there to bring the interagency together to develop options for the president to pursue US goals and objectives," she said. "I think it really was a good process." General McKenzie, then serving as director of the Joint Staff, thought it was the "best crafted strategy document" of the Trump administration.[29]

The review definitely bore McMaster's stamp. "McMaster came in, he framed out the policy review [and] dictated the framing," Miller recalled, much like Riedel had done in March 2009. His critics thought his strong views may have compromised his ability to run an impartial process. McMaster (and his successor, John Bolton) "wanted to be principals in the process rather than manage the process. They were more like a Brzezinski than they were like a Scowcroft," said Colin Jackson, comparing Jimmy Carter's and George H. W. Bush's national security advisors. "These guys were not faceless. They didn't want to be faceless. They wanted to have an argument."[30]

---

[28] Senate Foreign Relations Committee, "The Administration's South Asia Strategy on Afghanistan," February 6, 2018, 35. Pence, *So Help Me God*, 255–256.

[29] Coates, Curtis, McKenzie, and Jackson, interviews by author.

[30] Jackson, interview by author.

It's clear that McMaster had an opinion about Afghanistan and was advocating for it, but that isn't a problem by itself. In fact, it is the second of the two jobs a national security advisor has: to advise the president on the best course of action. The problem comes if the national security advisor neglects the process or blocks opposing views, as Susan Rice did. But unlike Rice, McMaster ran a process to allow all viewpoints, including his own, to surface, rather than trying to prevent a process from happening in the first place – evidently what Pompeo and Mattis would have preferred. Another difference was that, within Trump's inner circle, McMaster's view was the unconventional wisdom that would have otherwise been shut out of conversation, while Susan Rice's view reinforced Obama's and thus fed confirmation bias and groupthink. "We needed to present the president with the withdrawal option" – Trump's preferred option – "and others that were based on the realities of the region," McMaster later wrote.[31]

One reason Mattis worked hard to undermine McMaster was because McMaster was intent on fleshing out Trump's preferred option of complete withdrawal, an option both Mattis and McMaster opposed but one that McMaster believed was important to include in the discussion. McMaster was walking a tightrope, trying to obey the orders of his commander-in-chief while preserving America's position in South Asia. "The president wanted out of Afghanistan, so the strategy that HR [McMaster] came up with was a way of encapsulating that and putting it into a context that was transferable, translatable, understandable by the people that were going to do it," thought General Joseph Votel. "You can't just pick up and leave."[32]

McMaster's most important contribution was simply to care about Afghanistan. No one else wanted to make it a priority. The administration could have allowed the existing strategy to simmer along for a few months before announcing a final withdrawal. McMaster would not tolerate that in part because, uniquely among the policymakers I spoke to, McMaster brought a moral focus to the discussion. "I felt as if the war had become unethical because it no longer met the test of just war theory as laid out by Thomas Aquinas," he said. "We were no longer orienting our efforts on a just end in the war." He felt a moral urgency to getting Afghanistan right. Aside from Obama's Nobel speech, no other official that I am aware of invoked the just war tradition in thinking about America's longest war, which is a damning indictment of our national security establishment – and the institutions of higher education that train them. McMaster's critique is similar to the one I levied against Obama in Chapter 8: that America

---

[31] McMaster, *Battlegrounds*, 162.   [32] Votel, interview by author.

had given up on trying to achieve peace and justice in Afghanistan, resigning itself and the Afghans to endless conflict because it offered cheap insurance against terrorism. It worked, more or less, but it was morally indefensible.[33]

Trump was widely criticized for his decision. His base, which supported his call to end "endless wars," felt betrayed. "Bannon's chief objection was the lack of realism," Woodward reported. "You can't have him sitting there talking about victory. There's not going to be a victory,'" Bannon said (another example of how Bannon and Biden paralleled each other). Democrats criticized him because the opposition party always criticizes the party in power, but also because the party was already moving to embrace Biden's position on the war. Trump hated getting criticism from all sides. "That was a hard one," Trump said of the decision. "It's the graveyard of empires." Pompeo could see the writing on the wall. "I knew that day that this speech would not be the last word on Afghanistan," he wrote.[34]

Trump's backtracking was evident even in the official NSC memo codifying the strategy. It did not, in fact, reflect McMaster's full preferences and telegraphed the administration's future direction. "The goal in Afghanistan was to 'reshape the security environment,'" according to Woodward's reporting, "to limit the Taliban's military options and 'encourage them to negotiate a political settlement that reduces violence and denies safe haven to terrorists.'" The memo did not echo the president's language about victory either. "Stalemate likely to persist in Afghanistan" it said, and "Taliban likely to continue to gain ground," and "Win is unattainable." The Obama administration's misunderstanding of victory had become the accepted wisdom for both the military and the Trump administration. "I don't think any of us thought we were going to defeat the Taliban," McKenzie said. "As long as you can keep the government of Afghanistan up and running," that was good enough, and "we didn't think there was a way to win in the traditional military sense."[35]

Vice President Mike Pence made a surprise trip to Afghanistan in December 2017, months after the president announced his Afghanistan strategy. He addressed the troops in the same hangar at Bagram Airbase Obama had six years previously. "As one nation and one people, we vow to win this war on our terms on this soil," he said. "We are staying in that fight and will see it through to the end." He quoted from Trump's earlier speech,

---

[33] McMaster, interview by author.
[34] Woodward, *Fear*, 259. Pompeo, *Never Give an Inch*, 368.
[35] Woodward, *Fear*, 258–259, 260. McKenzie, interview by author.

repudiated "arbitrary timetables," touted how the administration had "lifted the restrictions that limited the effectiveness of our armed forces" and "put Pakistan on notice." Subtly echoing Bush more than Trump, Pence praised the soldiers because they had helped Afghanistan "liberate its people" and said the Afghan people "have never lost their love of freedom." He concluded, "I believe that victory is closer than ever before." Victory meant that "Afghanistan will be free and America will be safe."[36]

It was the sort of speech Bush could have and should have given in 2001 or 2002, the sort of speech I wanted to hear Obama give at the start of the surge in 2009. But by late 2017, the words rang hollow – not because Pence was insincere or the words were wrong, but because the context around the words had changed so dramatically. America had surged and withdrawn. It had tried to negotiate peace and failed. It had (briefly) tried to rebuild the Afghan government and mostly failed. It had liberated Afghanistan from the Taliban, but then watched inept, or even complicit, as an incompetent kleptocracy took its place. All that might have been surmountable with a fresh administration and a new-found dedication to victory, but it was clear to many observers, including Pompeo and others within Trump's inner circle, that Trump had no enthusiasm for his declared strategy. It was a striking parallel with Obama: both started out using the language of victory and endorsed a new strategy only to back away and lose faith prematurely. We'd seen this movie before. The troops in the hangar were markedly less energetic than they had been six years ago. Trump never let go of his original instinct to withdraw, and it only took a couple months for those instincts to reassert themselves.

THE ROAD TO DOHA

"I think there was instantaneous buyer's remorse," thought Colin Jackson. "This was McMaster and Mattis' strategy, that's whose strategy it was." It was not Trump's strategy, and Trump was impatient. "We started seeing in spring of 2018, into the summer, definitely a President who was becoming frustrated, wanted more results from the strategy than he was seeing," recalled Lisa Curtis. "We're being beaten, and [the Taliban] know they're beating us," Trump told the NSC in November 2018, "My strategy was wrong, and not at all where I wanted to be. We've lost everything. It was

---

[36] "Vice President Pence Addresses Troops in Afghanistan," C-SPAN, December 21, 2017. www.c-span.org/video/?438888-1/vice-president-pence-addresses-troops-afghanistan.

a total failure. It's a waste. It's a shame. All the casualties. I hate talking about it." Trump referred to his August 2017 speech as "that stupid speech," according to Bolton.[37] In McMaster's telling:

> The strategy did not last. Those who were deeply skeptical about America's long war in Afghanistan convinced President Trump to abandon it. Soon after I departed the White House in 2018, those who misunderstood the nature of the war, underappreciated the threat, and were ideologically predisposed toward disengagement from "forever wars" convinced him that a sustained and sustainable military effort in Afghanistan was futile and wasteful.[38]

"What was particularly tragic was that the Trump administration strategy announced in August 2017 was working," McMaster wrote. "The Taliban was under significant military pressure and no longer could simply wait out the US withdrawal time line." McMaster's claim is how he defends the early Trump administration against the record of the later Trump years. He was right that his strategy, especially the increased tempo of airstrikes and the new hard-line stance toward Pakistan, had changed the landscape of the war for the better, though it still lacked any approach to rebuilding the Afghan government.[39]

But Trump and Pompeo were impatient to go home. "We went to Afghanistan to defeat al-Qaida there, and we did," Pompeo claimed in his memoir. Whether the new strategy was working or not was irrelevant; the strategy itself wasn't necessary because the United States had already won, which was Pompeo's excuse to argue for getting out (foreshadowing Biden's argument in 2021).[40] Getting out meant, once again, trying to negotiate with the Taliban. Some officials claim that negotiations were part of the 2017 strategy all along, despite McMaster's earlier opposition to them. "The ultimate goal of this strategy was a negotiated settlement," claimed Colin Jackson. "The idea was that putting the Taliban on their back foot on the battlefield, bringing them to the point where they were willing to negotiate, was part of the strategy." That seems to be reading Trump's later endorsement of negotiations backward in the 2017 strategy. "Someday, after an effective military effort, perhaps it will be possible to have a political settlement that includes elements of the Taliban in Afghanistan," Trump said in his August 2017

---

[37] Jackson and Curtis, interviews by author. Bolton, *The Room Where It Happened*, 215–216, 219.

[38] McMaster, *Battlegrounds*, 164. [39] McMaster, *Battlegrounds*, 166–67.

[40] Pompeo, *The Room Where It Happened*, 362. Llorens, interview by author.

speech, "but nobody knows if or when that will ever happen." That was the most Trump was willing to say in public. The following January, Trump was more direct: "We do not want to talk to the Taliban." McMaster later wrote that, because of the escalation, "the United States had set conditions for its entering a future negotiating process from a position of strength, not desperation," with a notable emphasis on a "future."[41]

In any case, Trump and Pompeo came to focus on negotiations as the main effort in 2018 after losing faith in the 2017 strategy. "Mike, you have to talk with [the Taliban]," Trump told Pompeo in May 2018, months after firing McMaster, "they'll be there long after we're gone." The administration had come to believe that the Taliban was a "Pashtun nationalist insurgency," as Alice Wells told Congress in late 2019, which, if true, reinforced the sense that they were an inextricable part of Afghanistan that could not be defeated. (It was a striking parallel to how critics came to view the Vietcong and North Vietnam as truer embodiments of the Vietnamese nation.) Regardless, Trump and Pompeo replicated the Obama administration's error of turning to negotiations after military escalation rather than in tandem with it. Obama and Trump both almost got the timing right – synchronizing diplomacy with military pressure – but both missed the window for reaching out to the Taliban by a matter of months.[42]

Part of the problem was that, while Trump wanted out, he wasn't eager to deal with the Taliban. "A major part of our mission became supporting a negotiated settlement to the conflict," recalled General Joseph Votel, and that mission:

> was very clear to me as articulated by the secretary of defense and the chairman [of the joint chiefs], and not so much by the president. We didn't really have all that many discussions about this. This isn't a topic that he wanted to talk about much, frankly. I think the Secretary and others had been successful in convincing him that we needed to be a little bit more deliberate in this."[43]

Because Trump was not enthusiastic about talking to the Taliban, he delayed appointing a lead negotiator. The special representative for Afghanistan and Pakistan – the role held by Richard Holbrooke, Marc Grossman, and Jim Dobbins in earlier years – was supposed to be the

[41] Jackson, interview by author. McMaster, *Battlegrounds*, 166–167. Arul Louis, "No Talks with Afghan Taliban," *The Week (International)*, January 30, 2018.

[42] Pompeo, 371. House Foreign Affairs Committee, "The Trump Administration's Afghanistan Policy," September 2019, p. 48.

[43] Votel, interview by author.

point person for negotiations. Laurel Miller was in the position in an acting capacity in 2017 but, as an Obama appointee, on her way out, and the role was vacant in early 2018. Miller's departure is an interesting "what if." She had been an early advocate of negotiations. "I was arguing we need to put the peace process at the front because Washington is going to wake up one day ... and say, 'what the hell are we still doing in Afghanistan?'" she warned. Could earlier negotiations, when the United States had greater leverage, have been more successful? Then again, she viewed negotiations as an alternative rather than a complement to military operations. Regardless, "I don't think we anticipated that it would take that long for the administration to identify who their negotiator is going to be," Votel said. While the military waited for a diplomatic partner, "operations did become more kinetic ... because we were trying to keep pressure on the Taliban" and "compel them to come to the table."[44]

In September 2018, Trump found his man in Zalmay Khalilzad – the same Khalilzad who served on Bush's NSC, who became his special envoy and then ambassador to Afghanistan from 2002 to 2005 and the US permanent representative to the UN in 2007. It was an unlikely paring: Khalilzad, a Muslim born in Afghanistan who immigrated to the United States and became a respected member of the foreign policy establishment, working for the president who had called for a ban on immigration from Muslim nations and regularly derided the "deep state" and railed against establishment foreign policy. Khalilzad had coauthored the Atlantic Council report with Ambassador James Cunningham in 2015 calling on Obama not to withdraw that was cosigned by dozens of senior foreign policy professionals. No better example of "the establishment" could be found.

On another level, the pairing worked. Khalilzad, despite his establishment credentials, has a reputation for working outside regular channels. That is part of his success but also why he meshed with the freewheeling Trump administration. Rumors – or perhaps conspiracy theories – circulated over the years that Khalilzad aspired to return to his native land and run for president of Afghanistan someday, or that he aimed to work for energy companies and broker a deal with the Taliban to cash in on Afghanistan's mineral wealth, or possibly both. True or not (the first rumor seems more plausible to me, the second less), they suggest something about Khalilzad that probably resonated with Trump: a reputation for thinking big, imagining opportunity, and aggressively pursuing success regardless of conventional niceties. In early 2017, a reporter asked

---

[44] Miller and Votel, interviews by author.

Khalilzad about his interest in serving in the Trump administration, weeks after Trump's call for a ban on Muslim immigration. "If the president thought I could help the United States, I have told people I would be more than happy, if the country needs me, I am available," he replied.[45]

When Khalilzad joined the administration as the newly retitled special representative for Afghanistan reconciliation, "a judgment had been made that the war was not going well," Khalilzad told me, "that we were losing ground." As for the president's new strategy, "that also has not succeeded." Trump reminded Khalilzad "that staying in Afghanistan to nation build and state build had been a mistake, that it was costing too much, that the US stakes did not justify the level of effort." Khalilzad had tried to convince Bush and Rumsfeld in 2003 that solving America's problem required helping the Afghans solve their problems. Fifteen years later, even Khalilzad seemed to have given up that hope.[46]

Trump believed that Afghanistan was no longer important because jihadist groups had proliferated and dispersed and were therefore not as important as other issues, such as the rise of China – which made the American role in Afghanistan more trouble than it was worth. Trump was right that terrorist groups had proliferated and dispersed – but South Asia endured as a unique nexus of overlapping jihadist networks far more important than far-flung groups in Indonesia or Nigeria. South Asia also held special historical resonance as the place where jihadists had defeated the Soviet Union and formed al-Qaida, and from which they had struck America. American policymakers consistently underplayed Afghanistan's significance in their eagerness to minimize our commitment and get out.

Trump gave Khalilzad clear negotiating instructions. Khalilzad was to get an agreement with the Taliban that stipulated: "[1] withdrawal of forces, [2] no terrorism, [3] commitment from all Afghan sides [to] a political settlement . . . and [4] a ceasefire." Left unspecified, to the consternation of other policymakers and to the detriment of the ultimate agreement, was any mechanism for holding the Taliban accountable to their end of the deal; how firmly linked withdrawal would be to the other aspects of the deal; and whether "withdrawal" left room for a stay-behind force. On top of those ambiguities, negotiations took place against the backdrop of the freewheeling, unconventional nature of Trump's White House and the absence of

---

[45] "Zalmay Khalilzad on Middle East Policy and the Trump Administration," C-SPAN, February 5, 2017. www.c-span.org/video/?422837-4/zalmay-khalilzad-middle-east-pol icy-trump-administration.

[46] Khalilzad, interview by author.

a regular decision-making process. Others in the interagency were never informed about Khalilzad's negotiating instructions. "Whatever direct instructions he got from Pompeo [or] the president, he wasn't sharing those with the team," recalled Colonel Lujan, who had left the NSC and was now detailed to Khalilzad's staff. "I would be shocked if any such instructions existed," said Victoria Coates, one of many who complained that the process was opaque.[47]

Coates' comment illustrates an important truth to keep in mind about Trump administration officials' recollections about the road to the Doha agreement. The dust has settled on most of the big decisions earlier in the war, and officials' interviews, memoirs, and journalists' accounts can be collated to assemble a roughly accurate picture. Many Bush and Obama officials were willing to admit their own mistakes and bring them out into the light of day for inspection and retrospective education. The dust has not settled on the Trump administration; he was running for reelection at the time of this writing. Trump administration officials are not in a confessional mood and, especially when it comes to Doha and the final withdrawal, seemed eager not to admit or share blame, but to point fingers.

[47] Khalilzad, Lujan, and Coates, interviews by author.

14

2018–2020

Doha

Over the course of 2018, Trump fired Tillerson, Mattis, McMaster, and Kelly. He moved Pompeo from CIA to the State Department and hired John Bolton as the new national security advisor. From mid 2018 to the end of his presidency, Trump acted with increasing independence and diminishing regard for the counsel of anyone except Pompeo. Trump "brought in people who were more pliable, and then he started galloping around, he started doing his own thing," thought Llorens. With a new team in place, Trump wrested control of Afghanistan strategy and handed it to his most loyal national security appointee as a political football with which to score points toward a future election. Trump's newly empowered foreign policy led to the Doha agreement with the Taliban and America's final defeat in Afghanistan.[1]

POMPEO'S WAR

The Doha negotiations had "absolutely nothing to do with the way the National Security Council process should work at all," John Bolton, McMaster's replacement as national security advisor, told me. A lawyer by training, Bolton served as an assistant attorney general in the Reagan administration and in several positions in the State Department in both Bush administrations – including a brief stint as the US permanent representative to the United Nations, an irony considering his low view of the United Nations. Bolton speaks with the precision characteristic of lawyers; his memoir reads like a carefully argued case not only for his views on foreign policy (many of which I agree with) but also for his innocence of any of the failures that happened on his watch. Bolton has a reputation as a savvy bureaucratic infighter, though he struck me as more exasperated than cantankerous.[2]

---

[1] Llorens, interview by author.   [2] Bolton, interview by author.

Bolton recalled how "on any given day, [Trump] might say, 'Let's get out entirely. Why can't we do that?' And there we'd have the same argument over and over again, not in any very structured way about what we should be doing." Bolton was ostensibly in charge of managing the national security process, but he gave up trying. "My own view was that the circumstances were such that if we tried to do anything in a coordinated fashion using the regular national security process, that it would just be spinning wheels." Perhaps taking McMaster's fate as a cautionary tale, Bolton chose not to fight Trump's character, temperament, and style. "The White House simply wasn't working the way anybody in living memory had experience of how it worked," thought Ambassador McKinley.[3]

That meant there was no process as Pompeo and Khalilzad took over the Doha negotiations and, critics claim, ran them independent of interagency oversight. Bolton spoke extensively on the point:

> Between Pompeo and Khalilzad, the negotiations went off by themselves. And there wasn't a lot of transparency with the rest of the interagency . . . This [was] a period of six, ten, twelve months where State just wouldn't cooperate. And sometimes Zal [Khalilzad] would show up for a deputy's meeting. Sometimes he wouldn't. Sometimes he would talk to us. Sometimes he would talk to the Pentagon. Sometimes he wouldn't talk to anybody. And Pompeo said, look, the president told me just to negotiate this, not to coordinate with anybody . . .
>
> The negotiations were just ripped out of the normal coordination process. And you know, you can speculate as to why. I think it's because Pompeo wanted responsibility for it alone and ultimately credit for it alone. Because he wanted to run for president. He wanted to deliver something Trump very much wanted, getting out of Afghanistan. I think everybody else involved was frustrated, including Khalilzad.[4]

Bolton and Pompeo did not get along and worked hard in their memoirs to blame each other. But Bolton isn't wrong about Pompeo's presidential ambitions. After leaving office, he formed a political action committee, visited and spoke in key states, and published a campaign-style memoir before announcing in April 2023 that he would not run for president. He apparently hoped the Doha agreement would be a key part of his legacy as secretary of state that he could point to on the campaign trail. Pompeo – not Trump – is the one who flew to Doha and had his photo taken with Taliban officials, an experience Pompeo called "personally sickening," yet one he endured anyway.[5]

---

[3] Bolton and McKinley, interviews by author.   [4] Bolton, interview by author.
[5] Pompeo, *Never Give an Inch*, 377.

"Pompeo becomes the overwhelming power player in foreign policy," said Colin Jackson, "particularly on Afghanistan after Mattis' departure." Pompeo graduated first in his class from West Point and served as an armor officer in West Germany in the final days of the Cold War. After the army, he picked up a Harvard Law degree; moved to Kansas; founded, led, and sold a successful aerospace firm; and ran for Congress. Elected in the Tea Party wave of 2010, Pompeo branded himself as a foreign policy expert with clear ambitions for higher office. In 2016, he warned Republican voters that Donald Trump would be an "authoritarian president" who ignored the constitution – before, like the rest of the Republican establishment, closing ranks behind him. Pompeo carefully cultivated the Trumpian style of polit-ics: pugnacious, unapologetic, spoiling for a fight with the press and with Democrats, and Trump rewarded him by appointing him as CIA director, then as secretary of state.[6]

It was an odd situation. "Once Mattis was removed, DoD was severely underpowered in influence terms," Jackson recalled, which meant "Pompeo and Zal [were] driving the deal" while the Department of Defense was "trying to pump the brakes," albeit "ineffectively." Mattis' relationship with the president had deteriorated steadily throughout 2018. Trump was enormously frustrated with what he saw at Mattis' broken promises and insubordination. "The president definitely had the impression – and I would say this was accurate – that Mattis was playing him for time and was not particularly interested in what the president wanted to do, but very, very sure of what Mattis wanted to do," Coates thought. In December, Trump announced by tweet that he was pulling US troops out of Syria. Mattis resigned in protest, offering to stay on long enough to help his successor; Trump peremptorily fired him.[7]

Trump came to blame Mattis for Afghanistan. "I gave you what you asked for. Unlimited authority, no holds barred," Trump told Mattis days before his resignation. "You're losing. You're getting your ass kicked. You failed." He kept up his complaints long after Mattis left. "He would continu-ally claim Jim Mattis talked him into deploying more troops, promising that the war would be over on his watch," according to Mark Esper, Mattis' successor. "In Trump's view, Mattis was a 'terrible' secretary of defense who duped him by promising victory on one hand and, on the other hand, warning that if we didn't fight the terrorists in Afghanistan, we would be fighting them in America." Trump complained to his cabinet later, "What's [Mattis] done for me? How has he done in Afghanistan?

<hr>

[6] Jackson, interview by author.   [7] Jackson and Coates, interviews by author.

Not so good. I'm not happy with what he's done in Afghanistan and I shouldn't be happy."[8]

But Trump was torn. "The first thing the generals tell you when you want to pull out, they say, Sir, I'd rather fight them over there than fight them over here," Trump said. "That's a hard line if you're sitting here and you have to make that decision." Mattis did not write a memoir of his time as secretary, has rarely spoken in public since he left office, and declined to be interviewed for this book. His side of the story is largely untold. "We must do everything possible to advance an international order that is most conducive to our security, prosperity, and values, and we are strengthened in this effort by the solidarity of our allies," he wrote in his resignation letter, but, "you have the right to have a Secretary of Defense whose views are better aligned with yours on these and other subjects." Trump did not view international order and alliances the same way. Ultimately, Bolton believed Mattis (and McMaster) were victims of their early success. "What seemed like success to Mattis and his colleagues, such as the August 2017 Afghanistan speech, were, in retrospect, mistakes," Bolton wrote. "Trump had been pushed far beyond where he wanted to go, and now he was overreacting in the other direction."[9]

With Mattis and McMaster out of the way, and Bolton choosing to keep his powder dry, Pompeo had free rein. With his backing, Khalilzad began meeting with the Taliban political office in Doha in late 2018. Alice Wells had held one round of negotiations with the Taliban July 2018, but there was little progress and no momentum. "The major change . . . was that Zal Khalilzad was approached by people who said they were representatives of the Taliban, who said they wanted to talk with him," recalled Bolton. Khalilzad's prior experience, language skills, reputation, and contacts made him a natural fit for the role, and negotiations picked up momentum, especially after he asked Pakistan to release Abdul Ghani Baradar, a cofounder of the Taliban, from house arrest. Baradar was a senior and respected leader within the Taliban's ranks. Khalilzad felt Baradar would be a more credible interlocutor who could deliver on whatever deal came out of the negotiation. Baradar promptly took up a role as the Taliban's deputy leader and head of the Doha political office.

---

[8] Esper, *A Sacred Oath*, 211. Woodward, *Rage*, 143.

[9] Woodward, *Rage*, 194. Bolton, *The Room Where It Happened*, 220. Mattis resignation letter, December 20, 2018. https://d3i6fh83elv35t.cloudfront.net/static/2018/12/mattis-letter2.pdf.

One incident could have stopped negotiations before they began but instead shed light on how the Taliban viewed them. In October, as negotiations were getting underway, an assassin broke into a meeting with General Scott Miller in Kandahar – but didn't try to kill him. Killing the top US general in Afghanistan would have derailed negotiations and provoked a strong American military response. Taliban leaders had scuttled negotiations in 2014 and 2015 after Omar's death, fearing talks would make them look weak, but in 2018, hard-liners no longer feared negotiations and did not seize the opportunity to derail them. Instead, the gunman assassinated Afghan general Abdul Raziq Achakzai, one of the most ruthless, effective, and widely hated anti-Taliban commanders in southern Afghanistan. It was a clear sign of whom the Taliban truly feared.

Talks in Doha continued despite ongoing violence. The added diplomatic momentum came with a price. Aside from Pompeo, DC was in the dark about what Zal was saying, offering, or promising. "Few in the DoD were aware of the arrangement" that Khalilzad was negotiating, Mark Esper later wrote. Khalilzad had a draft plan by mid 2019. "The contours of the plan briefed to me by Pompeo still lacked some key details and had little support across the interagency," said Esper. "I pressed Mike about circulating the draft for review."[10]

"From an NSC perspective, Zal was definitely a one-man show," recalled Coates. Lisa Curtis agreed. "Pompeo got very invested in the deal, and he ended up giving a lot of cover to Zal when Zal didn't want the rest of the interagency interfering in what he was doing," said Curtis. "He got protection for that from Pompeo . . . For whatever reason, there was just a decision made that there wasn't going to be the normal policy process." Esper thought Pompeo was trying to avoid White House micromanagement. "The NSC had a historical reputation for getting too much into DoD (and other departments') business," he said (echoing Gates' complaints). Pompeo believed that the NSC "didn't want to study the plan as much as kill it." Going through the interagency process would "'give Bolton and his team' a chance to 'dissect it,' and 'leak its shortcomings' to the media." Pompeo may also have kept negotiations out of the normal interagency process in mimicry of Trump's freewheeling management style and to push them forward more quickly, without the delay and hassle that had dragged out negotiations for years under the Obama administration. Pompeo claims that "we made sure that everyone was tied in at the right level," though he

[10] Bolton, interview by author. Esper, *Sacred Oath*, 212.

was referring mostly to military counterparts in theater. His only other comments on the process were to take potshots at Mattis and Bolton and note Khalilzad's "reputation for freelancing and secrecy."[11]

Khalilzad claims, first, that he did include the interagency; but second, somewhat contradictorily, that Pompeo told him not to. "On my insistence, we got a negotiating team that was interagency," he told me. "We had representatives on the team from the Pentagon. We had a two-star general representing the Department of Defense," and a civilian from the Office of the Secretary of Defense. "General [Scott] Miller, the commander of the forces in Afghanistan, participated in the negotiations. If he couldn't come, he would send people." Lisa Curtis from the NSC was occasionally included. After a round of negotiations, Khalilzad insisted, "there would be briefings given to the NSC, briefings given to a mini-principals group that the secretary of state would convene," or he would "brief the principals separately." Because Khalilzad had some interagency representation on his team, he didn't need to go through the interagency process in DC; he felt his office *was* the interagency process. "Deputies meetings didn't happen, interagency meetings didn't happen on a regular basis, because Trump had the White House work very differently," said Ambassador McKinley, who stayed involved in the process as a senior advisor to Pompeo. "That explains why the military and particularly General Miller became an integral part of the negotiation."[12]

At the same time, Khalilzad indicated to others that Pompeo had instructed him to exclude the interagency. Bolton recalled how "in a couple private conversations with Zal, he said, 'Look, I don't know what the story is here, but Pompeo tells me not to meet with you, not to meet with the Pentagon,'" and that "'if Pompeo knew I were here, I'd be in real trouble.'" Bolton recounted how Pompeo himself "said Khalilzad was under instructions – he left unstated by whom – to make a deal without outside supervision," which, to Bolton, "showed yet again how State was treating the rest of the national security team." Khalilzad, Pompeo, and Bolton were each eager to avoid blame for the process, if not the content, of Doha. Regardless, for whatever reason, Trump and

---

[11] Coates and Curtis, interviews by author. Esper, *Sacred Oath*, 213. Pompeo, *Never Give an Inch*, 371, 373.

[12] Khalilzad, McKenzie, and McKinley, interviews by author. General McKenzie, then commanding Central Command, thought it was a one-star general, not two-star, on the negotiating team.

Pompeo felt comfortable conducting negotiations with an enemy during wartime without consulting the national security advisor or the secretary of defense.[13]

TALKING WHILE WITHDRAWING, AGAIN

The principal strategic questions at stake in talks with the Taliban were: Would the United States withdraw completely or try to get the Taliban's agreement to a stay-behind counterterrorism force? Would the withdrawal be conditioned on the Taliban's commitment to sever ties with al-Qaida and deny them safe haven? Would the withdrawal be linked to the Taliban's commitment to open talks with the Afghan government? How tightly linked would the different parts of the agreement be? Would the US withdraw anyway, regardless of what the Taliban did? Was the end *withdrawal* or *peace*? Would the means include a stay-behind force or not?

The Taliban's principal demand and the central element of the eventual Doha agreement was the full withdrawal of US forces from Afghanistan. It was hardly something the Taliban needed to demand because Trump was demanding it too. "Everybody thinks that the President was telling Zal 'you've got to make a peace deal with the Taliban,'" said Lisa Curtis. "No, the President wanted out of Afghanistan, he wanted troops withdrawn." A peace deal was incidental, a useful way to smooth the path toward withdrawal – but withdrawal, not peace, was the goal. "The instructions were pretty clear ... which were to negotiate a way out of Afghanistan, yesterday, with the perennial threat that the president can make the decision, irrespective of what was happening in the negotiations," McKinley recalled, "so negotiations became an effort ... to at least have a framework for withdrawal that provided a timeframe for the Afghan Government to react, and for an orderly, not disorderly, US departure."[14]

In December 2018, Trump ordered Mattis to draw up withdrawal plans, signaling the final break with his August 2017 strategy. Immediately after Mattis resigned over Syria, Trump publicly announced his intent to withdraw 7,000 troops, about half the total, from Afghanistan, though he later relented on the timing. "He now didn't want to wait for Khalilzad but wanted to announce the withdrawal of US forces prior to the end of his second full year in office," wrote Bolton, because Trump thought he could avoid "owning" the war by withdrawing before the halfway point of his

---

[13] Bolton, interview by author. Bolton, *The Room Where It Happened*, 430, 431.
[14] Curtis and McKinley, interviews by author.

term. In August 2019, Trump again announced that he was withdrawing 5,000 US troops from Afghanistan. In neither case was the announced withdrawal in response to conditions on the ground nor concessions by the Taliban. "By the time I became secretary of defense in July 2019, Trump wanted out immediately," Mark Esper recalled.[15]

In January 2019, Khalilzad met with the Taliban political office in Doha. Baradar wasn't yet in Doha; the Taliban were represented by Sher Mohammad Abbas Stanikzai, a Taliban diplomat with lesser standing. Heeding Trump's intent, Khalilzad gave the Taliban what they wanted: an offer to withdraw US forces. "The first day of serious negotiations, Zal offers up half of US forces in return for CT assurances, ceasefire, this kind of thing," recalled Colin Jackson. "The Taliban say no. And then in the afternoon, he is like, well, what if we withdrew everybody?" Jackson was incredulous. "All the chips get played in a day, literally." By offering the principal bargaining chip up front, Khalilzad had nothing with which to demand a stay-behind force, an Afghan political settlement, or an enforceable, verifiable promise to sever ties with al-Qaida. Bolton and the Department of Defense were alarmed. "[Acting Defense Secretary Patrick] Shanahan and I worried that Khalilzad was giving away too much, not because he was a poor negotiator, but because those were Pompeo's instructions." Jackson agreed, worrying the deal would not protect the United States' "counter-terrorism equities" because "it would not provide for an enduring presence." "[Resolute Support Commander] Scott Miller and I, we were concerned that we were going to get sold out," said General McKenzie.[16]

Pompeo's willingness to offer full withdrawal at a time when the Taliban were militarily ascendant turned the negotiations from a last-ditch attempt to salvage the United States' most basic interests into a forum for arranging the terms of America's defeat. Pompeo claims otherwise, of course. He claims that he and General Miller had developed a tightly coordinated campaign to talk and fight simultaneously. "General Miller would let us know when the Taliban had moved too close to an important location. Zal

15 Bolton, *The Room Where It Happened*, 218. Esper, *A Sacred Oath*, 211. Thomas Gibbons-Neff and Mujib Mashal, "US to Withdraw about 7,000 Troops from Afghanistan, Officials Say," *New York Times*, December 20, 2018. www.nytimes.com/2018/12/20/us/politics/afghanistan-troop-withdrawal.html. Associated Press, "Trump Plans to Withdraw over 5,000 US Troops from Afghanistan," August 28, 2019, PBS. www.pbs.org/newshour/world/trump-plans-to-withdraw-over-5000-u-s-troops-from-afghanistan.

16 Jackson and McKenzie, interviews by author. Bolton, *The Room Where It Happened*, 221. See Malkasian, *The American War in Afghanistan*, 431–432, for corroboration of Jackson's account.

or I would contact Mullah Baradar, the Taliban's top political leader, and tell him he had two hours to fix it. If he didn't, we rained down fire on his people in the field until he got the message," Pompeo wrote. "It took only a couple such conversations and demonstrations to make clear that we were operating in tightly coordinated fashion to coerce the outcomes we sought from the Taliban." But if Pompeo and Miller had such leverage at their disposal, why weren't they able to use it to craft a better deal? I don't doubt that Pompeo and Miller did what Pompeo claims they did, only that the Taliban were as impressed as Pompeo thought they were.[17]

It's likely true that the uptick in airstrikes in 2017–2018 (which mostly predated Pompeo's appointment as secretary of state) helped pressure the Taliban to the negotiating table. But once there, the Taliban quickly saw that the United States was withdrawing its ground presence and had no intent or ability to compel them to make any real concessions. The Taliban's confidence translated into Doha's provisions. Those terms were hammered out over the next six months. The US would make a specific promise to withdraw all troops by a publicized deadline in exchange for which the Taliban made generic, nonverifiable, and unenforceable promises to sever ties with al-Qaida, deny safe haven to terrorist groups, and open talks with the Afghan government. The Taliban were happy to make such promises with the certainty that, after the US withdrawal, no one would have any means with which to hold them to their end of the deal. The Afghan government was not part of the negotiations and had not agreed to anything.

Trump replicated Obama's error of withdrawing troops and depriving himself of leverage while supposedly trying to negotiate with the enemy. Trump – author of *The Art of the Deal* – was giving away his principal bargaining chip for almost nothing in return. "Everyone knew, Talibs included, this is the most important [thing], that the president was anxious to leave," Khalilzad told me. "That, I'm sure, had [an] impact on negotiations, no doubt about that," almost exactly echoing what Grossman told me about Obama's timetable. The problem was as obvious as it had been a decade previously. "The central problem with the diplomatic strategy was that if the Taliban really thought we were leaving, they had no incentive to talk seriously," Bolton wrote, "they could simply wait as they had often done before and as Afghans had done for millennia. As the Taliban saying went, 'You have the watches, we have the time.'" Even Pompeo, Trump's most loyal advisor, saw the problem. "Each time President Trump talked of getting out, the Taliban became emboldened to wait out our departure

---

[17] Pompeo, *The Room Where It Happened*, 375.

without firing a shot." The Taliban had all the leverage. In October 2018, the Taliban told an Afghan government official that "they thought Trump would withdraw any day," and "they were waiting for that," and saw no need to negotiate.[18]

Secretary of Defense Mark Esper agreed:

> Getting all (or at least most) of our forces out of Afghanistan sooner rather than later became Trump's singular focus, not implementing the peace agreement. This was obvious to everyone, including the Taliban, I bet. As such, his words and decisions would squander our leverage with them and undermine the prospects for achieving an enduring peace in Afghanistan that would benefit the Afghan people and better safeguard America's long-term security.[19]

The problem with a full and immediate withdrawal was the same as it had been since 2002: if the United States left, al-Qaida and other jihadist groups would have space to reconstitute. In late 2019, Esper conferred with John Rood, the undersecretary of defense for policy, about the emerging plan to withdraw from Afghanistan. Rood shared "concerns about going to zero US troops. If we did that, he argued – setting aside an arbitrary date – then how would we be able to maintain a counterterrorism presence in the country?" Esper equivocated. "In my view, if the Taliban lived up to their end of the deal – broke with al-Qaida, denied them safe haven, and committed to keeping terrorist groups out of Afghanistan – then we shouldn't need a counterterrorism force there," he wrote, then equivocated again. "I thought that was unlikely to happen, though, which is where a 'conditions-based' catchall would once again kick in and allow us to suspend our departure (and even return troops)." Esper wanted to get the Taliban to agree to a conditions-based withdrawal so that he could keep US troops there if, as seemed likely, it proved necessary.[20]

Bolton shared their concerns. In Bolton's view, a full withdrawal "was clearly bad policy." He went on: "In theory, the US government opposed any such arrangement unless it was 'conditions based,' meaning we would go to zero only if: (1) there were no terrorist activities in the country; (2) ISIS and al-Qaida were barred from establishing operating bases; and (3) we had adequate means of verification." It's unclear who Bolton had in mind when he characterized this as the view of "the US government," as it was no longer

---

[18] Bolton, *The Room Where It Happened*, 221. Pompeo, *Never Give an Inch*, 374. Malkasian, *The American War in Afghanistan*, 427.

[19] Esper, *A Sacred Oath*, 232–233.   [20] Esper, *A Sacred Oath*, 216–217.

the view of the president or the secretary of state. Regardless, Bolton rightly saw the agreement Khalilzad had negotiated did not meet those criteria. "If the Taliban, ISIS, and al-Qaida concluded from the plain evidence of palpable US troop drawdowns that we were withdrawing ... what would those terrorists conclude from a piece of paper that expressly said we were going to zero by October 2020?"[21]

Trump, to his credit, recognized the logic and "worried that pulling down our numbers would indicate weakness." In March 2019, he asked Bolton and the military: "Do we weaken our hand in the negotiations by saying we're dropping our forces?" Bolton, inexplicably, said no: "I said it would not." I found this passage in his memoir so baffling I asked him to elaborate. "I just thought they were two separate things," he replied, referring to troop numbers and diplomacy. "In other words, we make a decision on what we think the appropriate US force level is . . . on the basis of what we thought was needed to carry out the missions." Force levels were a military issue to be decided based on military considerations, isolated from the diplomatic context. "I just thought that there was a disconnect between what we were doing and negotiations, so I didn't think it would hurt the negotiation." I find that explanation unpersuasive because elsewhere Bolton clearly showed that he understood the link between military and diplomatic strategies. As I noted earlier (p. 409), Bolton saw that "the central problem with the diplomatic strategy was that if the Taliban really thought we were leaving, they had no incentive to talk seriously."[22]

Bolton offered a convoluted chain of logic. "As for the US–Taliban meetings, I was less concerned than before about their substance, and therefore less exercised than the Pentagon, because I thought we had largely won the key battle in Trump's mind," Bolton wrote. "The United States would not be completely withdrawing from Afghanistan but would maintain a persistent troop presence for counterterrorism and other objectives." That proved not to be the case, but Bolton seems not to have been able to admit to himself where Trump was really heading with his Afghanistan strategy. But Bolton thought the logic still applied even if Trump wanted to go to zero troops because "even that decision didn't depend on the state of play in the talks. In short, the US military posture was no longer tied to the peace process." But the question was not whether the military posture was tied to the peace process, but whether the peace process would be hurt by the military posture. Bolton treated the military presence as the goal; the

---

[21] Bolton, *The Room Where It Happened*, 423, 424.

[22] Bolton, *The Room Where It Happened*, 424. Bolton, interview by author.

peace process might be mildly useful if it yielded an agreement that gave permission for the military presence, but Bolton was just as happy to keep the presence without an agreement. "Thus, in my mind, there was no particular pressure for Khalilzad to produce results and no real target date to finish the negotiations."[23]

Bolton did not care about the peace process on its own merits. "I really cared less about what Zal was doing. Not that there was an awful lot I could do about it, anyway," he told me. "The negotiations could continue. They could continue forever. As far as I was concerned, it just didn't strike me that we were ever going to get an agreement that would be acceptable to the United States." He knew it was bad strategy but expected it to fail so didn't waste time fighting it. Bolton never believed the Taliban would "carry out any commitments they made anyway, which was another reason I didn't care that much about it. You were negotiating over something that ultimately would not work." Meanwhile, "if continuing negotiations bought us time to prepare and then maintain a sustainable counterterrorism presence, then play on." Bolton was simply doing triage, choosing which bureaucratic battles to fight. That's understandable in 2018 and maybe early 2019 – you can't fight every bad idea you encounter in government – but as negotiations picked up steam, it became implausible to ignore the reality that Trump and the Taliban were taking the negotiations seriously and genuinely intended a full withdrawal. Bolton knew that was bad strategy; for Bolton not to care, he had to have been in denial about the reality of what was happening in the Oval Office and in Doha.[24]

If Bolton had cared a bit more, he might have forced himself to see more clearly where things were headed and thus might have tried harder to dissuade Trump. "For HR [McMaster], with his personal history, [Afghanistan] was a major focus. For Bolton, it just simply was less so," thought Victoria Coates. "It's not that he didn't care," but "he had higher priorities," like China and Iran, while "nobody owned Afghanistan in the administration, particularly after HR left." For Bolton, the die had already been cast. "Bolton was very clear-eyed on the Afghanistan issue but didn't consider it the thing he was going to fall on his sword over," thought Jackson. As for the effect of withdrawal on negotiations, "I didn't think it would help," Bolton said, "but I didn't think it made any difference at that point."[25]

[23] Bolton, *The Room Where It Happened*, 429–430. Bolton, interview by author.
[24] Bolton, interview by author.
[25] Bolton, *The Room Where It Happened*, 424. Bolton, interview by author. Coates, interview by author. Jackson, interview by author.

ABANDONING COUNTERTERRORISM

How could the United States leave Afghanistan but still claim to have defended itself against terrorism? The conundrum was simple to state and impossible to avoid. "We were long overdue for getting out of that conflict," wrote Esper. "That said, we really needed to make sure that Afghanistan never again became a safe haven for terrorists to plan, prepare, and conduct attacks against the United States." The two halves of that sentiment contradicted each other.[26]

The solution that Bolton and the military advocated was to leave behind a small counterterrorism force. Some Trump officials can be hard to pin down on whether they or the president ever intended a full and complete withdrawal of all US forces, or whether they supported a stay-behind counterterrorism force. At one level the point is academic: by 2018, the 8,000 or so troops left in Afghanistan *were* the stay-behind force. Obama had already withdrawn over 90 percent of the troops that had been in Afghanistan at the peak of the surge. In 2017, I moderated a talk with Afghan Ambassador Hamdullah Monib at a day-long forum at the New America Foundation. I asked him how he and Afghans felt about the possibility of the United States' withdrawal from their country. Did they want us to leave? "You've already left," he replied. The residual presence was a fraction of what it had been, and the dynamics of the war had fundamentally changed to reflect that reality.[27]

The Trump administration did not see it that way and continued to debate whether and how many troops might be left after a deal with the Taliban. The lack of agreement within DC meant that Khalilzad effectively had opposing sets of negotiating instructions. "While his instructions from Trump (or Pompeo, whomever) at that time were to get US forces to zero, he also had instructions from Trump to support counterterrorism capabilities," Bolton recalled. Khalilzad liked Bolton's solution: "The trick was how to get the Taliban and the Afghan government to agree we were going to zero on the existing mission, while simultaneously creating a modified mission to support counterterrorism capabilities."[28]

Pompeo made the division worse by being on both sides of it. "Whenever the team would remind [Trump] that counterterrorism concerns might

---

[26] Esper, *A Sacred Oath*, 208, 210.

[27] New America Foundation, "Special Operations Policy Forum 2017," November 15, 2017. www.youtube.com/live/qBJz2VQh6to?feature=share&t=18215.

[28] Bolton, *The Room Where It Happened*, 434.

preclude a total withdrawal from Afghanistan, he'd say: 'I got it. Do it like we did early on: CIA and small forces. They can bring in the bombers if the Taliban do something stupid,'" Pompeo wrote. Pompeo was sometimes very much part of that team. "Pompeo was successful in showing that withdrawing all US troops from Afghanistan – one of the president's longtime goals, even obsessions – would risk another 9/11 style attack," according to Bob Woodward. Pompeo wrote approvingly of his understanding of Trump's goal, including, "if necessary, maintain a small and quiet force to reduce risk of an attack on Americans." But, as noted earlier (see Chapter 13), Pompeo also wrote, "that [Trump's] instincts were right about getting every single uniformed soldier, sailor, airman, and marine out of the country."[29]

Pompeo was apparently reflecting Trump's own inconsistency. In December 2018, Trump was categorically intent on full withdrawal but then vacillated throughout 2019. Pence summarized the problem succinctly: "Trump had campaigned on a promise to bring the troops home. But he had also pledged to fight terrorism." Pompeo spoke to the first promise; Bolton and the military to the second. Bolton thought he had persuaded Trump to change his position and endorse an enduring presence at a meeting at the Pentagon in July 2019 (one of the reasons Bolton thought it was safe to ignore the negotiating track). But then Bolton learned Pompeo and Khalilzad "were still negotiating as if we were withdrawing entirely." Bolton was surprised. "I called Trump and said it was his decision whether to let Khalilzad and the State Department act with complete independence in the negotiations, but I thought it was dangerous for what Trump said he wanted. 'I don't even know who he is,' Trump replied of Khalilzad. 'Do what you think is best.'"[30]

The anecdote is illustrative of Trump's managerial style; he rarely stuck to his word and never treated a commitment as binding. Trump would seem to agree to a stay-behind force, then back off. "When Trump agreed to that – or at least we thought he agreed to it, it turned out it was no more an agreement than anything else Trump ever talked about," Bolton told me, "it would last twenty-four hours, and he'd go to something else." A few months later, at Trump's golf club in Bedminster, New Jersey, "Trump opposed a continuing US military presence in Afghanistan for two related reasons," Bolton wrote, "first, he had campaigned to 'end the endless war' in faraway places; and second, the sustained mishandling of economic and security

---

[29] Woodward, *Rage*, 121. Pompeo, *Never Give an Inch*, 366.
[30] Pence, *So Help Me God*, 254. Bolton, *The Room Where It Happened*, 213, 428.

assistance, inflaming his instinct against so much frivolous spending in federal programs."[31]

Bolton, like Esper, strongly supported a stay-behind force – he opposed the negotiations altogether but never tried to stop them – and tried to persuade Trump to make it a priority. "There was clearly a disjunction between the State Department's objective – zero US forces – and my (and the Pentagon's) desire to preserve counterterrorism and other capabilities," he wrote. "We hadn't started the wars and couldn't end them just by our own say-so." Bolton was echoing Leon Trotsky's famous aphorism: you may not be interested in war, but war is interested in you. Bolton suggested adopting "the fiction of saying our military forces devoted to fighting the Taliban would drop to zero, replaced instantaneously with a counterterrorism force that just happened to be the same size and the same people," if that was what it took to get both Trump and the Taliban to agree to an enduring US presence. "As long as we had [a military presence], we could scale it back up. We could continue the insurance policy." Pence agreed with Bolton, though most accounts do not highlight his role in the process. "I had always held the view that if we ended our mission in Afghanistan, some small force should be left behind to support counterterrorism efforts," he wrote in his memoir.[32]

The ambiguity worried the military. "There were a lot of concerns about what [negotiations] meant long term for the US presence on the ground," General Votel recalled. "At the beginning of this, I envisioned that we would always keep some amount of forces on the ground to work with the Afghan forces and continue to strengthen their backbone." But Votel saw which way developments were headed. It "became apparent over time that ultimately this would be a total withdrawal." The reality affected the battlefield situation. "I don't think the situation changed for the better during that period," Votel recalled. "We began to see the Taliban be much more aggressive in terms of what they were doing." Votel ascribed the Taliban's military aggressiveness to their diplomatic savvy. "I think that the Taliban recognized an inherent weakness in our strategies: the longer they play out American strategies, the better the opportunities are," he said. "I think they saw the opportunity, and I think they took it." The Taliban stretched out negotiations to give them time to make more battlefield progress: they knew how to coordinate diplomatic and military efforts better than the United States.[33]

[31] Bolton, *Room Where It Happened*, 213, 428. Bolton, interview by author.

[32] Bolton, interview by author. Bolton, 430. Pence, *So Help Me God*, 354–355.

[33] Votel, interview by author.

Bolton, Pompeo, and others were deluding themselves: Trump wanted out, as anyone not vested in the administration's success could see, and the Taliban would never agree to a stay-behind force. "We've got to get out," Trump told his NSC in November 2018. "My campaign was to get out. People are angry. The base wants out." His occasional vacillation notwithstanding, Trump was committed to full withdrawal. Because both principal actors wanted the unconditional withdrawal of all US forces, it was impossible for Khalilzad to tie the withdrawal to any meaningful conditions. Trump did want the Taliban to agree to sever ties with al-Qaida and pledge not to allow safe haven for terrorists. And most of the administration, aside from the president himself, also wanted to see the agreement conditioned on the Taliban starting negotiations with the Afghan government, which had been excluded from Khalilzad's talks in Doha. But without leverage, Khalilzad could only get weak, unenforceable promises on both counts. As the negotiations wore on, it became evident "that the Taliban were not going to give anything away at the table," Ambassador McKinley said.[34]

Khalilzad nonetheless persuaded himself it was possible. His "theory on the negotiation was [first] that we would make peace with the Taliban, the Taliban would break up with al-Qaida, and the Taliban would take care of ISIS-K in return for the US withdrawing large numbers of troops," said Colin Jackson, then, second, "we would strike a deal with a future Afghan government," a government that included Taliban representation. The Taliban couldn't agree to a US counterterrorism presence on their own, but they could and would as members of a coalition government.[35]

Jackson thought the theory was implausible. Khalilzad was "the only person in the room that believes those two postulates." Jackson thought that "no one ... believes that they're going to break up with al-Qaida," and "nobody believes that they're capable of dealing with ISIS-K on their own." Jackson thought the whole negotiating approach was flawed. "We're going to deal away the most important equity we have in an irreversible way by offering to give up all US and foreign troops and contractors and everybody, in return for a rhetorical, reversible commitment to not have bad things come out of Afghanistan." Others in the Defense Department had similar concerns. According to Esper, Rood, the undersecretary of defense for policy, felt "the agreement was heavy on commitment by the United States to withdraw its forces down to zero, but light on how the Taliban would

---

[34] Bolton, *The Room Where It Happened*, 216. McKinley, interview by author.
[35] Jackson, interview by author.

deliver on their obligations." Jackson drew the obvious conclusion. "This was a terrible, terrible negotiating strategy."[36]

Ultimately, the Doha agreement did not have a provision for a stay-behind US counterterrorism force. I asked Khalilzad about its omission.

> There was no agreement on a [stay-behind military] presence ... the Taliban were not willing to agree to that in any way to be mentioned in the text, because they believe any agreement on a presence would negate the legitimacy of their struggle and the cost that they had paid. Because if they agreed to a presence then why were they fighting all these years? The reason they were fighting was that they saw the presence as an occupation, so they didn't want to have any part of it. The only thing they were willing to say orally is that if there was a political settlement – and that was oral – then a new government that consists of all sides that was the result of the negotiations, then future security cooperation would be the decision of that government. But as Talibs negotiating with us, they would never, could never agree to an explicit understanding on a presence because they could never sell that. And that would undermine their legitimacy of the struggle and the sacrifices that they had made.[37]

Steve Coll also reported on the oral agreements, commitments the Taliban supposedly made in person but would not put on paper. US officials wrote them down in memoranda for the record without Taliban signatures. "The Taliban representatives said that they 'welcome continued US operations' against the Islamic State and al-Qaida," Coll reported. "If the US bombed the Islamic State, 'we will hang flowers around your neck,' they said; as for al-Qaida, they told the Americans, 'Kill as many as you want.'" Other Trump officials told me something similar, that the Taliban gave verbal assurances that they wanted to be America's counterterrorism partner and suggested that they would be cheaper partners than the Kabul government. Of course, in saying that they would allow US airstrikes, the Taliban were agreeing to something they could not prevent anyway, knowing they had no means to stop the US Air Force or its drones.[38]

As for the Taliban's supposed agreement to US operations against al-Qaida, the evidence suggests the Taliban was simply telling their American interlocutors what they wanted to hear. They were comfortable making such assurances because they had already assured al-Qaida the agreement was

---

[36] Jackson, interview by author. Esper, *A Sacred Oath*, 216.

[37] Khalilzad, interview by author.

[38] Steve Coll, "The Secret History of the US's Diplomatic Failure," *The New Yorker*, December 20, 2021.

meaningless. The two groups remained tightly knit. During a round of talks in February 2019, the Taliban "insisted that al-Qaʻeda was not behind the September 11 attacks and refused to condemn the group publicly," according to Malkasian. "They never really fully broke ties with al-Qaida," Robert O'Brien, Bolton's successor as national security advisor, told me. The Trump administration publicly admitted as much: "The Taliban have never repudiated their relationship with al-Qaida," Alice Wells, the assistant secretary of state for South and Central Asian Affairs, told the House Foreign Relations Committee in September 2019.[39]

Even worse: "The Taliban showed the deal before it was signed to al-Qaida, to Zawahiri" – al-Qaida's leader after bin Laden's death – "and got his approval and said, 'Don't worry about it. We'll remain allies,'" said Lisa Curtis. "The Taliban figured they were getting a good deal." So, apparently, did al-Qaida. That the Taliban consulted with al-Qaida and got their approval before signing the Doha agreement is so damning that it may sound implausible – it sounds like either a Hollywood script dramatizing the Taliban's villainy or an American warmongers' conspiracy theory to justify staying in the war – but Curtis was not revealing anything new, shocking, or classified: she was summarizing what the United Nations published in an open, unclassified report in May 2020. Khalilzad's lack of leverage affected all aspects of the agreement, including even the Taliban's promise to sever ties with al-Qaida – the United States' most important aim and the reason for the war in the first place. It is the single most damning fact of the twenty-year war: the Trump administration essentially negotiated with al-Qaida through its Taliban proxy and conceded their principal demand, a stunning low point for American diplomacy.[40]

Days before the Doha agreement was signed, Siraj Haqqani, the deputy leader of the Taliban and future interior minister in the new Taliban government, published an op-ed in the *New York Times*. If the Taliban wanted to denounce al-Qaida or ingratiate themselves with an American audience, here was an ideal opportunity. This would have been, presumably, the occasion for a public disavowal of terrorism and al-Qaida. Haqqani did nothing of the kind. Instead, Haqqani blamed the United States for the war. He deflected questions about the Taliban's record in power and its intent toward the Afghan government. He did not denounce al-Qaida or

[39] Khalilzad, O'Brien, and Curtis, interviews by author. Malkasian, *The American War in Afghanistan*, 435–436. House Foreign Relations Committee, "The Trump Administration's Afghanistan Policy," September 19, 2019, 32.

[40] United Nations, S/2020/415, May 27, 2020. Curtis, interview by author.

even mention the group by name. The key passage was weak, noncommittal, and toothless.

> We are also aware of concerns about the potential of Afghanistan being used by disruptive groups to threaten regional and world security. But these concerns are inflated: Reports about foreign groups in Afghanistan are politically motivated exaggerations by the warmongering players on all sides of the war. It is not in the interest of any Afghan to allow such groups to hijack our country and turn it into a battleground.[41]

Haqqani dismissed American concerns about terrorism – the Taliban never acknowledged al-Qaida's responsibility for the terrorist attacks of 2001 – but instead used the op-ed to defend the Taliban's supposed commitment to peace and to lecture his American audience about the importance of abiding by their end of the deal. It was a clear indication of who had won the war.

ABANDONING THE AFGHAN GOVERNMENT

The final element to the Doha agreement was intra-Afghan talks. Prior to 2019, the United States insisted that any talks with the Taliban must include and be led by the Afghan government. The Afghan government had the most skin in the game and would be most vulnerable after the withdrawal of US military forces. Negotiating separately would allow the Taliban to exploit division and play the Americans off their Afghan allies. But this would be another long-standing strategy that Trump threw out in his eagerness to get out of Afghanistan. "We weren't really empowered to incur friction in that relationship" between the US and the Afghan government, "until Khalilzad, when he was empowered to incur a lot of friction," Laurel Miller said. Khalilzad negotiated directly with the Taliban without an Afghan government representative with the aim of getting the Taliban to agree to a general ceasefire first, and to negotiate with the Afghan government at a later point.[42]

At the January 2019 round of negotiations, the two sides quickly agreed to a troop withdrawal in exchange for assurances on terrorism but stalled on the question of a ceasefire and intra-Afghan talks. In the months that followed, the Taliban stubbornly refused to accept a ceasefire with the

[41] Haqqani, "What We, the Taliban, Want," *New York Times*, February 20, 2020.
[42] Miller, interview by author.

Afghan government. They agreed to stop attacking the United States once the withdrawal was announced but pledged to continue fighting Kabul, regardless of whatever agreement they signed with America. The most Khalilzad could get was a promise that the Taliban would open talks with the Afghan government after the US–Taliban agreement had been concluded – which meant the Afghan government would be negotiating under the shadow of America's looming departure and the Taliban's continued violence. Some US military advisors to the negotiations wanted to walk out and end talks altogether when they realized the Taliban would not agree to a ceasefire with Kabul – it amounted to an admission of defeat – but Trump and Pompeo wanted an agreement, any agreement. "It was not clear if we had any true red lines," one officer reportedly said. Khalilzad had played his one chip and gotten a single (mostly symbolic) concession. He had nothing else.[43]

The Taliban's refusal to countenance a ceasefire with Kabul was coupled with a demand that the United States curtail its military support to the Afghan army. The Afghan military relied heavily on American air support. The Taliban demanded that stop. Khalilzad reportedly agreed to some form of limitation on US forces, putting the provisions in one of two classified annexes to the deal, though he insisted to me that "the US and coalition had the right to come to the defense of the Afghan forces if they were attacked by the Taliban." The restrictions and exceptions were vague and poorly understood by both sides, leading to uncertainty among the US and Afghan militaries about what the United States was allowed to do, under what conditions, for the remainder of the war. McKenzie felt the restrictions on "our ability to prosecute targets, our ability to support our Afghan partners on the ground" were the most objectionable aspects of the agreement.[44]

Intra-Afghan talks were probably the part of the agreement Trump cared about the least but Khalilzad the most. Trump had insisted repeatedly that he wasn't interested in nation building and considered the Afghan government almost on par with the Taliban as an obstacle to American interests. Khalilzad, by contrast, cared deeply about the fate of his birthplace. "I think that Khalilzad deserves some credit in trying to ensure that there would be two stages to negotiations to include the Afghan government," said McKinley. "But by 2018 the focus was very much on withdrawal, and the Taliban saw that and obviously tailored their approach to

---

[43] Coll, "The Secret History."

[44] Coll, "The Secret History." McKenzie, interview by author. Khalilzad, email to author, July 12, 2023.

negotiations to see what they could gain from the American focus on withdrawal." Khalilzad was dissatisfied with the ultimate shape of this part of the deal. "I would've liked to have a stronger linkage between withdrawal ... and the political agreement," he told me. "It wasn't explicit that we wouldn't withdraw" if the Afghans did not reach a political agreement, though Khalilzad strove to craft it in such a way that "it allowed us to interpret it [that way] if we wanted to." As subsequent events showed, neither Trump nor Biden wanted to.[45]

Khalilzad and others involved did their best to compensate for the president's disinterest. "Khalilzad, [Laurel] Miller, everybody else involved in those talks, [tried] to get an Afghan delegation together, which in effect represented the government as well as civil society and included women," McKinley recalled. "A tremendous amount of work went into that." It went nowhere. Khalilzad wasn't the only one who saw the problem. "I think the way it was written, unfortunately, did not connect the intra-Afghan talks and the comprehensive ceasefire," Lisa Curtis said. "It was like a lopsided negotiation, and there was really nobody fighting for the Afghan government's positions in the room." Why did the administration proceed anyway? Curtis felt "there was some wishful thinking about the Taliban" and their willingness to talk to the Afghan government. It was a classic case of trying to wish something into reality. "It seemed clear to me that they weren't interested in doing that, but I guess if you held out hope that they were, then you could say, let the agreement be signed." McKenzie, similarly, faulted Khalilzad for trusting the Taliban too much. "He would accept Taliban promises of future performance as holy writ, rather than something that ought to be tested every day."[46]

Bolton was alarmed but, again, did little to stop it. "There came a point where it was obvious that Zal was engaged in a full-blown negotiation for an agreement with the Taliban, where it was clear that the government of Afghanistan was being excluded," he said. "Now, there was no secret about this anymore. Everybody in Kabul knew what was going on. And I, and people in the Defense Department, made an effort to say, you know, this is not exactly the right way to do it. But those concerns were brushed aside entirely." It was the wrong way to do it because "if you're Taliban and you've already accomplished ... all of your major objectives, which is mainly getting the US and NATO out of Afghanistan, what possible reason

---

[45] Khalilzad and McKinley, interviews by author.
[46] Curtis, McKenzie, and McKinley, interviews by author.

do you have to negotiate with [Afghan president] Ashraf Ghani? I just think it's kind of self-evident."[47]

Bolton had little concern for the Afghan government on its own merits. "This wasn't a war about making Afghanistan, Iraq, Syria, or any other country, nicer, safer places to live. I am not a nation builder," he wrote, agreeing with Trump on this, if on little else. But Bolton understood that it wasn't in America's interest for the Taliban to renege on its promise, continue the war against Kabul, and take power. Bolton and the military likely had in mind the negotiations between the United States and North Vietnam, in which the United States negotiated directly with its enemy without including its ally. The resulting peace agreement allowed the United States to withdraw, but at the price of leaving the South Vietnamese out to dry. "It was inconceivable to me that you'd make a deal with your adversary and then give it to your ally and say, take it or leave it," Bolton told me. "And yet that's essentially what happened. I just, I didn't see that coming. I didn't think it was possible." Bolton's inability to conceive of what Trump was willing to do showed another layer of wishful thinking at work. Elsewhere, he commented that Pompeo's deal was "touchingly naive" about the Taliban, but Bolton showed a naivete about his own boss. "I assumed the gravity of his responsibilities would discipline even him," he wrote years later. "I was wrong. His erratic approach to governance and his dangerous ideas gravely threaten American security." That much had been clear to some observers long before.[48]

The administration's debate about the deal came to a head in August 2019 at Bedminster, when the deal was nearly ready for signature. Pompeo briefed the contents of the emerging agreement. "The Secretary of State was realistic about the proposal and presented a sober assessment of its prospects, adding that it was 'not a perfect deal' and he 'did not trust the Taliban,'" according to Esper. "When the conversation turned to me, I told the president that the DoD supported the plan, contingent on a conditions-based approach." It was an odd caveat: the agreement was not meaningfully conditions-based. Esper, like Bolton, seems not to have been able to admit what the Doha agreement really was. Bolton insisted to himself that the agreement was unrealistic and had no chance of being signed, and therefore could be ignored; Esper insisted that the agreement was conditions-based, and therefore could be endorsed, when political reality said otherwise.[49]

---

[47] Bolton, interview by author.

[48] Bolton, *The Room Where It Happened*, 213, 423, 426. Bolton, interview by author. Bolton, "Trump Is a Danger to US Security," *The Wall Street Journal*, January 31, 2024.

[49] Esper, *A Sacred Oath*, 220.

Bolton saw the problem with Esper's position. "I explained why a 'conditions-based' withdrawal, linked to US forces' going to zero, was inherently unlikely to see the conditions actually met," he said. "We could repeat the phrase 'conditions based' all we wanted, but in reality, this agreement would be regarded as pulling up stakes and getting out." That is why Bolton "had no doubt the Taliban were increasingly happy about the terms of the emerging deal, most of which I believed they had little intention of following." The administration couldn't agree if the agreement was meaningfully conditions-based or not. "We're both seeing the same words, but we're reading different documents," General McKenzie recalled. Those who favored the agreement claimed it was conditions-based, while those who opposed argued (rightly) that the language on conditionality was too weak. Bolton and Esper found common ground in their belief that "we couldn't trust the Taliban" and shared "concerns about the lack of an enforcement mechanism."[50]

It was a substantive and meaningful discussion that got close to the heart of the matter. But then Trump interjected. "In the middle of the discussion, the president proposed that we bring Taliban representatives to Washington for talks, even suggesting that the meeting could take place at Camp David," Pence wrote, "and asked for my opinion." For some reason, Trump thought it would be a good idea to have a signing ceremony on September 11, the 18th anniversary of the terrorist attacks, an extraordinarily tone-deaf suggestion. "We all sat there stunned for a moment, carefully looking around at one another, and then at him to see if the president was serious," Esper recalled. Pence threaded the needle. "I thought it was a bad idea but weighed my words carefully. 'Mr. President,' I said, 'we should reflect on who they are and what they've done and if they have truly changed. These people are animals,'" which was strong language from the even-keeled-to-a-fault Vice President. Pence, a congressman in 2001, was in the US Capitol on 9/11 and recounts in his memoir how the passengers of Flight 93 likely saved his life by bringing down the plane before it arrived in DC, which accounts for his visceral reaction to Trump's idea. "The Taliban had no place in the US capital, let alone the historic grounds of Camp David," Pence thought. The rest of the Principals unanimously backed Pence up.[51]

Trump endorsed the Doha agreement and emphasized his desire, like Obama's, to bring the troops home before the coming US presidential

---

[50] Bolton, *The Room Where It Happened*, 436, 431. Esper, *A Sacred Oath*, 224–25.

[51] Pence, *So Help Me God*, 355. Esper, *A Sacred Oath*, 225.

election. "Near the end of our meeting, Trump said he wanted any public statement we might release about the peace deal to say that the US would be at 'zero [troops] in October' 2020, just before the election," Esper wrote. "November 3, 2020, was the lens through which he viewed the agreement. It was an important takeaway for me." Esper records the observation as if it were a novel insight for him, which illustrates the yawning gap between some foreign policy professionals, like Esper, and the politicians who appoint them to high office. Trump suggested, "let's make a big deal about it, like it's a wonderful deal. If they do anything bad, we're going to blow their fucking country into a million pieces." Bolton drily commented in an aside, "I did not take this to be a well-thought-out military strategy, but simply typical Trump analysis.[52]

As word of the impending deal circulated, former US officials again became concerned that whatever progress the US and Afghanistan had made in the previous eighteen years would be quickly undone. Cunningham, who had led the Atlantic Council report calling on Obama not to withdraw in 2015, organized another effort at the Council. Signed by almost every former US ambassador to Afghanistan, the ensuing report warned that "it is not clear whether peace is possible." It counseled against trusting the Taliban's good faith, warned of the possibility of renewed civil war, insisted on keeping the Afghan government involved in the negotiations (that ship had long since sailed), and argued that "a major withdrawal of US forces should follow, not come in advance of [a] real peace agreement." If the United States withdrew any troops up front, it "should not go so far or so fast that the Taliban believe that they can achieve military victory. In that case, they will not make compromises for peace with other Afghan political forces." At stake was American security, but also American honor. "We must not betray all those who have believed our promises or stepped forward with our encouragement to promote democracy and human rights." The letter fell on deaf ears.[53]

The road to Doha suffered a speed bump when the Taliban escalated violence immediately before the agreement was to be finalized, including a car bomb in Kabul that killed one American soldier. Trump was outraged and, in lieu of blowing Afghanistan into a million pieces, canceled peace talks and tweeted that he had rescinded his invitation to Camp David, which was how most of the world found out about the invitation in the first place. The public blowback confirmed his advisors' fears about the inadvisability of

---

[52] Esper, *A Sacred Oath*, 223. Bolton, *The Room Where It Happened*, 434.
[53] Atlantic Council, "US–Taliban Negotiations," September 3, 2019.

the meeting, but the cabinet was simply relieved to have an excuse to kill the meeting for good. Bolton and others hoped and believed it had killed the peace process altogether. It did not; the process was back on track within a few months, with the Taliban now agreeing to a seven-day ceasefire with US forces to demonstrate their good faith. In Trump's earlier tweet, he asked: "What kind of people would kill so many in order to seemingly strengthen their bargaining position?" It was an odd question for someone who built his reputation as a cutthroat real-estate tycoon and bragged about his tough-minded deal-making prowess. What kind of people use force as leverage in wartime negotiations? The kind who win.[54]

THE DOHA AGREEMENT

Mike Pompeo and Abdul Ghani Baradar met in Doha and signed the "Agreement for Bringing Peace to Afghanistan" on February 29, 2020. The agreement is four pages long and envisions four parts to a comprehensive peace deal: the US military withdrawal; the Taliban's guarantee against terrorist safe haven; intra-Afghan talks; and a permanent ceasefire. The agreement insists that the parts are "interrelated," and specifically that the first two are "interconnected," which is the closest Khalilzad could get to making the withdrawal conditional on the Taliban's compliance. The deal obligated the United States to withdraw "all military forces" within fourteen months. The United States also promised to release 5,000 Taliban prisoners, which it had no power to do because prisoners were under Afghan, not American, jurisdiction. They, not having been a partner to the talks, had not agreed to anything. By making specific, measurable, and public commitments, the United States invited accountability from the international press and the UN, whose monitoring would be the *de facto* enforcement of the United States' end of the deal.[55]

The Taliban committed, on paper, that it "will not allow any of its members, other individuals or groups, including al-Qaida, to use the soil of Afghanistan to threaten the security of the United States and its allies." It promised to "prevent them from recruiting, training, and fundraising" and said it "will not provide visas, passports, travel permits, or other legal

---

[54] https://x.com/realDonaldTrump/status/1170469619154530305, September 7, 2019.

[55] State Department, "Agreement for Bringing Peace to Afghanistan," February 29, 2020. www.state.gov/wp-content/uploads/2020/02/Agreement-For-Bringing-Peace-to-Afgha nistan-02.29.20.pdf.

documents" to them. The mention of al-Qaida by name was a win for the Trump administration. "It took a long time to get to an agreement because the Talibs did not want to mention al-Qaida specifically," Khalilzad told me. That and the ceasefire against American forces seem to be the only concessions Pompeo's and Miller's supposedly tightly coordinated military-diplomatic campaign forced out of them – but the Taliban's commitments were otherwise weak, overbroad, and unenforceable. A tougher agreement, for example, might have delivered to the Taliban a list of specific individuals and groups by name and obligated the Taliban to establish a sanctions enforcement arm before the American military withdrawal. It might have obligated the Taliban to accept a UN monitoring team, or even an American intelligence presence, to ensure compliance. The Taliban would never have agreed to such provisions so long as they felt confident on the battlefield and assured of a unilateral US withdrawal, which is a good argument for why any deal under those circumstances was not in America's interest.

The press reported that the deal came with "secret annexes." I asked Khalilzad to clarify. "There were two implementing documents" that were classified, he said. The first "was on terrorism cooperation, what they would do, what they wouldn't do, details of how we would measure their compliance with their commitments." The Taliban didn't want it made public. The second contained details about the American military withdrawal (apparently including some restrictions on US support to the Afghan army), which was classified because the United States always classifies details about troop movements and operational plans. Khalilzad specifically denied that the annexes contained any provision allowing for a small, covert US counter-terrorism presence in Afghanistan, as some rumors suggested. The Trump administration can point to the first annex to claim that Doha did contain meaningful Taliban commitments that were specific and enforceable. If so, the document should be declassified (not even the special inspector general was able to get a copy). In the wake of the Taliban's victory, the entire Doha agreement became moot. Publicizing whatever details are contained in the annexes would not threaten any American interests any more than a triumphant Taliban in power in Kabul already does.[56]

"I supported signing it and still think it was the right path forward," Pompeo wrote in his memoir. He had no other option; he could not run from the agreement he had championed from start to finish. It is his albatross. Pompeo used his memoir to craft a defense strikingly similar to what Joe Biden would claim the following year. "By January 2017, the model

[56] Khalilzad, interview by author.

of American military engagement in Afghanistan that had been in place since 9/11 was no longer serving American interests well," he wrote, as if there had been a single model of American intervention since 2001. "President Trump wasn't confronting a tactical or operational failure, but a strategic one. For sixteen years, we had not adapted our strategy," he claimed. In fact, Bush and Obama regularly tried to adapt, usually too little and too late – but also, if anything, too often. It is striking how frequently policymakers in DC believed they needed to rethink everything and come up with a new strategy in Afghanistan – how quickly Obama decided the surge was not working, for example, and how quickly Trump believed the same about his 2017 strategy. Regardless, "in hindsight, it was unrealistic to expect that the United States could transform what is essentially still a premodern, tribal society into a pluralistic, rights-respecting, Western democracy," Pompeo wrote. "The president rightfully complained that our troops in those places were too often acting like policemen and social workers, not warfighters." For Pompeo, the Doha agreement was at least a genuine attempt at a new strategic approach not beholden to the same old conventional thinking that, he felt, had failed for nearly twenty years.[57]

Robert O'Brien, who succeeded Bolton as national security advisor, agreed with Pompeo. "I believe at the end of the day, we ended up with a pretty good deal," he said. He had not been part of the debates about the shape of the deal but felt "we had conditions that were explicit in the deal," and "the enforcement mechanism would be US power." The Trump administration believed the Taliban would ask for American help to combat ISIS-K. To O'Brien, that meant "we knew we'd have US troops in country for a long period of time, at a minimum, to secure our embassy and our counter-terrorism operations ... Moreover, we never planned on giving up Bagram air base." He expected Trump to argue that he had fulfilled his promise by withdrawing all but 2,500 troops, who would stay to guard the embassy and enable counterterrorism missions. O'Brien may have been unaware of the fierce debates on a stay-behind force the year before, but it is still odd that he would believe Doha allowed for a stay-behind force when even Khalilzad clearly understood it did not.[58]

Khalilzad is a bit more circumspect but still supports the deal. "I think it was good in the sense that, to me good means it was realistic," he told me. "And given that the president wanted to get out, his objective that the withdrawal will be safely done, what was delivered, there was a good agreement in that they won't attack us." For Khalilzad, the Taliban's promises

---

[57] Pompeo, *Never Give an Inch*, 377, 223, 346, 361, 366. [58] O'Brien, interview by author.

against al-Qaida made the deal worthwhile – and he would be right, if the Taliban's promises were worth the paper they were printed on. Khalilzad fell prey to wishful thinking because he badly wanted to see the end of the war. "My sense from my business in Afghanistan was that people were yearning for an end to the war," he said, "And our standing was not as good as it once was when I was ambassador over there. People had lost a great deal of confidence and they were less supportive of what we were doing." Time had run out for the Americans in Afghanistan. And though he wished Doha could have been tougher with more specific enforcement mechanisms, he believed it was worthwhile. "I do not believe that the Government is going to collapse, that the Taliban is going to take over," he assured Congress in the spring of 2021.[59]

Mark Esper tried to have it both ways. He was not "optimistic about its prospects," but "at least it started us down a different path than we had been on the past nineteen years," again, as if American strategy had followed a single path. "It was worth a try after nearly two decades of fighting" because "the only way the conflict in Afghanistan would ever end acceptably was going to be through a political agreement," which was true enough but not an excuse for this particular agreement. "This wasn't a great deal; it wasn't even a good deal. For me, though, it was a 'good enough' deal." Esper could only come to that conclusion because he continued to insist the deal was conditions-based. At a press conference after the signing, Esper said that "'this will be a conditions-based process' and that the standard for me was that 'Afghanistan again never becomes … a safe haven for terrorists to threaten America.'"

But the conditionality in the agreement – already weak – would only be meaningful if Trump was willing to enforce it. Not even Esper believed he was. "I never believed President Trump bought into the peace plan. He just wanted out of Afghanistan, saying so in nearly every meeting I attended with him on this topic," Esper claimed. "It was a main reason I would say publicly and repeatedly, as I did not long after the deal was signed, that not only was the deal a 'conditions-based agreement,' but if we assessed that the Taliban was not honoring it and 'if progress stalls, then our drawdown likely will be suspended, as well.'" But if Esper had no faith in Trump's intent to enforce the deal, on what basis could Esper make those guarantees and those threats? Esper could not enforce conditions without Trump's approval, and without Trump's approval nothing that Esper said about the deal

---

[59] Khalilzad, interview by author. Senate Foreign Relations Committee, "US Policy in Afghanistan," April 27, 2021, 18.

being "conditions-based" meant anything – and Esper knew it. Esper was freelancing his own foreign policy, trying to make Doha something it was not because he was pretending Trump was someone he was not. If Esper believed Trump had no intent to enforce the already-weak conditions in the deal, he had no business pretending it was conditions-based or endorsing it in the first place.[60]

Bolton opposed the deal from the beginning and repeatedly advised Trump against signing it, the only member of Trump's team to do so. He was adamant that the United States needed an enduring counterterrorism presence in Afghanistan, no matter what the state of diplomacy, and wanted a presence in the region as insurance against instability in Pakistan. But Bolton did not make opposition to the deal a high priority. He seems most interested in ensuring that Pompeo gets the bulk of the blame. "Pompeo tried to keep the whole thing between himself, Khalilzad, and Trump ... By keeping it so tight, Pompeo guaranteed he owned it entirely. That was fine with me. If that's what he and Trump wanted, they could have the political blowback to themselves," Bolton wrote. "There would be precious little 'credit' when the agreement collapsed, which even Pompeo told me he thought was inevitable." Bolton has convincingly won the argument: history will record that Pompeo championed the deal, Bolton did not, and Pompeo rightly gets the blame. That petty victory pales in comparison with the much greater defeat the United States suffered, which Bolton did not do all in his power to prevent.[61]

2020: IMPLEMENTING DOHA

After the deal was signed, "it was up to the United States side as the agreement went into implementation whether to enforce these condition-alities," which was difficult because the deal "didn't have enforcement mechanisms," McKinley said. Technicalities aside, three factors interfered with enforcement. First, the COVID-19 pandemic emerged and swept the globe weeks after Doha was signed. Just as the Iraq war took up the lion's share of the Bush administration's bandwidth and attention, COVID became all-consuming. "It affected everything," O'Brien recalled. "It became the driving force in the White House." As the Trump administration, already in campaign mode for the 2020 election, scrambled to respond

---

[60] Esper, *A Sacred Oath*, 218, 230–233.
[61] Bolton, *The Room Where It Happened*, 216, 437, 435, 436.

to the once-a-century pandemic, Afghanistan faded from attention. Second, the administration was already in transition. Bolton quit before Doha was signed and the interagency process ground to a halt. "After Ambassador Bolton left, there was never another deputies level meeting on Afghanistan," recalled Lisa Curtis.[62]

But third, despite what he said, Trump was not inclined to enforce the agreement anyway. He claimed otherwise, of course. White House Chief of Staff Mark Meadows recounted a phone call Trump held with Baradar in March, shortly after Doha was signed. "President Trump spoke with a calm authority that carried just a hint of menace, not unlike General George Patton during his famous speeches. He clearly stated the conditions that would need to be met before a single American soldier came home." Trump threatened escalation if "anything bad happens to America" and personally threatened Baradar's home village. O'Brien, who was on the call, felt that "Baradar was somewhat taken aback at how serious the president was explaining to him the consequences of what would happen if the Taliban breached the agreement."[63]

It was all bark and no bite. The UN report about the Taliban's continuing entanglement with al-Qaida was made public in May; Trump did nothing to slow or halt the withdrawal of US troops. The Taliban had promised to begin negotiations with the Afghan government in March; they did not actually begin until September and quickly went nowhere, which also did not lead Trump to reevaluate the deal. Trump completed the first phase of withdrawal, drawing down to 8,600 troops, by mid June, ahead of schedule, and down to 2,500 by the end of his term, well below the threshold to keep the Jenga tower standing, in full knowledge that the Taliban were not in compliance with their commitments. The only aspect of the agreement that the Taliban honored was to refrain from attacking US forces, which is what Trump cared about. "Our number one metric," for assessing the Taliban's compliance, "was: are Americans being killed," O'Brien said. Trump knows how to sound tough, but only selectively backs it up with action. He ordered the killing of Iranian General Qasem Soleimani, the head of the Qods Force of the Islamic Revolutionary Guard Corps, in January 2020 – far riskier than any strike against Baradar or the Taliban – which suggests his failure to make good on his threat to Baradar was a deliberate choice.

---

[62] McKinley, Curtis, O'Brien, interviews by author.

[63] Meadows, *The Chief's Chief*, 271. Pompeo, *Never Give an Inch*, 379, 382. O'Brien, interview by author.

"Khalilzad was disappointed: he had expected the Trump Administration to conduct a formal review of the Taliban's compliance with the Doha deal before withdrawing more troops, but it hadn't," Coll reported. Instead, Trump pushed for a full withdrawal. Esper objected and in November, just before the presidential election, wrote Trump "a classified letter opposing the withdrawal of US troops from Afghanistan." Trump abruptly fired him. In December, after the election, Trump signed a memo ordering the immediate and complete withdrawal of all troops from Afghanistan with no stay-behind force. It was rescinded, because it had not been vetted through the normal process and not even O'Brien knew about it, but again demonstrates Trump's comfort with full unilateral withdrawal regardless of conditions on the ground or the Taliban's compliance with the deal.[64]

Far from his promise that "not a single American soldier" would come home before the Taliban showed compliance, Trump withdrew some 12,000 American soldiers over the course of 2020 in full knowledge that the Taliban remained tied to al-Qaida and were not negotiating with Kabul in good faith. The Taliban did not uphold their end of the deal – and Trump and Pompeo knew it – but Trump withdrew almost all the remaining US troops anyway. Trump's withdrawals "did a tremendous amount of damage because that really emboldened the Taliban," thought Llorens. "In the second half of 2020 is when the Taliban already begins to engage and ramp up their offensive operations," when they saw Trump was going to withdraw without enforcing the deal.[65]

After the fall of Kabul the next year, Pompeo claimed that the administration was tough on the Taliban. "We never trusted the Taliban ... We made abundantly clear if they did not live up to that piece of paper, to the words they had put on the ground, we weren't going to allow them to just walk away from any deal they'd struck. We were going to go crush them," he told Fox News. "We didn't take the word of the Taliban. We watched their actions on the ground." In his memoir, Pompeo claimed they had "demonstrated an ability to draw down our forces in a conditions-based manner." There is no evidence for Pompeo's claims. In fact, sorties and airstrikes declined precipitously in 2020, halting almost entirely by May. They ticked up slightly in the second half of the year but still averaged a fraction of the number of strikes in 2018 and 2019. "After the signing of the US–Taliban agreement, US support for conducting airstrikes on the Taliban

---

[64] Coll, "Secret History." Woodward, *Peril*, 148. Llorens, McKenzie, and Lujan, interviews by author.

[65] Llorens, interview by author.

dramatically decreased, reducing the ANSF's ability to conduct offensive operations to combat Taliban threats," according to the special inspector general.[66]

Pompeo himself admits "the agreement we signed laid down set conditions for our departure. They were never met." How then can Pompeo claim that Trump conducted a conditions-based withdrawal? "Our national security team never recommended to President Trump that we pull out entirely." He (and O'Brien) makes much of the fact that Trump left office with 2,500 US troops still in Afghanistan. Pompeo is transparently shifting the goalposts. Trump had claimed the Taliban's compliance had to precede *any* American withdrawal. A meaningfully conditions-based withdrawal applies to the entire force, not just the last planeload. Pointing to the 2,500 remaining ignores the 12,000 Trump withdrew, emphasizing a technicality while overlooking the broader strategic reality. Trump empowered the Taliban by withdrawing over 80 percent of US troops while the Taliban were noncompliant with Doha: that, not the 2,500 remaining troops, is the main reality of Trump's Afghanistan strategy. Pompeo, Khalilzad, and others blame the Biden administration for poor implementation of Doha, but Bolton rightly thinks that is laughable. "That's just not true," he said, "it was perfectly foreseeable how it was going to play out." The Trump administration took no meaningful action to hold the Taliban accountable to its promises.[67]

Lujan, who worked on the agreement and believed in its conditionality, was heartbroken. "The theory was that we would have this four-month period," after the signing and before any serious withdrawals, "we could be evaluating the intel and watching what they were doing on CT," to monitor the Taliban's compliance, said Lujan, but, in retrospect, "I think we were starry eyed and naive thinking that the political leadership would look at that and make an informed assessment." Lujan had envisioned a long process of monitoring, pausing withdrawals, and continuing strikes on the Taliban when they violated the agreement, probably what Khalilzad had envisioned as well. Instead, "I think at the end of the day, both administrations wanted out, and the hardest thing to accept is that it feels like we ended up negotiating a surrender," not by intent, but because neither Trump nor Biden would enforce the conditions that Khalilzad and his team wanted to believe were there. Lujan felt used.[68]

---

[66] "Chris Wallas Nails Mike Pompeo over Trump's Complicity in Afghanistan," August 17, 2021. www.youtube.com/watch?v=L6e7K3B6FTM. Bolton, interview by author. SIGAR, "Why the Afghan Security Forces Collapsed," 12.

[67] Pompeo, *Never Give an Inch*, 383.   [68] Lujan, interview by author.

The worst part is that Doha was unnecessary. The "forever war" was affordable, sustainable, and successful at the bare minimum goal of keeping the lid on Afghanistan and preventing another 9/11. Trump officials make much of the fact that the Taliban stopped attacking American forces after Doha was signed; just six US servicemen were killed in action in 2020. But that was not a meaningful change from the previous seven years. Ever since the 2014 transition, most American forces had been off the front lines and, even with the heightened tempo of Special Forces' operations, averaged fewer than one killed in action per month for over 100 months. I did not like the "forever war" strategy, and I agree with McMaster's judgment that it was essentially unjust because it had abandoned Afghanistan to never-ending conflict with no thought to investing in lasting peace or justice there – but it was still more defensible, strategically and morally, than handing Afghanistan over to the Taliban.

In 2017, the military "could have preserved the impasse," Colin Jackson believed. It was a stalemate, but the United States had the better part of the stalemate. "Which side of the stalemate would you rather have? Would you rather control the vast majority of the population of Afghanistan and the growing part of Afghanistan – all five of the major cities, the provincial capitals? Or, would you rather own a bunch of mud huts in eastern and southern Afghanistan?" Compared to that, Doha was a "terrible deal from the outset . . . It didn't look after US equities on counterterrorism. It did not deliver a ceasefire and it did not deliver a political settlement." If the stalemate was eroding, as some observers thought, that was a solvable problem so long as the United States stayed.[69]

The US would not stay because Trump did not want to, regardless of what the Taliban did and irrespective of their relationship to al-Qaida. Ultimately, Donald Trump bears principal responsibility for Doha, including the strategic context in which negotiations took place. Most US officials involved with the deal negotiated in good faith and sincerely hoped for its success, but Trump's transparent intent to leave guaranteed its failure. "Baradar and his colleagues told Khalilzad and other members of the US delegation that they had been listening to Trump's comments and believed the United States would be leaving no matter what and therefore they did not have to offer concessions," Malkasian reported. Trump campaigned on getting out of Afghanistan and repeatedly and publicly announced his intent to withdraw, which undermined negotiations just as much as Obama's timetable had done. As a result, "we didn't really get a denunciation of al-Qaida from the

[69] Jackson, interview by author.

Taliban," McKinley observed, "we didn't get a formal cutting of ties to the international jihadist movement." McMaster, now retired from government service and freed to speak his mind, called it a "surrender agreement," and Ambassador Llorens thought it was "the worst diplomatic agreement I've ever seen," in his forty-year career.

While some critics may accuse McMaster or Llorens of hyperbole, I suggest the opposite: they do not go far enough. Trump's singular goal was to leave Afghanistan, a goal he pursued in full knowledge that it would aid America's enemies. It cannot be emphasized strongly enough that Trump approved a diplomatic agreement that al-Qaida endorsed, materially aiding their campaign of terrorism. Trump's harshest critics (including me) sometimes accuse him of acting treasonously on January 6, 2021. But if there was an occasion on which Trump came even closer to giving "aid and comfort" to the enemies of the United States, it came the year before, at Doha.[70]

---

[70] Khalilzad, interview by author.

15

2021

Defeat

The Trump and Biden administrations have spent an enormous amount of energy blaming each other for the final collapse. Pompeo excoriated Biden in his memoir, fully blaming him and claiming the Doha agreement had nothing to do with Afghanistan's subsequent collapse. In turn, the Biden White House released a twelve-page document in April 2023 with their version of events, placing blame on the Trump administration. In their mutual finger-pointing, they are both right: Trump signed the deal, and Biden implemented it. The special inspector general for Afghanistan reconstruction concluded that "the February 2020 signing of the US–Taliban agreement and the April 2021 announcement of the continuation of the withdrawal of US military and contractor personnel degraded [the Afghan army's] morale," leading directly to its collapse. Afghan army officers told SIGAR that "the agreement's psychological impact was so great that the average Afghan soldier switched to 'survival mode'" because "Afghan soldiers knew they were not the winners."[1]

Trump was determined to withdraw from Afghanistan irrespective of what the Taliban said or did, weakening the United States' diplomatic and military position to the point of collapse. Biden, despite having campaigned on a promise to undo Trump's legacy, inexplicably followed Trump's example and implemented Trump's strategy. Thanks to Trump, Biden inherited an extremely difficult situation – one he managed to make even worse. He played a bad hand badly. And he did so, in large part, because when he looked at Afghanistan, he saw Vietnam.

JOE BIDEN AND THE VIETNAM WAR

In 1973, Senator Joe Biden called the Vietnam War a "quagmire" and an "American debacle," already well-worn clichés for the war's critics, in one of

---

[1] SIGAR, "Why the Afghan Security Forces Collapsed," 6.

his first speeches on the subject. Biden was thirty years old, six months into his first term as US senator from Delaware, the youngest and most junior member of the body. Biden played it safe by following the cues of his party elders for whom Vietnam had become a symbol of everything wrong with America's role in the world. He approvingly entered into the Congressional Record a speech by Senator Frank Church. "When, as in Indochina, an extravagant military venture is not only costly but irrelevant to our defense and divisive and disruptive at home, our security is diminished in all of its dimensions," Church said. Two years later, Biden argued on the floor of the Senate that "our policy in Southeast Asia was mistaken; this policy stubbornly persisted in long after it should have been discarded."[2]

In April 1975, two weeks before the fall of Saigon, President Gerald Ford met privately with members of the Senate Foreign Relations Committee, including Biden. Days earlier, he had delivered an address to a joint session of Congress asking for emergency military aid for South Vietnam and authorization to use force to evacuate Americans and South Vietnamese. The North Vietnamese were advancing rapidly, and the collapse of the South seemed imminent without American help. Ford lobbied the Senate committee to approve his request and help the South Vietnamese avoid the worst. Biden objected. "We should focus on getting [Americans] out. Getting the Vietnamese out and military aid for the [South Vietnamese] are totally different," he told Ford. He supported doing anything necessary to help evacuate American citizens, but not Vietnamese refugees. "I will vote for any amount for getting the Americans out. I don't want it mixed with getting the Vietnamese out."[3]

In the following weeks, Biden raised an alarm, not about the North's advance on the South, but about Ford's decision to mobilize the US military to prepare for an evacuation of Americans and South Vietnamese. As the North closed in, Biden worried the situation was ripe for "another Tonkin Gulf Resolution" and "another war in Southeast Asia," accusing the Ford administration of using the impending crisis as a pretext for restarting the war. He opposed the passage of a $100 million "evacuation contingency fund" for fear it could be used

---

[2] Congressional Record, June 8, 1973, 18826, 18829. Congressional Record, April 23, 1975, 11465.

[3] "Memorandum of Conversation," April 14, 1975, document #232 in Foreign Relations of the United States, 1969–1976, Volume X, Vietnam, January 1973–July 1975. https://hist ory.state.gov/historicaldocuments/frus1969-76v10/d232.

to fund military operations against the North. He expressed agreement with Senator Floyd Haskell of Colorado, who had moments earlier opposed giving Ford authority to use force to evacuate allied Vietnamese. "I would suggest that if we want to launch a bloodbath in South Vietnam, the best way to do so would be to send in United States troops to get out South Vietnamese nationals," Haskell argued. Biden went even further; his objection was not simply that evacuating South Vietnamese refugees was impractical, dangerous, or difficult. He thought it was irrelevant. "I do not believe the United States has an obligation, moral or otherwise, to evacuate foreign nationals," he said, "The United States has no obligation to evacuate 1, or 100,001, South Vietnamese."[4]

On May 1, two days after the fall of Saigon, Biden gave no speech but endorsed and entered into the Congressional Record a brief remark by Irving Shapiro, chief executive officer of the DuPont Company and a Delaware resident. It seems to capture Biden's verdict on the war. "Our involvement in Vietnam was a tragic mistake which exacted a terrible toll in human life and suffering and physical destruction," Shapiro said. He criticized the war for "diverting resources which could have been better used to help solve pressing economic and social problems." Shapiro called for nation building at home. "Our resources should now be focused on such concerns as combatting inflation, reducing the ranks of the unemployed, hammering out of a national energy policy and developing better health care."[5]

Biden, as most Americans of his generation, was decisively shaped by the war. To him, the war was a mistake, irrelevant to American security. It was futile and could not have been won. The US military leadership was untrustworthy and untruthful. More, Biden felt the danger of getting sucked back in was greater than the danger of staying out. "My apprehension is that this bill has a potential of beckoning us back into Vietnam," he said by way of explaining his objections to the evacuation contingency fund. The danger to the Vietnamese was incidental and unimportant, and Biden felt no particular obligation to them (though he later voted in favor of a resolution welcoming refugees to America). The most important thing for Biden was summoning the will to leave. "Today in the Senate we can simply say in respect to Indochina: 'Enough.'"[6]

---

[4] Congressional Record, April 23, 1975, 11441, 11448, 11465.
[5] Congressional Record, May 1, 1975, 12736.
[6] Congressional Record, June 8, 1973, 11465–11466.

JOE BIDEN AND AFGHANISTAN

Biden did not let Vietnam affect every foreign policy issue he confronted. He voted against the 1991 Iraq War but then criticized George H. W. Bush for leaving Saddam Hussein in power. He criticized Bill Clinton for his slowness in stopping ethnic cleansing in the Balkans in the 1990s, and he voted in favor of the 2003 Iraq War. He positioned himself as a centrist, hawkish Democrat comfortable with the use of American power, a successful electoral strategy that worked for a generation of Democrats eager to avoid being seen as soft on national security. That explains why Biden was an early, vocal, and consistent champion of American efforts in Afghanistan, including reconstruction and nation building.[7]

In fact, he was among the strongest advocates of nation building and the most vocal critics of the Bush administration's refusal to do more. "We must do all we can to lead the world to assist the Afghans in the task of rebuilding their country, their society, and their lives," Biden said in December 2001, "We have to help lay that foundation so the Afghan Government does not slide back into warlordism and anarchy." Biden had been in the Senate for nearly thirty years; he was now the ninth-most senior senator and chairman of the Foreign Relations Committee, and his voice carried weight. His vision of nation building in Afghanistan was extensive, including "education in the schools for girls and boys alike," and "digging wells and irrigation canals and paving roads, establishing medical clinics, and clearing up the most heavily land-mined country on earth." That required an international military presence to enforce the peace, "a robust, combat-ready force able and fully authorized to establish safety and stability in Afghanistan." It was a point Biden would hammer home repeatedly over the next several years. "There is little prospect of meeting the next stage of needs in Afghanistan without a security force on the ground," he said.[8]

Biden visited Afghanistan soon after his speech. In March 2002, he asked the Senate: "Would America stay the course? After all our successful military actions, after all our promises on reconstruction, after all our commitments to prevent Afghanistan from relapsing into chaos and warlordism, would we really have the stomach to get the job done?" Biden, with presidential aspirations ahead, answered for America: "We can, we must,

---

[7] Greg Jaffe, "The War in Afghanistan Shattered Joe Biden's Faith," *The Washington Post,* February 18, 2020.

[8] Senate Committee on Foreign Relations, "The Political Future of Afghanistan," December 6, 2001, 1–3. www.govinfo.gov/content/pkg/CHRG-107shrg77065/pdf/CHRG-107shrg77065.pdf.

and we will." Biden laid out the logic for an enduring US presence in Afghanistan. He warned that "if Afghanistan returns to a state of lawlessness and disorder," the Taliban would return to power and "provide safe haven to any terrorists, drug-traffickers and violent insurgents willing to pay their price." In turn, "these terrorists will once again use Afghanistan as a base to launch attacks on the United States." The conclusion was obvious: "If we don't do the job right, mark my words: US troops will be right back in Afghanistan a year or two down the line."[9]

Over the next several years, Biden returned to these themes again and again. In early 2002, he called for "economic reconstruction, building political institutions, clearing minefields, creating the educational, medical, and other infrastructure necessary for long-term self-sufficiency." He warned that "Afghanistan is not-so-slowly falling back into chaos" and repeated his call to expand the International Security Assistance Force (ISAF) throughout the country. In mid 2002, he had already raised the point so often he felt like a "broken record." He praised Bush's speech calling for a Marshall Plan for Afghanistan and used it to criticize Bush for his failure to "back up our words with deeds." Biden cosponsored the Afghanistan Freedom Support Act of 2002 authorizing billions more in aid dollars.[10]

In 2003, Biden took aim at Rumsfeld. "In some parts of this administration, 'nation-building' is a dirty phrase," he said. "But the alternative to nation-building is chaos – a chaos that churns out bloodthirsty warlords, drug-traffickers, and terrorists." Later that year, he sharpened his critique. "Because there has been this overwhelming reluctance on the part of some in the administration to get involved in genuine, quote, 'nation-building,' we essentially elected a mayor of Kabul and turned the rest over to the warlords, and we're paying a price for it now." Biden understood the connection between reconstruction and security. "If the administration isn't willing to make good on President Bush's promise of a Marshall Plan for Afghanistan, we run the grave risk of seeing all our hard-won military gains evaporate." He presciently warned about the emergence of a "genuine guerrilla insurgency."[11]

[9] Congressional Record, March 21, 2002, S2247.

[10] Senate Foreign Relations Committee, "Afghanistan: Building Stability, Avoiding Chaos," June 26, 2002, 1–3.

[11] Senate Foreign Relations Committee, "The Reconstruction of Afghanistan: An Update," February 12, 2003, 11. Senate Foreign Relations Committee, "Afghanistan: In Pursuit of

In 2004, Biden again summarized his main point: "The reconstruction and stabilization of Afghanistan is a vital national security imperative of the United States. We cannot permit this country to again become a haven for terrorists." In March 2007, he called for a surge of US forces to Afghanistan.[12] In early 2008, while running for president, he warned bluntly that "we're not succeeding in Afghanistan." He called for "a significantly greater investment, including troops," and reconstruction. He continued banging on the drum for more development aid. "The battle against the Taliban is not going to be won with bullets and bombs alone. It's going to be won with roads, clinics, and schools." His comments were markedly more pessimistic than in earlier years, but he was not defeatist. "I believe the war in Afghanistan is winnable, but I don't believe we're winning."[13]

For seven years, Biden argued that the war in Afghanistan was vital to American security. He never questioned the need to fight the Taliban to defeat al-Qaida. He said that reconstruction was essential to winning the war and criticized the Bush administration for its refusal to embrace nation building. He warned that the Taliban would reconstitute and wage an insurgency if Afghanistan was not stabilized and urged the Bush administration to do all it could to prevent, and then to defeat, the insurgency. He repeatedly called for more aid, more troops, and more attention. He warned that if the United States abandoned Afghanistan, the Taliban would retake power and al-Qaida would regain safe haven. It was an inspiring, hopeful vision of what America could do and what we could be. In every particular, Senator Joe Biden was entirely correct.

With the mathematical precision of a contrapuntal fugue, Vice President and President Joe Biden became the perfect inverse of his senatorial self. What changed? The situation in Afghanistan changed, but it changed in ways that Biden himself had predicted and warned against. The question is not why Biden grew more pessimistic – every observer did. Rather, at some point, Biden changed more fundamental views: about the war's importance, about the connection between the Taliban and al-Qaida,

Security and Democracy," October 16, 2003, 4–7. www.govinfo.gov/content/pkg/CHRG-108shrg91915/pdf/CHRG-108shrg91915.pdf.

[12] Senate Foreign Relations Committee, "Afghanistan: Continuing Challenges," May 12, 2004, 10. www.govinfo.gov/content/pkg/CHRG-108shrg95973/pdf/CHRG-108shrg95973.pdf. Senate Foreign Relations Committee, "Afghanistan: Time For a New Strategy?" March 8, 2007, 1–3.

[13] Senate Foreign Relations Committee, "Afghanistan: A Plan to Turn the Tide?" January 31, 2008, 1–3. www.govinfo.gov/content/pkg/CHRG-110shrg45330/pdf/CHRG-110shrg45330.pdf.

and about the connection between rebuilding Afghanistan and American security. Why?

Three things changed. First, he became vice president. As president-in-waiting, Biden had to think of the war as a potential commander-in-chief, not a senatorial gadfly. Much of his stance on the war before 2009 was likely simple partisanship and posturing. Bush didn't like nation building, so Biden embraced it. Bush didn't want to send troops, so Biden called for their deployment. Bush prioritized Iraq, so Biden called attention to Afghanistan. Biden was hardly alone in doing so, though he had been among the most outspoken, consistent, and seemingly genuine in his desire to do more for Afghanistan.

Second, Biden met with Karzai in January 2009. Biden was known for his view that "all foreign policy is an extension of personal relationships." That's a common view of foreign policy among politicians, but no less juvenile for how widespread it is: because they get elected by glad-handing and back-slapping, they believe they can navigate the waters of inter-national politics the same way. That may be true among world leaders in other democracies, but tyrants, dictators, and terrorists enjoy manipulating democratic politicians who put so much weight on personal rapport (recall George W. Bush with Pervez Musharraf or Vladimir Putin). More to the point, it does not apply to leaders of fragile states who must navigate tribes, warlords, insurgents, and drug traffickers. When Karzai did not warm to Biden – Karzai's problems would not have gone away if he had – Biden lectured, insulted, and shouted at him (see Chapter 7). Biden came away convinced the relationship with Karzai – and thus, by extension, the entire war – was unsalvageable. If so, his own neoimperial behavior had made it so.[14]

Third, and most significantly, Vietnam came back. As vice president, Biden was surrounded by Jim Jones, Chuck Hagel, and John Kerry, all Vietnam veterans; Richard Holbrooke, who spent six years in Vietnam as a foreign service officer and never shut up about it; and Hillary Clinton, who had been an antiwar protester in her college days. The press started to raise the Vietnam analogy, and it was natural for Biden's mind to start working along the same track. Faced with a spiking insurgency, a corrupt and incompetent allied government, bitter recriminations with the allied head of state, and US military leadership calling for escalation, it would have been surprising if Biden, given his history, had *not* started to think about Vietnam.

---

[14] Rhodes, *The World as It Is*, 65.

In early 2009, just months after he had argued as a senator that the war was important and winnable, now Vice President Biden was "more convinced than ever that Afghanistan was a version of Vietnam," according to Woodward's account, and when Obama was about to order more troops he warned that the United States might get "locked into Vietnam."[15] And if Afghanistan was Vietnam, then the old lessons came back: The war was a mistake, irrelevant to American security. It was futile and could not be won. The US military leadership was untrustworthy and untruthful. And the danger of staying in was greater than the danger of getting out. This way of thinking about Afghanistan was not rooted in new facts, a fresh understanding, or another strategy review. It was the reflexive, uncritical impulse of an American politician known for "an approach to foreign policy that is guided largely by impulse and feeling rather than abiding philosophy."[16]

2021: THE FINAL MISTAKE

It took two months. A week after inauguration, Biden tasked Jake Sullivan, his national security advisor, to lead a strategy review on Afghanistan – by one count, the ninth strategy review of the war. The debates were familiar, the issues well worn. Little new could be said, though the administration reportedly took twenty-five NSC meetings over the following weeks to say it. The sole strategic question was whether the Biden administration would honor the Doha agreement or not, whether it would withdraw or seek to keep troops in Afghanistan. Biden made a show of asking for a "full review ... leaving no stone unturned, and making sure everyone and every argument was heard." It was hardly full: many Biden appointees at the State and Defense Departments below the cabinet level were still awaiting Senate confirmation and could not participate. Additionally, "longtime Biden aides like Secretary of State [Tony] Blinken and chief of staff [Ron] Klain knew Biden was determined to bring all the troops home. He had wanted out, ever since 2009," Woodward reported. "Biden wanted to make a big move: terminate the endless war." After the review, General McKenzie, now commander of Central Command, came to believe that from the outset, Biden "had made his decision. He had made a moral decision on this, it's what he wanted to do. He'd wanted to do it for years."[17]

---

[15] Woodward, *Obama's Wars*, 250.
[16] Jaffe, "The War in Afghanistan Shattered Joe Biden's Faith."
[17] Woodward, *Peril*, 334, 335. McKenzie, interview by author.

It wasn't entirely a foregone conclusion. The idea of a stay-behind force, tabled since mid 2019, was revived. Lloyd Austin, the secretary of defense, "believed there were strong military, intelligence and strategic arguments for keeping a small US force there." General Scott Miller, the last coalition commander, agreed and worried what a final withdrawal would do to the Afghan military. "US troops were providing important coordination of surveillance and intelligence that helped stabilize the Afghan government," the military thought. "Austin said the US presence also provided a situational awareness they could not get without being there." The troop presence was down to 2,500. "Our thinking was, hold at 2,500. That was my recommendation," McKenzie said, "and if you draw down to zero rapidly, then odds are the government's going to collapse."[18]

Austin proposed a second-best solution: a phased withdrawal "in three or four stages to provide leverage for diplomatic negotiations." Obama had already phased the withdrawal of 90,000 troops, and Trump phased the withdrawal of almost 12,000 more. It was Zeno's paradox as strategy: the United States would withdraw ever-smaller portions of its military but never completely leave, so that every generation of policymakers could simultaneously claim that they had both withdrawn and responsibly left a stay-behind force.[19]

Blinken started out supporting the withdrawal but, through the review, changed his mind. "His new recommendation was to extend the mission with US troops for a while to see if it could yield a political settlement. Buy time for negotiations," according to Woodward. He sent the suggestion to the Taliban to test the waters. They rejected the proposal and insisted the US abide by the fourteen-month timeline in the Doha agreement, which meant withdrawal by May. US officials scrambled for a last-minute diplomatic breakthrough in intra-Afghan talks, which had gone nowhere. Khalilzad, still in his role as special representative, proposed a grand bargain under a new constitution and a power-sharing agreement. The Americans' reflexive hope that diplomacy could change or avert military reality bespoke a refusal to see what was happening. The Taliban had launched a major offensive in Kandahar and Helmand at the same time they sat down to talk to Kabul, showing that they, at least, understood the link between military pressure and bargaining leverage.[20]

Biden pushed back. His "primary argument, the one that undergirded the debate, was that the mission had shifted from its original intent." The US went to Afghanistan to get al-Qaida. But Biden believed "the war had

---

[18] Woodward, *Peril*, 336, 339, 377. McKenzie, interview by author.
[19] Woodward, *Peril*, 336, 339, 377.   [20] Woodward, *Peril*, 336, 377.

expanded to a nation-building enterprise to defeat the religiously extreme Taliban," even though nation-building efforts had ended a decade earlier. Biden did not believe they needed to defeat the Taliban and "had a particular disdain for counterinsurgency, viewing it as a classic example of mission creep." The mission was to defeat al-Qaida, "not to deliver a death blow to the Taliban." As in 2009, Biden insisted "that the Taliban was not al-Qaida. The insurgency was part of an internal civil war and not the terrorist group threatening the United States." Biden fully understood the likely consequences of withdrawal. "Blinken even had heard Biden privately say in 2009 that the United States had to accept a brutal civil war if US troops withdrew. 'How bad can that be?' Biden had asked."[21]

Biden knew the counterarguments because he spent seven years making them in the Senate. "The alternative to nation-building is chaos," he had said in 2003, and "the reconstruction and stabilization of Afghanistan is a vital national security imperative of the United States," in 2004. Whether he had been disingenuous then and was finally being honest now, or the other way around – or, most charitably, whether he had simply changed his mind – is unknown and unknowable. A few voices within the administration raised concerns about women's rights, but they could not outweigh the president's conviction that the war had to end. After Biden announced his decision, Congress grilled Khalilzad about the implications of America's withdrawal for human rights in Afghanistan. He dodged and suggested the US and other donors would condition foreign aid on the Taliban's respect for human rights but finally replied, "Should we use the US troops to enforce particular values?"[22]

In February, the Afghanistan Study Group offered a different way forward. Cochaired by General Joe Dunford, the congressionally chartered bipartisan group of former senior officials included Hadley, Grossman, Flournoy, Dobbins, and others – much like the Atlantic Council report in 2015. It was established in late 2019 when details of the imminent Doha agreement began to circulate publicly. Now, on the eve of Biden's announcement, the group recommended that "the United States should explicitly reinforce the conditionality of final troop withdrawal" and noted that "the Taliban have fallen short of their commitments." They were right, but an air of unreality attached to the report; it was written in a business-as-usual manner, calling for more regional diplomacy, support

---

[21] Woodward, *Peril*, 335, 337, 381.

[22] "The Reconstruction of Afghanistan: An Update, February 12, 2003, 11. "Afghanistan: Continuing Challenges," May 12, 2004, 10. Senate Foreign Relations Committee, "US Policy in Afghanistan," April 27, 2021, 16.

to intra-Afghan peace talks, and for holding to the basic Doha framework rather than scrapping it altogether. It was still better than what the Biden administration was contemplating.[23]

Critics worried that the Taliban had not severed ties with al-Qaida. Senator Rob Portman of Ohio asked Khalilzad about it. Khalilzad claimed "the Taliban have taken several positive steps" but did not offer details. In the administration's strategy review, Biden claimed the United States could rely on "over-the-horizon" capabilities to attack al-Qaida and ISIS, meaning military forces stationed outside of Afghanistan. McKenzie reminded the NSC of the "profound questions of physics that affect your ability to target" from outside the country. Proximity always helps. The infamously botched Desert One mission in 1980 to rescue American hostages in Iran was an example of a failed over-the-horizon operation, while the Abbottabad raid in 2011 succeeded despite a crashed helicopter because they had backup stationed immediately nearby, in Jalalabad. "Over the horizon is very difficult," McKenzie argued. "How are you going to gather intelligence? . . . You're going to fly drones overhead? Well, you're not going to fly from Pakistan. So you're going to fly from where we're flying them now, which is the Gulf. So you're looking through a soda straw, your [human intelligence] network on the ground is going to dry up," and the United States would lose granular situational awareness.[24]

Biden's mistrust of the military played a large role in his thinking, a mistrust founded on his belief that the military had "jammed" Obama in 2009. "Biden privately reviewed Obama's eventual decision to add 30,000 US troops. He characterized it as a tragic power play executed by national security leaders at the expense of a young president."[25] Biden likened the military to a kid who selectively confesses a minor sin to hide a bigger one:

> It's like the Catholic school kid. They teach you about confession and the priest. In third grade, when you're learning to go to do penance. Now you can't go in there and say I stole the gold chain and fail to tell the priest there was a gold watch at the end of the chain . . . That's how these guys are. You've got to find out if they've got a goddamn gold watch at the end of the chain.[26]

---

[23] Afghanistan Study Group, "Final Report," 8. In 2013, a separate and unaffiliated group of scholars convened, also calling themselves the Afghanistan Study Group, and issued a report. They argued the war was peripheral to American interests and unwinnable and thus the United States should withdraw as soon as practical.

[24] Senate Foreign Relations Committee, "US Policy in Afghanistan," April 27, 2021, 22. McKenzie, interview by author.

[25] Woodward, *Peril*, 380.   [26] Woodward, *Peril*, 381.

Biden was concerned that if he stayed in Afghanistan, the military would find ways to ask for more troops. "If we have 3,000 troops there and they're attacked, you guys will come in and say okay, we need 5,000 more," he complained. If staying meant escalating, it reinforced Biden's inclination to withdraw altogether. He didn't believe Afghanistan was worth it – but more importantly, he did not trust the military's judgment. He feared military freelancing, distrusted the military's word, and believed the military would take over US foreign policy without his oversight. Biden believed his judgment about the 2009 surge had been vindicated; he had counseled against the surge and believed that it had failed – despite that the military component showed signs of success – which gave him more confidence to go against conventional military thinking in 2021. Biden shared Obama's belief that the bigger threat to American national security was not the Taliban, but the US military's desire to defeat them. As with Obama, the belief was rooted in America's history of military adventurism and the military's dishonesty during Vietnam. It was not rooted in a fair assessment of the war the United States was fighting in 2021 or the state of the US military in the modern era.[27]

The military, for its part, had been beaten into accepting the narrative of its own past duplicity. During Biden's strategy review, General Mark Milley, chairman of the Joint Chiefs of Staff, warned the other chiefs about the military's supposed insubordination in 2009. "Mullen, McChrystal and Petraeus, the uniform guys, had tried to box in a president," he told them. "You never, ever ever box in a president of the United States. You always give him decision space." Milley reviewed the rules senior officers should abide by in discussions with the president and other principals. "You don't play cute and you don't give your advice on the front page of *The Washington Post*. And you don't, you damn sure don't give it in speeches. You just don't do that. You give candid, honest advice. You give it in private and you give it to the president." Milley's rules are sound, but the attitude he conveyed was premised on a false understanding of what had happened in 2009 – an attitude that neutered the military's ability to speak candidly and forcefully about the likely consequences of Biden's decision in 2021. Being too subservient is as much a type of military politicization as being insubordinate.[28]

Biden announced his decision on April 14. "Biden told his advisers the decision was hard. But Sullivan did not think Biden anguished over it. Biden seemed at peace with his choice."[29] He declared victory, arguing that the United States had gone to Afghanistan "to ensure Afghanistan would not be

---

[27] Woodward, *Peril*, 339–340. [28] Woodward, *Peril*, 387. [29] Woodward, *Peril*, 386.

used as a base from which to attack our homeland again. We did that. We accomplished that objective," and "we went to war with clear goals. We achieved those objectives. Bin Laden is dead, and al-Qaida is degraded," foregrounding retribution as the foremost reason for the war. He argued that "the threat has become more dispersed, metastasizing around the globe," such that "keeping thousands of troops grounded and concentrated in just one country at a cost of billions each year makes little sense to me," minimizing South Asia's importance as a nexus for transnational jihadist networks. As such, he concluded, "it's time to end America's longest war." Obama had announced the end of the war in 2014, there were only 2,500 troops in Afghanistan in 2021, and virtually none engaged in ground combat against the Taliban. The war had long been over for the United States.

Biden noted the Doha agreement and the United States' commitment to withdraw by May. "It is perhaps not what I would have negotiated myself, but it was an agreement made by the United States government," he said, without noting that the Taliban were openly flouting their end of the deal. The Doha agreement would be one of the few policies from the Trump administration Biden did not repudiate. Biden promised to conduct the withdrawal "responsibly, deliberately, and safely," which subsequent events contradicted. He also promised "we'll not take our eye off the terrorist threat," reassuring Americans that "we'll reorganize our counterterrorism capabilities." Biden promised continued support for the Afghan army and police, who, he said, "continue to fight valiantly, on behalf of the Afghans, at great cost," comments that would stand in contrast to his accusatory tone later that summer. He anticipated criticism. "I know there are many who will loudly insist that diplomacy cannot succeed without a robust US military presence to stand as leverage," he said. "We gave that argument a decade," ignoring the failure of Obama and Trump to coordinate their military and diplomatic efforts. Armed diplomacy did not "get a decade" to prove itself; it never got a single day.[30]

THE FALL OF KABUL

Biden's speech was the first of several public statements he made about Afghanistan between April and August. He grew more defensive and his

---

[30] "Remarks by President Biden," April 14, 2021. www.whitehouse.gov/briefing-room/spee ches-remarks/2021/04/14/remarks-by-president-biden-on-the-way-forward-in-afghani stan/. I emailed the White House to request an interview with Biden. In response, I received an email repeating the same themes. Email to author, March 28, 2023.

comments more detached from reality as the Taliban offensive entered its final phase and panic set in across Afghanistan. On May 4, weeks after Biden's speech and just after the withdrawal deadline established by Doha, the Taliban launched simultaneous offensives in seven provinces. On the 11th, they captured a district just outside Kabul. By early the next month, the offensive had spread to most of the country's provinces. It was difficult for the US military and the intelligence community to follow the Taliban's progress because the United States had withdrawn most of its eyes and ears and because there were few battles to observe. The Afghan army, without American air support or embedded advisors, fled, and the Taliban cut deals with local powerbrokers, making the situation both fluid and opaque. In June, the US intelligence community revised downward its estimate of the Kabul government's survivability, judging the government was likely to collapse within six to twelve months of the American withdrawal. It had previously said Kabul might survive for up to two years.[31]

As the US military withdrew, it handed over much of its equipment to the Afghan army. Sullivan told his Afghan counterparts that the United States was committed – somehow – to supporting the Afghan army, even as it left. He pressed Biden to slow the pace of withdrawal and to reconsider the closure of Bagram Airbase, which he did – for four days, resuming on June 22. Biden capped troop levels at 650 to secure the embassy and one airport; the military had to choose between Kabul International Airport and Bagram. "You can keep Bagram at 2,500 [troops]. You can't keep Bagram at 650, you just can't do it," McKenzie said. At 3 am on July 2, American forces left Bagram, where I had been stationed nineteen years earlier, slipping out in the middle of the night so that their departure would not become a target for the advancing Taliban. Allied Afghan forces were unaware the Americans were leaving until they found the base deserted the next day, which was profoundly demoralizing. One senior Afghan official said the US departure from Bagram was "a clear signal to all [Afghan] forces that they are alone," and that "after they left our soldiers understood they were totally abandoned." A week previously, Biden met with President Ashraf Ghani in Washington, DC. "The most important ask I have for Afghanistan is that we

---

[31] The narrative in this section is drawn from Michael R. Gordon et al., "Inside Biden's Afghanistan Withdrawal Plan," *Wall Street Journal*, September 5, 2021. Gordon Lubold, "Afghan Government Could Collapse Six Months After US Withdrawal," *Wall Street Journal*, June 23, 2021. Reuters, "Timeline: The Taliban's Rapid Advance," August 15, 2021. Mark Mazzetti, "Intelligence Warned of Afghan Military Collapse," *New York Times*, August 18, 2021.

have a friend in the White House," Ghani said. "You have a friend," Biden replied.[32]

Faced with mounting criticism and alarm, Biden spoke on July 8. He repeated his arguments from April. "We did not go to Afghanistan to nation-build" – as if that was relevant anymore – and "It's the right and the responsibility of the Afghan people alone to decide their future and how they want to run their country." Protecting that right was the point of the Afghan constitution, which the Taliban had no interest in respecting. The Taliban's military conquest of the country was not an expression of the will of the Afghan people, nor would their authoritarian government be. Biden pledged diplomatic efforts "to pursue peace and a peace agreement that will end this senseless violence." The Taliban had already signed a peace agreement, and Doha proved to be the enabling condition of, not an obstacle to, the "senseless violence" of the Taliban's final offensive. Biden assured the Afghans that the United States would "take on the Afghan nationals who work side-by-side with US forces" and accelerate the Special Immigrant Visa application process. "There is a home for you in the United States if you so choose," he said, in what would prove to be a cheap promise.

Biden, echoing the Trump administration's staunchest defenders, claimed the Doha agreement was the reason US casualties had dropped to almost nothing. That was false – US casualties had dropped following the 2014 transition, not the 2020 Doha agreement – but he used the claim to argue that if he kept troops in Afghanistan in violation of Doha, fighting would resume, more Americans would be killed and wounded, and he would be forced to send more troops back in. Biden is probably right that staying would have meant more troops – Trump had drawn down the presence to a dangerous low of 2,500. But Biden ignored that even when there was no peace deal and the Taliban attacked US troops, from 2014 to 2020, they almost never succeeded.

A journalist asked Biden if he trusted the Taliban. Biden was offended. "Is that a serious question?" Yes, the journalist replied. "No, I do not," he answered. It was a reasonable question because Biden's strategy depended on the Taliban – who now had almost-unimpeded military control of the country – abiding by the promises they had made in the Doha agreement when the United States had no means to hold them accountable. Biden quipped that he trusted "the capacity of the Afghan military," which might

---

[32] McKenzie, interview by author. SIGAR, "Why the Afghan Security Forces Collapsed," 97. Coll, "The Secret History of the US Diplomatic Failure in Afghanistan." Jamal and Maley, *The Decline and Fall of Republican Afghanistan*, 136.

have been a serious answer if Biden had not withdrawn the embedded advisors and, most importantly, denied them American air support. Another journalist challenged Biden with the intelligence community's assessment that the government in Kabul was likely to collapse. Biden simply, and falsely, denied that was the case. Another journalist asked Biden if he saw parallels with Vietnam. "None whatsoever. Zero," he said. "The Taliban is not the North Vietnamese army. They're not remotely comparable in terms of capability," which was true. He added: "There's going to be no circumstance where you see people being lifted off the roof of an Embassy of the United States from Afghanistan."

Biden repeated that "it's up to the people of Afghanistan to decide on what government they want," but added, "not us to impose the government on them." With that comment, Biden implied that an enduring US military presence in Afghanistan was "imposing a government on them," but the Taliban's military conquest was "the Afghan people deciding on what government they want," which was the Taliban's own perspective on the war. I'm reminded of McMaster's observation about the "reversal of morality" he saw in some policymakers' view of the world.[33] "In many countries there is a deep ambivalence about military action today, no matter what the cause," Obama warned in his Nobel Lecture in 2009. "And at times, this is joined by a reflexive suspicion of America." One does not expect to encounter such suspicion from the Oval Office.

Two weeks later, on July 13, nearly two dozen diplomats cosigned a State Department dissent cable that disagreed with much of what Biden had said. A dissent cable is a formal channel for foreign service officers to register their opposition to American policy. It is rarely used. The cable noted the Taliban's rapid advances and the collapse of the Afghan security forces and warned the Afghan government would collapse soon after the American military withdrawal. It recommended urgent attention to the evacuation of civilians and Afghan allies from Afghanistan. Earlier, in May, Pentagon planners had tried to jump-start planning for a possible emergency evacuation of the embassy and of allied Afghans, "but White House officials asked that those issues be removed from the agenda, saying they should be discussed separately."[34]

---

[33] "Remarks by President Biden," July 8, 2021.

[34] Vivian Salama, "Internal State Department Cable Warned of Kabul Collapse," *Wall Street Journal*, August 19, 2021. See also Senate Foreign Relations Committee, "Examining the US Withdrawal from Afghanistan," September 14, 2021, 20. Gordon, et al., "Inside Biden's Afghanistan Withdrawal Plan," *Wall Street Journal*, September 5, 2021.

The bureaucrats at State and Defense were notably more realistic and aware of what was happening on the ground than Biden – or, at least, than Biden's public comments suggest. By the end of July, the Taliban were in control of half the country's districts. The intelligence community warned that if the Taliban seized cities, "a cascading collapse could happen rapidly and the Afghan security forces were at high risk of falling apart." Biden authorized more air strikes on the Taliban to slow their advance, but – as with so much in the Afghan war – it was too little and too late. The Afghan government worked up a plan to defend the capital but could not communicate it to their own military, having resisted earlier American pleas to consolidate the military to defend key cities. "They had a plan that on paper would've been a good staff college plan, but it never was transmitted to the force," McKenzie said. McKenzie had now taken command on the ground in Afghanistan, Miller having left the previous month. He believed the best-case scenario was that the Afghan government might survive until the following spring. "The worst case was it's going to happen pretty quick," but even then, "I didn't think it would happen in August." On August 3, the intelligence community revised its estimate downward again, warning of imminent collapse, possibly within weeks.[35]

On August 6, one provincial capital fell to the Taliban, catalyzing a bandwagon effect that took ten days to sweep the Taliban into power. The speed of their final march caught everyone, probably including the Taliban, completely off guard, exceeding even the intelligence community's most pessimistic estimates. (Perhaps not everyone: in April, Senator Mitt Romney expressed concern about the possibility of "imminent collapse," worrying "that as soon as we are gone, that the military runs, that the Government folds, that the Taliban takes over."[36]) Up until August 14, US officials pressed Ghani to send an empowered delegation to Doha to negotiate a peaceful transfer of power. Ghani initially agreed but, when the Taliban entered Kabul, fled. The Taliban agreed not to enter Kabul until a transition could be arranged, but – like the Northern Alliance in 2001 – did so anyway, claiming they had to prevent the city from descending into chaos.

On the 15th, the Taliban raised their flag in Kabul, and Chinook helicopters began evacuating American diplomats from the embassy in eerie parallel to the evacuation of Saigon in 1975, exactly as Biden had

---

[35] McKenzie, interview by author. Mazzetti, "Intelligence Warned of Afghan Military Collapse," August 18, 2021.

[36] Senate Foreign Relations Committee, "US Policy on Afghanistan," April 27, 2021, 13.

promised would not happen. Two weeks later, after the final evacuation, al-Qaida issued a public statement congratulating their Taliban allies on their victory. "We praise the Almighty, the Omnipotent, who humiliated and defeated America, the head of disbelief," it said. "We praise Him for breaking America's back, tarnishing its global reputation and expelling it, disgraced and humiliated, from the Islamic land of Afghanistan." It celebrated Afghanistan as an "impregnable fortress" and the "graveyard of empires."[37] After 7,268 days, America's war in Afghanistan was over, and the Afghan people's nightmare resumed.

"I believe that we gave it away, gave Afghanistan away and I remain heartbroken and not only because I believed in what we're doing," John Gastright, the Bush-era deputy assistant secretary of state, told me shortly afterward. "There are so many things that we did that were valuable and that have now already collapsed in a matter of weeks." The Taliban moved quickly to reestablish their emirate, including "expansive measures to bar women and girls from participation in public and political life," according to the State Department. They dissolved parliament and the government's electoral bodies, concentrating power in the Taliban's leadership council. They reestablished their infamous Ministry for the Propagation of Virtue and Prevention of Vice to "surveil the public and monitor compliance with Taliban-issued edicts and directives." They issued edicts against the media and "used force against protesters and journalists and suppressed political discussion and dissent." And some Taliban fighters indulged in a wave of reprisal killings, arbitrary arrests, and torture against former government officials, though the full extent was unclear as most international observers and journalists had left.[38]

***

Biden addressed the nation again the day after the Taliban took Kabul. He sounded defensive, even angry. He repeated his arguments from April and July, insisted "I stand squarely behind my decision," and shifted the blame for Afghanistan's fall to the Afghan military. "American troops cannot and should not be fighting in a war and dying in a war that Afghan forces are not willing to fight for themselves," he said. "We gave them every tool they could

---

[37] Thomas Joscelyn, "al-Qaida praises Taliban's 'historic victory' in Afghanistan," *Long Wars Journal*, August 31, 2021. See also Shishir Gupta, "Al-Qaida hails Taliban for Emancipating Afghans," *Hindustan Times*, August 20, 2021.

[38] State Department, "2022 Country Reports on Human Rights: Afghanistan." Gastright, interview by author.

need. We paid their salaries, provided for the maintenance of their air force ... We provided close air support." In fact, the United States had stopped providing close air support after Doha, and "the loss of US close air support allowed the Taliban greater freedom of movement and enabled its fighters to infiltrate and surround major cities across Afghanistan," according to the special inspector general. Nonetheless, Biden insisted: "We gave them every chance to determine their own future. What we could not provide them was the will to fight for that future."[39]

Biden's blame shifting ignored that the Afghan army had fought the Taliban for over ten years, including seven years in the lead, and lost 66,000 soldiers in combat, almost thirty times the number of Americans killed in the war. Biden himself had praised the Afghan army in April for "fight[ing] valiantly, on behalf of the Afghans, at great cost." The Afghan army collapsed quickly in the spring and summer of 2021 because Biden's speech had a crippling effect on their morale and because of the reality of military logistics. The Afghan army was widely dispersed in bases across the country that relied on helicopters for resupply. As the Americans withdrew, so did the military and contractor maintenance support for the Afghan helicopter fleet. Within months, the fleet was effectively grounded, and the troops in dispersed bases were stranded, running out of food, supplies, and ammunition, and slowly starving as the Taliban closed in. Their decision not to fight in those conditions is not a reflection on their willpower so much as their rationality. If you know that your army is not equipped to win the battle that's coming, why fight? It is an individually rational decision to save your life, a decision that, when multiplied, loses a war. Biden's finger-pointing was demeaning, ignorant, and unpresidential. If Trump had said the same thing, critics would have called it racist.

Biden was not done. He ended with an extended riff that repeated some of his favorite themes, but there was a new rawness. "I've argued for many years that our mission should be narrowly focused on counterterrorism – not counterinsurgency or nation building." That was technically true – Biden had made those arguments since 2009 – but overlooked his vocal championship of nation building for the war's first seven years. "I will not repeat the mistakes we've made in the past – the mistake of staying and fighting indefinitely in a conflict that is not in the national interest of the United States." Biden had not previously said so clearly, in public, that the war was not in America's interest, which is a hard thing for a soldier to hear

---

[39] SIGAR, "Why the Afghan Security Forces Collapsed," 12. "Remarks by President Biden," August 16, 2021.

his commander-in-chief say. He spoke dismissively, almost with ridicule, of "our decades-long effort to overcome centuries of history and permanently change and remake Afghanistan." Biden invoked, one final time, the old trope. "The events we're seeing now are sadly proof that no amount of military force would ever deliver a stable, united, and secure Afghanistan – as known in history as the 'graveyard of empires.'"

And, for perhaps the first and only time, he spoke aloud what he had likely believed for a decade. "I made a commitment to the brave men and women who serve this nation that I wasn't going to ask them to continue to risk their lives in a military action that should have ended long ago," he said. "Our leaders did that in Vietnam when I got here as a young man. I will not do it in Afghanistan." One month previously, he insisted there was "zero" parallels between Afghanistan and Vietnam. Now, it seemed, Afghanistan was Vietnam after all, and President Biden had the chance to follow Senator Biden's example: *We can simply say in respect to Afghanistan: "Enough."*

THE EVACUATION

Two weeks of chaos followed the American military withdrawal and the collapse of the Afghan government. Thousands of American and allied diplomats and aid officials remained in country, along with tens of thousands of allied Afghans eligible for Special Immigrant Visa (SIV) applications who had worked for the United States or other allies as translators, embassy workers, or in other capacities. Biden believed that he would have months, even years, to arrange an orderly evacuation. That was understandable, barely, in April, when the intelligence community had judged the Kabul government might survive for up to two years following the withdrawal, but became implausible within weeks of Biden's announcement.

Biden's team claims that he chose not to "broadcast loudly and publicly about a potential worst-case scenario unfolding in order to avoid signaling a lack of confidence in the ANDSF or the Afghan government's position." That's a legitimate concern, but he seems not to have realized that his April announcement had that effect anyway. "I was watching the announcement," recalled one Afghan provincial police chief. "And the Taliban are also watching. And after eight or nine minutes, the Taliban intensified their attacks immediately, in all different places." The Afghans understood the full implications of Biden's announcement, even if he did not.[40]

The Afghans were not the only ones. Senator Robert Menendez, chairman of the Senate Foreign Relations Committee, grilled Khalilzad about the administration's evacuation plans and the SIV process in late April, two weeks after Biden's speech. "A plan is being developed" is all Khalilzad could reply. The Biden administration claims his NSC "hosted dozens of high-level planning meetings, formal rehearsals of the withdrawal, and tabletop exercises to explore scenarios for an evacuation" in the spring and summer of 2021. That would be surprising in light of their other claims that they believed the Kabul government would not immediately collapse and their surprise at the speed of events. On the other hand, worst-case-scenario contingency planning is a routine part of military planning, and it is conceivable that some Biden officials tried to think ahead and plan for the worst (although the State Department later faulted both administrations for "insufficient senior-level consideration of worst-case scenarios" leading up to the collapse).[41]

Embassy Kabul was placed on "ordered departure" status in late April, which should have started the process of reducing the embassy's size, though the State Department later concluded it "did not result in a notable immediate reduction of the embassy's footprint." The Biden team listed various events, meetings, and taskings in April, May, and June preparing for an evacuation in their official narrative. None of that activity, however, was significant enough to impress the diplomats on the ground, who felt compelled to file their dissent cable in July. The people who would be tasked with overseeing the evacuation were most alarmed by the lack of preparation for it.[42]

In July, the administration made a conscious decision not to undertake "a massive airlift evacuation" of SIVs because it expected the US embassy in Afghanistan would be able to continue normal operations, including SIV processing and evacuations, after the withdrawal, again showing how detached from reality the White House's thinking had become. According

---

[40] White House, "US Withdrawal From Afghanistan," p. 6. www.whitehouse.gov/wp-content/uploads/2023/04/US-Withdrawal-from-Afghanistan.pdf. SIGAR, "Why the Afghan Security Forces Collapsed," 98.

[41] Senate Foreign Relations Committee, "US Policy on Afghanistan," April 27, 2021, 11.

[42] White House, "US Withdrawal from Afghanistan," 3–5. Quote on page 4. www.whitehouse.gov/wp-content/uploads/2023/04/US-Withdrawal-from-Afghanistan.pdf. State Department, "After Action Review," 11, 12.

to the Biden administration's own document, they chose not to initiate a formal noncombatant evacuation operation (NEO) as late as August 9, in the middle of the Taliban's ten-day sweep to Kabul: "NSC convened a senior interagency meeting on August 8, which unanimously recommended against beginning the NEO based on conditions on the ground. National security leaders met on August 9 and concluded conditions on the ground did not support triggering a NEO."[43]

Biden authorized the NEO on August 14 and sent 5,000 US troops back to Afghanistan to secure Kabul International Airport. For two weeks, as thousands of Afghans mobbed the airport and stood in lines outside the security fence, the US military began flying diplomats, refugees, and other evacuees out. "I flew to Doha on the 15th of August," McKenzie recalled, "met Mullah Baradar and his team and delivered the warning: we're going to evacuate, and if you guys get in our way, we're going to kill you." The Taliban agreed – why provoke the United States on its way out? – and helped keep order in Kabul. Americans suffered the humiliation of watching their compatriots become refugees whose safety was hostage to the Taliban's magnanimity in victory – televised for the world to see.[44]

In the midst of the chaos, thousands of Afghan civilians packed tightly together in an outdoor public space were too tempting a target. An ISIS suicide bomber blew himself up in the crowd on August 26, killing 170 Afghans and 13 American servicemen and wounding dozens more. Three days later, the United States killed ten Afghan civilians, including seven children, in a reprisal air strike gone wrong. It was an example of Biden's "over-the-horizon" counterterrorism strategy. As Austin had warned Biden earlier in the year, "'over-the-horizon' still denied the military and the intelligence services the critical situational awareness on the ground that has been so central to US capability." A year later, a US drone strike successfully killed Ayman al-Zawahiri in Kabul, which showed that Biden's over-the-horizon strategy could work, so long as Americans had a higher tolerance for errant raids and dead Afghan children. Zawahiri's presence in Kabul also vindicated the critics who warned that al-Qaida would return to a Taliban-controlled Afghanistan.[45]

The evacuation continued. "On military aircraft alone, we flew more than 387 sorties, averaging nearly 23 per day. At the height of this operation an aircraft was taking off every 45 minutes," according to Lloyd Austin, the defense secretary. "It was the largest airlift conducted in US history," which

---

[43] White House, "US Withdrawal from Afghanistan," 7.   [44] McKenzie, interview by author.
[45] Woodward, *Peril*, 378. McKenzie, interview by author.

is probably not true, considering the year-long Berlin airlift of 1948–1949. The military in Kabul and at Central Command worked day and night. "The month of August was just a blur to all of us," McKenzie said. Civilian aircraft and volunteers flew out untold thousands more. The administration boasted that it evacuated 124,000 people.[46]

How many Afghans were left behind? Most estimates suggest there were around 18,000–20,000 SIV applicants in Afghanistan in August 2021. Counting their family members, that amounted to some 80,000–100,000 Afghans eligible for evacuation, but "senior administration officials had not made clear decisions" about which "Afghan nationals would be included [or] how they would be prioritized" in an evacuation, according to the State Department's later review. Because the evacuation was chaotic, data on who made it out is sketchy. Most, it seems, were Americans, Europeans, and other allied officials, diplomats, and aid workers. As few as 3,000 SIV applicants and family members made it out in the initial evacuation, according to the Association of Wartime Allies; even the Biden administration claimed only 7,000 SIVs were evacuated. An unknown number of other Afghans, not in the SIV pipeline, were also evacuated because the chaos at the airport precluded careful triage.

Worse, after the fall of Kabul, tens of thousands more Afghans applied for the visa, with hundreds of thousands more family members. The full measure of America's disgrace is stunning: in the fall of 2022, after one year of the Taliban's rule, "more than 500,000 Afghans were waiting for SIV processing," according to the special inspector general for Afghanistan reconstruction. SIV applications took an average of 2.75 years to process. The Biden administration took steps to streamline the process in early 2021, but by late 2022 "at the current pace, it will take 31 years to relocate and resettle all SIV applicants," assuming, of course, that the Taliban let them leave at all.[47]

Pompeo claims he would have done better. "You can be damn sure that if I had been secretary of state in a second term, we would have put in place a system for granting visas and exfiltrating our friends months ahead of time." But there was no reason to wait for a second term to begin planning. He served as secretary of state for nearly three years, personally oversaw

---

[46] White House, "US Withdrawal from Afghanistan." www.whitehouse.gov/wp-content/up loads/2023/04/US-Withdrawal-from-Afghanistan.pdf.

[47] Association of Wartime Allies, "The Left Behind Afghans," February 2022, 1. SIGAR, "2023 High Risk List," 27–28. White House, "US Withdrawal from Afghanistan." www .whitehouse.gov/wp-content/uploads/2023/04/US-Withdrawal-from-Afghanistan.pdf. State Department, "After Action Review," 12.

negotiations for the US military withdrawal for over a year, and served as secretary for almost a full year after Doha was signed – and evidently never took steps to prepare for the evacuation or expedite SIV processing. O'Brien claims that the Trump administration didn't plan for an evacuation because they never planned to withdraw the last 2,500 troops in the first place and because they counted on NATO's 5,000 troops and associated contractors as well – which, as we've already seen, ignores the reality of what Trump was plainly bent on doing.

The Biden administration claims that "the departing Trump Administration had all but stopped SIV interviews," in part because of COVID restrictions, but also because of Trump's general antipathy to refugee resettlement and immigration. The State Department's After Action Review similarly noted that the Trump administration "made no senior-level or interagency effort to address the backlog or consider options for other at-risk Afghans despite its commitment to a military withdrawal." In the spring and summer of 2021, the Biden administration took steps to revive and streamline the SIV process. It added more personnel to visa processing and set up a task force but also broadened the eligibility criteria, which inadvertently contributed to a rush of applicants in the final days.[48]

Biden addressed the nation one more time on August 31, the day the evacuation ended. He touted the evacuation's success and claimed 100,000 Afghans were saved, which was an exaggeration by an order of magnitude. Contrary to his earlier assurances that the American withdrawal would be orderly and safe, he now said "there is no evacuation from the end of a war that you can run without the kinds of complexities, challenges, and threats we faced." He repeated a line he often used: "We succeeded in what we set out to do in Afghanistan over a decade ago. Then we stayed for another decade." For Biden, the United States set out to kill Osama bin Laden, nothing more; the rest of the war was meaningless. "This decision about Afghanistan is not just about Afghanistan. It's about ending an era of major military operations to remake other countries." Investing in lasting conditions of peace and justice was immaterial to American security, to long-term success against terrorism. He reiterated his belief that "trying to create a democratic, cohesive, and unified Afghanistan" was "something that has never been done over the many centuries of Afghanistan's history."[49]

---

[48] Pompeo, *Never Give an Inch*, 382. Gordon et al., "Inside Biden's Afghanistan Withdrawal Plan," *Wall Street Journal*, September 5, 2021. White House, "US Withdrawal from Afghanistan." State Department, "After Action Review," 13.

[49] "Remarks by President Biden," August 31, 2021.

In 1973, Biden had insisted, "I do not believe the United States has an obligation, moral or otherwise, to evacuate foreign nationals. The United States has no obligation to evacuate 1, or 100,001, South Vietnamese." Those Vietnamese, like the Afghan allies, were America's partners, allies, translators, aid workers, embassy staff, and more. By renouncing any obligation to the Vietnamese, and by leaving tens or even hundreds of thousands of Afghans behind, Biden signaled that the United States had no obligation to its allies, at all, of any kind, which is only a half-step away from denying any political morality whatsoever. Such a view of the world is startling in its cynicism and shortsightedness. In 2001, Biden argued eloquently that rebuilding Afghanistan was in America's interest. It was the best safeguard against al-Qaida's reemergence. But more than that, rebuilding Afghanistan was also an investment in international order, in lasting conditions of peace and justice, not just for Americans, but also for Afghans and for the world. It held out the promise of aligning America's interest with the international common good, the highest calling and greatest challenge of statecraft. When Biden abandoned the Vietnamese and the Afghans, he abandoned that calling, forsook any aspiration for justice and peace, and turned his back on a hopeful vision of what America could be.[50]

ASSIGNING BLAME

Who is to blame? Biden was right that the situation was untenable in early 2021. Trump's last national security advisor, Robert O'Brien, claimed that "when we left office in January 2021, Afghanistan was relatively stable; certainly, [it] was not in danger of falling." O'Brien was wrong; violence surged after Doha. It might have appeared stable because US forces were not involved in the fighting, but the Taliban intensified its offensive against Kabul, which the Trump administration no longer bothered to notice. The number of security incidents rose by 10 percent in 2020, according to UN numbers, to an all-time high. "This is the highest on record since the United Nations started documenting incidents in 2007," it reported: for the Afghans, the war was at an even greater intensity than during the surge. The Taliban launched offensives in southern provinces in the fall of 2020 that General Miller characterized as "violations in spirit, if not the written word" of Doha. In the final months of 2020, "violence spiked across Afghanistan, and civilian casualties rose by forty-five per cent," Coll

---

[50] Congressional Record, April 23, 1975, 11441, 11448, 11465.

reported. The Department of Defense noted in late 2020 that "violence levels in Afghanistan remained above seasonal norms," including several "major attacks." In October, the Taliban attacked the capital of Helmand Province and "fighting throughout the city displaced as many as 35,000 residents." Militants tried to assassinate Vice President Amrullah Saleh and Fawzia Kufi, a member of the Afghan peace delegation.[51]

"The situation in my view began to deteriorate once it became clear publicly to everybody ... that we were having a serious negotiation and Trump wanted to get out," Bolton thought. "It was at that point, if not before, that throughout Afghanistan, people began to see, good God, they may really get out. And that is when the situation really went off the cliff." The negotiation altered the psychological dynamic in Afghanistan. "It's not that all the provinces started falling," Bolton said, "but if everybody's looking around saying, the end state here is the US is really going to get out, it has an enormous impact." SIGAR agreed: "Many Afghans thought the US–Taliban agreement was an act of bad faith and a signal that the US was handing over Afghanistan to the enemy as it rushed to exit the country." Bolton thought the collapse was inevitable once Doha was signed. "I don't think people should have been surprised. I think that was baked in ... I think the government would have collapsed as soon as it absolutely became clear, we were leaving. It was over."[52]

Bolton is mostly right, but he overstates the case; nothing is ever inevitable. Trump had catalyzed a decisive shift in the Taliban's favor, but the war was not over. Biden acted as if he had no real agency. In his view, the collapse was inevitable; the US presence was unsustainable; the administration was boxed in by the 2020 peace deal with the Taliban; if the United States had repudiated the deal, the Taliban would have gone on the offensive and resumed killing US troops. And for what? Biden argued that we gave it our best for twenty years, proving that the mission was impossible. The rapid collapse only demonstrated that we were never going to succeed no matter how long we stayed. The Afghan army was still dependent on the United States, showing it never would have become independent. We achieved the most important thing: Osama bin Laden was dead. The Afghans must run their own country, we cannot stay there forever, we shouldn't try nation building, and we can keep an eye on al-Qaida from afar.[53]

---

[51] O'Brien, interview by author. DoD, "Enhancing Security," 3, 8, 9. UN, A/75/811 S/2021/252, p. 4. Coll, "The Secret History of the US Diplomatic Failure in Afghanistan."

[52] Bolton, interview by author. SIGAR, "Why the Afghan Security Forces Collapsed," 6.

[53] The following is drawn from Miller, "Afghanistan Didn't Have to End This Way," *The Dispatch*, August 13, 2021.

On the surface, these explanations make a compelling case. It is also a comforting case, because it washes our hands of responsibility for what happened next. As a strategic and humanitarian catastrophe unfolded – as al-Qaida regained safe haven, as Afghan women fell back under the Taliban's uniquely cruel tyranny, as Afghans fled the Taliban's near-genocidal oppression of political and religious dissidents – we could tell ourselves, "there's nothing we could have done." These myths function as an *ex post facto* explanation that we – the most powerful nation in the world – were powerless all along. It turns out we didn't fail because of bad decisions, strategic incompetence, or moral myopia. We failed because no one could have succeeded, because the mission was inherently impossible. No amount of strategic insight, troop surges, or Marshall-Plan-level reconstruction assistance could have made a difference in the graveyard of empires.

Of course, none of that is true. The collapse was not inevitable. It was the result of a long chain of strategic missteps and bad decisions, of which Biden's April announcement was simply the final one. None of those decisions were foreordained, and each could have been made otherwise. Even as Biden was constrained by his predecessors, he still had a choice. And he chose poorly. The US presence in Afghanistan was indefinitely sustainable. There was no significant antiwar movement to speak of, there was little domestic political pressure to withdraw, and no election hinged on Afghanistan. US troops faced low risks in Afghanistan, and the low casualty rate was not a function of the 2020 peace deal. The conflict in Afghanistan was very small, and US ground troops were not involved in direct combat in large numbers. The cost of keeping the Afghan army in the field was small compared to the cost of a Taliban victory. The intervention was not an unmitigated failure. No large-scale international terrorist attacks emanated from Afghanistan or Pakistan. The Afghan people broadly supported the country's democratic constitution. The Afghan economy showed regular, if uneven, growth. By virtually every metric of human development, Afghans were better off in 2021 than they had been twenty years earlier. "The twenty years that the United States was in Afghanistan were the best twenty years out of the last fifty that Afghanistan has had," Ambassador Bill Wood argued.[54]

The Afghan army fled rather than fight in 2021, which Biden used as proof that they were incapable of independent operations. But the Department of Defense did not claim the Afghan army was capable of independence in 2021; in fact, it said the opposite. Every six months, the

[54] Wood, interview by author.

Department reported to Congress on the Afghan army's progress, and every report noted slow improvement and enduring challenges, especially in high-skill and technical functions like intelligence, communications, maintenance, logistics, piloting, and airlift. In its final report to Congress, in late 2020, the Department noted the Afghan army's need to improve leadership, anticorruption efforts, logistics, accountability, training, budget execution, salaries, and more. The Afghan army's collapse vindicated, not Biden's pessimism, but the Department of Defense's accurate assessment of them. Biden chose to withdraw support from the Afghan army in full knowledge that they could not operate independently, then blamed the Afghan army for the predictable consequences of his own choice. Biden and other critics complain that if the Afghan army was still dependent on the United States after twenty years, it never would have been. There's a legitimate critique that the United States tried to build an Afghan army on an American model, but Biden's critique acts as if there had been *no* progress, which was not true, and comes troublingly close to a racist attitude that Afghans were somehow incapable of running their own military.[55]

It is easy to envision the counterfactual: If the United States had maintained a small presence (larger than what Trump left behind), it could have kept the Afghan army in the field indefinitely. At the very least, that would have kept the Taliban out of power and prevented al-Qaida and ISIS from regaining safe haven – which by itself would have been a better outcome than what Biden achieved. Staying would have given the Afghan army time to reach full independence, allowing for a more stable withdrawal – and, at most, staying might even have created time and space for the political situation in Kabul to sort itself out, for a fresh round of negotiations with better leverage against the Taliban, and for reconstruction and development to continue.

And the United States should have stayed because the mission was not achieved. The war was not – or should not have been – a war of revenge to kill a single terrorist. While bin Laden is dead, al-Qaida is not and, along with the Islamic State and a murderers' row of copycat jihadists, has regained safe haven in Afghanistan and Pakistan. The US presence kept jihadists on the run, in hiding, and focused on avoiding air strikes and special forces. In 2021, they regained room to breathe, which means room to plan, recruit, train, and fundraise.

Biden's explanations, dissembling, and justifications amounted to a body of myth. The myths about Afghanistan's collapse – that we were

---

[55] DoD, "Enhancing Security," December 2020, 19.

powerless and the mission was always inevitably doomed – denies the reality of the United States' agency. Our policymakers made specific strategic missteps that caused direct, avoidable harm, including Bush's light footprint, Obama's withdrawal timetable, Trump's peace deal, and Biden's withdrawal, each of which made a bad situation worse. Those decisions were made by politicians elected by and accountable to the US electorate, who largely ignored the war and enabled policymakers' strategic muddling for two decades.

That is why Biden's claim that the Afghans just had to start taking responsibility for their own country was so mendacious. He told a drowning man to take responsibility for swimming while taking away the life preserver the man had been clinging to. He overestimated the Afghans' ability to fight on their own while minimizing American responsibility for the crisis in the midst of which we abandoned them – all while preaching a soothing myth that there was nothing we could have done. Many Americans are eager to believe him because it is much easier, emotionally and cognitively, to believe in the myth of our powerlessness than in the reality of our own stupidity and moral cowardice.

ASSIGNING MORE BLAME

"I fear that the endless war could come back with a vengeance," David Petraeus told me. He's right. In 2016, I concluded an earlier book with this warning, and I see no reason to change my judgment:

> It is as certain as anything can be in the unpredictable world of global politics that the United States will find itself threatened again by chaos, tyranny, and violence emanating from the Middle East and South Asia, much of it sown by the US's earlier missteps and failures. The withdrawals from Iraq and Afghanistan are likely to be seen as the Versailles of the War on Terror: catastrophic diplomatic errors that made vain years of military sacrifice and sowed the seeds for future conflict.[56]

I fervently pray I am never vindicated. Yet, while the United States is rightly focused on the wars in Ukraine and Israel and the rise of China, al-Qaida and ISIS are reconstituting in their safe havens in Afghanistan, Pakistan, Yemen, Libya, and elsewhere. They openly speak of a centuries-long struggle. It strains credulity to think their war against us is over. I do not know

---

[56] Miller, *American Power and Liberal Order.*

when or where, but I consider it a near-certainty that jihadists will again seek to murder Americans and our allies at home or abroad – as many as possible, as publicly as possible, as destructively as possible. The Afghans are paying the steepest and most immediate price for the US withdrawal, but sooner or later we will pay a price too.

Whose fault is it? Who is responsible for losing Afghanistan? While this book has mainly focused on the *why* and the *how*, it is also worth answering *who* chose defeat in Afghanistan. I noted in the opening chapter that the four presidents bear ultimate responsibility for the decisions made on their watch, and this book apportions blame among them according to their various missteps. I am often asked who is most to blame. I dislike the question because there is no quantifiable unit of blame I can tally up. They each failed in different ways; understanding those qualitative differences is more important than trying to count up some fabricated measure of guilt.

I can answer a different question: who am I most disappointed in? The answer is: President Obama, because I had the highest expectations of him. If I have been more critical of the Obama administration, it is because Obama's initial promise was exactly right and because he oversaw the war longer than the other three presidents. The gap between initial promise and eventual execution was the largest for the Obama administration.

I had high expectations of Bush, but I temper those expectations with the novelty of the situation he faced in the immediate aftermath of 9/11. To his enormous credit, he admitted in his memoir that he was wrong about nation building, and he spent much of his presidency trying to catch up. Of course, Iraq overshadowed everything, but my unpopular opinion is that Bush's mistake wasn't invading Iraq, but invading Iraq too soon. Even a one- or two-year delay might have made a substantial difference to Afghanistan. At first, I felt bitterly disappointed by Biden because he had campaigned to undo Trump's legacy, but as I learned more about Biden's long-gestating views on Afghanistan, rooted in echoes of Vietnam, I came to see how futile it was to have expected anything of him in the first place. I expected Trump to lose the war, and he lived down to my lowest expectations, and I have little else to say except we got what we voted for.

Speaking of voters, it is important to note their role in the war. The four presidents each had their flaws, but presidents are simply politicians; they are accountable to, and reflections of, their voters. While I believe we need better policymakers, I do not think they are uniquely deficient; I think they are an accurate reflection of the nation they represent and, especially, the system of higher education that produces them. That should be both a rebuke and a challenge.

In early years, voters supported the war but largely did not care. In 2002 and 2003, voters supported going to war in Iraq. In 2004, voters listed "moral values" and the economy as their top concerns. Terrorism and Iraq came next; Afghanistan was not listed at all.[57] In 2008, as the financial crisis was unfolding, the economy was the top issue by a wide margin, with 58 percent of respondents listing it as their greatest concern. Iraq had fallen to 13 percent, terrorism to 2 percent; Afghanistan was again not listed.[58] In 2012, 3 percent of voters listed either Afghanistan or Iraq combined as their top issue.[59] Afghanistan did not feature prominently in the 2004, 2012, 2016, or 2020 presidential elections. Voters' inattention enabled policymakers' inattention, strategic drift, and lack of urgency.

Voters began to care more, and to grow more pessimistic, as the situation in Afghanistan began to deteriorate. They were evenly split about the surge and the timetable in 2009. But in July 2010, seven months after Obama's speech announcing the surge, 33 percent wanted to keep troops in for the duration, while 66 percent supported the timetable.[60] In 2014, for the first time, more Americans said the war was a mistake than otherwise.[61] In July 2021, on the eve of the final withdrawal, 70 percent of Americans favored Biden's plan to withdraw troops. Even when asked pointedly if they still supported withdrawal if it enabled "al-Qaida and other terrorist groups to establish operations in Afghanistan," 45 percent still agreed.[62] Voters' pessimism validated policymakers' conviction that the war needed to end, no matter the outcome.

In that context, it is unsurprising that four presidents consistently prioritized other things. They followed the will of the voters when they did

---

[57] Gallup, "Moral Values Important in the 2004 Exit Polls," https://news.gallup.com/poll/14275/moral-values-important-2004-exit-polls.aspx.

[58] Gallup, "Economy Runaway Winner as Most Important Problem," https://news.gallup.com/poll/112093/economy-runaway-winner-most-important-problem.aspx.

[59] Gallup, "Economic Is Dominant Issue for Americans as Election Nears," https://news.gallup.com/poll/158267/economy-dominant-issue-americans-election-nears.aspx.

[60] Frank Newport, "In US, More Support for Increasing Troops in Afghanistan," Gallup, November 25, 2009. Jeffrey M. Jones, "Americans Divided on Sending More Troops to Afghanistan," Gallup, October 8, 2009. Frank Newport, "Americans Tilt against Sending More Troops to Afghanistan," Gallup, September 25, 2009.

[61] Gallup, "American Split," July 26, 2021.

[62] Gallup, "American Public Opinion and the Afghanistan Situation," August 27, 2021. https://news.gallup.com/opinion/polling-matters/354182/american-public-opinion-afghanistan-situation.aspx.

not give Afghanistan the time, resources, or attention it needed. They obeyed electoral logic when they sought to kill terrorists even when it compromised the rest of the war effort. They were simply representing the American people when they brought the troops home before the mission was accomplished. The American people sent troops to war but did not care about their mission, then turned against it when their own inattention proved strategically catastrophic. They demanded the war's end – even when "ending" meant "losing."

"The insurgents cannot defeat us militarily," General Stan McChrystal correctly warned in his commander's assessment in 2009, "but we can defeat ourselves."

16

WHY DID WE LOSE?

Do not wage more than one war at once. Do not set withdrawal plans and timetables in advance, and do not announce them publicly. Do not establish conflicting and overlapping chains of command and parallel warfighting forces in the same war zone. Do not withdraw military forces before negotiating with your enemy. War and diplomacy go together: talking is not the opposite of war, it is a complement to it.

These are not, in fact, lessons of the war in Afghanistan. They are basic, obvious, commonsense truths of politics and strategy that we already knew before the war in Afghanistan but violated anyway. The war in Afghanistan should reinforce these lessons in American strategic thought for all time, though I somehow doubt it will. That we so willfully and freely made so many avoidable and stupid mistakes means that Afghanistan is a poor test case for anyone's theory about anything. Afghanistan doesn't disprove counterinsurgency or nation building because no counterinsurgency theorist and no nation-building advocate called for deadlines, conflicting chains of command, or multiple wars. If you want to prove or disprove a theory, pick a hard case that follows the theory closely before claiming vindication or disproof.

THE LESSONS OF AFGHANISTAN?

What can we learn from the war in Afghanistan? Shelves have already been written to answer that question. British strategist Hew Strachan emphasized the need to understand "the needs of coalition warfare."[1] David Petraeus found fault with our lack of strategic patience, insufficient and inefficient use of resources, ignorance of the "local and regional context," and more.[2] Jim Dobbins argued that "Afghanistan was lost long ago," by mistakes in the

[1] Strachan, "Learning Lessons From Afghanistan."
[2] Petraeus, "Afghanistan Did Not Have to Turn Out This Way," *The Atlantic*, August 8, 2022.

Bush and Obama administrations, including Bush's failure to invest in reconstruction and to recognize Pakistan's duplicity and his decision to invade Iraq.[3] A congressionally-chartered Afghanistan War Commission, modeled on the 9/11 Commission, convened in 2023 to investigate all aspects of the war and is due to deliver a report in 2026 or 2027 with its own conclusions.

Among the longer and most substantive explanations, the special inspector general for Afghanistan reconstruction offered seven key take-aways. Some are generic truisms – "Persistent insecurity severely undermined reconstruction efforts" – that are not wrong but hardly shed new light: no one was unaware that insecurity undermined reconstruction. Some are basically correct ("The US government continuously struggled to develop and implement a coherent strategy") even though the supporting reasoning is false ("While initially tied to the destruction of al-Qaida, the strategy grew considerably to include the defeat of the Taliban," which is the opposite of what happened). SIGAR also noted that the United States "created unrealistic timelines"; did not build sustainable institutions; rotated personnel too often; "did not understand the Afghan context"; and did not monitor and evaluate its own efforts, which are all true. A separate report focusing on the Afghan army again criticized personnel rotation, short timelines, poor coordination and oversight, corruption, a lack of sustainability, and the Afghans' recruitment policies.

More helpfully, SIGAR noted that there are "reasons to develop these capabilities and prepare for reconstruction missions in conflict-affected countries," because of the likelihood that "insurgent control or influence over a particular area or population is deemed an imminent threat to US interests." Bolton rightly reminded Trump of Trotsky's truism: you may not be interested in war, but war is interested in you. Today, we might say: you may not be interested in counterinsurgency and nation building, but insurgents and failed states have an interest in us. We don't get to choose what threatens us. Turning a blind eye just because a threat is especially complicated or because we've failed in the past to meet that kind of challenge will only allow the problem to fester and metastasize. Unfortunately, SIGAR dodged the hardest question about the "nature and range of the investment necessary to properly prepare for these campaigns."[4]

---

[3] Dobbins, "Afghanistan Was Lost Long Ago," *Foreign Affairs*, August 30, 2021.
[4] SIGAR, "What We Need to Learn," vii–xi, 96, 97. SIGAR, "Why the Afghan Security Forces Collapsed."

Defense intellectuals have chimed in with their assessments, sometimes with overbroad and uninformed conclusions. Anthony Cordesman argued that "the US should not assume other nations and cultures can be transformed in the face of evidence to the contrary," a widespread view which has almost nothing to do with what the United States did or assumed about Afghanistan. There's a germ of truth – we should not assume our ability to rebuild broken state institutions under unrealistic, public deadlines – but it is buried under hyperbole characteristic of many scholars and critics in the aftermath of the war. More helpfully, Cordesman criticized the wild swings in the level of funding for different programs. "Program turbulence is inevitable in wartime, but this level of turbulence almost ensures that many forms of aid would fail – and fail after massive investment."[5]

Counterinsurgency theorist David Kilcullen, who advised the State Department during the war, gets some things right and some things wrong. "Western withdrawal from Afghanistan went hand in hand with a narrative of defeat, repeated so often it became a self-fulfilling prophecy," he argued, rightly. On the other hand, he wrongly suggests that the "objectives of constitutionalism, centralizing power and promoting democracy never matched Afghan (or, equally importantly, regional) realities," which is certainly not what the Afghans who signed the Bonn Accords thought. He rightly notes that "the war was not inherently unwinnable," but progress "within the resource and timeframe parameters" set by policymakers was "often unachievable."

Like others, he argues that "there was no integrated plan linking the military defeat of the insurgency with development and improved governance," that there was no "theory of victory," which is only partly true. There was occasionally such a plan and a theory: the strategy reviews before 2009 articulated the theory, and McChrystal's COIN campaign was the most well-developed plan to implement it. But the plans on paper were rarely matched with the time, money, and troops they called for, at least not consistently, because of policymakers' lack of strategic patience and because of the nature of bureaucracy.[6]

For Chris Kolenda, the wars in Iraq and Afghanistan show the dangers of pursuing "decisive military victory." Kolenda is a firm advocate of the view that wars like Afghanistan cannot end in unconditional surrender; he argues that negotiations should have driven US strategy. But to succeed in

[5] Cordesman, "The Lessons of the Afghan War That No One Will Want to Learn," CSIS, June 15, 2022, 4, 7. www.csis.org/analysis/lessons-afghan-war-no-one-will-want-learn.

[6] Kilcullen and Mills, *The Ledger*, 53, 72–73, 266.

that kind of endeavor, policymakers need to end their "fixation" on decisive victory; decentralize decisions to an interagency command; and "right-size the military's role in the policy and strategy process." A major theme is policymakers' outsized concern with the military aspects of war in a way that crowded out discussion and scrutiny of diplomacy and reconstruction, which were the aspects of war concerned with long-term victory.[7]

Does process matter? At the outset of this project, I expected to conclude that the formal mechanisms of the interagency process and the NSC system had a lot to do with the failures of the war. My interviewees were essentially unanimous: the interagency process is terrible, especially for a complex operation like Afghanistan. "A slow-motion train wreck tragedy," is how Vikram Singh described the war and the decision-making process. It is odd, then, that the national security establishment unanimously pays ritual homage to Brent Scowcroft, national security advisor for George H. W. Bush and the architect of the modern interagency system. By all accounts, Scowcroft was a consummate professional who gave excellent advice to Bush about how to manage the end of the Cold War. But he also created and bequeathed to the government an interagency process and structure that has generally served us poorly for the past three and a half decades.[8]

That said, I'm not persuaded fixing the process guarantees better decision-making. "My caricature is that the Bush administration was policy without deliberation and the Obama administration was deliberation without policy," Ambassador Jim Dobbins quipped. But neither model guarantees success, and neither is solely responsible for failure. I'm temperamentally inclined toward more formal processes and structured debate – I'm a university professor who teaches graduate seminars – but I recognize there are times for decisive action and rapid decisions. I would only add: the Trump administration in its last two years was neither policy nor deliberation, and that does guarantee failure.[9]

I am also not persuaded that another strategy review is always the right answer. By my count, there were nine major reviews of Afghanistan strategy over twenty years. Many were necessary, and some were better than others, but some of them were a waste of time, a prolonged paperwork exercise, because what the war needed wasn't necessarily a new or better strategy, but more competent and serious execution (and more resources). "Instead of asking whether the problem lies in some mix of funding, procedures, and

[7] Kolenda, *Zero-Sum Victory*, 358–364.   [8] Singh, interview by author.
[9] Dobbins, interview by author.

troops – all of which would require additional money and people – to implement the strategy already decided, the search is launched for a new idea," Neumann wrote. "Ideas are more easily come by than money and soldiers ... In the Afghan case I believed that without fixing numerous problems of implementation, the search for new strategy would do little beyond absorb time and create overlapping organizations." Some strategy reviews actively harmed the process, omitted key issues, worsened tensions between the military and the civilians, and reinforced policymakers' mistaken beliefs and preformed judgments. "Strategy review" can be a beguiling name for "groupthink," or, worse, "pooled ignorance."[10]

I agree with many of these initial lessons from the war. I want to take the discussion one step further. In Chapter 1, I argued we lost the war because of habits of thinking refracted through the nature of bureaucracy. I want to expand on those themes by reflecting on the nature of strategy and the nature of bureaucracy. Together, they suggest culminating lessons about statesmanship and the art of statecraft.

STRATEGY

The central strategic question of the war – of any war – was about the relationship between ends, ways, and means. Even framing it that way, however, was a challenge. "The only professional group that does real strategy is the military," Lute reflected. Civilian policymakers almost entirely lack education or experience with strategic thinking. "There is a heavy burden on the military for strategy development," which meant that the military component of strategy got the most attention. The goal (or end) was never unclear: defeat al-Qaida, deny safe haven, and prevent future attacks. It was muddled by Bush's decision to call it a "war on terror." All four presidents prioritized killing terrorists, which is what the military is best at and which was important, but often came at the expense of the longer-term goals: denying safe haven and preventing future attacks.[11]

It was hand-wringing over those longer-term goals that engendered nine strategy reviews over twenty years. How do we deny safe haven without permanently garrisoning the Khyber Pass? How do we prevent future attacks without adopting a permanent state of war? The answer, as I have emphasized throughout this book, should have been nation building. Build an Afghan army to deny safe haven on their own. Build an Afghan government

---

[10] Neumann, *The Other War*, 168. [11] Lute, SIGAR interview.

to control that army. Invest in an ally in South Asia to help provide early warning of jihadists' activities in the region where they most closely interact and overlap. Nation building was the means; defeating al-Qaida, permanently denying safe haven, and ensuring they do not come back was the end.

Most policymakers understood this, at some level, which is why we did not leave Afghanistan in 2002. Bush admitted in his memoir that his opposition to nation building had been a mistake. Rumsfeld and Feith ruminate in their memoirs about the need to do more to help the Afghans so that the United States would not be on the hook forever. Obama understood and gave voice to the same ideas in his first strategy review. Biden, in the Senate, was a forceful and eloquent advocate for nation building. Many policymakers at various points throughout the war had the right strategic concept. "For those who might contend that we shouldn't have engaged in nation building, I would ask, once you have intervened as we did, how else do you help build the forces and capabilities that allow you to hand off crucial tasks – such as denying sanctuary to terrorists, securing the population and infrastructure, and running the country and its myriad institutions?" Petraeus asked. "Nation building was not just unavoidable; it was essential."[12]

But the concept was imperfectly and inconsistently articulated, lacked widespread buy-in, and did not impose a sense of prioritization among its component parts. At some level, the debate wasn't *whether or not* to do nation building, but *how much* and *which parts*. The Afghan army was obviously necessary. Was the Ministry of Women's Affairs? Building roads was clearly necessary. Were rural medical clinics? These are legitimate questions, and there should have been a whole-of-government, interagency plan answering these questions. But the civilian policymakers' narrow focus on the military component of American strategy left the civilian component adrift.

Absent a coherent strategy, two imperatives collided. The military impulse is to do as much as possible, as quickly as possible, for as long as possible. As soon as a generation of military officers internalized the logic of counterinsurgency – the military counterpart to nation building – they pushed to do as much as possible for as long as possible, which is how we got the surge, COIN doctrine, $150 billion of reconstruction assistance, and a twenty-year war. That is why we had the seeming oddity of military officers like Petraeus and McChrystal, as well as Pentagon leaders like Gates and Carter, pushing for more nation building than many civilians.

Against the military impulse was the impulse from the Office of Management and Budget, from Congress, and from politicians more

---

[12] Petraeus, "Afghanistan Did Not Have to Turn Out This Way," *The Atlantic*, August 8, 2022.

concerned with polling than with victory in war – to say nothing of the opposition from "realists" who thought nation building and counterinsurgency were intrinsically impossible no matter the number of troops and amount of money thrown at it. The impulse from this crowd was to do as little as possible for as short a time as possible. Even the ones who bought into the logic of nation building wanted to do it on the cheap, quickly, and surgically targeted at select parts of the state. They wanted to conserve resources and give to the war the minimum amount needed to kill al-Qaida and maybe avert a collapse of the new Afghan government, but not much more. Their impulse is how we got years of neglect in the Bush administration, the withdrawal timetable from Obama, a premature judgment to abandon counterinsurgency, the Doha agreement from Trump, and the withdrawal from Biden. Every one of those decisions was rationalized as a necessary concession to the constraints of time or money. By that route policymakers rationalized themselves into defeat.

The question of *how much* nation building is an important discussion to have. My inclination is with the military: do everything and surge from day one. When you are sending troops to kill, fight, and die, you give them everything they need and more. You don't go to war on a shoestring budget. If it is important enough to go to war over, it is worth spending the money on. There is, of course, a risk in the "do everything" approach. Gates was right: the war effort did need a stronger sense of prioritization among its many component parts. I would simply want to err on the side of doing too much rather than too little.

But instead of engaging with this debate, critics like Gates regularly refuted a straw man when they explained that we couldn't turn Afghanistan into a rich-world paradise or a "Central Asian Valhalla" or a "Jeffersonian democracy." Trump and Biden grew almost clownish in their ritual denunciations of nation building, as if that were a relevant talking point years after we had given up such aspirations. Tony Blinken, the secretary of state, in explaining Biden's decision to withdraw, claimed that "somewhere along the way, with the best of intentions, we also sought to remake the country and, in effect, to use military force to remake another society."[13] It was the Afghans who decided at Bonn in 2001 to readopt their own democratic constitution of 1964.

Critics complained about the excessive zeal of American nation building efforts, but the problem was not that we did too much, but that, at first,

---

[13] Senate Foreign relations Committee, "The US Withdrawal from Afghanistan," April 27, 2021, 47.

we did too little. The United States did almost no nation building for the first five years. For the next five years, when we did try, we were too late and too rushed and put ourselves under unrealistic deadlines. Then, we abruptly gave up and reverted to a pared-down counterterrorism mission that Obama and Trump sustained for the rest of the war. Michael O'Hanlon of the Brookings Institution has it right. "We varied our strategy and effort too much over the years, largely ignoring Afghanistan at first, then rushing a surge to try to make up for lost time. Ultimately, once we had a sustainable strategy we then pulled the plug altogether very quickly – and unnecessarily."[14] On balance, with foreign aid and nation building, earlier, lower, slower, and longer is better than later, faster, bigger, and shorter.

Terminology contributes to the problem. When people think of "nation building" they think of abstractions like national identity and social cohesion, and they rightly argue that outsiders cannot build those things for the Afghans. Fortunately, Afghans had a robust sense of national identity already – arguably stronger than most postcolonial states whose borders were drawn by imperial whim. In academic circles, scholars prefer to talk about "state building" or "reconstruction" or "stability operations" to indicate a more limited aspiration to rebuild functioning governing institutions and to restore public order, which is what the international project in Afghanistan aimed at, and it was certainly realistic.

There are reams of scholarly work, including my own, on what causes success or failure in development, foreign aid, and stability and reconstruction operations.[15] As a dutiful scholar, my answer is: "it depends." It's easier to build discrete institutions with specified functions, like a central bank, and to rebuild physical infrastructure, like roads and power lines. It is much harder to build systems, like the judicial system, much less abstractions, like the rule of law. Building an army and police force fall in between; they are discrete institutions, but they are large, involve tens of thousands of people, and require a combination of hard and soft skills. We succeeded in building a light infantry force capable of defeating the Taliban in any tactical situation. We succeeded in building Afghan special forces that might have been the rival of our own. We failed to build a rural police force that could handle land disputes and drug traffickers. Kilcullen, summarizing decades of scholarship and experience, argues that reconstruction efforts "need to be more consultative than prescriptive, they need to be organic rather than based on a template, political not technical, less quantitative than qualitative, and

---

14 O'Hanlon, "Preliminary Verdict."   15 Miller, *Armed State Building.*

strategically intentioned rather than simply tactically focused."[16] This would have been a helpful focus of discussions. Instead, it too often deteriorated into caricatured talking points about how impossible it is to make Afghanistan into a "Jeffersonian democracy."

Why didn't we get this right? Nation building is messy, abstract, hard to measure, frustrating, and feels only indirectly relevant to American security because it was the ways and means, not the end. It's no fun, it's not sexy, and policymakers don't like overseeing it. By contrast, killing terrorists is easy to understand, gives an immediate measure of success, seems more "realistic," and is directly relevant to American security. It is also glamorous – think of all the spy and war movies and TV shows from the past twenty years – and bureaucrats in charge of counterterrorism are powerful, influential people. You can vicariously be a member of SEAL Team 6 playing *Call of Duty: Modern Warfare* on PlayStation; there are no videos games starring the administrator of the US Agency for International Development. *Zero Dark Thirty* is a prestigious Oscar-nominated war drama about the hunt for bin Laden and the Abbottabad raid, while the most prominent show set during the Afghan counterinsurgency campaign – the Netflix show *War Machine* – is a bumbling, poorly made satire.

John Brennan, who served as the director of the National Counterterrorism Center and later as the CIA director, described the various efforts as concentric circles: counterterrorism in the middle, counterinsurgency the next circle out, and nation building the furthest. I found his discussion of the relationship between them illuminating. Here is the Obama administration's senior-most official responsible for combating terrorist groups across the globe sharing his frustration that counterterrorism undermined counterinsurgency and nation building.

> I was putting counterterrorism in the center because that was the most specific and the least complicated of the objectives. Not that it wasn't difficult to achieve, but it was defined, it was known what we were doing there. Counterinsurgency was a much more challenging, difficult, complex undertaking. And nation building, more amorphous than any ... I put CT in the middle just because it is easier to cabin its targets, its goals, its objectives. And I think it was easier to assess progress ... But what frustrated me, I think, throughout my career was too often CT came at the expense of the other efforts ... It's maybe easier to do, and the effort, attention, energy, resources are dedicated to it because you can measure its success more readily than the others.

---

[16] Kilcullen and Mills, *The Ledger*, 89.

Brennan shared an anecdote about US efforts to work with Yemeni security forces to combat terrorists. The US could train individual soldiers in tactical skills, but trainers found it was pointless so long as Yemen remained a failed state. But no one wanted to talk about capacity building or civilian–military relations or human resources management. "Those were things that were not seen as the really attractive things to do," Brennan said. "The institutional flaws of these host government services led people to take the more expedient path that was more satisfying and cathartic," that is, direct kinetic operations to kill or capture terrorists. The other route involved "winning the hearts and minds and other things," but those operations "are more difficult to measure. And I think for a lot of folks in the intelligence community, as well as in the military, they're less attractive. They're less exciting."[17]

Policymakers are human; they drift toward what is easiest, what is comprehensible, what is countable, and what is glamorous. They could also tell themselves that killing terrorists was the goal, the whole reason we were there in the first place, which was true. But that created strategic pathologies. Every administration prioritized short-term, immediate counterterrorism operations, even when they actively hurt long-term reconstruction or state-building operations that were also necessary to make victory permanent. That is why the United States ended up fighting a forever war, and why we ultimately failed. For the bulk of the twenty-year war, we successfully killed terrorists without addressing the broader social, cultural, and political context from which they sprang. We ended up with a pile of dead terrorists, the Taliban back in power, and al-Qaida given room to reconstitute. That is the fruit of the "realistic," "counterterrorism-only" strategy. We are gone, but the context remains, and so do the terrorists. The critics of nation building got their way, and we lost the war.

The main intellectual error was confusing ends with ways and means. Because countering terrorists was the end, policymakers felt that killing terrorists had to be the ways and means. It sounds obvious and intuitive, but – like children playing chess – it is a childish strategy. Soldiers on the ground even mocked the CT-only strategy as "mowing the grass," a Sisyphean effort that showed success for a day until the grass grew back. Nation building is treating the lawn, not mowing the grass. It is landscaping the yard, not endlessly weeding the same patch of ground. Nation building was not a distraction, mission creep, or charity. It was the necessary and essential means for long-term victory, and four presidents' neglect of it accounts for our defeat.

---

[17] Brennan, interview by author.

BUREAUCRACY

"Amateurs talk strategy, professionals talk logistics," General Omar Bradley once said. As big as the problems were with the overall strategy in Afghanistan, it was only the beginning of what went wrong. Strategy is just words on paper until you translate it into specific orders and tasks to various departments and agencies, each authorized and funded by a line item in a budget. Those departments and agencies are the implementers, the people and institutions that perform the actions that make up US foreign policy. Even when policymakers in Washington got the words on paper right, getting those people and those institutions to do the thing that policymakers wanted them to do proved extraordinarily difficult. The behavior of bureaucracy and the logistics of implementation are another plotline in the story of America's defeat.

Bush liked to say that, as president, he was "the Decider." He's half-right: the president is ultimately responsible for the decisions he makes. But Bush's moniker implies that, once a decision is made, the issue is off the president's plate and into the hands of the implementers while the president moves on to the next heroic decision. The president is not only the decider-in-chief but also the chief executive officer, responsible for overseeing the operations of the executive branch. The president appropriately delegates most of this to cabinet secretaries and on downward to deputy, assistant, and under-secretaries. But war, statecraft, and diplomacy are, by their nature, intera-gency affairs that require an integrated perspective that no cabinet secretary has.

Lute summarized the prevailing model: "Make the decision, record it in a summary of conclusions, roll it out in a presidential speech or some variant to that path, and then presume that the government is going to implement itself." The model is broken. "It doesn't work like that. There's a huge gap between decision making and decision implementation." War is among the most complex and difficult things that governments under-take. Presidents cannot hand off oversight to anyone else, not even the national security advisor. "It's very difficult for a president in the modern age to have the bandwidth and [to] focus on one problem when there's so many other issues, economic, social, political issues going on," Peter Lavoy said. "They just don't really have the time and attention to deal with this."[18]

---

[18] Lute and Lavoy, interviews by author.

But that failure of focus and bandwidth is a fault of executive management, not a function of the problem itself. Among the four presidents, Bush – a two-term Texas governor – was the most experienced in executive leadership. He made his share of mistakes, but a constitutional lawyer, a real-estate developer, and a lifetime senator fared no better. Presidents must impose focus on themselves first, and then onto the discussion around them. Winston Churchill is famous as a good orator, but he was also an administrator, immersed in the details and overflowing with paperwork. In wartime, presidents must be immersed in the details; they must become experts in their wars.

"Practicalities involve details, and details are not sexy. Details are not for heroes and visionaries. They are gladly left to the career bureaucrats," Dov Zakheim wrote. "This attitude pervades the Washington policy community."[19] Ambassador Roland Neumann agreed. "Implementation strikes me as so often a key piece that our academic discussions don't pay enough attention to," he told me, and he wrote in his book that "making policy without paying attention to implementation is a bit like sailing near reefs without a lookout." Much of his book is a case study in navigating, using, and overcoming bureaucracy to get things done.

> The business of moving from ideas to shaping government action is fascinating. It is a far more incremental matter than it is one of laying out a grand idea and having everyone jump up and salute. Real policymaking isn't like that. Rather, one has to start talking and writing, use conversations to build alliances, shift the specifics of ideas to incorporate the thoughts of others, and take advantage of opportunities to move forward. In this way, what starts as a limited conception of one or a few persons gradually becomes the accepted common wisdom, lacking specific authorship (which some would resist) and more a matter that everyone sees as obvious and needing action. It is absorbing work and an endless study of human nature.[20]

That's how it should work. But there was a persistent "unseriousness" to America's war in Afghanistan, especially to implementation, in Eliot Cohen's words. Cohen dismissed questions about strategy and argued that the United States' main problems were with implementation. I disagree – there were plenty of big strategic errors – but Cohen is correct that even if we got the strategy right, something else was amiss. Cohen does not mean that

---

[19] Zakheim, *A Vulcan's Tale*, 2.
[20] Neumann, *The Other War*, xii, 135, and interview by author.

we were unserious about Afghanistan because of Iraq – because he thinks we were unserious about Iraq too. "The federal government was just not serious about waging these wars," he said, "The question is [about] the quality of the people who are conducting the fight and the willingness and ability of the institutions to adapt to the challenges that they faced. And we were lacking that." The United States fought much larger wars in the past and did not find them prohibitively complex. The invasion of Normandy in World War II involved more troops in a single day than were ever deployed during the entire war in Afghanistan, and they undertook the most complex and largest amphibious assault ever attempted in history.[21]

I think of Quinn's anecdote about the State Department's inability to buy helicopters for the counternarcotics effort (Chapter 6). I find it remarkable – not to say baffling and infuriating – that helicopter procurement defeated the United States. The problem was not limited to helicopters, or the counternarcotics effort, or the State Department. I heard similar anecdotes from too many people relating to different eras of the war and different agencies and departments. Feith made a related point when recalling the funding and authorities for training the Afghan army and police in 2002 and 2003. "Linking up the spending authorities was an administrative nightmare that consumed many weeks. Waiting for funding and managing the paperwork exasperated our forces," he wrote. "The task of quickly creating an army from scratch for a newly liberated country – afflicted by political instability and ongoing violence – was a hard enough assignment without having to maneuver through the legal intricacies of a hodgepodge funding apparatus."[22]

Among those scores of bureaucracies at work in Afghanistan, one stood out: the US military. Because the military controlled the overwhelming majority of resources, "it is hardly surprising that military considerations became predominant," according to Bob Komer, the author of the Vietnam-era reflection on bureaucracy. "Military aid proved the line of least resistance."[23] The US military and the intelligence community are the richest and most powerful collections of bureaucracies on earth. That makes them the most professional, the most capable, and therefore the tool that policymakers reach for most often, whether they are the most appropriate tool or not. The 2009 strategy review focused almost exclusively on the military surge to the exclusion of the civilian surge or a diplomatic strategy. After the 2014 transition, the war became nothing but rote military

---

[21] Cohen, interview by author.   [22] Feith, *War and Decision*, 151.

[23] Komer, *Bureaucracy Does Its Thing*, 38.

activity – mowing the grass, killing insurgents, training the Afghan army – with almost no serious civilian counterpart. US foreign policy is overmilitarized not because of a secret plot by the military to box in presidents but because it is the only bureaucracy that Congress adequately funds.

The intelligence community, though it shared in the military's primacy in budgets and strategic considerations, was not always on target. "The kinds of intelligence most needed in Vietnam were simply alien to the standard institutional repertoires of most US and [Vietnamese] intelligence services involved," Komer wrote. That remains true; the intelligence community knows how to study large, conventional opponents like the Soviet Union or, today, China, but was playing catch-up against tribal insurgents and terrorist networks. "We focused on order of battle and neglected insurgent infrastructure," Komer said.[24] Studying insurgencies and nations requires a different kind of knowledge, one focused on people, history, culture, and religion. The intelligence community improved dramatically in this respect, though it took four or five years to get there.[25] But the US national security establishment broadly – especially the State Department – is still intellectually hamstrung, stuck in an epistemic bubble defined by the norms of elite, secular, professional institutionalism. They have a very hard time understanding that most of the world is not like them.

The State Department was perhaps the most maddening actor. State "made no effort to assert managerial primacy, to control our military effort on political grounds," Komer wrote. In theory, the State Department is the senior US agency on the ground overseas, and it is the voice of overall US policy – which means that it should have been the advocate for long-term American goals (denying safe haven permanently) and the strategy required to achieve them (nation building), over against the military's short-sighted counterterrorism operations. But in Vietnam, State was guilty of "near-abdication of any executive responsibility for the US effort." In Afghanistan, Ambassador Bill Wood felt that "the State Department managed to spectacularly not step up to the challenge."[26]

On paper, because State is the lead civilian agency of the US government overseas, it should have been the lead nation builder, or at least the main

---

[24] Komer, *Bureaucracy Does Its Thing*, 59.

[25] This was a major theme of a 2010 report, "Fixing Intel: A Blueprint for Making Intelligence Relevant in Afghanistan" (CNAS, 2010). The report is quite good, despite the later activities and reputation of its author, General Michael Flynn, after his retirement.

[26] Komer, *Bureaucracy Does Its Thing*, 61. Wood, interview by author.

coordinator of nation-building efforts. But the State Department is not a nation-building agency. "The Department of State is supposed to lead reconstruction efforts, but it lacked the expertise and resources to take the lead and own the strategy in Afghanistan," according to the special inspector general for Afghanistan reconstruction. It is perhaps unfair to blame State for failing to do something that it simply does not do, like blaming your toddler for not doing the grocery shopping or graduating from college. "Vietnam further demonstrates that the way in which an organization will use its existing capabilities is governed largely by its own internal goals, performance standards, and measurement and incentive systems," Komer wrote, "even when these conflict with the role it is assigned." None of the State Department's internal goals, incentives, or missions lined up with the task of counterinsurgency or nation building. You can't expect, and should not trust, a bureaucracy to do something it is not set up to do because, "a hallmark of bureaucracy is reluctance to change accepted ways of doing things. Bureaucrats prefer to deal with the familiar," Komer wrote, "It is more comfortable and convenient to continue following tested routines, whereas to change may be to admit prior error – a cardinal bureaucratic sin." Some scholars and policymakers have suggested reforms – Ambassador Tony Wayne suggested creating a specialized "cone" in the State Department's career tracks to recognize service in expeditionary environments – and Rice and her successors made some efforts to change those incentive structures (changing performance evaluation standards, for example) though it seems, as always, to have been too little, too late.[27]

There are three possible responses to the nature of bureaucracy. First, you can try to force the bureaucracy to change and do the novel, difficult mission it is not prepared to do, in full knowledge of how difficult and maddening it will be. That is what Bush did with the surge in Iraq, and that example illustrates just how hard and rare it is and how much bandwidth it takes. It requires constant accountability, and it is exhausting and inefficient. Presidents typically can only do this for one issue in their entire presidency. Bush chose Iraq; Obama chose health care; Trump chose nothing; and Biden claimed he had no choice at all.

The second response is to create a new bureaucracy. Some observers called for a permanent, standing, nation-building agency. A new nation-building bureaucracy is probably not the right answer because there are not enough nation-building emergencies to keep such an agency occupied (more likely, it would find excuses to get involved in any failed state,

---

[27] Komer, *Bureaucracy Does Its Thing*, 65, 15–16. SIGAR, "What We Need to Learn," VIII.

anywhere, whether it is relevant to American security). Bush tried to create a Civilian Response Corps of volunteer civilians who would be mobilized in case of a nation-building emergency; it was later killed by budget cuts.

More intriguingly, McChrystal's vision for ISAF, as I understand it, was to turn it into a custom-tailored institution for counterinsurgency and the chief node in a network for nation building. McChrystal had read Komer's report on bureaucracy, handed it around to his team, and (like Petraeus) made a study of American performance in the Vietnam War.[28] That is why his first recommendation was to change ISAF's "operational culture," to focus less on itself and more on the Afghan people. McChrystal's vision for ISAF was almost certainly the best chance at changing the dynamic of bureaucracy and, coupled with his counterinsurgency strategy, the best opportunity to win the war. It probably would have taken a half-decade to fully mature, well beyond Obama's timetable.

The third response is to accept the limits of bureaucracy, which also means accepting the bureaucracy's primacy in defining the goal. If you can't fight or replace the bureaucracy, it will assert its ability to redefine your intent. That is what the US chose in Afghanistan. Bush focused on Iraq, which means the bureaucracy ran Afghanistan. "In Iraq we do what we must," which meant that Bush forced his vision on the bureaucracy, but "in Afghanistan we do what we can," which meant that the administration allowed bureaucratic inertia to take its course. The 2006 strategy review succeeded in redefining the strategy and pushing bureaucratic inertia in a different and better direction, but with the president's attention still focused on Iraq, the bureaucracy simply absorbed and appropriated the new direction to show activity with little progress on a larger budget. Obama changed bureaucratic incentives in a different way, with his withdrawal timetable. The worst effect of the timetable, aside from undermining negotiations with the Taliban, was how it skewed bureaucratic incentives. The goal was not victory; it was withdrawal. There was no incentive to think or plan beyond one or two years. Even as Obama poured billions of dollars into reconstruction efforts, bureaucratic autopilot was set to the timetable, and other considerations fell by the wayside. Obama seems not to have considered the managerial implications of his timetable. Trump's negotiations with the Taliban had the same effect.

In Chapter 4, I conceded that this is the most powerful argument against nation building: we are incompetent. "Everybody was doing things they didn't know how to do because nation building is something that no

---

[28] McChrystal, email to author, July 28, 2023.

agency is structured to do," said Ambassador James Dobbins, one of the foremost champions of nation building and author of a handful of studies on the subject. Critics of nation building treat that as the final word on the subject. I respond: what is the alternative? The alternative in Afghanistan was to give in to the nature of bureaucracy – and look how that turned out. Critics of nation building defend their stance as one of "realism," of accepting the constraints of reality. In a sense they are right: they are accepting what our bureaucracy is presently capable of doing.

But I believe the "realists" have drastically underestimated what we can change. McChrystal's approach was an effort to change that part of reality, to create an institution tailored to our national security needs, and it was premised on the belief that we could do that, that we could win the war. Do we want our abilities – our incompetent bureaucracy – to define our national interests? Or should we go the other way around: start with our national interest and go get the abilities we lack? "I do not buy into the 'graveyard of empires' argument that said we couldn't have done it, because I think that's a dodge, it's an excuse that lets us off the hook, because we can say that it was impossible," McChrystal concluded.

STATESMANSHIP

Some common themes emerge from these lessons about strategy and bureaucracy. For the most part, our policymakers did not lack for intelligence, credentials, hard work, patriotism, or goodwill. But in addition to all those, the statesman, stateswoman, and strategist also need wisdom to take the long view; prudence to discern what is practical; persistence and fortitude in implementation; courage to overcome groupthink pride, and bureaucratic resistance; and temperance and humility to toil in unglamorous details. Above all, the strategist must have a passion to pursue justice and peace. These are character traits, not educational credentials or textbook lessons. The solution to our endemic problems with poor decision-making begins but does not end with more classroom learning. Statesmen and stateswomen need wisdom, courage, temperance, and justice.

Wisdom. I am reminded of Reinhold Niebuhr's serenity prayer. "God grant me the serenity to accept the things I cannot change, courage to change the things I can, and the wisdom to know the difference." In the American foreign policy landscape, self-styled "realists" have too much serenity and not enough courage: they tend to overestimate the things they cannot change. Liberal internationalists and so-called neoconservatives have an excess of courage and not enough serenity: they tend to overestimate the things they can change. It's the wisdom to know the difference that policymakers need. Bush overestimated what he could change when he launched a second war before finishing the first. He underestimated what he could and should change by avoiding nation building. Obama, similarly, lost sight of what he could change when he lost faith in his counterinsurgency strategy – but also overestimated what he could change under an arbitrary and public withdrawal timetable. Trump overestimated his ability to change the Taliban's strategic calculus; Biden underestimated his ability to stop their march to Kabul. In every case, they judged wrongly about what they could change and what they couldn't. They lacked wisdom.

Strategy is hard. It demands almost impossible levels of knowledge, judgment, and foresight. Policymakers must know a lot about the part of the world they are working in. The lowest levels in the bureaucracy know the most because they can specialize; the higher one ascends, the greater responsibility and breadth one has, but the less one is able to know about everything within one's purview. The most senior decision-makers are, by definition, the most ignorant. "While the president's foreign policy team collectively brought with them decades of experience, none of the princi-pals and very few senior presidential appointees had a feel for the histories, cultures, and emotions that drove the politics of the broader Muslim world," Zalmay Khalilzad wrote in his memoir. Years later, Ambassador Neumann made a similar observation. "I found people badly informed about the reality of the situation; the public personalities were shockingly so."[29]

But more than knowledge, policymakers need mature judgment, what Aristotle called "prudence" or "practical wisdom," a knack for knowing how to navigate the world, for discerning what works and what doesn't. You only get this kind of judgment through long experience in your field. This is what the best senior policymakers bring to the table, and it is why they are the right people to make big decisions despite their relative ignorance about specific crises; they compensate for their lack of knowledge with the good judgment to listen to a wide range of advisors. The best decisions emerge from a dialogue between the junior specialist and the senior generalist. The specialist brings a granularity of expertise; the generalist brings a wider perspective and maturity of judgment.

The best shortcut to good judgment – and to a healthy foundation of expertise and knowledge – is to read history, which is where American foreign policymakers tend to be glaringly deficient. Reading history is

---

[29] Khalilzad, *The Envoy*, Kindle location 2078. Neumann, *The Other War*, 170.

vicarious experience. When you read history, you benefit from the mistakes others have made. You go through the process of thinking through a decision in the moment, along with the historical actors. Read enough history and you develop the feel for what works, the knack or instinct or sixth sense that helps you know when an idea passes the smell test and when it does not. Withdrawal deadlines, for example, do not pass the smell test. But reading history also helps you gain some degree of empathy with even bad decisions and so come to understand how you yourself could make the same mistakes. Reading history induces humility. Reading history broadens your horizons and breaks you out of the groupthink of your decade, your generation, and the small group of professors and scholars you happen to have taken classes from or whose books you read in college.

I do not mean, when a crisis happens, you should skim one or two books and a clutch of articles on the internet. That is how a generation of policy-makers and pundits learned to say "graveyard of empires" and congratulate themselves on becoming sophisticated students of Asian lore. A little knowledge of history is almost worse than none; it gives you a dangerous level of confidence without the competence to back it up. "No one in Washington knows anything about Afghanistan," Richard Holbrooke once told a colleague. "And what they do know is mostly wrong."[30] Laurel Miller warned against not only ignorance, but our ignorance about our own ignorance. She warned about "the failure to appreciate how little the conditions were understood and, therefore, the lack of a firm basis for confidence." America exhibits a grand strategic Dunning-Kruger effect: the least competent have the most confidence because we aren't even aware of how little we know and thus have no reason for humility. "Recognize how much you do not know," Miller told Congress.[31] Despite the widespread mockery he earned for it, Rumsfeld was correct to warn against the "unknown unknowns." Steeping yourself in history should convince you of your own ignorance, not give you punchy talking points for your next media appearance. It should be about crafting what Eliot Cohen calls "the historical mind," not mining the past for tidbits to use in debate.[32]

Courage. It takes courage to take the long view. "We're an impatient culture. We want things done now," Ronald Neumann observed. That was reflected in the military's planning process. "It's a back-planning process

---

[30] Packer, *Our Man*, 444.

[31] Miller, "Afghanistan 2001–2021." www.crisisgroup.org/asia/south-asia/afghanistan/afghanistan-2001-2021-us-policy-lessons-learned.

[32] Cohen, "The Historical Mind."

from the end state" that demands specific, measurable, concrete objectives. But "what if your end state is 20 years out there and vague? . . . That doesn't fit in the planning process." A generation of consultants and MBAs sold the government on emulating the private sector. But the private sector is driven by quarterly earnings reports and daily ups-and-downs of share prices. The public interest does not have quarterly earnings and cannot be reduced to a single dollar value that fluctuates on a daily or hourly basis. We cannot measure progress in war by counting corpses or balancing budgets. The defeat of an insurgent network, a terrorist group, or – hardest of all – a totalitarian ideology will have milestones, like the Taliban's 2001 fall from power or bin Laden's death in 2011. But real victory looks different: as the front cover of *The Economist* memorably challenged after the Abbottabad raid, "Now, Kill His Dream." Nazism wasn't defeated only by the fall of Berlin, but by the long slow process of denazification and building German democracy over the following generation.[33]

Such efforts take time, something our enemies know. "If you look at the Taliban, or look at al-Qaida, or another enemy like that, where they say, 'Hey, we're going to win. I don't care if it takes a hundred years, I don't care if it kills all of us and our kids and our kids' kids, that's what we're going to do,'" Stan McChrystal reflected, "we can't even comprehend that anymore. We can't get our minds around it, and if we could, we'd be much more effective." It takes courage to face up to the reality of such a challenge, and it takes wisdom to think about foreign policy over a much, much longer timeframe, something that American strategic culture undermines. "For far too long, and with far too few exceptions, American policymakers of both parties and all political philosophies have been shackled to their in-boxes," Zakheim wrote. "Their focus is on the immediate, the must-do; they devote little time to considering the long-term consequences of their short-term policies."[34]

The US managed to win World War II without email, PowerPoint, or video teleconferences, and without the relentless, never-ending-news-cycle sense of urgency they reinforce – and hasn't won a war since those technologies became ubiquitous. Ryan Crocker testified to the US Congress that "there is a single overarching problem that is at the root of what we have seen in Afghanistan and elsewhere. It is the failure on our part to demonstrate strategic patience."[35] David Petraeus agreed. "Our foundational

---

[33] Neumann, interview by author.

[34] McChrystal, interview by author. Zakheim, *A Vulcan's Tale*, 170–171.

[35] Crocker, "Afghanistan 2001–2021." https://carnegieendowment.org/2021/11/17/afg hanistan-2001-2021-US-policy-lessons-learned-pub-85814.

mistake was our lack of commitment," he said. "We never adopted a sufficient, consistent, overarching approach that we stuck with from administration to administration, or even within individual administrations."

In some sense, we do need grandiose aspirations and Churchillian vision – not to achieve in time for the next election, but as guiding principles, as orienting frameworks, as the basic polestar toward which we patiently steer the ship of state decade after decade. We need them because we need inspiration to persist in the day-to-day grind against bureaucratic inertia, enemy violence, and everyday realities. When Thomas Jefferson described America as an "Empire of Liberty" and John F. Kennedy pledged to "pay any price" to "secure the survival and success of liberty," it was grandiose and even hubristic, but it also gave coherence and consistency to America's role in the world. It takes a kind of intellectual courage to formulate and articulate that kind of vision against the resistance of naysayers and "realists." The words are aspirational, but aspiration is how we challenge ourselves to strive and persist when success seems distant. Bush's Marshall Plan speech, Obama's Nobel Lecture, portions of Trump's 2017 Afghanistan speech, and most of Biden's senatorial orations on Afghanistan approached this, but each backed off for different reasons.

Temperance. At the same time, the strategist needs humility to engage in the daily grind of implementation. Implementation is boring, thankless, and unglamorous. It takes humility, patience, discipline, and perseverance to get it right. Another word for the right virtue is temperance: the moderation of one's appetites. You must temper your pride, impatience, and eagerness for the limelight. "The politics of high policymaking is sexy, alluring, and magnetic," Zakheim wrote. "The politics of implementation, of translating intentions into reality, on the other hand, is hard." Policymakers most concerned with headlines and history books focus their attention on the sexy and magnetic stuff. Grinding into the details requires you to temper that urge, impose humility and patience on yourself. If you are a glutton for excitement, fame, or power, you will fail at implementation.

"Any plan for the longer term must of necessity include a plan of implementation. Implementation is something policymakers consistently prefer to leave to others, however, without clarifying who those others might be or how they might obtain the necessary resources to carry out the plan," Zakheim wrote. "Such an attitude is disastrous in the context of conducting an American occupation overseas." Zakheim is right to describe that as an "attitude." It is not an intellectual error so much as a characteristic or habit of being dismissive about details. I see this in my students' attitude toward research. Because all knowledge is already known, catalogued and ready on the internet, there is no need for them to have it in their brains. They'll Google when they need to know something but otherwise can't be bothered with the details. That attitude is equal parts ignorant and arrogant – and when applied to grand strategy, catastrophic.[36]

To implement policy well, policymakers must know about the US government's capabilities, budget process, legal authorities and restrictions, and history. Getting all that knowledge is the point of graduate school, and there is another book to be written about how the shortcomings of American higher education threaten the foundations of American national security. But I am also struck by policymakers' ignorance of the history of US policy and strategy; that is, they weren't just ignorant about Afghanistan, they were ignorant about what the United States did or did not do in the recent past, such details passing beneath their notice. That ignorance hurt their ability to think through what worked and what didn't, and thus to make good decisions in the present. Each new administration came into office with only the vaguest, most caricatured understanding of what the United States had been trying to do in Afghanistan earlier in the war, shaped by the media's shallow and context-free reporting, and rarely took time to understand.

For example, I am struck by how universally Trump administration officials justified their positions by invoking a false or incomplete version of history. That's clearly true with Trump, who never had a close relationship with truth or history. But Pompeo and Esper did so as well when they said Doha was something new after twenty years of trying the same thing and failing. They should have known better: the United States did not persist in a single strategy for the duration of the war. O'Brien argued Trump was right to stop "trying to turn Afghanistan into Sweden," when Obama had abandoned nation building almost a decade earlier. Even Bolton, the most experienced foreign policy professional among them, did the same when he rejected the 2017 approach. "It was based on an argument that had been repeated for twenty years," he said, arguing that if it hadn't worked by then, it would not do so now.[37]

The irony is that Bolton's preferred strategy – ignore nation building and focus on counterterrorism – is what Obama and Trump had endorsed for a decade. "The strategy should have been, we're not going to solve the question in Afghanistan," Bolton said. "We're not going to defeat the Taliban, but we're going to bring a sufficient measure of stability with an adequate ongoing counterterrorism presence so we can prevent what we're mostly concerned with, which is terrorist attacks on the United States." That

---

[36] Zakheim, *A Vulcan's Tale*, 294, 171, 2.   [37] Bolton, interview by author.

was the United States' strategy for the second half of the war. Bolton could have been quoting Obama, Trump, or Biden.[38]

It is cliché to observe American policymakers' ignorance about Afghanistan. That's true, but it only scratches the surface of their historical amnesia. US policymakers did not even know the history of their own decisions. It wasn't so much that the left hand and the right hand did not know what each other were doing – though that was true – as it was the case that the left and right hands of today had no awareness of what they had done yesterday and acted as if they needed to reinvent everything from scratch, every day. Policymakers regularly used their faulty understanding to prematurely reject policies before they had a chance to prove success and to justify increasingly erratic and irresponsible experiments in foreign policy.

Here is where character and temperance come into play. Historical amnesia is not simply a function of ignorance; it is often born of a presumptuous confidence that the past does not matter. Just as wisdom and humility seem to go together, so do their opposites. The difference between good and bad strategic thinking and decision-making rarely has anything to do with Republican or Democrat and is only partly a function of intelligence or education. It seems to require a combination of intellectual curiosity, personal humility, and stubborn courage. You have to ask questions, lots of them, to the point of impertinence and annoyance, to get at an issue from all sides and to whatever degree of depth is possible. Rumsfeld, in particular, was good at that, and most of the participants in most of the strategy reviews did it well enough. But, unlike Rumsfeld, you must ask with humility, with genuine understanding of your own need to learn, in a way that allows the other participants to learn from the dialogue. Arrogant policymakers are poison to strategic deliberation, which is why the strategic thinker also needs stubborn courage. While they need humility about their own judgments, they need to confront and forcefully (but professionally) challenge other policymakers' ignorance, arrogance, groupthink, complacency, or cognitive bias.

Humility and temperance are the rarest virtues in Washington. Hubris ruins policymaking. Rumsfeld was extraordinarily intelligent, driven, knowledgeable, and detail-oriented. As the secretary of defense in the aftermath of the Vietnam War, he should have been the ideal candidate to oversee the department again during two counterinsurgencies. That he failed is a flawless illustration of another truth: intelligence and hard work are not enough. Everyone working at senior levels of government is intelligent and

---

[38] Bolton, interview by author.

highly credentialed. Rumsfeld did not lack insight; he lacked humility. He was hardly the only one. Trump had Rumsfeld's arrogance with none of the brilliance, drive, or expertise. Obama had a self-assurance reinforced by an admiring media and by his dramatic and rapid ascent to the White House. Biden had the self-confidence of a lifetime politician validated by getting elected and reelected for fifty years.

I am not suggesting that moral failure always leads to strategic failure, like a morality play or Greek tragedy. Arrogance drives failure through specific causal mechanisms. Arrogant policymakers make judgments and decisions by themselves; they lack the wisdom, refinement, and accountability gained through debate with others. Arrogant policymakers are intellectually blind, certain of their own judgments such that listening to others is a waste of time. They fall prey to groupthink in a group of one. They are isolated and unable to learn from or even recognize their mistakes. They ultimately makes themselves a fool.

Justice. Finally, it takes personal integrity and a passion for justice to simply care enough. "We almost never took this war seriously enough," General David Barno told me. "There just wasn't any real concern that if we don't do this right, we're going to pay a high penalty . . . I don't think that we actually ever worried about losing the war in Afghanistan." Except for occasional bursts of attention in 2001, 2009, and 2017, there was rarely a sense of urgency, a felt need to get things right *or else.* "I think we don't believe that losing carries the cost that it does," McChrystal said. "I was really surprised that nobody gave a damn about Afghanistan when I got into the administration," H. R. McMaster told me.[39]

I have a strange mixture of admiration and contempt for the American policymaker. When I think of the scores of colleagues I worked with and talked to over the decades about Afghanistan, I admire the public-spiritedness, intellect, hard work, patriotism, and eagerness to do good that characterizes virtually everyone who works in government on both sides of the aisle. But when I think of the institutions we work in, the incentives they set up and the pathologies they reinforce, and how little resistance we put up to them, it's a different story. Virtually everyone knew that the war in Afghanistan was always going poorly – yet almost no one put their career on the line for it. One diplomat made an offhand comment to me to the effect that *we knew we were losing, but that was above our pay grade. We kept doing our jobs and hoped things would work themselves out.* That perfectly

---

[39] Barno, McChrystal, McMaster, interviews by author.

encapsulates *bureaucrat* in all its worst connotations: passive complicity with bureaucratic drift toward failure, which I find contemptible.

Public servants should pound tables and throw chairs when lives, wars, and justice are on the line. Ambassador Ronald Neumann and General H. R. McMaster are the only officials I am aware of who essentially ended their careers trying to get Afghanistan right. Not a single Biden official resigned in protest over the fall of Kabul. I am struck by how many Obama officials now claim to have opposed the timetable all along. One diplomat told me, "in our private discussions there were considerable reservations about the idea that the entire surge had been done on a timeline ... I think everyone privately felt that this was a strange way to do business." Private reservations do not change policy or win wars. If there was such widespread opposition to the timetable, they should have raised hell, resigned in protest, or filed a dissent cable, as diplomats did a decade later over Biden's withdrawal and evacuation plans.

The imperative to give a damn extends to presidents. Presidents must care about the wars they lead, and that needs to be evident in how they talk about it. Presidents need to use the language of justice and victory. When presidents talk to the public and to the American soldier, they should not talk like scholars or professors. Ambassador James Cunningham found fault with "a series of administrations [who] never wanted to explain to the American people what it is that we were actually doing in Afghanistan and why we were doing it."[40]

The "why" requires a moral language. Wars are moral contests; they only possible justification for killing another human being is if the killing is a necessary act to rectify an injustice, defend public order, and achieve peace. If it is just to fight, it is just to win, and our presidents should talk like they believe it. This is not crusading; it is recognizing that, done right, war serves justice. Bush spoke this language, but mostly about Iraq. Trump got this right – once, in August 2017 – and then fired his entire national security team and lost the war. Biden never talked like this at all. Obama talked like this – once, in July 2008, on the campaign trail – and evidently didn't mean it. His worry that talking about victory glamorizes war is such a non sequitur I have trouble even knowing how to critique it. Victory in a just war glamorizes justice, not war.

More than intelligence or education, statesmen and stateswomen need character. They need wisdom, courage, temperance, and justice. That these happen to be the four cardinal virtues of classical antiquity may be

---

[40] Cunningham, interview by author.

a coincidence or may be providential. Or perhaps it suggests that the lessons that emerge from this sprawling twenty-year saga transcend the war that inspired them; that these lessons are no temporary or passing ephemera, that they are not quirky authorial idiosyncrasies. Perhaps these are timeless truths of statecraft, enduring principles about how to wield power in service of a just and lasting peace among nations.

STATECRAFT

If that is true, such timeless principles do not apply only to the individual policymaker. They apply to the nation we serve. American foreign policy should be characterized by wisdom, courage, temperance, and justice; our role in the world should serve those principles. Our grand strategy should take the long view, be practical and aware of our limits yet also courageous and visionary, fearless and uncompromising in the face of obstacles. Above all, it must aim at justice – which means it must serve American interests, but it must do so with an awareness of how our interests are entwined with others.

This is an unpopular thing to say in an era when half the country insists we need to put "America First." I don't disagree with that sentiment: I simply argue that the way to truly put America first is to take the longer view; to recognize that America exists within a community of nations; and that those nations have a great deal of influence over how and whether we will be able to secure our interests. Again, the proof is in the pudding: we tried the other version of "America First," lost the war, and al-Qaida regained safe haven. America is more at risk, and al-Qaida is stronger today than before.

To return to Reinhold Niebuhr, the twentieth-century theologian I invoked in Chapter 1, our grand strategy must be other-directed as much as self-directed. Our national interests are entwined with the national interests of other nations. We must define and pursue our interests with an awareness of how it affects others. We must make justice, fair play, and peace among nations central to our foreign policy. We must choose to define our interests as coterminous with the international common good. We must change who we are until what's good for us is good for the world – or, at least, good for other nations guided by similar values – and vice versa. That is the only moral defensible option.

It is also the only strategically defensible option. Critics might dismiss my conclusion as moralistic finger-wagging. This book is primarily concerned with strategy; what has morality to do with it? Academic "realism" claims morality has no place in discussions of national security. "Realism" equates wisdom with accepting constraints, never challenging them, and it neglects courage and justice entirely, which is why it offers such a shrunken, vapid, morally empty vision of America's role in the world. The "realist" view about why we lost Afghanistan is the mirror image of mine: we lost, they say, because of too much moral aspiration, not too little. The war in Afghanistan proves nation building is foolish, impossible, and irrelevant.

It should be clear from the narrative of America's war in Afghanistan that political morality has everything to do with good strategy. We lost because of poor strategy rooted in short-term, self-absorbed, "realistic" thinking. We fought with no thought for long-term peace, justice, or conciliation. Just war aims at peace, as Augustine argued in the fifth century AD. Every act of warfare must be oriented toward achieving a better peace. Augustine advised that as a moral imperative, but it is also good strategy. Fighting with no thought for how your war will end or how the war will translate into peace is immoral, but it is also stupid. Just war must be other-regarding, which is precisely what counterinsurgency and nation building demanded. A lasting peace in Afghanistan was the precondition for permanently denying safe haven to al-Qaida, the means to achieving al-Qaida's permanent, strategic defeat. That required an other-regarding strategy of investing in justice and peace, not only a self-regarding strategy of killing terrorists. A just strategy is, over the long run, the most effective strategy.

If this is true, the art of statecraft must begin with a proper understanding of who we are and what our role in the world should be. Foreign policy is downstream of national identity. Presidential leadership, at its best, speaks to the higher angels of our nature, articulating a hopeful vision of America as an exemplar of liberty and equality, wielding its unrivaled power in the service of a just and lasting peace. Truly following that long-term vision would mean adopting and implementing an other-regarding strategy rooted in universal human aspirations. As one president argued, "all people yearn for certain things: the ability to speak your mind and have a say in how you are governed; confidence in the rule of law and the equal administration of justice; government that is transparent and doesn't steal from the people; the freedom to live as you choose."

Those words were not spoken by anyone in the supposedly neoconservative cabal of the Bush administration, but by Barack Obama in his address at Cairo University, Egypt, in 2009. "These are not just American ideas; they are human rights. And that is why we will support them everywhere," Obama said. He boldly exhorted his Arab and Muslim audience: "You must maintain your power through consent, not coercion; you must respect the rights of minorities, and participate with a spirit of tolerance and compromise; you must place the interests of your people and the legitimate workings of the political process above your party." And he highlighted the importance of free religion. "People in every country should be free to choose and live their faith based upon the persuasion of the mind and the heart and the soul."

These are not simple platitudes, talking points for diplomats or boiler-plate for bleeding-heart humanitarians. "The instruments of war do have a role to play in preserving the peace," Obama reminded his audience while accepting the Nobel Peace Prize in 2009. The ideals of justice and peace should animate wartime strategy. Just war is the necessarily violent response to those who would violently disrupt a just peace. If war does not defend, achieve, or restore a just peace, it is mindless murder. We must plan backward from the vision of peace and justice we want to achieve through warfare. And a just peace should embody the principles of freedom that Obama articulated. "Peace is not merely the absence of visible conflict. Only a just peace based on the inherent rights and dignity of every individual can truly be lasting," he said. Combating terrorism was the initiating cause of the war in Afghanistan, but winning required restoring and defending the rights and dignity of the Afghans, which should have been the just peace we sought at the end of our military operations.

Critics are right to warn against a spirit of utopianism and crusading. But those are lessons we have learned too well: we should be equally on guard against nihilism, passivity, and dishonor. "In many countries there is a deep ambivalence about military action today, no matter what the cause," Obama warned (though he succumbed to this very thing). "And at times, this is joined by a reflexive suspicion of America." Between the dangers of utopianism, on the one hand, and nihilism, on the other, is what Niebuhr called Christian Realism and what others have called conservative inter-nationalism: a stance of recognizing the immovable evils of the word while not avoiding our inescapable responsibility to strive for justice. "We do not have to live in an idealized world to still reach for those ideals that will make it a better place," Obama argued. "We can acknowledge that oppression will always be with us, and still strive for justice."

That requires hope. Our foreign policy – our grand strategy, our national identity, our very lives – must be founded on hope, or we will wither. "Realism" is a hopeless, nihilistic vision of the world: it correctly observes that we live in a brutal, dog-eat-dog world yet offers no other advice than to be the biggest dog. We need more. "It will not be enough to make the world safer. We must also work to make the world better," Bush said in 2002.

"America seeks hope and opportunity for all people in all cultures." Like Obama, Bush did not match his words with action, but the vision was there. And the vision was hopeful. "Let us reach for the world that ought to be," Obama said in his Nobel Lecture, "that spark of the divine that still stirs within each of our souls." Hope is a necessary, though not sufficient, condition for victory. Hope, by itself, would not have won the war; but everything else, without hope, lost it. The story of the war in Afghanistan is the story of our losing hope.

In these presidential visions, America, the most powerful nation in the history of the world, can be an exemplar of freedom and equality; it can put its enormous power in the service of justice and peace; it can align its national interest with the international common good. After 9/11, that became a vision of America going to war for a just cause and liberating an oppressed people whose freedom would mean our security. It is too late for Afghanistan, but we always face the perennial question of our role in the world. The goal is not mere victory, but a *just* victory and a lasting peace. Losing that hope would be the final defeat from our long war in Afghanistan.

Sustaining such hope, on the other hand, is how we find meaning despite defeat, how we carry on, how we live that our honored dead shall not have died in vain.

Bibliographic Essay

Interviews: I am grateful to the following officials who sat for on-the-record interviews for this book (listed alphabetically by last name): Richard Armitage, David Barno, John Bolton, Richard Boucher, John Brennan, Ash Carter, Victoria Coates, Eliot Cohen, Ryan Crocker, James Cunningham, Lisa Curtis, Jim Dobbins, Eric Edelman, Jeff Eggers, Karl Eikenberry, Andrew Erdman, William Fallon, Douglas Feith, John Gastright, Robert Gates, Bob Grenier, Marc Grossman, Stephen P. Hadley, Chuck Hagel, Tony Harriman, Colin Jackson, Jim Jones, Zalmay Khalilzad, Chris Kolenda, Peter Lavoy, Hugo Llorens, Fernando Lujan, Doug Lute, Stan McChrystal, Ken McKenzie, David McKiernan, Michael McKinley, H. R. McMaster, Dan McNeill, Laurel Miller, Ronald Neumann, Robert O'Brien, Rick Olson, Leon Panetta, David Petraeus, Maureen Quinn, Mitchell Reiss, Condoleezza Rice, Barney Rubin, Frank Ruggiero, James Shinn, Mitchell Shivers, Vikram Singh, Ashely Tellis, Joseph Votel, Tony Wayne, Larry Wilkerson, Bill Wood.

I also used interviews from two other sources. First, the Miller Center's George W. Bush Oral History project at the University of Virginia (https://millercenter.org/the-presidency/presidential-oral-histories/george-w-bush) is cited in the text by the last name of the interviewee followed by "Bush Oral History." (Columbia University houses the Obama Oral History Project and only just started publishing interviews as my work on this book concluded.) Second, interviews conducted by the special inspector general for Afghanistan reconstruction are available through the *Washington Post*'s *Afghanistan Papers* project (www.washingtonpost.com/graphics/2019/investi gations/afghanistan-papers/documents-database/). They are cited in the text by the last name of the interviewee followed by "SIGAR interview."

Some former officials were unavailable or unwilling to sit for an interview. Bush and Obama declined invitations. Both have written insightful memoirs, though Obama's second volume, covering his second term, has not been published yet. Trump's office did not respond to my invitation, and he was busy running for a second term and avoiding jail, not writing a memoir, during this project. Biden's office responded with an email touting his success in managing the withdrawal. Among the other principals: Don Rumsfeld passed away two months before I started this project; Colin Powell passed away four months later, before I could establish contact with him, and sadly left behind no memoir of his time as secretary of state, though I did hear a rumor that he had started one. Susan Rice and John Kerry were serving in the Biden administration and declined or did not respond to invitations to speak to me during this project. Unfortunately, their memoirs are sparse on Afghanistan. Jim Mattis graciously declined my invitation and appears to have no plans to write a memoir of his time as secretary of defense. Tom Donilon, Hillary Clinton, and Rex Tillerson did not respond to repeated requests for an interview. Clinton's memoir has more detail than Kerry's or Rice's; Donilon and Tillerson seem unlikely to write theirs. I remain interested in speaking to any official involved in the war in hopes of someday updating this work in a new edition.

Official Reports: The UN secretary general began issuing quarterly reports on "The situation in Afghanistan and its implications for international peace and security" in 1996, after the Taliban first came to power. They are cited in the text using the United Nations' notation system (e.g., A/56/6810-S/2001/1157) along with the date and page number. The US Department of Defense issued twenty-six biannual reports between 2008 and 2020, first entitled "Report on Progress towards Security and Stability in Afghanistan" until the 2014 transition, and "Enhancing Security and Stability in Afghanistan" thereafter. They are cited in the text as "Report on Progress" or "Enhancing Security," along with the date and page number. The special inspector general for Afghanistan reconstruction (SIGAR) issued fifty-two quarterly reports from October 2008 to the end of the war (and continued to issue them after the fall of Kabul), which are cited in the text as "SIGAR Quarterly Report," along with the date and page number. Collectively, these sources are the best official narratives available in English representing the American and international side in the war in Afghanistan.

Document Archives: Donald Rumsfeld's memoir is unique: he cajoled the Department of Defense into declassifying hundreds of pages of his memos during his time as secretary of defense. The papers are available at www.ru msfeld.com and represent the earliest look at the archival record of the Bush administration (though Rumsfeld's selection of what to declassify is itself a matter for scrutiny). Other primary source documents are available at

George Washington University's National Security Archive (nsarchive.gwu
.edu), with special reading rooms related to Afghanistan here (https://nsarc
hive.gwu.edu/project/afghanistan-taliban-project) and here (https://nsarc
hive.gwu.edu/briefing-book/afghanistan/2021-08-19/afghanistan-2020-20
-year-war-20-documents).

Congressional Testimony: There are tens of thousands of pages of
congressional hearings and testimony related to Afghanistan from 2001 to
2021. I have cited Congressional testimony by committee name, name of the
hearing, date, and page number. Hearing transcripts and committee
reports can be found here (www.govinfo.gov/browse/committee).

Speeches, News, Polls: Where I have quoted from presidential speeches
or used contemporary news source or public opinion polls, I have put the
full citation in the footnote. I have not included those sources in the
bibliography.

Online Data: I used a wide array of data that is readily available online.
These are generally cited in the text with the originating organization's
name, the name of the dataset or webpage, and a web address.

- The Brookings Institution collected a wide range of data in its periodic
  "Afghanistan Index," updated regularly between 2005 and 2020 (www.br
  ookings.edu/afghanistan-index/).
- The Asia Foundation first polled the Afghan population in advance of the
  2004 presidential election and thereafter conducted annual surveys from
  2006 to 2019, the best (and almost only) source of information about
  public opinion in Afghanistan. The reports were taken down from the
  Foundation's website after the Taliban's seizure of power, but many
  university libraries and other organizations host copies.
- The New America Foundation maintains an online database of reported
  drone strikes in Pakistan (www.newamerica.org/international-security/r
  eports/americas-counterterrorism-wars/the-drone-war-in-pakistan/).
- USAID maintains an online portal with data on US foreign assistance to
  every state in the world since World War II (www.foreignassistance.gov/).
- The World Bank calculates several "governance indicators" to measure
  the quality of governance around the world (https://info.worldbank.or
  g/governance/wgi/).
- Transparency International publishes an annual "Corruptions
  Perception Index" ranking all countries in the world by the amount of
  perceived corruption in their public institutions (www.transparency.org/
  en/cpi/2022).

- The United Nations Office of Drugs and Crime (UNODC) publishes an annual Opium Survey with reams of statistics on poppy cultivation and opium and heroin production in various states, including Afghanistan (www.unodc.org/unodc/en/data-and-analysis/statistics/surveys.html).
- The Uppsala Conflict Data Program (at Uppsala University, Sweden) is the largest dataset on organized violence that I know of (www.pcr.uu.se/research/ucdp/).

BOOKS AND JOURNAL ARTICLES

Andres, Richard. "The Afghan Model in Northern Iraq." *Journal of Strategic Studies*, Vol. 29, No. 3 (2006): 395–422.

Andres, Richard B., Craig Wills, and Thomas E. Griffith Jr. "Winning with Allies: The Strategic Value of the Afghan Model." *International Security*, Vol. 30, No. 3 (2006): 124–160.

Art, Robert, Timothy W. Crawford, and Robert Jervis (eds.). *International Politics: Enduring Concepts and Contemporary Issues*. 14th ed. Rowman & Littlefield, 2023.

Barfield, Thomas. *Afghanistan: A Cultural and Political History*. Princeton University Press, 2023.

Barry, Ben. *Blood, Metal and Dust: How Victory Turned into Defeat in Afghanistan and Iraq*. Bloomsbury Publishing, 2020.

Bearden, Milton. "Afghanistan, Graveyard of Empires." *Foreign Affairs*, Vol. 80, No. 6 (2001): 17–30.

Beath, Andrew, Christia Fotini, and Ruben Enikolopov. *Randomized Impact Evaluation of Afghanistan's National Solidarity Programme: Final Report*. World Bank, 2013.

Benjamin, Daniel, and Steven Simon. *The Age of Sacred Terror: Radical Islam's War against America*. Random House Trade Paperbacks, 2003.

Berntsen, Gary, and Ralph Pezzullo. *Jawbreaker: The Attack on Bin Laden and al-Qaida. A Personal Account by the CIA's Key Field Commander*. Crown, 2006.

Betts, Richard K. "Is Strategy an Illusion?" *International Security*, Vol. 25, No. 2 (2000): 5–50.

Bhatia, Michael, Kevin Lanigan and Philip Wilkinson. *Minimal Investments, Minimal Results: The Failure of Security Policy in Afghanistan*. Afghan Research and Evaluation Unit, 2004.

Biddle, Stephen. "Afghanistan's Legacy: Emerging Lessons of an Ongoing War." *The Washington Quarterly*, Vol. 37, No. 2 (2014): 73–86.

Biddle, Stephen D. "Allies, Airpower, and Modern Warfare: The Afghan Model in Afghanistan and Iraq." *International Security*, Vol. 30, No. 3 (2006): 161–176.

Biddle, Stephen. "Ending the War in Afghanistan: How to Avoid Failure on the Installment Plan." *Foreign Affairs*, Vol. 92, No. 5 (2013): 49–58.

Biddle, Stephen, Fotini Christia, and F. Alexander Thier. "Defining Success in Afghanistan: What Can the United States Accept." *Foreign Affairs*, Vol. 89, No. 4 (2010): 48–60.

Blehm, Eric. *The Only Thing Worth Dying For: How Eleven Green Berets Fought for a New Afghanistan*. Harper Collins, 2011.

Bolger, Daniel P. *Why We Lost: A General's Inside Account of the Iraq and Afghanistan Wars*. Houghton Mifflin Harcourt, 2014.

Bolton, John. *The Room Where It Happened: A White House Memoir*. Simon & Schuster, 2020.

Bradley, Rusty, and Kevin Maurer. *The Lions of Kandahar: The Story of a Fight Against All Odds*. Bantam Books, 2011.

Bush, George W. *Decision Points*. Crown, 2010.

Byman, Daniel L. "Friends Like These: Counterinsurgency and the War on Terrorism." *International Security*, Vol. 31, No. 2 (2006): 79–115.

Chandler, David C. *Empire in Denial: The Politics of State-Building*. Pluto, 2006.

Chandrasekaran, Rajiv. *Little America: The War within the War for Afghanistan*. Vintage, 2012.

Chayes, Sarah. *The Punishment of Virtue: Inside Afghanistan after the Taliban*. University of Queensland Press, 2006.

Cheney, Richard B., and Liz Cheney. *In My Time: A Personal and Political Memoir*. Simon & Schuster, 2011.

Chollet, Derek. *The Long Game: How Obama Defied Washington and Redefined America's Role in the World*. Public Affairs, 2016.

Clarke, Richard A. *Against All Enemies: Inside America's War on Terror*. Simon & Schuster, 2004.

Clinton, Hillary Rodham. *Hard Choices*. Simon & Schuster, 2014.

Cohen, Eliot A. "The Historical Mind and Military Strategy." *Orbis*, Vol. 49, No. 4 (2005): 575–588.

Coll, Steve. *Directorate S: The CIA and America's Secret Wars in Afghanistan and Pakistan*. Penguin, 2018.

Collins, Joseph J. *Understanding War in Afghanistan*. National Defense University Press, 2011.

Cordesman, Anthony. *Learning the Right Lessons from the Afghan War*. Center for Strategic and International Studies, 2021.

Cramer, Christopher and Jonathan Goodhand. "'Try Again. Fail Again. Fail Better?'." In Jennifer Milliken (ed.), *State Failure, Collapse and Reconstruction: Issues and Responses*. Blackwell, 2003: 885–909.

Dam, Bette. *A Man and a Motorcycle: How Hamid Karzai Came to Power*. Ipso Facto, 2014.

Dobbins, James. *After the Taliban: Nation-Building in Afghanistan*. Potomac Books, 2008.

Dobbins, James. *Foreign Service: Five Decades on the Frontlines of American Diplomacy*. Brookings Institution Press, 2017.

Dobbins, James, John G. McGinn, Keith Crane, Seth G. Jones, Rollie Lal, Andrew Rathmell, Rachel M. Swanger, and Anga R. Timilsina. *America's Role in Nation-Building: From Germany to Iraq.* RAND Corporation, 2003.

Dobbins, James, Seth G. Jones, Keith Crane, Andrew Rathmell, and Brett Steele. *The UN's Role in Nation-Building: From the Congo to Iraq.* RAND Corporation, 2001.

Donati, Jessica. *Eagle Down: The Last Special Forces Fighting the Forever War.* Hachette UK, 2021.

Eikenberry, Karl W. "The Limits of Counterinsurgency Doctrine in Afghanistan: The Other Side of the COIN." *Foreign Affairs*, Vol. 92, No. 5 (2013): 59–74.

Esper, Mark. *A Sacred Oath: Memoirs of a Secretary of Defense during Extraordinary Times.* William Morrow, 2022.

Ewans, Martin. *Afghanistan: A Short History of Its People and Politics.* Harper, 2002.

Fairweather, Jack. *The Good War: Why We Couldn't Win the War or the Peace in Afghanistan.* Hachette UK, 2014.

Farrell, Theo. *Unwinnable: Britain's War in Afghanistan.* Random House, 2017.

Farrell, Theo, and Antonio Giustozzi. "The Taliban at War: Inside the Helmand Insurgency, 2004–2012." *International Affairs*, Vol. 89, No. 4 (2013): 845–871.

Feith, Douglas J. *War and Decision: Inside the Pentagon at the Dawn of the War on Terrorism.* Harper, 2008.

Franks, Tommy, and Malcolm McConnell. *American Soldier.* HarperCollins, 2004.

Gall, Carlotta. *The Wrong Enemy: America in Afghanistan, 2001–2014.* Houghton Mifflin Harcourt, 2014.

Gates, Robert M. *Duty: Memoirs of a Secretary at War.* Knopf, 2014.

Giustozzi, Antonio. *Koran, Kalashnikov, and Laptop.* Columbia University Press, 2008.

Goodson, Larry P. "The Lessons of Nation-Building in Afghanistan," in Francis Fukuyama, ed., *Nation-Building: Beyond Afghanistan and Iraq.* The Johns Hopkins University Press, 2006: 145–172.

Gopal, Anand. *No Good Men among the Living: America, the Taliban, and the War through Afghan Eyes.* Metropolitan Books, 2014.

Gopal, Anand. *The Battle for Afghanistan: Militancy and Conflict in Kandahar.* New America Foundation, 2010.

Grenier, Robert L. *88 Days to Kandahar: A CIA Diary.* Simon & Schuster, 2016.

Grossman, Marc. "Talking to the Taliban 2011–2012." *Prism*, Vol. 4, No. 4 (2014): 21–37.

Hadley, Stephen J., Peter Feaver, William Inboden, and Meghan O'Sullivan, eds. *Hand-Off: The Foreign Policy George W. Bush Passed to Barack Obama.* Brookings Institution Press, 2023.

Hayden, Michael V. *Playing to the Edge: American Intelligence in the Age of Terror.* Penguin, 2017.

Isby, David. *Afghanistan: Graveyard of Empires: A New History of the Borderland.* Pegasus Books, 2010.

Jamal, Shuja, and William Maley. *The Decline and Fall of Republican Afghanistan.* Oxford University Press, 2023.

Jones, Seth G. *In the Graveyard of Empires: America's War in Afghanistan.* WW Norton & Company, 2009.

Jones, Seth G. "The Rise of Afghanistan's Insurgency: State Failure and Jihad." *International Security*, Vol. 32, No. 4 (2008): 7–40.

Kerry, John. *Every Day Is Extra.* Simon & Schuster, 2019.

Khalilzad, Zalmay. *The Envoy: From Kabul to the White House, My Journey through a Turbulent World.* St. Martin's Press, 2016.

Kilcullen, David, and Greg Mills. *The Ledger: Accounting for Failure in Afghanistan.* Hurst Publishers, 2021.

Kolenda, Christopher D. *Zero-Sum Victory: What We're Getting Wrong about War.* University Press of Kentucky, 2021.

Komer, Robert W. *Bureaucracy Does Its Thing: Institutional Constraints on US-GVN Performance in Vietnam.* RAND Corporation, 1972.

Kushner, Jared. *Breaking History: A White House Memoir.* Broadside Books, 2022.

Landler, Mark. *Alter Egos: Hillary Clinton, Barack Obama, and the Twilight Struggle over American Power.* Random House, 2016.

Lykke, Arthur F., Jr., "Defining Military Strategy," *Military Review* (Jan./Feb. 1997): 183–186.

Malkasian, Carter. *The American War in Afghanistan: A History.* Oxford University Press, 2021.

Mann, James. *The Obamians: The Struggle inside the White House to Redefine American Power.* Penguin Group USA, 2013.

McChrystal, Stanley. *My Share of the Task: A Memoir.* Penguin, 2014.

McMaster, Herbert Raymond. *Battlegrounds: The Fight to Defend the Free World.* Harper, 2020.

Meadows, Mark. *The Chief's Chief.* All Seasons Press, 2021.

Miller, Paul D. *American Power and Liberal Order: A Conservative Internationalist Grand Strategy.* Georgetown University Press, 2016.

Miller, Paul D. *Armed State Building: Confronting State Failure, 1898–2012.* Cornell University Press, 2013.

Miller, Paul D. *Just War and Ordered Liberty.* Cambridge University Press, 2021.

Mutawakil, Wakil Ahmed. *Afghanistan and Taliban.* Byeralai Pohaneon Lray, 2005.

Neumann, Amb Ronald E. *The Other War: Winning and Losing in Afghanistan.* Potomac Books, 2009.

Niebuhr, Reinhold. *The Essential Reinhold Niebuhr: Selected Essays and Addresses.* Yale University Press, 1986.

Obama, Barack. *A Promised Land.* Crown, 2020.

Obama, Barack. "Renewing American Leadership." *Foreign Affairs*, Vol. 86, No. 4 (2007): 2–16.

O'Neill, Robert. *The Operator: Firing the Shots that Killed Osama Bin Laden and My Years as a SEAL Team Warrior.* Scribner, 2017.

Owen, Mark, and Kevin Maurer. *No Easy Day: The Autobiography of a Navy SEAL. The Firsthand Account of the Mission That Killed Osama Bin Laden.* Dutton, 2012.

Packer, George. *Our Man: Richard Holbrooke and the End of the American Century.* Random House, 2019.

Panetta, Leon, and Jim Newton. *Worthy Fights: A Memoir of Leadership in War and Peace.* Penguin, 2014.

Pence, Mike. *So Help Me God.* Simon & Schuster, 2022.

Pompeo, Mike. *Never Give an Inch: Fighting for the America I Love.* Broadside, 2023.

Rashid, Ahmed. *Descent into Chaos: The US and the Disaster in Pakistan, Afghanistan, and Central Asia.* Penguin, 2008

Rhodes, Ben. *The World as It Is: A Memoir of the Obama White House.* Random House Trade Paperbacks, 2019.

Rice, Condoleezza. *No Higher Honor: A Memoir of My Years in Washington.* Crown, 2011.

Rice, Condoleezza. "Promoting the National Interest." *Foreign Affairs,* Vol. 79, No. 1 (2000): 45–62.

Riedel, Bruce. *The Search for al-Qaida: Its Leadership, Ideology, and Future.* Rowman & Littlefield, 2010.

Rice, Susan. *Tough Love: My Story of the Things Worth Fighting For.* Simon & Schuster, 2019.

Rosen, James. *Cheney One on One: A Candid Conversation with America's Most Controversial Statesman.* Simon & Schuster, 2015.

Rumsfeld, Donald. *Known and Unknown: A Memoir.* Penguin, 2011.

Rumsfeld, Donald H. "Transforming the Military." *Foreign Affairs,* Vol. 81, No. 3 (2002): 20–32.

Sanger, David E. *Confront and Conceal: Obama's Secret Wars and Surprising Use of American Power.* Crown, 2012.

Schroen, Gary C. *First In: An Insider's Account of How the CIA Spearheaded the War on Terror in Afghanistan.* Presidio Press, 2005.

SIGAR, *What We Need to Learn: Lessons From Twenty Years of Afghanistan Reconstruction.* Department of Defense, 2021.

Stanton, Doug. *Horse Soldiers: The Extraordinary Story of a Band of US Soldiers Who Rode to Victory in Afghanistan.* Simon & Schuster, 2010.

Strachan, Hew. "Learning Lessons From Afghanistan." *Parameters,* Vol. 49, No. 3 (2019), 5–10.

Strmecki, Marin. "Afghanistan at a Crossroads." Briefing, August 17, 2006. Available through the Rumsfeld Library. https://library.rumsfeld.com/doclib/sp/456/2 006-08-17%20from%20Marin%20Strmecki%20re%20Afghanistan%20at%20a% 20Crossroads%20Briefing.pdf.

Suhrke, Astri. *When More Is Less: The International Project in Afghanistan.* Columbia University Press, 2012.

Tenet, George, and Bill Harlow. *At the Center of the Storm.* HarperCollins, 2007.

Tyler, John A. *Afghanistan Graveyard of Empires: Why the Most Powerful Armies of Their Time Found Only Defeat or Shame in This Land Of Endless Wars.* Aries Consolidated LLC, 2021.

Vaishnav, Milan. "Afghanistan: The Chimera of the 'Light Footprint.'" *Significant Issues Series – Center for Strategic and International Studies,* Vol. 26 (2004): 244–262.

Vickers, Michael G. *By All Means Available: Memoirs of a Life in Intelligence, Special Operations, and Strategy.* Knopf, 2023.

West, Bing. *The Wrong War: Grit, Strategy, and the Way Out of Afghanistan.* Random House Trade Paperbacks, 2012.

Whitlock, Craig. *The Afghanistan Papers: A Secret History of the War.* Simon & Schuster, 2021.

Woodward, Bob. *Bush at War.* Simon & Schuster, 2002.

Woodward, Bob. *Fear: Trump in the White House.* Simon & Schuster, 2018.

Woodward, Bob. *Obama's Wars.* Simon & Schuster, 2011.

Woodward, Bob. *Rage.* Simon & Schuster, 2020.

Woodward, Bob, and Robert Costa. *Peril.* Simon & Schuster, 2021.

Zaeef, Abdul Salam. *Taliban: From Kandahar until Mazar.* Hurst, 2011.

Zakheim, Dov S. *A Vulcan's Tale: How the Bush Administration Mismanaged the Reconstruction of Afghanistan.* Rowman & Littlefield, 2011.

Index

9/11 terrorist attacks, 37, 38, 39, 51, 418, 419, 423
  al-Qaida and, 39, 45

Abbottabad raid, 149, 261, 263, 275, 345, 445, 475, 486
Abdullah, Abdullah, 213, 350, 351, 352
Abizaid, John, 128
Abu Sayyaf, 44
Accelerating Success, 109, 110, 111, 125, 129, 132, 137, 154, 162, 163, 164, 185, 188, 194, 206, 254
Adams, John, 135
Adams, John Quincy, 135
Afghan government. *See also* corruption
  agreements with, 349
  and the Bonn Accords, 75, 313
  capacity building, 215
  Central Narcotics Tribunal, 341
  coalition envisioned, 306
  collapse of, 450, 451, 454, 460
  communication with, 314, 328
  corruption in, 161, 188, 233, 339–343
  and the Doha negotiations, 419–425
  exclusion from Doha negotiations, 409, 416, 419, 421
  failures of, 289, 295
  fragility of, 87
  High Peace Council, 304
  interim, 76
  under Karzai, 190
  as kleptocracy, 339, 340, 341, 395
  losing control, 369
  and the military surge, 263
  Ministry of Transportation, 331

negotiation with the Taliban, 303, 304, 416, 419, 420, 424, 430
  and the peace process, 314
  popular support for, 141
  post-Taliban, 80
  rebuilding, 12, 296, 396
  stabilization of, 443
  taking responsibility, 290
  and the Taliban, 60, 249, 314, 315, 318, 350, 407
  Taliban participation in, 306, 416
  as thugocracy, 338
  and UN peacekeeping, 168
  US support for, 92, 253, 337, 438, 471, 473
  warlords invited into, 118
  weakness of, 137, 138, 139, 294
  Zalmay's confidence in, 428
Afghan Interagency Operations Group, 104
Afghan Local Police, 178, 287, 474
Afghan National Army, 109, 111, 167, 171, 175–180, 258, 262, 282, 330, 332, 349, 351, 447
  assistance for, 188
  assuming responsibility, 368
  blamed by Biden, 452
  capability gaps, 355
  collapse of, 435, 448, 450, 451, 453, 461
  dependence on US, 329, 460, 462
  difficulties encountered by, 468
  enforcing the Doha agreement, 449
  fighting the Taliban, 354, 453
  lack of readiness, 359, 361, 367
  purpose of, 93
  special forces, 179

Afghan National Army (cont.)
  support for, 1, 420, 448, 461, 471, 472
  taking over US bases, 360
  and the Taliban, 369
  training by US, 2, 92, 93, 128, 158, 163, 176,
    177, 178, 187, 189, 199, 328, 352, 365,
    367, 373, 479
  US aid for, 14
  US equipment given to, 448
Afghan National Auxiliary Police, 178
Afghan National Development Strategy
    (ANDS), 187
Afghan Police, 92, 94, 109, 111, 167, 171,
    175–180, 188, 262, 351, 447
  capability gaps, 355
  collapse of, 450, 451
  corruption in, 176
  creation of, 2
  training by US, 178
  training for, 127, 163
  US aid for, 14
Afghanistan. *See also* Kandahar; Kabul
  1964 constitution, 13, 75, 81, 111
  al-Qaida in, 236
  in the American imagination, 4–10
  and the British Empire, 53, 84, 142, 214
  civilian surge in, 253, 258, 264–269, 274,
    296, 304, 305, 336, 479
  compared to Iraq, 330
  compared to Vietnam, 218
  constitutional government, 108, 195, 349
  democracy in, 11, 12, 14, 21, 26, 73, 75, 76,
    91, 107, 113, 134, 141, 196, 203, 215, 328,
    359, 469
  diplomatic surge in, 305
  economy of force mission, 104
  education in, 272
  elections in, 102, 113, 154, 161, 185, 186,
    202, 205, 210–213, 233, 342, 349–352, 354
  evacuation of, 450, 451, 454–459
  as failed state, 20, 22, 86, 94, 132, 133, 157,
    185, 290, 320–326
  governance in, 184–191
  as graveyard of empires, 6, 9, 53, 56, 82,
    142, 214, 384, 394, 452, 454, 461
  High Peace Council, 313
  military history, 6

  military surge in, 1, 24, 29, 33, 228, 238,
    239, 240, 241, 243, 250, 254, 255,
    258–264, 273, 277–282, 296, 297, 305,
    315, 321, 324, 330, 332, 340, 389, 395,
    440, 446, 465, 479
  modern constitution, 1, 13, 111–115, 207,
    300, 304, 307, 389, 449, 461, 473
  regime change in, 50, 56
  Russia in, 214
  as safe haven for terrorists, 12, 22, 26, 37,
    39, 45, 56, 107, 108, 130, 233, 253, 355,
    383, 394, 409, 410, 413, 416, 425, 428,
    439, 440, 461, 462, 463, 492, 493
  and the Soviet Union, 53, 84, 142
  stabilization of, 17, 23, 26, 71, 88, 109, 126,
    129, 131, 132, 142, 163, 206, 207, 225,
    266, 271, 349, 440, 444
  troop presence in, 167, 411
  US aid to, 14, 20, 83, 88, 90, 91, 94, 106,
    108, 109, 113, 130, 142, 152, 167, 199,
    251, 265, 271, 335, 337, 351, 389, 444
  US goals in, 70, 91, 355
  in US popular culture, 5, 7, 8, 9
  US withdrawal under Biden, 1, 23, 218,
    257, 442, 443, 444, 447, 448, 460, 463,
    469, 473
  US withdrawal under Obama, 1, 8, 13, 23,
    199, 228, 237, 238, 242, 243, 244, 248,
    251, 258, 282, 291, 292–296, 297, 318,
    320, 321, 327, 329, 330–334, 352, 353,
    354, 360, 362, 364, 378, 413, 443, 463
  US withdrawal under Trump, 23, 407, 408,
    410, 411, 412, 414, 415, 416, 419, 423, 424,
    425, 426, 430, 431, 432, 435, 443, 458
Afghanistan Compact, 113, 187
Afghanistan Freedom Support Act (2002),
    108, 439
Afghanistan Papers, 10–15, 91
Afghanistan reconstruction. *See also* Provincial
    Reconstruction Teams (PRTs)
  abandonment of, 338
  Afghan responsibility for, 81
  and American security, 108, 441, 444
  approach to, 33
  attempts at, 26
  Biden's support for, 438, 440, 459
  under Bush, 5, 269

Bush's neglect of, 468
challenges of, 131
civilian efforts, 267, 268, 273, 336
consequences of neglect, 139
and counterinsurgency, 164, 339
and counterterrorism, 333
as distraction, 19
as international effort, 92, 93
debate over, 216
economic, 439
efforts to improve, 161
Eikenberry's support for, 235
failure of, 17, 32, 126, 352, 374, 395
failure to invest in, 389
funding for, 1, 11, 13, 23, 29, 88, 95, 188, 472, 482
goals of, 14, 22, 328
in Helmand, 272
importance of, 107, 130
insecurity as deterrent to, 468
insufficient, 180
international assistance for, 187
investment in, 109
Kajaki Dam, 272
limited effort, 338
long-term operations, 476
need for, 95, 142, 233
neglect of, 14, 158
Obama's support for, 208
under Obama, 228, 269
planning for, 12, 129, 132, 266
popular dissatisfaction with, 141
positive results, 125
postwar agreements, 349
recommendations for, 366
rhetoric about, 14
security for, 207
stagnation of, 71
under Trump, 23
UN involvement in, 74, 76
US aid for, 258, 265, 270, 271, 330, 331
US commitment to, 82
US involvement in, 88
Zakheim's assignment for, 152
Zalmay's view of, 84
Afghanistan Reconstruction Trust Fund (ARTF), 76

Afghanistan Study Group, 444
Afghanistan war. *See also* War on Terror
2010 review of progress, 286–291
Abbottabad raid, 149, 261, 263, 275, 345, 445, 475, 486
Afghan casualties, 368, 453
assigning blame for losing, 459–466
battle for Kunduz, 64
Battle of Shahi-kot, 3, 70
Battle of Wanat, 193
debate over approach, 51–56
decrease in violence and casualties, 261
defeatist approach to, 253–257
defining the mission, 229
effect on Pakistan, 348
end of, 352–357, 363, 442–447
fall of Kabul, 447–454
as forever war, 14, 257, 368, 373, 379, 385, 433, 463, 476
goals of, 12, 22, 26, 38, 39, 40, 45, 83, 236, 251, 253, 372, 385, 386
Konduz offensive, 365
loss of faith in, 211
McMaster's influence on, 381–387
Obama's initial approach to, 197–201, 206–210
Obama's influence on, 374–378
Obama's strategy, 249–253
policy mistakes, 467
psychological aspects of, 221
public perception of, 292
timetable for, 236–244, 250, 277–282, 333
unique demands of, 24
US casualties, 193, 210, 255, 258, 368, 433, 449
US support for, 465
veterans of, 131
as war of retribution, 197, 372, 447
Afghanistan War Commission, 468
Agha, Tayeb, 303, 312, 313, 321
Ahmed, Mahmud, 58
aid dependency, 82, 83, 87
Albright, Madeleine, 364
Alexander the Great, 53
Allen, John, 272, 279, 292, 330
as commander of ISAF, 330, 331, 332

al-Qaida. *See also* bin Laden, Osama
9/11 terrorist attacks, 37, 39, 45
in Afghanistan, 37, 71, 89, 410, 456, 461, 462, 463, 476, 492
Arab Brigade, 50
association with the Taliban, 18, 22, 26, 44, 45, 46, 48, 49, 50, 51, 65, 68, 77, 133, 207, 228, 229, 300, 305, 388, 407, 409, 416, 417, 418, 428, 430, 431, 433, 440, 445, 452
containment of, 410
counterterrorism against, 232
defeat of as goal, 26, 27
distinction from the Taliban, 444
drone strikes against, 311, 312
and the Haqqani Network, 276
hunt for, 168
intelligence against, 39
in Iraq, 158, 219
jihadism and, 43
leadership of, 56
opposition to, 18
and Pakistan, 100
Pakistan's cooperation against, 58
in Pakistan, 145, 146, 148, 206, 234, 274, 276, 347
pressure on, 70, 374
resurgence of, 367
revenge on, 159
in South Asia, 399
surveillance of, 23
as threat, 5, 207
US war against, 1, 11, 12, 22, 24, 26, 38, 40, 45, 51, 57, 65, 67, 72, 73, 74, 158, 160, 174, 194, 197, 199, 203, 206, 227, 228, 236, 249, 261, 263, 276, 294, 300, 331, 333, 335, 347, 349, 354, 359, 362, 371, 372, 373, 396, 417, 440, 443, 445, 462, 468, 471, 473
ambiguity bias, 25
Anglo-Afghan wars, 6
Arabs, 158
Armitage, Richard, 41, 47, 54, 57, 73, 76, 103, 275
Assad, Bashar al-, 374
assassinations, 119, 134, 147, 313, 369, 405, 460

attempted, 58
Atlantic Council, 364, 398, 424, 444
Atwah, Muhsin Musa Matwalli, 56
Augustine, 493
Austin, Lloyd, 443, 456
Authorization for the Use of Military Force (AUMF), 37
axis of evil, 74

Bagram Airbase, 2, 3, 72, 111, 137, 291, 328, 394, 427, 448
Balkans, 87, 88, 130, 310, 322, 438
Balkan wars, 297
Baluchistan, 96, 100, 276, 312, 344, 370
Bannon, Steve, 386, 394
Baradar, Abdul Ghani, 404, 408, 409, 425, 430, 433, 456
Barakzai tribe, 4
Barfield, Thomas, 4
Barno, David, 90, 94, 102, 103, 110, 111, 113, 121, 122, 128, 170, 332, 490
assessment of the war, 126
counterinsurgency plans, 164
on military command, 171
on PRTs, 110
Barry, Ben, 21
Bearden, Milton, 6, 9, 53
Bergdahl, Bowe, 303, 319
Berntsen, Gary, 55
Betts, Richard, 251
Bhutto, Benazir, 147, 277
Biddle, Steve, 21, 261
Biden administration
Afghanistan strategy, 28, 445, 455
blaming Trump administration, 435
and the Doha agreement, 432, 442
evacuation of Afghanistan, 454–459
members of, 33
records of, 36
SIV reviews, 458
Biden, Joe, 108
in Afghanistan, 438
Afghanistan strategy, 1, 14, 23, 286, 287, 289, 292, 331, 370, 435, 438–442, 443, 446, 460, 461, 462, 464, 465, 473, 484, 489
assessment of the war, 290, 291

blamed for mishandling Afghanistan, 435
on civilian evacuation, 459
claiming victory, 446
counterinsurgency strategy, 234, 235
counterterrorism strategy, 232, 233, 246,
    252, 255, 259
criticisim of Rumsfeld, 439
and the Doha agreement, 447, 449
and the evacuation, 454, 456
and Ghani, 449
and Karzai, 314, 441
mistrust of the military, 203, 228, 243, 246,
    247, 257, 288, 361, 386, 442, 445
negativity of, 292, 370, 375
opposition to Afghanistan war, 229, 230,
    231, 244, 250, 334, 394, 421
opposition to nation building, 473
opposition to the Vietnam War, 435–437,
    441, 464
as president, 35, 440, 442, 454, 481, 490,
    491
as presidential candidate, 440
as senator, 435, 436, 454, 472
speeches regarding Afghanistan, 447, 452,
    453, 458
support for nation building, 441
support for reconstruction, 440
supporting the war in Afghanistan, 439,
    440
on the Taliban, 449
as vice president, 198, 202, 203, 237, 278,
    440, 441
on Vietnam, 217, 218
withdrawal from Afghanistan, 257, 361,
    396, 426, 432, 463
bilateral security agreement (BSA), 349, 350
bin Laden, Osama, 47, 158
    death of, 56, 263, 275, 294, 328, 345, 352,
        372, 447, 458, 460, 462, 486
    hunt for, 7, 39, 55, 159, 196, 197, 371, 475
    and Mullah Omar, 50, 51
    in Pakistan, 97, 149
    and the Taliban, 48, 49, 51, 64
Black, Cofer, 48
Blinken, Tony, 442, 443, 444, 473
Blue Mosque (Kandahar), 133

Bolger, Daniel, 19
Bolton, John, 368, 392, 404, 405, 407, 408,
    416, 425, 460, 468, 488
    Afghanistan strategy, 412
    counterterrorism plans, 251, 413, 414, 415
    on the Doha negotiations, 402, 429
    as national security advisor, 401, 402
    on negotiation with the Taliban, 404, 406,
        409, 411, 412, 421, 422, 423, 424
    resignation of, 430
    on Trump, 414
    on withdrawal from Afghanistan, 410
Bonn Agreement, 75, 117, 342
Bonn conference, 59, 60, 74, 75, 116, 191,
    313, 316, 469
Bonn Process, 45, 70, 71–76, 81, 86, 102, 111,
    113, 129, 161, 185, 473
Bosnia, 80, 89, 191, 310
Boucher, Richard, 41, 78, 122, 185, 186
Bradley, Omar, 477
Brahimi, Lakhdar, 59, 74, 112
Brennan, John, 230, 242, 243, 252, 255, 328,
    340, 360, 373, 475, 476
    as Homeland Security Advisor, 229, 232
    in Afghanistan, 354
    on Pakistan, 345, 346
Brzezinski, Zbigniew, 84, 392
Bureau of International Narcotics and Law
    Enforcement Affairs (INL), 127
bureaucracy, 29–33, 131, 153, 161, 170,
    221, 269–274, 308, 469, 471, 477–483,
    491
    in Afghanistan, 186
    antiterrorist, 371
    competitive, 266
    counterterrorism, 172, 174
    international, 191
    military, 31, 172, 173, 174, 179
    opposition to, 221
    provincial, 270
    US, 382
    in the US–Pakistan relationship, 347
Burns, Nicholas, 104, 170
Bush administration, 401
    and Afghan governance, 184–191
    and the Afghanistan constitution, 112

Bush administration (cont.)
  Afghanistan strategy, 14, 23, 40, 45, 46, 50,
    51, 57, 64, 67, 68, 70, 78, 90, 92, 105, 124,
    129, 132, 133, 142, 143, 156, 157, 160,
    161, 163, 174, 197, 229, 262, 271, 334,
    370, 371, 373, 470, 473
  at the Bonn conference, 75, 76
  counterinsurgency efforts, 167, 174, 180,
    188
  and counterterrorism, 156–160
  focus on counterterrorism, 41, 131
  criticism of, 20, 91, 249, 438
  decision-makers in, 33
  use of drones, 311
  failures of, 131, 132, 133
  fighting corruption, 339
  and Iraq, 101
  in Iraq, 191
  Karzai and, 211
  missed opportunities for peace, 59
  nation building by, 235
  opposition to nation building, 56, 80, 87,
    440
  overtures to the Taliban, 45–51, 68
  and Pakistan, 47, 58, 97, 145, 147, 149, 346
  and peace building, 160
  progress made by, 191
  records of, 36
  and the Taliban, 121, 125, 156, 300
  and the warlords, 183, 342
  warlord strategy, 117, 119
Bush, George H. W., 41, 162, 392, 438
  administration of, 214, 401
Bush, George W., 195
  Afghanistan strategy, 3, 5, 11, 13, 14, 39, 46,
    50, 51, 54, 73, 151, 154, 155, 162, 372,
    427, 463, 464, 468
  bureaucracy of, 153
  Camp David meeting, 49, 54
  and the Cold War, 470
  errors of, 175
  foreign policy, 374
  invasion of Iraq, 1
  and Iraq, 441, 481, 482, 491
  and the Iraq War, 366
  on Iraq, 101, 105, 155
  on Islam, 43

  Karzai and, 211, 212
  Marshall Plan speech, 90, 106, 129, 131,
    215, 439, 487
  memoir, 53, 194, 195
  and the Middle East, 43
  and Musharraf, 441
  on nation building, 80, 106, 389, 441, 464,
    472
  and Pakistan, 100, 148
  on Pakistan, 97, 144, 146, 346, 349
  and Putin, 441
  as president, 35, 37, 38, 41, 195, 477, 482,
    491, 494
  Rice's advice to, 165
  speech to Congress, 46, 47
  staff changes, 166, 167
  State of the Union address (2002), 74
  on war, 199
  War on Terror, 37, 41, 43, 44, 45, 52, 471

Cambodia, 191, 310
Camp Chapman, 210
Campbell, John, 360, 367, 369
Capacity Development Program (CDP), 186
Card, Andy, 80
Carr, E. H., 25
Carter, Ash, 262, 268, 269, 278, 318, 338, 353,
    355, 366
  on nation building, 472
  on negotiation with the Taliban, 321
  on Pakistan, 348
Carter, James "Jimmy," 392
Casey, George, 209, 235
ceasefire, 399, 408, 419, 425, 426, 433
Center for the National Interest, 379
Central Command (CENTCOM), 55, 128,
    168, 171, 172, 192, 193, 260, 278, 309
Chamberlain, Wendy, 45, 47, 57
Chandrasekaran, Rajiv, 19
Chayes, Sarah, 18, 62, 118
Chechens, 158
Cheney, Dick, 38, 41, 53, 79, 162
  in Afghanistan, 137
  on Iraq, 105
  on Pakistan, 100
  support for war, 49
  on the Taliban, 50, 77, 78

as vice president, 41
China, 399, 412, 463
Chollet, Derek, 237, 242
Christian Realism, 494
Christians, 363
Christopher, Warren, 286
Church, Frank, 436
Churchill, Winston, 366, 478
CIA
  in Afghanistan, 54
  casualties at Camp Chapman, 210
  district assessments, 260
  and the military, 328
  partner with Northern Alliance, 120
  pessimistic assessment of Afghanistan, 354
  Special Activities Division, 54
  and the Taliban, 48, 319
civil rights, 112
civilian casualties, 19, 139, 140, 209, 211, 220,
    262, 350, 456
  in Pakistan, 275
Civilian Response Corps, 482
Clarke, Richard, 46
Clausewitz, Carl von, 122
Clinton administration
  Plan Colombia, 181
  staff, 286
Clinton, Hillary, 120, 162, 208, 213, 214, 218,
    228, 230, 231, 248, 296
  Afghanistan strategy, 286, 287, 322, 324
  on counterinsurgency, 229, 234, 263
  vs. Eikenberry, 235, 285
  Holbrooke and, 234, 298, 304
  and Karzai, 314
  on nation building, 268
  as presidential candidate, 366, 379, 380
  as secretary of state, 51, 202
  speech to Asia Society, 304
  and the Taliban, 300, 306, 313
  timetable for the war, 242, 243
  on troop withdrawal, 293
  and Vietnam, 441
Clinton, William "Bill," 52, 333, 364, 375, 438
Coalition Provisional Authority, 191
Coalition Support Funds (CSF), 144
Coates, Victoria, 381, 392, 400, 403, 405, 412
cognitive biases, 25

Cohen, Eliot, 155, 162, 163, 164, 177, 478, 485
Cold War, 194, 347, 470
Coll, Steve, 66, 77, 96, 118, 155, 158, 159, 171,
    172, 417, 431, 459
Collins, Joe, 21, 110
Colombia, 87, 130, 181
Combined Joint Special Operations Task
    Force–Afghanistan (CJSOTF-A), 168
Combined Joint Task Force 180, 2
Combined Security Transition
    Command–Afghanistan (CSTC-A), 171
commander's emergency response program
    (CERP), 189
Conflict Resolution Cell, 301, 302
Conway, James, 282
Cordesman, Anthony, 21, 469
corruption, 1, 17, 18, 23, 82, 120, 139, 140,
    141, 161, 188, 192, 211, 216, 233, 241,
    283, 334, 335, 339–343, 389
  drug-related, 180, 342
  in the justice sector, 184
  of the Karzai family, 211, 338
  and the police, 176, 184
counterinsurgency, 2, 22, 45, 91, 93, 94, 109,
    121, 123, 160, 164, 175, 206, 216, 232
  abandoning, 473
  alternative to, 301
  attempts at, 26
  Barno's plans for, 164
  Biden's views on, 444
  Bush administration, 167, 189
  campaign against, 122
  challenges of, 174
  and counternarcotics, 183
  vs. counterterrorism, 14, 22, 111, 163, 172,
    229, 232–236, 244, 250, 252, 253, 272,
    371, 373, 475
  criticism of, 295
  debate over, 216
  as distraction, 19
  vs. economic development, 271
  emphasis on, 207
  failure of, 18, 20, 28
  focus on, 13, 472
  goal of, 232
  importance of, 221, 254, 475
  impossibility of, 22

counterinsurgency (cont.)
  impressionistic, 111
  lack of commitment to, 257
  long-term, 373
  McChrystal's campaign, 8, 259, 482
  and nation building, 268
  need for, 26, 29, 220, 322, 468
  vs. negotiation, 301
  Obama's approach to, 224, 247, 248, 255
  and Obama's timetable, 291
  Obama's view on, 371
  opposition to, 235, 473
  in Pakistan, 276
  by police, 178
  political component, 122, 124
  purpose of, 26
  reconstruction and, 339
  resistance to, 171
  in Riedel's review, 208
  and state building, 138
  strategy for, 23
  successful efforts, 20, 191, 287
  support for, 227, 228, 309
  supporting counterterrorism, 263
  against the Taliban, 228, 232
  troops for, 251
  US Army manual, 138, 165, 167
  in Vietnam, 29, 110
counternarcotics, 26, 92, 161, 180–184, 216
  aerial eradication, 184
  and counterinsurgency, 183
  cutting or burning, 183
  funding for, 181
  lack of success with, 184
counterterrorism, 14, 19, 69, 139, 160, 168,
    169, 216, 224
  abandoning, 413–419
  against al-Qaida, 148, 229, 232
  attempts at, 26
  autonomy of, 174
  bureaucracy of, 172, 174
  Bush administration and, 41, 156–160
  clandestine, 168
  vs. counterinsurgency, 14, 22, 111, 163,
    229, 232–236, 244, 250, 252, 253, 272,
    371, 373, 475
  and the Doha agreement, 417

effectiveness of, 263
focus on, 74, 88, 89, 131, 160, 488
as focus, 371, 372, 453
as goal, 70
goals of, 224
importance of, 158, 323, 475
McChrystal's views on, 260
as nation building, 372
vs. nation building, 204
need for, 26
NSC's recommendation for, 287
Obama administration's approach, 373
Pakistan and, 98
pared-down mission, 474
postwar, 353, 360, 367, 410, 411, 412, 413,
    415, 427, 429, 433, 447, 456
prioritizing, 26, 91, 159, 373
relationship to governance and
    reconstruction, 333
requirements for, 267
security requirement for, 387
short-term, 373, 476
support for, 227
supported by counterinsurgency, 263
Taliban's view of, 417
troops for, 251
US strategy, 374
and the warlords, 120
COVID-19 pandemic, 429
Crimea, 359
Crocker, Ryan
  as ambassador, 89, 97, 213, 260, 279, 319,
    353
  Congressional testimony, 486
  on reconstruction, 94, 272
  signing the Atlantic Council report, 364
  on the Taliban, 344
Cuba, 40
Cunningham, James
  as ambassador, 11, 334, 336
  assessment of the war, 354, 356, 360, 491
  Atlantic Council report, 364, 365, 398,
    424
  on nation building, 335
  on Obama's timeline, 281, 325, 329, 330,
    331, 332, 354, 366
  on the Taliban, 318, 329

Curtis, Lisa, 392, 395, 405, 406, 407, 418, 421, 430
Cyrus the Great, 13

Dam, Bette, 62
Dayton Accords, 297
Delmore effect, 25
Desert One mission, 445
disarmament of illegally armed groups (DIAG), 118
disarmament, demobilization, and reintegration (DDR) effort, 92, 122
dissent cable, 450, 455
Dobbins, Jim
  and the Afghanistan Study Group, 444
  on aid to Afghanistan, 88, 89, 91
  as ambassador, 59, 73, 277, 314, 316
  assessment of the war, 20, 78, 467, 470
  at Bonn, 74, 75
  in Doha, 317
  on the end of the war, 354
  on Karzai, 350
  on nation building, 95, 126, 132, 273, 483
  negotiation with the Taliban, 316, 317, 318, 319, 350
  on Obama's timetable, 326
  on Pakistan, 344, 346
  on reconstruction, 92
  signing the Atlantic Council report, 364
  as Special Representative for Afghanistan and Pakistan, 271, 303, 309, 316, 376, 397
Doha agreement, 23, 326, 400, 401, 473
  accountability for, 449
  and the Afghan government, 419–425
  and the Biden administration, 442, 447
  compliance with, 431
  and counterterrorism, 413–419
  implementation of, 429–434, 443
  negotiations, 402–407
  praise for, 449
  public circulation of, 444
  questions for negotiation, 407–412
  signing of, 435
  substance of, 425–429
Donati, Jessica, 359, 360, 361, 362, 367, 370
Donilon, Thomas, 201, 205, 236, 240, 252, 259, 286, 292

Dostum, Abdul Rashid, 116, 118
drone strikes, 147, 148, 229, 276, 348, 353, 370, 417, 456
  in Pakistan, 145, 148, 311
drug trafficking, 4, 20, 116, 119, 137, 139, 140, 141, 161, 181, 184, 211, 340, 439, 441. *See also* opium production
  counternarcotics and, 180–184
Dunford, Joe, 268, 333, 368, 386, 444

East Timor, 191
economic development, 26, 31, 90, 109, 139, 164, 207, 268, 271, 274, 383
Edelman, Eric, 38, 60, 98, 127, 135, 150, 159, 164, 171, 176, 177
Eggers, Jeff, 340, 347
Egypt, 88
Eikenberry, Karl
  as ambassador, 20, 208, 210, 233, 235, 265, 285
  assessment of the war, 177, 255, 264
  Clinton's dislike for, 285
  counterinsurgency strategy, 234, 295
  disagreement with McChrystal, 285
  on Germany's police training, 94
  governance concerns, 235
  and Karzai, 314
  on Obama's timetable, 279
  on Pakistan, 347
  reconstruction strategy, 235
  replaced by Crocker, 213, 272
  as US commander, 20, 93, 100, 134, 139, 150, 159, 164, 169, 185
  videoconference with, 239
Eisenhower, Dwight, 194
Emanuel, Rahm, 246
Enhanced Partnership with Pakistan Act, 199, 274
Erdmann, Andrew, 32, 104
Esper, Mark
  on leaving Afghanistan, 413, 415, 423, 424, 428, 431
  on negotiation with the Taliban, 410, 423, 488
  as secretary of defense, 403, 405, 408, 410, 422, 428
European Command (EUCOM), 171

Fairweather, Jack, 51
Fallon, William (Bill), 55, 103, 143, 151, 170,
    177, 185, 190
Farrell, Theo, 138
Fayaz, Malawi Abdullah, 134, 136
Feaver, Peter, 154
Federally Administered Tribal Areas (FATA),
    96, 148, 312, 370
Feith, Doug
    on Afghan security forces, 479
    and the Afghanistan constitution, 112
    on aid to Afghanistan, 109
    assessment of the war, 44, 85, 86, 101
    on the Bonn Process, 87
    on challenges of Afghanistan, 126
    counterterrorism approach, 79
    internal memo, 89
    on international cooperation, 92
    memoir, 80, 107, 472
    on nation building, 86, 108, 334
    on Powell, 42
    on reconstruction, 107
    on the Taliban, 48, 49, 67, 79
    on terrorism, 39, 40
    on warlords, 119
Finn, Robert, 339
Flournoy, Michèle, 209, 223, 270, 364, 444
Focused District Development program,
    178
Ford, Gerald, 162, 436
Foreign Service, 128, 129, 135, 217, 218, 297,
    376, 441
    dissent cables, 450
Foreign Terrorist Organizations, 40
Fox, David, 63
Franks, Tommy, 49, 53, 55, 91
friendly fire, 173

Gall, Carlotta, 19
Gastright, John
    on aid for Afghanistan, 110, 152, 153
    assessment of the war, 92, 100, 104, 107,
        289, 452
    on corruption, 139
    on the drug trade, 181, 182, 184
    and Musharraf, 98, 100
    on Pakistan, 135, 144, 147
    on the Taliban, 123
    on warlords in Kabul, 116
Gates, Bob, 405, 473
    in Afghanistan, 337
    Afghanistan strategy, 334
    assessment of the war, 191, 231, 242, 253,
        255, 259, 291, 473
    background and experience, 214
    on Biden in Afghanistan, 211
    on Biden's plan, 233
    on Biden's opposition, 292
    on the bureaucracy, 271
    on capacity building, 266
    changing commanders, 222
    on civilian aid to Afghanistan, 266
    on civilian casualties, 262
    on the civilian surge, 265
    Congressional testimony, 267
    on corruption, 120, 339
    on counterinsurgency, 229, 235
    on counternarcotics strategies, 183, 184
    on counterterrorism, 233
    disagreement with Biden, 286, 287
    firing McKiernan, 21
    Flournoy's memo to, 270
    goals for Afghanistan, 215, 216
    on governance, 185
    on Iraq, 151, 155
    on Karzai, 212
    and Lute, 385
    on Lute's plan, 206, 230
    on McChrystal's interview, 283
    on McKiernan's troop request, 202
    memoir, 174, 199, 216, 259, 278, 285, 286
    on military command, 175
    on military vs. White House, 246
    on nation building, 472
    National Intelligence Estimate, 192
    on negotiation with Taliban, 305, 306, 307,
        308, 309, 315, 317, 320, 326
    and Obama, 204, 205, 206, 208, 214, 215,
        223, 225, 245, 246, 248, 252, 254, 292
    on Obama, 199
    on Obama's timetable, 237, 238, 239, 240,
        241, 243, 280, 281, 287
    on Pakistan, 146, 149, 344, 346, 348
    on reconstruction, 273

as secretary of defense, 126, 133, 150, 167, 172, 173, 200, 215, 219, 228
on the timetable for withdrawal, 327
on US withdrawal, 331
George W. Bush Presidential Library, 3
Germany, 92, 94, 486
  embassy in Kabul, 369
  US presence in, 353
Ghani, Ashraf, 350, 352, 422, 448, 451
Giustozzi, Antonio, 136, 138
Goldberg, Jeffrey, 374, 375, 377
Goodson, Larry, 4, 94, 95
Gopal, Anand, 19
governance, 184–191, 338, 389, 469
  and counterterrorism, 333
  efforts to improve, 161
  under Ghani, 352
  improving, 184, 263
  investment in, 224
  lack of, 230, 235, 264
  pessimism regarding, 334, 335, 338
  vs. terrorism, 264
  tribal, 342, 343
  US aid for, 258
  warlords and, 342
  weak, 139
Graham, Lindsey, 211
Green Berets, 159, 168, 177
Grenier, Bob, 49, 62, 78
  meeting with Osmani, 48
Grossman, Marc
  and the Afghan Study Group, 444
  in Afghanistan, 142, 214, 233
  communication with Karzai, 313
  negotiation with Taliban, 312–315
  on Obama's timetable, 278, 326, 409
  plan for prisoner exchange, 319
  on reconstruction, 32
  signing the Atlantic Council report, 364
  as special representative, 397
Guantanamo Bay, 303, 319
Gulf War (1991), 52

Haass, Richard, 12, 13, 82, 174
Hadley, Steve
  and the Afghanistan Study Group, 444
  on aid to Afghanistan, 87, 102, 106

assessment of the war, 72, 129, 130, 142, 154
background and education, 162
on Bush's Afghanistan strategy, 52
on governance, 188
on the intelligence community, 162
on Iraq, 152, 155
on McKiernan's troop request, 202
memos for Lute, 193
on nation building, 82
as national security advisor, 151, 162
NSC review, 163, 164, 167
on Pakistan, 58, 145, 146, 147, 150, 157
preparing for the Obama administration, 3, 194, 195
signing the Atlantic Council report, 364
strategy review (2006), 154
on the Taliban, 60, 67
Hagel, Chuck, 316, 319, 333, 338, 355, 364, 376, 441
Haiti, 89
Haqqani Network, 97, 146, 148, 150, 276, 320, 344, 345
Haqqani, Siraj, 418, 419
Harriman, Averell, 209
Harriman, Tony, 104, 118, 158, 187
Haskell, Floyd, 437
Hayden, Mike, 58, 146, 159
Hazaras, 17, 73, 113
helicopters, 134, 182, 331, 368, 451, 453, 479
Helmand, 138, 173, 259, 260
  reconstruction in, 272
  Taliban attack on, 460
  town of Marja, 288
Hizb-i-Islami, 122
Holbrooke, Richard
  assessment of the war, 230
  on the civilian surge, 270
  and Clinton, 234
  death of, 273, 304
  as diplomat, 297, 310, 325
  on ignorance, 485
  and Karzai, 314
  on Karzai, 212
  Lute and, 298
  on negotiation with Taliban, 298, 299, 300, 302, 308, 317, 323

Holbrooke, Richard (cont.)
  on Pakistan, 275
  prior experience, 297
  as special representative for Afghanistan
    and Pakistan (SRAP), 208, 212, 213, 397
  unpopularity of, 308
  on Vietnam, 218
  Vietnam experience, 441
Hosseini, Khaled, 7
hubris, 295, 374, 375, 489
human rights, 13, 74, 75, 112, 306, 349, 389,
  424, 444, 493
humanitarian aid, 88
Hussein, Saddam, 152, 157, 438
hyperbolic discounting, 25

imperialism
  avoiding, 83
  cultural, 82, 83, 85, 380
Independent Directorate of Local
  Governance (IDLG), 187
India, 100, 347
Indian Embassy, 137
Indonesia, 399
internally displaced persons (IDPs), 95, 369
International Security Assistance Force
    (ISAF), 31, 76, 89, 117, 138, 167, 168,
    172, 260, 262, 288, 330, 331, 337, 356,
    439, 482
  and the Afghan elections, 350
  critique of, 220
  drawing down, 369
  new operational level headquarters, 209
  and OEF, 167–175
  US forces separate from, 174
Inter-Services Intelligence (ISI), 96, 97, 98,
    99, 345
Iran, 104, 156, 412
  hostages in, 445
  support for terrorism, 39, 40
Iran-Contra, 319
Iraq, 81, 87, 191, 310, 379, 441, 491
  Afghanistan compared to, 330
  as distraction, 5, 7, 21, 23, 96, 104, 133,
    150–156, 166, 192, 208, 318, 365, 479,
    482
  invasion of, 24

military surge in, 154, 156
Obama and, 374
reconstruction in, 389
Shia autocracy in, 363
sponsoring terrorism, 40
stability in, 226
strategy review, 223
success in, 334
surge in, 131, 150, 153, 193, 229, 366, 392,
  481
US aid to, 88, 95, 110, 337
US invasion of, 1, 103, 105, 157, 160, 464,
  468
in US popular culture, 7
US withdrawal from, 363, 463
war in, 4
Iraq War (2003–2011), 71, 150, 160, 199, 215,
    218, 284, 438, 469
  American support for, 105
  as distraction, 101–105, 109
  disagreements over, 200
  end of, 259
  and the Obama administration, 375
  Obama's opposition to, 197, 200
  surge in, 309
  US support for, 465
  veterans of, 131
Iraqi army, 177
ISIS, 363, 371, 380, 410, 445, 462, 463
  pressure on, 374
ISIS-K, 416, 427
Islam, 43
  Deobandi, 16
  Hanafi, 16
  Shia, 17, 363
Islamic Emirate, 140, 316, 317
Islamic law, 11
Islamic Revolutionary Guard Corps, 430
Islamic State, 360, 363, 367, 417, 462. See also
    ISIS; ISIS-K
Islamists, 43, 44
Israel, 144, 463
  US aid to, 88, 110, 337
Italy, 92

Jackson, Colin
  assessment of the war, 433

on the Department of Defense, 403
on Khalilzad's negotiation with the
  Taliban, 408, 416
on McMaster and Bolton, 392, 412
on McMaster and Mattis, 395, 396
on Pompeo, 403
on Trump's policymaking, 387, 390
on Trump's South Asia strategy, 392
Jalil, Mullah, 62
Japan, 42, 92, 118, 125, 144
Japanese internment camps, 43
Jefferson, Thomas, 487
jihad, 58, 134, 135, 140, 156
jihadism, 42, 44, 158, 374
jihadists, 8, 14, 18, 22, 147, 156, 276, 363, 365,
  374, 384, 399, 410, 434, 447, 462, 464,
  472
Johnson, David, 117
Joint Special Operations Command (JSOC),
  168
Jones, James (Jim)
  advising Biden, 441
  and Holbrooke, 209, 212
  and McChrystal, 222, 225, 231
  as national security advisor, 3, 170, 195,
    252, 260
  and Obama, 298
  on Obama's timetable, 242, 279, 332
  under Obama, 201, 202, 206, 209, 218, 222
  on Pakistan, 345
  replaced by Donilon, 286, 332
  signing the Atlantic Council report, 364
  as Supreme Allied Commander in Europe,
    169
  on the Taliban, 236
  on Vietnam, 217
  as Vietnam veteran, 217
Jones, Seth, 139, 261
just war, 157, 197, 377, 393, 491, 493, 494

Kabul. See also Afghan government
  Afghan government in, 143, 185, 215
  Afghan security forces in, 261
  al-Qaida in, 456
  American embassy in, 455
  anti-corruption task force, 382
  Biden's visit to, 211

chief of police, 134
civilians in, 265, 266
destruction in, 94, 116
evacuation from, 457
fall of, 34, 55, 431, 447–454, 491, 497
German embassy in, 369
Holbrooke's visit to, 212
Kerry's visit to, 213, 351
NATO headquarters, 210
Northern Alliance in, 73
peacekeeping in, 75, 76, 89, 168, 169, 456
police academy in, 94
Serena Hotel, 137, 358
and the Taliban, 320
Taliban attacks on, 73, 365, 383, 422, 456,
  459
Taliban in, 134
Taliban leaving, 74, 75, 224
terrorist violence in, 134, 358, 365, 424
US embassy in, 89, 98, 135, 152, 213, 265,
  289, 354
US forces in, 360
war in, 137, 191, 193
warlords in, 116
Kabul–Kandahar highway, 125
Kajaki Dam, 272
Kandahar
  Blue Mosque, 133
  capture of, 260
  chief of police, 119, 369
  evacuation of, 61, 63
  fall of, 12, 55, 75
  Gates' visit to, 338
  governor of, 118
  negotiations over, 66
  Ruggiero in, 265, 269
  Sarposa Prison, 178
  suicide bombing in, 137
  surrender of, 61, 62, 64
  Taliban in, 48, 59, 320, 443
Karzai administration, 124
Karzai, Ahmed Wali, 3, 211
Karzai, Hamid
  and Biden, 211, 441
  at Bonn, 60
  and the BSA, 350
  communications with, 62

Karzai, Hamid (cont.)
on counternarcotics efforts, 184
on counternarcotics strategies, 184
criticism of, 210, 271
criticism of US, 225
Eikenberry's critique of, 285
election of, 63, 113
family of, 338
improving governance, 187
and Holbrooke, 212
as interim leader, 75, 77, 78
and the Kajaki Dam, 272
lack of trust in, 234, 340, 343
meeting with Biden, 203
meeting with Taliban, 61, 62, 63, 65, 66
negotiations process, 312–315
and the Obama administration, 211, 212,
213
Obama's dislike for, 292
objecting to US negotiation with Taliban,
314
on Pakistan, 99
and the Pashtuns, 61
on the peace process, 314
and Petraeus, 285
request for troops, 93
responsibilities of, 250
second inaugural address, 327
support for, 76
taking ownership, 238, 241
and the Taliban, 62, 121, 125, 300, 315
as unreliable partner, 350
US assistance for, 106, 107, 117, 119
on US negotiation with Taliban, 304, 313,
316, 317, 324, 443
and the warlords, 118
weaknesses of, 189, 190, 211, 212
Kayani, Ashfaq, 344
Kelly, John, 385, 386, 401
Kennan, George, 209
Kennedy, John F., 487
Kerry, John, 150, 316, 335, 350, 376, 441
and the Afghan elections, 351
in Afghanistan, 213
as secretary of state, 213
on the Senate foreign relations committee,
214

key terrain districts (KTDs), 288, 289
Khalilzad, Zalmay
on aid to Afghanistan, 106, 107, 200
as ambassador, 110, 111, 112, 113, 117,
123
assessment of the war, 72
Atlantic Council report, 364, 398
background and experience, 84
on Biden's speech, 455
on the Bonn process, 59
Congressional testimony, 444, 445
counterinsurgency plans, 164
disappointment of, 126
and the Doha agreement, 326, 443
on the Doha agreement, 426, 427, 432
Doha agreement consequences, 431
Doha negotiations, 402–407, 408, 409, 411,
412, 413, 416, 417, 418, 420, 421, 425,
433
governance concerns, 235
and Karzai, 190
on the Loya Jirga, 76
on the need for diplomats, 128
on Pakistan, 99, 144
as special presidential envoy for
Afghanistan, 84
as special representative for Afghanistan
reconciliation, 399
on stabilization, 142
on the Taliban, 123
chosen by Trump, 398–400
Khan, Fahim, 116, 118
Khan, Ismail, 3, 118
Khyber Pakhtunkhwa Provinces, 96
Kilcullen, David, 50, 66, 469, 474
Kissinger, Henry, 84, 162, 302
Klain, Ron, 442
kleptocracy, 339, 340, 341, 395
Kolenda, Chris, 280, 304, 323, 324, 325, 340,
469
Komer, Robert (Bob), 29, 30, 31, 32, 128, 177,
270, 479, 480, 481, 482
Korean War, 285
Kosovo, 80, 89, 174
Kufi, Fawzia, 460
Kurds, 363
Kushner, Jared, 385

Latin America, 377
Lavoy, Peter
  on Afghan good enough, 335
  assessment of the war, 263, 264, 270, 279, 365, 375
  on the bureaucracy, 270, 477
  on the end of the war, 361, 362, 363
  leading 2015 review, 361
  on negotiation with the Taliban, 298, 299, 369, 370
  on Obama, 377
  on Obama's attitude toward the military, 248
  on Obama's timetable, 240
  on Pakistan, 276, 277
  on the peace process, 321
  on the postwar situation, 358
  on Riedel's review, 204
  roles of, 32, 148
  strategy under Trump, 392
  on the Taliban, 232, 320
  on timetable for withdrawal, 362
  on US postwar presence, 382
  on withdrawal from Afghanistan, 360
Law and Order Trust Fund for Afghanistan (LOTFA), 76
law of triviality, 25
Lebanon, 319
Levin, Carl, 243
liberal internationalism, 27
Liberia, 130
Libi, Abu Laith al-, 56
Libya, 40, 379
  bombing of, 41
  reconstruction in, 389
  as terrorist safe haven, 463
Lincoln, Abraham, 391
literacy training, 176
Llorens, Hugo, 325, 367, 371, 383, 388, 390, 391, 401, 431, 434
Loya Jirga, 76, 112
Lujan, Fernando, 355, 360, 362, 400, 432
Lute, Doug
  on the 2009 strategy review, 228
  in Afghanistan, 288
  as ambassador to NATO, 209, 357
  assessment of the war, 171, 223, 233, 253, 271, 286, 287, 288, 289, 290, 291

background and education, 166
  on bureaucracy, 477
  and the chain of command, 172
  on chain of command, 219
  Conflict Resolution Cell, 301, 302, 309
  on the end of the war, 357
  and Gates, 288, 385
  on governance, 188
  on Green Berets, 177
  on Grossman, 312
  Holbrooke and, 298
  on Karzai, 314, 315
  on McChrystal's report, 245, 259
  on McKiernan's firing, 209
  on McKiernan's troop request, 202
  memos from the NSC, 193
  on military vs. White House, 247
  on negotiation with the Taliban, 299, 301, 313, 314, 315, 321
  in the NSC, 288
  on Obama's strategy, 255
  and Obama, 205
  preparing for Obama, 200
  strategic implementation plan, 230, 231
  strategy review, 192, 194, 195, 204, 206, 216, 254
  on strategy, 471
  on the timeline, 238
  as war czar, 166
  White House role of, 208
  on withdrawal from Afghanistan, 294

MacArthur, Douglas, 249, 285
Mahmud Ahmed, 47, 49, 57
Malkasian, Carter, 4, 15–18, 51, 66, 418, 433
  on the Taliban, 140
Mansour, Mullah Akhtar, 320, 370
Marshall Plan, 90, 106, 129, 130, 131, 199, 215, 439, 487
Marshall, George, 91
Massive Ordinance Air Blast (MOAB), 391
Mattis, Jim, 384, 385, 386, 388, 393, 401, 403, 406, 407
  Afghanistan strategy, 395
  firing of, 403, 407
  resignation letter, 404
McCain, John, 200, 243

McChrystal, Stanley, 490
  Afghanistan report, 227
  assessment of the war, 31, 175, 255,
    283–284, 323, 336, 367, 483, 486
  on Biden's proposal, 233
  as chief of staff, 141
  counterinsurgency campaign, 8, 259, 469
  counterinsurgency strategy, 228, 229, 235
  counterterrorism campaign, 233, 260
  on defeating the enemy, 231, 232, 466
  expectations of, 290
  firing of, 283–284, 309, 323
  on governance, 264, 266
  in Iraq, 219
  as ISAF commander, 128, 168, 173, 208,
    260, 262, 311, 373, 388, 482
  London speech, 246, 247
  on McKiernan's troop request, 201
  on nation building, 472
  on negotiation with Taliban, 302, 309, 323
  and Obama, 446
  on Obama'a approach, 255
  on Obama's timetable, 241
  opposition to Obama, 246
  on Pakistan, 348
  pressure on, 278
  progress reports, 288
  protection for civilians, 262
  on reconstruction, 265
  replacing McKiernan, 210, 219
  report on Afghanistan, 222, 223, 224, 225
  report on the war, 245, 254
  on the Riedel review, 223
  Rolling Stone article, 283–284, 285
  on size of force, 217
  strategy report, 245
  troop request, 228, 229, 231, 233, 234, 236,
    245, 250, 251, 252, 332
  videoconference with, 239
McColl, John, 219
McKenzie, Kenneth, 219, 278, 392, 408, 421,
    423, 442, 445, 448, 451, 456, 457
  Afghanistan strategy, 394
McKiernan, David, 119, 159, 169, 170, 172,
    192
  at the 2008 review, 193
  on the Afghan Army, 179

assessment of the war, 193, 222, 245, 268
  on the drug trade, 181
  firing of, 208, 209, 219
  as IASF commander, 178, 204, 214
  troop request, 201, 202, 203, 205, 216, 222,
    223, 244, 245
McKinley, Mike, 307, 358, 359, 402, 406, 407,
    416, 429
  on Pakistan, 274
McMaster, H. R., 120, 219, 341, 342, 404, 412,
    433, 450, 490, 491
  Afghanistan strategy, 392–394, 395
  background, 382
  Camp David meeting, 387
  firing of, 401
  Trump disagreeing with, 384
  and the war in Afghanistan, 381–387
McNeill, Dan, 78, 81, 94, 101, 102, 106, 110,
    130, 158, 167, 170, 173, 219
Meadows, Mark, 430
Mearsheimer, John, 25
medical evacuations, 328, 331
Mehsud, Baitullah, 146, 276
Mehsud, Hakimullah, 276
Menendez, Robert, 455
Middle East, 377
Miller, Laurel, 267, 321, 372, 390, 392, 419,
    426
  as Deputy Special Representative, 316, 317,
    318, 319
  Doha negotiations, 421
  on ignorance, 485
  on McMaster, 382, 383
  on negotiation with the Taliban, 322, 323,
    384, 398
  on the postwar situation, 358
  on the timeline for withdrawal, 327, 332
  on Trump, 389, 391
  on withdrawal from Afghanistan, 364
Miller, Scott, 369, 405, 406, 408, 443, 451, 459
Milley, Mark, 446
Milosevic, Slobodan, 52
Mohammad, Khalid Sheikh, 56, 58
Mojaddedi, Sibghatullah, 4, 123
monarchy, 76
Monib, Hamdullah, 413
Morgenthau, Hans, 25

Mullen, Mike, 151, 153, 202, 219, 222, 239
  assessment of the war, 245
  Congressional testimony, 247, 259
  on Bush's priorities, 215
  on counterinsurgency, 228, 229
  on McKiernan's firing, 209
  and Obama, 246, 446
  on Obama's timetable, 240
  on Pakistan, 345
  timetable for the war, 243
Musharraf, Pervez, 46, 47, 57, 58, 96, 97, 98, 100, 144, 145, 146, 274, 277, 441
Muslim immigration ban, 380
Muslims. *See* Islam
Muttawakil, Wakil Ahmed, 77

Naqib, Mullah, 62
nation building, 19, 26, 74
  abandonment of, 14, 23
  Biden's approach to, 230, 438, 439, 453, 472
  bureaucracy and, 130
  Bush's approach to, 106, 196, 464, 472
  challenges of, 474
  and the civilian surge, 266
  and counterinsurgency, 22, 373
  and counterterrorism, 267
  counterterrorism as, 372
  criticism of, 10, 12, 473
  as cultural imperialism, 380
  failure of, 18, 28, 337
  funding for, 13
  as goal, 69
  governance and, 186
  Holbrooke's view on, 298
  at home, 437
  importance of, 468, 471, 476
  impossibility of, 22
  inattention to, 180
  as issue, 229
  lack of, 13, 235
  lack of training for, 273
  limited approach to, 14, 371
  need for, 26, 111, 206
  Obama's approach to, 204, 215, 335, 336, 371

  opposition to, 25, 54, 56, 80–87, 107, 132, 157, 189, 190, 237, 241, 266, 267, 334, 380, 389, 420, 440, 473, 483
  as priority, 373
  purpose of, 26
  question of how much, 473
  successful, 20
  support for, 5, 438, 483
  Trump's opposition to, 29
National Intelligence Estimate (NIE), 192
National Solidarity Program, 186, 337
National Unity Government (NUG), 352
nationalism, 380
NATO
  in Afghanistan, 169, 170, 191, 221, 251, 259, 318, 359, 364, 365
  attack on headquarters in Kabul, 210
  in the Balkans, 310
  Chicago summit, 349
  Lisbon summit, 327
  Lute as ambassador to, 209
  in Pakistan, 275, 277
  UK summit, 349
  Warsaw summit, 365
NATO Training Mission–Afghanistan (NTM-A), 171
neoimperialism, 377
nepotism, 335
Neumann, Ronald E.
  on Afghan security forces, 94
  on Afghanistan, 161, 164, 471
  on aid to Afghanistan, 126, 129, 153, 181, 185
  as ambassador, 135, 152, 491
  assessment of the war, 129, 135, 176
  on counterterrorism, 158
  on the drug trade, 180
  governance concerns, 235
  on Karzai, 190
  memoir, 135, 182, 187, 484, 485
  on the need for funding, 137
  on Pakistan, 100
  on policy implementation, 478
  signing the Atlantic Council report, 364
  on the Taliban, 136
Neumann, Ronald G., 135

#NeverTrump movement, 380
New America Foundation, 311, 413
Nicholson, John, 368, 383, 386
Niebuhr, Reinhold, 27, 483, 492, 494
Nigeria, 399
nihilism, 494
Nixon, Richard, 294, 302, 310
noncombatant evacuation operation (NEO), 456
North Korea, 40, 156
North Vietnam, 302, 310, 397, 436. *See also* Vietnam
North Waziristan, 344
Northern Alliance, 3, 50, 54, 60, 64, 72, 73, 76, 87, 93, 113, 116, 118, 120, 140, 306, 351, 451. *See also* warlords

O'Brien, Robert, 418, 427, 429, 432, 458, 459, 488
O'Hanlon, Michael, 12, 20, 21, 474
O'Sullivan, Meghan, 166
Obaidullah, Mullah, 61
Obama administration, 124, 132
  on Afghan reconstruction, 338
  Afghanistan strategy, 13, 14, 23, 91, 107, 197, 210, 214, 217, 228, 230, 245, 253, 292, 299, 312, 315, 328, 335, 336, 338, 343, 355, 356, 359, 367, 371, 381, 394, 464, 470
  bureaucracy hurdles, 269–274
  civilian aid to Afghanistan, 265
  and the civilian surge, 268
  counterinsurgency strategy, 174
  counterterrorism strategy, 371, 373, 475
  criticism of, 20
  decision-makers in, 33
  dislike for Holbrooke, 308
  drawdown plans, 376
  use of drones, 311, 312
  and Karzai, 211
  Karzai and, 211, 212, 213
  on nation building, 235, 236, 267
  negotiation with the Taliban, 303, 304, 306, 313, 316, 317, 383, 397, 405
  opposition to timetable, 491
  and Pakistan, 275, 277, 345
  vs. the Pentagon, 244–249, 284

  pessimism of, 337
  preparations for, 194, 200
  records of, 36
  and the Riedel review, 245
  staff changes, 286
  and the Taliban, 68, 300, 320, 323, 348, 386
  on troop withdrawal, 292–296
  view of Vietnam, 217
Obama Doctrine, 377
Obama, Barack
  2010 review of progress, 286–291
  in Afghanistan, 291, 328
  Afghanistan strategy, 1, 6, 11, 13, 14, 33, 120, 197, 198, 200, 203, 208, 210, 214, 223, 224, 226, 227, 228, 229, 230, 232, 235, 236, 241, 245, 247, 248, 249–253, 254, 255, 289, 292, 324, 329, 335, 356, 371, 372, 376, 389, 390, 409, 427, 447, 464, 472, 484, 488
  approach to foreign aid, 254
  approving request for more troops, 205
  assessment of the war, 197, 199, 291, 377
  background, 198
  and the Bush administration, 195
  Cairo University address, 493
  campaign rhetoric, 200, 203, 222, 224, 225, 280, 333, 375, 378, 491
  counterterrorism strategy, 474
  criticism of, 8
  on drone strikes, 311
  ending the war, 353, 354, 357, 359, 360, 363, 447
  endorsing the Riedel review, 215
  errors of, 175
  exit strategy, 366, 375, 382
  firing McChrystal, 283–284, 309
  Holbrooke and, 298
  inaugural address, 201
  inauguration of, 3
  increasing troops, 442, 445
  influence on war in Afghanistan, 374–378
  and Iraq, 363, 374
  Mattis's critique of, 385
  on McChrystal's report, 224, 225
  on McKiernan's troop request, 202
  memoir, 224, 225, 226, 236, 237, 249, 484
  mistrust of the military, 377

on nation building, 236, 389
National Security Council meeting, 201
Nobel Prize speech, 256, 372, 393, 450, 487, 494, 495
opposition to Iraq War, 200
on Pakistan, 274, 346, 349
postwar strategy, 365, 367, 370
as President, 35, 239, 248, 481, 490
and the Riedel review, 207
as Senator, 197
strategy review, 3
and the Taliban, 324
timetable for withdrawal, 23, 236–244, 250, 252, 258, 277–282, 290, 293, 305, 325, 326, 327, 330, 333, 340, 343, 358, 361, 362, 364, 365, 366, 367, 378, 409, 413, 433, 463, 465, 473, 482, 491
tribute to Holbrooke, 304
on Vietnam, 218
on the War in Iraq, 197
and the War on Terror, 197
West Point speech, 249
Odierno (General), 279
Office of the Coordinator for Reconstruction and Stabilization, 131
Olson, Rick, 271, 278, 323, 328, 340, 345
Omar, Mullah, 47, 48, 49, 50, 51, 62, 63, 64, 65, 66, 67, 78, 97, 134, 135, 138, 207, 303, 310, 313, 320
death of, 405
Operation Anaconda, 70
Operation Deliberate Force, 310
Operation Enduring Freedom (OEF), 171
and the ISAF, 167–175, 330
Operation Mountain Resolve, 111
opium production, 180, 181, 183, 263. *See also* drug trafficking
organized crime, 341
Osmani, Mullah, 48, 49

Pace, Peter, 64
Packer, George, 201, 208, 212, 213, 234, 255, 267, 298, 300
Pakistan, 45, 47, 73
and al-Qaida, 100, 236
and the Bush administration, 3
drone strikes in, 311

as Major Non-NATO Ally (MNNA), 144
and the Obama administration, 197, 275
as safe haven for Taliban, 199
as state sponsor of terrorism, 346
and the Taliban, 123, 133, 135, 143–150, 156, 274–277, 388
Taliban in, 310
as terrorist safe haven, 98, 99, 133, 139, 143, 144, 146, 148, 149, 150, 156, 160, 195, 206, 227, 229, 233, 234, 274, 292, 294, 311, 344, 346, 348, 356, 370, 390, 462, 463
Trump's strategy, 390, 396
untrustworthiness of, 1, 57–59, 96–101, 145, 157, 274–277, 343–349, 468
US aid to, 88, 144, 149, 199, 275, 344, 346, 349
violence in, 147
Pakistan People's Party, 274
Pakistani Army, 275
Pakistani Taliban, 145, 147, 148, 275, 277, 344, 345. *See also* Taliban
Panetta, Leon, 120, 228, 252, 287, 307, 325, 338, 354, 355, 360
background, 333
on corruption in the Afghan government, 340, 342
signing the Atlantic Council report, 364
on tribal governance, 343
Paris Peace Accords, 302, 310
Pashtuns, 16, 47, 53, 54, 61, 73, 75, 76, 80, 96, 113, 189, 190, 212, 397
patronage networks, 335, 339
Patterson, Anne, 229
Patton, George, 284, 430
peace building, 1, 132, 160
peacekeeping, 69, 80, 89, 137, 168, 175
by European allies, 170
Pence, Mike, 387, 392, 414, 415, 423
in Afghanistan, 394
Pentagon
vs. the Obama administration, 244–249, 284
Pentagon Papers, 10
personalistic rule, 335, 342
Petraeus, David
at the 2008 review, 193

Petraeus, David (cont.)
addressing corruption, 341
assessment of the war, 291, 463, 467, 486
on the Balkans, 310
as CENTCOM commander, 260
as commander of ISAF, 173, 219, 260, 309, 330, 332
confirmation hearing for CIA, 293
Congressional testimony, 267, 293, 336
on counterinsurgency, 167, 228, 229, 263, 321
on the end of the war, 353, 354
expectations of, 290
as ISAF commander, 309
and Karzai, 285
and the KTD focus, 289
on McKiernan's firing, 209
McMaster as advisor to, 382
on nation building, 267, 268, 472
on negotiation with Taliban, 309, 311, 323, 370, 388
and Obama, 246, 446
on Obama's commitment to the war, 289
on Pakistan, 149, 276
pressure on, 278
progress reports, 288
public comments, 246
troop withdrawal strategy, 237, 239, 240, 244, 279, 292, 293, 295, 325, 329, 330, 331
on Vietnam, 310
Philippines, 44
Plan Colombia, 130, 181
Poland, 88
Pompeo, Mike, 384, 385, 386, 393, 394, 395, 400, 416, 431
Afghanistan strategy, 396
blaming Biden, 435
on the Doha agreement, 432
Doha negotiations, 402–407, 408, 409, 413, 414, 422, 426, 488
on the evacuation, 457
on negotiation with the Taliban, 309, 397
presidential aspirations of, 402
signing the Doha agreement, 425, 426, 429
in the State Department, 401
and Trump, 403

Portman, Rob, 445
Powell Doctrine, 54
Powell, Colin, 39, 41, 47, 54, 73, 78, 80, 82, 275, 385
on aid to Afghanistan, 88
on Iraq, 103
on nation building, 82
on Pakistan, 57, 99, 100
on the Taliban, 67
on Vietnam, 217
press freedom, 263
Priebus, Reince, 384, 386
prisoner exchange, 319, 323
private security forces, 118
Provincial Reconstruction Teams (PRTs), 15, 110, 111, 125, 128, 164, 167, 330, 336
PTS (*Program Tahkim-e Sulh*), 122, 123, 124, 207
Putin, Vladimir, 381, 441

Qanuni, Yunis, 4
Qatar, 303
Taliban in, 316, 317, 318, 320
Qatar, Emir of, 312, 313, 314, 318
Quetta Shura, 97, 148, 320
Quinn, Maureen, 182, 183, 184, 479

Rabbani, Burhanuddin, 313
Rabia, Abu Hamza, 56
Rashid, Ahmed, 19, 96
Raziq, Abdul Achakzai, 119, 405
Razzaq, Abdur Akhundzada, 61
Reagan, Ronald, 4, 41, 401
realism, 25–28, 85, 193, 216, 374, 483
academic, 492
Christian, 494
lack of, 394
prudential, 375
refugees, 70, 95, 436, 437, 456, 458
Resolute Support, 357
Rhodes, Ben, 198, 239
Ricciardone, Frank, 234
Rice, Condoleezza, 48, 52, 53, 54, 60, 81, 92, 122
on Afghanistan, 125, 163
on aid for Afghanistan, 109
on counternarcotics efforts, 182

on Iraq, 102, 103
memo for Bush, 125
memoir, 58, 72
on NATO's involvement, 170
on Pakistan, 97, 144, 146, 149
on reconstruction, 132
as secretary of state, 162, 165, 481
on the Taliban, 123, 135
on the warlords, 119, 130
on women's rights, 112
Rice, Susan, 360, 361, 362, 363, 370, 393
Riedel, Bruce
    strategy review, 204, 205, 206, 207, 208,
        215, 220, 222, 223, 224, 225, 227, 229,
        236, 245, 250, 254, 290, 356, 392
Rodman, Peter, 170
Romney, Mitt, 333, 451
Rood, John, 410, 416
Roosevelt, Franklin, 43
Rubin, Barney, 4, 92, 282, 297, 317, 325, 341
Rubio, Marco, 380
Ruggiero, Frank, 265, 269, 288, 303, 305, 312,
    321, 322
Rumsfeld, Donald, 40, 58, 175, 372, 399, 485,
    489
    Afghanistan strategy, 53, 56, 68, 158, 165,
        334
    on aid to Afghanistan, 109, 129, 131, 158
    bicycle metaphor, 85
    Biden's criticism of, 439
    advice to Bush, 54
    on challenges of Afghanistan, 126
    on civilian vs. military agencies, 165
    on counterinsurgency, 111
    and the Defense Department, 131
    on defense transformation, 52, 54
    firing of, 167
    on imperialism, 83
    internal memo, 90
    on Iraq, 102
    memoir, 39, 80, 81, 85, 107, 204, 472
    on nation building, 83, 334, 380, 389
    on NATO's involvement, 169
    opposition to peacekeeping, 89
    on Pakistan, 97, 99
    and peace building, 132

and the Pentagon, 41
Petraeus's assessment for, 330
and Powell, 385
press conference, 63–69
on PRTs, 110, 128
on reconstruction, 107
and Strmecki, 108, 162
on the Taliban, 48, 65, 66, 67, 163
and Vietnam, 217
on the war in Afghanistan, 121
on the War on Terror, 41, 42
on warlords, 117
Russia. *See also* Soviet Union
    in Afghanistan, 214
    Crimea invasion, 359

Salang Tunnel, 331
Saleh, Amrullah, 4, 460
Sanger, David, 210
Sarposa Prison, 178
Sayyaf, Abdul Rassul, 116
Schelling, Thomas, 299
Schultz, George, 41
Scowcroft, Brent, 162, 363, 392, 470
Serbia, 52, 310
Shaheen, Jeanne, 389
Shahi Kot, Battle of, 3, 70
Shahryar, Ishaq, 13
Shanahan, Patrick, 408
Shapiro, Irving, 437
Sharif, Nawaz, 277
Sharif, Raheel, 344
Shea-Porter, Carol, 267
Shelton, Hugh, 52
Sherzai, 63
Shibh, Ramzi bin al-, 58
Shinn, Jim, 124, 127, 160, 172
Shirzai, Gul Agha, 3, 118
Short, Mike, 310
Sierra Leone, 130
Singh, Vikram, 243, 251, 266, 269, 270, 312,
    322, 324, 356, 371, 376, 470
    on Pakistan, 275
Snowden, Edward, 359
Solarium exercise, 194
Soleimani, Qasem, 430

South Korea, 353

South Vietnam, 32, 177, 217, 422, 436, 437. *See also* Vietnam

Soviet Union. *See also* Russia

in Afghanistan, 53, 54, 84, 90, 142, 182, 217, 399

U-2 spy plane incident, 347

Soviet–Afghan war, 5, 6, 17, 57, 94, 97, 108, 215, 343, 347

Spanta, Rangin Dadfar, 4

Special Immigrant Visa (SIV) program, 449, 454, 455, 457, 458

Special Inspector General for Afghanistan Reconstruction (SIGAR), 10, 30, 33, 127, 279, 369, 426, 432, 435, 453, 457, 468, 481

Special Operations Command (SOCOM), 168

Special Operations Forces (SOF), 168

special operators, 169

Srpska, 310

Stanikzai, Sher Mohammad Abbas, 408

state building. *See* nation building

statesmanship, 28, 483

and courage, 485–487

and justice, 490–492

and temperance, 487–490

and wisdom, 483–485

Strachan, Hew, 467

Strategic Implementation Plan, 236

Strategic Partnership Agreement (SPA), 113, 349

strategy reviews, 87. *See also* Riedel, Bruce

2003, 206

2006, 154, 161, 162, 175, 206, 249–253

2007, 161

2008, 191–196

2015 review, 358–362

under Biden (ninth), 442, 446

under Bush, 3, 12, 28

conclusions of, 26, 28, 161, 253

fall 2009, 253

for Iraq, 155

Lute's review, 192, 194, 195, 204, 206, 216, 254

under McMaster, 382

under Obama, 3, 29, 227, 289

recommendations of, 364, 366

relative value of, 470

Riedel's review, 204, 206, 254

Strengthening Peace Program, 122

Strmecki, Marin, 31, 99, 108, 109, 129, 162, 163

Sudan, 40

Suhrke, Astri, 140

suicide bombings, 134, 137, 147, 210, 358, 369, 456

Sullivan, Jake, 442

Sullivan, John, 389, 392, 446, 448

Suhrke, Astri, 141

surveillance, 23, 177, 443

Syria

civil war in, 359, 374

reconstruction in, 389

sponsoring terrorism, 40

US withdrawal from, 403, 407

Tajiks, 16, 17, 73, 113, 351

Taliban. *See also* Doha agreement

accomplishments of, 16

Afghan, 148, 276, 277, 312, 344

Afghan fight against, 354

and the Afghan government, 350

in the Afghan government, 416

and Afghan identity, 15, 16, 18

in Afghanistan, 3, 76–80, 121, 234

airstrikes against, 451

association with al-Qaida, 22, 26, 44, 45, 46, 47, 48, 49, 50, 51, 65, 68, 77, 133, 207, 228, 229, 300, 305, 388, 407, 409, 416, 417, 418, 428, 430, 431, 433, 440, 445, 452

American view of, 5

amnesty for, 121, 324

Arab Brigade, 50, 56

attack on Navy SEALs, 134

and bin Laden, 47, 48, 49, 51, 64

collapse of, 48, 59

counterinsurgency against, 2, 45, 232, 234, 236

decision not to defeat, 338

defeat of, 93

departure of, 89

disrupting elections, 113

distinction from al-Qaida, 444
Doha agreement, 326, 407, 414, 423, 425
Doha agreement conditions, 426
and the drug trade, 181, 184
emirate of, 452
empowerment of, 27
failure of negotiations with, 320–326
fall from power, 12, 37, 45, 55, 56, 68, 70, 75, 116, 122, 174, 486
good vs. bad, 121
in Helmand, 138
inflexibility of, 125
insurgency of, 22, 61, 69, 133, 137, 138, 140, 143, 150, 156, 158, 160, 161, 163, 170, 207, 256, 332, 367, 444
intelligence against, 39
as Islamic Emirate, 316, 317
jihad of, 134, 135, 140, 156
killing Fayaz, 134
Konduz offensive, 365
leadership of, 320, 370
military offensive, 163, 443, 448, 449, 451, 459, 460
Ministry for the Propagation of Virtue and the Prevention of Vice, 16, 452
negotiation and the military, 307–312
negotiation with, 1, 21, 23, 24, 33, 61, 62, 63, 64, 65, 76, 124, 209, 250, 252, 297, 298, 299, 300–304, 321, 323, 326, 329, 369, 370, 376, 383, 388, 396–400, 415, 482
negotiation with Afghan government, 416
negotiations with Grossman, 312–315
and the Northern Alliance, 54
and Obama's timetable, 278, 281, 282
oral agreements, 417
overthrow of, 1, 129
overtures to, 45–51, 68, 77
and Pakistan, 57
in Pakistan, 96–101, 123, 133, 143–150, 156, 195, 199, 229, 274–277, 310, 311, 344, 347, 348, 370
Pakistan sympathy for, 59, 145
Pakistani, 145, 147, 148, 275, 277, 344, 345
possible surrender of, 66, 67
pressure on, 312, 374, 396, 398
publicity on negotiation with, 304–307

in Qatar, 303, 316–318, 320
reconciliation with, 121–125, 207, 208, 250, 252, 300, 302, 305, 309
removal of leaders, 324
resurgence of, 93, 95, 133–137, 358, 369
return to power, 87, 132, 138, 476
Rumsfeld's press conference, 63–69
sanctions for, 77
as state sponsor of terrorism, 43, 44
taking over Kabul, 451
terrorist attacks by, 365
as terrorist organization, 78
as threat, 5, 377
UN sanctions, 64
unfavorable view of, 140
untrustworthiness of, 431, 449
US bombing of, 391
US demands to, 46, 50
US war against, 11, 15–18, 26, 37, 42, 44, 45, 49, 51, 57, 67, 79, 109, 160, 174, 198, 208, 220, 228–232, 236, 244, 247, 248, 249, 256, 261, 294, 332, 347, 354, 368, 374, 376, 377, 440, 444, 468
victory of, 68
Taliban for Karzai, 77
Taliban Military Commission, 313
Taliban Political Commission, 313
Talibs, 101, 409, 417, 426
Task Force Shafafiyat, 341, 342
Taylor, Maxwell, 29
Tea Party, 403
Tellis, Ashely, 98, 100, 104
Tenet, George, 39, 47, 48, 53, 54
terrorism
    international, 18
    state sponsors of, 12, 39, 40, 43, 45, 56, 69, 79, 346, 372
    US approach to, 27
    war against, 56
terrorist violence, 358, 365, 377, 380, 439. *See also* suicide bombings
Tillerson, Rex, 382, 387, 401
Trotsky, Leon, 415, 468
Truman, Harry, 249, 285
Trump administration
    Afghanistan strategy, 23, 107, 381, 392, 394, 396, 400, 401, 413, 458, 470

Trump administration (cont.)
  blaming Biden administration, 435
  decision-makers in, 33
  and the Doha agreement, 401
  Doha negotiations, 422
  false version of history, 488
  negotiation with al-Qaida, 418
  negotiation with the Taliban, 303
  opposition to nation building, 380
  records of, 36
  South Asia strategy (2017), 387–395
  staff changes, 401
  and the Taliban, 68, 418, 431, 432
Trump, Donald, 368
  Afghanistan speech (2017), 487
  Afghanistan strategy, 23, 384, 386, 388, 390,
    391, 394, 395, 396, 399, 404, 407, 409,
    410, 411, 414, 416, 419, 421, 432, 435,
    447, 460, 464, 484, 488
  approach to counterterrorism, 474
  believability of, 34
  Capitol insurrection, 434
  and the Doha agreement, 23, 427, 433, 447,
    449, 463, 473
  election of, 34, 381
  exit strategy, 432, 433, 434, 435
  foreign policy vision, 379, 380, 381, 384
  Khalilzad appointment, 398, 399
  managerial style, 414
  on nation building, 389, 420, 473
  negotiation with the Taliban, 1, 397, 482
  Pakistan strategy, 390, 396
  and the peace plan, 428
  as president, 35, 481, 490, 491
  as presidential candidate, 380
  South Asia Strategy, 29
  suspending aid to Pakistan, 149
  views on Afghanistan, 379
  war rhetoric, 391

Ukraine, 463
United Kingdom, 92
  counternarcotics effort, 180
  in Afghanistan, 309
military operations in Afghanistan, 272
United Nations, 74, 136
  and the Afghan elections, 113, 350

  in Afghanistan, 78, 142, 187, 191, 210
  aid assessment, 88
  and the Bonn conference, 74, 75, 87
  Bush's address to, 105
  and the ISAF, 117, 175, 357
  peacekeeping force, 168
  Resolute Support mission, 357
  security incident reports, 369, 459
  state building efforts, 130
  unclassified report, 418
United Nations Assistance Mission in
    Afghanistan (UNAMA), 76
United States
  Agriculture Department, 191, 273
  Commerce Department, 188
  Defense Department, 79, 93, 108, 126, 127,
    131, 152, 163, 165, 182, 189, 261, 282,
    287, 319, 332, 355, 368, 391, 403, 406,
    416, 421, 422, 442, 451, 460, 461
  Department of Homeland Security, 229
  Justice Department, 188, 273
  Office of Management and Budget, 31,
    152, 158, 472
  popularity of in Afghanistan, 143
  State Department, 11, 104, 127, 128, 131,
    163, 166, 182, 188, 189, 209, 218, 235,
    266, 270, 273, 287, 304, 319, 323, 360,
    415, 442, 450, 451, 452, 455, 458, 479,
    480
  Treasury Department, 64, 188, 273
US Agency for International Development
    (USAID), 127, 186, 188, 189, 266, 268,
    270, 273, 336, 337
US Air Force, 391
US Army. *See also* Green Berets
  in Afghanistan, 142
  counterinsurgency manual, 138, 165, 167,
    309
  increasing size of, 154
  Operation Enduring Freedom, 168
  Pakistan operations, 149
  rotation of commanders, 171
  separate from ISAF, 174
  Special Forces, 159, 168
US Marines, 154, 173, 175, 177
utopianism, 25, 83, 85, 217, 494
Uzbeks, 16, 17, 73, 113, 158, 351

Vickers, Mike, 99, 148, 311
  assessment of the war, 260
Vietnam, 81, 82, 85, 162, 213–218, 255, 437, 482. *See also* North Vietnam; South Vietnam
  Afghanistan compared to, 11, 31, 55, 128, 177, 217, 218, 248, 270, 376, 435, 441, 450, 454, 464, 480
  Biden's opposition to, 435–437, 441, 459
  bureaucracy in, 32, 481
  counterinsurgency in, 9
  Holbrooke in, 297
  intelligence needed in, 480
  negotiation with, 310, 422
  and the Pentagon Papers, 10
  US perceptions of, 446
  US withdrawal from, 294, 302, 436
  veterans of, 19, 29, 135, 333, 376, 441
village stability operations, 259
Vines, John, 171
Vitter, David, 243
Votel, Joseph, 329, 364, 366, 368, 373, 393, 397, 398, 415

Waddell, Rick, 387
Waltz, Kenneth, 25
Wanat, Battle of, 193
War on Terror, 22, 37, 38–45, 51, 52, 69, 70, 77, 91, 125, 133, 158, 196, 197, 298, 463, 471
  and Coalition Support Funds, 144
  goals of, 79
  Pakistan and, 58, 99, 100
  and the Taliban, 46
  victories in, 56
warlordism, 18, 117, 119, 140, 343, 351, 438
warlords, 71, 93, 109, 113, 116–121, 136, 137, 139, 141, 161, 178, 306, 342, 343, 439, 441. *See also* Northern Alliance
  and the Bush administration, 183
Washington, George, 4, 249
Wayne, Tony, 72, 104, 265, 269, 274, 278, 289, 330, 337, 341, 481

weapons of mass destruction, 74
Wells, Alice, 389, 397, 404, 418
West, Bing, 19
Wilkerson, Larry, 41, 49, 78, 82, 103
Wilson, Woodrow, 25, 27
Wolfowitz, Paul, 67, 83
women
  in Afghanistan, 269
  in the Afghan constitution, 112, 389
  democracy and, 380
  education for, 338
  inclusion of, 421
  oppression of, 18
  and the Taliban, 17, 60, 306, 452, 461
  voting rights for, 13
women's rights, 13, 112, 306, 307, 380, 444
Wood, Bill, 158, 167, 169, 171, 172, 175, 182
  as ambassador, 187, 191, 193, 211, 461, 480
  in Colombia, 181
  on corruption, 176
  on counternarcotics efforts, 183, 184
  on governance, 189
  on Karzai, 190
Woodward, Bob, 48, 52, 53, 101, 223, 394, 414, 442, 443
  on the Bush administration, 50
  on McMaster, 384
  and Obama, 227, 237, 242, 246, 248, 442
  on Obama's strategy, 255
  on Trump, 387
World Bank, 75
World Trade Center, 2

Yazidi, 363
Yemen, 463, 476
Yugoslavia, 297

Zakheim, Dov, 89, 95, 139, 152, 180, 189, 478, 486, 487
  on aid to Afghanistan, 153
Zarqawi, Abu-Musab al-, 219
Zawahiri, Ayman al-, 56, 159, 418, 456
Zubaydah, Abu, 58